Lincoln's
Informer

Lincoln's Informer

Charles A. Dana and the Inside
Story of the Union War

Carl J. Guarneri

University Press of Kansas

For my students

Excerpts from the Tribune Association Minute Book, 1849–1860, appear courtesy of the
John Hay Whitney and Betsey Cushing Whitney Family Papers at Yale University Library.

Published by the University Press of Kansas (Lawrence, Kansas 66045), which was
organized by the Kansas Board of Regents and is operated and funded by Emporia State
University, Fort Hays State University, Kansas State University, Pittsburg State University,
the University of Kansas, and Wichita State University.

Library of Congress Cataloging-in-Publication Data

Names: Guarneri, Carl J., 1950– author.
Title: Lincoln's Informer : Charles A. Dana and the inside story of the Union war
   / Carl J. Guarneri.
Description: Lawrence, Kansas : University Press of Kansas, [2019] | Includes
   bibliographical references and index.
Identifiers: LCCN 2019006707
   ISBN 9780700628469 (cloth : alk. paper)
   ISBN 9780700628476 (ebook)
Subjects: LCSH: Dana, Charles A. (Charles Anderson), 1819–1897. | United
   States. War Department—Officials and employees—Biography. | War
   correspondents—United States—Biography. | Lincoln, Abraham,
   1809–1865—Friends and associates. | Stanton, Edwin M. (Edwin McMasters),
   1814–1869—Friends and associates. | Espionage—United
   States—History—19th century. | United States—History—Civil War,
   1861–1865—Secret service. | United States—History—Civil War,
   1861–1865—Campaigns. | United States—Politics and government—1861–1865.
Classification: LCC E467.1.D162 G83 2019 | DDC 973.7092 [B]—dc23
LC record available at https://lccn.l oc.gov/2019006707.

British Library Cataloguing-in-Publication Data is available.

Printed in the United States of America

10 9 8 7 6 5 4 3 2 1

The paper used in this publication is recycled and contains 30 percent postconsumer waste.
It is acid free and meets the minimum requirements of the American National Standard for
Permanence of Paper for Printed Library Materials Z39.48–1992.

Contents

Maps and Illustrations

Maps

Illustrations

Acknowledgments

Plans for this book were hatched three decades ago as a sort of sequel to my history of the antebellum communitarian movement, *The Utopian Alternative* (1991). In the course of writing that book I had learned that Charles Dana, after living at Brook Farm and working at the *New York Tribune*, had a colorful, important, and overlooked Civil War career. I resolved to unearth it. Years of teaching, monograph and textbook writing, and professional obligations intervened, and my Dana project became a cautionary tale for any scholar who plans to write a quick little book in their so-called spare time. It is a pleasure to finally acknowledge many of the people and institutions who helped me on the journey toward finishing my not-so-quick or little book.

Like other travelers in Civil War territory, I have relied on a massive corpus of scholarly histories and biographies that continues to accumulate yearly. This book's extensive notes and bibliography are, beyond their usefulness to readers, expressions of gratitude to the authors of those works, even when I dispute their evidence or judgments. In addition, many scholars and writers personally provided me with information and encouragement. Decades ago, William Freehling, Willie Lee Rose, Ron Walters, and Gerald Linderman grounded me expertly in the Civil War era during graduate school at the University of Michigan and Johns Hopkins University. "The snitch!" Linderman exclaimed when I first broached working on Dana, and after that he followed my work with interest and good will. John Higham urged me, as always, to expand my subject outward toward big themes in nineteenth-century history. Janet Steele, a fellow Higham student, was already working on a study of Dana's journalism when I conceived this project. I told her about a few manuscript sources I had discovered, and I benefited far more when her 1993 book, *The* Sun *Shines for All*, examined Dana's Gilded Age career as a prominent New York newspaperman.

When I resumed research on Dana after a long hiatus, I made new friends and found generous mentors. Michael Fellman set a stirring and always provocative example of migrating from antebellum reform to Civil War history; he offered camaraderie and encouragement along with large helpings of opinions on Lee, Sherman, Reconstruction, and other topics. Steven Woodworth graciously agreed to review drafts of my battlefield chapters. His encyclopedic knowledge not only saved me from several factual errors but also made me refine my interpretive judgments of persons and events. Thomas Mallon's dark novel *Henry and Clara* (1994) showed how secondary characters could illuminate Lincoln and his times. Tom forwarded references to Dana that he came across in the archives and on several occasions buoyed me with his enthusiasm for the project. Alfred Habegger, author of a biography of Henry James, Sr., shared information on the Macdaniel family and Dana's relation with James. Leslie Rowland, director of the groundbreaking Freedmen and Southern Society project at the University of Maryland, sent me copies of the unpublished segment of Dana's testimony before the American Freedmen's Inquiry Commission. Robert Wilson, editor of *The American Scholar* and biographer of Mathew Brady, offered valuable insights about Brady and good guidance about the world of trade publishing. Charles Postel informed me about a source of digitized newspapers I had overlooked. Gary Gerstle, Nick Guyatt, Andrew Preston, and the American history group at the University of Cambridge granted me visiting scholar status, providing not just library privileges but hospitality and advice as I completed the book's first draft in the spring of 2017.

Colleagues at Saint Mary's College of California followed this project over the years and helped in specific ways to move it along. Fellow historians Paul Flemer, Ben Frankel, Gerald Henig, Brother Charles Hilken, Ronald Isetti, Katherine Roper, Gretchen Lemke-Santangelo, Myrna Santiago, Aeleah Soine, and Elena Songster read early chapter drafts and offered constructive commentary. David Alvarez of the Politics Department shared his expertise on ciphers and cryptography. Librarians Allegra Porter and Steve Stonewell acquired essential sources through Interlibrary Loan. Kate Wilson assisted me in scanning nineteenth-century illustrations. Sue Birkenseer kept our Civil War stacks current, and she and Sarah Vital played pivotal roles in building an SMC Library website that features Civil War letters and diaries. Heidi Donner took the lead in securing a Lee and Grant exhibit for the Saint Mary's Museum of Art; she and Mike McAlpin trumpeted my Civil War scholarship to the public. Carl Thelen of IT Services turned out to be a seasoned Civil War reenactor with much to teach me about camp life and military equipment.

Saint Mary's has also been generous in its financial support. Two semester-long sabbaticals gave me time to complete my research. Funds from the

College's Filippi Endowment for History sent me to distant archives, allowed me to walk the battlefields Charles Dana trod, and defrayed expenses related to images, permissions, and publication. The Saint Mary's Faculty Development Fund also supported archival research and conference presentations.

I am also grateful for the help of student research assistants. Carrie Beth Holt unearthed documents from the National Archives on Richard Montgomery, the intrepid and not altogether trustworthy Union spy. William Lane's excellent research in the *Chicago Republican* and *New York Sun* over the course of two summers laid a solid foundation for my chapter on Dana's postwar career. Zephyr Snyder, Alyssa Sisco Ginn, and Deirdre Riley worked with me to decipher and interpret Civil War letters and diaries in Saint Mary's Special Collections. This book's dedication recognizes the curiosity and passion of these students and numerous others in my history classes over the past four decades.

In ways big and small, the following friends and relatives helped me to research and think about this book; their interest also bolstered me during fallow months: Andy Rotter, Padma Kaimal, Barbara Steinson, John Schlotterbeck, Stewart and Rita Jacoby, John and Tina Gillis, Tom Dublin, Kitty Sklar, Jay Gordon, Eric Vermilion, Kathy Dalton, Anthony Rotundo, Alicia Rivera, Helen Amritraj, Paul and Joann Guarneri, Theresa and Joseph Gould, Kevin McCoy, George and Alice Weller, Steve Weller, and Diane Giddis. Ann Grogg, a peerless editor who guided my work on a US history textbook, taught me to trim paragraphs to their nimble essence—a lesson I have often honored in the breach. Literary agent John W. Wright, introduced to me by Paul Finkelman, turned out, astonishingly, to be the same "Mr. Wright" who had taught me world history as a high school freshman a half-century earlier. After reading a prospectus and sample chapters he gave me indispensable advice on next steps. Stalwart members of my Bay Area book group—Greg Anderson, Bob Berring, Bruce Budner, Wayne Canterbury, Eric Danoff, and Gerald Eisman—served gamely as stand-ins for that mythical target of all authors, the "general reader." Their comments on draft chapters were enormously helpful, and their suggestions for incorporating personal details about Dana shaped my revisions.

I am grateful to librarians at archives across the country who gave me research leads and access to materials. Staff members at the Library of Congress and National Archives, the preeminent Union Civil War repositories, were unfailingly helpful. Special thanks also go to staff members at the Allegheny College Library, Duke University Library, Ohio Historical Society,

Cornell University Library, Historical Society of Pennsylvania, Kansas State Historical Society, and Syracuse University Library, all of whom provided copies of documents from afar. Serving on fellowship panels for the National Endowment for the Humanities and the Massachusetts Historical Society took me to Washington and Boston to double-check familiar sources and to discover new ones. The Huntington Library in San Marino, California, arranged a hospitable stay and proved a rich source of Civil War materials.

At the University Press of Kansas, Joyce Harrison expressed immediate enthusiasm for the project, then proved she meant it by quickening the timeline to a contract. As the book moved through production, Kelly Chrisman Jacques, Michael Kehoe, and Colin Tripp contributed their expertise with efficiency and tact. Historians Michael Burlingame and Harold Holzer, who reviewed the manuscript, offered essential corrections and helpful guidance for the final revision. Jon Howard copyedited the manuscript with a light but sure touch. George Skoch, an expert Civil War cartographer, graciously agreed to a tight schedule, then proceeded to turn my sometimes murky ideas and instructions into beautifully clear and informative maps.

Finally, there is my immediate family, whose short bursts of curiosity and longer bouts of patience have sustained me during research and writing. My daughters, Anna and Julia Guarneri, were initially baffled by my newfound Civil War obsession but gradually accepted it with bemusement ("Who's winning?" they asked when Civil War journals arrived) and even with interest, especially after it became clear that slavery and emancipation stood at the topic's center. My sons-in-law, Jeff Rechler and John Connor, were indulgent and insightful during discussions of nineteenth-century life. My wife, Valerie Weller, asked probing questions and suggested penetrating answers about Dana and the Civil War. I now owe her the undistracted attention that too often went missing as this book neared completion.

Introduction: "The Eyes of the Government at the Front"

On the night of May 4, 1864, General Ulysses Grant's massive federal army lumbered across the Rapidan River to begin its climactic advance against Robert E. Lee's Confederates defending Richmond. Back in Washington, two harrowing days passed without word from the front. One visitor observed President Abraham Lincoln "sickening with anxiety" as he awaited dispatches in the War Department telegraph office. When a congressman asked how Grant was faring, Lincoln replied gamely: "Well, I can't tell much about it. You see, Grant has gone to the Wilderness, crawled in, drawn up the ladder, and pulled in the hole after him, and I guess we'll have to wait till he comes out before we know just what he's up to."[1] Tormented by the silence, Lincoln and his secretary of war, Edwin Stanton, decided to send Stanton's trusted deputy, the newspaper veteran Charles A. Dana, to the front as their confidential reporter.

Dana was at a diplomatic reception when a messenger summoned him to the War Office. He arrived in evening dress to find Lincoln and Stanton conferring soberly. How soon could he start for Grant's headquarters? the president asked. A half-hour, Dana responded, and in that time a special train was readied at Alexandria with a cavalry escort. Meanwhile Dana (in his own words) "got into my camp clothes, borrowed a pistol, and with my own horse was aboard the train . . . that was to take me to Alexandria." Just then a second messenger arrived to recall him to the War Department. Galloping back, Dana found Lincoln draped in the same chair. The president was having second thoughts. Since Lee's whereabouts were still unknown and Jeb Stuart's cavalry was rampaging above the Rapidan, Lincoln was reluctant to expose Dana to the risk of capture or harm. Unruffled, Dana replied that with his mounted escort he was "strong enough to fight" or, if necessary, "equipped to run." If he started out right away he might reach Grant's rear guard by daylight. Lincoln leaned forward. "Well now, Dana," the president said with a twinkle in his eyes, "if you feel that way, I rather wish you would. Good night, and God bless you."[2]

This wasn't the first time Lincoln and Stanton had sent Dana to the front, nor would it be the last. When doubts had arisen about Grant's competence during the campaign on the Mississippi in 1863, they asked Dana to investigate. He remained with Grant's army for three months, sending dispatches through the siege and surrender of Vicksburg. When later that year General William Rosecrans moved slowly to expel the Confederate army from Tennessee, Dana joined Rosecrans in time to experience the shattering Union defeat at Chickamauga. After Grant and George Thomas replaced Rosecrans, Dana stayed through the Battle of Chattanooga as a reporter and liaison to Washington. In July 1864, when the Confederate general Jubal Early mounted a surprise raid on Washington, Grant sent Dana from Virginia to advise him on defense of the capital. In the spring of 1865, when Grant's Overland Campaign culminated in the fall of Richmond, Stanton commissioned Dana to report on the Union occupation. Finally, when Jefferson Davis, fleeing south, was captured in Georgia, Dana was sent to oversee his imprisonment while Union war leaders decided his fate.

Charles A. Dana was the kind of behind-the-scenes operator that a historical novelist—or a conspiracy theorist—might invent. Vigilant and efficient, he moved inconspicuously through the Union's camps and corridors of power, observing and advising—and sometimes scheming—but largely remaining in the background. Nearly half of his time with the War Department was spent in the field, usually accompanying an army on campaign. As befit a no-nonsense newspaper man, Dana filed reports that were clear and concise, enlivened by vivid detail and peppered with quick and decisive judgments. His confidential letters and telegrams bristle with information and insights about the war's inner workings. According to the custodian of the Union war records, they constitute "the most remarkable, interesting, and instructive collection of official documents relating to the Rebellion."[3]

Dana didn't just record history; he made it. He intervened at decisive points to change government policies on the cotton trade, to lobby Congress for legislation crucial to Lincoln's administration, and to thwart Confederate "dirty tricks" operations hatched in Canada. Dana's observations of major Union generals and campaigns were used to inform the public on the progress of the war, to guide war leaders' military moves, and to promote or demote army officers. His reports convinced Washington officials that their most competent generals were Grant and Sherman, proved that General John A. McClernand should be reassigned, doomed the bewildered Rosecrans after Chickamauga, and advised that Grant and Thomas should take over his army. Victims of Dana's confidential criticism lambasted him as an informer or betrayer, but

Stanton told Dana his telegrams were "a great obligation, and are looked for with deep interest," and Lincoln valued him as "the eyes of the government at the front."[4] In a poll of leading modern historians, Dana was named among the "Twenty-five Most Influential Civil War [Figures] That You've Probably Never Heard Of."[5]

Dana's wartime reporting built upon a fifteen-year newspaper apprenticeship. In the 1850s he rose to managing editor of Horace Greeley's *New York Tribune*, the nation's largest-circulation newspaper and a beacon of the Republican-oriented Free Soil movement. As the sectional struggle over slavery escalated, Dana took increasing control of the paper's operations and editorial line. More militant than his politically erratic boss, Dana led the *Tribune*'s charge against proslavery forces in Congress and the Kansas Territory. After Lincoln's election he steered the *Tribune* away from Greeley's flirting with "peaceable secession" toward demanding all-out war to restore the Union. Three months after Confederate cannons blared at Fort Sumter, it was Dana's "Forward to Richmond!" editorials that prodded Lincoln and his cabinet into the fateful Union advance on Bull Run.

Dana's *Tribune* career demonstrated the growing power of the press in the Civil War era. National newspapers like the *Tribune* escalated the sectional conflict as they covered it; they established alliances with party politicians and government officials, and they provoked changes in war policies and strategies through their editorials and reporting.[6] Dana remained an impatient critic of the Union's sluggish military response until Greeley, fearing a repeat of the Bull Run debacle, forced him to resign in 1862. Within months, Secretary Stanton appointed him as a special agent and later as assistant secretary.

When not at the battle front, Dana managed a heavy workload at the War Department as Stanton's deputy. His Washington duties were as adventurous and significant as those at the front. Dana investigated cases of fraud and disloyalty, supervised a cohort of Union spies, worked for Lincoln's reelection in 1864, lobbied to pass the Thirteenth Amendment, assisted Stanton as Lincoln lay dying, and gathered evidence to implicate Confederate leaders in a grand conspiracy to assassinate the Union president. Between his stints at the front and the nation's capital, few men had such a varied experience of the war or enjoyed such close relations with those in charge of the government and army. No one played as important a role as a shaper of wartime events from the shadows.

The range of Dana's experience means that to trace his activities during the national crisis is to reconstruct an inside history of the Union war. Dana's government service clarifies continuing controversies of the campaigns in Vicksburg, Chattanooga, and Virginia, especially relating to Generals Grant, Rosecrans, and Thomas. His commentary offers new views of the debate over emancipation, wartime policies on civil liberties, and Lincoln's assassination. His observations reveal a confidant's reflections on the personalities, leadership skills—and the flaws—of Union heroes Lincoln, Stanton, and Grant. Taken as whole, Dana's Civil War career also suggests one answer to the perennial question of why the conflict ended as it did.

The task of explaining why the North won the Civil War—putting aside the even more contentious question of why the South lost it—has occupied generations of historians. Virtually all agree that sizable credit must go to the skilled political leadership of Lincoln, which Dana grew to appreciate more and more as he saw it up close. But Lincoln could not win the war by himself; when his two-year ordeal of finding a fighting general was ended by Grant at Vicksburg (with a major assist from Dana), the Union's fortunes received a decisive boost. Once the right leaders were in place in the cabinet and the army, attention turned to a third factor, more prosaic but increasingly vital as the war dragged on: the ability to harness the North's huge advantages in manpower and resources and direct them efficiently toward victory.

More than half a century ago, the historian Allan Nevins described the momentous transition from an "improvised war" to an "organized war" that enabled the Union to prevail.[7] Mobilizing men, materials, and technology, the North marshaled its superior resources to win what became a war of attrition against the South. Stanton's War Department was the epicenter of this seismic shift in planning and organization. His appointment in 1862 provided the major shock, and he assembled a team that forged the policies and conducted the business of the colossal military enterprise. The group included several dynamic and effective administrators among the assistant secretaries and bureau chiefs, including Thomas Scott, Peter H. Watson, Montgomery Meigs, Lewis B. Parsons, Joseph Holt, and of course Charles A. Dana. These hardworking, capable second-level figures gave the Union a clear and decisive organizational advantage over the Confederacy.

Like the single-minded Stanton, Dana exemplified the North's relentless will to win by all means necessary and its ability to manage the Union's resources to bring the war to a successful end. Dana played a major role in stretching the government's powers of arresting citizens suspected of disloyalty and in harnessing the technology of telegraphs and railroads to organize military and electoral victories. His wartime career shows how much this organizing was *improvised* as Stanton rapidly built up the War Department's offices and procedures, sent associates on inspection tours, and created the role of roving reporter at the front for his deputy. It is worth noting that Jefferson Davis and Richmond authorities received no such reliable, independent reports from the military front; their absence stoked feuding among Confederate generals and led Davis to make disastrous decisions about military appointments and dismissals.

Dana's insider role and his unflinching judgments made him controversial, then and now. Close wartime associates concluded that Dana was a "great man" and an unsung hero of the Union victory, while those pricked by his sharp pen impugned him as "an infamous libeler" and "the meanest of all knaves and scoundrels."[8] The divide echoes through modern Civil War studies. Biographers who admire Edwin Stanton commend Dana as his indispensable assistant while scholars critical of the autocratic war secretary paint Dana as his wily henchman. The most dramatic contrast emerges between historians of the Vicksburg campaign, who praise Dana's support at a key juncture in Grant's career, and historians of Chickamauga, who almost unanimously condemn Dana as Rosecrans's unfair executioner.[9]

The Dana that emerges from these pages is not a villain, but neither is he an unblemished hero. Ambitious, shrewd, and opinionated, he promoted the cause of Union and emancipation forcefully, but not without revealing flaws of judgment and temperament. To advance his aggressive brand of antislavery Unionism, and not incidentally to further his career, Dana attached himself to a series of prominent patrons—Greeley, Stanton, and Grant—and rose to power by their side. At the War Department and as the administration's private reporter, Dana made mistakes. His investigation of quartermaster corruption at Cairo, Illinois—examined in chapter 5—exonerated an obvious fraudster and well-connected Lincoln appointee, with disastrous consequences. Dana readily accepted unlikely stories that smeared political opponents, failed generals, or Confederate officials. He was prone to repeating camp gossip, making hasty judgments, and tossing aside scruples to promote his views. Yet although Dana rode self-assurance to the brink of arrogance, he was also a sharp observer who was right most of the time. While leaving the tarnished reputations of several well-meaning Union generals in his wake, he rendered the hard judgments that saved thousands of Union soldiers' lives. Like the reporters he hired for the *Tribune*, Dana called the shots as he saw them without fear or remorse, and his dispatches to Stanton and Lincoln hastened the Union's day of vindication.

Absorbed by his daily duties, Dana kept no diary, saved few documents, and never wrote up his Civil War experience. Three decades after Appomattox, a fellow editor noted ruefully that Dana was "the one man who knows most about the inside war movements and has said least of all the men connected with the government."[10] That was about to change.

In 1897 some segments of Dana's Civil War story were pieced together by the young muckraking journalist Ida Tarbell. Assigned by *McClure's* magazine to ghostwrite the aging editor's memoirs, Tarbell interviewed him, then wrote a series of articles that was published as Dana's *Recollections of the Civil War* (1898). The book became a standard source for historians and Civil War buffs and has been quoted widely. In fact, Dana wrote nothing for the memoir and vetted fewer than two of its twenty chapters before he died. Tarbell's book was a biographical essay disguised as a memoir.[11] Told in the first person and advertised as written by Dana, it was a patchwork of Dana's wartime documents and later recollections stitched together by Tarbell, using her own inferences as well as information from Grant's memoirs and other histories. Her account is marred by chronological gaps and factual errors, in addition to events that the aged Dana misremembered. Worse still, Tarbell mistook the context and significance of key wartime episodes involving Dana and Lincoln. Despite its questionable provenance and spotty reliability, *Recollections of the Civil War* has been used by historians for more than a century, supplying them with anecdotes about Lincoln and Grant and satisfying them that they had read Dana's authentic Civil War story, even after it emerged in the 1930s that Tarbell was the real author.

Like many memoirs, Dana's ersatz version preempted biographers, and the absence of a trove of personal papers also deterred later researchers. In 1907 Dana's wartime colleague James H. Wilson compiled a deeply admiring biography that is important for including unique Civil War anecdotes and now-lost letters. No other book on Dana's Civil War has appeared in print in a hundred-plus years, although he makes cameo appearances in many studies of wartime journalism and military campaigns as well as biographies of Grant, Lincoln, and other Union leaders.[12]

Taking the full measure of Dana's Civil War career has required consulting many new or neglected archival sources as well as combing through published histories and documents. For Dana's stint at the *Tribune*, through careful analysis of editorials and correspondence I have been able to distinguish Dana's distinctive voice and views from those of his editorial chief, Greeley. To understand Dana's subsequent government duties, I excavated thousands of War Department reports, letters, and telegrams in the National Archives, many written or signed by Dana. These and other materials revealed a string of activities overlooked by historians and allowed a close assessment of Dana's field reports about Union battles and military officers. For the most part I have relegated my disputes with other historians and corrections of Ida Tarbell's ghostwriting to the endnotes; but a few episodes are so important and controversial that they merit deeper discussion in the text.

Dana's Civil War was a story of personal and national triumph, but his postwar career featured a sudden turnabout and made a troubling contrast. Dana's political course during and after Reconstruction—covered in chapter 17 and the book's epilogue—mirrored the defeat of the Radical Republicans, but Dana went much further in retreating from his wartime idealism, abandoning his commitment to freed people's equality, and reconciling with the South's resurgent white racism. Breaking abruptly with President Grant, ostensibly over his administration's corruption, Dana gained notoriety as editor of the *New York Sun*, a lively, Democratic-leaning paper obsessed with uncovering fraud and entertaining readers. For thirty years Dana ran the *Sun* as his sparkling and deliberately provocative precursor to the tabloids, cultivating sensation and publicity more than editorial consistency. Over time, Dana's Civil War career became eclipsed by his postwar journalistic prowess, biting and unpredictable as it was.

Although Charles Dana is remembered now—if at all—as the newspaper genius behind the postwar *Sun*, the Civil War years saw his most consistent, honorable, and effective intervention in public life. Dana's wartime activities deserve to be recounted accurately and in full, not simply for the light they shed on his own hidden role but also for their insights into the war's momentous events and the major Union leaders he knew and assisted.

1 "The Responsible Editor of the *Tribune*"

"The republicanism of the Continent has come to a focus at the corner of Nassau and Spruce Streets," journalist James Parton declared on a visit to New York City in 1854. He had in mind a particular newspaper office fronting Printing House Square, a grimy, five-story box that advertised its tenant in five-foot gilded letters above the cornice: "THE TRIBUNE."[1] Unlike its neighboring rival papers, which were geared to providing information or entertainment, the *Tribune* aimed to enlighten, advise, and improve. Horace Greeley, its colorful founder and editor, infused the paper with a progressive spirit and guided readers to his favorite causes: honest government, temperance and dietary reform, a protective tariff, western homesteads and worker cooperatives, and—with growing insistence in the 1850s—the struggle to contain slavery.

The *Tribune*'s blend of Whig Party policies and social reform did not always sit well with local political leaders, but it announced Greeley's national ambitions. As railroads sped the paper's delivery it became the nation's most influential sheet. The *Tribune*'s weekly edition enrolled 200,000 subscribers in the rural North. If each copy was read by five people, as Greeley estimated, his exhortations touched more than a million citizens. The paper, one of Greeley's travel writers reported, "is next to the Bible all through the West." Not all who read the *Tribune* were impressed: because Greeley promoted antislavery and controversial reform "isms" his paper had a distinctly sectional appeal. It was, a New England reporter quipped, "the best beloved and best hated paper in the country—the paper that is sworn at in South Carolina, and sworn by in Ohio."[2]

By the 1850s the eccentric Greeley had become a folk hero whose rise from a poor family farm in New Hampshire through journeyman printing to editing his own paper in New York was celebrated as an American success story. After producing Whig Party campaign sheets in Albany and New York, Greeley launched the daily *Tribune* in April 1841 with funds borrowed from friends and political associates. Its circulation rose steadily as Greeley

The *Tribune* building, as seen from New York's City Hall Park in the 1850s. Library of Congress Prints and Photographs Division.

jousted with rival editors and antagonized the novelist James Fenimore Cooper, who won $200 in a libel suit but gave Greeley publicity worth much more. Greeley's reputation as a crusading idealist was enhanced by his disheveled, Dickensian appearance: wisps of graying hair protruded from his chin and the sides of his bulbous, balding head; his skin was ghostly pale; and he shuffled through New York's streets in mud-splattered boots and a drooping white coat whose pockets were stuffed with notes to himself. Easily recognizable, Greeley evoked titters from spectators and became a natural target of cartoonists.[3]

So successfully did Greeley impart a friendly and fighting tone to the *Tribune* that readers believed "Uncle Horace" wrote every column, "including shipping news," one of his reporters joked. Some historians have made the same mistake. In truth, the *Tribune* was far from a one-man operation. By the mid-1850s it had more than thirty paid correspondents and nearly a dozen associate editors. Unstable in his moods, unfamiliar with the world beyond America, and prone to ride reform hobbyhorses, Greeley required rounding out. Fortunately, he surrounded himself with a talented group of writers, many with better educations and steadier nerves than their boss. They constituted, according to one authority, "the most brilliant staff yet to serve on an American newspaper." To James Parton, their give-and-take exemplified the "republicanism" the *Tribune* practiced internally while it broadcast political Republicanism to the nation. The man responsible for bending the efforts and egos of these men to the task of producing a daily paper was not Greeley; it was his chief deputy, Charles A. Dana. If Greeley was president of the Republic of the *Tribune*, Dana was prime minister.[4]

Greeley's Manager

One morning in 1854 Parton ascended the *Tribune*'s ink-stained stairs to the third-floor editorial rooms.[5] To his right, a small inner office appeared, dusty and green-carpeted, with a sofa against the wall and a large bookcase filled with reference works. Greeley's desk sat by the window overlooking City Hall and the bustling square. Like Greeley himself, it was genially unkempt, piled with letters, clippings, and proof sheets, and topped by shelves with manuscripts nearly falling out—all presided over by "a large bronze bust of Henry Clay, wearing a crown of dust." Across the room, another desk was "in perfect order," cleared except for a neat stack of foreign letters awaiting perusal. It belonged to Dana.[6]

At mid-morning, Parton wrote, "Mr. Dana enters with a quick, decided step [and] goes straight to his desk." Parton's sketch of Dana was brisk like the man:

> In figure, face, and flowing beard, he looks enough like [the Hungarian patriot] Louis Kossuth to be his cousin, if not his brother. Mr. Dana, as befits his place, is a gentleman of peremptory habits. It is his office to *decide*; and, as he is called upon to perform the act of decision a hundred times a day, he has acquired the power both of deciding with dispatch and of announcing his decision with civil brevity. . . . He is an able, and, in description, a brilliant writer; a good speaker; fond and proud of his profession; indefatigable in the discharge of its duties; when out of harness, agreeable as a companion; in harness, a man not to be interrupted.[7]

Standing five feet, ten inches, Dana impressed others as taller due to his slim build and erect posture. Beneath his broad forehead Dana scanned the room alertly with deceptively kindly bluish-gray eyes. He gave a nod to his boss's callers, then dispatched reporters and answered queries from associate editors in a deep baritone that struck listeners as imperious, whether intended or not. At his desk Dana read letters from the paper's correspondents, penned requests for politicians' speeches, and sent instructions to the *Tribune*'s Washington bureau.

Greeley joined Dana at the office after noon, Parton reported. After pronouncing the morning issue's successes and shortcomings in his high-pitched voice, he settled down to receive callers and read his correspondence. At five o'clock the pace of activity quickened. Greeley scrawled the next day's lead editorial in a crazy, irregular script that the *Tribune* compositors miraculously deciphered. Dana edited reports from the Washington bureau and correspondents in Europe. Collecting the day's harvest of essays and editorials, Dana spotted room to squeeze in a comment on a senator's speech or dash off a riposte to a rival newspaper.

By eleven at night Greeley had left, and Dana received from the foreman a list of articles ready to run. As he finalized the *Tribune*'s contents, Dana kept in mind Greeley's preferences and consulted his own. At the last minute he might excise a too-conciliatory paragraph from Greeley's editorials, include gossip from Washington, or add text to "put the cracker" to an opinion piece. Greeley had hired a junior editor and staff members with more pointed political agendas and stronger antislavery opinions than his, and he faced the consequences. "I never opened the paper in those days without a terror as to what they might make me say after eleven o'clock at night," he recalled. By midnight the paper was "locked up" and sent to a team of compositors. Dana donned his coat and departed.[8]

Since 1849 Dana had been the *Tribune*'s managing editor, the first to hold that title in American journalism. Dana hired and supervised the paper's writers, reporters, and office staff; commissioned its articles; and determined its day-to-day content. He also selected copy for the all-important weekly edition, which circulated widely beyond the Appalachians. Dana's relations with the *Tribune*'s editors, reporters, and correspondents were friendly but exacting, and his terse replies to queries set the pattern of efficiency that successors learned to imitate. Dana once defined a managing editor as "a being to whom the sentiment of remorse is unknown." Endowed with steady work habits and executive self-assurance, he called the shots as he saw them and rarely looked back. Business was quickly dispatched and correspondence discarded: "It has not been my practice to preserve letters after the subjects on which they were written have been disposed of," he explained to an inquirer. Although this habit frustrated later biographers, it kept Dana's mind clear, his desk tidy, and the *Tribune* on deadline.[9]

Staff of the *New York Tribune* in the late 1840s: *Standing, left to right*: music critic
William H. Fry, managing editor Charles A. Dana, and assistant editor Henry J. Raymond
(later editor of the *New York Times*). *Seated, left to right*: financial writer George H. Snow,
literary critic and travel writer Bayard Taylor, editor Horace Greeley, and literary editor
George Ripley. Library of Congress Prints and Photographs Division.

Dana's relationship with Greeley was more complicated. Though a strong
character, the managing editor harnessed his ambitions to Greeley's quest for
influence and hewed his opinions to his boss's shifting editorial line. Dana
learned to read Greeley's mind, handle his temper, and keep the *Tribune*
on course through his mood swings and ideological gyrations; meanwhile,
Greeley's warm heart and faith in reason kept Dana's killer instincts in check.
When their views were aligned, the two admired each other's strengths and
offset each other's weaknesses. Patience was neither man's strong suit, but
each mustered enough to make the relationship work. Tensions arose periodically, however, when the managing editor imprinted the *Tribune* with his
more combative tone and agenda.

This happened more frequently as the years went by. Ambitious for political
office, Greeley gradually relinquished daily oversight of the *Tribune*. In the

early 1850s Greeley's winter lecture tours and political campaigning pulled him away for months—"a full third of the time," by his own estimate. Over the next few years, he crowded his calendar with lobbying in Washington, attendance at conventions, two trips to Europe, and one to the American West. Dana took charge while Greeley was away. Most of the time his boss approved, but Greeley was less pleased when Dana set aside his letters to make way for breaking news, a more hard-hitting piece, or a juicy scandal. *Tribune* reporters were well aware of Dana's growing influence, and one began calling him "the Prince Regent." Competing newsmen soon pointed to Greeley's nominal deputy as "the really responsible editor of the *Tribune*." One introduced Dana to readers as "a smart, active, driving, go-ahead man, very much liked by his friends, and not very bitterly hated by his enemies," and concluded that Dana's skill had brought the *Tribune* its "unexampled prosperity." There followed a few biographical hints. Dana was "a man very fond, in his youth, of distractions," who became "very remarkable in his middle age for his practical talent in business." These veiled references were about all most readers knew about Dana's personal journey from Transcendentalism to the *Tribune*.[10]

From Utopia to Journalism

By personality if not station, Charles Dana was born to command. Direct and concise, he stood poles apart from the meandering and fussy Greeley. His correct attire and dignified manners contrasted with Greeley's slapdash outfits and social obtuseness. His hearty baritone overpowered Greeley's scratchy falsetto, and he was better read than his chief, whose sporadic schooling ended at age thirteen. Much credit for sustaining their partnership was due to Dana's willingness to play second fiddle to Greeley and his tact at performing that role. Yet the two men also shared a rural New England background and reform enthusiasms that fostered mutual respect and made the *Tribune* their joint obsession.

Born in 1819 in small-town New Hampshire, Dana was the eldest of four children in a family disrupted by illness and economic reverses. Charles's father, Anderson Dana, was a petty merchant who failed repeatedly in business. In the early 1820s he moved the family to western New York, where he ran a warehouse on the Erie Canal and then an unsuccessful farm. When Charles's mother, Ann, died of malaria in 1828, his father took the children to Vermont, where he divided them among relatives. At the age of nine Charles was placed with a maternal uncle, and at twelve he was sent to Buffalo to work as a clerk in the dry goods store of another uncle. Meanwhile, Dana's father remarried, started a new family in Ohio, and did little for his first set of children beyond sending an occasional scolding letter.[11]

Dana was a venerable New England name. As a young man, Charles was painfully aware of the gap between his birth family's circumstances and those of his notable ancestors and successful living relatives, including Richard Henry Dana, Jr., the author of *Two Years Before the Mast*. Dana was determined to make a name for himself. In Buffalo he joined a circle of aspiring, literate young men who shared their discoveries at the Young Men's Association and a "coffee club." One member, Austin Flint, a Harvard graduate and medical doctor, took a special interest in his education. Dana's relationship with Dr. Flint began a decades-long pattern of latching onto rising patrons to advance his career—a practice he would continue with Horace Greeley, Edwin Stanton, and Ulysses Grant.

An exceptionally curious reader, Dana spent most evenings studying history, literature, and languages, at which he was gifted. He learned Greek, Latin, and the local Seneca dialect, and he later picked up several European tongues. Encouraged by Flint, he prepared himself for college, and not long after the Panic of 1837 forced his uncle's store to close, Dana entered Harvard. At the end of his first term he ranked seventh in a class of seventy-four, no small feat for a largely self-taught youth. The next term proved more difficult. He found mathematics tough going, and when his money ran out he was forced to take a leave of absence. To economize, he stayed with relatives and then taught school in Scituate, Massachusetts. Dana managed to return to Cambridge, but another leave of absence, granted for ill health in June 1841, ended his Harvard education. His eyesight had deteriorated from studying by gaslight. For the rest of a busy life filled with newsprint, Dana complained of eyestrain and avoided nighttime reading when possible.[12]

Dana left Harvard with a wellspring of knowledge in languages, history, and literature that he drew upon in his journalistic career. He developed an economical prose style that favored direct Anglo-Saxon words over Latinate circumlocutions—quite different from the florid effusions of his Harvard mentors. Perhaps most important, his student encounter with the philosophical ferment of transatlantic Romanticism lured Dana to social activism. At Harvard Dana escaped from the suffocating Congregational orthodoxy of his upbringing into the fresh breeze of liberal theology. "There is certainly a movement going on in philosophy which must produce a revolution in politics, morals, and religion," he reported to Flint in 1840. He was stimulated by Ralph Waldo Emerson's lectures, admired Thomas Carlyle's reform tracts, and appreciated the "boldness, freedom, and philanthropy" that Transcendentalism introduced into scripture-bound religion.[13]

One Transcendentalist, George Ripley, led the "fraternal" faction of the movement, which rejected Emerson's insistent individualism in favor of co-operation and social justice. In 1840 Ripley resigned from his ministry in Boston to organize a communal experiment that aimed "to insure a more nat-ural union between intellectual and manual labor [and] guarantee the highest mental freedom by providing all with labor adapted to their tastes and tal-ents." The Brook Farm Association was launched early the next year when Ripley purchased a farm nestled on rolling hills eight miles up the Charles River from Harvard. With its congenial philosophy and circle of Harvard graduates, Brook Farm offered a welcome refuge from Dana's interrupted studies. His idealistic and pragmatic sides might be harmonized by "living justly and purely," working at the community's farm and school, and mini-mizing expenses. Dana applied by letter to Ripley and joined the group by September 1841.[14]

Dana's clerkship in Buffalo added up to modest practical experience, but his energy and executive temperament stood out among Brook Farm's knot of ministers and dreamers. Ripley appointed Dana director of finances and soon became dependent on him to organize daily tasks. According to one ob-server, Dana was "the best all-around man at Brook Farm—a good teacher, editor, and farmer," although he "was held not to be quite so zealous or un-selfish for the faith as were some of the others." The qualifier referred to Dana's ambition and his interest in making Brook Farm "pay" to relieve his indebtedness.[15]

Brook Farmers later recalled the twenty-two-year-old Dana as "a handsome man, . . . so slender as to seem tall. He had a firm, expressive face, regular and clear cut, a scholar's forehead, auburn hair, and a full beard. . . . Strong of purpose and lithe of frame, he conveyed the impression of force, whether he moved or spoke." Dana had a natural dignity that commanded respect. He spurned the blue-gray belted frocks that Brook Farm's young men sported and instead "dressed like a well-to-do young farmer."[16] When not attending to business or waiting tables, Dana taught Greek and German at Brook Farm's school. He acquired the nickname "Professor," earned by his decorum, cor-rect language, and high standards. Yet Dana was far from humorless. "Social, good-natured and animated, he readily pleased all with whom he came in contact," one Brook Farmer remembered. A cache of surviving gossipy let-ters indicates that Dana joined in the teasing and flirting that preoccupied the community's younger set.[17]

As a community officer, Dana left the farm periodically to publicize the venture and to build alliances with other reformers. At conventions of the "Friends of Reform" in Boston, he mingled with the abolitionists William Lloyd Garrison and Frederick Douglass. After Texas was annexed as a slave state in 1845, antislavery feeling surged among Brook Farmers. Dana and several others attended protest meetings in Boston's Faneuil Hall.[18]

On a fundraising trip to New York, Dana first met Greeley, who had established the *Tribune* the year before. Dana explained Brook Farmers' idea of a community animated by Christian sharing. Greeley sympathized but warned Dana that a few selfish parasites would be enough to sow discord. In later years the idea of Greeley urging Dana to be less dreamily idealistic would strike either as a ludicrous role reversal. But in the 1840s Greeley had taken up the social mathematics of Charles Fourier, the French utopian theorist, whose "scientific" communal blueprint claimed to channel self-interest to the common good. As streamlined by Albert Brisbane, Fourier's chief American disciple, Fourierism, or "Association," as it was labeled, called for several hundred individuals to purchase shares in a joint-stock community, or "phalanx," where workdays would be pleasantly varied and compensation distributed according to a complex formula that rewarded capital, labor, and skill in precise proportions. Fourier's scheme, Greeley told Dana, would achieve communal harmony "by having a rampart of exact justice behind that of philanthropy."[19]

Greeley and Brisbane launched a propaganda offensive to convert Brook Farm to the Fourierist creed, and the residents were intrigued. What one critic derided as the "unnatural union of Transcendentalists and Phalansteries" went surprisingly smoothly. Once they Christianized Fourier's vocabulary, the Brook Farmers saw affinities between their idealism and his philosophy of "attractive industry" and social harmony. An alliance with the Associationist movement provided capital, drew working-class recruits, and evolved Brook Farm from an elite private retreat into the propaganda center of a national movement.[20]

Dana hesitated at first but then enthusiastically embraced Fourierism. He helped frame Brook Farm's new constitution and preached Association at New England meeting halls and labor conventions. He wrote dozens of essays, editorials, and reviews for *The Harbinger*, the movement's weekly journal, which in June 1845 transferred its headquarters from New York to Brook Farm.[21]

Without knowing it, Dana was preparing for his career at the *Tribune*. His direct prose style was honed by *The Harbinger*'s weekly deadline, and his book reviews revealed a critical temperament that reined in his Romantic idealism. Fourier's doctrine gave Dana a hammer, and all naysayers looked to him like a nail. One target was his former teacher Emerson, who preached an "extreme individualism" that "sunders the man from his fellows, and even doubts whether it is necessary that he should have any fellows at all." Abolitionist friends who refused to condemn "wage slavery" were called out for practicing selective compassion, since chattel slavery was "only an elder sister of the same monstrous family." From the outset Dana relished argument over persuasion and took more delight in attacking than advocating positions.[22]

Brook Farm's "Hive," the three-story farmhouse where most of its single residents resided, offered Dana a relaxed version of student life at Harvard, with the added bonus of including young women. Among friends and amid communal meals and coffee parties, Dana found surrogates for the familial ties he lacked. Separated from his siblings at an early age, Dana had developed little attachment. His younger brothers Junius and David went their own ways, Junius to live near their father in Ohio, David to work in Boston, and the three had little contact. The exception was Dana's younger sister Maria, whom he convinced to join Brook Farm in 1844.[23]

That same year the Macdaniels, a progressive family from Georgetown, DC, associated with the community. Eunice, the family's younger daughter, was described by Dana's friend James Wilson as "an attractive and spirited girl, with black and sparkling eyes, and a slight but erect and energetic figure." An admirer at Brook Farm noted her "quick, nervous, volatile" temperament and charming Southern accent. Twenty years old, Eunice aspired to an acting career.[24] Before long, gossip swirled around a budding romance between Charles and Eunice, and on March 2, 1846, they were secretly married in New York City. The wedding's mysterious circumstances and the couple's absence from Brook Farm left an unpleasant taste. Dana's explanation to fellow Brook Farmer John Dwight did little to clear up the mystery: "You will be surprised at this and indeed . . . it was entirely unexpected to me," Dana wrote. "For obvious reasons connected with E's private movements which then seemed to require her to stay for some time in New York it [the wedding] was entirely private."[25]

Three weeks later Brook Farmers hosted a poorly attended wedding party. Dana's comrades were troubled by his secret ceremony as much for its violation of communal sharing as for the nasty speculation it invited. Dana had chosen private love over Associative ideals. This was hardly unusual: one chronicler counted fourteen couples who formed friendships at Brook Farm and eventually left the Hive for the marital nest. Shortly after Dana married

Brook Farm. Oil painting by Josiah Wolcott, c. 1847, with the "Hive" on the extreme right and ruins of the burned phalanstery on the hillside at the center, below the square structure. Bridgeman Art Images. Massachusetts Historical Society, Boston, MA, USA/Bridgeman Images.

Eunice, his sister Maria was wed to Eunice's brother Osborne Macdaniel. Yet Charles was a special case because he was Ripley's right-hand man. His elopement marked him to fellow communitarians as one "who will probably not stop here long."[26]

To make matters worse, while Charles and Eunice were away in New York, Brook Farm met disaster. One day after the wedding, the community's nearly completed phalanstery, or communal dwelling, burned to the ground, ignited by a basement stove. Dana returned from New York to suggest that the community eliminate all industries but the school and farm. This and other reorganization plans were floated among residents and creditors, but Brook Farmers could not recover and the community slowly disbanded.

Dana continued to write for *The Harbinger* in the summer of 1846, but he had no interest in holding out at the farm. By July he and Eunice had moved to Boston. Still burdened by debts and needing a "tolerable living" as a married man, he sounded out Greeley, but the New York editor offered him a low-paying place as a proofreader and translator of foreign journals. Dana then turned to Elizur Wright, editor of the *Boston Daily Chronotype* and a Fourierist fellow traveler, who hired him to edit city news and clip exchanges, and who allowed him to write editorials and arrange the paper's contents in his absence.[27]

Eventually Greeley came up with a new offer for Dana to work as the *Tribune*'s city editor for ten dollars a week. Early in 1847 Charles moved to New York to assume the position, and Eunice joined him shortly thereafter.[28] That fall Greeley recruited George Ripley as his literary editor. Together with Margaret Fuller, whose letters from Europe had begun to appear in the *Tribune*, the Brook Farmers' shift from utopia to journalism enhanced the paper's literary reputation and Greeley's reform credentials.

Before the year was out Greeley raised Dana's pay to fourteen dollars a week, a measure of his talent and usefulness. Dana, meanwhile, thrived amid the bustle and anonymity of New York as he had not at cloistered Brook Farm. "Here in this great city, where solitude and the intensest activity can exist together," he told a country cousin, "I feel myself in a good measure at home. My element is action." In a rare moment of self-reflection, he acknowledged that his brisk manner inhibited close relationships: "All the fire in me is devoted more to the business of going ahead than keeping folks warm, though if they are not afraid to come near me and are travelling my way I can do something at that too." Brusque and barely civil when on the street or the job but flashing unexpected warmth to associates and friends, Dana, despite his Yankee origins, epitomized the emerging profile of a New Yorker.[29]

On March 4, 1847, the day Ripley met with Brook Farm's creditors to dissolve the community, Eunice Dana gave birth in New York to the Danas' first child, a girl named Zoe. Eunice had put aside hopes for an acting career to manage a house and grow a family. "My wife is dear, noble, generous, and clear-sighted," Dana reported to a female friend. There were adjustments both partners had to make. Years later, Dana confided to a friend that the first year of a marriage "is apt to be the least happy." There is "a collision of little points of character and a difference of tastes which is afterwards actively avoided, or absorbed, or overlooked." Another adjustment concerned Dana's long hours at the office. Although he was busy at the *Tribune* well into the night, Eunice bore his absence "like a heroine." He soon tested her patience by going away much longer.[30]

Revolutions and Respectability

When news of the February 1848 revolution in France reached America, Dana and his fellow Fourierists hailed it as "the greatest political event of modern times." The overthrow of Louis-Philippe for the Second Republic represented more than a political upheaval; it was a social revolution that promised economic justice to the masses. Eager to witness the events, Dana convinced Greeley to have him cover the revolutions in weekly letters to the *Tribune*, at ten dollars per letter. He made similar deals with a few other American papers, including *The Harbinger* and *Chronotype*. Some historians credit Dana with launching the first syndicated correspondence in American journalism, but in fact he took care to craft unique letters tailored to each paper's interests.[31]

Dana arrived in Paris during the bloody June Days, when French workers attacked the Provisional Government for closing the National Workshops. Dana roamed the streets, providing graphic accounts as the National Guard suppressed the insurrection. When the violence subsided he sketched journalistic portraits of the leading socialist figures and reported on speeches by Victor Hugo, Adolphe Thiers, and Alexis de Tocqueville. In early October Dana headed to other countries where republican uprisings had erupted. In Cologne he met Karl Marx, whom he described as having "the strongest . . . and most accomplished intellect which . . . approached the labor problem from a workman's point of view." From there, Dana proceeded to Frankfurt, Berlin, and Vienna. Back in Paris in December, he covered the election of Louis Napoleon, the great emperor's nephew, to president of the Republic, a sign that the revolutionary fervor had been tamed. In late January 1849 he set sail for New York, having seen "plenty of revolutions" and charted their demise. The income from his letters supported his young family in New York, and he came back "only sixty-three dollars out for the whole trip," he recalled.[32]

The European experience left a strong imprint. Sensing how remote utopian communalism was from workers' real needs, Dana returned "no longer a Fourierist." Impressed by Pierre-Joseph Proudhon's program, he praised interest-free "mutual banks" and cooperative stores and workshops. He had come back "freed from all exclusive devotion to any special method of helping the world into a better case," he told friends. "A sincere blow struck anywhere" would bring progress.[33] That blow might involve force. When a Fourierist colleague called the European revolutions a mistake and decried their violence, Dana responded angrily. France's uprising was preferable to a peace dominated by reactionaries. "The privileged and powerful, by whatever name they are called, do not yield their privileges except as they are compelled."[34]

Dana was no Marxist. Revolutionary violence was legitimate to topple kings, but after that the ballot should eliminate monopolies and enact economic reforms. Still, the European revolutions reinforced Dana's longstanding hatred of privilege. They convinced him that aristocratic elites would not voluntarily disband and acclimatized him to violence against them. If a climactic war should erupt in Europe between despotism and aristocracy on one side, and political liberty and "social freedom" on the other, as Dana predicted, he made it clear to *Tribune* readers where his loyalties lay. Over the next decade Dana mapped this dire scenario onto the United States, where Southern slave owners were provoking an analogous showdown. Despite its republican institutions, the United States was not so different from Europe.[35]

In addition to highlighting politics as an arena of social struggle, the 1848 revolutions sharpened Dana's journalistic skills. Reporting from the scene, he cultivated a participant-observer method of sketching incisive descriptions, ferreting out hidden motives, and offering quick judgments. The American journalist, Dana wrote, "is no dull analyzer; . . . [h]is enthusiasm . . . concentrates itself upon persons and deeds and makes him almost a part of the occurrence he describes. His element is action and his method rapidity." Over the next fifteen years these techniques enlivened Dana's *Tribune* articles and produced his valuable Civil War reportage for the Union government.[36]

Dana's reports from Europe showed that he had matured into a shrewd and often skeptical judge of character. His eyewitness assessments punctured "the illusions and halos of distance." Louis Napoleon was not "a man of sufficient intellect and character to be capable of genuine sincerity"; he would "rather be Emperor than President." Republicans and leftists were not spared: Alphonse de Lamartine uttered only glittering generalities, and Louis Blanc was fatally indecisive. In short, Dana saw "all sorts of intrigue and stupidity" at work among the parties.[37] It is going too far to say that Dana's European experience transformed him into the cynical, misanthropic editor of the post–Civil War decades. But glimpses of the crooked timber of humanity in Europe began to erode his trust in public figures.[38]

More immediately, the revolutions opened a connection between the *Tribune* and Karl Marx. In 1850 Dana invited Marx, exiled in London, to become a foreign correspondent. Dana needed letters with European news, and Marx, crammed with his family into a dingy Soho apartment, desperately needed money. "The situation was quite different when Dana knew us in Cologne," Marx's wife Jenny told a friend. "Such a comfortably situated American has no idea how . . . ten shillings, coming at the right moment, can often rescue one from a horrifying situation." Dana initially hired Marx to write a series of articles on the German revolution, which his collaborator Friedrich Engels produced. After that, Marx and Engels averaged two letters a week on European affairs for the next several years. About three-quarters were written by Marx, initially in German translated by Engels, later in Marx's rapidly improving English. For the next decade the *Tribune* was Marx's main source of income as he struggled to write socialist treatises and fend off his landlord and creditors.[39]

Marx was a brilliant and acerbic polemicist who pulled no punches against bourgeois reformers as well as conservative "villains." Dana tolerated his dismissal of liberal nationalists such as Louis Kossuth because he offered unique insights. "Mr. Marx has very decided opinions of his own," Dana told *Tribune* readers, "with some of which we are far from agreeing; but those who do not read his letters neglect one of the most instructive sources of information on the great questions of current European politics." Dana printed portions of Marx's and Engels's letters (especially Engels's) as unsigned editorials, a practice they initially encouraged. "For 8 weeks past," Marx gloated to his collaborator in December 1853, "Marx-Engels have virtually constituted the editorial staff of the *Tribune*."[40] Increasingly Marx complained that he was underpaid and frequently overdrew his account. Still, he and Engels relished the chance to place their views on an astonishing range of subjects before the American public: not only the European revolutions but also the Taiping Rebellion in China, British Rule in India, Russian expansion, European labor movements, English parliamentary debates, and developments in military technology. The *Tribune* solidified its place as the most cosmopolitan American newspaper by commissioning such commentary, and Dana burnished his reputation by appropriating it for his editorials.

While Marx cursed capitalism for his penury in London, his friend at the *Tribune* dove with gusto into New York's competitive race. Due to the city's national prominence, Dana exulted, "my best ambition has open to it the widest sphere of action and influence." Dana poured his energies into the *Tribune*. He took the lead in improving the paper's format and separated advertisements from news columns. His special province, the foreign correspondence, he pronounced "first rate." "Your letters are a great card," he wrote Bayard Taylor in Stockholm, then added the names of Marx in London and "a whole tribe of new men in various localities." The *Tribune* is "far better in every respect than ever." With multiple voices heard in its pages, it "ceases to be the paper of any one person"—a pointed reference to Greeley—and has "become a great public organ."[41]

Dana's financial fortunes grew with his responsibilities. His salary rose gradually from $25 to $40 and then $50 per week by the outbreak of the Civil War. It was supplemented by the *Tribune*'s semiannual stock dividends. In 1849 Greeley turned the *Tribune* into a joint-stock association—a mechanism both Fourierism and capitalism endorsed—divided into 100 shares at $1,000 each. Five shares were set aside for Dana, who purchased them with a combination of cash and dividend credits.[42] "I regard the property as unequalled," he confided to a friend, "as good as real estate, or better." To take advantage, he borrowed money from his well-heeled Fourierist friend Henry James, Sr. (father of the novelist) to raise his total to ten shares by mid-1854. During good years the paper's dividends tripled his earnings.[43]

Still, Dana's household budget remained tight and debts accumulated. He borrowed from *Tribune* associates and was slow to repay. "The fact is," he explained to James Pike in 1856, "the bills for last six months' household expenses pile up awfully for a young father of a family." Things soon got worse. In the fall of 1857 railroad and currency speculation in Europe and America crashed in a financial panic and depression. "I never witnessed anything like it," Dana wrote Taylor, who was touring Europe. "There is ruin everywhere. . . . Banks all stopped, merchants failed, factories closed, workers turned out of employment." The *Tribune* suspended dividends for a year and Dana scavenged for funds.[44] "Retrenchment is the order of the day," he told friends. "We don't expect to live in that high and luxurious style which in the days of vanity we did too much delight in." The Danas reduced their household staff and took in boarders. Throughout the 1850s, partly because of the swings of the economy, Dana was habitually concerned about money, even while his income allowed him to live in middle-class comfort if not luxury.[45]

Home ownership became a badge of Dana's respectability. In 1856 the Danas purchased 90 Clinton Place (now East 8th Street), a brick townhouse in a tree-lined neighborhood that was gradually being encroached upon by commercial buildings. About a mile up Broadway from the *Tribune* office, it was close to Washington Square and the Astor Library. Eunice became a skilled household manager, directing servants and keeping a close eye on expenses. She ran a tight ship, but Dana's letters to friends suggest that their marriage was a happy one.[46]

Settled into a comfortable home, by the late 1850s Dana was able to entertain a circle of journalistic friends, including George Ripley, Henry James, Sr., Parke Godwin, George W. Curtis, Thomas Hicks, Richard Henry Stoddard,

Charles Dana in the mid-1850s, flanked by artist Thomas Hicks (*left*) and author George William Curtis, Brook Farm associates who also sought their fortunes in New York City. Lithograph after photo by Mathew Brady. Print Collection, Miriam and Ira D. Wallach Division of Arts, Prints, and Photographs, New York Public Library, Astor, Lenox and Tilden Foundation.

and Frederick Law Olmsted. Most were aspiring New York artists or literati, and several were veterans of the Fourierist movement. E. L. Godkin, longtime editor of *The Nation*, later recalled Dana's "pleasant evening receptions . . . to which I was glad to be invited." Dana's Brook Farm background, Godkin wrote, "was a feather in his cap with the numerous *fidèles* that thronged his parlors."[47]

Above all, Dana delighted in his children. Coming from a broken family, Dana was determined to be a good father. No child under his roof would be sent away or scolded for having an independent mind. By August 1854 three more Dana children had arrived: Ruth, Paul, and Eunice, called "Minnie" by her parents. Dana's frosty Fourierist critique of the selfish and unhappy "isolated family" melted in the warmth of the domestic hearth. "There's no delight like that in a pack of young children—of your own," he wrote James Pike. "Love is selfish, friendship is exacting, but this other affection gives all & asks nothing. The man who hasn't half a dozen young children about him must have a very mean conception of life." Most summers Eunice and the children escaped the heat of the city by retreating to a cottage on the Connecticut shore. On Sundays Dana found the place a "cool and delightful" refuge from the *Tribune* office. He drove the children around in a one-horse wagon, sailed with them on Long Island Sound, gathered shells and berries, and spent evenings "gazing into the sky with the whole tribe about me."[48]

For weekday respite from home and office and to maintain physical vigor, Dana took up daily horseback riding, a ritual made more picturesque when the first winding drives of Central Park were opened in 1860. Dana became an assured horseman and occasionally a participant in horse races. His riding habit spread to other *Tribune* staff and became so well known that a New York humor magazine printed a cartoon claiming that he had established a "hossback" club, a pun that poked fun at his loyal backing of Greeley for political office.[49]

After several years at the *Tribune*, Dana's daily routine was set and his personality merged with his profession until the two seemed indistinguishable. Walt Whitman, a fellow journalist and avid people-watcher, often encountered Dana walking briskly down Broadway to the *Tribune* office. Whitman sketched him as "a straight, trim-built, prompt, vigorous man, well-dressed with strong brown hair, beard, and mustache, and a quick, watchful eye. He steps alertly by, watching everybody . . . a man of rough, strong intellect, tremendous prejudices firmly relied on, and excellent intentions."[50]

During one such encounter in 1855, Whitman showed Dana a private letter from Ralph Waldo Emerson that praised the fledgling poet's just-published *Leaves of Grass* as "the most extraordinary piece of wit & wisdom that America has yet contributed." Dana had written a favorable *Tribune* notice of *Leaves of Grass* a few months earlier—the first review to appear in print. He persuaded Whitman to let him publish in the *Tribune* what became the most famous letter in American literature. "I greet you at the beginning of a great career," Emerson gushed, an endorsement whose value both the newsman and the poet understood. Whitman stamped the quotation on the spine of *Leaves of Grass*'s second edition. All this occurred without permission from Emerson, who was understandably annoyed, but it gave a huge boost to Whitman's visibility and reputation.[51]

At this stage of his career, Dana, unlike Whitman, was more interested in financial stability than literary acclaim. Dana's anthology of short verse, *A Household Book of Poetry*, provided some royalties. Including within one volume "whatever is truly beautiful and admirable among the minor poems of the English language," the collection appeared in 1858, sold briskly, and was revised in 1866 and 1882. Catering to the genteel tastes of middle-class readers, Dana included poems of several *Tribune* colleagues, but he found Whitman's verses too unpolished to qualify. "Lord, how the omitted poets growl over it," Dana wrote a friend, perhaps with Whitman in mind. Only the last edition included half a dozen short offerings by Dana's rough-edged friend.[52]

Dana's most ambitious publishing venture was the *New American Cyclopedia*. This "popular dictionary of general knowledge" was a joint project of Dana and his Brook Farm mentor George Ripley. They wrote few articles but decided upon entries, solicited contributions, supervised editorial associates, and kept the enterprise on schedule. To fill its pages, Dana recruited Greeley, George Bancroft, Theodore Parker, Ralph Waldo Emerson, Richard Henry Dana, Frederick Law Olmsted, Orestes Brownson, and other luminaries as contributors. Knowing that Karl Marx was desperate for funds, Dana hired him for the *Cyclopedia*. Together, Marx and Engels contributed more than sixty articles on history and military affairs, earning two dollars per printed page.[53]

The first volume appeared in 1858; the other fifteen were released over the next five years. Critics pointed out that the reference work was not comprehensive or deep, like the esteemed *Encyclopedia Britannica*, but it provided a convenient reference guide filled with up-to-date subjects of American interest. The initial volumes sold less than spectacularly in the wake of the 1857–1858 slump: the publisher sent out between five thousand and ten thousand copies, Dana reported. Eventually the completed set netted Dana and Ripley an annual income of several thousand dollars; but those royalties did not accrue until after the Civil War.[54]

Although neither Dana nor Ripley had become wealthy, during the 1850s both Brook Farm veterans left behind the social radicalism of communal experiments for newspaper journalism and middle-class respectability. In other ways their lives diverged. For the next three decades, Ripley settled comfortably into his position on the *Tribune* as the dean of American book reviewers. He was, James Parton noted, "a gentleman of sound digestion and indomitable good humor" who believed that "anger and hatred are seldom proper, and never pay."[55] Decorous, generous, and a bit stodgy, Ripley retired from social activism to enjoy the secluded life of a genteel man of letters. Dana, meanwhile, remained energetic and opinionated and became increasingly engaged in politics. In partnership with Greeley, the *Tribune*'s junior editor injected his fighting spirit into the mounting sectional quarrel over the fate of slavery and, with it, the future of a divided nation.

2 "A Party against the Slave Power"

By the mid-1850s Charles Dana and Horace Greeley's attention became riveted on the struggle between free and slave states over slavery's expansion and its hold on the national government. Both editors agreed that the *Tribune* should stand against the machinations of the "Slave Power" in Washington and Kansas, but differences in journalistic styles and political tactics complicated their partnership.

Dana, ever the agitator, wanted the *Tribune* to awaken indifferent readers, shake up smug politicians, and not flinch "because what we have to say will be offensive to nine-tenths of the world." He preached this creed to the paper's contributors, especially in wisecracking letters to James S. Pike, the Maine abolitionist he hired as the paper's Washington correspondent. Pike's slashing attacks on proslavery politicians and their Northern allies delighted the managing editor: "They were great & good, and stirred up the animals, which you as well as I recognize as one of the great ends of life." Pike and allied *Tribune* correspondents were, an associate wrote, "resolute, brilliant, capable, [but] . . . not above setting things on fire for the fun of seeing them burn." Dana encouraged their antislavery outbursts and became associated with the "unbending radicals." Meanwhile, Greeley grew more cautious, anxious to woo opponents into coalitions and incurably ambitious for public office. Dozens of fretful letters to Dana expressed Greeley's frustration with his sharp-tongued adjutant when his more combative voice reverberated through the *Tribune's* columns.[1]

Despite temperamental differences with his superior, during the antislavery struggle Dana generally adopted Greeley's editorial line. Sometimes he was persuaded that Greeley was right; other times he kept the peace by respecting Greeley's prerogative as chief editor. Even when Greeley's absences and lax oversight gave Dana leeway to voice his opinions, they were most often Greeley's own sounded in a harsher key. Not until Lincoln's election and the secession crisis did the two men's personality clash produce deep political disagreement.

Change of Allegiance

At the beginning of the 1850s neither Greeley nor Dana was preoccupied with slavery. The *Tribune*, pledged to the Whig Party, promoted its program of tariffs and economic modernization. Greeley added favorite causes like temperance and free homesteads in the West to lend the Whigs a progressive tint; Dana's distinctive addition was worker cooperatives, whose plans he brought back from Paris in 1849. Still influenced by Fourierist thinking, the editors claimed to find the North's cutthroat "wage slavery" as troubling as bondage in the South.

The *Tribune* did, however, take a firm stand against the extension of slavery into territories acquired from the Mexican War. In 1850 Henry Clay introduced a series of measures to save the Union from a fatal division over the issue. Greeley and Dana sat among the spectators during Senate debates on the Compromise of 1850. They applauded New York senator William Seward when he invoked a "higher law than the Constitution" to condemn slavery, and they initially opposed the Compromise and its provision for local control in the New Mexico territory as a scheme to "plant slavery on Free Soil."[2]

Yet in the summer of 1850 the *Tribune* shifted course to align with "Cotton" rather than "Conscience" Whigs. President Zachary Taylor died suddenly and was succeeded by New York's Millard Fillmore, a conservative Whig. Greeley, believing party unity essential, parted company with antislaveryites. Behind Greeley's back Dana criticized Daniel Webster for endorsing the Compromise and promised Pike to "hit 'em hard" in the *Tribune*. But Greeley set the editorial line, and he declared that by admitting California as a free state and thwarting Texas's grab of New Mexican lands, the Compromise was essentially a Northern victory, even though it countenanced extending slavery in the New Mexico and Utah territories, and despite the fact that both editors detested its tough provision against fugitive slaves.[3]

The *Tribune* editors swallowed hard in 1852 when the Whigs nominated the war hero Winfield Scott, who supported the Fugitive Slave Law. Privately Greeley considered Scott an "aristocratic, arbitrary ass" and repudiated his proslavery views, but he and Dana pumped Scott in the *Tribune*. Dana urged Pike to write "sharp, slashing & spicy" articles on the Democratic aspirants, but added, "the Whigs we must hold our tongues about, . . . though I should like to have a bout at them too." The Whig Party was declining, in part from rifts dating from the Compromise of 1850, and Scott's nomination did little to revive it. Dana told Pike he expected Scott to be "licked" by the Democratic candidate, Franklin Pierce, who triumphed easily. "I am ready for that [defeat]," Dana wrote, and have "set about sharpening my knives and getting out my war-paint, and practicing the battle-yell for the sharp work and joyous which is to come after."[4]

The post-election fight turned on the growing sectional divide over slavery. Northerners' bold resistance to the new Fugitive Slave Law pleased Greeley and Dana and encouraged them to toughen their editorial stand. Just a few doors down from the *Tribune* building on Nassau Street, Sidney Howard Gay, editor of the *National Anti-Slavery Standard*, ran a busy Underground Railroad operation that assisted hundreds of runaway slaves in transit to freedom farther north. The *Tribune*'s editors were aware of Gay's activities, and they used their paper's office to collect contributions for the defense of captured fugitives. *Tribune* editorials proclaimed the abolitionists' right to speak out and even scolded Greeley's hero Clay for scoffing at Northern opposition to slave-catching. In 1858 Greeley and Dana hired Gay as an assistant editor, and he continued to aid fugitives right up to the Civil War.[5]

In the interim, slavery's westward expansion, not the fate of its fugitives, became the *Tribune*'s galvanizing issue. In June 1852 Dana gave a lecture on slavery before a Chicago audience, his most extended statement on the subject. Its text is now lost, but Dana's friend James H. Wilson had a copy and summarized its contents. Dana strongly affirmed his opposition to the westward spread of slavery, and he assured listeners that the institution, once checked, would wither in the border states and concentrate in the cotton South. Even there, the efficiency of free labor and the march of moral progress would gradually snuff it out. Dismissing the prospect of a mass slave uprising or a reactionary revolt by secessionists, Dana declared that "the United States will extinguish slavery before slavery can begin to extinguish the United States."[6]

Events soon shook that confidence. Stephen Douglas's Kansas-Nebraska Act of 1854, in defiance of Greeley and Dana's Free Soil program, opened the remaining Louisiana territory north of the Missouri Compromise line to slavery under its "popular sovereignty" provision. When Douglas, known as the "Little Giant," steered his bill through Congress, Greeley mournfully removed the American flag from atop the *Tribune* building. He labeled the law a fraud perpetrated on the American people by the Slave Power, a coterie of proslavery Southerners and their Northern allies. Pike sounded the alarm to *Tribune* readers: "The revolution is accomplished and slavery is King!"[7]

Dana and other insiders later recalled that Greeley sank into a hopeless funk after the law passed. He doubted it could be reversed and "told his associates he would not restrain them, but as for himself, he had no heart for the strife." As a result, the *Tribune*'s vigorous campaign against the Kansas-

Nebraska Act was "fought with his consent . . . but with very little active aid and little encouragement." Instead, it was Dana, with his colleague Pike and the *Tribune*'s Kansas correspondents, who led the charge.[8]

Greeley's political instincts remained conservative; he hoped the Whigs would adopt the Free Soil position even while they split along sectional lines over Douglas's law. For a decade Greeley had hewn to an uneasy alliance with the "Albany Dictator," New York Whig Party boss Thurlow Weed, and his protégé Seward. Their interests often coincided, but Greeley's commitment to reform sowed discord, and a series of blows weakened the alliance. Over time, Seward and Weed became convinced that the white-coated idealist was temperamentally unfit for office. Increasingly they turned to the more conservative *New York Times*, founded by Greeley's former employee Henry J. Raymond in 1851, as a reliable ally.[9]

The climactic break came during the Kansas-Nebraska uproar, when Weed rejected Greeley's bid to become New York's governor, handing the nomination to the party's anti-immigrant faction over the Free Soilers. Adding insult to injury, Weed chose Raymond for lieutenant governor, signaling his shift of patronage from the *Tribune* to the *Times*. Greeley was devastated by the snub, but his deputy Dana sensed an opportunity for their paper to guide the emerging political realignment. "The Whig Party being annihilated beyond redemption," he advised, "the *Tribune* becomes an independent paper in a position to wield a power which no partisan journal could hope for." Greeley penned a long, bitter letter to Seward in which he listed his grievances and declared the "firm of Seward, Weed and Greeley" dissolved. Years later, Greeley revealed that he sent the letter only after Dana had read it and steeled his nerve.[10]

Abandoning the Whigs, Dana and then Greeley became cheerleaders for the nascent Republican Party, a political coalition formed expressly to keep slavery out of the territories. In June 1854 Dana traveled on a Great Lakes steamboat to Chicago and proceeded to Iowa, where he and the *Tribune* correspondent Adam Gurowski assessed prospects for an "anti-Nebraska" party. Not long after, Greeley, his fight returning, attended organizing conventions in Pittsburgh and Philadelphia, which he saw as "the beginning of a National movement designed to unite all the opponents of Slavery Extension" for the election of 1856.[11]

In the Republicans' promotion of "free soil, free labor, and free men" Dana found a fitting successor to his radicalism of the 1840s. Instead of assailing the shortcomings of free-labor capitalism, he was now defending it against its proslavery enemies; but in other ways the distance from Fourierism was not great. The utopian socialists had called for free western lands, and Dana and

Greeley injected this program into the Republican agenda. More important, by opposing slavery's extension Dana championed opportunity for common freemen. His resentment of reactionary elites and class privilege—a product of his humble origins and European experience—now targeted the South. When he described slavery as "despotism" and slaveholders as aristocrats, Dana mapped his class analysis of the revolutions of 1848 onto American society, where the struggle between freedom and oppression crystallized over western expansion. The urgent mandate to stop the spread of slavery supplanted the distant dream of organizing a perfect society. It became, according to his friend Wilson, "the chief aim of Dana's life, the central subject of his thoughts and actions, and he threw himself into it with all his energy and determination."[12]

The Politics of Antislavery

While the Whig Party declined and the upstart Republicans organized, a third party vied for voters in the North and Upper South. The American Party, or Know-Nothings—so-called because they originated among secret organizations—exploited Protestant fears over the rising tide of Irish Catholic immigrants and mounted campaigns against local political machines. The new party achieved a stunning success in the 1854 elections by capturing offices in several Northern states and electing seventy-five congressmen. Mindful that the slavery issue could split them, the Know-Nothings avoided it by broadcasting patriotic rhetoric and urging obedience to existing laws.

Greeley and Dana saw an opportunity to exploit the Know-Nothings' discomfort over slavery, but characteristically they took opposite tacks. Dana went on the offensive. He assured Pike that "the Know-Nothings shall never be mentioned again in the *Tribune*, except to give 'em a devil of a whack. . . . It's war, and there's no use talking peace." At a St. Patrick's Day dinner in New York, Dana spoke "as one whose Americanism dates from the rock of Plymouth": "[It is] a disgrace, not merely to our country, but to our century, that the accident of birth under this or that sky, should be made the standard of fitness for citizenship."[13]

With Greeley on an extended European trip, Dana plotted to siphon off the nativists' antislavery followers to the Republicans. There could be no neutrality on slavery's expansion, the *Tribune* declared before the American Party convened in Philadelphia. Dana hired Samuel Bowles, editor of a Massachusetts Republican paper, to infiltrate the convention, which was exposed anonymously in the *Tribune*. Dana gleefully baited the nativists by suggesting that the *Tribune*'s mole was a Jesuit priest in plain clothes.[14] A contingent of Northern delegates repudiated the Americans' platform, which upheld the Kansas-Nebraska Act. Dana praised these "Know-Somethings" as "high-souled men, and not cringing, heartless doughfaces," and advised them to join the Republicans "in an all-powerful and effective party against the aggressiveness of Slavery." When they defected he exulted to Pike that "the Know-Nothings, thank God, are in their graves." The victory declaration proved premature, for the American Party carried the fall 1855 elections in New York and Massachusetts.[15]

Greeley also aimed to weaken the Know-Nothings, but he favored conciliatory tactics and "fusion" over Dana's confrontational methods. Fresh from Europe, Greeley began a four-month sojourn in Washington to report to the *Tribune* and to promote Nathaniel Banks for Speaker of the House. A Massachusetts politico, Banks was a mildly antislavery Know-Nothing and a former Democrat, the kind of candidate Greeley believed could lure defectors from those parties to the Republicans and build their strength in Congress for the fight over territorial slavery.

The long struggle over the speakership frayed Greeley's nerves and exposed his frustration with Dana's bellicose tactics. The high-strung editor sent dozens of carping letters pleading with Dana over management of the *Tribune*. Greeley "had a complaining way, generally amusing from its quaintness," an associate recalled, but it was "apt to become petulance" if not mollified. With a flash of insight, Dana once traced the "querulous, helpless tone of feeling" that Greeley adopted when things did not go his way to childhood deprivations he never outgrew.[16]

"What would it cost to burn the Opera House?" Greeley snarled when Dana crowded out his political reports with a gossipy feature. "If the price is reasonable have it done and send me the bill." Greeley's temper changed daily as he canvassed the Capitol's corridors for votes and checked the *Tribune*'s reportage. He praised some of Dana's editorials, thanked him for inserting friendly material, and pronounced the new Saturday supplement "glorious." But the main note he sounded was exasperation. Dana used the *Tribune* columns to bludgeon Banks's opponents, who, he charged, were obstructing the cause of freedom by allowing proslavery gangs in Kansas to intimidate free-state settlers. Greeley, anxious to solicit opponents' support, howled. "If you were to live fifty years and do nothing but good all the time you could hardly atone for the mischief you have done," he scolded. "I write once more to entreat that I may be allowed to conduct the *Tribune* with reference to the mile that stretches either way from Pennsylvania Avenue. It is but a small space, and you have all the world besides." As Greeley lobbied a Banks opponent he claimed to be "in constant terror of seeing him guillotined in the next *Tribune*." In actuality, it was Greeley who was in danger: Dana's editorial stabs at one of Banks's more vocal opponents, Congressman Albert Rust of Arkansas, prompted him to assault Greeley with a cane outside the editor's Washington hotel. Yet Greeley was so eager to conciliate Democrats that he asked Dana not to publicize the incident.[17]

Dana promised penance and apologized for typesetters' mistakes, but he quickly backslid. "You wrote me that you would assail no member of Congress without first consulting me," Greeley pouted, "yet not a week elapsed before you come down in full force" on another Democrat who was a lobbying target. Dana told Pike he wished Greeley would be "hotter & sharper" with opponents, "but you must take men as the Lord makes 'em; and the Lord made Horace with a kind heart."[18]

It took nine weeks and 133 ballots to get Banks elected. Greeley, who exaggerated his influence and the *Tribune*'s, blamed Dana for prolonging the ordeal. When a congressman said he would have voted for Banks except for Dana's attacks, Greeley resorted to melodrama: "Of course I am not supposing the false knave would have done it at all; but you have given him . . . an excuse for not doing it, and the *Tribune* has to bear the credit of beating Banks—for to-day, certainly, perhaps forever." The next day, February 2, 1856, Banks was elected. Dana was forgiven for the time being, and Greeley's deputy again learned to take his boss's self-pitying plaints with heaps of salt.[19]

"Free Soil, Free Men, and Frémont"

Greeley stayed on in Washington to lobby for Congress to seat a free-state delegate from Kansas, where Douglas's bill had opened a free-for-all between proslavery and antislavery partisans. By early 1856 guerrilla warfare erupted between rival territorial governments, and President Pierce pledged armed support for the proslavery regime. What the *Tribune* called "Bleeding Kansas" became the focal point of mounting sectional conflict.

Because of Greeley's lecture tours, Dana had editorial charge of the *Tribune* during the crisis, and he made the most of it. He pledged that "all other issues will be postponed or subordinated till Kansas shall have been fully delivered from her oppressors." As the conflict escalated into violence Dana gave it global significance: upon it "hangs the prospects of republican government in the world," he told a crowd gathered at New York's Broadway Tabernacle.

The territorial battle between freedom and despotism was an American version of the European revolutions of 1848. "The eyes of all nations are turned here" as they had been to Europe eight years earlier.[20]

The crisis in Kansas propelled Dana and the *Tribune* to a new level of political involvement. Dana arranged for the abolitionist James Redpath, a rabid, restless Free Soil partisan, to cover events in Kansas. Redpath had been secretly sending dispatches to the *National Anti-Slavery Standard* and the *Tribune* describing conditions in the slave South; once redirected to Kansas, he labeled the territory's proslavery rule a "Reign of Terror" and urged *Tribune* readers to support the free-state advocates. Redpath himself took part in armed skirmishes against proslavery guerrillas: a photograph from this period shows him sitting on a barrel with a rifle in his right hand and a copy of the *Tribune* in his left.[21] Back in New York, the *Tribune* served as a clearinghouse for Kansas donations; Dana's local committee alone raised more than $20,000 in funds and clothing.[22] In June 1856 the paper's proprietors subscribed $1,000 to "the general movement for Free Kansas" and another $1,000 to the Republican National Committee. An additional drive raised money to arm the Kansas free-staters through the New England Emigrant Aid Company. "The guns have gone forward, and one of these days we shall certainly have a good fight there," Dana wrote Pike. He jokingly offered to nominate Pike for brigadier general.[23]

Greeley, who supported the Kansas free-state movement, nevertheless became alarmed by his deputy's hot rhetoric. He urged Dana "not to allow anything to get in [the *Tribune*] which seems impelled by hatred of the South or a desire to humiliate that section." He still hoped to win over non-slaveholders to the Republicans' anti-extension platform. "Charge Dana not to slaughter anybody, but to be mild and meek-souled like me," Greeley wrote Pike—perhaps the *Tribune* associate least likely to follow such advice.[24]

In fact, Dana was toning down Pike's threats, borrowed from Garrisonian abolitionists, that the North would secede from the South, which were intended to scare slaveholders into submission or else cause a separation. In Pike's case, this strategy was fueled by a virulent Negrophobia, which Dana abhorred, that envisioned a crescent of "Africanized" Gulf states cast from the Union.[25] "You are wrong to talk of disunion," Dana told Pike. Thrashing the proslaveryites could be done "more effectively in the Union than out of it" by winning in Kansas and securing the White House. Dana paid Pike for his letters but kept them out of the *Tribune*. "If you will come around to our side & help hang the southern fools," he wrote Pike, "I dare say you can get into the [Republican] church again. How would you like a foreign mission?"[26]

Dana was dangling in front of Pike potential spoils from the hotly contested presidential contest of 1856. Passing over Douglas as too controversial, the Democrats turned to Pennsylvania's James Buchanan, a reliable doughface and an overseas diplomat during the Kansas crisis. Dana thought the Republicans should choose a military man and early on pointed to the western adventurer John C. Frémont, who eventually secured the nomination. His odds looked promising. The Know-Nothings had been split by slavery into sectional wings, as Dana had hoped; their Northern organization endorsed Frémont and the Southern one nominated former president Fillmore. The Republican coalition counted Old Whigs, Free Soil Democrats, and antislavery Know-Nothings among supporters. Even the New York Whigs, with Weed's belated blessing, had merged into the new party.

These developments struck Dana as signs that the Republican nominee had "great elements of popularity & success." Buoyed by Frémont's prospects, the *Tribune* editors published a campaign biography and several pamphlets. "Frémont is the man for us . . . and the only one," Dana wrote Pike, who had favored Supreme Court Justice John McLean. "Besides *he is the true metal*, and that I'll swear to, and more than that, if he is elected, *his Cabinet will be made up of our sort of men*." That included Greeley, who was angling to become Postmaster General.[27]

The Republicans were short of funds. Anxious to maintain business as usual, "the rich men here, who used to give to the Whigs, are now for Fillmore and Buchanan," Dana reported from New York. Doing his best to compensate, Dana threw himself into the campaign. He had never been "so absorbed by a single object," he told friends. He headed his Manhattan ward's pro-Frémont "Rocky Mountain Club" and gave more than a dozen speeches at Republican clubs in New York and Connecticut, touting "Free Territory for Free Men, and Frémont."[28] Dana was "astonished at the depth & ardor of the popular sentiment." "It is a great canvass," he wrote Pike, "for genuine inspiration 1840 couldn't hold a candle." During the campaign the *Tribune*'s aggregate circulation soared to a record 280,000. "The tide is rising with a rush as it does in the Bay of Fundy," Dana wrote his friend from Maine, "and you'll hear an awful squelching among the hogs and jackasses when they come to drown." If every free state voted for Frémont, as Dana predicted, "the Pathfinder" would be the next president.[29]

Dana's forecast proved too optimistic, but not by much. Frémont ran remarkably well, carrying eleven of the sixteen free states. Fillmore siphoned enough votes from the Pathfinder in Illinois and New Jersey to give them to Buchanan, who also took every slave state but Maryland. If the Republicans had taken Pennsylvania and Indiana or Illinois, Frémont would have entered the White House instead of Buchanan.

"We are beaten," Dana wrote Bayard Taylor in Europe, "but the power exhibited by this new and unorganized party is astonishing." Downplaying the Know-Nothings' spoiler role, Dana saw the Republicans' proper target in the Slave Power's continuing rule. "The attempt to found a party upon either Protestantism or nativism will always fail, and always ought to fail," he wrote Henry C. Carey. "Neither the Pope nor the foreigners ever can govern the country or endanger its liberties." In contrast, "the slave breeders and slave traders do govern it, and threaten to put an end to all other government than theirs. Here is . . . an issue on which we will as surely succeed in the long run, either directly or indirectly, as there is such a thing as truth and right."[30]

Dana and Greeley set out to broaden the Republicans' appeal by pressing an economic program featuring a homestead law, federal support for internal improvements, and a protective tariff—an updated version of Henry Clay's old "American System." The economic theme continued when the Supreme Court declared in the Dred Scott case that Congress could not outlaw slavery in the territories because the Fifth Amendment forbade taking a person's property without their consent. Dana saw the decision as a declaration of class warfare by slave owners: "It is a war upon free labor, it is a war upon non-slaveholders, whom the Court seeks to deprive of the power to protect themselves against the competition of slave labor." This charge complemented the *Tribune*'s strenuous efforts to publicize Hinton Helper's *Impending Crisis*, a popular tract published a few months after the decision in *Dred Scott* that argued that slavery blocked economic mobility for the South's nonplanter whites.[31]

Amid the firestorm over *Dred Scott*, President Buchanan's attempt to resolve the Kansas question provoked a rebellion in his own party. Backing a proslavery constitution approved by a local plebiscite that Free Soilers boycotted, Buchanan pressured Congress to admit Kansas as a slave state. Here Stephen Douglas drew a line: he opposed the corruption of popular sovereignty and chafed at slaveholders' stranglehold over Democrats. Douglas's stand infuriated Southerners, but it drew praise from antislavery Republicans who had cursed the "lying little villain" for his Kansas-Nebraska Act. Among them was Horace Greeley.[32]

Overnight, it seemed, Douglas became one of the *Tribune*'s favorites. On the Kansas question, Greeley declared, Douglas's course had not been "merely right—it had been conspicuously, courageously, eminently so." Greeley hoped to lure Northern Democrats to switch parties, or at least to drive a wedge between the Democrats' Northern and Southern wings by strengthening Douglas. He tilted toward supporting Douglas for reelection to the Senate over the Republican nominee, Abraham Lincoln. It was a slight that bedeviled relations between Greeley and Lincoln, who complained that the *Tribune* editor was wronging him by supporting "a veritable dodger" over a true Republican. At election time, Greeley withheld a direct endorsement of either candidate: "We *know* that Mr. Lincoln will prove an excellent Senator if elected; we *believe* Mr. Douglas cannot henceforth be otherwise."[33]

What about Dana? By this time he had concluded that Greeley's promotion of Nathaniel Banks for House Speaker had been a mistake; in his view, the Massachusetts opportunist had turned on Republican backers. No doubt Dana felt Douglas would do the same. Greeley fretted that his lieutenant would not toe the line. "I wish you would keep Dana advised in my absence at the West," Greeley wrote Schuyler Colfax. "He is shrewd, but green in politics, and don't keep his eye close enough to the field. I know how to favor the Douglas rebellion without weakening his Democratic standing, and shall continue to write, but there will be occurrences that need to be seized on the instant." In the end, Dana went along with Greeley's strategy of fattening Douglas in 1858 for the kill two years later. As Dana explained to Pike, "Douglas hasn't a chance at Charleston [the Democrats' 1860 convention site], and we crack him up, and call him the Dictator of the Democracy in order to render it all certain for him."[34]

Illinois Republicans won the popular vote, but Douglas controlled the state legislature and was reelected over Lincoln. Greeley's strategy bore fruit. Nearly two dozen Northern Democrats voted to submit the proslavery constitution to a local referendum; Kansas voters turned it down, vindicating Douglas, embarrassing Buchanan, and enraging Southern Democrats. As things turned out, Douglas's victory set in motion a sectional split in the last remaining national party.

Anticipating this, Greeley and Dana put a premium on unifying the Republicans for the next presidential campaign. Eager to nationalize their party's following, they stressed the party's conservatism. The *Tribune* promised no interference where slavery already existed, and Greeley even pledged to accept a slave state if it came in through legitimate popular sovereignty. To appease the Know-Nothings, Greeley called for a new registry law and a one-year interval between naturalization and the right to vote. This conservative turn spawned talk of nominating Greeley for governor in 1858, but Thurlow Weed again blocked the move.[35]

Angered but undeterred, Greeley resumed his conservative campaign, and Dana toed the line when Greeley left for California in the summer of 1859. His editorials called for antislavery Democrats, Know-Nothings, and former Whigs to rally under the Republican banner. Coalition was the Republicans' birth cry in 1854, Dana declared, and it would be the winning formula in 1860. Dana had come around to Greeley's view that fusion with the Know-Nothing remnants would benefit the cause. When his friend Pike expressed dismay about courting former foes, Dana defended his conversion: "I have simply pursued, and that with greater moderation and I think with greater caution than he exhibited, the course which Mr. Greeley started upon. I think he was right, & I think I have been right too."[36]

Dana, Greeley, and "Honest Abe"

The *Tribune*'s conservative turn dictated its approach to the 1860 presidential election. Again, as with Banks and Douglas, Dana went along with Greeley, partly to respect rank but also because he agreed that the Republican nominee had to attract independent voters in Pennsylvania, Indiana, and New Jersey, swing states where Frémont had fallen short.

William Seward was not the man. Greeley and Dana acknowledged that the New York senator was well qualified and pledged to support him if nominated. But the *Tribune* editors shunned Seward, in part for his connection with the unsavory Weed, whose protégés' plundering habits at Albany and Washington would taint Seward's candidacy. Dana warned Pike that attacking the Seward-Weed connection in print would violate "the Napoleonic principle of washing your dirty clothes in private," but he and Greeley circulated their objections through conversation and correspondence.[37] Most important, the *Tribune* editors judged that Seward did not have wide enough appeal among Northern voters to win. Seward's poor standing with the Know-Nothings—he had supported public aid to Catholic schools as governor—and his association with antislavery radicalism after his "Irrepressible Conflict" speech of 1858 would turn away conservative voters. "There is no question that if we are to be beaten, Seward is the best man to run," Dana told Pike.[38]

Dana personally preferred Salmon P. Chase. The Ohio governor was a former Free Soiler and Democrat and an ostensibly clean politician. Chase had swallowed his disappointment in 1856 and campaigned tirelessly for Frémont, proving to Dana that he was "ten times as much of a man" as Seward, who had delayed until near the election. Dana learned later that the Germans who held the balance of power in several midwestern states opposed Chase. Casting around for alternatives, Dana pronounced Nathaniel Banks "impossible" and the shady Senator Simon Cameron of Pennsylvania "a joke."[39]

Among the names Republicans floated, neither Dana nor Greeley seriously considered Abraham Lincoln. Dana knew little about him. Greeley, recalling the gangly freshman congressman he met in 1848 and the debater who challenged Douglas a decade later, remained unimpressed. Greeley began to warm to Lincoln after he came to New York to give a major antislavery address at the Cooper Institute in late February 1860. Greeley sat on stage while Lincoln documented with legalistic precision how the founding generation had empowered Congress to restrict slavery's expansion westward. The *Tribune* published Lincoln's speech the next day, and an accompanying editorial gushed that no one since the days of Clay and Webster had "made such an impression on his first appeal to a New-York audience."[40] Historians mark the Cooper Institute address as the event that vaulted Lincoln to national prominence: it was "the speech that made Lincoln president." Yet in the weeks after its report the *Tribune* made few editorial references to Lincoln, and even these suggested that Lincoln was a second-tier figure who would promote the Republican ticket but not be on it.[41]

By early 1860 Greeley had picked his own dark horse: Edward Bates of Missouri. This former congressman and onetime judge was a most unlikely and unpromising candidate: a stodgy old-line Whig, a former slaveholder, and the most conservative of the Republicans' presidential aspirants. But Bates filled much of Greeley's calculated bill for a "proper candidate." He was a westerner from a border-South slave state, a supporter of Fillmore in 1856 who might attract Know-Nothing votes, a quiet opponent of the Kansas-Nebraska Act, and solid on the tariff and internal improvements. Once Greeley coaxed Bates into endorsing the Republican plank on containing slavery, he had his nominee.[42]

Strangely, it required little effort from Greeley to lift his managing editor onto Bates's makeshift bandwagon. Dana's friends James Pike and Fitz Henry Warren, ardently antislavery *Tribune* correspondents, were stunned. "Horace is kinky," Warren confided to Pike, "but what has obfuscated Dana?" Warren was sure that Dana held his tongue to keep his job. He swore that hell would freeze over before he—and Dana, he thought—"volunteered to advocate a Southern man for the presidency." He added to Pike, "Don't read this to Dana."[43]

Dana, however, put aside his qualms and agreed that Greeley's man was the expedient choice. There was "no doubt as to Judge Bates's principles on the question of the superiority of Freedom over Slavery," Dana declared in the *Tribune*, citing Bates's freeing his own slaves and his opposition to Kansas-Nebraska. Privately, Dana explained that Bates met all potential Republican voters halfway. He was a conservative who could be supported by "the Old Whigs and Americans [Know-Nothings] of all the doubtful free states, and by the abolitionists of the others." With any other nominee the Republicans would face "the Fillmore split over again." "With Seward we are surely beaten," he told Pike, "[but Bates] may be elected. No one else can. That is the beginning, middle and end of the story."[44]

This time the *Tribune* editors miscalculated. Bates was barely acceptable to most Republican leaders and the first choice of few. In early May, border-state Whigs joined with conservative Know-Nothings to nominate John Bell of Tennessee and Edward Everett of Massachusetts. Desperate to preserve the Union, they patched together a Constitutional Union Party that conjured the spirit of Henry Clay but had no specific compromise to offer. The new party seized the conservative center and undermined Greeley's rationale for choosing Bates. Dana was despondent: "I reckon there is now nothing serious in the way of Seward's nomination," he wrote Pike. "We shall now have a straight candidate, an enthusiastic canvass, and a sure defeat at the end of it."[45]

Despair shifted abruptly to optimism when the Democratic Party split over slavery, following the script Dana and Greeley had sketched. In April 1860 the Democrats met at Charleston; when Stephen Douglas secured the majority the Deep South delegates, who demanded a federal guarantee of slavery in the territories, walked out. The same drama played out at Baltimore weeks later. In the end, the Democrats offered opposing candidates to the public, Douglas for the Northern wing of the party and John Breckinridge for the Southern. The election took shape as a four-way contest, offering the Republicans a golden chance at victory.

In mid-May the Republicans gathered in Chicago inside a huge temporary frame structure dubbed the "Wigwam." Seward was the clear front-runner, but caucuses were organized for Chase, Cameron, Lincoln, Bates, and a scattering of others. Greeley arrived several days early, shuffling around the convention hotels in his trademark white coat, accosting delegates and declaring that Seward could not be elected and Bates should be considered. Thurlow Weed, who controlled the New York delegation, had shut Greeley out, but the wily editor arranged to fill a vacancy from Oregon. Greeley spent much time working on the platform committee, but he made his distaste for Seward clear as he circulated among state delegations.

As the balloting drew near, Greeley was disappointed by Bates's unpopularity and Seward's opponents' inability to unite. Just before midnight on May 17 he wired the *Tribune* that Seward would probably be nominated. On the convention floor the next day, Greeley watched as Seward led the field on the first ballot but fell sixty votes short of a majority. The pivotal states of Illinois and Indiana favored Lincoln, and on the next ballot Seward's opponents, led by Pennsylvania, began to rally around the Rail-Splitter. By the third ballot enough delegates switched to declare Lincoln the winner. Greeley emerged from the Chicago fight with half a victory: his hoped-for groundswell for Bates never materialized, but his rival Seward had been defeated in a dramatic upset.[46]

While Greeley rode the rails back to New York, Dana published a long editorial that touted the Republican nominee's career. "Honest Old Abe" was a nickname that reflected Lincoln's "perfect integrity" and the affection of midwestern voters, but not his age: at fifty-two he was still—unlike Bates—"in the full vigor and bloom of manly maturity." Dana redirected praise he had previously issued to Bates. Zealous Free Soilers would like Lincoln, Dana declared, but "the moderation of his character . . . [and] the conservative tendencies of his mind" commended him to every Republican faction. A difference was that Lincoln was a "Man of the People" who had been "raised by his own genius and integrity from the humblest to the highest position"; for this he would be hailed by the masses. Lincoln's election, Dana concluded in the slang of the day, was "*a thing that can be done*," and he urged the party faithful to get to work.[47]

Greeley remained stubbornly tepid toward the nominee. In a signed editorial published shortly after his return, he acknowledged that "there is no truer, more faithful, more deserving Republican than Abraham Lincoln," but then he backpedaled: "When all the world is raining bouquets on the successful nominee, so that, if he were not a very tall man, he might stand a chance to be smothered under them, . . . I . . . reiterate that I think Judge Bates . . . would have been the wiser choice." It was a grudging endorsement at best.[48]

Greeley had failed to get Bates on the ticket, but he was delighted to have played a part in scuttling Seward's nomination. Reaction came swiftly from the Albany machine and New York journalists who had backed the state's favorite son. Weed fumed that Greeley's meddling had "misled many fair-minded men." The *Times*'s Raymond charged that Greeley had been plotting revenge against Weed ever since they had parted ways. Greeley's campaign against Seward's bid and Weed's resentment of it escalated their private rift into an open feud between Greeley's reform wing and the Seward-Weed faction, an inside war that divided New York Republicans for the next decade.[49]

"Back from Chicago." "Mrs. Greeley" returns from the 1860 Republican convention as a mourner shedding crocodile tears for William H. Seward while Charles Dana hands over an African American child labeled "Tribune": "While you've been taking care of our dear baby, I've done for Aunt Seward—she's a goner! . . . Poor thing! She was too good for this world!" *Frank Leslie's Budget of Fun*, July 15, 1860. Courtesy HarpWeek LLC.

Weed also took aim at Dana. The *Albany Evening Journal* accused Dana of personal hostility to Seward. Weed's evidence was obscure: a proposal Dana had endorsed after Frémont's defeat in 1856 to unite Republicans around his renomination in 1860. Dana replied that the "manifesto" in question "was hostile to nobody but the Democratic party." He had always received "exceeding kindness and courtesy" from Seward, but he opposed his nomination because he thought him unelectable. Dana slyly dropped a hint about other considerations "connected with the peculiar state of things at Albany, and the possibility of its transfer to Washington"—the corruption issue—but did not elaborate. In any case, Lincoln's majority in New York was "beyond all peril, whether from open foes or pretended friends."[50]

The *Tribune* rallied its readers behind the Republican ticket. Greeley and Dana collected Lincoln's speeches and the Republican platform in a speaker's manual, and the paper published so many campaign supplements—twelve-page issues on Saturdays—that the trustees called a meeting to complain. Dana defended the practice, Greeley seconded him, and the trustees gave in.[51] Greeley aimed his editorial pen on Stephen Douglas, whom he considered the most prominent candidate and the one most dangerous to Republicans. To those who took the word of "Uncle Horace" as gospel, the main contest was between the Republican platform—which Greeley claimed to have personally crafted—and Douglas, the "eminent Squatter-Sovereign."[52]

Dana was more certain of Republican victory than he had been in 1856. He predicted that Lincoln would carry New York by 30,000 votes.[53] Dana was also more enthusiastic than Greeley about Lincoln, in part because he sensed victory, but also because he warmed to Lincoln's biography. In an ironic twist, Greeley's Harvard-educated lieutenant seemed to appreciate Lincoln's rise from obscure origins more than his boss, whose background more closely resembled Lincoln's. Greeley's egotism apparently kept him from sharing the limelight with the Rail-Splitter. Perhaps he felt there was room for only one self-made hero in the *Tribune*'s columns. Perhaps, too, Greeley failed to recognize the patronizing tone of his annual exhortations to western audiences. Whatever the reason, Greeley never relinquished his condescending view of Lincoln as a backwoods, rather mediocre politician who was not up to the challenge of an impending civil war.

Dana felt otherwise, and his admiration grew as he became familiar with "Honest Abe." Speaking to New York's "Wide-Awakes," young Republicans who conducted torch-lit parades through the city's streets, Dana praised their "infusion of new life and strength into the old political ranks," and he added an encomium to Lincoln:

> They had for a candidate and an example a man who had always been wide awake; who through an unhelped life, had struggled on, determined to make for himself a name, till he has reached a position where he will be the next President. Not only his example, but also the principles he holds, have stimulated the young men of our country . . . [to] be on the side of freedom and right.

Lincoln's career, Dana declared in the *Tribune*, "proves our doctrine [of free labor] sound. He is Republicanism embodied and exemplified."[54]

While Dana was not a polished political orator, he spoke plainly and forcefully at Republican rallies. He worked a boisterous crowd for Lincoln and his running mate Hannibal Hamlin on Lower Manhattan's Bowling Green and addressed German Republican associations in their native tongue. He gave a rousing speech at a Cooper Institute rally to boost his friend Frederick Conkling over the Democratic congressional incumbent, Tammany Hall's John Cochrane. Dana told the fired-up audience that Cochrane was known for three things: "incomparable slackjaw," "readiness to eat dirt at every command of the conspirators for the extension of slavery," and "constant support of every scheme of administrative corruption." A few days before the election, Dana served as an honorary officer for a mass meeting of 10,000 Republicans at Union Square, where Seward gave a speech graciously promoting Lincoln.[55]

After Republican victories in Pennsylvania and Indiana in October, Dana declared Lincoln's election a fait accompli. Thinking the same way, prominent Deep South Democrats began to threaten secession. There the *Tribune* drew a line in Dana's unmistakable editorial voice. Three weeks before election day, he warned that the victorious Republicans would tolerate no talk of disunion. "To undertake to browbeat the North out of her convictions by threats of rebellion and revolution, is to renounce the whole machinery of popular elections, and convert our country into another Mexico or New-Granada, where each election is expected to be followed by a civil war between those who carried it and those who were defeated." Advocates of secession were "traitors . . . to the vital principle of representative institutions." If they were foolhardy enough to follow through on their threats, Northerners would close ranks to ensure that "the Union will in no case be shattered."[56]

On election night, a crowd assembled on the sidewalk in front of the *Tribune*'s bulletin board. As returns came in, a clerk climbed out to the second-story ledge to record them in chalk. One story above, Dana and Greeley opened the windows to hear the crowd cheering the latest results. They watched as the torch-bearing Wide-Awakes marched along Park Row and a band played in front of City Hall.[57] At midnight the presses began rolling with the news of Lincoln's election. "Honest Abe" took New York by 50,000 votes over the Douglas–Breckinridge fusion ticket, nearly twice the spread Dana had predicted. Lincoln carried all the free states except New Jersey, where the Republicans split delegates with Douglas Democrats. Breckinridge took nine states in the Deep South. The Upper South was divided among Bell, Breckinridge, and Douglas, who won only Missouri. Lincoln won just under 40 percent of the popular vote, but he captured the Electoral College by a large majority. The Republicans had learned the lesson of 1856: their presidential candidate needed no Southern votes if he could carry both the Northeast and Midwest.

Greeley looked on the Republicans' victory as a "conspicuous and glorious triumph." He did not expect "political harmony and quiet" right away, he told *Tribune* readers, but he was convinced that the secessionist agitation would "gradually and surely subside into peace." Even as contrary evidence accumulated, Greeley continued to believe that the loyal Southern unionist majority would calm the region's secession fever.[58]

Within a week of the election, the South Carolina legislature called a convention to consider what to do next. Its members argued that the Northern states had "denounced as sinful the institution of slavery" and denied the "rights of property" of slaveholders in the territories. They warned that the incoming president would wage war on slavery "until it shall cease throughout the United States." On December 20 their "Declaration of Causes" was ratified, and South Carolina officially dissolved its connection with the United States.[59]

While South Carolina's delegates deliberated, Greeley editorialized that if the cotton states decided to leave the Union they should be allowed to "go in peace." Contradicting Dana's preelection ultimatum, he declared that if secession was white Southerners' popular will, and if South Carolina could convince other states to join it, peaceful separation was preferable to the horrors of war. "Whenever a considerable section of our Union shall deliberately resolve to go out," Greeley wrote, "we shall resist all coercive measures designed to keep it in. We hope never to live in a republic, whereof one section is pinned to the residue by bayonets."[60]

As the crisis over slavery escalated through the 1850s, Charles Dana, tempering his more combative personality, had adopted Horace Greeley's conservative tactics and seconded his endorsements of doubtful antislavery men like Banks, Douglas, and Bates. But when slave states began leaving the Union after Lincoln's election, the two men's temperamental differences flared into an obvious editorial rift.

3   "Forward to Richmond!"

In February 1861 Albert D. Richardson, an adventurous young reporter fresh from a stint in gold rush Colorado, proposed that the *Tribune* send him to New Orleans to cover the secession movement. Entering the editorial office, he found Charles Dana at his desk sorting the day's mail: "Two or three glances appeared to decide the fate of each [letter]. . . . Some were ruthlessly thrown into the waste-basket. Others, with a lightning pencil-stroke, to indicate the type and style of printing, were placed on the pile for the composing-room." Hardly looking up, Dana warned Richardson that "two of our correspondents have come home within the last week, after narrow escapes. We have six still in the South; and it would not surprise me, this very hour, to receive a telegram announcing the imprisonment or death of any one of them." Richardson was determined to go and asked how long he should stay. "While the excitement lasts, if possible," came the answer. Finally Dana raised his head and leaned back in his chair. "Do you know how long you *will* stay? You will be back here some fine morning in just about two weeks." That was the *Tribune*'s hard-boiled managing editor speaking.[1]

Richardson took Dana's dare. Through a friendly New Orleans newspaper editor he was certified as a New Mexico Democrat and attended the Louisiana State Convention. Relying upon memory, he reproduced for *Tribune* readers the inflated rhetoric of secessionist hotheads, reserving praise for the brave resistance of a few Unionist delegates. After the convention ratified the Confederate constitution Richardson moved on to report on the Mississippi secession gathering at Jackson.[2]

Covering the secession movement was dangerous business for Dana's reporters. No Northern newspaper was so reviled in the proslavery South as the *Tribune*. A Texas sedition law declared it a felony to receive the paper, and Southern postmasters routinely returned it stamped "Undeliverable." Yet no paper featured more firsthand reports during the secession winter. Dana's reporters knew that they risked being banished, imprisoned, or perhaps hanged if discovered. All traveled in disguise: as rebel sympathizers, mercantile agents, or foreign tourists. Their letters were addressed to cooperating commercial houses or police inspectors in New York, then forwarded to the *Tribune*, where reports on secession conventions and war preparations were extracted from what appeared to be business correspondence or financial drafts. Particularly sensitive paragraphs were written in cipher.[3]

For all the derring-do of the *Tribune*'s secret correspondents, their reports were not as consequential as the paper's editorials. Atop page four, Dana and his chief Horace Greeley had to advise the public and politicians what stand to take toward secession once it became fact. Should the North let the South desert the federal union in peace? Should Republicans compromise on the issue of slavery to keep wavering border states in the Union, and perhaps to lure the Lower South back in? Would secession result in war if the North insisted that the South remain tethered to the United States?

"No Concessions to Traitors!"

For a decade Greeley had been blithely assuring Southerners that they could secede from the Union if they really wished. He could afford to be nonchalant because he was convinced it would never happen. Secession, Greeley proclaimed, was a threat that the South's vocal minority of "fire-eaters" issued to win concessions from Northern politicians. When South Carolina followed through on its supposed bluff, Greeley was taken aback but stuck to his principles. Southerners were free to "deliberately vote themselves out of the Union," and the Union had no right to force a wayward state to return. Coercion was probably unconstitutional and would surely result in war. Greeley had no stomach for the death and destruction of armed conflict, and a civil war would be "the most hideous of all wars."[4]

As Southern disunionism took hold, Greeley began to equivocate, tightening the conditions for separation. He declared South Carolina's defection unconstitutional unless other states departed with it. When other slave states voted to join South Carolina, he proclaimed their conventions unrepresentative and too hastily elected. The historian David Potter suggested that Greeley had been bluffing all along: he "had no more idea of dividing the Union than Solomon had of dividing the infant." Other scholars argue that Greeley's offer was sincere but based on his confidence that an independent Confederacy would be short-lived. Greeley's pronouncements could support either view, but at bottom they relied on a misplaced faith in Southern patriotism.[5]

Sincere or not, Greeley's talk about "peaceable secession" worried Republicans determined to stanch the Union's bleeding. President-elect Lincoln wrote Greeley in December to discourage disunionist rhetoric, and his political scout George C. Fogg told Dana the *Tribune*'s editorials were alienating Northern readers. On December 22, 1860, Fogg reported to Lincoln that he had a long talk with Greeley and Dana: "Hereafter the *Tribune* will contain no nonsense in favor of 'peaceable secession,' but will be in harmony with the great patriotic heart of the country."[6] The same day, Greeley penned a less reassuring reply to Lincoln. He declared again that a single state could not secede from the Union, but a group of seven or eight "large enough and strong enough to maintain a national existence" did have the right, as long as they followed a deliberative process. The Union might "slide" but it could be reconstructed in a few years. The "only real danger" was compromise on slavery in the territories. Lincoln found little comfort in the *Tribune* editor's vagaries. Both men nonetheless shared the belief that there were powerful pro-Union elements in Southern states waiting to assert themselves. If Republicans bided their time, cooler heads would prevail and Southerners would back off from secession.[7]

Dana nursed no such illusions. He had no greater firsthand knowledge of the South than did Greeley or Lincoln, but he believed their confidence in Southern Unionism was misplaced. Dana had witnessed revolutions in Europe, and he smelled a reactionary one among the proslaveryites. The secessionists were in earnest and in control of Southern white opinion. No matter how it came, secession was a dangerous reality that the North had to confront. In the face of this threat Greeley's notion of peaceful separation was hopelessly naive.

At the outset Dana's dissent from his boss was covert. As make-up editor of the *Tribune*'s weekly edition, Dana excluded many of Greeley's "peaceable secession" editorials from the most widely circulated version of the paper. More direct opportunities to assert his own views arose when Greeley handed the editorial reins to his associate. The longest hiatus occurred when Greeley embarked on a five-week lecture tour in mid-January 1861. During this critical period the Confederate government was formed, controversy arose over federal property in the South, and compromise schemes were introduced in Congress. Greeley mailed editorials back to New York City on peaceable secession and the horrors of war, but according to the *Tribune*'s night editor, Dana suppressed them. He was busy redirecting the paper's policy. It was a tricky business—to take over the paper unobtrusively, to shift its editorial tone, and to avoid angering Greeley. But Dana carried it off, partly because Greeley finally realized that his peace overtures were alienating his Republican backers.[8]

Dana's confrontational voice reverberated through the *Tribune*'s editorials. The Constitution protected Southerners' free speech, but "acts of resistance to the lawful General Government" were a different matter. Federal courts, postal buildings, and forts belonged to the American public, not to the states, and revenues must be collected at all ports. Even the Southern slave owner Andrew Jackson had proclaimed the president's duty to maintain the authority of the Union against nullifiers and secessionists, with force if necessary.[9]

Examining the issue under the head, "The Alleged Right of Secession," Dana argued that leaving the Union was nothing less than treason. The states were bound by an irrevocable federal Constitution and by their shared history. Citizens from both sections had fought or paid to acquire new territories, and Southern states could not walk off with their joint property. Slave states were not, as Greeley had written, "erring sisters" who might be allowed to "depart in peace"; they were traitorous brothers who were trying to abscond with the family inheritance. Northerners must preserve the Union as a guarantor of freedom and prosperity for future generations. This was the least they could do to be worthy of their ancestors.[10]

Many politicians of the era, including Lincoln, cast their generation as metaphorical "sons of the Founders" charged with preserving the sacred patrimony. For Dana this language struck a deep—if unacknowledged—emotional chord. His devotion to the "Founding Fathers," like Lincoln's, may have served as a surrogate for his own missing father. Dana's rage against secessionists probably gained force from his resentment of his father for breaking up the family and, in effect, seceding from his children after he remarried. Preserving the Union from usurpers avenged the "House Divided" of Dana's own childhood.[11]

Secession also tested Northerners' manhood, and they (and Dana) would prove that it remained intact by saving the Union. Contemporaries often described the decisive, deep-voiced Dana as "virile" and "manly," especially in contrast to his fickle, squeaky-voiced boss, who was frequently caricatured in political cartoons as a woman. During the secession crisis Dana and Greeley seemed to step into the gendered stereotypes their bearing and reputations had prepared for them, with Greeley pleading for peace and Dana girding for war.[12]

Propelled by a deep-seated, emotional unionism, Dana swept aside Greeley's constitutional quibbles for plain talk about political power. Politicians from the South had controlled the executive and judicial branches for a generation; it was time to yield to the more populous North. By not acknowledging Lincoln's victory, Dana charged, South Carolina was replacing America's constitutional system with the "Mexican system of rebellion" through bullets rather than ballots. The Union had to resist this counterrevolution at all costs, for a democratic government must have "the power of self-preservation."[13]

In any case, the facts of geography made dividing the Union impossible, Dana argued. Fugitive slaves would flee northward and prompt a government crisis. The Mississippi River was so vital to midwestern commerce that the federal government had to control it. As separate nations, the North and South would hotly dispute their boundaries and the western territories. And the United States could surely not tolerate any move by a Southern confederacy to establish ties with foreign and hostile powers. When rumors warned of a secessionist plot to seize Washington, Dana reminded readers that the capital was sandwiched between slave states. These realities guaranteed that war would break out if Southerners were allowed to secede.[14]

It would be a brief war, Dana assured *Tribune* readers. Early in 1861 he sketched the scenario for a powerful sectional siege. The Union navy would blockade the Southern coast, forcing the Rebels either to suffer economic privation or to route tobacco and cotton through the prosperous North. Many Southerners would clamor to rejoin the Union, but if the Confederacy sent troops northward, loyal Union men would rise up to crush them. In March Dana joined New York politicos at a breakfast for the *London Times* correspondent William Howard Russell. When a speaker warned that England might dispute a blockade, Dana told Russell that "the President could open and shut ports as he pleased." Dana's confidence in the Union's might whetted his appetite for war and distanced him from the squeamish Greeley.[15]

When proposals were aired to keep the peace by compromising on slavery or conceding federal property, Dana returned to common ground with Greeley, although his rhetoric was several degrees hotter. His editorials accused the lame-duck president, James Buchanan, of treason for failing to reinforce Fort Sumter and other federal strongholds in the South. If the Rebels wished to avoid war, they must return federal forts and arsenals to their "rightful owners." Meanwhile, Republicans should support no concessions to lure secessionists back or to keep the border slave states in tow. In January 1861 a proposed Thirteenth Amendment worded by Seward was introduced that prohibited Congress from interfering with slavery in states where it existed. This merely codified most politicians' and jurists' understanding of the constitutional boundary between state and federal powers. The *Tribune* called the proposal an example of "mistaken magnanimity" but saw it as harmless. "If the South is satisfied with that," Dana wrote Schuyler Colfax, "they are satisfied with a trifle that must seem ridiculous to all sensible men." The amendment passed through Congress and went to the states, but it did little to calm secessionist fever.[16]

Real concessions were out of the question. "No sir-ree!" Dana declared to Colfax, "I will never propose any compromise whatever." Lincoln assured Greeley during a brief interview in Springfield that he opposed any deal that might extend slavery. In the *Tribune* Dana praised the president-elect for holding the line and denounced Republicans who attended a peace conference in Virginia. While Lincoln stood firm, "his aides and his lieutenants waver and open their lines in the face of a desperate enemy." When Seward urged senators to conciliate the South, Dana quoted his earlier speeches against compromise.[17]

A menu of measures introduced by the Kentucky senator John Crittenden gained support among congressmen who hoped to settle the slavery issue short of war. The main provision extended the Missouri Compromise line westward to California; slavery would be forbidden in territories above the line and permitted below it. Dana denounced the Crittenden proposal. It would scuttle the Republican platform, void the November election, and open Mexico and Central America to proslavery adventurers. "If we compromise," Dana warned Republicans, we may keep the border states with us but we will have "neither a Government, nor a Union, nor a Republican party."[18]

In mid-February a new *Tribune* masthead made its debut in large bold type: "NO COMPROMISE! NO CONCESSIONS TO TRAITORS! THE CONSTITUTION AS IT IS." Dana led the *Tribune*'s editorials with it for two weeks. When Greeley returned he did not complain or remove it. Dana's diatribes against treason, the defeat of compromise measures, and the mounting crisis at Fort Sumter had changed Greeley's attitude. Now he believed that a show of Union force was the only way to quell secessionist sentiment.[19]

Shortly before Greeley returned to New York, Lincoln passed through the city on the way to the Washington inaugural. Dana watched the procession of carriages to the Astor House not far from the *Tribune* office. Thousands of spectators lined the streets of a city that had given Lincoln only a third of its votes. The impressive turnout showed Dana "how strong and undaunted is the feeling of regard the people entertain for the Union." The next day Lincoln breakfasted with two dozen wealthy Seward-Weed supporters, while members of Greeley's faction won only a brief audience. Still, Joseph Nye, a New York politician in the Seward-Weed camp, fretted. He told Seward that Greeley's associates tried to "induce [Lincoln] to believe that all of the Republicans were for war." Nye was disgusted: "Imagine Greel[e]y booted & Spurred with Epaulets on his Shoulders and with a whetted blade in his hands marching at the head of a column. . . . The idea . . . is too ridicul[o]us to be thought of."[20]

Ridiculous or not, Greeley had joined his managing editor in girding for war. Greeley sat behind Lincoln during his inaugural address, half-expecting it to be interrupted by the crack of a rifle shot aimed at the president. The *Tribune* praised Lincoln for assuring the South that the Constitution would be upheld and Union property secured. The question of legal secession had been bypassed, and the Union was faced with a de facto Confederate government. The *Tribune* advised against attacking the South but insisted that Lincoln reinforce Fort Sumter. If the secessionists resisted, the war would be one of self-defense.[21]

"Let us know once for all whether the Slave Power is really stronger than the Union," Dana had written months earlier. By April the Northern majority had come around. With Greeley nodding approval, Dana beat the war drums again: "Let this intolerable suspense and uncertainty cease! The Country, with scarcely a show of dissent, cries out—If we are to fight, so be it."[22] On April 6, 1861, Lincoln sent a messenger to notify South Carolina authorities that he would dispatch a relief ship to Fort Sumter to offload food but no men or ammunition. Six days later, the rebel government ordered local commanders to fire on Fort Sumter before the ship arrived. Lincoln had maneuvered Confederates into firing the first shot, underscoring Unionists' conviction that secession was a rebellion against legitimate national authority. After two days of relentless bombardment, the federal garrison surrendered. Miraculously, no soldiers were killed in the battle that began the bloodiest war in American history.

On April 13 the *Tribune* announced that Fort Sumter had been fired upon. After years of threats and subterfuge the Slave Power had "inaugurated in blood its more direct and manly efforts to subvert the Federal Constitution and Government, and build up a Slaveholding Oligarchy on their ruins." Dana conveyed palpable relief and a somber confidence: the fight had finally come and with it the determination to defend the Union. "Fort Sumter is lost," he declared, "but Freedom is saved." "The territorial integrity and the political unity of the nation" would be preserved, no matter the cost.[23]

The Battle over Spoils

Even as the specter of civil war hung over Republicans, many were preoccupied with the spoils of office. In early 1861 Washington became a mecca for patronage seekers. The customary postelection feeding frenzy was heightened by new circumstances: It was the Republicans' first-ever presidential victory; many federal officials had defected to the Confederacy; and the Republican coalition had several factions to placate. Petitioners besieged the president-elect, swarming like flies around a patient horse. Republican leaders, complained sometime *Tribune* correspondent Adam Gurowski, a Polish expatriate who worked as a translator in the State Department, "look to create engines for their own political security, but no one seems to look over Mason and Dixon's line to the terrible . . . spreading fire of hellish treason."[24]

The indictment was not totally fair. To Dana and his allies the contest for offices and the struggle over the Union were entwined. If key positions in the administration went to candidates who were soft on slavery or disposed toward compromise, the Union would be endangered. In New York, the divide between "conscience" and "compromise" Republicans coincided with the rift between factions led by the *Tribune* men and the Seward-Weed coalition. The overlap made New York's Civil War politics even more rancorous than usual as both sides claimed they were saving the Union by advancing their candidates.

Everyone assumed that Seward would give up his Senate seat to take a position in the new cabinet, although Dana and Greeley preferred to send him on a foreign mission. Rejected at Chicago because he was too radical, Seward actually leaned far more than Lincoln or the *Tribune* editors toward conciliating the South. Although he avoided taking public stands, his patron Weed printed trial-balloon editorials approving the extension of the Missouri Compromise line to the Pacific.[25] The *Tribune* denounced the idea, and Dana told Republican congressmen who visited his office that Weed was voicing Seward's ambition "to make a great compromise like Clay and Webster." As the rumor spread, a caucus of Republican senators became alarmed and interrogated Seward. On December 5 he issued a blanket repudiation of Weed's position and all compromise schemes. Lincoln felt that this closed the matter, and three days later he offered Seward the State Department. Dana's attempt to tar Seward with the brush of compromise was on target, but it failed to keep him out of the cabinet.[26]

Weed delivered a second blow to the *Tribune* editors in the contest to replace Seward as senator. Weed's choice was the New York City lawyer William Evarts, but Greeley, incurably hungry for office, sought the position. Dana went to work loyally and energetically. He puffed Greeley in the *Tribune* and traveled to Albany with the legal scholar David Dudley Field and New York City congressman Frederick Conkling to lobby legislators. When the New York legislature caucused on February 4 Greeley moved ahead of

Evarts but lacked a majority due to a stubborn block of votes for the former state supreme court judge Ira Harris. Weed, determined to block Greeley, swung his support to Harris, and the man Weed boasted he had "invented" became Seward's successor. Weed gloated that he had "paid the *first install-ment* on a large debt to Mr. Greeley." Greeley masked disappointment by claiming victory over the Weed machine, and Dana was furious. Both vowed revenge.[27]

While the Senate contest was heating up, Dana and his circle of New York Republican Radicals, which included Field, George Opdyke, and Parke Godwin, set to work lobbying for Salmon Chase to have Treasury. Chase, Dana editorialized, was adept in economic matters, and his firmness was needed in the secession crisis. Privately, Dana urged Chase to accept the posi-tion: "I do not refer to the slavery question, though I don't underestimate that, but to the plunder question"—stopping Seward and Weed's "thieves." Chase, who wore a morally punctilious façade to hide—unsuccessfully—his burn-ing ambition, protested that while he did not seek an appointment, if asked he would set aside "personal inclination" for his "obligation to the cause and its true and faithful friends."[28]

As Lincoln, mulling over a place for Simon Cameron, strung Chase along, he became more openly ambitious. Chase asked Opdyke to consult with Greeley and Dana and send a New York delegation to meet with Lincoln. Opdyke, Hiram Barney, and Greeley called upon the president-elect in Springfield to press Chase's appointment and to oppose Cameron's. Dana reported that the New Yorkers were sending letters for Chase and, believ-ing Cameron "disposed of," predicted victory. Again he urged Chase, whose "immoveable will" was the ideal antidote to Seward, not to refuse the post.[29]

On the night of February 24 Lincoln arrived in Washington secretly. He set up office in Willard's Hotel. Gathered in a nearby suite, Greeley, Field, Barney, and James Wadsworth lobbied Republican insiders for Chase and against Cameron. By the end of February Lincoln decided to take *both* men— Chase at Treasury and Cameron at the War Department—and to appease New Englanders by giving a place to Connecticut's Gideon Welles. According to Dana, who joined the group for the inauguration on March 4, the full cabinet slate was not revealed until the next day, when Opdyke and Greeley were del-egated to sound out Lincoln at the White House. When they returned, Greeley burst into the New Yorkers' room at the Willard. "Dashing his dilapidated hat upon the table," Dana recalled, Greeley "screamed in a tone half way between a squeak and a war-whoop, 'You may bet your pile on Old Abe!'" The anti-Seward group had gained four out of seven cabinet posts: Welles, Bates, and

Montgomery Blair in addition to Chase. All shouted for joy, and Wadsworth rang for tumblers.[30]

With barely a pause, the New York Radicals set to work on local federal appointments. Up for grabs were postmasterships, US Attorneys for the District of New York, treasury agents, and customs officials. By the Civil War the Customs Collector of the Port of New York had become a lucrative sinecure and a powerful source of patronage. Most of the post's 1,200 employees were political appointees, and its salary of $6,000 plus an estimated $20,000 earned through fees made it the plumpest of the "Fat Offices of New York."[31]

To Dana and the New York Radicals these appointments were Chase's "first test of strength" against Seward. Dana sent the Treasury secretary a barrage of requests. Opdyke should be appointed customs collector and Henry B. Stanton surveyor. No aspirant for US Attorney would match the Dana-Greeley man in working "for the stoppage of the slave trade." There was talk that Dana was being considered for a postmastership, but he apparently took himself out of the running.[32]

To bolster the New Yorkers' cause, Chase arranged for a delegation to call at the White House shortly after the inauguration. It was Dana's first personal encounter with Abraham Lincoln. The other delegates were Wadsworth, Opdyke, and Thomas B. Carroll. Wadsworth spoke for the group, urging that one faction not control New York patronage. The meeting was interrupted twice by a servant announcing that Mrs. Lincoln wanted to see her husband immediately. Wadsworth proposed that the delegates pay their respects to the First Lady. Mary Todd Lincoln granted them a brief interview and icily informed them that she never interfered with her husband's political affairs—a claim that no one believed. Lincoln, mortified by the interruption, told his callers to make up a list of recommendations. He knew that neither faction of New Yorkers had gone to Chicago to nominate him, but he appreciated the Republican Radicals (whom he called "reformed Democrats") for their campaign support and wished to avoid a party split. "One side shall not gobble up everything," Dana remembered Lincoln saying. He would "apply the rule of give and take." Dana came away impressed by the president's fairness: "We all felt that he meant to do what was right and square in the matter."[33]

In a few days Lincoln appointed Hiram Barney the New York customs collector. Dana was disappointed for Opdyke but proclaimed it a victory over Seward and Weed because Barney was Chase's man. Over the next month, amid the escalating crisis over holding federal forts in the South, callers besieged the White House clamoring for patronage posts. Lincoln compared himself to "a man so busy in letting rooms in one end of his house that he

cannot stop to put out the fire . . . burning in the other." Greeley, Field, and
Carroll followed up on the New Yorkers' visit, and Lincoln invited Barney to
Washington to confer. Barney and Thurlow Weed met, like seconds in a duel,
to frame a protocol on appointments between Chase and Seward. Finally, after receiving the advice of all parties, Lincoln divided up the New York appointments on April 15. It was the day after Fort Sumter surrendered to the
Confederates.[34]

Lincoln hesitated to give the Port Surveyor position to the Radicals because, in his words, it would put "two big puddings on the same side of the
board." But Stanton was eventually named Deputy Collector and the Free
Soiler Isaac Henderson Naval Agent. Nevertheless, Seward-Weed candidates
were given the majority of the customs offices. Although Lincoln attempted
a reasonable balance of interests, in the end he deferred to the state's delegation in Congress, as was the custom, and it was dominated by Seward-Weed
men. Barney, meanwhile, proved too friendly to the Albany machine for the
Radicals' tastes. Dana protested to Chase when Barney hired a dodgy *Herald*
reporter with a proslavery past and gave three upstate posts to Seward and
Weed men. For the duration of the war the distribution of New York patronage was a source of worry to Dana and a nagging headache for Chase
and Lincoln. Each appointment opened a skirmish in the contest between
Republican factions and, by implication, the war to crush the Southern rebellion.[35]

Bull Run

After the rebel guns roared across Charleston harbor at Fort Sumter, Dana
became an even more indispensable member of the *Tribune*'s staff. While
Greeley had little knowledge of military matters, Dana had pored over text-
books on military operations from the American Revolution to Napoleon. He
kept a large map of the United States on his office wall; there he familiarized
himself with rivers and railroads and followed troop movements.[36]

In the heady days after the fall of Sumter, both men sounded the war cry
with gusto. The *Tribune* praised the "sublime uprising of the unanimous and
devoted people" as a revival of republican virtue: "Yesterday we were esteemed a sordid, grasping, money-loving people, too greedy of gain to cher-
ish generous and lofty aspirations. Today vindicates us from that reproach,
and demonstrates that . . . the fires of patriotic devotion are still burning."
Furious that Southern leaders had violated the beloved Union, Dana urged an
aggressive, even vengeful war. The North should aim "not merely to defeat,

but to conquer, to subjugate" the Rebels, leaving "poverty at their firesides" and "privation in the anxious eyes of mothers and the rags of children."[37]

Dana and Greeley turned up the heat on Lincoln. Within days, the *Tribune* moved from counseling patience with the new administration to prodding it insistently, finally charging that it had "hesitated, temporized, waited" since the inauguration. Lincoln's call for 75,000 volunteers was inadequate; the *Tribune* advised raising it to half a million. Instead of placating the border states, Lincoln should force them to choose between loyalty and treason. The city of Baltimore, where a pro-Confederate mob had attacked Union soldiers on their way to Washington, should be leveled. Liberal with their advice, the *Tribune*'s editors offered a six-point strategy for Union victory that included the military occupation of Maryland, declaration of martial law in rebellious states, a reward for the arrest of Jefferson Davis, and—most important—an "advance upon Richmond and the armed holding of that city."[38]

Dana brought the *Tribune*'s mounting impatience to a fateful climax when primary responsibility for directing the paper shifted to him. In mid-May Greeley gashed his knee with an ax while trimming trees at his Westchester County farm. The wound healed slowly, forcing him to stay at home for several weeks. While Greeley chafed at Chappaqua, Dana roused *Tribune* readers for a decisive military offensive. On the morning of June 26 a new slogan blazed in bold italics atop the *Tribune*'s daily editorials and then ran for a week:

THE NATION'S WAR CRY: FORWARD TO RICHMOND!!
The Rebel Congress Must Not be
Allowed to Meet There on the
20th of July
BY THAT DATE THE PLACE MUST BE HELD
BY THE NATIONAL ARMY

Responsibility for the din rested with Dana, but the slogan itself was the brainchild of Fitz Henry Warren, the *Tribune*'s feisty Washington editor whom Dana hired after his friend James Pike was appointed minister to the Hague. Formerly the militant antislavery editor of an Iowa newspaper, Warren charged that the administration had no intention to suppress the rebellion and was still pursuing "the old harlot of a compromise." When Seward issued a strong denial, Warren dared him to break up the Union army camps in Alexandria and advance upon Richmond. The next day Dana adopted the

"Forward to Richmond!" call, which fit both his militant mood and his penchant for eye-catching editorial slogans.[39]

"What in the world is the matter with Uncle Horace?" a vexed Lincoln asked the *Tribune*'s bureau chief. "Why can't he restrain himself and wait a little?" Greeley, nursing his wounded knee at home, claimed he did not want the war hurried but "quietly pressed to a righteous conclusion." At the same time, he was suspicious of Lincoln's apparent temporizing. By not restraining Dana he gave tacit approval to his course. Years later, Greeley declared that while the "Forward to Richmond!" war cry was Dana's doing it was "just what should have been uttered."[40]

Appropriate or not, Dana's war cry hit home. It was immediately reprinted in the *Chicago Tribune* and circulated through the North. Senator Lyman Trumbull introduced a resolution calling for an attack on Richmond by Dana's deadline. Reporters spied Dana's editorial on war secretary Cameron's desk and noticed that Seward carried a folded copy of the *New York Tribune* to a meeting with Lincoln. Warren was summoned to a conference at the White House and told that the Union offensive was about to open. On the following day, June 29, General Winfield Scott's objection to a hasty advance was overruled by the cabinet. Historians often generalize that Lincoln succumbed to the pressure of "northern newspapers" or "the press" for a march on Richmond, but the main journalistic goading had come from Dana at Greeley's *Tribune*.[41]

Retribution came swiftly for Dana's attempt to play military adviser. On July 22, Dana's lead editorial announced victory at the Battle of Bull Run, but the *Tribune*'s war news told a different story. General Irvin McDowell's army had begun well at Manassas, but when Confederate reinforcements arrived they prompted a Union retreat that devolved into a panicked, headlong rout. Blue-clad soldiers staggered on foot back to Washington, leaving behind a trail of artillery, baggage, dead horses, and wounded men. The grim reality of combat mocked the *Tribune*'s confident rallying cry.[42]

Dana was unrepentant. Barely pausing for breath, he lashed out at scapegoats. The blood of Northern men, the *Tribune* declared, had been "needlessly shed": the Bull Run debacle stemmed from months of government paralysis and incompetence. Swinging wildly, Dana called for immediate replacement of the entire cabinet. From Washington Warren advised him that General Scott was the villain for failing to coordinate the attack. Dana picked up Warren's refrain, blaming Scott in private correspondence to prominent Republicans, then in *Tribune* editorials, for "the shipwreck of our grand and heroic army." The tune caught on. When Frank Blair, Jr., sounded out

Republican politicians and editors in New York in early August, he found that "Dana and everybody that I talked with . . . are convinced of the entire incompetency of old Scott."[43]

Only in hindsight did Dana's "Forward to Richmond!" editorial campaign appear foolhardy. The Union battle plan had been sound, and its green troops fought bravely through most of the day. The primary blame lay with General Robert Patterson, who failed to hold General Joseph E. Johnston's troops in the Shenandoah Valley, and McDowell, who advanced too slowly to attack General P. T. Beauregard's troops before Johnston reinforced them. No matter: the *Tribune* had led the fatal charge, and now it was barraged from all sides by its foes. The New York papers quickly blamed their rival for Bull Run, fingering Greeley's abolitionist convictions and Dana's snarling "conceit." "Field-Marshal Greeley" was caricatured as a military strategist giving orders to General Scott in *Harper's Weekly*, and the next issue featured him jumping on Lincoln's desk to dismiss the cabinet. Lincoln's private secretary John Hay, surveying the press, found that most papers indicted the *Tribune* as "the sole cause of the defeat, in its foolhardy persistence that an advance should be made forthwith on Richmond." Even the *Tribune* faithful joined the scolding chorus as letters of condemnation inundated the paper, their writers canceling subscriptions.[44]

Greeley was wracked with anguish and remorse. He spent seven sleepless nights after Bull Run, then took to bed for another week with an attack of "brain fever." "Dana tells me that Greeley is completely broken down and the next thing to being insane," Frank Blair reported to his brother in the cabinet. "He says that [Greeley's] first idea was peaceable separation, that he Dana prevailed upon him to go for the war policy and the disaster at Manassas unhinged his mind and prostrated him entirely. . . . [He] sent for Dana and made him promise to conduct the Tribune in the way he had marked out & retired to the country."[45]

From his sickbed Greeley scribbled a half-crazed letter to Lincoln, calling himself "hopelessly broken" and promising to second any movement the president initiated, including an armistice with the Rebels. On July 25 the *Tribune* printed Greeley's meandering semiapology for the "Forward to Richmond!" fiasco. The slogan was not his, nor "in any wise suggested or prompted" by him, and he "would have preferred not to iterate it," but he agreed with its sentiment. Similarly, he had not written the article demanding cabinet changes but seconded it. McDowell's blundering had doomed the Union army, but Greeley was willing to play the scapegoat if necessary.

DICTATOR GREELEY dismisses the Cabinet, and Warns Lincoln that he will stand no more Nonsense.

"A decimated and indignant people demand the immediate retirement of the present Cabinet from the high places of power, which, for one reason or another, they have shown themselves incompetent to fill. The people insist upon new heads of Executive Departments."—*New York Tribune, July 23.*

"Dictator Greeley dismisses the Cabinet." Although Horace Greeley was blamed after Bull Run for overstepping his bounds, the *Tribune*'s July 23 editorial demanding cabinet resignations, which is quoted below the cartoon, was penned by Charles Dana. *Harper's Weekly*, August 10, 1861. Special Collections and College Archives, Musselman Library, Gettysburg College.

Finally, henceforth he would "bar all criticism in these columns on Army movements, past or future." Bending to the storm, the *Tribune* would devote itself to rallying the public behind the war.[46]

Ten days later Fitz Henry Warren resigned from the *Tribune* and took up a Union sword to atone for his errant pen. Dana, however, made no apology. There is no record of a heated argument between Greeley and Dana over the incident, as the rival *Herald* alleged. In covering for his managing editor, Greeley had made his displeasure clear enough. Behind Dana's back Greeley was more direct. All Dana had written about the military's management of the war was "the naked truth," he told one shareholder, "yet the Tribune should not have said it—certainly not in the *tone* it too often held." When Sam Wilkeson at the *Tribune*'s Washington bureau suggested that Greeley take a longer rest, Greeley reminded him: "You know well that no one can manage a newspaper for another in such a crisis as this, and I am peculiarly unfortunate in this respect. I must stay about the Tribune now or let everything go to destruction."[47]

For a time everything did seem to be going to destruction. The *Tribune*'s circulation took a dive after Bull Run. Readership of the weekly plummeted from 215,000 to 189,000 by October; the daily went from 72,000 to 51,000. By then the Sunday edition was discontinued for lack of advertising. Meanwhile, rivals gained: the *Times* nearly reached the *Tribune*'s total circulation by the end of the year, and the *Herald* doubled it. To economize, Dana cut out war maps and switched to cheaper newsprint. The trustees took out a bank loan, temporarily cut salaries by 10 percent, and discontinued dividends for the foreseeable future. Greeley, heartbroken, lamented to a friend that "through the faults of several, mainly mine, the Tribune *as a power* is broken down."[48]

The paper's misfortune coincided with a wider economic downturn. There was "general & increasing dissatisfaction" with the progress of the war, Dana reported to Pike in November. With little faith in the Union military, Northerners balked at subscribing to war bonds and many employers laid off workers. Greeley had recovered from the shock of Bull Run but still "regard[ed] everything as lost & nothing but disaster in store for the country." For Dana the war had finally hit home: curtailing dividends forced his family to retrench. "Instead of four servants there are only two & everything else in proportion; and our house is but an instance of what is done in every other." As bills went unpaid Dana tried to relocate his family to their summer cottage in Connecticut and rent out the family's Manhattan house, but he found no takers. Several weeks later he confided to Pike: "I am on the verge of total collapse & expect to come out without a copper." His family had "come down mightily," with "scarcely a dollar . . . for clothes since the war began; & not a cent for anything else that could be avoided." He had offered his house on Clinton Place to its previous owner at a loss and expected to be refused. Unless things got better he would try again to rent it out and seek cheap rooms elsewhere. Dana, Greeley's editorial usurper, had paid the price for the "Forward to Richmond!" debacle.[49]

4 "A Printing House Divided"

By the end of 1861 things seemed to be getting better. As Northern morale rebounded, so did the economy and the *Tribune*. In the fall Dana worked as steadily as ever, Greeley regained his old verve, and both kept Greeley's promise after Bull Run to avoid criticizing military developments—as Dana told Charles Sumner, to "tell no more truth than he can afford." The *Tribune* editors applauded minor Union victories in western Virginia. They agreed with their London correspondent Karl Marx that Union authorities should release the Confederate envoys whom an overzealous naval officer had illegally removed from the British ship *Trent* in the Caribbean. They even stood by their archrival William Seward as the secretary of state smoothed over the incident with England. When a Massachusetts regiment passed through New York on its way to Virginia, Dana saluted them at a public dinner: "We feel that they are contending not merely for us, not merely for our country, but for the most . . . sacred cause that can inspire the heart of man." As much as possible, the *Tribune* editors submerged their differences with the Lincoln administration over the conduct of the war and rallied public support.[1]

Sifting Generals, Awaiting Victories

The major exception was Lincoln's treatment of General John C. Frémont. In the summer of 1861 Lincoln appointed Frémont to command the Department of the West, covering all US territory from the Mississippi to the Rockies. From his headquarters in St. Louis Frémont was supposed to drive Confederate forces from the divided state of Missouri. But the Pathfinder quickly became an embarrassment. Union defeats at Wilson's Creek and Lexington were attributed to Frémont's failure to send timely reinforcements while he lingered in St. Louis to supervise construction of elaborate fortifications. On August 30, Frémont issued a proclamation freeing the slaves of citizens in his department who resisted the Union government. Lincoln, fearing its impact upon Kentucky and unwilling to turn the war into an attack on slavery, annulled the order. Finally, reports circulated that Frémont spent lavishly on his entourage and allowed contractors to overcharge the government. In late October, after War Department investigators and a House committee on contracts reported that Frémont's operations were chaotic and corrupt, Lincoln ordered him relieved.[2]

The *Tribune* editors leaped to Frémont's defense when news of his removal reached New York. In a string of editorials they excused waste and fraud in his department as beneath the attention of a general who had to mobilize loyal troops rapidly and save an embattled state from encircling rebel armies. Frémont had done the best he could under adverse circumstances, Dana told James Pike, and the administration wrongly "ordered back his army from the very face of the enemy it was undertaking to crush." For months the *Tribune* pressed the administration for redress. Dana wanted badly to believe that Frémont was the fighting general so needed to crush the slaveholder rebellion. Blinded by the Pathfinder's mythic past and his antislavery proclamation, he failed to see that Frémont possessed little talent beyond a genius for self-promotion.[3]

Despite the noise over Frémont, Lincoln was pleased enough with the overall restraint of the *Tribune* after Bull Run that he arranged an informal alliance. Two of the president's intermediaries, journalist James R. Gilmore and Pennsylvania Republican Robert J. Walker, agreed to leak government news to Greeley in return for editorial backing of Lincoln's administration. Concluded in late November 1861, the secret arrangement began a public honeymoon that continued for several weeks. Dana reflected this upbeat mood when he reported to Pike that "on the whole there is as much progress as any reasonable man ought to expect."[4]

By early 1862, however, the *Tribune* began to revert to its customary stance as a critical watchdog over the conduct of the war. Not enough inside news was reaching the paper through Gilmore and Walker to justify the editors' pledge of allegiance. Greeley, meanwhile, had lost patience with Lincoln, whom he believed inadequate to the crisis. At first determined that the war to preserve the Union should not target slavery, Greeley was becoming convinced that abolition should become an essential war objective. Destroying slavery would redeem the nation's moral honor and deal a fatal blow to the rebellion. Under Greeley's leadership the *Tribune* joined congressional Radicals in praising Secretary of War Simon Cameron's proposal to use runaway slaves against their masters. Seizing upon congressional legislation aimed at confiscating the "property" of Rebels, Greeley pushed Lincoln to discard his cautious border-state approach to emancipation.[5]

Although Dana joined Greeley in advocating emancipation as a military necessity, he had a stronger sense of the constraints facing Lincoln. In January 1862 Dana told Pike that the president was "quite up with the majority of the people" on emancipation. Most Northerners still opposed freeing and arming slaves, but the tide was turning, thanks in part to the danger of Britain's intervention, Dana thought. He applauded Lincoln's message of March 1862 urging Congress to offer compensation to Union slave states (Delaware, Maryland, Missouri, and Kentucky) that adopted an emancipation plan. Lincoln's timing was just right, Dana editorialized: had he made the announcement earlier it would have seemed desperate, but thanks to General Grant's recent victories in Tennessee it was issued from strength.[6]

Dana's chief quarrel with Lincoln was the president's apparent inability to manage his subordinates. Among cabinet officials, Seward was constantly bidding to become prime minister, Cameron did not rein in corrupt suppliers, and Navy Secretary Gideon Welles was suspected of securing contracts for his brother-in-law. Yet "Abe hangs on to all his men, as if he were afraid that the dismissal of anyone must tumble down the whole house." Dana lashed out at Cameron's order of December 1861 that stopped state governors from sending units to the front and handed over recruits to the regular army. Ending the practice of forming local regiments "seems to us a great blunder," the *Tribune* editorialized. When Cameron wrote Dana defending the change, Dana replied that the plan "will utterly fail." Fortunately, the new policy was scaled down and did not replace prior practice.[7]

Another wayward Lincoln "subordinate" was Mary Todd Lincoln. Dana was appalled that the First Lady spent lavishly on White House dinners and decorations while common Northerners endured the hardships of war. His letters spread stories of Mrs. Lincoln securing military appointments and contracts for White House favorites, accepting gifts from politicians in return for promises to influence her husband, and conspiring with staff to fund her aristocratic lifestyle, all behind the president's back. In December 1861 Mrs. Lincoln leaked an advance copy of the president's annual address to Congress, perhaps in exchange for money, and the *New York Herald* published excerpts. Dana judged things had improved the next month when Lincoln dumped Cameron and "set his foot down" on Mrs. Lincoln's machinations.[8]

The most damaging insubordination, to Dana's mind, was the procrastination of the Union army's self-proclaimed savior, General George B.

McClellan. A handsome West Pointer and then railroad engineer from Pennsylvania, McClellan campaigned for Douglas in 1860, sharing the Little Giant's loyalty to the Union and hatred of abolitionists. Commissioned as a major general, McClellan achieved minor Union victories in western Virginia that, coupled with his reputation as an expert in logistics, vaulted him to prominence. In August 1861 the *Tribune*'s editors, still on their best behavior after Bull Run, applauded McClellan's promotion to command what later became the Army of the Potomac. Dana sent *Tribune* reporter Bayard Taylor to interview the "young Napoleon," whom he found "cool, firm, prompt, determined, and self-reliant"—just the energetic professional the army needed.[9]

Late in 1861 cracks surfaced in the *Tribune* editors' patience. They expressed frustration that none of the 660,000 Union soldiers enlisted were ready "to advance upon the rebels *somewhere*," although, remembering Bull Run, they wanted it understood that the *Tribune* "neither asks nor advocates a movement of the Army of the Potomac." As the year came to an end without significant Union victories the *Tribune* began to air doubts about McClellan's resolve. Some 140,000 Union troops in Virginia had marched and drilled endlessly without a sign of forward movement. Dana reported to Pike that Washington insiders were questioning McClellan's competence. Republican Radicals, led by Benjamin Wade and Thaddeus Stevens, "say he does nothing & can't manage so big an army." Dana was reserving judgment, but he was convinced that McClellan was "at heart a believer in slavery": "When Frémont issued his famous proclamation McClellan was determined at once to issue another . . . on the other side of the question, but his personal friends had the sense & the firmness to stop him." A few days later the *Tribune* featured Dana's charge that several top Union generals were soft on slavery and did not want the Confederates "too severely whipped."[10]

After two more months of waiting, the *Tribune*'s junior editor again complained of McClellan's "delays and procrastinations." While McClellan gave audiences to admirers in Washington, a contingent of his army sent to occupy an abandoned Confederate position at Centreville, Virginia, discovered that its imposing defenses consisted largely of dummy wooden cannons camouflaged behind earthworks, so-called Quaker guns. Bayard Taylor, who broke the story for the *Tribune*, reversed his earlier positive impression of McClellan and reported from "Camp Disappointment" that McClellan's army had been made "a laughing-stock to the whole civilized world." Called to testify before the Joint Committee on the Conduct of the War in March 1862, Taylor told congressmen that without McClellan's exaggerated caution the Confederate force at Manassas would have been captured long ago.[11]

This View of the Block (*split*) out of which "THE WOODEN GUNS" were made, showeth how the Editors do sometimes make things up out of their own Heads.
[*Vide N. Y. Tribune.*]

"View of the Block (Split) Out of Which 'The Wooden Guns' Were Made."
The *Tribune*'s story of the sham batteries at Centreville was corroborated by witnesses, but George McClellan's supporters discredited it. Here Horace Greeley splits a block with an axe imprinted with the head of Bayard Taylor, revealing Greeley and Dana's carved faces. This shows "how the Editors do sometimes make things up out of their own Heads." *Harper's Weekly*, April 19, 1862. Special Collections, Saint Mary's College of California.

Reporting the War

Taylor's congressional testimony indicated how influential and eagerly read wartime reportage had become. Begun with reporters' impromptu feats of pluck and daring, the *Tribune*'s coverage of the Civil War became a matter of efficient organization and intense competition. Greeley's paper and its New York rivals rapidly expanded operations. Washington bureaus were reinforced, dozens of reporters were sent to the military zone, and telegraphers, stenographers, and extra presses transferred dispatches into print. The public appetite for news led to separate daily editions of the same paper: a few days after Fort Sumter Dana announced that the *Tribune* would publish an evening edition for the duration of the war. When important military or political news arrived, all the major papers produced "extras" and hired special trains to deliver them to outlying towns.[12]

All this cost a small fortune. In March 1861 the *Tribune* trustees authorized Dana to spend $7,500 a year for Washington correspondence. When Dana hired Fitz Henry Warren as his capital chief, the *Tribune* claimed his salary was "double that of an average governor." Special correspondents at the front were not much cheaper: "Early news is expensive news, Mr. Greeley," reporter Charles A. Page explained. "If I have the watermelons and whiskey ready when the officers come along from the fight, I get the news without asking questions." These outlays were augmented by the cost of messengers, telegraphic fees of at least $40 per news column, and payments to informers. After bottoming out after Bull Run, the *Tribune*'s circulation and revenues recovered. Still, Greeley and Dana could not match the resources mustered by James Gordon Bennett at the *Herald*, who spent more than a half-million dollars on war coverage. The *Tribune* faced a constant uphill fight to "score a beat" over its rivals. As a newsman, Dana believed the outcome of events less important than reporting it first, for even military defeats could be turned into journalistic triumphs.[13]

From his desk in New York Dana commanded the *Tribune*'s "bohemian brigade" of special correspondents. He was "as grimly peremptory and brief in his official orders . . . as the General commanding in a hotly-contested battle," a colleague recalled. The "specials" Dana assembled in the war's first year numbered fewer than twenty compared to the *Herald*'s thirty, but the *Tribune*'s had more journalistic experience and stronger antislavery credentials. What Dana's army lacked in money it had to compensate for in ingenuity, inside connections, and accurate writing. Dana scribbled orders for his reporters to follow the major armies and sniff out the next battlegrounds. He kept track of them with pins on the large map hung on his office wall.[14]

When a campaign ended or a battle story had to be rushed into print, field reporters returned to the *Tribune*'s Washington bureau to file copy. In a small one-story building on 14th and F Streets opposite Willard's Hotel, they encountered Warren and his assistant, the nervous, bespectacled Adams S. Hill. After Warren enlisted in the army Dana recruited Samuel Wilkeson to head the office. An imposing figure with a high forehead and flowing beard, Wilkeson brought political savvy and insider connections to the job: he had edited Thurlow Weed's *Albany Evening Journal* before defecting to the *Tribune*. Wilkeson and Hill were expected to transmit Washington scuttlebutt, promote the paper's views on political and military issues at the capital, and obtain useful documents and other "scoops." Dana and Greeley, convinced that the war's outcome hinged on the *Tribune*'s lobbying, believed that fighting it was as much a political as a military battle.[15]

So was reporting it. Even before the armies collided, Dana battled fluctuating and sometimes arbitrary government censorship. Shortly after Fort Sumter, the War Department, worried about Confederates' awareness of troop movements, detailed a censor to review all telegrams sent from Washington. Dana cooperated begrudgingly, but he protested when a story he was told to excise was allowed to appear in Baltimore papers. By June Dana and the New York editors learned that reporters could circumvent telegraphic censorship by sending their accounts by mail or express. The next month Dana printed so much information about Union preparations for an advance in Virginia that General Scott issued an order declaring that no military news could be telegraphed without his headquarters' approval. Facing protest from Washington correspondents and telegraph companies, Scott rescinded the order just before reporters accompanied the army to Bull Run.[16]

When field generals tried to muzzle *Tribune* reporters, Dana's reaction was belligerent. At Fortress Monroe General Benjamin Butler, complaining that his plans reached the enemy, issued an order expelling from his department anyone revealing proposed troop movements. Dana snapped back: "Whose fault is this? . . . If officers, in violation of military law and personal confidence, are weak enough to tattle, shoot them or hang them, we do not care which; but to suppose that paid men, sent expressly to obtain information, will not use it when obtained, is to exhibit a fatuity unworthy of a Major General." Dana professed "to print a newspaper [which] . . . if we understand the meaning of the word, is a paper containing news."[17]

Dana's tirades against censorship resumed in October when Secretary of State Seward, anxious to suppress negative battle news and cabinet disagreements, issued a gag order forbidding all wires from Washington related to "the civil or military operations of the government." In January 1862 the House Judiciary Committee opened hearings investigating telegraphic censorship. The *Tribune*'s Wilkeson and Hill were star witnesses. Both testified that their dispatches detailing cabinet debates over the *Trent* affair and proposals to arm escaped slaves were suppressed. Wilkeson had been forbidden to send wires "damaging to the character of the administration, or any individual member of the cabinet, or . . . the reputation of the officers charged with prosecution of the war." Always wary of the moderate Seward, Dana and Greeley saw his order as protection of "doughface" officers too soft on slavery and West Pointers like McClellan too slow to attack the Rebels.[18]

When the House hearings ended, the War Department, under the new secretary Edwin Stanton, took charge of monitoring telegraph messages. Dana acknowledged the need to censor information about pending military operations: "If it is necessary to kill the Press in order to save the Nation, so be it!" But he warned in the *Tribune* that the responsibility for suppressing accurate reports "will be a fearful one, and *it will rest wholly on the Government.*"[19]

At Bull Run the *Tribune*'s specials faced their first serious test, and the results were mixed. E. H. House witnessed the opening cannonade, pieced together reports that rebel ranks were breaking, and began sending off news of victory. In a few hours he and other reporters were overrun by panicking spectators, horses, and soldiers in wild retreat. Thinking the Union army would reorganize at Centreville, House spent the night there only to find in the morning that the Federals had fled to safety within the capital. Meanwhile, Adams Hill's telegram to Dana about the retreat was suppressed by the government's censor. The *Tribune* was beaten by the *Herald*, whose reporter rode back to Washington overnight and filed the first story revealing the grim truth. Nevertheless, the *Tribune* lingered for nearly a week to present the most comprehensive and accurate account of the battle available.[20]

The Bull Run experience of sometimes late but more reliable military news proved to be the *Tribune*'s norm. Dana's corps of reporters was too scattered to cover every point of engagement. Better educated and more professional than the *Herald*'s frantic news gatherers, the *Tribune* specials were "far less concerned with scoring beats than getting it right," according to one authority. Dana relied on their judgment and integrity for honest reports. "New as I was in journalism," George Smalley recalled, "Mr. Dana gave me a free hand." The managing editor "liked . . . to assign a man to duty and judge him by the result; which meant that the man was left free to work out his own salvation; or damnation, as the case may be." The system produced independent journalism and built good relations between Dana and his reporters. Smalley did not recall ever receiving a reprimand from Dana, though he remembered complaints from Greeley. Dana solidified his specials' loyalty by refusing to reveal their names when aggrieved parties threatened a libel suit.[21]

Occasionally Dana's patience ran out. *Tribune* specials were constantly reminded of rising telegraph expenses and instructed not to clad their battle scenes in the *Herald*'s purple prose. After the Army of the Potomac won a rare victory, the *Tribune* man began his wire: "To God Almighty be all the glory! Mine eyes have seen the work of the Lord and the cause of the righteous hath triumphed." Dana sent a sharp reply: "Hereafter, in sending your reports, please specify the number of the hymn and save telegraphic expenses." For all his insistence upon accuracy over speed, Dana was annoyed when the *Tribune* was scooped. "Mr. __, you were disgracefully beaten this morning," he once remarked casually in hearing distance of the entire *Tribune* staff. No doubt some field reporters got the same treatment by post. In April 1862 Dana's successor, Sydney Howard Gay, anxious for fresh battle news, berated a special at the Virginia front for a report that arrived eight days after the battle: "I pray you remember the *Tribune* is a *daily news*-paper — or meant to be, — & not a historical record of past events." Dana would have put it more bluntly than Gay, "a man of soft manners and heart."[22]

The *Tribune*'s most important war "beats" were political rather than military. The paper's best energies had always gone into editorials and Washington news, and multicolumn congressional reports crowded out letters from the front. Dana had close ties with Treasury Secretary Chase and influential Republican senators such as Charles Sumner, Ben Wade, and William Pitt Fessenden. The *Tribune* printed exclusive excerpts from their letters and speeches as well as items they leaked. Other public officials were farther from the paper's orbit, or even prewar enemies, but they were wooed through calculated flattery. To curry favor with Navy Secretary Welles, Dana urged his Washington bureau to "soft-soap" critical reports on the Naval Office. Government officials, he wrote Adams Hill, "have stomachs most greedy of praise, and are able to digest it in the thickest possible form." (Two decades later, Dana took his own advice to heart when he sought a favor from Democratic presidential also-ran Samuel Tilden: "It seems to me that in our day there have been three statesmen who have had the genius to rule men through their intellects. I mean Bismarck, Disraeli, and Tilden.")[23]

Secretary of War Cameron, a Pennsylvania boss allied with Thurlow Weed, was hounded by charges of corruption and waste. Cameron came under the *Tribune*'s fire for failing to bring order to the Union's chaotic military mobilization. Despite this, Dana and his staff drew Cameron close through flattery and favorable notices. Wilkeson sent letters to the *Tribune* praising Cameron's performance and forwarded the clippings to the secretary. Dana's editorials joined the campaign, saluting Cameron's "vigilance, wisdom, and practical ability" in "guard[ing] the public interests while providing for the sudden expansion of the military."[24]

These tactics resulted in special favors and exclusive scoops for the *Tribune*.

When the reporter George Smalley was refused passage on a Union warship in South Carolina, he telegraphed Secretary Welles, explaining that Dana had ordered him to Port Royal. "The effect of Mr. Dana's name was magical," Smalley discovered, and the commodore was ordered to give him a berth. In October 1861 Cameron sent a directive to the War Department's chief censor that he "neither suppress nor alter the telegrams of Mr. Samuel Wilkeson." Meanwhile Wilkeson was named the government's official European telegraphic agent, making him the first to see the Union's foreign publicity. The same month, Wilkeson accompanied Cameron as an adviser on a tour of the scandal-ridden western departments. In that capacity he confided to the *Tribune* editors that Frémont, who had "surrender[ed] the Commissariat and Quartermaster's department of an army of 70,000 to a gang of the damnedest villains," would soon be removed.[25]

Returned to Washington, Wilkeson used his War Department connections to send Dana three more important scoops. Two were official documents that Lincoln himself had not yet seen. The first, General Lorenzo Thomas's confidential report on the western trip, described Frémont as a general "more fond of the pomp than the realities of war," advocated his replacement, and criticized General William T. Sherman as "gloomy." Dana obtained permission from the War Department before publishing it. This arrangement suited both parties: For Cameron, the leak helped prepare the public for the two generals' dismissal; for Dana, although he was not happy about Frémont's impending downfall, at least the *Tribune* was the first paper to report it.[26]

Wilkeson's second coup was to obtain General Charles P. Stone's report of the controversial Union defeat at Ball's Bluff on the Potomac River, during which Lincoln's friend, the Oregon senator Edward Baker, was killed. The defeat provoked Radical Republicans to establish the Joint Committee on the Conduct of the War, which made Stone its first target. When Stone's official report appeared exclusively in the *Tribune*, Dana and Greeley's New York competitors were outraged. They sent emissaries directly to Cameron arguing that if the government was going to leak secret information "it belongs equally to all." In November 1861 Cameron agreed to new arrangements by which all official department documents would be delivered to the Associated Press's agent in Washington "for prompt and simultaneous transmission" to all Northern papers.[27]

Yet his special relationship with the *Tribune* continued. In December rumors circulated at the capital that Cameron had quarreled with the president by suggesting in his annual report that federal armies moving into the South should free and arm the slaves. This was a position Lincoln thought premature, politically dangerous, and improper for the secretary to announce without consulting his chief. The president ordered the undelivered copies of Cameron's report seized and had the offending passages excised.

This story lay behind Wilkeson's third scoop, which he mailed to Dana to circumvent the government's telegraph censor. Wilkeson reported that Lincoln's cabinet voted 4 to 3 against Cameron's proposal, and he provided the text of Cameron's original report while other New York papers printed the redacted version distributed by the Associated Press. The episode set off an explosion that propelled Cameron out of the War Department and into the foreign service. Whether Cameron had truly been converted by abolitionists or—more likely—was attempting to win the support of Republican Radicals to save his job, he had created an open break with the president. In January 1862 Lincoln, after clocking off a tactful interval, gratified Cameron's "desire for a change of position" and appointed him minister to Russia.[28]

Dana and Greeley, heartened by Cameron's new antislavery convictions, heaped praise upon the departing secretary. The editors ran a lithograph of Cameron and Frémont, linking the pair as wronged heroes, the victims of profiteering contractors and corrupt subordinates. Dana sent a note via Wilkeson congratulating Cameron on the appointment to St. Petersburg—and thanking Cameron for allowing him to nominate *Tribune* reporters Bayard Taylor and E. H. House as legation secretaries.[29]

By the anniversary of Fort Sumter it was clear that the war had worked revolutionary changes in the *Tribune*. Eyewitness accounts of the battles were telegraphed to New York by armies of specials. Advertising, shipping information, and reviews remained, but they were overshadowed by space devoted to national news. Foreign correspondence was cut back: Dana, under pressure from Greeley, suspended Karl Marx's contributions for several months. Editorials continued to trumpet Greeley and Dana's views on page four, but the first business of newspapers had emphatically become the news. As if to symbolize the shift, on April 10, 1862, the *Tribune* moved the day's news permanently to the front page, displacing paid announcements and advertisements. Yet it was not Dana who proposed the change, but his successor, Sidney Howard Gay; two weeks earlier, Greeley had abruptly forced Dana to resign.[30]

"Flung Out of My Career"

"My dear Pike," Dana wrote his friend at The Hague, "I have got a strange story to tell you, and you must let me tell it in some detail." On March 27

Dana learned from Sidney Gay that a movement to oust him had spread among the *Tribune* owners. Greeley privately told two stockholders that "either Mr. Dana or he must leave." The paper's trustees decided that Greeley was "more necessary to the concern," and Dana was advised to resign or be dismissed.[31]

Dana was as stunned by Gay's revelation "as if he had told me I was about to be shot for treason." He sent an emissary to Greeley to see if he could stay with the paper in another capacity—this was the trustees' preference, too. No such arrangement was possible, he was told, so he resigned. The trustees passed a resolution praising Dana's "conscientious devotion to the duties of his post" and his "noble and endearing qualities," and they awarded him six months' salary as severance pay. Without warning or explanation, Dana's career at the *Tribune* was over.[32]

In the next few days Greeley compounded his subterfuge with cowardice. He told the trustees it was "a damned lie" that he had issued an ultimatum, professed confidence in Dana's loyalty, and sent word indirectly that he could stay as an editorial writer. Greeley never spoke to Dana nor wrote him to clear up the alleged misunderstanding. Dana concluded that Greeley "is glad to have me out, and that he . . . set on foot the secret cabal by which it was accomplished."[33]

Dana's reaction evolved from bewilderment to anger. He "avoids us all, is very dark, wounded, and is very bitter in his complaints," a colleague reported. Among his *Tribune* coworkers only George Ripley protested his dismissal. Above all, Dana viewed his dismissal as a personal betrayal by Greeley, whose reason, he told Henry Carey, "I cannot fathom. I had rendered him great services and had never stood in his way. Political advancement for myself I had always refused, so as not to interfere with his ambition." Dana of course did not mention his episodes of covert editorial independence, if not insubordination, toward Greeley.[34]

Looking back years later, Dana declared that "the real reason" Greeley had him dismissed was that "while he was for peace I was for war, and that as long as I stayed on the Tribune there was a spirit there which was not his spirit—that he did not like." This was an overstatement, but with a strong core of truth. As Greeley admitted to another publisher, "*I* am the one who would have let the Rebels go in peace if they would have so gone—he was always for making them stay and behave themselves." War exposed the fault lines in their partnership and heightened their clash of temperaments. Dana's forthright stand made the vacillating Greeley uncomfortable. He acquiesced in Dana's "Forward to Richmond!" editorials, but after Bull Run he was unnerved and exchanged the paper's fighting spirit for a less "decided" tone.[35]

Dana had tried to follow the new policy, but his differences with Greeley eventually resurfaced. Historians have failed to explain why Greeley waited nine months after Bull Run to fire Dana. The evidence reveals that a rift over General McClellan early in 1862 shattered their truce. Both men grew impatient when McClellan kept postponing the Union army's offensive across the Potomac, but Greeley, still hounded by rivals for the "Forward to Richmond!" slogan, held his editorial tongue while Dana loosened his. The result, the *Tribune*'s critics noticed, was a journalistic "house divided against itself," with Greeley "the minority party." When Lincoln kept McClellan in charge after the advance on Manassas's "Quaker guns," Greeley asked readers to "let bygones be bygones," rally around the general, and "strengthen his hands as far as possible." Meanwhile, Dana's Washington correspondents accused McClellan of arrogance and incompetence, and Dana charged that he lacked a "warlike spirit" and was "more anxious for the preservation of slavery than for the exemplary crushing out of the rebellion." Greeley grew alarmed. He issued a stern warning to Sam Wilkeson to report only news from the capital and not to embed opinions in dispatches. For Dana, he had more than a warning in store.[36]

The *Tribune* had not fully recovered revenues and readership since the Bull Run controversy, and Greeley feared a fatal rerun. He could not be seen as rushing McClellan's army to its slaughter. A *Harper's Weekly* cartoon portrayed Greeley chained to the wall in a lunatic asylum, screaming "On to Richmond!! Down with McClellan!!" as the general watched in mock pity. *Vanity Fair* ran a variant of the same theme, a cartoon showing Greeley haranguing McClellan and Stanton while Dana egged him on. These images captured the nightmare churning in Greeley's fevered brain. The *Tribune* must no longer play the role of military adviser, and Dana, publicly recognized as its lead "warmonger," would have to go.[37]

Dana's *Tribune* associates secretly shared Greeley's concerns. "Dana's removal was an absolute necessity," Bayard Taylor wrote privately. Judicious editorial management meant eliminating "the vacillations between bitterness and inanity which have characterized the *Tribune*, and well nigh ruined it forever." The *Tribune* "is worn out with petulant snarling; it must have a little rest, to recover tone." Sidney Gay told Dana that the problem was "a radical incompatibility of character" between his strong will and Greeley's hesitance. Writing to others, Gay was more critical. Firing Dana was "a painful business" and associates were "sincerely sorry" for him, "but [we] saw that it was imperative inasmuch as Dana is Dana, and Greeley, Greeley. Even if it were

ASSAULT BY THE PRESS-GANG
ON TWO WELL-KNOWN PUBLIC CHARACTERS.

"Assault By the Press-Gang on Two Well-Known Public Characters." Edwin Stanton and George McClellan stand arm in arm while badgered by New York editors who push for an offensive in Virginia: (*left to right*) William Cullen Bryant of the *Evening Post*, Charles Dana in fisticuffs, and Horace Greeley. "On to Richmond" is written on the paper Greeley holds. Cartoon by H. L. Stephens in *Vanity Fair*, March 15, 1862. Special Collections and College Archives, Musselman Library, Gettysburg College.

possible to change the former's will, it was clearly impossible to bestow upon him the gift of *judgement*."[38]

By 1862 the terms of Dana and Greeley's partnership had changed. Greeley, Dana sensed, began to fret over "the importance which . . . I had attained in the concern." Dana had emerged from his boss's shadow into public light. Greeley was "weary of seeing letters sent to me by leading men, senators, Congressmen, cabinet ministers &c about things already said in the paper, or which they desired to have said. . . . He was weary also of seeing other papers speak of me as an essential part of the *Tribune*." More was at stake than petty jealousy: Greeley's power play was about who controlled the *Tribune*'s editorial policy. As Dana's imprint grew due to his expertise in military matters and Greeley's long absences, continued reliance upon him meant losing the paper as Greeley's mouthpiece. The mild-mannered Sidney Gay, Dana's replacement, posed no such threat. "Mr. Greeley knows what he wants to say," Gay scolded a Washington correspondent who had veered into editorializing after Dana left. "If Dana could have remembered that Mr. Greeley was the *responsible* editor his head would have been safe on his shoulders at this moment."[39]

Reaction to Dana's firing was swift. Newspapers throughout the North carried notices that praised Dana for his skill and professionalism. Democratic and Republican papers agreed that the change was made to "remove the intensely radical tone which had attached to the editorials under Mr. Dana," but opinions divided along partisan lines over whether the decision was sound. Karl Marx was not pleased. Dana immediately wrote Jenny Marx that the *Tribune* would take no more contributions from her husband. Only later did Marx and Engels learn from the London papers that Dana had left on account of "differences of opinion" with Greeley. "This old jackass with the face angelic [Greeley] thus seems to be responsible for everything," Engels complained.[40]

Greeley, resuming active management, was free to pursue his own editorial course. The humorists at *Vanity Fair* quickly noticed that hints of defeatism crept into the *Tribune*'s columns. "The old dog again begins to insinuate his old tricks" of letting the Rebels go, one writer charged, while a red-hot Unionist "Devil" announced, "I have stopped taking the *Tribune* since Dana left it. It has ceased to be interesting." As the *Tribune* reeled from crisis to crisis, Greeley's mood swings demonstrated how much the paper had benefited from Dana's consistently militant Unionism. Greeley continued his editorial crusade for emancipating Southern slaves as a military necessity, but by 1863 he was again wearied by Union defeats and began floating peace proposals. His erratic course caused the *Tribune*'s Washington mainstays Wilkeson and Hill to resign in exasperation, and the paper's reputation plummeted among stalwart Republicans committed to Union victory. At the war's end a *Tribune* trustee who had voted for Dana's dismissal sent him an apology: "If I had known then what I know now as to Mr. Greeley's state of mind in relation to the war, I would sooner have let him go off, as he threatened to do, than sought your removal to retain him."[41]

These sentiments came too late to do Charles Dana any good. Nearly forty-three with a family of five to support, he was "flung out of my career," he complained to Henry Carey. Due to the *Tribune*'s decreased profits, Dana had to sell his ten shares of stock for $30,000, a third less than they would have fetched the year before. He estimated that if he were to settle with his creditors, he would be worth no more than $10,000—a buffer against financial disaster but not enough to provide income. What he would do for a living, he had "no idea."[42]

His reputation in newspaper circles brought immediate offers. One feeler came from Greeley's archrival James Gordon Bennett at the *Herald*. After his firing Dana caused a stir by talking with Bennett and airing complaints about the sale of his stock. When Bennett set Dana's grievances in print, Greeley charged Dana with "making war upon the *Tribune*" and asked the trustees to cancel his severance pay. They refused, although they were miffed by Dana's "uncivil" behavior.[43]

An alternative scheme had Dana wresting control of the *Albany Evening Journal* from Thurlow Weed, then combining that paper with his friend Thomas B. Carroll's Republican sheet and making the new journal the official state printer. This would catapult Dana to the head of New York's anti-Weed faction, "wielding a great influence and making a great deal of money." The project remained at the speculative stage, and Greeley, worried for the *Tribune*, helped kill it by telling the state treasurer that Dana was "too ultra" to satisfy the Albany government's tastes.[44]

One way or another Dana supposed he would "gravitate back into journalism," although he vowed not to "connect myself again with any establishment where there are twenty masters." In fact, it would be more than three years before Dana worked for another newspaper. Meanwhile he found himself in the service of the administration he had criticized in the *Tribune* for not winning the war. The gadfly was about to become an insider.[45]

5 "Several Propositions"

"I have had several propositions, but none that exactly suits," Charles Dana wrote a friend after his resignation. After serving for a turbulent decade and a half as Horace Greeley's right-hand man, Dana eventually found a more approving patron in the new war secretary, Edwin Stanton. But Dana's route to Washington proved more circuitous than he expected, detoured by assignments in the West and frustrating false starts.[1]

Dana, Stanton, and "War in Earnest"

The intense, irascible little man Lincoln chose as Simon Cameron's successor was a mystery to Dana, as to many Washingtonians. Bespectacled and asthmatic, with a long, flowing beard, Stanton looked like a reclusive Talmudic scholar. Yet behind his kindly eyes burned fierce determination and a pugnacious temperament, qualities that vaulted him to national renown as a trial lawyer and, in the waning months of the James Buchanan administration, an appointment as Attorney General. As Lincoln's cabinet considered Cameron's successor, Stanton won the support of its bickering triumvirate of Salmon Chase, William Seward, and Cameron by having a past varied enough that each found grounds for a prospective alliance. Stanton's early antislavery connections pleased Chase, and his clandestine role in stiffening Buchanan's attitude toward South Carolina satisfied Seward, who was his secret channel to congressional Republicans during the secession crisis. Cameron could be placated by being replaced with a former Pennsylvania Democrat. Stanton courted the favor of all three with wily behind-the-scenes maneuvers and an ingratiating "versatility" in answering queries.[2]

On the question of slavery Stanton kept his cards close to his vest; in fact, he seemed to play with a different hand according to the occasion. Publicly, Stanton was silent on slavery while his appointment was being considered. Privately, he voiced divergent opinions. With McClellan Stanton favored a cautious, border-state approach, but he approved and even strengthened

Secretary of War Edwin Stanton in 1862. From a carte de visite. Library of Congress Prints and Photographs Division.

Cameron's annual report recommending that slave runaways be recruited and armed. "Can you tell me," Dana wrote Senator Charles Sumner, "what Stanton's sentiments really are about slavery?" It was a question no one could answer with certainty.[3]

There was no doubting Stanton's zeal for prosecuting the war. On this issue Dana immediately sensed an ally in Stanton. Both wanted the Confederates' rebellion crushed, and they were quick to suspect disloyalty among Northerners less obsessively committed to victory. Both suspected that behind the pomp and procrastination of General McClellan—formerly a friend of Stanton—lay a fatal unwillingness to fight. As the Union army drilled endlessly, Stanton and Dana were drawn together by their determination to prod its commanders to attack. Stanton looked to Dana for editorial support, Dana to Stanton for a military reveille. Unlike Dana's wooing of Cameron, his budding friendship with Stanton was not simply convenient to the *Tribune*; it forged a partnership of two forceful men who saw eye to eye.

When Stanton's appointment was announced on January 20, 1862, Dana penned a *Tribune* editorial that opened their correspondence. Union success depended upon clearing Washington of the rebel spies, slack military officers, and rapacious contract-jobbers tolerated by Cameron, Dana wrote, and Stanton was just the man for the cleanup. Stanton replied with a letter of thanks and promised a thorough housecleaning: "As soon as I can get the machinery of the office working, the rats cleaned out, & the ratholes stopped we shall *move*." Ten days later, Dana declared that the public was fed up with the "policy of 'wait-and-get-ready'" and wanted "war in earnest." Stanton concurred: "Instead of an army stuck in the mud on the Potomac," he told Dana privately, "we should have . . . one hundred thousand men venting upon Nashville & sweeping rebellion and treason out of Kentucky & Tennessee with fire & sword. . . . We have had no war; we have not even been playing war." The main problems were his own department, which was "still poisoned with treason, or helpless from imbecility," and the lack of a "military genius" to command the armies.[4]

Dana and Republican Radicals had a longstanding candidate for the latter post: John C. Frémont was still without a command. When Frémont arrived in Washington to face the Joint Committee on the Conduct of the War, Dana pronounced the charges against him "groundless." The committee's chairman, the Radical Republican Ben Wade, seemed to agree; he wrote Dana that "the investigation has proceeded far enough to convince me beyond a doubt that . . . [Frémont] was sacrificed by a weak and wicked administration to appease the wrath of an indignant people." Frémont's military rivals in Missouri had engineered his dismissal, Dana claimed. Frémont may not be "a great general," Dana wrote Pike, but "considering the paucity of the means given him he did the very best he could." Dana aired these complaints to Stanton and pressed him to give Frémont a second chance.[5]

"If Gen. Fremont has any fight in him, he shall (so far as I am concerned) have a chance to show it, and I have told him so," Stanton replied. In March the committee began to interrogate witnesses hostile to Frémont, but Dana and Greeley obtained Frémont's testimony and published it with supporting documents in a spread that covered thirty columns of the *Tribune*. Radical Republican newspapers considered it a complete vindication of their hero. Faced with political pressure, Stanton and Lincoln decided to appoint Frémont to a new command in the mountainous areas of Virginia, Kentucky, and Tennessee—a minor post, but enough to satisfy Dana and most of Frémont's partisans.[6]

Stanton's responsiveness to Frémont's backers and his unrelenting work habits helped him win over Radical Republicans and editorial warhawks like Dana. The joint committee invited Stanton to secret sessions to discuss plans to root out military cowardice and corruption. Stanton collapsed from overwork less than a month after taking office but was back at his desk in a few days, assuring Dana that he "never enjoyed more perfect health." "Stanton was entirely absorbed in his duties," Dana later recalled, "and his energy in prosecuting them was something almost superhuman." Subordinates who did not find his example infectious were threatened with replacement. When Stanton took hold of the War Department, Dana wrote, "the armies seemed to grow."[7]

In February, news of Grant's capture of Fort Donelson came to Dana's desk from a *Tribune* reporter at Fortress Monroe, who heard of it from exchanged Union prisoners. For once the *Tribune* managed to scoop its rivals on military news. Dana put out an extra and placed the story on page one beneath a woodcut of the flag. His editorial praised Stanton as "the Minister who has organized the victory." Stanton rushed to correct him. In letters to the *Tribune* the secretary deflected praise onto the "gallant" western soldiers and officers. There were two keys to winning battles, Stanton wrote: The first was "the spirit of the Lord that moved our soldiers to rush into battle"; the second was "boldly pursuing and striking the foe." Stanton's criticism of McClellan's stalling was implied but obvious.[8]

The *Tribune* exchange was widely reprinted and evoked a strong reaction. "No high official in my day has written a dozen lines half as weighty and telling," the New York patrician George Templeton Strong wrote in his diary. Not everyone agreed. Writing as an anonymous Washington correspondent, Lincoln secretary John Hay bristled that "Dana, that demon of discord whose excess of bile always makes him most miserable when others are most happy, took it into his head to throw an apple of contention into the feast by ascribing the sole merit of victory to one man [Stanton]." McClellan's supporters charged that Stanton had "sold out to the Tribune & [was] thwarting McClellan in every possible way."[9]

As part of this public relations war a pro-McClellan reporter wrote that in a recent speech Stanton had credited Union successes in the West to McClellan's "gigantic and well-matured" plans. Dana was skeptical and sent the story to Stanton. It was "a ridiculous and impudent effort to puff the general," Stanton fumed, "by a false publication of words I never uttered." Stanton assured Dana that they shared the same opinion of McClellan: "Was it not a funny sight to see a certain military hero in the telegraph office at Washington last Sunday organizing victory, and . . . capturing Fort Donelson *six hours after* Grant and Smith . . . had victorious possession! It would be a picture worthy of *Punch*."[10]

Out of patience, Stanton issued a private decree: McClellan, he told Dana, "has got to fight or run away; and while men are striving nobly in the West, the champagne and oysters on the Potomac must be stopped." Lincoln agreed, and on January 31, 1862, the president issued Special War Order No. 1 commanding the Army of the Potomac to advance directly toward Richmond by Washington's birthday (February 22). McClellan proposed an elaborate flanking assault upon the Confederate capital by troops to be transported by steamer to the Yorktown Peninsula. Lincoln and Stanton reluctantly assented, but not until April 1 did McClellan embark upon the disastrous Peninsula Campaign.[11]

Just after Dana dispatched reporters to accompany McClellan, he lost his position on the *Tribune*. A few weeks later he visited Washington and toured the Bull Run battlefield, but his real mission was to sound out opportunities in government. There was talk of a diplomatic position, since several of Dana's *Tribune* colleagues were already in European posts; but he preferred not to leave the country during the crisis.[12] The most promising lead came from Dana's new friend Stanton, who told him they shared "one heart and one mind in this great cause" and confided his intention to hire him in the War Department.[13] A month later an opportunity arose. It was not what Dana had sought: a temporary rather than permanent post, one that took him not to the corridors of power in Washington but to a distant river town on the winding Mississippi. But it got his foot in the government's door.

"A Regular System of Fraud"

Cairo, Illinois, was a damp, uninviting town of great strategic importance. Located at the confluence of the Mississippi and Ohio Rivers, it sat on a marsh protected by levees from the great rivers' overflow. Cairo had new life pumped into it by the Civil War. By 1862 it was the Union's most important river port in the West, the staging ground for General Grant's efforts to split the Confederacy in two. From its docks Union gunboats were dispatched on expeditions up the Ohio and Tennessee Rivers, and Union armies on both sides of the Mississippi—in Kentucky, Tennessee, and Missouri—received their supplies and munitions.

When the British novelist Anthony Trollope visited in February 1862, he found the town's streets "absolutely impassable with mud" and donned high boots to negotiate its plank sidewalks. Up the Ohio River Trollope witnessed a test-trial of Union mortar-boats that failed when their bottoms leaked. Thirty-eight of these costly vessels had been purchased, a "spectacle of reckless prodigality," Trollope judged, but also a testament to the "smartness of the contractor who had secured to himself the job of building them."[14]

The problem of rapidly outfitting the mushrooming Union army led to improvised, irregular supply procedures and, as Trollope suspected, enticing opportunities for corruption. There was growing evidence that quartermaster operations at Cairo were being managed incompetently and perhaps dishonestly. In May 1862 Dana accepted an assignment from Stanton to serve on a temporary fact-finding body. "By direction of the President," the official charge read, "a commission has been appointed consisting of Messrs. George S. Boutwell, Stephen T. Logan and yourself, to examine and report upon all unsettled claims against the War Department at Cairo, Illinois, that may have originated prior to the first day of April 1862." Boutwell, once a Free Soil governor of Massachusetts, and Logan, a former law partner of Lincoln, were to meet Dana in Cairo in mid-July to begin their work. Dana welcomed the opportunity to supplement his *Tribune* severance pay with a stipend of eight dollars a day; more important, he hoped the appointment might lead to a regular job offer from Stanton. Through the commission Dana made important military and political contacts, but it proved a thornier assignment than he had imagined.[15]

The problems at Cairo dated from the summer of 1861, when Reuben B. Hatch was appointed assistant quartermaster with the rank of captain. Lincoln himself had requested Hatch's appointment as a favor for an old friend. Hatch was the younger brother of Ozias M. Hatch, a political crony of Lincoln who had helped secure his nomination at Chicago and formed a circle of Republicans who advised Lincoln on appointments and fought pro-Confederate influences in Illinois. Captain Hatch, put under military arrest in February 1862, was accused of using illegal purchasing methods and defrauding the government through inflated billing on vouchers issued for supplies.[16]

The transactions Dana's commission was asked to untangle were complicated, but Hatch's ties to prominent Illinois Republicans and to the

White House made this an especially ticklish case. Another complication was that the investigation arose from three different sources: the House of Representatives, General Grant, and the War Department. This division of labor caused delays, duplications, and omissions, and at times it put the investigators at cross-purposes. All the while, Lincoln lurked in the background as Hatch's patron, and eventually the commander in chief was given the last word on how the case should proceed.[17]

In July 1861 Congress formed a House committee to inquire into contracts relating to war operations. Testimony presented at Cairo alleged irregularities under Captain Hatch such as long delays in the settling of accounts, use of his clerk as a middleman, and diversion of government horses to Hatch's own farm. There the matter stood until mid-December, when the *Chicago Tribune* printed a story that local lumber dealers were instructed to fill out false bills to cover the Cairo quartermaster agent's "commission." Grant, then commander at Cairo, sent an aide to Chicago to investigate. His inquiries established that Hatch and his clerk Henry Wilcox had overbilled the government and may have split the profits with the lumbermen. Grant had Hatch and Wilcox arrested and quartermaster records seized.[18]

Meanwhile, Quartermaster General Montgomery Meigs ordered Grant to submit outstanding claims at Cairo to a War Department commission convened in St. Louis to examine military contracts, with Frémont as its primary target. Commission members found strong indications that transactions in coal, ice, and lumber were tainted with fraud. Perhaps to cover his tracks, Hatch regularly had his clerk sign the vouchers for him, a practice that in itself was illegal. The commissioners recommended that no Cairo vouchers be paid without an investigation of claimants under oath.[19]

Meigs also urged Stanton to dispatch an attorney to investigate the allegations against Hatch. Stanton sent Assistant Secretary Thomas A. Scott, a former Pennsylvania Railroad executive who could be counted on to penetrate the fog of army contracts. In February 1862 Scott reported to Stanton that "the condition of affairs under Q. M. Hatch was about as bad as could well be imagined." Testimony from contractors had uncovered "a regular system of fraud": vouchers billing the government for lumber, hay, oats, and ferryboat rentals were inflated over costs, and "the difference, it is supposed, was to belong to the Quarter Master's Department *as perquisites*." Scott also reported that a few days after Hatch's arrest two of his ledgers were found dumped in the river. He recommended that Hatch's accounts be handed over to a competent officer who would settle all claims.[20]

Around the same time, the House Committee on Contracts, alerted by

Stanton, held hearings in Chicago that exposed Hatch's practice of overcharging for lumber to skim a "commission." Hatch compounded the fraud with a cover-up. He met secretly with the lumbermen to renegotiate their contracts in an attempt to paper over the deals, then hid his clerk Wilcox at a relative's farm to evade government investigators. The House report concluded that Hatch had "combined with other parties to defraud the government and put money directly into his own pocket."[21]

Thus, by the spring of 1862 four separate investigations presented evidence of Hatch's involvement in irregularities and fraud at Cairo. Lincoln, meanwhile, came under pressure from his Illinois friends, who sought a quick resolution that would exonerate Hatch. Lincoln asked Judge Advocate General John F. Lee if he as president could order a court-martial; Lee advised him not to interpose. Ozias Hatch and Illinois governor Richard Yates wrote Lincoln that the charges against the quartermaster were "*frivolous* and without the shadow of foundation in fact." Lincoln again asked Lee for an opinion, declaring: "I also personally know Capt. R. B. Hatch, and never, before heard any thing against his character." Lee consulted Meigs, who replied that it would be "highly improper" to pass over the charges until Hatch was cleared of wrongdoing.[22]

As the case dragged on, the options narrowed to two: a court of inquiry into the allegations against Hatch, or a commission to examine and settle the Cairo claims. Stanton and Meigs left the decision to Lincoln but made their preference clear: A court would sit for a long time and divert too many officers from military duties; and contract claims had to be resolved if supplies for a summer offensive were to be procured. A commission could settle all outstanding claims and could also produce evidence to resolve the question of a court-martial. Lincoln agreed. In April he wrote Stanton to inform him and to suggest possible appointees for the commission.[23]

Two months later Stanton appointed Dana, Boutwell, and Logan. The group convened in Cairo on June 18; they set up quarters in a shed on the levee and organized a mess with the officer in command. Their situation was "disagreeable to an extent that cannot be realized easily," according to Boutwell. The summer heat was torrid, dead animals littered the ground, and every evening they endured a collision of thunderstorms over the two rivers. Almost immediately Logan resigned due to illness and was replaced by Shelby Cullom, another Lincoln crony. Despite the heat the commissioners worked hard; they met almost daily until July 31. According to the sketchy minutes that survive, two-thirds of the meetings were spent examining individual claims presented by contractors and other aggrieved parties, with Captain Hatch present much

of the time. On July 12 Boutwell ceded the chairmanship to Dana, who over-
saw the final two weeks of testimony and preparation of the commission's
report.[24]

All told, 1,696 claims were examined, amounting to nearly $600,000. The
value of those approved and certified for payment was $451,105. Most of the
claims rejected were for requisitions made by armies in the field against citizens with inadequate documentation or whom the commissioners found disloyal. Of the claims accepted, most were credited at face value. "A very small
percentage of the claims were rejected because of fraud," Dana recalled. "In
almost every case it was possible to suppose that the apparent fraud was accident." Astonishingly, Dana and the commissioners found no evidence of
wrongdoing by Hatch. The full reason may never be known, since the Cairo
Commission's report disappeared from the War Department archives without
being printed. But the surviving files suggest some answers.[25]

Part of the problem lay in the Cairo Commission's ambiguous mandate.
Were the commissioners merely to deal with outstanding claims, or were
they to undertake a sweeping investigation of quartermaster operations?
Should they investigate allegations of fraud if the relevant claims were not
presented? Although their course was not consistent, Dana and the commissioners mainly stuck to settling claims. Hatch's attorney argued that his client
should not be asked to testify on the general management of the Quartermaster
Office but only on particular claims. No claims were submitted relating to the
controversial lumber and ice transactions, but Hatch was allowed to insert
statements into the record that inflated prices were "a business necessity" and
he received no kickbacks.[26]

At times the Cairo Commission seemed to take its investigative role seriously. Two of Hatch's clerks were examined under oath on business prac-
tices in his office. The Cairo Commission conducted a reasonably thorough
investigation of shoe and boot contracts, in which they found no evidence to
sustain allegations of a 5 percent premium to secure the deal. According to
Dana, the Cairo Commission also looked into the charge that Hatch destroyed
incriminating ledgers but found he had no access to them after his arrest. The
ledgers discarded in the Ohio River were simply a crude attempt to keep accounts early in Hatch's service. In short, Dana informed Meigs, "it was the
unanimous conclusion of the Commission that there was no evidence before
it to prove him [Hatch] other than an honest man."[27]

Yet even by the loosest of standards no thorough investigation had been undertaken. The commissioners did not interrogate Hatch's clerk Wilcox; they
did not review testimony before the House committee; and they failed to

check the discarded ledger books against extant vouchers. For the vast majority of claims they simply accepted Hatch's sworn certification "as to their correctness and legality."[28] There is little doubt that Hatch was guilty of fraud in the lumber deals, and it was obvious that he ran his office in a haphazard and sometimes illegal fashion. But Dana and his colleagues did not find—nor did they look hard for—evidence to indict him. Beyond the priority they gave to settling claims, were there other factors at work? Did Hatch's connection to Lincoln produce a too-friendly inquiry?

Stanton no doubt felt some political pressure to acquit Hatch, but it is hard to imagine him meekly acquiescing, given his prickly independence in other cases Lincoln referred to him. One of the commissioners (Logan) had been suggested by the president, but Dana and Boutwell were the war secretary's choices and were known for tough stands against corruption. It is also hard to imagine Dana on his first assignment trying to please Stanton with a lackluster investigation. The two men fully expected to sustain the charges against Hatch and were pleasantly surprised by their findings. "There is rascality in some of the [western] Quartermasters I am pretty certain," Dana wrote a friend, "but generally the business of the army is honestly done. Charges of fraud, as I have ascertained, dwindle when you come to sift the evidence." Years later Dana remembered that finding so little corruption in a case "where the charges seemed so well based . . . was a source of solid satisfaction to every one in the War Department."[29]

Obviously, Dana and his colleagues cut Hatch enormous slack as an inexperienced quartermaster and a Union loyalist operating in a border-state region. The irregularities they found—unauthorized signatures and deceptive vouchers—Dana dismissed as mistakes "by green volunteer officers who did not understand the technical duties of making out military requisitions and returns." High prices had to be offered suppliers because Hatch had to run his department without cash for several months. Hatch, Grant later explained to Lincoln, "offered his services to his country early in the war, . . . was placed from the start in one of the most trying positions in the Army," and faced the resentment of contractors who were paid late, a position "embarrassing and dangerous to his reputation even without a fault being committed by himself." It was nearly the same argument Dana and Greeley had used to defend Frémont's lavish expenditures in Missouri.[30]

When Reuben Hatch was exonerated, his Illinois supporters wrote Lincoln asking that he be released and remanded to duty. Lincoln passed the requests to Meigs, who remained suspicious and delayed Hatch's release until the president ordered it six weeks later.[31] In January 1864 Lincoln, bowing to

Ozias Hatch's patronage request in an election year, asked Stanton to appoint Reuben Hatch a quartermaster in the regular army: "I know not whether it can be done conveniently, but if it can, I would like it," the president told the war secretary. Meigs again was the main obstacle. Lincoln's secretary John Nicolay asked Dana to remind Meigs that the commissioners had found Hatch innocent. Dana's letter "removed a painful impression from my mind in regard to Hatch," Meigs wrote, and in March 1864 Hatch was promoted to chief quartermaster of the Army's XIII Corps.[32]

Hatch's subsequent army career justified Meigs's hesitation and betrayed Dana's and the other commissioners' vote of confidence. Soon he was in trouble again; this time it was a matter not of dollars but of life and death. Assigned with Grant and Lincoln's endorsement to the Department of the Mississippi at Vicksburg, Hatch became a prime contributor to the *Sultana* disaster of April 27, 1865, in which a steamboat jammed with 2,400 Union veterans, many returning from Confederate prisons, exploded and sank near Memphis, killing more than 1,800 persons. The *Sultana*'s certified capacity was less than 400, but Hatch and others allowed it to be overloaded even though two other transport steamers were available at Vicksburg. Testimony indicated that a possible kickback from the steamboat's owners influenced Hatch and his subordinates. Experts contend that the overcrowding likely caused the *Sultana*'s boilers to overheat and explode. After the incident Hatch testified briefly before investigators, denying responsibility. Hatch narrowly escaped a court-martial, but General Meigs stripped him of his quartermaster duties. He was honorably mustered out in July 1865.[33]

Although its trail of evidence went back to the Cairo Commission's report and to Lincoln's intervention on Hatch's behalf two years later, the *Sultana* tragedy was eclipsed by the Lincoln assassination and manhunt and escaped close political scrutiny.[34] Dana and his fellow commissioners did not fix their findings to please Lincoln, but their lax examination of Reuben Hatch's behavior at Cairo, and Lincoln's eagerness to use patronage appointments to please his Illinois backers, inadvertently led to the worst maritime disaster in US history prior to Pearl Harbor.

Despite the Cairo Commission's heavy workload, Dana managed to get away from Cairo a few times. In early July, taking a steamboat downriver to Memphis, he met General Ulysses Grant for the first time. The occasion was a Fourth of July celebration to which military officers, government officials, and newspapermen were invited. At dinner Dana sat between Grant and his chief of staff, Major John Rawlins. Dana knew that Grant's reputation was under a cloud for lack of vigilance at the Battle of Shiloh in April, where his

The steamboat *Sultana* photographed April 26, 1865, on the Mississippi at Helena, Arkansas, overloaded with Union soldiers, the day before the boat's boilers exploded and it sank, killing more than 1,800 men. Library of Congress Prints and Photographs Division.

troops had been surprised by a morning attack and suffered serious losses before driving the Rebels back. But Dana found Grant imperturbable, giving the "pleasant impression . . . of a man of simple manners, straightforward, cordial, and unpretending." After the meal Dana proposed a toast to "Honest Abraham Lincoln." When others offered toasts to the victor of Fort Donelson and the band struck up "See the Conquering Hero Comes," Grant rose to say that he "dropped speech-making when he donned his uniform." He would rather "talk" the way he had at Donelson. Dana's admiration for the taciturn general grew deeper in the year ahead. They would be together again the next Independence Day, celebrating the fall of Vicksburg.[35]

In late July Dana joined his fellow Cairo commissioner Boutwell for another trip down the Mississippi, this time at Lincoln's behest. In the face of pressures from runaway slaves and congressional Republicans, the slow-moving president had decided to take a momentous step toward undermining the Confederacy. On July 22 Lincoln presented to the cabinet his draft of a preliminary Emancipation Proclamation warning Confederates that he would free slaves in rebellious areas after a short interval. The cabinet urged Lincoln to wait for a military victory before announcing his decree. Even then, Lincoln worried that Union military officers in the West and the border states would oppose the measure and perhaps resign in protest. "There are fifty thousand bayonets in the Union armies from the Border Slave States," he told a delegation of Chicago clergy at the White House. They might "go over to the rebels" in reaction to an emancipation decree. Anxious for reassurance, Lincoln sent word to Dana and Boutwell to test the sentiments of leading officers in Kentucky and Tennessee.[36]

Setting out from Cairo, they stopped at various river ports to interview Union soldiers. At Columbus, Kentucky, a group of officers came aboard and were prompted by Dana and Boutwell to speak. General Grenville Dodge, a former railroad executive whom Lincoln had met during a tour of Iowa in 1859, spoke up for freeing the slaves. Dodge was already employing nearly a thousand "contrabands" in building military railroads and working in the camps. He believed in "using the negroes as much as possible" to suppress the rebellion, he told Dana and Boutwell. "They should be freed," since they were "the mainstay of the South, . . . raising all the crops" while white Southerners left for the army. Most officers present applauded Dodge's speech. Dana asked Dodge to put his views in writing and took them to Stanton, who passed them to Lincoln. Dodge's testimonial contained "everything that we desired," Dana reported. Through this channel Lincoln received crucial reassurance about the potential impact of an emancipation decree.[37]

A Series of Setbacks

Dana delivered the Cairo Commission's report to Stanton in the first week of August, then returned to New York. Even before the group adjourned, Boutwell was appointed Commissioner of Internal Revenue. Dana hoped that Stanton would be impressed enough with his service to offer him a position. Meanwhile, he could spend time with his family—he planned to guide his children, in birth order, through Dante's *Divine Comedy*. And beyond the family hearth there was work to do.[38]

One task was to finish the *American Cyclopedia*, whose volumes had been dribbling out since 1858. The sixteenth and final installment was published in 1863, with an essay on Martin Van Buren by Dana himself. Critical reception was mixed. The curmudgeonly Adam Gurowski, a contributor, declared that "people ought to be warned and preserved from such a heap of stupendous ignorance and bad faith." *Knickerbocker* magazine appreciated the encyclopedia's concise entries and its tone of sober factuality. Whatever the critics said, Dana and Ripley had guessed correctly that the American middle class wanted to own and display a symbol of their—and the nation's—arrival. By

January 1863, 14,000 sets had been printed, although many subscribers in the slave states had stopped their payments. Sales of this first American encyclopedia merited a revised edition in 1873, and by 1882 Appleton's had sold almost a million and a half volumes of both editions. Dana's share of the profits amounted to some $90,000. These royalties eventually made Dana a wealthy man, but little of this income materialized until after the war.[39]

Republican politics also continued to occupy Dana. He visited Washington frequently in the second half of 1862, observing Congress, confiding with decision makers, and sounding out job prospects. When not in Washington he sent letters to Chase and Stanton expressing opinions on appointments and policies. During the fall campaign Dana solicited Lincoln's intervention to thwart an irregular bid among dissidents in New York City, a revolt he attributed to troublesome Seward-Weed appointees in the Customs House. The regular candidate, Dana's friend Frederick Conkling, was safely reelected after Dana gave several speeches on his behalf.[40]

The feud between the Seward-Weed and Radical Republican factions in New York intensified with each election. In the fall of 1861 the *Tribune*'s attacks charging Weed with corruption and war profiteering had hit their mark when George Opdyke, a wealthy clothing merchant and ally of Dana, was elected mayor. Dana gloated that Weed's power as the boss of New York politics was gone. During the 1862 gubernatorial campaign the anti-Weed faction again smelled victory. Weed favored the War Democrat John A. Dix, while Dana, Greeley, and their allies backed James S. Wadsworth, a western New York patrician and Radical Republican. In a stunning reversal for Weed, Wadsworth was nominated on the first ballot and the convention adopted a platform supporting Lincoln's emancipation policy. But the *Albany Evening Journal* endorsed Wadsworth belatedly, and Weed made only a half-hearted effort to get him elected. When the November canvass ended with the Democrat Horatio Seymour as governor, Dana and his friends blamed Weed and his faction for sabotaging Wadsworth's ticket.[41]

Dana and his allies petitioned Lincoln, Stanton, and Chase for retaliation against the Weedites but met with little success. The most tantalizing opportunity for the Radicals to get even—and a chance for Dana to reenter the newspaper business—came in late 1862 when Weed decided to sell the *Albany Evening Journal*. Rebuffed by his party on the recent nominations, at odds with Lincoln on emancipation, and tired of being attacked as the "Lucifer of the Lobby," Weed decided to yield control after thirty years at the state capital's largest newspaper. Dana hoped his faction could supplant Weed's as New York's political kingmakers, and he coveted the *Journal*'s lucrative state printing contracts. He put together a credible bid to buy the paper. Determined to hold a controlling interest, Dana offered $30,000 for five-eighths of the *Journal* and 10 percent of the paper's job office. Negotiations continued until Weed refused to take Dana's New York City house in payment. A scramble for funds ensued. Dana obtained $10,000 in pledges at a small meeting of friends in New York City, and he wrote to Gerrit Smith and other Republican notables to raise more.[42]

In the end the deal fell through. Weed sold his interest to his current partners, including Seward's son Frederick. The *Evening Journal*'s staff disliked Weed's opposition to emancipation, and Weed's partners respected Dana's editorial abilities, but they anticipated "frequent collision" with Dana on political matters. The Albany boss settled for readier cash and more politically compatible successors. Disappointed, Dana announced his "narrow escape" to Pike and cried sour grapes: newspapers, he said, were a poor investment due to the wartime inflation of paper prices.[43]

Between his friend Wadsworth's electoral defeat and his own failed bid to buy Weed's paper, Dana suffered a third setback when he fumbled an opportunity to join Stanton's staff. In mid-November Assistant Secretary of War Peter Watson summoned Dana to Washington. Dana expected another investigative assignment, but when he arrived at the war office Stanton offered him the position of second assistant secretary. Stanton's brother-in-law Christopher Wolcott, the incumbent, was seriously ill. There were indications that Watson himself would not stay on after his one-year term expired early in 1863. Noting these probable vacancies, Lincoln secretary William Stoddard wrote that "these posts are not lucrative, and so laborious that no man, properly qualified, would accept either of them, except from patriotic motives." Dana took Stanton's offer without hesitation, and the war secretary considered the matter settled.[44]

Out on the street Dana ran into Charles G. Halpine, an Irish American newspaperman and sometime poet better known by his pen name, "Miles O'Reilly." Dana told Halpine about his appointment, and when Halpine passed the news along to Washington correspondents it appeared in the New York dailies and was clipped by papers from Boston to San Francisco. The leak annoyed Stanton, who was adamant about controlling the flow of news from his department, and he abruptly withdrew the offer. It happened so quickly that the retractions in New York dailies ran simultaneously with notices of Dana's appointment in many out-of-town sheets. Dana and Stanton parted amicably, but he was embarrassed enough not to discuss the incident with friends.[45]

Public events combined with these career setbacks to leave Dana discouraged. At the end of 1862 he told Pike he felt "heavy hearted about the country." The Union military seemed to be "drifting to hopeless destruction." The Army of the Potomac had been crushed at Fredericksburg, and western forces were mired in Mississippi mud. Dana had just returned from Washington, drawn by reports of a major cabinet change. Congressional Radicals had conspired to oust Seward from the cabinet, but they were thwarted when Lincoln maneuvered to obtain Chase's resignation as well and then rejected both. Dana reasoned that the cabinet truce could not hold for long without military victories. In New York the Republican Party was "hopelessly broken." Seward and Weed, after helping to elect a Democratic governor, were now "mak[ing] war on the 'radicals' more than on the rebels."[46]

The multiple disappointments of late 1862 created a vacuum for Dana's energies, and into it rushed his reawakened obsession with financial security. As the year closed, Dana joined a venture to get rich through the cotton trade.

Once the war broke out, cotton was "no more a king in the South," Adam Gurowski declared, "but the temptation . . . to dirt and vileness for many, even once tolerably honest men in the North. Cotton licenses, cotton contracts, cotton speculations, . . . [are] the bait held out by Satan to ruin men's souls and drag them with hurricane velocity into perdition." Charles Dana was one of a wide assortment of Northerners, including his nemesis Thurlow Weed, who were enticed to trade cotton across the lines. By late 1862 Dana's *Tribune* salary had run out. His failure to purchase the *Albany Evening Journal* attracted him to a profit-making scheme that might enable him to "take hold of [a newspaper] independently." By procuring cotton from Union-occupied areas in the Mississippi Valley Dana would also be helping the country—so he was told by his friend, Secretary Chase. Reopening the trade could relieve shortages in Northern mills and keep England from allying with the Confederacy.[47]

Patriotic or not, it was perfectly legal. In July 1861 Congress gave the president permission to license commercial trade with the rebellious states under supervision by the Treasury Department. In February 1862 Lincoln authorized a "partial restoration" of trade, which allowed exchanges where federal authority had been reestablished by military occupation. Trade followed the flag with spectacular—and often unsettling—results. As Union armies moved down the Mississippi they opened the gates to a huge, fantastically profitable business in cotton. If private traders with passes could get hold of cotton seized by the army or buy it from willing planters, they could sell bales in Memphis or Cincinnati for ten times the purchase price.[48]

In pursuit of such rewards Dana entered into a partnership with Roscoe

Conkling of Utica, later a United States senator, and George W. Chadwick, a New York businessman. Dana and Conkling each invested $10,000; Chadwick contributed his expertise as buyer and manager. Despite his recent flap with Stanton, Dana procured letters from the war secretary commending him to the region's generals. In early January 1863 Dana and Chadwick traveled to Memphis. They set up headquarters in the Gayoso Hotel, where Grant and his wife Julia also kept rooms, and began scouting opportunities. Dana used Stanton's letter of endorsement to procure a pass from Grant authorizing him to travel "through all parts of this Military Dept."[49]

Then, quite suddenly, Dana underwent a change of heart. As he conversed with army officers who ran a side business in cotton and walked Memphis's streets overrun with civilian middlemen, Dana decided that the cotton trade should be stopped. It is easy to be skeptical about Dana's about-face. The fact that his opportunities for profits were more "occasional" than expected probably eased the way. Grant may have criticized the trade when Dana first approached him, and he could rise in Grant's eyes by agreeing. But it appears that Dana was genuinely shocked by the extent to which the trade preoccupied Union soldiers. He drafted a letter to Stanton advising that abolishing the permit system had become a "military necessity":

> The mania for sudden fortunes made in cotton, raging in a vast population of Jews and Yankees scattered throughout this whole country, and in this town almost exceeding the numbers of the regular residents, has to an alarming extent corrupted and demoralized the army. Every colonel, captain, or quartermaster is in secret partnership with some operator in cotton; every soldier dreams of adding a bale of cotton to his monthly pay. I had no conception of the extent of this evil until I came and saw for myself.[50]

Dana proposed that private purchasers be excluded from occupied areas and army quartermasters purchase cotton at a fixed price, then ship it northward for sale at public auction. With market prices covering the costs, the operation would become self-supporting; it would also free up thousands of army men consumed with cotton mania for the critical business of war.

Before Dana sent the letter to Stanton he took it to Grant. It was common knowledge that the general hated cotton traders, whom he called a "gang of thieves." When his own father turned up with three business partners from Cincinnati—who happened to be Jewish—and asked for permits, Grant issued General Orders No. 11 in December 1862 expelling all Jews from his department within twenty-four hours. Protests quickly reached the White

House, and Grant was forced to revoke his anti-Semitic decree. By showing Grant his letter against the trade, Dana could showcase his patriotism and add Grant's authority to his advice for Stanton. Not surprisingly, Grant agreed with Dana's assessment of the cotton trade, except for the sentence imputing corruption to every officer, which Dana admitted he did not intend literally. When Dana offered to go to Washington and "endeavor to get it [the cotton trade] stopped altogether," Grant readily agreed.[51]

Toward the end of January 1863 Dana followed his letter to the capital, where he impressed his and Grant's views upon Stanton and other administration leaders.[52] By this time the cabinet had discussed the cotton trade more than once and Lincoln had heard many reports that military officers "connive and share in the profits." Like Dana and Grant, he came to believe that the army in the West was "diverted from fighting the rebels to speculating in cotton." Dana's report probably played a role in Lincoln's proclamations of March 31 and April 2, 1863, which revoked previous trading privileges in occupied Confederate areas and required strict adherence to Treasury Department regulations. An order from Stanton restricting military involvement in the trade was even closer to the spirit of Dana's advice.[53] But not until the spring of 1864, when military authorities in Memphis issued drastic orders requiring permits of all travelers and outlawing all trading vessels, was the cotton trade in Tennessee effectively halted. By then, between twenty and thirty million dollars had been gained by the Confederacy in the exchange, and absorption with cotton trading had cost the western army a third of its strength, by Grant's estimate.[54]

One reason the flow of cotton across the lines eventually slowed was that its chief producers defected. As Grant's army and Sherman's zigzagged down the Mississippi, rebel planters fled inland and slaves from local plantations worked their way northward behind the Union lines. Treated as "contrabands," they found work in camps organized by Grant's appointee, John Eaton. By the time Dana arrived, thousands of these refugees, just declared free by Lincoln's Emancipation Proclamation, had been herded into camps two miles outside Memphis, cordoned off so effectively that Dana recalled years later seeing few blacks on the city's streets at the time.[55]

Dana on Emancipation

Dana's wartime attitude toward slaves and emancipation must be pieced together mainly from private evidence, but the record is clear enough: Greeley scribbled most *Tribune* editorials that advised Lincoln to free slaves owned by Rebels and enlist them in the Union army; but his managing editor ran them and seconded their sentiments. Writing to James Pike in January 1862, Dana regretted that "those who would oppose arming the negroes are more numerous than the friends of that measure." Two months later he served as an honorary officer of a mass meeting at the Cooper Institute that pressed Lincoln and Congress to adopt emancipation as a measure to win the war and remove its root cause.[56]

After his forced resignation from the *Tribune* Dana lacked a public forum for his views, but private evidence from the summer of 1862 indicates his zeal for making emancipation official Union policy. Dana's use of General Dodge's testimony to encourage Lincoln toward emancipation is one example; another comes from the reminiscences of Lincoln's Illinois crony, Leonard Swett, concerning an August 1862 visit to the White House. While the president was discussing arguments for and against a proclamation, he showed Swett "a dozen or more letters from Dana of the Tribune to the general effect that all the men in the Administration were a set of 'wooden heads' who were doing nothing and letting the country go to the dogs." These were likely not letters but clippings of Dana's biting *Tribune* editorials; but they established Dana's association with the pro-emancipation lobby in Lincoln's mind.[57]

In September 1862 Lincoln announced his intent to emancipate the slaves of rebel owners at the end of the year unless the Confederates quit the war. On the basis of a letter to Seward that is misattributed to Dana, several historians have asserted that Dana had serious qualms about Lincoln's proposal or even opposed it.[58] In fact he strongly supported it as a way to crush the rebellion as well as to bring justice on behalf of slaves. Like Lincoln and many Republicans who had not been prewar abolitionists, Dana believed the war made presidential emancipation legally possible and militarily desirable. Declaring blacks in the rebel states free would ruin Southern agriculture, prevent England and France from recognizing the Confederacy, and—most important to Dana—enable the Union army to enroll thousands of former slaves eager to destroy their masters and liberate their fellows.[59]

Just before the Emancipation Proclamation took effect, Dana expressed his disgust to Pike that "a very large minority of the northern people still love slavery & hate negroes with a zeal surpassing all their other passions." Dana lumped in this group not only Democrats but also conservative Republicans like Weed, whose faction, he warned Stanton, was scheming to remove him from the cabinet and "defeat the emancipation policy."[60]

Dana viewed Lincoln's decision to free Southern slaves on January 1,

1863, as fitting punishment for the Rebels' "great crime." Initially he meant the crime of secession, but by the time the Emancipation Proclamation had taken effect he acknowledged that slaveholding itself was the root cause of the sectional war. Sounding very much like an abolitionist, he told Pike that the Army of the Potomac's galling defeats may have been "a necessary chastisement of Providence" for a slaveholding republic. At New York Dana presided over a Republican banquet on Washington's birthday convened to endorse Lincoln's emancipation edict. His toast hailed it as "a military act necessary for the National defense, but none the less memorable in history as wiping off an infinite blot from the fair name of the American people."[61]

By mid-1863 Charles Dana had come to see the South's acquiescence in emancipation as an essential precondition of national reunification. His friend James Pike heard rumors in Europe that Lincoln would revoke the Emancipation Proclamation for Confederate states that might rejoin the Union. Dana dismissed them and labeled this scenario a "calamity." He was convinced that Northerners would no longer tolerate a "House Divided" over slavery and would govern the South "for fifty years if necessary by military power" to prevent it. Still, during the war the long-term consequences of black emancipation concerned Dana—and nearly all Republicans—far less than its immediate contribution to Union victory.[62]

6 "Mr. Stanton's Spy"

On April 13, 1863, Charles Dana wrote to a friend in Europe from Milliken's Bend, Louisiana, on the banks of the Mississippi. He was troubleshooting for Lincoln and Stanton again:

> You will ask what the deuce I am about away down here with Vicksburg almost in sight, and Grant's big army stretched up and down the river, its white tents affording a new decoration to the natural magnificence of these broad plains. Well, I am here as a "special commissioner" of the War Department, a sort of official spectator and companion to the movements of this part of the campaign, charged particularly with overseeing and regulating the paymasters, and generally with making myself useful. With the generals, big and little, . . . I am on friendly terms, and of course see and know all the interior operations of this toughest of tough jobs, the reopening of the Mississippi.[1]

The day before, Dana got his first good look at Vicksburg from a gunboat chugging downriver under a flag of truce to exchange prisoners. "It is an ugly place . . . with its line of bluffs commanding the channel for fully seven miles and battery piled above battery all the way." Still, he was upbeat about Grant's chances. "Like all who really know the facts, I feel no sort of doubt that we shall before long get the nut cracked."[2]

"This Toughest of Tough Jobs"

Vicksburg was indeed a tough nut, but cracking it was essential to winning the war. Dubbed the "Gibraltar of the West," the city commanded the Mississippi River from its position atop a line of 200-foot bluffs on the east bank. Nature also protected the city against land invasions, since approaches by road were thwarted by bayous, swamps, and ravines. Its location made the city essential for the Union to seize. Situated roughly midway between Memphis and New

Orleans, both under Union control, it became the focal point for the Federals' attempt to patrol the entire Mississippi. "Vicksburg is the key," Lincoln told Admiral David Porter. "This war can never be brought to a close until that key is in our pocket."[3]

The job of grabbing it belonged to Ulysses Grant. A plain, taciturn man of medium height, Grant had found in the Civil War a potential cure for his life's disappointments. Graduated from West Point with an undistinguished record, he served as a quartermaster during the Mexican War. Later assigned to posts in the Pacific Northwest, Grant became lonely and bored and took to drink, initiating a lifelong struggle with alcohol. After he resigned in 1854 to avoid a dishonorable discharge, Grant stumbled badly at making a living in business and farming. When the Civil War broke out, he had been reduced to an assistant in his family's leather store in Galena, Illinois. Cynical relatives nicknamed him "Useless."

Yet Grant proved calm and confident in battle, and he possessed the determination and strategic insight to succeed where other Union generals failed. His ascent from colonel of an Illinois regiment to command of the Army of the Tennessee was capped by triumphs at Forts Henry and Donelson, but it stalled at Shiloh when his troops appeared unprepared for a Confederate attack. In the summer of 1862 Grant was restored to command with the directive to capture Vicksburg. Success would put to rest lingering doubts about his abilities and habits; failure would confirm them and set back the Union campaign in the West.

To approach Vicksburg, Grant first tried advancing southward along the Mississippi Central Railroad from Tennessee while his subordinate, General William T. Sherman commanding the XV Corps, attacked Vicksburg's northern defenses. The campaign met with failure after Sherman's troops took heavy losses at Chickasaw Bayou. Undaunted, Grant moved his headquarters to Young's Point, Louisiana, at a loop of the Mississippi fifteen miles upriver from Vicksburg. From there he tried no fewer than four other approaches early in 1863. Two were canal and river excavations intended to bypass Vicksburg's batteries in order to move troops and supplies south of the city for an uncontested crossing. Two others tried to reach Vicksburg from the north by transporting troops through the labyrinthine shallow waterways of the Mississippi Delta to Haynes' Bluff, high ground that might force the city's evacuation.

These projects kept Grant's army busy during the winter, which was off-season for combat, but they made Grant look more desperate than enterprising. Despite a huge expenditure of time and manpower, none approached success. Privately Grant admitted that he was "much perplexed." "Heretofore I have had nothing to do but fight the enemy," he wrote his wife, Julia. "This time I have to overcome obstacles to reach him."[4]

Stalled by external barriers, Grant did a better job of fending off an internal threat in the form of the ambitious General John A. McClernand. A prominent Illinois Democrat and a friend of Lincoln who cast his lot early with the Union, McClernand was rewarded by the president with appointment to an independent command on the Mississippi River. Although he had no military training, McClernand was a quick learner and fearless fighter. When it became apparent that McClernand had designs to mount his own attack on Vicksburg, Grant took charge. He appointed McClernand to lead the XIII Corps, one of the three mobile corps under his command. McClernand protested loudly to Washington authorities. Grant wrote General in Chief Henry Halleck, calmly explaining that he and his fellow generals distrusted the green McClernand's ability to "conduct an expedition of the magnitude of this one successfully," but assuring Halleck that he would "cheerfully submit to and give a hearty support" to whatever his superiors ordered. Grant's decision stood; his tactful army politics won out over McClernand's heavy-handed political lobbying. He had neutralized McClernand's threat, but he was left with the problem of having to rely on a politically connected corps commander whose ability he questioned and who plotted constantly to take his place.[5]

If Grant's stalled engineering projects and the devious McClernand were not enough to bedevil him, rumors about his drinking circulated through Washington in early 1863. Some were instigated by McClernand's allies in an attempt to undermine Grant; others were spread by newspapermen pumping up their favorite generals. One of the latter wrote Treasury Secretary Chase that "our noble army of the Mississippi is being *wasted* by the foolish, drunken, stupid Grant." It was easy to detect self-interested motives in such charges, but endless repetition seemed to give them credibility. The deeper problem they purported to explain was undeniable: "This campaign is being badly managed," General Cadwallader Washburn complained to his brother Elihu, Grant's Illinois congressman and champion at the nation's capital. "The truth is, Grant . . . is frittering away time & strength to no purpose." Astonishingly, Congressman Washburne shared the letter with Chase, who showed it to Lincoln. Even Grant's political patron was losing faith in his protégé.[6]

Lincoln, however, steadfastly supported Grant. "I think Grant has hardly a friend left, except myself," he confided to John Hay. "What I want is generals who will fight battles and win victories. Grant has done this, and I propose to stand by him." Still, the president fretted. It was not just the lack of good news from Vicksburg that bothered him, but the lack of any news at all. Grant's updates to Washington averaged one terse message per week. "General Grant is a copious worker, and fighter, but a very meagre writer, or telegrapher," Lincoln complained to another general. In January the president was reduced to pleading with General John A. Dix in Virginia for news about the West: "Do Richmond papers have *anything* about Vicksburg?" For a while Lincoln considered sending General Butler to report on operations on the Mississippi.[7]

Mr. Stanton's Spy

In March Lincoln and Stanton decided on a different stratagem. They needed continuous and reliable reports about Grant from a disinterested party rather than a military man. Looking for someone to serve as the government's eyes and ears, they turned to Charles Dana, no doubt at Stanton's suggestion. Dana's newspaper experience commended him, and his trips to Cairo and Memphis certified his commitment to Union success. Summoning Dana to Washington, Stanton offered to make him a special commissioner of the War Department. As Dana later described it, the secretary and president wanted information to "settle their minds as to Grant." Grant's competence was the key question, to be demonstrated by progress in moving on Vicksburg. Information on his personal habits, especially drinking, was secondary but also important. Dana's job, Stanton told him simply, was "to report to me every day what you see."[8]

Dana readily accepted. To disguise his mission, his "ostensible function" was to investigate the pay service of the western armies. Grant had recently complained to Washington about long delays in paying his soldiers, so this seemed a plausible cover. Dana's letter of commission ordered paymasters to furnish him with information and military officers to offer "assistance, courtesy, and protection." Enclosed was a draft for one thousand dollars and identical letters of introduction to several commanders in the West, including Grant.[9]

Dana left New York on March 16, instructed to gather information at each stop and await further orders at Memphis. At Cairo and again at Columbus, Kentucky, Dana wired reports containing little information on affairs downriver. It was a measure of Lincoln's thirst for news that Stanton forwarded these unedifying dispatches to the White House.[10] From Columbus Dana took a boat to Memphis, where he arrived on March 23. Lincoln had already sent

General Stephen Hurlbut, the local commander, a barrage of anxious questions, and Hurlbut shared with Dana the sketchy information he had gleaned about Grant's operations from boatmen passing upriver and from Confederate newspapers. "This is not so well informed a place as I hoped to find it," Dana told Stanton.[11]

For the next nine days Dana sent Stanton regular dispatches from Memphis. At the War Department he had been taught a simple code known as a "transposition cipher" that he used throughout the war, often serving as his own clerk. After writing out his message in lines divided into a number of columns, Dana transmitted the columns as scrambled sentences. A keyword indicated the number of columns and the route through them the recipient should follow. Extra and decoy words were inserted, and a list of code words was used to denote persons, places, time, and numbers. Vicksburg's code was "Cupid" or "Oakum"; among Dana's aliases were "Spunky," "Squad," "Baltic," "Bellows," and, later in the war, "Raven" and "Rebel."[12] Using this cipher, Dana sent Stanton more than seventy reports in the next hundred days, most steamed upriver to Cairo then wired to Washington. Dispatches from Memphis took two or three days to reach Stanton, while news from Grant's headquarters at Milliken's Bend took four or five; return times were similar. On the Mississippi, Washington authorities did not enjoy the rapid telegraphic communication with the front as in Virginia. This made Dana's presence as their representative nearly as important as his reporting, since he was on hand to advise commanders or approve their plans on short notice.[13]

The news at Memphis confirmed that Grant's engineering projects were not going well. The canal dug to bypass Vicksburg refilled with mud when water rushed in and eroded the banks. Another dredging project, from Lake Providence to the Tensas River, was being hindered by overhanging trees and underwater snags. Meanwhile, the Yazoo Pass approach from Vicksburg's north had been halted by Confederate artillery planted at Fort Pemberton, a makeshift earthwork constructed at the junction of the streams that formed the Yazoo. There appeared to be one bright spot. On March 27 reports reached Memphis that Sherman's men and Porter's gunboats had taken a route through Steele's Bayou and landed regiments near Haynes' Bluff. Days later, Dana learned that this operation had bogged down far short of its destination and Porter had to be rescued by a detachment of Union infantry.[14]

Having "tried unsuccessfully every conceivable indirect means of attacking Vicksburg," Grant was reported to be considering a direct assault up its cliffs. Dana was skeptical, and when Grant's superintendent of railroads came to Memphis on April 2 Dana learned that Grant had rejected it. Instead, Grant

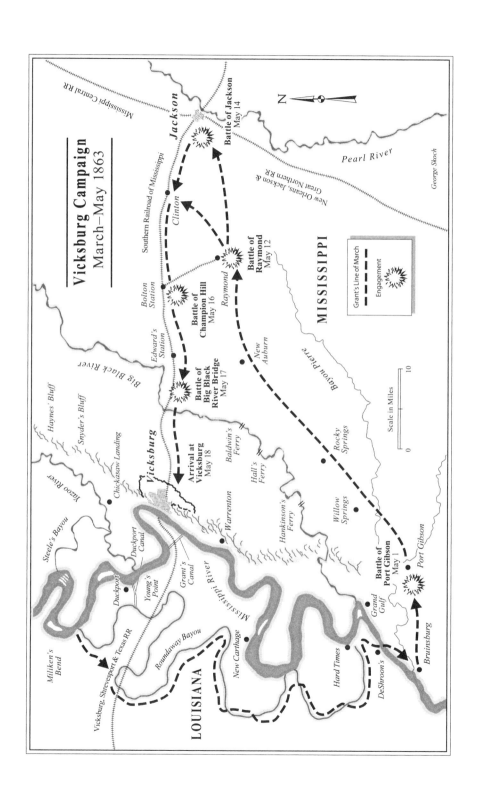

Vicksburg Campaign
March–May 1863

N

Mississippi Central RR

Southern Railroad of Mississippi

New Orleans, Jackson & Great Northern RR

Jackson

Battle of Jackson
May 14

Clinton

Pearl River

George Skoch

Battle of Raymond
May 12

Raymond

Bolton Station

Battle of Champion Hill
May 16

Edward's Station

Big Black River

Battle of Big Black River Bridge
May 17

Arrival at Vicksburg
May 18

Vicksburg

Haynes' Bluff

Snyder's Bluff

Chickasaw Landing

Yazoo River

Steele's Bayou

Duckport Canal

Duckport

Young's Point

Grant's Canal

Warrenton

Baldwin's Ferry

Hall's Ferry

Hankinson's Ferry

Mississippi River

MISSISSIPPI

New Auburn

Bayou Pierre

Rocky Springs

Willow Springs

Port Gibson

Battle of Port Gibson
May 1

Grand Gulf

Bruinsburg

DeShroon's

Hard Times

New Carthage

Roundaway Bayou

LOUISIANA

Milliken's Bend

Vicksburg, Shreveport & Texas RR

Scale in Miles

0   10

Grant's Line of March
Engagement

had a new plan. He ordered his men to dig a new cutoff, the Duckport Canal, designed to connect to bayous that rejoined the Mississippi more than thirty miles below Vicksburg. Because only narrow supply boats could negotiate this passage, Grant proposed to "float empty transports past Vicksburg in the dark" while his troops marched down on the Louisiana side to a point where they could be transported across the river to advance on Vicksburg. Dana relayed the new plan to Stanton.[15]

The news ramped up Dana's impatience to join Grant. "Let me suggest that I should be much more useful farther down the river than here," he wired Stanton, who gave him the go-ahead: "You will proceed to General Grant's headquarters, or wherever you may be best able to accomplish the purposes designated by this Department. You will consider your movements to be governed by your own discretion without any restriction."[16]

By the time Dana reached Grant's headquarters at Milliken's Bend on April 6, his mission was no secret. Word had reached camp, probably from officers who shuttled between Memphis and Milliken's Bend. Grant's chief of staff John Rawlins held a conference to announce the visit. Some staff members resented the intrusion of an "informer." "Dana was about as popular in camp as a case of measles," Grant's cipher operator Samuel Beckwith recalled. "We knew why he had come and the role he was playing, and the knowledge did not engender any warm-hearted enthusiasm for him among us." William S. Duff, Grant's hot-headed artillery chief, proposed to throw the "government spy" into the Mississippi.[17] This kind of behavior would have likely gotten Grant sacked, but a calmer approach prevailed. Rawlins declared that Dana should be treated with respect as Stanton's representative and no information withheld. Staff officers realized that Grant's fate hinged on the reports Dana sent to Washington. The best policy was to win his trust and let him see that Grant was the right man to lead this campaign. As a result, Dana was welcomed and admitted to headquarters as an equal to the highest staff officers. He slept on a riverboat while bedding was procured, and then he occupied a tent next to Grant's, with orderlies put at his service and a place reserved for him at the officers' mess table.[18]

Grant, remembering Dana from the cotton-trade episode a few months earlier, received him cordially and took him into his confidence. Within hours Dana sent details of Grant's daring plan of operations to Stanton. Fifty barges would transfer the whole army on the cutoff via Roundaway Bayou to New Carthage below Vicksburg, while half a dozen transports ran Vicksburg's batteries and provisioned the army after it crossed the Mississippi around Grand Gulf. Moving eastward, Grant's army would threaten Vicksburg until "the enemy will be compelled to come out and fight." Grant was confident that Vicksburg would be taken, whether as the result of fighting or "from the starvation of the garrison."[19]

Grant's openness and confidence impressed Dana from the outset. The general was quite unlike the ambitious, crafty politicians Dana had learned to distrust at the *Tribune*. He was "the most modest, the most disinterested, and the most honest man I ever knew," Dana later recalled, "with a temper that nothing could disturb, and a judgment that was judicial in its comprehensiveness and wisdom." Searching for words to capture Grant's combination of ordinariness and greatness, Dana described him as "not an original or brilliant man, but sincere, thoughtful, deep, and gifted with courage that never faltered." Despite Grant's reputation for keeping to himself, Dana found him "a social, friendly man, . . . fond of a pleasant joke and also ready with one; but liking above all a long chat of an evening, and ready to sit up with you all night, talking in the cool breeze in front of his tent."[20]

For his part, Grant found Dana helpful and companionable. Dana's daily reports freed him from the chore of composing frequent telegrams to Washington. Dana rarely showed his dispatches to Grant before sending them, but alongside Dana's personal observations they reflected information circulating at headquarters and reported Grant's views. Grant learned to trust Dana's judgment and called on his assistance. At the front, he employed Dana as a courier, scout, inspector, and adviser; with the authorities in Washington, he relied on Dana as a conduit of information and increasingly as an advocate. As early as April 10 Grant asked Dana to recommend a staff officer's promotion to Lincoln. Two days later, he assured Halleck that the administration would "receive favorable reports of the condition and feeling of this Army . . . from all who have been sent from Washington to look after its welfare."[21]

Collaboration between the general and the journalist was eased by the rustic conditions of camp life. Dana was an excellent horseman with no fear of danger, always eager to ride off to observe operations or inspect construction projects. He shared the privations of an army on the move without complaint. Around evening campfires at headquarters, Dana could be counted on for humorous anecdotes or incisive judgments. Grant "seemed to take special pleasure in [Dana's] company both in camp and on the march," a staff officer wrote. By the campaign's end Grant referred to Dana in letters as "my friend."[22]

Nevertheless, both men kept a respectful distance, not just to preserve the civilian-military divide. Dana deferred to Grant's rank and military experience, while Grant was not entirely comfortable with Dana's education and

Generals Ulysses S. Grant, William T. Sherman, James B. McPherson, and George H. Thomas (*clockwise from upper left*). Library of Congress Prints and Photographs Division.

verbal ease. Dana's ability to converse with just about every foreign-speaking Union soldier he encountered amazed Grant. "Dana was in a certain sense a revelation to Grant," a staff officer recalled, and "to those of us who were younger. He was not only genial, unaffected, and sympathetic in his manners, but far and away the best educated and most widely informed man that any of us had up to that time ever met." Dana's learning elevated the conversation at headquarters, but it could also come across as conceit and prevent closer friendships.[23]

There were two notable exceptions. During the Vicksburg campaign Dana and John Rawlins, Grant's assistant adjutant general, were frequently together in camp. A handsome, rudely educated lawyer from Grant's hometown, Rawlins was Grant's friend and watchdog, especially devoting himself to keeping him away from liquor. Rawlins's poor command of written English and "rough style of conversation" separated him from the suave Dana. "He bossed everything at Grant's headquarters," Dana recalled, "swearing and scolding." But Rawlins had an endearing side, too. A bashful widower, he endured teasing good-naturedly during his anxious courtship with Mary Emma Hurlbut, a young Connecticut governess at Vicksburg. Despite Rawlins's limitations Dana found him "one of the most valuable men in the army." Dana believed him straightforward, "perfectly fearless," and entirely devoted to Grant. Over time, the two had something else in common: both were shortchanged when Grant in later life downplayed their significant role in his rise and gave them cursory notice in his memoirs.[24]

Dana found in young Colonel James Harrison Wilson the closest kindred spirit among Grant's staff officers. Born in Illinois, the slim, nervous Wilson attended college for a year before his appointment to West Point. He was twenty-five when he joined Grant's staff in November 1862, a brash, outspoken engineer. Known to most friends as "Harry" but always called "Wilson" by the older Dana, he was initially leery of Dana as a "genteel informer" but soon recognized him as a mentor whose experience was instructive and whose influence might boost his career. Dana, meanwhile, found Wilson a helpful guide to explain army operations or to accompany on inspection tours. On their frequent rides the two men enjoyed conversing about literature and history as well as assessing the campaign's men and events. Both were self-confident and impatient with slow-moving colleagues, and they reinforced each other's critical views. At times their voices blended: Wilson assisted Dana, who suffered from eyestrain in dim light, by writing his dispatches from dictation in the evening, and Dana jotted entries in Wilson's journal

Brigadier General John A. Rawlins, photographed by Mathew Brady. Library of Congress Prints and Photographs Division.

Major General James H. Wilson, photographed by Mathew Brady. Library of Congress Prints and Photographs Division.

when Wilson was away from headquarters. Decades later, after a long career in the military and business, Wilson became Dana's admiring biographer.[25]

Among Grant's corps commanders Dana had limited contact with General James B. McPherson and even less with McClernand. But the shrewd Sherman cultivated his support. "Mr. Dana is here I suppose to watch us all," Sherman confided to his brother John, a senator representing Ohio, but especially as "a kind of spy on [Grant's] movements." Dana discovered that Sherman was a "first-rate talker" and enjoyed his feverish monologues. "I have seen a good deal of [Dana] and feel assured he knows many things he never did before," Sherman wrote his brother. This included bringing Dana up to speed on the campaign's history and geography and inviting him to witness an exchange of prisoners. Less tactfully, Sherman lectured Dana on his current hobby-horses: the villainy of newspapers—a perennial theme with the general—his disagreement with Grant's plan to approach Vicksburg from the south, and the incompetence of General McClernand.[26]

In Sherman's view, "newspaper clamor" had raised expectations that would undo Grant. He suspected Dana had been sent from Washington for "impressing on Grant the necessity of achieving something brilliant" after the campaign's long delays, and he blamed popular impatience whipped up by newspaper editors for pushing Grant to undertake unnecessary risks. Sherman may have been aware of Dana's role in the *Tribune*'s "Forward to Richmond!" fiasco, but he chattered on, telling his brother (and no doubt Dana) that he saw "the same old Bull Run Mania" at work pushing Grant's army "to destruction."[27]

Sherman considered such alarmist language appropriate because he judged Grant's plan to take his army south of Vicksburg a fatal mistake. The roads and canals involved were precarious, and once across the river Grant's army would be cut off from its base. Sherman's preference was to retry the northern approaches, but because such moves would be seen as retreat he knew his advice was falling on deaf ears. Dana reported Sherman's dissenting views to Stanton, adding hopefully that the general would eventually "tend . . . to the conclusion of General Grant."[28]

As Grant's plans matured it became clear that he would assign a primary role to McClernand in his move south. Sherman opposed this, too. By the time Dana arrived, Sherman had fixed his opinion that McClernand was unfit for command and consumed by "a mean, gnawing ambition, ready to destroy everybody who could cross his path." Dana absorbed this critical view of McClernand and formed an opposite one of Sherman. As he observed Sherman's skillful handling of troops, Dana's admiration soared. In turn,

Sherman's suspicion of Dana eased when he learned that Stanton's spy "remarked to one of Grant's staff incidentally that he was better pleased with me than he could have possibly expected."[29]

Another facet of Dana's education at Grant's headquarters was his first close-up view of plantation life. To chart the progress of Grant's construction projects, he often rode with Colonel Wilson, who supervised bridge-building on bayous that meandered through fertile lowlands dotted with cotton plantations. "The plains stretch far back from the river," Dana wrote a friend, "with the mansions of the owners embowered in roses, myrtles, oaks, and every sort of beautiful and noble tree, and the negro huts cluster near them." "During the eight days that I have been here," he confided, "I have got new insight into slavery, which has made me no more a friend of that institution than I was before." Dana and Wilson often stopped at plantation houses to spend the night; they were received hospitably because they provided letters that protected the property from Union raids. After bridging Roundaway Bayou on the Louisiana side of the Mississippi they boarded at a stately plantation whose mistress was the "charming and accomplished" Mrs. Junias Amis. Except for the master's absence, the hardships of war had not yet reached this enclave. The cook prepared broiled chicken, bacon, and hominy muffins so tasty that the Yankee guests recalled them fondly decades later. But Dana's dominant impression was revulsion over the disparity between masters and slaves. "Though I had seen slavery in Maryland, Kentucky, Virginia, and Missouri," he wrote a friend, "it was not till I saw these plantations, with all their apparatus for living and working, that I really felt the aristocratic nature of it" and its "infernal baseness." Dana and Wilson learned with satisfaction that the Amis slaves, who had been properly subservient during their visit, soon gathered their belongings and followed the Union army to freedom.[30]

Despite Sherman's opposition, Grant remained "dead set" on his plan to move his army south of Vicksburg for a river crossing, Dana reported. On April 13 the levee protecting work on the new canal was cut. Dana watched with others as the Mississippi's waters poured into the canal, but the flow was not deep enough for barges, and trees and stumps blocked the passage. Additional dredging might turn the roads that paralleled the route to mud. "It now appears that the canal and road cannot both be relied upon," Dana told Stanton. Coached by Wilson, Dana advocated bypassing the canal, and Grant agreed. He decided to push the troops forward by road to New Carthage while the transports ran Vicksburg's batteries.[31] There was another important change, Dana reported, made to placate Halleck and Lincoln. After occupying Grand Gulf, most of Grant's army, instead of moving up the Big Black River toward Vicksburg's rear, would continue downriver to join General Nathaniel Banks in capturing Port Hudson, 240 river miles south. The combined federal forces would then proceed against Vicksburg.[32]

Dana had serious doubts about this diversion, but to his mind the biggest hitch in the plan was that Grant entrusted the leading role in his army's southward march to McClernand. Sherman, Wilson, and Admiral Porter bent Dana's ear about the politician-general. One night they gathered around Grant's campfire to discuss the campaign. Sherman and Porter complained that McClernand was not up to his assignment and was "still intriguing against General Grant," but Grant, Dana wrote, "would not be changed." Dana conveyed Grant's reasoning to Stanton: McClernand was senior in rank to the others and had endorsed Grant's plan from the outset; his troops were best positioned to lead the advance; and he was "an especial favorite of the President" and ought to be given a chance.[33]

Grant's decision may have been good politics, but Dana saw little value in risking the campaign to score points with Lincoln, and he told Grant so. "I have remonstrated, so far as I could properly do so, against intrusting so momentous an operation to McClernand," he reported to Stanton. The war secretary, sensing trouble, scolded his special agent for overstepping his bounds: "Allow me to suggest that you carefully avoid giving any advice in respect to commands that may be assigned, as it may lead to misunderstanding and troublesome complications." Dana replied that Stanton's directive would be "scrupulously observed even in extreme cases," thereby implying that McClernand was one. Grant's decision stood, but Dana's reports planted seeds of doubt about McClernand in Stanton's mind and perhaps Lincoln's.[34]

Despite Grant's decision on McClernand, Dana remained optimistic. Parts of the scheme might miscarry but "the chances all favor its execution." The spirit of the troops was "all that could be desired," he told Stanton, and Grant's officers were warming to his plans. Dana wrote a friend that before his letter reached New York, news would arrive that Grant had taken Grand Gulf and Port Hudson.[35]

Running the Batteries and Crossing the Mississippi

Just before ten o'clock on the night of April 16, Dana watched with Grant's staff and family members from the top deck of the headquarters steamer as the Union flotilla, led by Admiral Porter's flagship *Benton*, cast loose its moorings. Barely visible on a moonless night, "a mass of black things detached itself from the shore," Dana observed, and floated silently toward the middle of the river, "showing neither steam nor light." The Union vessels were spaced at intervals of about two hundred yards. "First came seven iron-clad turtles and one heavy armed ram; following these were two side-wheel steamers and one stern-wheel, having twelve barges in tow. . . . Far astern of them was the one carrying ammunition." Enemy scouts had been watching. When the gunboats rounded the hairpin turn upriver from Vicksburg, orange flashes burst from the upper forts and cannons boomed along the entire four-mile gauntlet. Buildings on both shores were set on fire to light the floating targets for rebel gunners. The river took on a gorgeous red glow, and the roar of cannons from land, returned by fire from the Union gunboats, punished the ears. Grant watched impassively, smoking the inevitable cigar. Ten-year-old "Buck"—Ulysses, Jr.—sat on James Wilson's lap, pulling him closer with every explosion until ordered to bed. Dana stood nearby, tabulating cannon discharges; he counted 525 in ninety minutes. It may have been the contrast between Wilson's warmth and Dana's detachment that led Julia Grant to tell her husband she "did not like" Dana.[36]

One of the transport steamers, the *Henry Clay*, caught fire and was abandoned by its captain and crew. Otherwise there was little damage. By mid-night the guns had fallen silent, and at 2:30 A.M. the last of the transports arrived at New Carthage, thirty-five miles downriver from Vicksburg. The next morning Dana rode there with Grant and Wilson. "We found the squadron there, all in fighting condition," Dana told Stanton, "though most of them had been hit." Remarkably, no crewman had been killed.[37]

Determined to press his advantage, Grant returned with Dana to Milliken's Bend and ordered six transport steamers, each loaded with rations, readied for running the batteries. Volunteer crews were sought from General John Logan's division, and the eager response impressed Dana. On April 22, a cloudy night, the transports set loose with a barge tied to each side and bulwarks of hay, cotton, and pork barrels constructed on deck. Dana summarized Grant's orders: the ships "were to drop noiselessly down with the current from the mouth of the Yazoo, and not show steam till the enemy's batteries began firing, when the boats were to use all their legs." Again Dana watched from Grant's headquarters deck. One of the transports, the *Tigress*, was hit and sunk and a handful of men were wounded. The others emerged battered but repairable.[38]

The next day Grant, accompanied by Dana, shifted his headquarters to Smith's plantation near New Carthage. McClernand's XIII Corps, 12,000 men, was encamped nearby and expected to be ready to cross on April 24; Sherman's XV Corps remained at Young's Point to screen Grant's move and

REAR-ADMIRAL PORTER'S FLOTILLA ARRIVING BELOW VICKSBURG ON THE NIGHT OF APRIL 16, 1863—IN THE FOREGROUND GENERAL W. T. SHERMAN GOING IN A YAWL TO THE FLAG-SHIP "BENTON."

"Rear-Admiral Porter's Flotilla Arriving below Vicksburg on the Night of April 16, 1863." Porter's flagship *Benton*, on the right, leads the line of ships past Vicksburg's batteries. From *Battles and Leaders of the Civil War* (New York: Century Co., 1888), 3:521.

pretend to threaten Vicksburg from the west. At this juncture Dana's warnings about McClernand began to look like accurate prophecies. On April 26, the day planned for the attack on Grand Gulf, Dana steamed with Grant down to McClernand's embarkation point; they found only half of McClernand's men, and steamboats and barges were "scattered about in the river as if there was no idea of the imperative necessity of the promptest move possible." Grant ordered McClernand to begin moving men onto the boats. Instead, and much to Grant's annoyance, McClernand reviewed a brigade of Illinois troops with that state's Governor Richard Yates and ended with an artillery salute, against orders to conserve ammunition for battle. When darkness came, Dana found that "not a single cannon or man had been moved."[39]

By the morning of April 29, all of McClernand's men had finally been moved to Hard Times Landing, where they were joined by 6,000 of McPherson's troops. They prepared to cross the river once Grand Gulf's guns were silenced. At 8 A.M. Admiral Porter's seven gunboats, led by his flagship *Benton*, approached the batteries on the bluff, and for the next five hours a fierce duel was waged between the Confederate cannons and the Union ironclads swirling in the currents below. Dana watched with Grant, Governor Yates, and others from a tug beyond the Confederate gunners' range. The Union gunboats fired "now at long range, seeking to drop shells within the parapet, now at the very foot of the hill, within about two hundred yards, endeavoring to dismount its guns by direct fire," Dana reported. Either way they could not take out the Confederate guns, and they absorbed many direct hits.[40] After the battle Dana boarded the *Benton* with Grant. The boat's armor had been pierced repeatedly, and seven sailors on the gun deck were killed. Years later Grant remembered being "sickened" by the sight of the mangled and dying men. Porter himself was wounded slightly when a shell fragment struck his neck. All told, seventy-five federal sailors were killed or wounded and one gunboat was put out of action.[41]

Unable to silence the Confederate batteries, Grant called on his alternative plan, which was to debark the troops and march them downriver along the west bank to DeShroon's Plantation, the new point of embarkation. By this time all of McClernand's corps and three divisions under McPherson were on the scene, raising Grant's effective force to more than 20,000 men.

To those who had accompanied him during the stalled projects of winter, Grant seemed a new man, infused with energy and riding at a gallop. On the evening of the Grand Gulf firefight, as he rode beside Grant on the levee to DeShroon's, Dana saw the commander's horse stumble. "I expected to see the general go over the animal's head, and I watched intently, not to see if he was hurt, but if he would show any anger," he recalled. Grant, an expert horseman, remained in the saddle. "Pulling up his horse, he rode on, to my utter amazement, without a word or sign of impatience. . . . [T]hough I was with Grant during the most trying campaigns of the war, I never heard him use an oath."[42]

That night, Porter's transports ran the batteries at Grand Gulf and caught up with Grant's army on shore. An escaped slave informed Grant that he could land at Bruinsburg, just below the mouth of Bayou Pierre. It was sixty miles from Vicksburg, with two inland river crossings between, but, as Dana wrote, it was "the first point south of the Grand Gulf from which the highlands of the interior could be reached by a road over dry land." On the afternoon of April 30 Dana reported that all of McClernand's men had crossed to Bruinsburg or were boarding boats, but he took another jab at the general, who had delayed things by forgetting to issue his troops their three-day ration of food and ammunition: "Had any other general . . . held the advance, the landing would certainly have been effected at daylight." What Dana did not add was that had any other Union general but Grant moved his army to the Confederate-held side of the Mississippi, his anxiety would be palpable. Instead, Grant felt "a degree of relief scarcely equaled" in the war. At long last, he wrote, "I was on dry ground and on the same side of the river with the enemy."[43]

Determined not to lose time, Grant pointed his troops eastward toward Port Gibson, where he planned to cross Bayou Pierre and take Grand Gulf from the rear. Dana had to play catch-up. By Grant's orders all space on the crossing vessels was reserved for fighting men and their officers. Artillery and supplies had to wait, as did observers, reporters, and nonessential soldiers. With the latter went Dana's already flimsy cover for his mission. "I have to report that the paymasters have finished their work and gone," Dana wrote Stanton, "and henceforth any shrewd person can see that I am not attending to their transactions."[44]

Leaving his horse and baggage behind, Dana did not cross the Mississippi until the morning of May 1. From Bruinsburg he tramped on foot, following the sound of guns up the steep hills along the Bayou Pierre. He hitched a ride in a quartermaster's wagon and came to a field scarred by signs of a fight. Dana approached a small white house with vine coverings, an improvised field hospital. In the yard, he was stopped in his tracks by "a heap of arms and legs which had been amputated and thrown into a pile outside." He had seen body parts before, most recently on the *Benton*, but not in such horrible profusion.[45]

Resuming the trail, Dana caught up with Fred Grant, the general's feisty twelve-year-old son, who had joined his father at the front and accompanied the army downriver. Fred had been left asleep on a steamer at Bruinsburg with orders to remain, but when he awoke he slipped away on foot to find the army. After joining forces, Fred and his temporary guardian "foraged together until the next morning," Dana recalled. They procured two old white carriage horses that had been captured by Union officers. They rigged a pair of worn-out saddles taken from a farmhouse and were given an old coach bridle and a parlor rug to use as a saddle cloth by a friendly slave whose owner had fled. The pair rode toward Port Gibson, Grant's temporary headquarters. The sight of the youngster sporting his father's sash and sword on a huge draft horse drew laughs from foot soldiers; Dana and his companion in ragged regalia evoked Don Quixote and Sancho Panza. When they arrived at headquarters Grant smiled at their not-so-grand entrance, "mounted on two enormous horses, grown white from age, each equipped with dilapidated saddles and bridles." The general was pleased with their pluck. Dana rode the sorry plantation horse for four or five days until Grant commandeered a fine mount for him from a captured Confederate officer. The new horse remained with Dana through the campaign and Grant frequently inquired after it.[46]

On to Vicksburg

By the time Dana reached headquarters, the 8,000 Confederates sent from Vicksburg by General John Pemberton to harass the Federals had been pushed back across Bayou Pierre toward the Big Black. Grant followed, but his army was compelled to wait overnight while the bridge the Rebels destroyed was replaced. The night was cool and the troops encamped on the plantation grounds around them. As Dana slept on the damp grass, his head on his saddle, he turned to the side and saw Grant doing the same, without even a blanket. Here was a different kind of general, Dana mused, one who did "without tents and every comfort" and woke up ready to move. Surely he was destined to accomplish great things.[47]

Grant was eager to establish Grand Gulf as his supply and communications base. The next day, May 3, Dana, Rawlins, and Wilson rode there with him, and Dana used the wires to update Stanton for the first time in three days. Grant had so far brought 23,000 men across at Bruinsburg, Dana told Stanton. Sherman's corps, after making its feint near Chickasaw Bluffs, had hurried overland past Vicksburg and would join Grant momentarily. Moving into the enemy's territory would draw Pemberton out of Vicksburg, Grant believed, and the Confederates would "endeavor to bring on the decisive battle within the next ten days."[48]

Grant overestimated Pemberton's resolve. For a host of reasons, Pemberton failed to concentrate his forces against Grant. Sherman's diversion had deceived him into leaving troops to guard Vicksburg's northern approaches. Meanwhile, the Union colonel Benjamin Grierson led a spectacular cavalry raid down the spine of central Mississippi that distracted Pemberton while Grant's forces crossed the Mississippi. Even more important, Pemberton's units failed to coordinate their movements with the other Confederate army in Mississippi. General Joseph Johnston had been sent by Confederate President Jefferson Davis to supervise Confederate operations in the West. Early in May Johnston came down with 3,000 men from Braxton Bragg's army in Tennessee and assembled reinforcements from Georgia, South Carolina, and elsewhere into a force designed to harass Grant's army from the rear. An able strategist and career-long counterpuncher, Johnston believed that defeating Grant's army was more important than saving Vicksburg; he urged Pemberton to come out from the town and join him to pin Grant between their armies. Pemberton, meanwhile, had received a dispatch from Davis that he interpreted as an order to stay in Vicksburg and hold it. Born in Pennsylvania but siding with his wife's Virginia family, Pemberton was sensitive to doubts about his Confederate loyalty and eager to please President Davis. He would not move the bulk of his men from the city until Johnston attacked and weakened Grant. As each waited for the other to make the first move, Johnston and Pemberton wasted precious time. While Grant assembled men to outnumber their combined armies, his campaign benefited from the fact that those armies never did combine.[49]

Grant saw the potential for a similar game of indecision and delay on the Union side, but with Dana's assent he declined to play it. At Halleck's urging, Grant had planned to detach troops to help General Banks take Port Hudson before the combined armies moved on Vicksburg. But at Grand Gulf he received word that Banks, then on the Red River, could not reach Port Hudson until at least May 10 and would bring fewer than 15,000 men. Refusing to squander the initiative against Pemberton, Grant made a momentous decision that Dana transmitted approvingly to Stanton: "General Grant intends to lose no time in pushing his army toward the Big Black Bridge and Jackson, threatening both and striking at either, as is most convenient. As soon as Sherman comes up and the rations on the way arrive, he will disregard his base and depend upon the country for meat and even for bread." To wait for Banks's cooperation against Vicksburg would give the enemy crucial time to reinforce and fortify. To seek approval of his new course from the cautious Halleck would be similarly fatal. Grant would act immediately and explain later.[50]

Grant knew that his plan defied existing doctrines of warfare, which prescribed concentration of forces and scorned living off the land. Sherman, not yet the general who marched to the sea in Georgia, advised Grant to create a dependable supply route, but Grant disagreed. Grant also knew that Halleck, who not only fought by the book but wrote it—his *Elements of Military Art and Science* was often consulted by Civil War generals—would be miffed. (Neither Grant nor Dana was aware that Lincoln also privately considered Grant's plan mistaken.) Yet there *was* a high government official at hand who backed Grant's idea and could assure Washington leaders about it. Dana agreed that Vicksburg should take precedence over Port Hudson. He, too, believed that Halleck was overcautious and should be ignored. Dana's approval gave Grant official cover for his change of plans.[51]

Dana not only advocated Grant's eastward dash; he found it invigorating to accompany an army marching into enemy territory. "Campaigning I found very agreeable and very wholesome, and came back from my three months' experience in tents and on horseback much better in health than I went," he later told a friend. Dana's fascination with camp life is evident from a letter to his son, Paul, written after he rejoined Grant on the Big Black River:

Away yonder, in the edge of the woods, I hear the drum-beat that calls the soldiers to their supper. It is only a little after five o'clock, but they begin the day very early and end it early. Pretty soon after dark they are all asleep, lying in their blankets under the trees, for in a quick march they leave their tents behind. Their guns are all ready at their sides, so that if they are suddenly called at night they can start in a moment. It is strange in the morning before daylight to hear the bugle and drums sound the reveille, which calls the army to wake up. It will begin perhaps at a distance and then run along the whole line, bugle after bugle and drum after drum taking it up, and then it goes from front to rear, farther and farther away, the sweet sounds throbbing and rolling while you lie on the grass with your saddle for a pillow, half awake, or opening your eyes to see that the stars are all bright in the sky, or that there is only a faint flush in the east, where the day is soon to break.

By then a wagon train arrived with camp equipment and Grant could establish a routine. "Living in camp is queer business," Dana told his son. "I get my meals in General Grant's mess, and pay my share of the expenses. The table is a chest with a double cover, which unfolds on the right and the left; the dishes, knives and forks, and caster are inside. Sometimes we get good things, but generally we don't. . . . The cooking is not as clean as it might be, but in war you can't be particular about such things."[52]

On May 7 Grant's headquarters was moved from Hankinson's Ferry to Rocky Springs, six miles east. Over the next four days McClernand's and McPherson's corps advanced toward the railroad connecting Vicksburg and Jackson, with McClernand's forces on the left hugging the Big Black and McPherson's veering eastward toward Raymond. On May 10 Dana wired Stanton that Grant ordered Sherman to destroy the bridge at Hankinson's Ferry. "You may not hear from me again for several days," Grant warned Halleck, speaking more for Dana, since he had sent only two terse telegrams in a week. The rear guards of Grant's army were abandoned and its communications cut. Sporadic trains of supply wagons brought ammunition and rations from Grand Gulf, but otherwise the Union forces were on their own.[53]

During the next ten days Grant's army was constantly marching and nearly always fighting, fanning out and then concentrating, pushing to the northeast and northwest. Grant "was a most agreeable companion on the march and in camp," Wilson recalled, "plain and simple in his manners, kind and considerate to the officers and men of his staff." Dana was also in his element. Advancing with the army, Dana retained his role as observer but also volunteered to "do staff duty," much to Grant's delight, "riding and working night and day." Wilson kept a journal in which he and Dana tracked their activities. Together, they carried Grant's orders to his commanders; noted the country's resources of water, crops, and cattle; reconnoitered the roads; interrogated Confederate deserters and civilian informers; supervised construction of Union bridges; and observed the chief battles.[54] Dana learned more about military operations than he had in two years of reading. It was not always easy. He rode thirty or forty miles a day, and "more than one night," he recalled, "I bivouacked on the ground in the rain after being all day in my saddle." Once, Dana slept on the pew of a church, borrowing the Bible from the pulpit for his pillow. Despite the hardships, he relished the adventure. Dana later told Wilson that these were the most exciting ten days he had ever spent.[55]

Leaving Rocky Springs on May 10, Grant and his staff followed the army and positioned their headquarters at its center, halfway between McClernand and McPherson. Just west of Raymond on May 12, McPherson's corps of 11,000 was met by about 4,000 men under General John Gregg. After a three-hour fight McPherson drove the Confederates back. When Grant found out, he sent Wilson and Dana with verbal orders for McPherson to push on the next morning to Clinton, seven miles northeast on the Vicksburg & Jackson Railroad, to place his corps between Pemberton's army and Johnston's. The messengers found McPherson flush after his victory but determined not to expose his corps further. He wanted written orders from Grant. Wilson and Dana whirled their horses about and galloped through the dark to Grant's camp, where the general wrote out the order. Mounting fresh horses, they returned to McPherson before midnight. McPherson obeyed but did not reach Clinton until three the next afternoon, too late to cut off the Confederates' retreat.[56]

Because Grant was improvising, his staff could influence his orders as well as carry them. Grant's plan was to break the railroad at Clinton, then head west to Vicksburg. But as Dana and Wilson rode back to Grant's camp they agreed that Grant should continue east to take Jackson, the state capital, a major railroad crossing and a center for rebel operations against Grant's rear. After sounding out Rawlins, they took the idea to Grant, who that night wrote new orders for Sherman and McPherson to converge on Jackson. On the afternoon of May 14 Sherman and McPherson launched a combined attack just west of the capital against 11,000 men led in the field by Gregg. Sherman's men broke through first, and the Bluecoats drove the Rebels back into the city's works and then into a full evacuation. The Federals suffered 440 casualties, Confederates lost more than 500, and Johnston's army retreated north along the Canton road.[57]

In the evening Grant and his staff, joined by Dana, entered the Mississippi capital. They spent the night at the Bowman House hotel, which Johnston had just vacated, enjoying comfortable beds and Southern food. The next morning the proprietor made it clear that he preferred "Yankee money," an indication to Dana that Southerners were losing faith in their cause. As he and Wilson traversed the country they had seen few young men capable of bearing arms and found war-fatigued civilians "rendering Grant the most valuable assistance" so that "something [could be] saved by the Southern people out of the otherwise total and hopeless ruin." Sagging Confederate morale lifted the Union soldiers' spirits, and the business of marching and fighting—"a great improvement on digging canals and running batteries," Dana remarked—also helped.[58]

At Jackson Dana was handed a dispatch from Stanton that had found its way along the Union lines. Written on May 5, shortly after Dana's complaint that McClernand was holding up Grant's crossing, it communicated the assurance Dana had sought: "General Grant has full and absolute authority to enforce his own commands and to remove any person who by ignorance in action or any cause interferes with or delays his operations." Dana's reports had smoothed the way for Grant to replace McClernand without resistance from the War Department or the White House. Grant did not act immediately, but his relations with McClernand remained distant. He rarely saw the general and relied on Wilson and others to transmit messages. Dana hoped that Grant was simply biding his time, waiting for McClernand to behave badly enough that no one would question his dismissal.[59]

There was other important news at Jackson. Grant learned from a Union spy that Pemberton had been ordered by Johnston to march out of Vicksburg to attack the Federals. Grant turned McPherson's corps around to join McClernand in meeting the enemy. Sherman remained in Jackson temporarily to tear up the railroads and destroy remaining property of use to Confederates. Dana stayed behind to observe the work, including the torching of a cotton mill that churned out tent cloth with "c.s.a." woven in each bolt.[60]

On the morning of May 16 Dana rejoined Grant in Clinton. There they learned from railroad employees that Pemberton had moved 22,000 men eastward along the Vicksburg & Jackson line to Edward's Station. This was the move Grant had been awaiting: the rebel turtle was peeking out of its shell. Grant ordered Union forces to rush west along the railroad, and he and his staff followed. When Grant and Dana reached Sidney Champion's plantation two miles east of Baker's Creek, they found Pemberton's men curled in a strong semicircle on a wooded ridge. General A. P. Hovey's division of

McClernand's corps drew up in a line of battle on each side of the road that faced the ridge and awaited the approach of the remaining Union divisions.

By noon the two sides' sporadic skirmishing escalated into the Battle of Champion's Hill. Dana scribbled entries in Wilson's journal that documented the battle's ebb and flow as experienced by Grant and his staff. They had gathered in the shade of Sidney Champion's front yard, the general giving orders and calmly puffing on his cigar. Messengers brought news that the Union divisions led by Generals Hovey, Marcellus Crocker, and Logan bore the brunt of the hard fighting with successive attacks on the north side of the Confederate hill. Around four o'clock these men carried the heights and took more than a thousand prisoners. A half-hour later Dana rode with Grant and Rawlins along the crest from which the Confederates had been driven. "The evidences of a terrific struggle are abundant," Dana recorded. "It is certain that the enemy is in full retreat—the whole height is abandoned."[61]

Amid the Union victory Dana saw its human costs. At one spot on the hill, Dana and Rawlins were surveying the torn-up ground and the dead and dying men lying all about, when a wounded Confederate soldier, forty-five or fifty years old, lifted himself on his elbow and called out: "For God's sake, gentlemen, is there a Mason among you?" Rawlins dismounted and knelt by the dying man, who gave him letters and other mementos to send to his wife in Alabama. Dana remained on the field until dark conversing with officers. Close to midnight he rode forward to Grant's makeshift headquarters, the porch of a small house that had served as a Confederate field hospital. Entering the cottage, he was confronted by a distraught soldier blinded by a Union bullet to the head. "Kill me! Will someone kill me?" he pleaded. "It will be mercy to do it . . . don't let me suffer!" Dana procured the surgeon, who examined his case but pronounced it hopeless. Before morning the man died.[62]

More than 2,400 Union soldiers fell at Champion's Hill, a third from Hovey's division. Pemberton lost more than 3,800 men. Despite the high Union casualties, Champion's Hill was a major victory that weakened Pemberton's forces and sent most of them reeling toward Vicksburg. (A division under General William Loring escaped to join Johnston.) By retreating toward the city, Pemberton relinquished the idea of a junction with Johnston's men. Grant's only regret was that his whole force had not been used to destroy Pemberton's army. Logan's move to the Union right left a path of retreat open to the Confederates, and McClernand, who Dana noted "had no serious fighting" in the battle, failed to block it despite repeated orders to advance. Had McClernand acted promptly, Grant wrote, "Pemberton could [not] have escaped with any organized force." The delay was one more count in the silent indictment Grant was compiling against his subordinate.[63]

The pursuing Federals forced Pemberton to move his main contingent across the Big Black River. Dana was up at daylight on May 17 and off with Grant to the front. When they arrived they found that Pemberton had built impressive defenses. Earthworks were constructed over cotton bales to make a stand on the bottomlands on the east bank of the river. The Confederate rifle pits were protected by felled logs and a difficult bayou. Another rebel line was deployed on the heights on the west side of the river. Despite this formidable defensive position, the Union troops met only halfhearted resistance at the Battle of Big Black River. Most of Pemberton's men were on their way back to Vicksburg; the regiments covering them had lost faith in their commander and also had retreat on their minds. At mid-morning Dana spoke with a runaway slave named Monk, who had overheard Confederate general Martin Green declare that Pemberton "had sold the army" and that the best course was to "vaccinate [evacuate] back to the entrenchments at Vicksburg and pile the last bluejacket there."[64]

A few minutes later General Michael Lawler, in his shirtsleeves, led a daring dash through the knee-deep water of the bayou on the Confederate left, which served as a ditch fronting the rebel works. Climbing up the entrenchments, Lawler and his men carried the rifle pits and sent the enemy fleeing. The Confederates scrambled across the river and burned the railroad bridge behind them, abandoning eighteen guns and more than 1,700 prisoners. Dana considered Lawler's charge "one of the most splendid exploits of the war." Riding to the captured ground, he found the corpulent Lawler sitting on a log, his face covered with sweat and smoke, brewing a pot of coffee on a campfire. The Rebels were still dropping shells close by, and flames from the railroad bridge rose in the distance. Dana shook Lawler's hand, and the general recounted his maneuver, which Dana reported to Stanton as "most gallant."[65]

Grant's men had to construct new crossings to keep up the pursuit. That evening, Dana joined Wilson as they helped build three floating bridges made from "cotton bales, gin-houses, pontoons, and railroad-bridge materials" collected by the army. After midnight, Dana rode to Sherman's pontoon bridge at Bridgeport, several miles north. There he watched with Grant and Sherman as the troops marched over the swaying boards, guided by the light of pitch pine bonfires. Shortly after 9 A.M. on May 18 Dana crossed over the rebuilt railroad bridge at the battle site and rode with Grant to join Sherman, whose head start brought his men more quickly to Vicksburg's defenses.[66]

Grant's first concern was to establish a line of supplies with his original base on the Mississippi above Vicksburg. On the afternoon of May 18 Dana, at Sherman's headquarters, recorded that General Frederick Steele opened artillery fire on the bluffs on Vicksburg's north. The next morning the Union troops took possession of the Confederate forts between Chickasaw Bayou and the city. Sherman had the pleasure of occupying the bluffs that had repulsed his attack the previous December. There he turned to Grant at his side and ate crow: "Until this moment I never thought your expedition would be a success. I never could see the end clearly; but *this* is a campaign—this is a success [even] if we never take the town."[67]

At 6 P.M. on May 20 Dana recorded with satisfaction that the first supply train had arrived from Chickasaw Landing. Able to send to Stanton his first dispatch in ten days, he penned a brief summary of Grant's "great and momentous victory" at Champion's Hill, the Battle of Big Black River, and the capture of Vicksburg's northern hills. Dana singled out Generals Hovey, Crocker, Lawler, and Steele for special commendation. Stanton, eager to get good news to the public, released Dana's telegram to the newspapers. Grant now had Vicksburg closely invested, Dana told Stanton (and unwittingly, the Northern public), and "probably the town will be carried today."[68]

His prediction was overly optimistic. Grant's three corps had advanced up to the edge of Vicksburg's defenses, with Sherman's troops on the Union right, McPherson's in the center, and McClernand's on the left. Although not yet complete, the encirclement of Vicksburg was in reach. Believing that the Confederates had been demoralized by their losses, Grant ordered an assault on May 19. Sherman's corps, which carried most of the attack, gained a bit of ground, but his men were shot down in clusters by the cannon and musket fire that poured down from the Confederate ramparts. It was the same all along the line, and Grant's army lost nearly 1,000 men. "The enemy holds out obstinately," Dana recorded in Wilson's journal. Pemberton's men were "encouraged by the hope of re-enforcements" and bolstered by fighting behind Vicksburg's stout defenses.[69]

The next two days were spent strengthening the Union position. Grant still hoped to capture Vicksburg while his troops had their blood up and before Johnston's 10,000 men could come to Pemberton's aid. He ordered a general attack along the whole Union line for the morning of May 22. Following the customary artillery barrage, at exactly 10 A.M.—in a wartime innovation, the corps commanders had synchronized their watches—the Union troops moved out and then the bugles sounded for the assault. The Union soldiers did their best, but they were easy targets for the artillery and musket fire from the Confederate works, which felled them in waves. By 2 P.M. Dana recorded that "the assault has failed." McPherson and Sherman had not carried any of the rebel works. There was one exception: "It is reported that McClernand has secured a position within the rebel entrenchments. [Isaac] Quinby is ordered to re-enforce him."[70]

Dana's entry hinted at a developing disaster, the blame for which he would lay squarely at McClernand's feet. McClernand had sent a message to Grant that he had gained the enemy's entrenchments "at several points" and needed reinforcements. Another message from McClernand claimed to have "part possession of two forts" and urged a renewed push along the line. From his position Grant could not see the success McClernand reported, but he sent him Isaac Quinby's division of the XVII Corps and ordered Sherman and McPherson to renew the assault. The move proved costly. Two more hours of Union casualties were stacked up without gaining any ground.[71]

By overconfidence, elation in the heat of battle, or a ravenous quest for glory, McClernand had overstated his men's breakthrough. Sherman concluded that at best McClernand had pierced a few outlying lunettes where his men were still "at the mercy of the Rebels behind the main parapet." When the truth reached headquarters Rawlins burst into profanity and Grant's face took on a "grim glowering look of disappointment and disgust."[72]

That evening Dana carefully copied McClernand's battlefield messages in Wilson's journal, as if documenting evidence for the prosecution. The next morning he wrote Stanton that "McClernand's report was false, as he held not a single fort, and the result was disastrous." The official Union toll was 3,052 casualties, a thousand of which, Dana estimated, were suffered after the assault was renewed. Grant told Halleck that "Gen. McClernand's dispatches misled me as to the real state of facts and . . . caused us to double our losses for the day." McClernand's messages had indeed done damage, but they also gave Grant cover for his blunder of ordering a second day's assault on Vicksburg's almost impregnable fortifications.[73]

Two days after the failed assault Dana secretly updated Stanton. On May 23 Grant "had determined to relieve General McClernand, on account of his false dispatch," but Grant still hoped for a peaceful way out. Perhaps he feared that the Illinois politician would call for a damaging inquiry into Grant's decision to order the assault. Perhaps Grant blamed himself for not overseeing McClernand more closely. In any case, "he changed his mind, concluding that it would be better on the whole to leave McClernand in his present command till the siege of Vicksburg is concluded, after which he will induce McClernand to ask for a leave of absence." Dana was not pleased with this nonsolution. "My own judgment," he added—although Stanton had

Major General John A. McClernand, photographed by Mathew Brady. Library of Congress Prints and Photographs Division.

expressly told him to withhold it—"is that McClernand has not the qualities necessary for a good commander, even of a regiment."[74]

Despite the festering sore of McClernand, Dana had good reason to be optimistic. Vicksburg was being surrounded, the Union supply lines were humming, Grant's army was "in the best of spirits," and measures were being taken to prevent Pemberton's reinforcement. The repulsed assaults proved "the necessity of a more protracted investment," Dana told Stanton, but "there is no doubt of the final result."[75]

Grant had made victory possible by moving rapidly. In twenty days after crossing the Mississippi, Grant's army marched more than 200 miles, fought and won five battles, took the state capital and destroyed its wares, drove the Confederates back into Vicksburg, and enclosed the city. Grant's quick movements and shifts of direction left his Confederate opponents bewildered, prevented their junction, and allowed him to defeat them separately. In retrospect, Dana judged this three-week push of marching and fighting "the most brilliant campaign of Grant's career." As Washington's on-the-scene representative, he could share some credit. More than the "official spectator" he called himself at the campaign's outset, Dana served as a reliable government reporter and a trusted assistant to Grant. His dispatches kept Stanton and Lincoln informed about Grant's movements, explained his plans, and projected confidence in his success. At the same time, he assisted Grant as a courier, inspector, and adviser, and he interceded at Washington to neutralize the threat of McClernand and to stifle potential disagreement over bypassing Port Hudson. More and more, Dana saw Grant as the fighting general the Union desperately needed, and he committed himself to championing his cause with Stanton and Lincoln.[76]

Back in Washington, as authorities anxiously awaited General Robert E. Lee's next move after the crushing Union defeat at Chancellorsville, Virginia, the news from Grant's campaign provided welcome relief. Lincoln carried transcriptions of Dana's wires back to the White House. Stanton gleefully circulated Dana's long-awaited update of May 20 from "the rear of Vicksburg" to cabinet members. It was now "pretty certain," Stanton told them, "that Grant will capture the place and Pemberton's army also." At their next meeting Lincoln and his cabinet expressed confidence in Grant, according to Navy Secretary Gideon Welles. The president, who followed Grant's campaign on a map affixed to a tripod in his office, was maturing into a shrewd military strategist. After reading Dana's reports Lincoln offered a seasoned assessment to a friend: "Whether or not Gen. Grant shall or shall not consummate the capture of Vicksburg his campaign from the beginning of this month to the twenty-second day of it, is one of the most brilliant in the world." Despite the lavish praise, that "whether or not" showed that Lincoln knew there was work ahead. Vicksburg, although surrounded, had not yet capitulated. A prolonged siege would be necessary, and since Grant remained a "meagre writer or telegrapher," Lincoln and Stanton counted on Charles Dana to report its progress.[77]

7 "At the Side of the Conqueror"

Vicksburg's land defenses were as formidable as its riverside heights. On the city's east side a segmented, kidney-shaped arc of fortifications curved clockwise from the Mississippi's shore two miles north of town to the riverbank an equal distance south of town. Along that arc centuries of erosion formed an irregular line of ridges separated by ravines and gullies. Confederate engineers constructed small forts and ramparts on the ridges, with deep rifle pits connecting the main works. Passage through the ravines was obstructed by thickets, felled trees, and pointed logs placed in a menacing line. These defenses easily withstood the Union assaults of May 19 and 22 and were poised to resist future attacks as well.

Mounting the Siege

Once Ulysses Grant understood this, he ordered the Army of the Tennessee to settle down to a siege. Columns of Union troops fanned out to form a fifteen-mile semicircle hemming in Vicksburg and blocking all roads to it, while navy boats patrolled the river from a safe distance below the citadel. Earthworks and rifle pits were dug in front of each corps, punctuated by platforms for batteries. The town was bombarded by cannons and mortars almost daily to weaken its defenses and wear down morale. If bombarding or exploding mines under Vicksburg's works failed, Grant was prepared to starve out the enemy.

Meanwhile, too proud to admit defeat in the assaults of May 22, Grant had not asked for a flag of truce to bury the Federals killed. Instead, the Confederate general John Pemberton offered a cease-fire three days later because, as Charles Dana reported to War Secretary Edwin Stanton, decomposing corpses were causing the Confederate garrison "great annoyance by their odor." While the dead were retrieved Grant's engineers looked over the ground between them and the enemy, planning their forward trenches. Confederate deserters told Grant's men that supplies of food and ammunition in Vicksburg were dwindling. Dana estimated that Pemberton could hold out for no more than thirty days.[1]

Inside the city, Pemberton put his troops on half rations and set them to strengthening the city's defenses. Some civilians had evacuated, but many who remained dug caves into the sides of hills and ravines, giving the city the look of a prairie dog village. In the dim interiors the cave-dwellers watched their diet decline. At first bacon and beef were available to supplement corn-bread, but as the days wore on, bread made from pea flour appeared and residents began killing mules and rats for meat.

Compared to their Confederate counterparts, Union soldiers were well provisioned. Some honeycombed the hills with protective caves, but most rotated shifts between living in camps to the rear and manning the forward trenches. The Federals had established a secure supply line on the Mississippi, and nearby farms and brambles supplemented their rations with fresh fruit. Dana encountered soldiers returning to camp "with buckets full of mulberries, blackberries, and red and yellow wild plums." The wooded hills behind the lines afforded respites of pure air and shade, and the deep ravines that divided them abounded in springs of unpolluted water.[2]

Dana lived at Grant's headquarters during the siege, occupying a high, shaded bluff behind Sherman's lines at the one o'clock spot on the Union semicircle. The location was safe and comfortable, beyond the range of Confederate artillery. A charming letter to his daughter Ruth described the outlook from his tent:

> It is real summer weather here, and, after coming in at noon to-day from my usual ride through the trenches, I was very glad to get a cold bath in my tent before dinner. I like living in tents very well, especially if you ride on horseback all day. Every night I sleep with one side of the tent wide open and the walls put up all around to get plenty of air. Sometimes I wake up in the night and think it is raining, the wind roars so in the tops of the great oak forest on the hillside where we are encamped, and I think it is thundering till I look out and see the golden moonlight in all its glory, and listen again and . . . it is only the thunder of General Sherman's great guns, that neither rest nor let others rest by night or by day.[3]

On typical days Dana inspected the Union works, visited hospitals, or checked Grant's supply base at Chickasaw Landing. "He knew from personal observation every foot of the country between the Yazoo and the Mississippi on one side and the Big Black on the other, as well as every road and path which traversed it," recalled James Wilson, who often accompanied him.

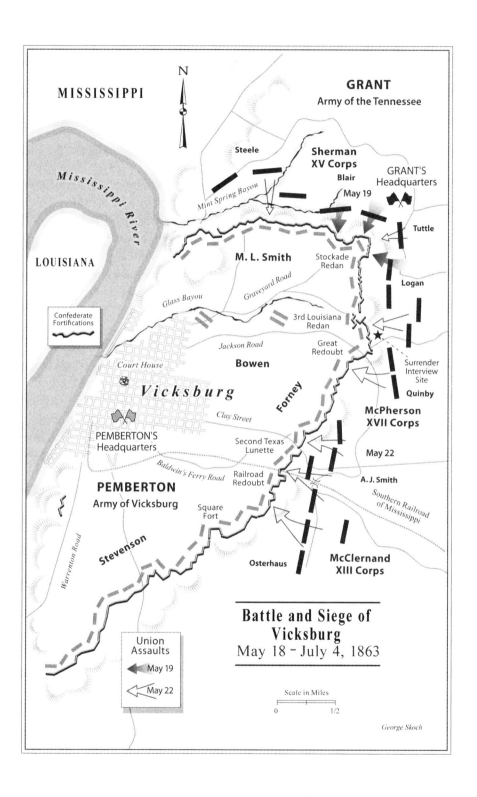

MISSISSIPPI

N

GRANT
Army of the Tennessee

Mississippi River

Steele

**Sherman
XV Corps**

Blair

May 19

GRANT'S
Headquarters

LOUISIANA

Mint Spring Bayou

M. L. Smith

Stockade
Redan

Tuttle

Logan

Confederate
Fortifications

Glass Bayou

Graveyard Road

3rd Louisiana
Redan

Jackson Road

Bowen

Great
Redoubt

Court House

Vicksburg

Surrender
Interview
Site

Quinby

Forney

Clay Street

PEMBERTON'S
Headquarters

**McPherson
XVII Corps**

Second Texas
Lunette

May 22

Baldwin's Ferry Road

Railroad
Redoubt

A. J. Smith

PEMBERTON
Army of Vicksburg

Square
Fort

Southern Railroad
of Mississippi

Warrenton Road

Stevenson

Osterhaus

**McClernand
XIII Corps**

Union
Assaults

May 19

May 22

**Battle and Siege of
Vicksburg**
May 18 – July 4, 1863

Scale in Miles

0   1/2

George Skoch

Their rides could last well into the evening. Dana estimated that in one night he passed 20,000 men asleep on their guns, curled into a variety of grotesque positions. Deep trenches protected soldiers from enemy fire, but the sound of Dana and Wilson's horses' hoofs attracted enemy pickets. One shot seriously wounded an orderly who accompanied the pair.[4]

Once the Union trenches advanced to within seventy yards of the Confederate lines, Dana's evening rounds actually became less dangerous. Enemy soldiers began fraternizing, trading newspapers and small presents between the lines. Opposing sentries established a makeshift truce that allowed Dana to pass without incident, and he greased the negotiations by bringing tobacco or coffee to exchange. By daylight, however, the hills around Vicksburg were exposed and potentially deadly, scanned constantly by Confederate sharpshooters. In late May Dana went on foot to a rise overlooking the town and soon heard bullets whizzing by. He hesitated briefly, considering which way to face while lying down, then unceremoniously hit the dirt. Afterward he became more cautious in venturing beyond cover.[5]

Behind the lines the roads were free of rebel guerrillas; there Dana joined sorties with Grant and his staff to view army outposts or just to make a breeze on a hot day. Returning from an outing to the Yazoo River, the party took an ill-advised shortcut and came to a muddy edge of an impassable lagoon. As darkness approached, they decided to build a log road across the sludge. Grant watched with approval as Dana pitched in to help drag large driftwood logs into position. In less than half an hour the men constructed a forty-foot corduroy passage that took them over the flats and back to camp. Dana relished the achievement, which signaled that he had practically become a member of Grant's staff.[6]

He had not, however, relinquished his role as the government's informant. Knowing that Stanton and Lincoln would be interested, Dana sent them pen portraits of Grant's corps generals. His letter has been lost, but its tenor can be gleaned from his dispatches, surviving letters, and postwar recollections.

Sherman's forces anchored the Union right, which coursed from the Mississippi along the heights northeast of town and stretched north to protect Grant's supply line. Everything Dana saw during the siege heightened his admiration for the sharp and impulsive general. Sherman "always liked to have people about who could keep up with his conversation," and he backed up his words with deeds, according to Dana, who portrayed him as a dynamo. Dana saw Sherman's "amazing activity and vigilance pervading his whole force" as they constructed defenses. Although Sherman had criticized Grant's campaign plan, he performed his role dutifully and mounted the siege with speed and skill.[7]

Dana described James McPherson, whose men occupied the Union center facing Vicksburg, as a tall, handsome, and gentlemanly officer with dark, deep-seated eyes, a medium-length beard, and dark complexion. Dana heard McPherson express anger a few times during the Vicksburg campaign, most vividly when he described McClernand's behavior or complained that his corps was unduly exposed to danger; but Dana usually seconded McPherson's judgments.[8]

Dana noted that among Grant, Sherman, and McPherson — all West Pointers and Ohioans by birth — "the utmost confidence and cordiality" prevailed. Dana's relationship to all three was similarly collegial. Dana "was far from being an emotional man," wrote his friend Wilson, "but he made no effort to conceal the feelings of affection and respect with which he looked upon these splendid soldiers," who exemplified "the best training of the regular army."[9]

McClernand, the political general whose troops covered the Union left sweeping down to the Mississippi, was the odd man out. About him Dana had already given Stanton an earful, and his drumbeat of criticism kept McClernand under discussion at the War Department. From Dana's arrival, when he heard McClernand badmouthing fellow officers, he developed a strong distrust that mounted as McClernand neglected daily operations for personal advancement. Like many politicians Dana had sized up for the *Tribune*, McClernand had been schooled in Congress to "look after himself." Dana understood that Lincoln looked after McClernand, too, for the general's popularity in Illinois could serve "the greater good of the cause." But Lincoln's friendship encouraged McClernand to believe that he served at the president's pleasure, not Grant's, stoking his defiance of orders and impatience to rise. Dana believed that his ambition and outsized ego disrupted the campaign.[10]

Each commander's siege trenches gave Dana an indication of his competence. While Sherman and McPherson pushed their lines forward relentlessly, McClernand, who faced the weakest segment of the Confederate line, lagged so much that he delayed Grant's plans for another attack. "His trenches are mere rifle-pits, 3 or 4 feet wide," Dana complained to Stanton, "and will neither allow the passage of artillery nor the assemblage of any considerable numbers of troops."[11]

Stanton appreciated Dana's assessment of Grant's commanders as much as his updates on the siege. "Your telegrams are a great obligation, and are looked for with deep interest," he wired on June 5. "I cannot thank you as much as I feel for the service you are now rendering." For all his gruffness Stanton had a soft spot for valued assistants, and he fretted over Dana's safety. To allow Dana to be exchanged if captured, Stanton gave him an on-the-spot army appointment as an assistant adjutant general with the rank of major.

Although Dana never used the title or rank and later asked that his nomination be withdrawn, the brevet recognized his potential exposure to danger as he immersed himself in Vicksburg operations.[12]

By the end of May the threat of a Confederate breakout from Vicksburg could be dismissed. After completing a circuit of the lines Dana reported to Stanton that the remaining gaps on the Union left were small enough that "the enemy cannot either escape by that route or receive supplies." "Nothing can save the town," he concluded, "except the arrival of heavy reinforcements." This was exactly what Grant feared. Captured correspondence and Confederate informers revealed that General Joseph Johnston was gathering troops for an attack on the rear of Grant's lines. Rumor had it that Johnston had collected 40,000 soldiers from Braxton Bragg's army in Tennessee and other sources. Grant thought the number exaggerated, but he worried that Johnston was planning to pin the Federals against the Vicksburg defenses. To be ready on two fronts, Grant needed more men. When General Banks failed to reply to his request for reinforcements, Grant asked Dana to go in person to add the War Department's clout. Dana got as far as Grand Gulf when he met a courier returning with Banks's statement that he could not spare any men. In fact, Banks asked Grant to send 10,000 men to help him capture Port Hudson.[13]

Returned to Grant's headquarters, Dana wired an urgent appeal for Stanton to push reinforcements from Tennessee, Kentucky, or Missouri. Like Grant, Dana believed that Vicksburg should take priority over Port Hudson, which would inevitably fall after Vicksburg was taken. Even if Union troops had to be drawn from Tennessee, the payoff would be worthwhile: "Better retreat to Nashville than retreat from the hills of Vicksburg." In reply, Stanton assured Dana that "the emergency is not underrated here." Compared to whiners like McClellan and William Rosecrans, Grant asked for additional men so infrequently that, when he did, Washington authorities listened. In short order Union divisions were sent from the Department of the Missouri and General Ambrose Burnside's corps at Knoxville to supplement those on their way from Memphis.[14]

"General G. Intoxicated!"

Once the tedious task of inching the siege forward became the daily routine, Dana and Wilson noticed that an air of "lassitude and depression" hovered over headquarters. This feverless fatigue found its way to Grant, who appeared sluggish and was advised to take extra rest. Grant resisted, partly from concern that reinforcements under Johnston might arrive before Vicksburg succumbed. Thinking that the Confederates would try to threaten Haynes' Bluff, about fourteen miles northeast of his headquarters, Grant sent a force under General Nathan Kimball up the Yazoo toward Satartia and Mechanicsburg to prevent their advance. On June 4 news arrived that Johnston's army had taken Yazoo City, fifteen miles northeast of Satartia. Grant pondered withdrawing Kimball's forces, then decided, despite feeling under the weather, to assess the situation himself. He invited Dana to go along. On the morning of June 6 the two men set out on horseback with a small cavalry escort toward Haynes' Bluff, where they would board the small steamer *USS Diligence* and proceed upstream to Satartia.[15]

Grant carried a letter in his pocket from his chief of staff John Rawlins, who suspected that Grant had been treating his condition by hitting the bottle. The night before Grant departed, Rawlins found him at his tent ringed by officers drinking wine and urging the general to join in. Rawlins figured from Grant's slurred and halting speech that he had participated. He withdrew to his tent and penned a stern warning to Grant to stay on the wagon: "Had you not pledged me the sincerity of your honor early last March that you would drink no more during the war, and kept that pledge during your recent campaign," Rawlins wrote, "you would not to-day have stood first in the world's history as a successful military leader. Your only salvation depends on your strict adherence to that pledge."[16]

With Dana at Grant's side, Rawlins handed the letter to the general the next morning before the two departed for Satartia. Grant pocketed it and ignored it. Soon after the boat started, Grant "became ill and went to bed," Dana reported to Stanton. Decades later, writing after Grant died, Dana admitted that his dispatch had been couched in euphemism. As the *Diligence* steamed upriver the general got "as stupidly drunk as the immortal nature of man would allow." Grant had a tendency to drink when bored, Dana wrote, and he had chosen a "dull period in the campaign" to go on a binge that did not "interfere with any important movement that had to be directed or attended to by him." "General G. intoxicated!" Wilson scribbled in his diary. He was not present but was told the essentials by Dana upon his return and "many a time" in the following months.[17]

Dana's belated candor about Grant's behavior was more convincing than his excuse for him. The expedition to Satartia was no joyride but rather a serious inspection tour intended to protect Grant's rear lines. The presence of Confederate troops not far off added an element of genuine danger. It is also puzzling that Grant chose to get drunk in the presence of a War Department agent who had been sent to report on him. The most likely explanation for the episode is that Grant was still feeling unwell and tried to right himself with a strong drink or two. As Wilson later wrote, Grant "fell sick, and thinking a drink of spirits would do him good, took one with the usual unhappy result."[18]

Colleagues familiar with Grant disputed how frequently he indulged in liquor, but most agreed that it took few drinks to get him besotted. Grant's military career alternated long teetotaling stretches with periodic lapses. Despite Rawlins's best efforts, it was very easy for officers to obtain alcohol. "This is an awful country for drinking whiskey," Dana wrote a friend. "I calculate that on an average a friendly man will drink a gallon in twenty-four hours." Dana drank moderately and claimed to "suffer in public estimation for not doing as the Romans do."[19]

While Grant slept off his drunken stupor, the *Diligence* chugged up the Yazoo until it encountered a pair of federal gunboats coming downstream two miles below Satartia. The boats' commanders told Dana that General Kimball had withdrawn his men southward after hearing that the Confederates had occupied Yazoo City. Satartia was no longer in Union hands, making a trip there unsafe. Dana awakened Grant to receive new orders, but the general was "not in a condition to conduct an intelligent conversation," Dana later explained. Completely out of character, Grant left the next step to Dana, who ordered the steamer back to Haynes' Bluff. His decision probably saved Grant from being captured. The next morning, June 7, a brigade of Texas cavalrymen reached Satartia, plundered the abandoned Union camp, and probed southwest to overtake the retreating Federals. They would have easily overpowered Grant's escort.[20]

That same morning on the *Diligence*, Grant "came out to breakfast fresh as a rose, clean shirt and all, quite himself," Dana recalled. He had no memory of the night before. "Well, Mr. Dana," he said, "I suppose we are at Satartia now." "No, general," Dana replied, "we are at Haynes' Bluff." When Dana told Grant what had happened, he had no quarrel with Dana's decision, but he wanted to track the Confederates' movements. He ordered a cavalry detachment to go back toward Mechanicsburg to link up with Union troops under Kimball and to report on Johnston's whereabouts. Because he lacked officers nearby he asked Dana to accompany it.[21]

Riding north in the rain on bad roads, Dana and the other horsemen got within ten miles of Mechanicsburg but found no signs of an enemy force, nor did they encounter Kimball's men. The country, Dana noted, was "broken, wooden, unpopulous, with a few streams," and its fields were stripped of corn; Johnston could not move troops through it without taking all his supplies, he reported reassuringly. When Dana's contingent got back to Haynes' Bluff about midnight, they found that Kimball's troops, taking a different route, had arrived there hours earlier.[22]

While Dana was out reconnoitering with Grant's cavalry, the general recuperated aboard the steamer and returned to headquarters. At least that was what Dana surmised. According to another account of June 7, however, Grant resumed his drinking in spectacular fashion. Sylvanus Cadwallader, a reporter for the *Chicago Times* who was a fixture at headquarters, had gone to Satartia ahead of Grant. Cadwallader later claimed that he encountered Grant's steamer on the return trip and joined the general, but he gave the trip a very different ending. In his telling, at Haynes' Bluff Grant procured whiskey, began drinking again, and proceeded downstream to Chickasaw Bayou. There Cadwallader found Grant downing whiskey on a sutler's boat and steered him toward his escort to headquarters. But the tipsy Grant resisted: mounting an aide's horse, he tore off at full speed through the woods. When the horse finally slowed down with Grant reeling atop, Cadwallader caught up with the general, talked him out of the saddle, and procured an ambulance to return him safely to headquarters, where they arrived around midnight.[23]

Cadwallader's tale, penned in the 1890s and not published until 1955, has served as a lightning rod for Grant's critics and defenders. Civil War historians, including Grant's biographers, have split quite evenly on accepting Cadwallader's story as authentic. Some find it consistent with Grant's long history of drinking problems; others point out that it was written from memory three decades after the war and cast the reporter in suspiciously grandiose terms as Grant's rescuer. The epic bender Cadwallader describes does not resemble Grant's known binges, which typically left him in a sleepy stupor. Cadwallader also had a motive to embellish his story, or perhaps concoct it outright, since he was angered that Grant gave so little credit in his *Memoirs* to Rawlins, whose curbs on Grant's drinking he believed essential to the general's success.[24]

The most damaging charge against Cadwallader is the absence of corroborating evidence from documents or witnesses. Dana, whose story is grounded in wartime dispatches, later swore that Cadwallader had not accompanied Grant on the expedition. Of the two remembrances, Dana's is by far the more credible and consistent with other evidence about dates and locations.[25] Yet there may be something to Cadwallader's story. Even if he was mistaken about the first day of the Satartia trip, his account of Grant's spree the next day might account for the general's unusually sluggish return from Haynes' Bluff to headquarters, a trip of fourteen miles that took from noon until late at night. Dana, who was hunting for Kimball on June 7, was in no position to refute this part of Cadwallader's tale. It may also be revealing that after the episode Grant accorded Cadwallader special privileges at headquarters and treated him practically as a member of his staff. This confidential relationship, confirmed by a testimonial letter from Grant and another from his staff that praised Cadwallader's "discretion" and "delicacy" in reporting events, offers circumstantial evidence that he had buried *some* potentially embarrassing news story in his journal.[26]

Whatever the case, Dana's testimony was damning enough on Grant's conduct and potentially to his reputation. Grant had resorted to liquor directly after Rawlins warned him against it, become drunk in the presence of Stanton's emissary, and incapacitated himself on an inspection tour during a critical campaign. Dana confided details of the episode to Wilson. Through him, and perhaps Cadwallader, whisperings circulated through the camp. Yet Dana wrote nothing about it to Stanton and lied about Grant's behavior. When rumors reached Washington about Grant's binge and another bout in August that allegedly caused a serious fall off his horse while visiting Banks in Louisiana, Dana denied them. He told public men in the capital and at New York that Grant "doesn't drink."[27]

There may have been one crucial exception. Long after the war, Dana wrote that he privately shared "the facts" about Grant's drinking with Stanton and Lincoln when he returned to Washington in August 1863. They agreed that infrequent binges "did not disqualify him for successful command" and even considered promoting him to head the Union armies. A few days later Lincoln told a White House visitor—John Eaton, Grant's supervisor of the freedmen's camps—the famous story of his response to congressmen who complained that Grant "sometimes drank too much": if they found out what brand of whiskey he drank, he would distribute it to the other generals.[28]

Spreading word about the Satartia episode would have given Grant's critics a field day and fueled calls for his resignation. Convinced that Grant was essential to Union victory, Dana was willing to overlook the general's lapses. He also counted on Rawlins—without whom, he wrote, "Grant would not have been the same man"—to prevent repeat performances. Dana's cover-up saved Grant's job, and he kept a public silence about Grant's wartime drinking bouts for as long as the general lived.[29]

Relief for Grant but Not Pemberton

Dana resumed his daily updates to Stanton upon his return from Satartia. Although the siege progressed steadily, the presence of Johnston's men east of

Grant's army and the threat of General Kirby Smith invading from across the Mississippi continued to concern Grant. In mid-June Grant ordered Sherman to plant two divisions at Haynes' Bluff in case Johnston attacked from the northern approach to Vicksburg. Dana reported that fortifications capable of withstanding 50,000 troops were being completed there. The Mississippi River defenses were less sure. After visiting Admiral Porter, Dana learned that two dozen Union gunboats were patrolling the Mississippi above and below Vicksburg. These might be enough to deter a large-scale invasion from the west, Dana judged, but a small Confederate force might manage to cross somewhere.[30]

In fact, while Dana and Grant were on the Satartia trip a serious threat had come from the west. Hoping to disrupt Grant's supply lines, on June 7 Kirby Smith sent a force of 3,000 Confederates under General Richard Taylor against a 1,400-man Union garrison at Milliken's Bend, fifteen miles up-river from Vicksburg. The great majority of the Union defenders were former slaves, recruited when the Emancipation Proclamation took effect months earlier. Badly outnumbered, they were initially overrun but rallied and fought the attackers to a stalemate, often in hand-to-hand combat at the levee that held back the Mississippi. Eventually, two Union gunboats opened fire from the river and drove the Confederates off.

The Confederates had charged while yelling "No quarter!" and wounds showed that many Union deaths had come from bayonet stabs or musket butts to the head. General Taylor reported that around fifty blacks were captured, and some were apparently sold into slavery. There were rumors of even worse treatment. Dana heard from Porter, who was not there, that the Confederates had hanged some black soldiers taken prisoner. This prompted Grant to threaten retaliation against Confederate prisoners, but Taylor denied the report and Grant dropped the matter.[31]

Milliken's Bend was a small battle and a costly Union victory, with 652 federal casualties compared to 186 Confederates. It gained its significance as a failed Confederate attempt to relieve Vicksburg, and even more so from the valor displayed by the Union's African American soldiers. Together with Banks's assault on Port Hudson ten days earlier, it was among the first Civil War battles in which large numbers of black soldiers came under fire. They performed admirably. General E. S. Dennis told Dana it was the hardest fighting he had ever seen. "It is impossible," Dana quoted Dennis, "for men to show greater gallantry than the negro troops in this fight."[32]

Milliken's Bend vindicated the government's policy of arming former slaves, which Dana had been urging since late 1861. Visiting the site after the battle, he told Stanton that "the sentiment of this army with regard to the employment of negro troops has been revolutionized by the bravery of the blacks" in combat. "Prominent officers, who used in private to sneer at the idea, are now heartily in favor of it."[33] Dana did not mention Grant as one of those converts, but Milliken's Bend played a key role in bringing the general into line with Dana and the administration on this highly charged issue.

Unlike Dana, Grant was not an early supporter of arming Southern blacks. When the idea was discussed in 1862, Grant, by his own admission, was "bitterly, very bitterly, opposed." He doubted whether contrabands could be disciplined into good soldiers, and recruiting them, he feared, would inflame Southern whites. In the spring of 1863, when Halleck and Stanton informed him that Union generals were expected to recruit freedmen, Grant pledged soldierly obedience rather than personal assent. When black regiments were readied he relegated them to guard supply lines and garrison forts so as to free white soldiers for combat.[34] After Milliken's Bend, Dana's enthusiasm for black combat soldiers rubbed off on Grant and moved him from skepticism to warm support. The manpower shortage looming at Vicksburg also helped. In the weeks after Milliken's Bend, Grant and General Lorenzo Thomas stepped up recruitment of freedmen and filled several newly authorized black Union regiments. Lincoln heard from Dana that Grant was finding these added forces indispensable as he stretched his lines around Vicksburg.[35]

By mid-June veteran Union reinforcements were also streaming into federal camps, and they plugged a gap in the lines south of Vicksburg, effectively sealing the city. A few Confederate deserters were nevertheless able to cross into Union lines, and Dana joined in questioning them. They confided that the garrison inside Vicksburg was worn out and beginning to despair of Johnston's relief. Since Confederate gunfire had tapered off, Grant reasoned that the Rebels must be running low on ammunition as well as morale. Dana's dispatches to Stanton became ebullient: on June 14 he predicted the imminent surrender of Vicksburg and queried Stanton about his next assignment.[36]

The next day the Confederates opened a strong artillery fire on the Federals' center, postponing the Union celebration. Dana rode with Wilson, Sherman, and McPherson to the brow of a hill where they could follow the projectiles' arc from firing to the point of impact, which opened craters three yards in diameter. When the cannon fire turned toward them, the Union commanders sat calmly on their mounts, "discussing the work of the batteries, apparently indifferent to the danger."[37]

Sherman's and McPherson's lines crept so near the enemy that Grant began to ponder another assault. The chief obstacle, by Dana's reckoning, again was McClernand, whose trench lines were too far back. Although Grant had put off relieving the Illinois general, he was losing patience. At this opportune moment, McClernand handed Grant an excellent excuse: a bombastic congratulatory address he delivered to his men after the failed assault of May 22 and then sent to newspapers. McClernand claimed most of the credit for the Vicksburg campaign, asserted that he had held two rebel forts for several hours, and implied that the attack faltered due to lackluster support from other commanders. A printed copy of the speech reached Grant's headquarters, accompanied by complaints from Sherman and McPherson. Its content promoted division among his generals, and its publication without Grant's permission violated army regulations.[38]

In Grant's view, McClernand had schemed to usurp his superior's place, made multiple operational blunders, and poisoned relations between corps commanders. After McClernand refused to disavow his address, Grant sacked him and appointed General Edward O. C. Ord in his place. Dana's friend Wilson, who had once threatened fisticuffs with McClernand when the general tossed aside an order from Grant, had the pleasure of waking McClernand early on June 19 and presenting him with the notice. "Well, sir, I am relieved!" McClernand exclaimed after he read the order. Then, understanding Wilson's likely reaction, he blurted out: "By God, sir, we are both relieved!"[39]

In a long telegram Dana, who had done much to prepare Stanton for this day, announced the firing and forwarded the letters between Grant and McClernand that led to it. McClernand's address was the occasion of his removal, not its cause, Dana assured Stanton: "That cause, as I understand it, is his repeated disobedience of important orders, his general insubordinate disposition, and his palpable incompetence for the duties of the position." Dana added another reason Grant had confided to him: if Grant should become disabled, McClernand was next in command, and Grant feared that his incompetence and hostile relations with Sherman and McPherson would prove disastrous for the campaign.[40]

McClernand's dismissal, which Grant told Dana was "better than 10,000 reinforcements," gave him the freedom to detach troops to find Johnston, whose numbers and whereabouts remained a puzzle. Reports from spies claimed that Johnston's army was on the move east of Vicksburg, and Sherman took 30,000 men to engage him. On June 26 Dana visited Sherman's camp at Bear Creek and found him well prepared to repel an attack. His men dug rifle pits, blocked important roads, and watched fords on the Big Black. By moving his men rapidly and visibly, Sherman "produces the impression that his forces are ten times as numerous as they really are." There were no signs of Johnston's army, but Dana filed another glowing report on Sherman's soldierly qualities.[41]

Meanwhile, Johnston, who had accumulated 32,000 men, abandoned the idea of attacking Grant from the east and began moving his men toward the southern end of the federal line to flank the most imposing works. Always tentative, he floated July 7 as the target date for an attack to divert Grant's men while Pemberton tried to escape Vicksburg. Grant was unaware of Johnston's plans, but he decided to probe Vicksburg's defenses before the rebel armies could coordinate. On June 20 he ordered an artillery attack on the town. Two hundred cannons fired for six hours. Through their field glasses Union officers could glean that buildings had been hit and some cannons disabled, but Dana concluded, with Grant and his generals, that the Rebels were holding fire and that a federal assault would not succeed.[42]

By this time the two armies' lines were so close that a race was under way to tunnel mines under each other's works. Dana reported the disappointing results. On June 25 McPherson's men sprung a mine that blasted a crater in the rebel earthworks thirty-five feet in diameter, but it did not reach the main part of the fort. After failing to establish a position on the new ground, the Federals gave up. A second mine exploded near the first on July 1; it killed dozens of Confederates, but McPherson's men again could not capture the fort. Meanwhile the Confederates countered with a mine of their own on Sherman's front, which destroyed a tunnel his men were digging.[43]

Surrender

The long siege, intense heat, and ritual exchange of cannon fire produced listlessness among the Union men, Dana reported. The belief that Vicksburg would soon capitulate sapped the Federals' enthusiasm for preparing an assault. When Grant held a council of war on June 30, his corps commanders advised waiting. Grant consented, but he confided to Dana that if the enemy did not surrender Vicksburg by July 6 he would storm it.[44]

Fortunately for the Federals, the stalemate was broken sooner. Under fire from Union artillery, the Confederates had lost nearly six times as many men as the Union since the attack of May 22, and survivors were worn down by sleeplessness and poor food. On the morning of July 3 the Confederate general J. S. Bowen crossed the lines bearing a letter from Pemberton to Grant. To "save the further effusion of blood," Pemberton requested an armistice for the capitulation of Vicksburg, asking Grant to appoint three commissioners to meet three of Pemberton's own to discuss terms. Grant replied that his

GENERAL GRANT.   MASTER FRED. D. GRANT.   CHARLES A. DANA,
ASSISTANT SECRETARY OF WAR.
UNION HEADQUARTERS, JULY 3. GENERAL GRANT RECEIVING GENERAL PEMBERTON'S MESSAGE.
FROM A SKETCH MADE AT THE TIME.

"Union Headquarters, July 3. General Grant Receiving General Pemberton's Message." From a sketch by Theodore R. Davis. In the background Ulysses Grant reads the request for a surrender conference at his tent under the flag; in the foreground Grant's son Fred visits Charles Dana. *Battles and Leaders of the Civil War* (New York: Century Co., 1888), 3:532.

only terms were unconditional surrender—the formula he had used since Fort Donelson—but offered an interview later that day. At three o'clock Grant advanced to meet Pemberton on the Jackson road between the lines. Dana was with Grant, along with some staff members and all corps commanders except Sherman, who was tracking Johnston's force. Grant wore a plain, dusty uniform. Pemberton, attired in an elegant officer's outfit, was accompanied by General Bowen and an aide, Colonel Lewis Montgomery.[45]

It must have been a bitter moment for the Confederate general, Dana reflected. As a northern man Pemberton "not only suffered the usual pangs of defeat, but he was doubly humiliated by the knowledge that he would be suspected of treachery by his adopted brethren." To surrender Vicksburg to Grant was damaging enough, but to give the Union a key victory so close to July 4 was to pour salt on the Confederates' wounded pride. Pemberton later claimed he had hoped to secure better terms on the national holiday due to "the vanity of our foe," but more likely he feared his men could not resist the assault that many anticipated that day. Dana's telegrams and diary jottings reflect statements from deserters that Confederate soldiers expected either an attack or surrender on the Fourth of July.[46]

Pemberton arrived at the meeting late and in a testy mood. Grant had served in the same division with Pemberton in the Mexican War and greeted him as an old acquaintance, but Pemberton wanted no cordiality. Dana, who kept his distance with Rawlins and Wilson, could see that Pemberton was "much excited, and impatient in his answers to Grant." Later he learned that Pemberton vowed not to lay down arms without receiving favorable terms. "I can assure you, sir, you will bury many more of your men before you will enter Vicksburg," Pemberton told Grant. To break the impasse it was suggested that subordinate officers discuss terms, acting like the "commissioners" Pemberton had proposed. While McPherson, A. J. Smith, Bowen, and Montgomery conversed, Grant and Pemberton moved to the earthworks nearby and sat down to an awkward conversation. After a while the officers brought Grant Bowen's proposal that the Confederates be paroled and allowed to march out of Vicksburg with their weapons, food, and servants. Grant rejected it but promised to make a counteroffer.[47]

Back at his headquarters Grant conferred with his corps and division commanders. In his memoirs Grant claimed that he dropped his demand for unconditional surrender over his generals' opposition. Dana's telegrams reveal the opposite: it was Grant's commanders who persuaded *him* to relent. All but one favored a parole plan proposed by McPherson. They had strong arguments. Paroling the Confederates would free Grant's army for further operations instead of guarding and transporting so many prisoners, and it would reserve the Union's steamboats for military use—a point driven home by Admiral Porter. Grant mulled it over and gave way. He informed Pemberton that after his men signed paroles they could leave. Officers could take their side arms, clothing, and a horse, and the rank and file their clothes. After more haggling Pemberton accepted Grant's terms.[48]

"Vicksburg has capitulated," Dana announced in a dispatch to Stanton on the Fourth of July. The message missed the fast boat for Memphis, so it and a terse announcement by Grant reached the War Department on July 8, a day after the government learned of Vicksburg's fall from Admiral Porter's wire to Navy Secretary Welles. But Dana's telegram, which contained the surrender correspondence and explained Grant's reasons for paroling the rebel soldiers, was the first to outline Grant's terms. The initial response from Washington was cautious. Halleck feared that Pemberton's parolees would immediately rejoin the ranks, and he ordered Grant to retain them until further orders. But it was too late: Grant had already transferred them to the Confederate parole agent. On July 10 Halleck reported that the Washington authorities had reconsidered and authorized Grant to do as he saw fit.[49]

Whether Dana agreed with Grant's generous terms is open to question. In his telegram to Washington Dana called the parole arrangement logical and the argument against it—Grant's—"one of feeling only." Yet his friend Wilson later claimed that Dana "did not personally favor paroling the surrendered army." Wilson believed Grant's terms "unnecessarily lenient" and may have realigned Dana's views with his own in retrospect. At the time, all of Dana's recorded sentiments favored parole. When he circulated among defeated soldiers in Vicksburg he found them eager to return home; he believed the majority would never serve again. This prediction proved accurate, but Wilson's opposition was partly vindicated when some of the parolees were later recaptured at Chattanooga.[50]

At ten o'clock on July 4, Confederate troops marched out of Vicksburg and stacked arms in front of their works. Dana reported that Pemberton and his staff briefly watched from the parapet of the central fort. Below them, Union soldiers lined the sullen parade without cheering, respecting the fraternity of combatants. The rebel officers "had mostly . . . the look of men who had been crying all night," according to Dana. A Missouri officer bawled as he followed his men to their lines after they surrendered their colors. The troops then marched back to the city to sign their paroles.[51]

An hour later Grant entered the city, with Dana and staff officers riding "at the side of the conqueror." Their first stop was Pemberton's headquarters, a brick house on whose porch the Confederate general, still fuming, awaited the Union commander. Grant dismounted in his dusty field clothes, and Pemberton, in dress uniform, received him with even more "marked impertinence" than at their previous interview, according to Dana. No one offered Grant a seat, and when he asked for water he was told to fetch it inside from some slaves. ("No coldness among *them*," a Northern reporter noticed, "but eager rivalry in serving him.") Grant's officers were visibly angry, but Dana marveled that the general bore the shunning "like a philosopher" and, understanding that Pemberton's cold shoulder was a response to humiliation, treated him with gentle courtesy. Dana drew a broader lesson about differences between democratic and aristocratic ways: "Northern manners are less showy and splendid than Southern chivalry, but sounder and better."[52]

Dana next rode with Grant and his staff to the Vicksburg courthouse, where Logan's men lowered the Confederate flag and raised Union colors in its place. From there Dana followed Grant down to the river and walked the gangway onto Porter's flagship, where all enjoyed a round of handshaking, congratulations, and wine. Amid the festivities Grant was the only one who did not imbibe; he sat in his chair with a look of calm satisfaction and puffed on a cigar.[53]

Taking Stock

Looking back a few weeks later, Dana hailed Grant's "splendid campaign" as a major turning point. "The Mississippi is all regained," he gloated to a friend, and the lands west of it had been taken out of the war. Dana had heard from the Confederate general E. W. Gantt of Arkansas, who surrendered during the siege, that the rebellion in his home state was nearly over and the slave system permanently disrupted. Grant's army took nearly 31,000 captives at Vicksburg, an irreplaceable loss for the Confederates and more than the 20,000–25,000 Rebels Grant and Dana had estimated were penned in the city. An additional 6,000 soldiers had been captured during the campaign, about the same number killed or wounded, along with 66,000 small arms and two hundred cannons. Only old men and young boys were left to fight, as implied by Jefferson Davis's proclamation calling out men up to age forty-five. "How can a population of five millions of whites keep full the ranks of an army of 400,000 men?" Dana asked his friend James Pike as he contemplated the Rebels' decline.[54]

The Federals lost relatively few men for a prolonged offensive campaign. Including the failed assaults of May 19 and 22, fewer than 10,000 Union soldiers were killed or wounded after Grant's armies crossed the Mississippi. With that daring ploy, Grant pioneered a new kind of campaign in which soldiers were constantly on the move, living largely off the land and striking the enemy in a lightning-quick succession of battles. Dana emphasized that the plan of circling to the south and east of Vicksburg was Grant's "own conception, and execution, [and] . . . was opposed by Sherman, McPherson and in Washington." After the war, he used the Vicksburg campaign to combat the legend of Grant as an unimaginative bulldog who simply hurled his numerically superior troops against the enemy: Vicksburg was won "by the most brilliant and original strategy, by rapid marching, judicious combination and self-reliance."[55]

In Washington, news of Vicksburg's fall produced, according to the normally dour Gideon Welles, "spontaneous gatherings, firing of guns, ringing of bells, and general gratification and gladness." Compared to the mixed feelings engendered by General George Meade's repulse of Lee at Gettysburg—also on the Fourth of July—and his failure to prevent Lee's escape, Vicksburg was an unambiguous victory and a welcome antidote. "I cannot, in words, tell you my joy over this result. It is great—Mr. Welles—it is great!" Lincoln threw his arm around the navy secretary. A few days later Welles found Lincoln stretched out on a sofa in Stanton's office, despondent over word that Lee had recrossed the Potomac unmolested. Stanton showed his visitors Dana's tally of men and materials captured at Vicksburg, and happiness returned.[56]

Grant's reputation soared. General Halleck, no great friend, congratulated the hero of the hour and told him he had been promoted to major general. "Old Brains" compared Grant's campaign favorably to Napoleon's surrounding the Austrian army at Ulm. Most important, Grant had won over the president. "The Father of Waters again goes unvexed to the sea," Lincoln exulted in a letter intended for a Republican rally at Springfield. In a personal note of thanks to Grant, Lincoln appended a surprising apology: "When you got below [Vicksburg], and took Port Gibson, Grand Gulf and vicinity," the president confided, "I thought you should go down the river and join Gen. Banks; and when you turned Northward East of the Big Black, I feared it was a mistake. I now wish to make the personal acknowledgment that you were right, and I was wrong." Dana, who had argued against ordering Grant away from Vicksburg to aid Banks in Louisiana, shared in Grant's vindication.[57]

Grant, meanwhile, was busy with plans to reassign his forces. On July 5 Dana wrote on his behalf, requesting instructions about the general's next move. Grant had "no idea of going into summer quarters" and was eager to resume the offensive. Halleck, always cautious, advised that before organizing another campaign "it will be best to clean up a little" by pursuing Johnston and consolidating Union control over Arkansas and northern Louisiana. Grant acted before Washington's response arrived, dividing his army as needed. Sherman moved his troops across the Big Black in pursuit of Johnston, retaking Jackson from the Confederates and again destroying anything of military use. Grant's IX Corps was sent to rejoin Burnside in an effort to hold East Tennessee, and a division of the XIII Corps was dispatched to aid Banks at Port Hudson. On July 9, shortly before the federal division arrived, the Confederates surrendered the city and 6,000 men, clearing the Mississippi of rebel guns for good.[58]

In the course of a day the Union soldiers at Vicksburg switched from offense to defense. Dana reported that they set about destroying the approaches they had recently built, and the tedious process of issuing paroles for Confederate soldiers began. A momentous but largely unforeseen question that arose was what policy to adopt toward Vicksburg's black population. The terms of surrender did not permit Confederate officers to take servants with them when they departed, but some protested that faithful slaves wished to accompany white families. Dana described Grant's decision to McPherson, who stayed behind to oversee the occupation. Grant wanted Vicksburg's blacks "to understand that they are free men." If any expressed a desire to accompany whites to Confederate territory their case should be examined skeptically, and if their decision was deemed voluntary, no more than one servant per family would be allowed. Even this concession was revoked by McPherson when he discovered widespread abuses by Confederate soldiers. Stanton, who had fretted early in the campaign that Grant's officers were returning slaves to their masters, was reassured that the occupation was aligned with emancipation policy.[59]

With Vicksburg's surrender Dana's mission came to an end. He left on July 6 and headed upriver to Helena, Arkansas, where he reported on General Benjamin Prentiss's recent triumph over a larger rebel army under General Theophilus Holmes. From there Dana steamed to Cairo, where one more task remained. At the military telegraph Dana was handed a dispatch from Stanton urging him to continue his "sketches" of officers in Grant's army. Stanton had found Dana's impressions of Grant's corps commanders helpful and wanted more. At Cairo Dana penned two long reviews of Grant's line and staff officers. Designed to provide Stanton and Lincoln with assessments of soldiers who might come up for promotions or reassignment, these handwritten letters offered thumbnail portraits and snap judgments that sorted men into columns of fitness and unfitness as efficiently as if Dana were arranging newspaper copy. Frank and confidential, they abandoned nuance and pulled no punches. Not surprisingly, they were not placed in the War Department's files or published in the official Union records.[60]

Dana summoned Grant's generals to inspection first. In his negative column, Jacob Lauman was found "totally unfit to command," and E. A. Carr exhibited "a critical, hang-back disposition." Jeremiah Sullivan, recently assigned to Grant's headquarters, had been "doing nothing with more energy and effect than he would be likely to show in any other line of duty." Among those allegedly over their head were A. J. Smith, a good division officer who "should not be intrusted with any important independent command," and Francis J. Herron, who, though energetic, lacked "the first great requisite of a soldier, obedience to orders."[61]

Officers who led troops gallantly to the front fared better. A. P. Hovey, an Indiana lawyer, devoted himself to soldiering "as if he expected to spend his life in it." He was one of Grant's best officers, although—Dana recalled

Hovey's pique over the official press release after Champion's Hill—"too anxious about his own personal renown." John Logan was "heroic and brilliant" on the battlefield but unreliable away from it. Unqualified praise was reserved for a fortunate few, usually good fighters and strict disciplinarians: Thomas Ransom, a fine engineer and brave general; Grant's fellow townsman John E. Smith, who was becoming "a better and better general every day"; and W. S. Smith, a "first-rate schoolmaster."[62]

Dana's sketch of Michael K. Lawler, the portly Irishman whose brigade had led the charge at Big Black Bridge, was his most colorful: "Lawler weighs two hundred and fifty pounds, is a Roman Catholic, and was a Douglas Democrat. . . . He is as brave as a lion, and has about as much brains; but his purpose is always honest, and his sense is always good." Lawler was no observer of protocol: "Grant has two or three times gently reprimanded him for indiscretions, but is pretty sure to go and thank him after a battle." Because of Lawler's temper Dana nicknamed him "The High Dominie Dudgeon," and the witty barbs they exchanged at headquarters delighted listeners. At Washington Dana intervened to squelch a disciplinary charge against Lawler, declaring him "a splendid old fighter, with only two grains of discretion" and his offense an excusable mistake.[63]

Dana's second letter covered staff officers. As befit McClernand's poor judgment, his staffers were mostly incompetent and his artillery chief "an ass." By contrast, Sherman's coterie was small and efficient, while McPherson's group was "the most complete . . . and in some respects the most serviceable in this army." Finally, there was Grant's staff, which Dana called "a curious mixture of good, bad, and indifferent . . . a mosaic of accidental elements and family friends." Grant's chief of staff John Rawlins had good judgment and was an indispensable watchdog over Grant's habits, but he was too slow at army business and could not "write the English language correctly." Colonel James Wilson, who passed the fluency test, was a man of "remarkable talents and uncommon executive power" who "will be heard from hereafter." Grant's judge advocate, Theodore Bowers, quartermaster J. D. Bingham, and new chief engineer Cyrus Comstock were excellent men. But his medical head, Madison Mills, was too quarrelsome and his artillery chief William Duff incompetent. Both were kept on, Dana told Stanton, because "it is one of [Grant's] weaknesses that he is unwilling to hurt the feelings of a friend." This flaw would return to haunt Grant during his postwar presidency.[64]

Dana also saw no use for Grant's numerous aides, most of whom were "idle loafers" when no battle was on. Colonel Clark Lagow was a "whiskey-drinking, useless fellow." (Four months later, when Lagow hosted an all-night drinking party at headquarters, Grant allowed him to resign.) Two aides were personal friends of Grant's, and another his cousin. "The army would be better off if they were all suppressed," Dana judged: "If General Grant had about him a staff of thoroughly competent men, disciplinarians and workers, the efficiency and fighting quality of his army would soon be much increased."[65]

Dana's report cards were virtuoso performances, remarkable for their range and unblinking self-confidence. No fewer than eighty men were described and evaluated in letters written from memory on consecutive days. James Wilson, perhaps indulging his own vanity, claimed that "in no case did Dana do injustice or give a false or exaggerated impression" and judged the portraits accurate predictions of success and failure. This was true in most cases, but Dana tossed a few mistakes and grudges into the mix. Despite Dana's criticism, Herron proved an able commander after Vicksburg in Mississippi, Texas, and Louisiana, and A. J. Smith earned promotions for his leadership under Generals Banks, Sherman, and Thomas. Meanwhile, W. S. Smith, one of Dana's favorites, put his career under a cloud by ignoring Sherman's orders during the Meridian Campaign in Mississippi of February 1864. Dana's animus against Duff may have come from Rawlins, who discovered that Duff had supplied Grant with liquor in camp.[66]

Despite some questions about accuracy and bias, Dana's gallery of cameos proved useful as Stanton weighed personnel matters. Dana's praise for Logan and Frank Blair, Jr., as the most able of Lincoln's political generals boosted their military careers. On the other side of the ledger, Stanton remembered Dana's criticisms of Grant's staff when he recommended its overhaul the next year. Stanton's reliance on the letters reflected his growing confidence in Dana. Early in the campaign he had warned Dana not to give advice about personnel matters; by its end he asked for as much as possible. In a final irony, Dana's letters said nothing at all about officers in the paymaster's department, whose operations had been the excuse for his "investigation" of Grant's army.[67]

Throughout the siege, Dana proved his worth to Stanton with his clear and concise reports, assurances of eventual Union victory, and sharp judgments of men and events. Meanwhile, the influence Dana gained in Washington proved invaluable to Grant, who by sharing information with Dana won an important advocate in government councils. In short, Dana served both Grant and the administration effectively as a confidant and liaison, and the trust he built with Stanton and Lincoln furthered his own prospects for a permanent government appointment.

James Wilson's admiring assessment was formed firsthand. Charles Dana "did all in his power to remove the prejudice against Grant" from Lincoln and Stanton's minds and to replace it with confidence. "He did this without concealing or minimizing the peculiarities of the general, or of his staff, or of his subordinate commanders," Wilson added. "His position was a delicate one, but he filled it with such tact and ability as to satisfy the Government, to strengthen the hand of Grant, and at the same time to win his personal friendship." Because Dana grew to admire Grant and share his opinions, there was little conflict between his role as "Stanton's spy" and Grant's "writer and telegrapher." Relations between Lincoln and Stanton and their top western general, critical to the Union's success, were cemented by Dana's work as a go-between. As a consequence, the Federals' day of victory moved closer as measurably as the Union lines had at Vicksburg.[68]

8   Interlude: "Some Duty Not Yet Explained"

Charles Dana's reports from Vicksburg in 1863 established his value as a roving agent for Secretary of War Edwin Stanton and President Lincoln, who were often in the dark about realities at the front. But Stanton's department at Washington also needed attention. His staff was buried in piles of paperwork generated by mushrooming military operations. Succumbing to the workload, Stanton's chief assistant, Peter Watson, announced his intention to resign. Dana would make an ideal replacement. At the same time, Generals George Meade in Virginia and William Rosecrans in Tennessee were preparing offensives before winter, and Washington authorities could use independent reports on both of these balky commanders. While Stanton pondered Dana's next assignment, Dana left Cairo on July 14 to rejoin his family in New York for a few days, then reached Washington on July 19.[1]

Grant's Man at the Capital

At the capital Dana found Union war leaders pleased about Vicksburg but distraught over Meade's failure to pursue and capture Robert E. Lee's Army of Northern Virginia after the rebel defeat at Gettysburg. Dana was initially more forgiving. No doubt a vigorous pursuit "seasonably made" would have corralled Lee's entire army, he told James Wilson, but Meade's corps commanders, he was told, had opposed pursuing Lee when Meade polled them. A week later, perhaps after Stanton's disappointment rubbed off on him, Dana took a harsher line. "Had Meade finished Lee before he had crossed the Potomac, as he might have done & he should have done," he wrote his friend James Pike, "we should now be at the end of the war."[2]

Soured on Meade, Lincoln and Stanton considered naming Grant to head the Union Army of the Potomac. Dana, along with General in Chief Henry Halleck, advised against the move. Dana gave two main reasons. First, Grant had learned the capabilities of the western army and its officers, the local roads and rivers, and the land and its resources; he would have to start over in the eastern theater. Second, Grant would face resentment among the eastern army's already contentious officers as an outsider brought in over the heads of soldiers promoted from within.[3]

In the end, Meade was kept on. Grant, relieved to learn that he had been spared the transfer, penned Dana a letter of thanks: "Gen. Halleck and yourself were both very right in supposing that it would cause me more sadness than satisfaction to be ordered to the command of the Army of the Potomac." After repeating most of the arguments Dana had used, Grant concluded with his shaky spelling: "I feel very greatful [*sic*] to you for your timely intercession." Dana shared the letter with Stanton and Lincoln, who read it "with great satisfaction."[4]

Some of that satisfaction stemmed from Grant's soundness on emancipation and the use of African American troops, two major concerns of Lincoln and Stanton. At Stanton's prompting, Grant had established a board of examiners to purge his own Army of the Tennessee of vocal anti-emancipation officers. "Slavery is already dead and cannot be resurrected," Grant told his congressman, Elihu Washburne. "I never was an Abolitionist, [n]ot even what could be called anti slavery, but . . . it became patent to my mind early in the rebellion that the North and South could never live at peace with each other except as one nation, and that without Slavery."[5]

With Dana's nudging and the brave performance of African American troops at Milliken's Bend, Grant had dropped his misgivings about arming former slaves. In July Stanton sent General Lorenzo Thomas on his second recruiting trip to the Mississippi Valley. Dana assured Lincoln of Grant's cooperation: "Mr Dana understands you as believing that the emancipation proclamation has helped some in your military operations," the president wrote Grant. "I am very glad if this is so." In an interview with John Eaton, Grant's superintendent of contrabands, Lincoln went further: Dana, he heard, had told listeners that Grant claimed he "could not have taken Vicksburg had it not been for the proclamation." Lincoln guessed—correctly—that Dana's point had been stretched as it circulated, and he doubted that Grant made "so strong a statement." But Lincoln was pleased enough to repeat the claim, in slightly qualified form, in a message to a pro-Union rally held in his hometown of Springfield.[6]

Grant responded to Lincoln by expressing "hearty support" for arming blacks and pledging to assist Thomas's recruiting efforts. Echoing the president, he declared that former slaves "will make good soldiers and taking them from the enemy will weaken him in the same proportion as they strengthen us." Writing separately to Grant, Dana emphasized that it was critical to enlist Southern blacks because many Northerners were avoiding conscription through commutation or disability. There was another reason: "There is a large party whose effort is to bring the seceded states back with the same leaders and the same slavery with which they went out." Enlisting "a powerful negro force . . . from among the former slaves" would counter this plot. Rumors were circulating that the Emancipation Proclamation would be suspended for any rebel state agreeing to return to the Union. "No such thing will be done by this administration," Dana assured his friend Pike, and "as a safeguard against such a calamity hereafter, the work of subsisting and arming the Southern Negroes is being prosecuted with all possible energy." Dana predicted that 100,000 black Union soldiers would be in the field by the end of the year, the same figure Lincoln used in writing to Grant.[7]

Dana also registered his support for equal treatment of African American soldiers, who were paid less than their white counterparts and had to serve under white officers. On August 10 the black abolitionist leader Frederick Douglass visited Washington to convince Lincoln and the cabinet to equalize conditions for African American Union soldiers and to protect them against enslavement if captured. After touring Capitol Hill, Douglass headed to the War Department with Samuel Pomeroy, the Radical Republican senator from Kansas. Their first stop was Dana's office. Dana had befriended Douglass two decades earlier when the newly escaped slave visited Brook Farm, and they had exchanged views during the *Tribune*'s Free Soil campaigns. After hearing from Douglass about his mission, Dana escorted him downstairs and introduced him to Stanton.[8]

Scowling behind the standing desk in his receiving room, Stanton greeted Douglass as brusquely as everyone else. "Every line in Mr. Stanton's face told me that my communication with him must be brief, clear, and to the point; that he might turn his back on me . . . at any moment," Douglass recalled. Douglass explained his grievances, then added a personal plea to treat African American recruits just like their white counterparts. Stanton warmed as he sensed Douglass's sincerity and intelligence. He admitted that the administration had appeased popular prejudice but assured Douglass that justice would ultimately be done. Stanton proposed that Douglass travel to the Mississippi Valley to recruit black volunteers and even promised him a military commission—an appointment that would signify the administration's support for black officers. Within days, however, Stanton decided that he had leaped ahead of administration policy. Although the secretary approved

Douglass's transportation to Vicksburg and a modest salary, his commission as an officer never arrived.[9]

General Grant did not go on record on the question of equal pay for black soldiers, but his assent to emancipating and recruiting the South's slaves reassured congressional Republicans. To solidify support for Grant, Dana puffed him among leading politicians: "I tell everybody that he is the most disinterested, and the most honest man I have ever known," Dana wrote Elihu Washburne. Since returning to the capital Dana had met "hundreds of prominent and influential men" and had sung Grant's praises to all. That included covering up Grant's problems with alcohol. "To the question they all ask: 'Doesn't he drink?'—I have been able, from my own knowledge to give a decided negative." Senator Henry Wilson, chairman of the Senate Military Committee, had a long conference with Dana, whom he considered "a man of talent and a good judge of men." Dana spoke "in the most glowing terms of Grant," Wilson reported to Washburne. "He tells me that Grant is modest, true, firm, honest and full of capacity for war." Equally important to Wilson, Dana relayed that Grant "is in favor of destroying the cause of this civil war— of overthrowing Slavery and that his army is deeply imbued with the same feeling."[10]

Dana brought back from Vicksburg a success story everyone wanted to hear. In New York he recounted the campaign to members of the elite Union League Club. George Templeton Strong, a wealthy Republican attorney and prolific diarist, noted that Dana was "the object of a concentric fire of queries, which he answered very intelligently and clearly." Dana told attendees that the rebellion in the Southwest had been smashed and that Arkansas would "secede from secession and return to her normal condition"—overoptimistic assessments he had absorbed at Grant's headquarters. Dana recounted for New York Republicans the "snobbishness and arrogance" displayed by Confederate general John Pemberton and his staff during the surrender of Vicksburg. Again, in response to a question about the Union general's habits, he asserted flatly that "Grant doesn't drink."[11]

Summing up his reflections on Grant's character, Dana sent Pike an appraisal that he no doubt shared with Stanton. Grant reminded him of Zachary Taylor, the Mexican War hero elected president. "He has the same absolute honesty, the same directness of purpose, and the same dogged determination." Grant combined "sure and sufficient" mental powers with "transparent sincerity," a combination he shared with "Old Rough and Ready" but that was rarely seen among men in power. Grant the soldier differed from Taylor in one critical respect, Dana confided: he "has no political aspirations and I don't believe he could be brought to have any." This was music to the ears of Lincoln loyalists.[12]

Vicksburg sealed the administration's confidence in Grant as a military strategist and a fighting general; Dana's meetings in Washington cleared up lingering doubts about the general's character, habits, and political ambitions. Together with Rawlins's interviews, which presented Grant's side of the McClernand story, these lobbying efforts smoothed Grant's eventual rise to the top of the Union army; they also spurred McClernand's reassignment far away at the Texas-Mexico border.[13]

The status of Grant's other lieutenants was also at issue. Despite a shortage of brigadier generalships to give out, Grant was able to secure promotions for a handful, including Sherman and McPherson. John Rawlins, not a West Pointer or a line officer, required a special effort; Grant asked Halleck for his promotion as a favor. Dana reported to Grant that it went through. Privately, Dana expressed one reservation: "The truth is that the adjutant's department in the Department of the Tennessee has never been well administered," he told Wilson. Dana wrote Rawlins to warn him of "a storm brewing against him" at the War Department unless he gave up his adjutant duties, which included writing orders, maintaining correspondence, and keeping records. Grant felt the warning gusts. Once Rawlins was promoted, Grant made him his chief of staff and replaced him as assistant adjutant general with his aide Theodore Bowers.[14]

Riots and a Respite

In late July Dana returned to New York City. Two weeks earlier it had been the site of draft riots that ranked among the worst mob outbreaks in American history. A stronghold of the Democratic Party, the city had not met its quota of enlistments and became one of the first to be subjected to the federal draft. On July 11 the draft authorities began selecting names by lot, and two days later the explosion erupted. Thousands of Irish workers and other war dissenters rampaged through the streets, set fire to the draft office, looted factories and stores, and ransacked the homes of prominent Republicans. One cluster of rioters stormed Mayor George Opdyke's recently established rifle factory at 21st Street and Second Avenue, broke in and distributed the guns, then torched the building. Another angry group gathered at the *Tribune* building, where they smashed windows and trashed furniture on the first floor before the city police and employees of the *Tribune* and *Times* fended them off. Horace Greeley escaped by walking calmly through the howling crowd. The next day, despite warnings that his presence would invite a mob attack, Greeley insisted on coming to work, and he scribbled his editorials before exiting the back door in the evening.[15]

The mob's main target was the city's black residents, whom they blamed for the war and competition for jobs. Bloodthirsty gangs of rioters lynched at least a dozen African Americans and burned down the city's Colored Orphan Asylum. The New York governor Horatio Seymour, a Democrat who opposed the Lincoln administration's policies, cut short his vacation to calm the rioters. Addressing the crowd at City Hall Park as "Dear friends," he called the draft unconstitutional but urged citizens to leave the streets and forgo violence. Not until the fourth day of rioting, when several Union regiments arrived from Gettysburg, was the mayhem brought under control. About 120 people were killed and hundreds more were wounded or injured.[16]

Dana was convinced that Seymour had fueled the outbreak by denouncing emancipation and conscription. The governor considered using the state militia to close down the draft, Dana believed, but was "too great a coward" to execute the scheme, especially with federal troops on the way. "When the pinch comes," Seymour "lacks the courage for the revolution his friends have planned." His dander up, Dana wanted leaders of New York's "Copperhead Democracy" not just discredited but eliminated. "Nothing could be more useful just at this moment than a regular attempt at civil war and secession in New York," he told Pike. "The restoration of national unity can hardly be thought complete until some of these northern friends of slavery have been punished by powder and ball."[17]

Dana conceded that his former boss Greeley had acted "with great coolness and courage" during the riots, but the *Tribune* editor's vacillating stance on the war still looked like cowardice to his former deputy. Early in 1863 Greeley, shaken by the Union defeat at Fredericksburg, had met confidentially in Washington with Henri Mercier, Napoleon III's minister to the United States, to encourage a French plan to mediate an end to the war. Greeley's initiative probably violated federal laws against private citizens conducting diplomacy. It also exposed the crusading editor's naïveté, for while Greeley envisioned an armistice that would preserve the Union, the French had in mind an agreement to divide it in two and further their imperial plans in Mexico.[18]

Greeley's "idea of settling our difficulties by the intercession of L[ouis] Napoleon I will never forgive him for," Dana told his friend Pike, by then an experienced diplomat. Dana saw in Greeley's plan an updated version of the editor's delusion of "letting the wayward sisters go." He was sure that the

"The Meeting of the Friends, City Hall Park," 1863. This biting political cartoon shows New York Democratic governor Horatio Seymour addressing the draft-rioters as "Dear Friends" while they lynch African Americans and attack the *Tribune* building in the background. Library of Congress Prints and Photographs Division.

Northern public regarded peaceful separation in 1863 as they had two years earlier: "The strongest sentiment of this people," Dana wrote a friend abroad, is "for the preservation of the territorial and political integrity of the nation at all costs." In practical terms, this meant that "they prefer to keep up the existing war a little longer, rather than to make arrangements for indefinite wars hereafter." Still angry about the "explosion" with Greeley a year earlier, Dana told friends he never wanted to see him again. One day in mid-July they approached each other on the Broadway sidewalk, but according to Dana, Greeley averted his eyes. Again, the famous editor behaved like a coward.[19]

Dana noted ruefully that the New York draft riots had done nothing to increase the value of his house on Clinton Place, which he was trying to sell. It sat just a few blocks west of Tompkins Square, a staging area for some of the draft-rioters. Toward the end of July Dana escaped the city and joined his family for a short stay at their Connecticut cottage. He enjoyed the cooling breezes of Long Island Sound and played naval commander "in a fifteen foot sailboat full of children." After a fortnight he was supposed to return to the capital "for some duty not yet explained to me." "Very probably" he would be asked to take Peter Watson's place as Stanton's assistant.[20]

Unless he was lured by another offer, that is. In New York Dana was approached by a group of wealthy businessmen, including Mayor Opdyke and the millionaire banker Morris Ketchum. They were looking for someone to manage a large California gold-mining operation Ketchum had recently purchased and turned into a public company, with Dana's friend Opdyke as one of the owners. Ketchum's property was no ordinary mine. The Mariposa Estate covered seventy square miles and straddled California's famed Mother Lode, containing the state's largest gold holdings. It was originally a Spanish land grant that was acquired by General John C. Frémont two years before the gold rush. Its six mines had made Frémont rich and subsidized his runs for office. By 1863 Frémont was heavily in debt and sold out to Ketchum.

Opdyke and Ketchum offered Dana an annual salary of $5,000 for five years and a hundred shares of company stock each year. With a family of five to look after, Dana was tempted but decided against it. "Their proposal was handsome," he told Pike, "but not quite enough to make me feel like deserting the flag & going into private life. Very likely I made a mistake not to take it." The property's remoteness put Dana off, and he was reluctant to abandon the Union's epic struggle for survival. Dana checked with Stanton, who asked him to remain at the War Department as one of his assistants, and he agreed.[21]

In turning down the Mariposa position Dana dodged a frustration-filled western stint and a career cul-de-sac. In his place he recommended his friend Frederick Law Olmsted, the designer of New York's Central Park (along with his partner Calvert Vaux) and presently head of the Sanitary Commission, a charity that assisted Union soldiers. Olmsted endured two years steering the isolated, underproducing California mines through a series of financial crises before assigning the estate to creditors.[22]

Dana returned to Washington on August 10, stunned by the city's "infernal heat," and set to work as Stanton's assistant secretary. The prospect had its own set of misgivings, mostly related to the sedentary routine and Dana's weak eyesight. "I feel some dread of work in an office, and would much prefer the life on horseback and in the field which I enjoyed with you in

Mississippi," he wrote James Wilson. Still, Dana was an experienced and efficient desk man who acclimated easily to bureaucratic demands. He spent the remainder of August attending to War Department business, advising on army promotions, referring requests to the proper offices, and overseeing military contracts. Dana's signature appears below no official War Department correspondence that month, no doubt because Congress had not yet authorized his appointment.[23]

There was little time for his desk work to become routine. Within days Dana was again being considered for a field assignment with the Union army. The question was where. On August 18 Dana informed Grant that he was joining Meade's Army of the Potomac for several weeks. On the same day, he wrote Pike that he would be dispatched to "look after matters in the army of Gen. Rosecrans." Stanton was evidently still deciding.[24]

Meanwhile, the war secretary sent Dana back to New York City to make certain that the draft lottery, which had been postponed by the July riots, proceeded peacefully. The Union general John Dix, who had replaced the aging and ineffective John Wool as commander of the New York district, warned that Governor Seymour's request for further postponement might rekindle riots, and he asked the War Department for more soldiers. On August 19 all of Dix's available men were stationed at the provost marshal's offices and other key public spaces, and navy ships stood on alert around Manhattan. That morning the drawing of names began. "There is not the least disturbance in any part of the city," Dana wired Stanton just before noon. Although the troops sent by Stanton had not yet arrived, Dix had 10,000 soldiers on hand, and the state militia's cooperation convinced the locals that Dix had twice that number. The Union's strong military presence, combined with a deal worked out by Mayor Opdyke to fund substitutes for men essential to their families, kept the peace. The draft resumed without a hitch.[25]

After ten more days Dana's waiting game ended. Stanton and Lincoln decided to send him not to the Army of the Potomac in northern Virginia, which Meade was methodically preparing for a new offensive against Lee, but to Tennessee. After long delays, Rosecrans's Army of the Cumberland had resumed its southward march to clear the state of General Braxton Bragg's rebel troops.

9 "As Fatal a Name as Bull Run"

Edwin Stanton's soul was "always at white heat in his country's cause," Charles Dana recalled, to explain why he was so overbearing. True to form, Stanton wasted no time using Ulysses Grant's victory at Vicksburg to goad other Union generals. "We have just received information that Vicksburg surrendered to General Grant," he wired General William Rosecrans on July 7. With Grant victorious and Robert E. Lee's Army of Northern Virginia defeated at Gettysburg, "you and your noble army now have a chance to give the finishing blow to the rebellion. Will you neglect the chance?" There was, in truth, more than zeal for victory involved in Stanton's prodding: he was venting six months of accumulated frustration at Washington as Rosecrans's promising drive against Confederate general Braxton Bragg's Army of Tennessee bogged down in delays and excuses.[1]

Edging toward Glory

A brilliant Ohio engineer who graduated fifth in West Point's class of 1842—much higher than Ulysses Grant the next year—William S. Rosecrans never lived up to his potential. Rosecrans—like Grant, William T. Sherman, and many others—resigned his commission when opportunities for advancement stalled in the 1850s. Turning to business, Rosecrans helped build one of the first oil refineries west of the Appalachians. In 1859 he was severely burned when an oil lamp exploded, and the scars left what looked like a permanent smirk under his auburn beard. The Civil War finally gave Rosecrans a chance to use his military skills, first under George McClellan in western Virginia and later under Grant in Mississippi. His successful defense of Corinth, Mississippi, against an assault by Confederates in October 1862 earned Rosecrans his own army. He took charge of Don Carlos Buell's troops, renamed the Army of the Cumberland, with orders to move against the rebel troops under Bragg in the center of Tennessee.[2]

General William S. Rosecrans, photograph by Mathew Brady. Library of Congress Prints and Photographs Division.

If President Lincoln and Secretary of War Stanton expected another Grant in Rosecrans they were sorely mistaken. "Old Rosy" was genial but volatile, possessing a temper that could startle its victims, especially if they knew of his reputation for piety (Rosecrans had converted to Catholicism at West Point). Troubled, like Sherman, with a restless mind, Rosecrans lacked Sherman's power of concentration in battle, let alone the steadiness of Grant. Rosecrans's main shortcoming was his insistence on biding his time. A shrewd tactician, he preferred outmaneuvering the enemy to outfighting him. This led to delays while preparing his troops for complex operations, constant appeals for more soldiers, and capturing enemy territory instead of combatants. As Grant backed General John Pemberton's army into Vicksburg in May 1863, Washington leaders urged Rosecrans to push south to prevent Confederates from sending troops to relieve Pemberton. Because he did not, Bragg detached thousands of men under Johnston to threaten Grant's forces from the rear.[3]

On June 24 Rosecrans finally moved his men south, distributing them through several mountain gaps, bypassing Bragg's Confederates and forcing them to withdraw from their supply depot at Tullahoma and retreat across the Tennessee River at Bridgeport. In just over a week and at the cost of fewer than six hundred casualties the Federals had almost cleared Bragg out of Tennessee. Rosecrans eagerly awaited public acclaim, but his timing was unlucky. Within days his achievement was overshadowed by the monumental Union victories at Vicksburg and Gettysburg. Piqued by Stanton's dispatches announcing these triumphs, Rosecrans cautioned the war secretary against overlooking his victory "because it is not written in letters of blood." "The contemptuous silence with which our success was treated," he told General in Chief Henry Halleck, "has produced a feeling that the Secretary is unjust." Rosecrans's bruised ego added to grievances over Washington's refusal to supply him with more cavalry, and he became convinced that Stanton and Halleck were plotting against him.[4]

What happened next added to his resentment. Believing that Bragg's men were in disorganized retreat, Washington leaders urged Rosecrans to keep after the Rebels. The Union objective was Chattanooga. A shabby town of some 3,000 residents settled on a flat at a bend in the Tennessee River, Chattanooga was overlooked by the 1,700-foot summit of Lookout Mountain to the south and the 500-foot elevation of Missionary Ridge to the east. Gaps between these outcroppings of the Cumberland Mountains gave Chattanooga its strategic importance. It formed the junction of three of the South's major railroads, one from Virginia, another from Memphis and Nashville, and a third

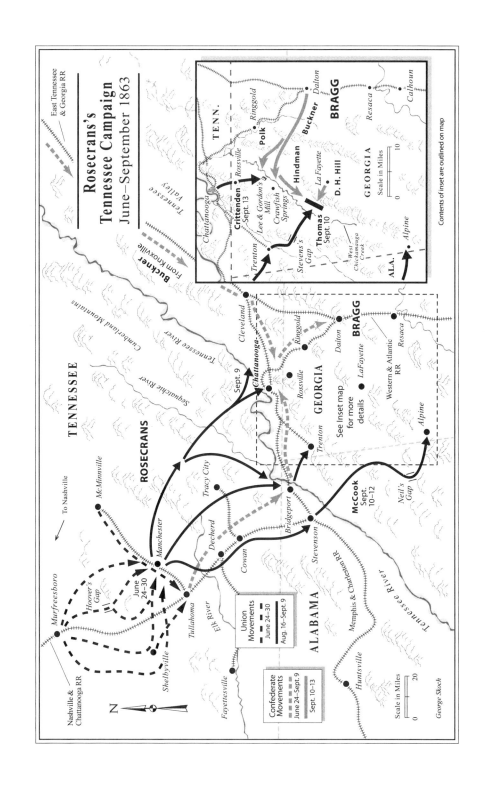

Rosecrans's
Tennessee Campaign
June–September 1863

East Tennessee
& Georgia RR

TENN.

Ringgold

Dalton

BRAGG

Resaca

Calhoun

Polk

Buckner

Hindman

LaFayette

D. H. Hill

GEORGIA

Scale in Miles

0   10

Chattanooga

Rossville

Crittenden
Sept. 13

Lee & Gordon's
Mill

Crawfish
Springs

Thomas
Sept. 10

West
Chickamauga
Creek

Trenton

Stevens's
Gap

Alpine

ALA.

Contents of inset are outlined on map

From Knoxville

Buckner

Tennessee
Valley

Cumberland Mountains

Tennessee River

Sequatchie River

Cleveland

Chattanooga

Sept. 9

Ringgold

Dalton

BRAGG

Rossville

GEORGIA

LaFayette

Resaca

See Inset map
for more
details

Trenton

Western & Atlantic
RR

Alpine

TENNESSEE

McMinnville

To Nashville

ROSECRANS

Tracy City

Manchester

Decherd

Cowan

Bridgeport

Stevenson

McCook
Sept.
10–12

Neil's
Gap

Murfreesboro

Hoover's
Gap

June
24–30

Tullahoma

Elk River

Shelbyville

Fayetteville

ALABAMA

Memphis & Charleston RR

Huntsville

Tennessee River

Nashville &
Chattanooga RR

N

Union
Movements
June 24–30
Aug. 16–Sept. 9

Confederate
Movements
June 24–Sept. 9
Sept. 10–13

Scale in Miles

0   20

George Skoch

connecting to Atlanta and the Atlantic and Gulf Coasts. A series of parallel valleys descended southeast from Chattanooga to Atlanta, making it the gateway to the Confederacy's heart. Once they grabbed Chattanooga, Union forces could split the Confederacy diagonally by penetrating into Georgia. This was the first stage of the "finishing blow" Stanton foresaw in his challenge to Rosecrans of July 7; the second was to destroy Bragg's army.[5]

Instead of being spurred to action by this prospect, Rosecrans dug in his heels for another six weeks. He could not move until railroads and bridges were repaired and his army was resupplied, he told Washington officials. General Ambrose Burnside's Army of the Ohio in northeast Tennessee had to draw his men nearer for support. Rosecrans claimed to need additional troops now that Johnston's army, driven off by Grant, could be returned to Bragg. Halleck sent the Ohio general a peremptory order to advance, assuring him that Stanton was not undermining him. Even Lincoln had to tell the by-now paranoid general that he was not "watching you with an evil eye."[6]

The Tullahoma Campaign brought Rosecrans to "the edge of glory," according to his biographer William Lamers. "Edging," or moving sideways, was Rosecrans's preferred mode as he held to a methodical war of maneuvering even as the conflict was evolving into a relentless war of destruction. Stanton gradually became convinced that Rosecrans was another blood-shy, procrastinating War Democrat on the model of George McClellan. Treasury Secretary Salmon Chase, a champion of the Ohio general, noted that as the summer came, Stanton's estimation of Rosecrans descended "to painful doubt and then to positive disapproval." Stanton's short fuse gave out in August, when the war secretary berated two of Rosecrans's military emissaries in his office, swearing that the general "shall not have another damned man."[7]

The message finally registered. Shortly afterward, Rosecrans began moving his troops, and Stanton turned to Charles Dana for help in monitoring the campaign. Stanton's written instructions mirrored his Vicksburg orders: Dana was to investigate problems in administrative operations and to transmit Union generals' views to Washington. He was told to proceed to Burnside's headquarters and then to Rosecrans's and confer with the military governor in Nashville. A new feature, prompted by Stanton's interview with Frederick Douglass, was the "particular attention" Dana was to give to "the condition of colored persons in the respective Armies, and in the region of country in which the Armies are operating." Dana's central task was left unwritten: as he had with Grant, he was to size up a commanding general about whom administration leaders had doubts and provide an independent, confidential voice assessing him and his army's operations.[8]

Dana set out from New York on September 1, but delays on railroads and steamboats overloaded with military cargo slowed his way. At Cincinnati he learned that it was impossible to visit Burnside's army, which was strung out along an irregular line toward Knoxville, with no secure route to Rosecrans. Continuing to Louisville, Dana examined evidence of contract frauds in the quartermaster's department and transmitted it to Washington, fulfilling one pretext of his mission.[9]

Dana next rode the rails to Nashville, where on the morning of September 8, 1863, he called on Andrew Johnson, the pugnacious War Democrat whom Lincoln had appointed military governor. It was Dana's first meeting with Johnson, and he was not impressed by the politician's gruff, plebian ways. Dana described him as "short and stocky, of dark complexion, smooth face, dark hair, dark eyes, and of great determination of appearance." Reaching for a jug on the floor by his desk, Johnson poured Dana a drink and took a bigger one himself. "I noticed that the Governor took more whiskey than most gentlemen," Dana recalled, "and I concluded that he took it pretty often."[10]

The whiskey loosened Johnson's tongue for a long interview that Dana reported to Stanton. Aware that his words would be relayed to Stanton, Johnson played up his antislavery views. Slavery in Tennessee, he declared, had been destroyed in fact and would be abolished legally by the new legislature. Johnson favored immediate emancipation, Dana reported, both as "a matter of moral right" and as the trigger for an influx of "industrious freemen" who would "repeople and regenerate the state." Johnson had *white* newcomers in mind, "freemen" rather than "freedmen"; he told Dana that Tennesseans were worried about the "status of the negro" after emancipation. Dana understood what this meant: despite his support for ending slavery, Johnson shared the fears and prejudices of the state's poor whites.[11]

Turning to military matters, Governor Johnson was pleased with Burnside's occupation of Knoxville two days earlier but complained that Rosecrans was advancing too slowly. Time was wasted in constructing useless fortifications that were a windfall for army suppliers. Rosecrans, the governor charged, had been manipulated by his ambitious chief of military police, William Truesdail, whom Johnson viewed as a rival for control over the occupied capital. Nashville's fortifications were indeed elaborate. With an afternoon to kill after talking with Johnson, Dana inspected the town's defenses. Three imposing forts were being built on the south side of the town; the central one, to be blasted out of a hill of limestone, might take two years to complete. Dana guessed that they would require a garrison of more than four thousand men. Eventually the constructions proved their worth: in December 1864 they anchored the ring of forts that deterred General John Bell Hood's Confederate troops from attacking, and the Rebels were routed on the city's outskirts.[12]

At Rosecrans's Headquarters

On September 9 Dana left Nashville for the front with General Gordon Granger of Rosecrans's army. They traveled by rail to Bridgeport on the Tennessee River, where the Nashville Railroad joined the eastward line to Chattanooga. The bridge across the river had been destroyed by Bragg's troops, complicating Rosecrans's supply situation. Dana estimated that it would take a month to replace the bridge and surmised that Rosecrans would concentrate his army at Chattanooga before pushing forward. The next morning he learned that the advance corps of Rosecrans's army had entered Chattanooga.[13]

Rosecrans had once more outmaneuvered his seemingly hapless Confederate counterpart. Setting out from Manchester, Rosecrans directed three of General Thomas L. Crittenden's divisions to feint a river crossing above Chattanooga while he sent General Alexander McCook's and General George Thomas's troops across the Tennessee at places south and west of the city. Bragg was unable to deploy his army against "the popping out of the rats from so many holes." Realizing that his defenses had been flanked and his rail connection southward was in danger, Bragg left the city to the Union invaders.[14]

Dana set out for Chattanooga on a route that paralleled the disabled railroad from Bridgeport to the foot of Lookout Mountain. He reached the city on the evening of September 11 and went straight to Rosecrans's headquarters, a two-story brick house that Bragg had just abandoned. Dana presented Stanton's letter of introduction, which declared that he was "a gentleman of distinguished character, patriotism, and ability, and possesses the entire confidence of the department." Dana, Stanton told Rosecrans, was sent to confer "upon any matters which you desire to have brought to the notice of this Department." Rosecrans read the letter and tossed it aside, bursting out "in angry abuse against the Government," as Dana remembered it. His requests for men and supplies had been ignored, and he accused Stanton and Halleck of doing "all they could to prevent his success." Taken aback, Dana cut him short: he was not sent to report Rosecrans's opinion of his superiors, but for "finding out what the Government could do to aid" the general.[15]

It was not an auspicious start to Dana's mission. Instantly he learned that Rosecrans lacked self-control and reflexively blamed his problems on Washington. Rosecrans's staff officers shared his resentments. Unlike at Grant's headquarters, no welcoming reception awaited Dana, who, according to a press observer, was viewed as a "bird of evil omen." Rumors circulated that Dana had come as Stanton's spy to "ruin Rosecrans." For the next six weeks Dana traveled with Rosecrans's entourage and boarded at headquarters, reporting confidentially to Stanton in the evening. Eventually a few staff members, including the chief of staff James Garfield, shared camp gossip and their views with Dana. But Stanton's agent formed no friendships like those with John Rawlins and James Wilson at Grant's headquarters. Suspicion of Dana also spread through the ranks. According to a *New York Herald* reporter, soldiers taunted Dana when he rode by in his civilian clothes, pretending to mistake him for a camp vendor, a class of parasites they despised. "Hey, old sutler, when are you going to open out?" they jeered.[16]

Once Rosecrans calmed down, he explained the army's situation to Dana. Reports from field officers seemed to indicate that Bragg was in full retreat toward Rome, Georgia, sixty miles below Chattanooga. For once, Rosecrans, brimming with confidence after his second flanking of the Rebels, was determined to act quickly. Instead of consolidating his hold on Chattanooga as Dana had forecast, he decided to pursue Bragg and destroy his army. His forces, already divided in three, were ordered to push through three mountain gaps staggered in a series south of Chattanooga.[17]

Dividing his army had worked twice before against Bragg, but the third attempt courted danger. Just before Dana met Rosecrans, a Confederate force of 15,000 men confronted a division of Thomas's corps and forced it back to Stevens's Gap. The encounter posed grave complications because the Federals were scattered over a line more than forty miles long. As Dana reported, for a while it seemed probable that Bragg had "abandoned his retreat on Rome and returned with the purpose of falling upon the different corps and divisions of our army . . . and destroying them in detail." The next morning was quiet, and Rosecrans convinced himself that Bragg had simply been covering his retreat. This was nearly a fatal guess, for Bragg was as capable of tricks as was the wily Rosecrans. He pretended to retreat headlong while concentrating his army southeast of Chattanooga for surprise counterattacks against isolated Union corps. Two divisions of Johnston's troops had arrived from Mississippi to bolster Bragg, bringing his forces to near equality with Rosecrans, and more men were on the way: after conferring with General Lee, Jefferson Davis detached two divisions from Lee's army—12,000 men—and sent them west under General James Longstreet.[18]

Fortunately for the Federals, their opponents were delayed and divided. Confederates from Virginia had to follow a roundabout route by train through the Carolinas to Atlanta that took nearly two weeks. Meanwhile, Bragg had two good chances to destroy pieces of Rosecrans's army, but his generals let him down. At McLemore's Cove on September 11 Bragg's subordinates mistakenly believed their armies were outnumbered and defied his orders to attack. An opportunity to surprise Crittenden's isolated corps was squandered on September 13 by General Leonidas Polk, who assumed a defensive position instead of attacking as Bragg had ordered.[19]

To supervise field operations Rosecrans left Chattanooga on the afternoon of September 13 for Thomas's headquarters, and Dana rode with him. Dana took heart in what the Union army had accomplished. "The difficulties of . . . crossing the Cumberland Mountains, passing the Tennessee, turning and occupying Chattanooga, traversing the mountain ridges of Northern Georgia, and seizing the passes which lead southward have been enormous," he wrote Stanton, "and can only be appreciated by one who has personally examined the region." Rosecrans's army had "gained a position from which it can effectually advance upon Rome and Atlanta, and deliver there the finishing blow of the war." Dana's high praise for the campaign and his requests for Stanton to bolster Rosecrans's mounted forces suggest that at this point, despite their testy introduction, there was little friction between him and Rosecrans. Dana endorsed the general's plans while Rosecrans wrote his wife that "Mr. Dana Asst Secy of War" was with him and "of great service to us."[20]

Things took a turn for the worse, however, when Bragg's stratagem became apparent and Rosecrans pivoted to defense. Skirmishes with rebel patrols suggested that the Confederates were massing east of Chickamauga Creek for counterattacks on the pursuing Federals. These and other "queer developments," Dana reported, indicated that Bragg was "playing possum." Without a firm idea of Bragg's whereabouts, Rosecrans gave urgent orders to abandon the pursuit and to concentrate the federal army near Lee and Gordon's Mills, thirteen miles south of Chattanooga. On September 16 Rosecrans established headquarters in a plantation house at nearby Crawfish Springs. There he awaited his men's arrival in mass. The question was whether his army could be reunited and prepared for battle before Bragg's men destroyed it in separate encounters.[21]

Disaster at Chickamauga

Rosecrans's three corps put in five days of hard marching before they joined up. The worst delay was caused by McCook on the Union right, who was unfamiliar with the roads and took a roundabout route to the rendezvous.

There were tense moments as Rosecrans and Dana awaited word at Crawfish Springs, but Dana was optimistic that the concentration would be "perfect" by September 17. It never became perfect, but it coalesced in the nick of time as the Federals edged sideways to connect and move closer to their supplies at Chattanooga. As it turned out, both armies were sidling northward and massing within a few miles of each other across Chickamauga Creek. Confederate and federal cavalry patrols made contact as Bragg's men crossed the creek to test the Union left above Lee and Gordon's Mills. "Sky cloudy, thermometer 62; perfect day for fighting," Dana reported on September 18. But delays in Bragg's troop movements and resistance put up by federal horsemen postponed heavy fighting to the next day.[22]

According to Dana, Rosecrans had not yet decided whether to launch an attack or wait for Bragg to make his move. Realizing that Bragg's men were massed to his north, Rosecrans opted for defense. He ordered Granger's reserve troops to block the route to Chattanooga and shifted Thomas's men north to prevent Bragg from getting between the federals and the city. By the morning of September 19 Thomas occupied the Union left, Crittenden held the center, and McCook was on the right.[23]

The expected battle began at 9 A.M. when Confederate cavalrymen under Nathan Bedford Forrest attacked Thomas. As the fighting spread southward to other sectors it became increasingly confused and disjointed. The area's heavy woods prevented generals from seeing their commands or the enemy's position, and both armies fought piecemeal. Brigades were thrown into battle under unfamiliar commanders, reducing unit cohesion. When it became clear that the battle was being fought to his left, Rosecrans rode north with his staff, moving headquarters to a three-room log cabin perched on a hill. It belonged to Eliza Glenn, whose husband had recently perished serving the Confederate army. The soldiers packed up the terrified widow's children and belongings on an oxcart and sent them to the rear. A field telegraph was hastily set up and connected to the main line from Chattanooga. Beginning at 1 P.M. Dana sent Stanton ten brief reports of the day's engagements. The earlier messages predicted Union success. "Decisive victory seems assured to us," Dana wired at 2:30 P.M. Two hours later he told Stanton: "I dare not say our victory is complete, but it seems certain." Once he realized the Confederates were holding their ground, Dana backtracked: it "appears to be an undecided contest, but later reports will enable us to understand more clearly."[24]

The truth was that Dana's contact with distant Washington was better than his and Rosecrans's knowledge of the Union soldiers' fate in the nearby fields. Despite the cabin's high ground, they saw almost none of the fighting, which raged in haphazard sequence at distant points that were heavily forested or hidden by smoke and thus "invisible to outsiders," as Dana reported. Rosecrans paced outside the cabin in high excitement, guessing locations of the firing by the sounds of shots and shells, receiving reports from couriers, and appealing to subordinates for news. At times Rosecrans issued orders to reposition troops, but for the most part his corps commanders were left to themselves.[25]

By day's end both armies had made small breakthroughs but were forced to pull back. Bragg's Confederates had pushed the Federals a few hundred yards west across portions of the Lafayette Road, but Rosecrans still controlled the path north to Chattanooga. At 7:30 P.M. Dana reported that the Union had the advantage in inflicting casualties and holding its ground: "The result of the battle is that the enemy is defeated in attempt to turn and crush our left flank and regain possession of Chattanooga. His attempt was furious and obstinate, his repulse was bloody, and maintained till the end. If he does not retreat Rosecrans will renew the fight at daylight."[26]

This was the optimistic party line at Rosecrans's headquarters that evening, seconded by staff member John P. Sanderson in his journal. Not everyone shared it. General John Palmer told a *New York Tribune* reporter at the telegraph table that his troops were "in good spirits, and ready for another fight," but he complained that they had been scattered and confused during the day's battle. "I have no hesitation in saying to you," he began with the reporter — and then noticing Dana down the table, raised his voice — "and I have no hesitation in saying to *you*, Mr. Dana, that this battle has been lost because we had no supreme head to the army on the field to direct it."[27]

Around nine o'clock that night Rosecrans convened his corps commanders at Widow Glenn's for a council of war. Each reported on the condition of their men and advised what to do next. All had gotten little or no sleep as the army shifted north. Dana remembered watching the burly General Thomas doze off repeatedly, awakening only to advise strengthening the left. Others counseled strengthening the right. Each time, Rosecrans asked in dismay where reinforcements would be taken from. Word came that Longstreet's Confederate reinforcements had arrived, and Rosecrans was convinced his forces were greatly outnumbered, much more than the actual Confederate infantry advantage (68,000 to 60,000). When discussion closed, Rosecrans gave his orders for the next day. Thomas was to draw in his lines and McCook to cover the Widow Glenn site; Crittenden was positioned between to give aid to either when necessary. Despite the optimism Dana transmitted to Stanton, apprehension seemed the dominant mood. Rosecrans's state of mind was evident from his instructions to Thomas, which urged him to "defend your position with the utmost stubbornness" but added that "in case our army should be overwhelmed it will retire on Rossville and Chattanooga."[28]

When this business was concluded, hot coffee, bacon, and crackers were brought out—the first nourishment most had received all day. McCook, who had a fine voice, entertained the assembly with "The Hebrew Maiden's Lament," a gloomy popular ballad. When the party broke up around midnight, Rosecrans, too overwrought to sleep, went outdoors and paced in his overcoat until dawn. Dana lay down to fitful slumber among a row of officers packed like sardines on the cabin's bare floor. The night was chilly and the wind whistled through gaps between the floorboards. When anyone turned over, the whole row of spooners was forced to rotate.[29]

At daybreak on September 20 a dense mixture of fog and smoke settled over the valley of Chickamauga Creek. As the sun rose the sky took on an angry reddish hue. Rosecrans rode off without breakfast to inspect and position the Union lines, with Dana in tow. After shifting General Philip Sheridan's and General Jefferson C. Davis's divisions northward to flank the Widow Glenn's cabin, he rode toward Thomas's command, where he gave orders to tighten the line. Returning to the center, Rosecrans was puffy-eyed and testy. He reprimanded General James Negley for moving his men prematurely, scolded General Thomas Wood for joining the line of battle too slowly, then exploded at McCook for leaving the Union right, in Dana's words, "elongated so that it was a mere thread." Agitated, Rosecrans was firing off too many orders too swiftly, some without the knowledge of corps commanders, others confusingly worded.[30]

On the Confederate side, Bragg's troops under General Polk began their advance on the Union left after 9 A.M. With the help of reinforcements and hastily constructed breastworks Thomas repulsed these assaults. Farther south, Rosecrans and Dana returned from their inspection at mid-morning and established temporary headquarters about a half-mile north of the Widow Glenn's cabin. The spot, on a knoll near the Dyer cabin, provided an open view of the terrain below. The morning had become warm, and for a brief interval the fields in their sight were quiet, with only the distant rumble of Thomas's fight disturbing the silence. Dana, who had slept little for three days, grew drowsy. He dismounted, handed his reins to his orderly, lay down on the grass, and dozed off.

Shortly after 11 A.M. Dana was startled awake by the roar of cannon and musketry booming at close range. Bolting upright, the first thing he noticed was Rosecrans making the sign of the cross. Turning toward the din, Dana

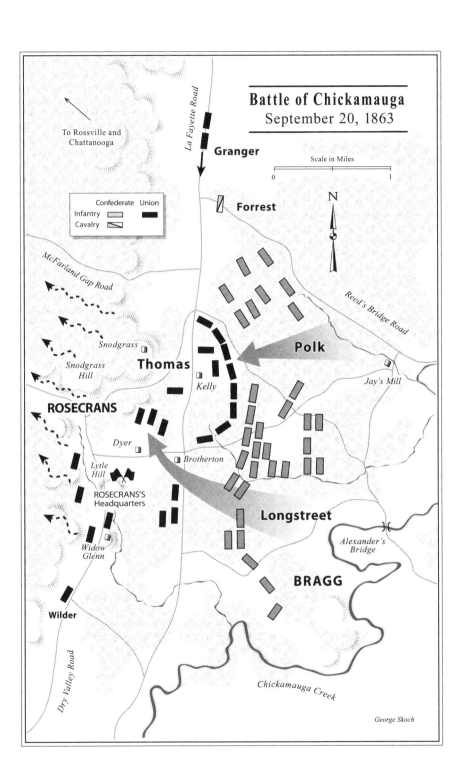

Battle of Chickamauga
September 20, 1863

To Rossville and
Chattanooga

La Fayette Road

Granger

Scale in Miles

0   1

Confederate Union
Infantry
Cavalry

N

McFarland Gap Road

Reed's Bridge Road

Polk

Snodgrass

Snodgrass
Hill

Thomas

Kelly

Jay's Mill

ROSECRANS

Dyer

Brotherton

Lytle
Hill

ROSECRANS'S
Headquarters

Longstreet

Alexander's
Bridge

Widow
Glenn

BRAGG

Wilder

Dry Valley Road

Chickamauga Creek

George Skoch

saw why: Confederate infantrymen were charging in his direction out of the woods into the open field three hundred yards downhill from headquarters. In the next twenty minutes Dana watched the thin Union lines confront "immense columns" of enemy soldiers, then break and scatter "like leaves before the wind." "Our soldiers turned and fled," he told Stanton. "It was wholesale panic." The Graybacks kept up their pursuit, and soon musket balls were whizzing past Rosecrans, Dana, and staff members. One bullet shattered an aide's hand as he stood beside Rosecrans. An order to mount was shouted. Dana jumped on his horse and, with his orderly, sought cover in the woods behind headquarters.[31]

Dana guessed that a hole had opened in the Union center. Rosecrans, frayed by fatigue and anxiety, had issued a fatal directive. Acting on a faulty report that troop movements had created a gap north of the Union center, Rosecrans sent a badly worded order directing General Wood to shift his men leftward to back up General Joseph Reynolds. This made no sense to Wood. For two days, however, he and McCook had been berated by Rosecrans for failing to follow orders perfectly. Without seeking clarification, they pulled men out of line to back up Reynolds while McCook summoned another division to replace them. The adjustment created a virtually undefended 600-yard opening in the Union center at the worst possible moment, just as General Longstreet was stacking 11,000 of his men four lines deep for an all-out assault.[32]

The massive Confederate charge swept across Brotherton Field at 11:15 A.M. It easily overpowered the thinned Union lines, whose men retreated in disarray to the west. There in the woods Dana encountered Horace Porter and James P. Droulliard, two of Rosecrans's staff officers who tried to rally the fleeing Union soldiers. "They would halt a few of them, get them into some sort of a line, . . . and then there would come a few rounds of cannon shot through the tree-tops over their heads and the men would break and run," Dana recalled. After twenty minutes the Confederates threatened to annihilate the improvised Union line, and Porter and Droulliard joined the wave of Federals breaking westward toward the base of Missionary Ridge.[33]

For a time Rosecrans remained with his staff officers on the wooded ridge behind headquarters. Shouting encouragement and waving his sword, Rosecrans "made all possible efforts to rally the broken columns," Dana wrote. Fearing the Union right was routed, he sent a messenger to Sheridan to confer on their next move. Sheridan's men, meanwhile, had hurried to meet the Confederate advance on a hill north of the Widow Glenn's cabin. Outflanked and outnumbered, they fought bravely but fell back after their commander, General William Lytle, was fatally wounded. Rosecrans failed to connect with Sheridan and was swept along in the panic. Accompanied by a cavalry escort, his chief of staff General Garfield, and a few other staff members, he headed up Dry Valley Road, intending to make contact with Thomas on the Union left. The small party wove their way through masses of fleeing Union wagons and foot soldiers that clogged the road as it headed north toward Rossville, where a gap opened the way toward Thomas. Amid his routed troops, Rosecrans rode in a stunned and distracted silence, praying to God for deliverance.[34]

Dana was not with Rosecrans on that desperate, mournful ride. Instead of fleeing with the Federals, he turned south under cover of the woods. Perhaps he was disoriented; more likely, he was seeking Sheridan's men, who had anchored the Union right. When Dana reached the Widow Glenn's cabin they were no longer there. By feeling his way southward behind the action Dana was inadvertently moving in the opposite direction from the momentum of battle. Approaching the end of the Union right, he was seriously at risk for capture.[35]

All was not yet lost for the Union, however. On the extreme right came the last of the Union reserves, the 39th Indiana Mounted Infantry, led by Colonel John T. Wilder. Dismounted and equipped with seven-shot Spencer repeating rifles, Wilder's brigade tore into the flank of General Arthur Manigault's oncoming Confederates and sent them retreating eastward. As Wilder considered his next move, he thought of charging his brigade north past the Widow Glenn's cabin, which was aflame from artillery fire, to hurl them against the rear of Longstreet's troops, who were threatening the Union divisions still on the field. His men would be dangerously outnumbered, but Wilder believed that with his superior firepower he could cut through the Rebels and reach Thomas's beleaguered defenders.[36]

At this moment Dana emerged from the woods. As Wilder later described it, a hatless, bearded, red-haired man in civilian clothes galloped up to him, hysterical and breathless. Dana demanded to know what unit Wilder commanded, then introduced himself as the assistant secretary of war. Dana told Wilder that the day was lost: in Wilder's paraphrase, "our troops had fled in utter panic; that it was a worse rout than Bull Run; that General Rosecrans was probably killed or captured." Wilder then explained his plan to fight his way to General Thomas.[37]

What happened next became the subject of controversy. Wilder wrote in his official report that Dana "strongly advised me to fall back and occupy the passes over Lookout Mountain to prevent the rebel occupancy of it." Decades later, Wilder claimed that Dana had been much more high-handed: he forbade

Wilder to make his projected counterattack and ordered him to withdraw. He also demanded that Wilder provide him a safe escort to Chattanooga.[38]

High civilian officials were not supposed to give orders on the battlefield, and none had done so since Secretary of State James Monroe reorganized a front line at the Battle of Bladensburg in the War of 1812. Whether it was couched as an order or strong advice, Dana's directive made an impression on Wilder, who called off the attack and arranged for scouts to guide Dana to safety. Wilder's troops turned to gathering wagons and artillery left behind by the Federals and convoyed them and dozens of ambulances carrying wounded Union soldiers up the Dry Valley Road to safety behind the federal lines.[39]

For the rest of his life Wilder insisted that Dana had prevented him from achieving a signal breakthrough at Chickamauga. Each time Wilder retold the story his plans became more developed and Dana's obstruction more dictatorial: "If I had been allowed to attack as I wished," he wrote forty-five years later, "it would have been fatal to Bragg's army." Colonel Smith Atkins, Wilder's subordinate, gave a particularly blunt assessment: "Wilder was daring and desperate; Dana, a coward and an imbecile."[40]

To be sure, Dana had behaved less than heroically. An unarmed civilian frightened by the panicked retreat, he likely overreacted. Decades later, Dana revised the story to cover his embarrassment. According to this version he told Wilder: "I have no authority to give orders, but if I were in your situation I should go to the left, where Thomas is." This was wishful fabrication, not faulty recollection, for at the time Dana believed Thomas's men were fleeing to Rossville with Confederates in pursuit.[41]

Still, Dana was not the first to tell Wilder to quit the battle. Lieutenant Colonel Gates Thruston, McCook's chief of staff, told Wilder that the Union line to his left had evaporated and, like Dana, advised him to withdraw to Lookout Mountain. General Sheridan, convinced that further resistance was futile, sent a directive to Wilder to "get out of there" and "fall back to the Chattanooga Valley." Wilder's brigade was "in the air," according to military slang—dangling on the right and cut off from retreating federal columns. Spencer rifles or not, they were in danger of being overtaken by the Confederates, who had a fresh brigade in reserve nearby. Wilder's claim that he could have turned the battle around was exaggerated bravado.[42]

Instead of the vainglorious Wilder, stolid General Thomas became the Union hero by holding his ground and minimizing the Union defeat. Consolidating mixed forces on Snodgrass Hill, Thomas rallied them to withstand multiple attacks from Bragg's entire army while other Union soldiers escaped to Chattanooga. Dana, who was told the details by Garfield the day after the battle, summarized them for Stanton:

> Thomas, finding himself cut off from Rosecrans and the right, at once brought
> his seven divisions into position for independent fighting. Refusing both his
> right and left, his line assumed the form of a horse-shoe posted along the
> slope and crest of a partly wooded ridge. He was soon joined by Granger from
> Rossville . . . and with these forces firmly maintained the fight till after dark. Our
> troops were immovable as the rocks they stood on. The enemy hurled against
> them repeatedly the dense columns which had routed Davis and Sheridan in the
> morning, but every onset was repulsed with dreadful slaughter.[43]

The heroic stand by the "Rock of Chickamauga" saved Rosecrans's army. "There is nowhere in history a more astonishing instance of victory snatched from the very jaws of disaster," Dana wrote later. At the moment, however, no one knew for certain whether Thomas's men had held or were retreating. When Rosecrans reached the crossroads village of Rossville he decided that Garfield should find Thomas and report his situation while the commander returned to Chattanooga to organize its defenses. Exhausted, emotionally spent, and fretting about losing the city, Rosecrans did not understand the implication of abandoning his men during battle. No other Civil War battle involved the flight of the commanding general from the field, and Rosecrans would live to regret his decision.[44]

Rosecrans reached Union headquarters in Chattanooga after 3:30 P.M. on the day of the battle. Worn out and broken in spirit, he wrote a series of orders designed to protect the army's supplies and the city's defenses. After hearing from Garfield that Thomas had fended off all Confederate attacks on Snodgrass Hill, he sent a dispatch telling Thomas to gather his forces and conduct an orderly retreat. Without a clear view of the battlefield or any thoughts of resuming the offensive, he accepted defeat.[45]

Meanwhile, Dana made his way over Missionary Ridge and galloped up the Chattanooga Valley road to the city. He found the escape route clogged with "a disordered throng of fugitives" that included "baggage-wagons, artillery, ambulances, negroes on horseback, field and company officers, wounded men limping along, Union refugees from the country around leading their wives and children, mules running along loose, squads of cavalry—in short, every element that could confuse the rout of a great army." To Dana's disgust, this included "a major-general commanding an army corps"—a reference to the hapless McCook, who had failed to find the route to Thomas and decided to join Rosecrans in the city.[46]

Arriving at Chattanooga half an hour after Rosecrans, Dana wired the first news of the day's debacle to Washington. "My report today is of deplorable importance," he began. "Chickamauga is as fatal a name in our history as Bull Run." Relying on what he had seen of the battle and rumors that coursed among retreating soldiers, Dana wrote that the entire Union army had left the field, some brigades in confusion, others in orderly retreat. Rosecrans and several subordinates had returned to Chattanooga and "our wounded are all left behind." Dana estimated total Union casualties and prisoners at over 20,000—they would prove to be around 16,000—and ended on a foreboding note: "Enemy not yet arrived before Chattanooga. Preparations making to resist his entrance for a time."[47]

Unfortunately for Dana and for Northern morale, this alarming report quickly reached Northern newspapers. The army telegraph operator at Nashville cracked Dana's code and spread the news. An Associated Press agent in Louisville picked up the report, including Dana's comparison of Chickamauga to Bull Run, and the story ran in several cities. Dana later claimed it was the only instance when one of his dispatches was leaked before reaching Washington. The timing was terrible, and Dana was furious. He opened an investigation that pinpointed the Nashville office and urged Stanton to "deal with your faithless subordinates who betrayed me." He suggested that Stanton provide him with a new cipher, but no changes were made beyond substituting new code words.[48]

Back in Washington, a stunned Stanton sent Dana's dispatch to President Lincoln at the Soldiers' Home. Lincoln rode back to the War Department to begin a sleepless vigil. Three hours after Dana's wire the two men received one from Rosecrans no less gloomy: "We have met with a serious disaster; extent not yet ascertained. Enemy overwhelmed us, drove our right, pierced our center, and scattered troops everywhere."[49]

As reports arrived from the front Dana tempered his initial alarm. In the evening he wrote Stanton that "having been myself swept bodily off the battle-field by the panic-struck rabble," he had given "too dark a view of our disaster." Davis and Sheridan were routed, but Thomas still held the Union left and was being reinforced by Granger and remnants of other commands. Mounted units were intact and assisting in evacuating the wounded. Dana also put in a good word for Rosecrans: "I can testify to the conspicuous and steady gallantry of Rosecrans on the field." He had tried to rally the broken Union columns, and Dana could find "no fault in the disposition of his forces."[50]

Dana's dispatch did nothing to brighten Stanton's dim view of Rosecrans, and even Lincoln struggled to keep his composure. Just after midnight the president telegraphed Rosecrans to "be of good cheer. We have unabated confidence in you and your soldiers and officers." Lincoln counseled him to "save your army by taking strong positions until Burnside joins you, when I hope you can turn the tide." Minutes later, the president wired Burnside to "go to Rosecrans with your force without a moment's delay." When Burnside replied that he had sent his men to capture a nearby guerrilla outpost, the telegraph office staff overheard Lincoln swear. At dawn on September 21 the president trudged into the little bedroom of his secretary John Hay. "Well, Rosecrans has been whipped, as I feared," he sighed.[51]

Rosecrans believed himself whipped long before Lincoln heard about it. Despite pleading from Garfield and Granger to organize a counteroffensive, his thoughts turned to saving Chattanooga rather than defeating Bragg's battered army. After conversing with Rosecrans, Dana reported that the army would "fall back to the strongest line of defense, for the purpose of defeating [the] enemy's design of regaining Chattanooga and the Tennessee." That line did not include the Rossville gap. Rosecrans heard from Garfield that Rossville was vulnerable to being flanked and not a strong position to defend against the Confederates. His nerves rattled, Rosecrans mistook the movements of Nathan Bedford Forrest's cavalry for an all-out Confederate advance on Chattanooga. He ordered Thomas to retire to Chattanooga under cover of darkness and all federal troops to concentrate at the town's defenses.[52]

Around noon on September 21 Garfield returned to headquarters and regaled Dana with details of Thomas's splendid fight. Dana relayed the story to Stanton, commending the entire "body of heroes." Thomas "seemed to have filled every soldier with his own unconquerable firmness," and Granger "raged like a lion wherever the combat was hottest with the electrical courage of a Ney." The comparison to Napoleon's field marshal at Moscow was fanciful, since Granger stayed back from the front lines at Snodgrass Hill. The reference so befuddled the War Department's telegraph operators that Dana had to recode and resend it.[53]

"Our Dazed and Mazy Commander"

At Chattanooga Rosecrans settled into an abandoned house a safe distance from rebel shellfire, and Dana found a room for himself. Both men spent the next few days making preparations to defend against a Confederate attack, pleading with Washington for reinforcements, and sorting out what had happened. By midnight on September 21 the entire army had returned to Chattanooga. Rosecrans hastily arranged outer and inner lines for the city's defense. Yet his resolve had been shaken and he vacillated between deciding to hold the city and ordering a retreat across the Tennessee. Dana's telegrams charted Rosecrans's polar mood swings. "If you have any advice to give, it should come tonight," Dana implored Stanton on September 22, hoping for an order to hold the city. No such order came, but Dana soon reported that Rosecrans had "determined to fight it out here at all hazards." Lincoln and Stanton were left wondering whether Rosecrans's "stampede" was over.[54]

There was actually little danger of a rebel attack. After the battle Bragg was more intent on purging dissident subordinates than pursuing the retreating Federals. His attempt to relieve General Polk sparked a firestorm of infighting that was quelled only after Jefferson Davis visited the Army of Tennessee to defend Bragg and negotiate several minor transfers. Meanwhile, confident that his superior numbers and strong position around Chattanooga could compel Rosecrans's surrender, Bragg decided to starve out the Union forces rather than attack them.[55]

In the lull that followed, a more resolute mood took hold at Union headquarters. By September 23 Dana concluded that Chickamauga had been a tactical but not a strategic victory for the Rebels, who had "suffered quite as severely as we have." In fact, Confederate losses of men killed, wounded, and missing numbered more than 18,000, compared to Union losses of approximately 16,200. Despite the ignoble Union retreat, the campaign's main objective—possession of Chattanooga and the Tennessee River—had been accomplished.[56] To make it stick, the Union troops dug in. "The labors of this army for [the] last forty-eight hours have been herculean," Dana wired on September 24, sending telegraph operators once more to their dictionary. He had ridden the lines with Thomas, whose men were digging with gusto. "When the inner fortifications are completed, 10,000 men could hold this place against the world." "Have no further doubt about this place," Dana assured his superiors.[57]

To cement the Union's hold on Chattanooga and to counter Bragg's reinforcements from Lee, Dana sounded an urgent call for additional soldiers. "No time should be lost in pushing 20,000 to 25,000 efficient troops" to Bridgeport to supplement Rosecrans's 35,000 effectives at Chattanooga, Dana told Stanton. If they arrive soon, "this place—indispensable alike to the defense of Tennessee and as the base of future operations in Georgia—

will remain ours." More resolute than Rosecrans, Dana estimated that Union forces could hold out for fifteen to twenty days with their present resources.[58]

Stanton, to his credit, put aside his disgust with Rosecrans and responded with energy. "Every nerve is being strained to strengthen General Rosecrans and his gallant army," he assured Dana. If Rosecrans could hold out for half that time, reinforcements would reach him. Yet Stanton seemed to promise more than he could deliver. Burnside, Dana complained, had "done nothing" to send help, and Sherman would take weeks to reach Chattanooga, in part because Grant had belatedly received Halleck's telegram requesting the move.[59]

On the night of September 23 Stanton sent messengers to Lincoln, Halleck, and various cabinet members, rousing them to attend a council of war. He proposed to send 20,000 men from the Army of the Potomac to reinforce Rosecrans and insisted it could be done in five days. After a protracted debate, Stanton, backed by Seward and Chase, prevailed over Lincoln's and Halleck's reservations. At 2:30 A.M. orders were issued for two army corps in Virginia under General Joseph Hooker, along with 3,000 horses and mules, to be rushed to Tennessee. An hour later Stanton wired Dana with the news, declaring that 15,000 of Hooker's men would reach Nashville in less than a week.[60]

Backed by the cooperation of War Department agents and Northern railroad officials, Stanton nearly made his deadline. On September 25 Hooker's soldiers began filing into boxcars at Manassas Junction. Transferred to the B&O Railroad, they chugged westward and switched lines to traverse Ohio and Indiana. Ferried across the Ohio River, they boarded trains from Louisville to Nashville. Dana, eager to report their arrival, went with one of Rosecrans's staff officers to Nashville. He arrived on September 29, hours before the advance cars reached the capital. The next day, only five days after Hooker's men started their nearly 1,200-mile journey, Dana joined some of the first arrivals on an overloaded train to Bridgeport, Alabama, on the Tennessee River southwest of Chattanooga. The last leg was the slowest: caught in a huge downpour, the train took more than twenty-four hours to cover 120 miles. By October 3, eight days after the first soldiers departed, the entire XI Corps had debarked at Bridgeport and the XII Corps passed through Nashville. Hooker set up headquarters at Stevenson, near Bridgeport. Stanton and his collaborators had used the North's efficient rail and telegraph network to orchestrate the longest and fastest transport of a large body of troops in military history before the twentieth century.[61]

As the danger of Confederate attack receded, Dana pieced together what had happened at Chickamauga and transmitted to Stanton a list of the disaster's causes. First was the "great numerical superiority of the enemy." With the addition of Longstreet's corps, the Confederates outnumbered the Union men by more than 10,000. (Dana wisely withheld from Stanton Rosecrans's staff members' "denunciations fierce and strong . . . against the Secretary of War for not reinforcing this army.") Second, the Union lines had been stretched too far, a mistake that Dana believed was the shared responsibility of Rosecrans and McCook, who had moved his men too slowly into position. Finally, there was Rosecrans's mistaken order that created the gap in the Union center.[62]

Dana believed these problems might not have been fatal if "that dangerous blunderhead McCook" had shown more fighting spirit. While Sheridan and Davis stayed to rally their men—a partial truth—McCook and Crittenden "made their way here and slept here all night, and did not look after their troops till Monday." Stanton had already decided whom to blame. "They need not shuffle it off on McCook," he fumed when Dana's message was deciphered. "I know the reasons well enough. Rosecrans ran away from the fighting men and did not stop for 13 miles." McCook and Crittenden "made pretty good time away from the fight to Chattanooga, but Rosecrans beat them both."[63]

Stanton's pulse, as usual, was quicker than others. Rosecrans still had supporters in the army, the cabinet, and the White House. When he rode the Union lines defending Chattanooga back on September 22 the troops had given him a round of cheers. Talk of replacing him was premature. Meanwhile, Union leaders demanded that some heads roll, and McCook's and Crittenden's would do.[64]

Neither was a stellar commander. Alexander McCook, one of seven Ohio brothers who joined the Union army, was a coarse blusterer who affected a rough-and-ready persona but failed in battle at Perryville and Stone's River before his disgrace at Chickamauga. Thomas L. Crittenden, from a powerful Kentucky family, was the only corps commander in Rosecrans's army who had not attended West Point. Dana believed him brave and gentlemanly but too quick to defer to experienced men. The implication, echoed by some historians, was that Crittenden should have intervened to block Rosecrans's fatal order.[65] After the battle, Dana reported, four division commanders, including Sheridan and Palmer, revealed that they could no longer serve under such incompetent superiors and threatened to resign. Other officers, from Garfield and Wood to Colonel Emerson Opdyke of Ohio, approached Dana unbidden to confirm the soldiers' "unanimous sentiment" against the generals.[66]

Stanton took the case immediately to Lincoln, who signed an order relieving McCook and Crittenden and directing them to Indianapolis for a court of inquiry. Their corps were consolidated and Granger was given command. To avoid the impression of censuring the troops, Dana suggested that officials justify the consolidation by citing the necessity of merging depleted units. The court of inquiry eventually held both generals blameless for the Confederate breakthrough at Chickamauga and declined to censure them for leaving the battlefield. McCook's flight was simply "an error of judgment," the court concluded, while Crittenden had done "everything he could" to rally his troops before following Rosecrans to Chattanooga. Despite the acquittals, both men's reputations suffered. McCook was not given another frontline command in the war, and Crittenden, later moved to Grant's army in Virginia, fought under a shadow.[67]

For Dana, it was a short step from condemning corps commanders for leaving the field to blaming Rosecrans for the same thing. Dana's dispatches at the end of September sounded his first serious criticisms of the commander. Rosecrans was unwilling to remove McCook and Crittenden due to "the defects of his character," he wrote. "He is a temporizing man" too loyal to subordinates. Another factor may have been his own sense of guilt: Rosecrans's excuse of returning to oversee Chattanooga's defense "cannot entirely clear him either in his own eyes or in those of the army," Dana surmised. Repeating complaints he heard from officers such as Garfield, Dana confided that Rosecrans's "faulty management on the field" and premature retreat dealt his subordinates' respect for him "an irreparable blow."[68]

For the first time Dana broached the subject of replacing Rosecrans: "If it be decided to change the chief commander," Stanton should name "some Western general of high rank and great prestige, like Grant." Three days later he threw General George Thomas's hat in the ring: "There is no other man whose appointment would be so welcome to this army." Thomas was governed by a stern sense of duty that led him to side with the Union instead of his native Virginia, and it colored every move of his large, sturdy frame. Six feet tall, well over two hundred pounds, full-bearded, and deliberate in speech, Thomas projected steadiness, solidity, and integrity, if not brilliance. Dana considered him "a man of the greatest dignity of character" and like many others compared him to George Washington.[69]

Stanton shared Dana's dispatch with Lincoln, who read it to William Seward and Gideon Welles. Seward wanted Rosecrans relieved; Welles took note that Lincoln had "clearly lost confidence" in Rosecrans and agreed that Thomas should replace him. But Lincoln demurred. Rosecrans's flanking maneuvers against Bragg in Tennessee were "the most splendid piece of strategy he knew of," he told his advisers. Rosecrans deserved another chance.[70]

Like Dana, Stanton preferred Thomas: "The merit of General Thomas and the debt of gratitude the nation owes to his valor and skill are fully appreciated here, and I wish you to tell him so," he wired Dana. "It was not my fault that he was not in chief command months ago." On October 4 Dana visited Thomas's headquarters to convey the message. Thomas was taken aback. He told Dana he was grateful for the expression of confidence and admitted that he coveted an independent command; but if he took over Rosecrans's army it would appear he had intrigued against him. A few days later Thomas told Dana through an intermediary that he would consent to any command outside the department but refuse to become Rosecrans's replacement.[71]

Over the next week Dana muted his criticism of Rosecrans. Thomas's refusal left few viable alternatives. Dana was also preoccupied with coordinating Rosecrans's corps changes and reporting work on Chattanooga's fortifications and supply lines. Quartermaster General Montgomery Meigs, diverted from a western inspection tour, helped to inventory supplies and supervise the transport of animals. Several appointments improved the quality of Rosecrans's staff. Dana noted particularly the arrival of General William F. "Baldy" Smith as Rosecrans's new chief engineer, whom he expected to energize bridge and road repair. The optimistic tone of Dana's daily dispatches from October 3 to 11 contradict accusations by many historians that his attacks on Rosecrans escalated in response to Stanton's encouragement.[72]

Still, the momentum at Washington was swinging against Rosecrans. The clincher was his failure to solve the Federals' precarious supply situation in the face of Bragg's siege. Shortly after Chickamauga Rosecrans ordered his troops to abandon Lookout Mountain and to destroy the wagon road that wound along its side to the Tennessee River. Garfield and Granger had protested, claiming the position could be held by relatively few troops, but Rosecrans prevailed. The withdrawal enabled Bragg's army to control the river and roads between Bridgeport and Chattanooga, disrupting the Union supply line.[73]

Dana considered the abandonment of Lookout Mountain as disastrous as Rosecrans's mistaken battle order at Chickamauga. It left only one route from Chattanooga to obtain supplies, a sixty-mile wagon road that took a tortuous route north to climb the rugged high plateau of Walden's Ridge, then turned south to follow the Sequatchie River from Jasper to Bridgeport. Difficult to traverse in dry weather, the road became a muddy quagmire when violent rainstorms arrived in early October. Passage slowed to a crawl and sometimes stopped entirely as mules sank in the mud up to their bellies and wagons dumped cargo to free their wheels. Travelling this route on October 9, Dana suffered a spill. The muddy shoulder gave way under his horse's hind feet and Dana tumbled with his mount down a fourteen-foot bank, rolling over together in the sandy bottom. He was lucky to emerge with nothing worse than a bruised shoulder and a cut on his head from the horse's hoof. Under such conditions it took two weeks for wagon teams to reach Chattanooga from Bridgeport, and hundreds of wagons were stalled or abandoned.[74]

To relieve the growing supply crisis Rosecrans hoped to retake Lookout Mountain using Hooker's reinforcements. But when Hooker's men arrived, he could not deploy them near Chattanooga for lack of food. Casting for solutions, Rosecrans and his staff concocted elaborate plans, including building a steamboat to ply the river and preparing a new road on the north bank. These projects were set in motion, with General Meigs on hand to give advice, but they progressed at a snail's pace.[75]

Amid this activity Rosecrans appeared unfocused and irresolute. By October 12 Dana could hold his tongue no longer. He lambasted Rosecrans in a long private wire to Stanton. "It is my duty to declare," he wrote,

> that while few persons exhibit more estimable social qualities, I have never seen a public man possessing talent with less administrative power, less clearness and steadiness in difficulty, and greater practical incapacity than General Rosecrans. He has inventive fertility and knowledge, but he has no strength of will and no concentration of purpose. His mind scatters; there is no system in the use of his busy days and restless nights. . . . Under the present circumstances I consider this army to be very unsafe in his hands.

Again he suggested that Thomas replace Rosecrans.[76]

Lincoln continued to resist. "When Dana's long dispatches, ruthlessly criticizing or commending our generals, were being deciphered," a War Department telegraph operator recalled, "Lincoln waited eagerly for the completed translations which he would usually read aloud with running comments, harsh criticisms being softened in the reading." Lincoln valued Dana's reports, but he held out hope that Rosecrans would rally and was wary of doing him an injustice.[77]

The president had to weigh other considerations, including army cohesion, home-front morale, and political fallout. The last was especially critical in early October as a contentious election campaign in Ohio, Rosecrans's home state, headed toward its climax. Clement L. Vallandigham, the "King of the Copperheads," had been arrested by Burnside for a speech obstructing the war effort, then banished by Lincoln to the Confederacy. Escaped into

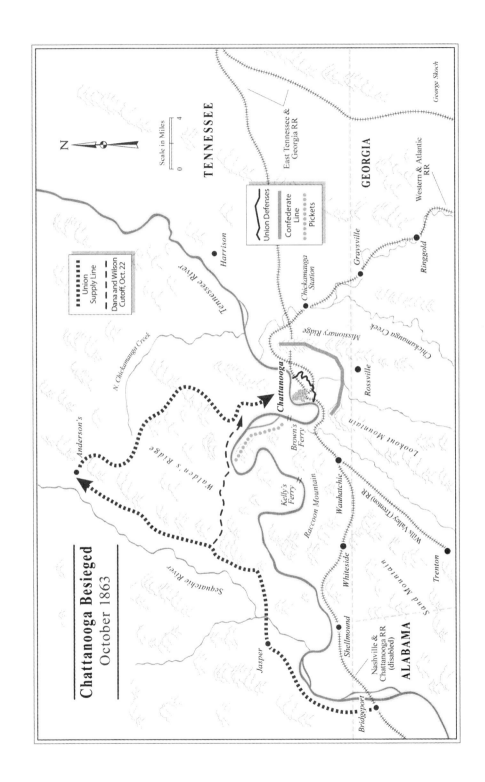

Chattanooga Besieged
October 1863

Canada, Vallandigham was nominated by Ohio Democrats to run for governor against the Republican candidate, John Brough. A Vallandigham victory would badly compromise Ohio's loyalty and encourage obstructionists across the North. Lincoln told Gideon Welles that he was watching the Ohio race with "more anxiety . . . than he had in 1860" when he was elected president.[78]

Removing Rosecrans before the election might alienate Ohio voters or even tempt the Democratic general to ally with the administration's enemies. Such an about-face seemed improbable, but several insiders told Dana it could happen. The *New York Tribune* reporter Henry Villard learned from Rosecrans that his official report on Chickamauga would "show up" Washington authorities, who, he claimed, had forced him to take the offensive without adequate troops or supplies. Dana passed this gossip to Stanton, raising suspicions that Rosecrans, like McClellan, would make his disagreements with the administration public and political. Rosecrans fed those suspicions by suggesting to Lincoln that he offer a general amnesty to Confederate soldiers as a way to end the war. If this proposal were made public, Lincoln replied, it would look like "a confession of weakness and fear" by the Union. Stanton, as usual, took greater offense: he scowled at Rosecrans's suggestion and saw it as the first step toward "recommending an armistice with a view of agreeing on terms of peace"—exactly the Peace Democrats' position.[79]

The voting began on October 9, with soldier votes coming in later. By October 14 it was clear that the Republicans had won comfortably. The Ohio soldiers in Rosecrans's army had done their part to defeat the Copperheads: Dana reported that 90 percent had voted for Brough over Vallandigham (the final figure was 95 percent). "Ohio has saved the Union," Lincoln telegraphed Governor David Tod. It had also cleared a major obstacle to Rosecrans's removal.[80]

From October 14 to 18 Dana sent a series of increasingly alarming telegrams to Washington that catalogued the deteriorating conditions in Chattanooga. Work on the city's fortifications had all but stopped due to constant rain. The road from Bridgeport, which Quartermaster General Meigs called "almost impassable," was strewn with dead animals, and surviving teams had to be doubled to plod through the mud. Along the city's defenses the battery horses were too weak to move cannons, and in a few days most would be dead. Meanwhile, soldiers' rations had been cut from three-quarters to half. Due to the food shortage, Dana warned, "it will soon become necessary for all persons except soldiers to leave" the city. On October 15 Stanton was shocked to have his emissary ask matter-of-factly: "Shall I then return to Washington or endeavor to make my way to Burnside?"[81]

Rosecrans talked about leaving Chattanooga if Bragg's men succeeded in building pontoons and crossing the river north of the city. "Nothing can prevent the retreat of this army from this place within a fortnight," Dana told Stanton on October 16, "except the opening of the river." An attack on Lookout Mountain could not be mounted until Hooker's forces were consolidated and horses and wagons arrived from Nashville. By Dana's estimate, this would take several weeks. Meanwhile, Rosecrans waited and asked Halleck for more cavalry, bemoaning that "our future is not bright."[82]

The crisis seemed to paralyze Rosecrans, and Dana's criticism was biting: "In the midst of all these difficulties General Rosecrans seems to be insensible to the impending danger, and dawdles with trifles in a manner which can scarcely be imagined." Rosecrans had wasted part of ten days compiling his official report of Chickamauga, then became occupied with mapping the country between Chattanooga and Knoxville. "Meanwhile," Dana complained, "with plenty of zealous and energetic officers ready to do whatever can be done, all this precious time is lost because our dazed and mazy commander cannot perceive the catastrophe that is close upon us, nor fix his mind upon the means of preventing it."[83]

Dana's telegram of October 16 forced the issue in Washington. Brandishing it, Stanton pressured Lincoln to make a move. Poor coordination had been hamstringing the Union's western armies—Burnside's failure to reinforce Rosecrans was only the latest example—and Lincoln and Stanton had been considering Dana's suggestion that Grant be assigned to command at Chattanooga. The solution that emerged in a closed cabinet session on the evening of October 16 was to combine Grant's transfer to Tennessee with reorganizing all the western armies under his lead. Whether Grant's appointment meant retaining Rosecrans as commander of the Army of the Cumberland was another question. Stanton, Seward, and Chase argued for removing Rosecrans. Lincoln concluded from Dana's telegrams that ever since Chickamauga Rosecrans had acted "confused and stunned like a duck hit on the head." But for personal and political reasons the president wanted someone else to fire him. He would leave the decision to Grant.[84]

After the cabinet meeting, orders were drawn up creating the Military Division of the Mississippi, placing all Union armies between the Alleghenies and the Mississippi under Grant. Halleck ordered Grant to Louisville, where an "officer of the War Department" would deliver instructions. Still in crutches from his fall at New Orleans while visiting General Banks, Grant was told to prepare for immediate operations in the field. The War Department emissary turned out to be none other than Stanton. On route to Louisville, the secretary's train from Washington and Grant's from Cairo converged on Indianapolis, where on October 18 the two men met for the first time. Stanton handed Grant two orders signed by Lincoln. Both placed Grant in charge of the newly created Division of the Mississippi; one retained Rosecrans as commander of the Army of the Cumberland; the other replaced him with Thomas. Stanton made clear his own preference for the Rock of Chickamauga, but Grant needed little prodding. Although he considered Thomas too slow, Grant believed him a brave and compliant corps commander, whereas he concluded from commanding Rosecrans at Corinth that he "would not obey orders." Grant quickly chose Thomas. That night John Rawlins issued Grant's orders making the change.[85]

Grant and Stanton proceeded to Louisville and the Galt House, where they discussed plans for western campaigns. Stanton continued to receive telegrams from Dana. His dispatch sent from Chattanooga on October 18 declared that "our condition and prospects grow worse and worse." After reviewing the problem of impassable roads and the desperate hunger of men and animals, Dana minced no words: "If the effort which Rosecrans intends to make to open the river should be futile, the immediate retreat of this army will follow." If the army abandoned Chattanooga, it would probably "fall back like a rabble, leaving its artillery, and protected only by the river behind it." Dana added a qualifier that was alarming enough: "If, on the other hand, we regain control of the river and keep it, subsistence and forage can be got here, and we may escape with no worse misfortune than the loss of 12,000 animals."[86]

Dana set out on the morning of October 19 to join Stanton in Louisville. That evening Grant, accompanied by his wife, Julia, attended the theater while Stanton stayed behind to nurse a cold. When the general returned at eleven o'clock he found Stanton "nervous and excited," pacing the floor in his dressing gown and waving a dispatch from Dana in the air. Stanton showed Grant the telegram, which, Grant wrote in his memoirs, warned that "that unless prevented Rosecrans would retreat" and advised "peremptory orders against his doing so." In another account Grant went further, recalling that Dana told Stanton that Rosecrans "had given orders to his army to retreat, and that such a retreat would be disastrous not only to that campaign but to the Union."[87]

There is a great deal of confusion over this telegram. No Dana dispatch of October 19 has been found in the Union records or other archives. Recollections by James Wilson and Grant's staff officer Adam Badeau, and even Grant's battle report in 1864, used conditional language to describe the telegram, which was surely the one Dana sent on October 18. Rosecrans "might" have to abandon Chattanooga and fall back across the Tennessee, they paraphrased Dana. But Ida Tarbell, who drew on Grant's *Memoirs*, twice inserted Grant's categorical wording when ghostwriting Dana's *Recollections*, and historians ever since have ignored Dana's actual phrasing in the wartime record.[88]

When he wrote Stanton on October 18 Dana knew that Rosecrans planned over the next few days to establish a supply depot at Williams Island down-river from Chattanooga; on departing for Louisville he expressed regret that he could not witness the attempt. Of the two alternatives—that Dana con-cocted what one historian labels "a deliberate lie" on October 19 to hasten Rosecrans's removal, or that Stanton assumed the worst from Dana's dark message of the day before (as Grant remembered it years later)—the second matches logic and the evidence.[89]

In any case, Dana's earlier wires to Stanton had already sealed Rosecrans's fate. Grant's order appointing Thomas was transmitted the night before and was read by Rosecrans on the afternoon of October 19. The alarming predic-tion Stanton and Grant derived from Dana's dispatch only added insult to in-jury. It also produced memorable words that were frequently reprinted. When Grant wired Thomas at 11:30 P.M. on October 19 to "hold Chattanooga at all hazards," Thomas immediately sent reassurance: "I will hold the town till we starve." The declaration appeared in newspapers throughout the North.[90]

As Dana rode the train north to Louisville he crossed paths with Grant, who was heading south to assess the situation in Tennessee. At the Nashville sta-tion Dana was accosted by one of Grant's staff members and led across the platform to his car. He was informed that Grant had been put in command and had replaced Rosecrans with Thomas. "I am going to interfere with your journey, Mr. Dana," Grant greeted him. "I want you to dismiss your train and get in mine." Reunited with the hero of Vicksburg, Stanton's agent would see the Tennessee campaign through to its end.[91]

Recollections and Recriminations

For its commanders, the Civil War involved four years of combat and forty more of mutual recrimination. While they lived, their military reputation, political advancement, and personal honor were at stake; for the future, they sought to bend the opinion of posterity in their favor. Historians took up the controversies when the generals fell silent, keeping them simmering in biog-raphies and campaign chronicles. Dana's role in Rosecrans's removal was his foremost contribution to these disputes.

Many Union figures shared responsibility for Rosecrans's fall, including

Stanton and Halleck, who expressed impatience with Rosecrans for months and pressured Lincoln to relieve him. Lincoln signed the necessary order, and Grant in the end chose Thomas over Old Rosy. For all that, it is clear that Dana's reports from the front played the leading role in shattering Union leaders' faith in Rosecrans.

Reporters on the scene portrayed Dana as the engineer of Rosecrans's dismissal. The *Herald*'s William Shanks wrote that the general fell "victim to the sharp eyes of the wide awake and energetic . . . Assistant Secretary of War." Since "Dana's denunciations were the only information which reached the Government from an authoritative source," the *Tribune*'s Henry Villard called them the decisive factor in Rosecrans's demise. Lincoln read Dana's dispatches avidly, and notes from cabinet meetings make it clear that they drained the president's confidence in Rosecrans. According to Gideon Welles, the delay and dysfunction Dana recorded convinced Lincoln that Rosecrans was "completely broken down" after the battle.[92]

Lincoln preferred to portray Rosecrans's fall as a self-inflicted wound. At a White House interview several months after Rosecrans was fired, James R. Gilmore, a New York journalist and Rosecrans ally, dismissed Dana as Stanton's hatchet man and pressed Lincoln for an explanation. "It was not Dana, it was Rosecrans's own dispatches" that doomed him, the president answered. Rosecrans's confused and gloomy attitude facing the siege showed he "was not up to the occasion." Lincoln made an essential point: Dana's bleak portrait might have been discounted if Rosecrans's own despairing reports did not substantiate it. Yet when Lincoln told Gilmore that "the army had lost confidence" in Rosecrans and "we could not have held Chattanooga three days longer if he had not been removed," he was precisely echoing Dana.[93]

According to Villard, Dana took credit for Rosecrans's dismissal in conversation a few months after the event.[94] Two decades later, when Dana had evolved into the fiercely partisan editor of the Democratic-leaning *New York Sun*, political considerations changed his story. Dana tried to shift the responsibility to James A. Garfield, the late Republican president, whose election he had strongly opposed.

As Rosecrans's chief of staff, Garfield had written privately to his political mentor, Treasury Secretary Chase, in July 1863 to complain that delays in advancing from Tullahoma were undermining the campaign. Rosecrans was "singularly disinclined to grasp the situation with a strong hand," he confided. After Chickamauga, Chase allegedly received another letter from Garfield declaring Rosecrans unfit to retain command. Recounting the episode, Chase told the meddlesome James Gilmore that he showed the second letter to Lincoln and read it aloud at the cabinet meeting where the decision was made to send Grant to Chattanooga. The politically ambitious Garfield had played a duplicitous game to cultivate a favorable image in Washington. His letters to Rosecrans and journalists praised his commander while his comments to Stanton, Chase, and Dana behind the general's back raised doubts about his fighting spirit and his troops' support.[95]

When Dana penned Edwin Stanton's obituary in 1869, he referred to this episode indirectly. Rosecrans's sacking was caused not by Stanton but Chase, who was alarmed by letters sent by "a military friend of high station" in Rosecrans's army. Dana told Rosecrans through an emissary that it was Garfield's betrayal that had caused his dismissal. His own telegrams to Stanton were merely "statements of the 'situation' as [I] . . . saw it, and in no way suggestive of your removal." Cabinet member Montgomery Blair seconded Dana's story, claiming that Garfield's letters "finally broke the camel's back and made even Chase consent to Rosecrans's removal."[96]

In 1882, a year after Garfield succumbed to an assassin's bullet, Dana obtained his July 1863 letter and reprinted it in the *Sun*. The damning post-Chickamauga letter that Chase, Dana, and Blair referred to never came to light, and after querying his predecessor as assistant secretary, Dana concluded that Chase had shown Lincoln Garfield's July letter. Even this appeared damning enough to convince Rosecrans that his chief of staff had undermined him. "I always thought that you were the cause of my removal," Rosecrans wrote Dana; "I now begin to think I have done you injustice all these years."[97]

This was misplaced penitence, for Dana, by 1882 more interested in peddling scandal than printing the facts, was also engaged in deception. Dana "now charges upon a dead man the dirty work of pen stabbing he was then committing himself," a rival editor fumed. If Garfield wrote letters to Chase disparaging Rosecrans after Chickamauga—and he probably did not—they may have lifted Chase onto the anti-Rosecrans bandwagon, but the rest of the cabinet was already aboard. Dana's onslaught of critical dispatches owned the lion's share of responsibility for destroying the administration's confidence in Rosecrans, as the general lived long enough to learn when they were published in the official Union war records in 1890.[98]

Dana's part in Rosecrans's removal drew strong criticism then and later. The fiercest rancor came from Rosecrans loyalists, who charged that Dana was doing the bidding of Stanton and Halleck and blamed all three for conspiring against Rosecrans. One Ohio officer told Rosecrans that "Dana is nothing but a respectable spy" for Stanton and that his meddling caused "the most intense disgust and hatred" in camp. General Granger and Colonel Sanderson of Rosecrans's staff nursed lifelong grudges against Dana that were fueled in part by the War Department's blocking their promotions; they believed Dana was sent by Stanton to "destroy Rosecrans." According to an embittered Rosecrans, even General Thomas had referred privately to Dana as one of "the traitors from Washington now in camp" plotting his removal. Many historians have repeated the charge that Dana maliciously undermined Rosecrans to serve Stanton's agenda.[99]

By contrast, Rosecrans's detractors hailed Dana as a hero. "*We are saved*," Ohio colonel Emerson Opdyke wrote his wife when he heard about Rosecrans's dismissal. "And for it, we are indebted to Mr C.A. Dana . . . [who] is entitled to the thanks of the whole Country." James Wilson and Baldy Smith credited Dana with rescuing the Army of the Cumberland from destruction, and Grant agreed. After he saw firsthand the trap Rosecrans had fallen into, Grant estimated that Chattanooga could have been supplied only a week longer: "It looked as if two courses were open: one to starve, the other to surrender or be captured." Even Sanderson, Rosecrans's ever-loyal aide, was shocked when he rode the Union lines a few days after his commander was sacked. "I find many men badly clad, without blankets or overcoats, and many horses & mules dying for want of food," he recorded privately. "The truth is, this army is in danger of starvation." He favored evacuating the city just as Rosecrans had contemplated.[100]

Stepping back from the hero-or-villain name-calling to examine the evidence, it seems clear that Dana's warnings to Washington arose from a cool assessment of Rosecrans's actions more than from personal prejudice. Dana had heard about recurrent problems with Rosecrans from Grant and Stanton before he arrived in Chattanooga, but he had not come to destroy the general. Even after Chickamauga, Dana continued to report favorably until Rosecrans could not shake off his indecision and defeatism. Rosecrans's unnerved and vacillating performance no doubt looked especially bad to Dana in contrast to the calm, resolute command of Grant at Vicksburg. This may have led him to exaggerate Rosecrans's failed leadership, but not by much, as a stack of corroborating evidence attests.

Some postwar critics, and historians who echo them, accused Dana of violating Rosecrans's confidence. Villard, the *Tribune* reporter, charged that Dana had breached military decorum: "[H]e deliberately drew the general into confidential communications, the substance of which he used against him," and "fell into the role of the informer without perhaps being conscious of it." No doubt Dana's dual charge as a government official sent to assist Rosecrans and to report confidentially to Washington put both men in an awkward position. The problem was Rosecrans's response. Like Grant before him, Rosecrans understood Dana's role, but unlike Grant he lacked composure, blamed Washington for his plight, and proved incapable of projecting efficiency and confidence.[101]

A final line of criticism asserted that Dana's reports reflected haste, prejudice, or misinformation. The Union general Jacob Cox wrote that Dana's dispatches "were not always quite just, for they were written at speed under the spell of first impressions, and necessarily under the influence of army acquaintances in whom he had confidence." This resulted in mistakes and inconsistencies in describing events and, in some cases, failure to question his sources' bias. This charge hits closer to home, for Dana reported to Stanton daily amid a busy campaign, basing much of his information on initial reports and camp gossip. Looking back later, Dana accepted this criticism but defended his course. He could not remember everything in his telegrams, he wrote Rosecrans: "No doubt there are passages in them which you will regard as having been unjust to you; many concerning which you will tell me, probably with justice, that I was entirely misinformed; some, perhaps, which you may think justify to some extent the resentment [of me] you speak of." Yet he denied having any animus against Rosecrans or doubts about his patriotism. Most important, Dana took nothing back. During his *Tribune* days Dana described a managing editor as a creature to whom remorse was foreign. When he brought this credo into government service he called the shots as he saw them and moved on.[102]

The truth was that Charles Dana was substantially correct in his assessment of Rosecrans's broken condition and the army's dire straits after Chickamauga.[103] His language was harsh and his claims sometimes exaggerated, but his reports to Stanton and Lincoln conveyed Rosecrans's breakdown vividly and wisely counseled his removal. What happened after Grant took charge in Tennessee demonstrated that Dana's warnings had been accurate and the alarm they sounded helped turn around the Union army's fortunes.

10 "Glory to God! The Day Is Decisively Ours"

In October 1863, after weeks of frustration with William Rosecrans's dithering, Charles Dana was pleased to be reunited with Ulysses Grant, whose aggressiveness and strategic skill might turn around the dire situation in Tennessee. The Army of the Cumberland was being starved out of Chattanooga and a detachment of rebel troops under the Confederate general James Longstreet was headed northeast to force the surrender of Ambrose Burnside at Knoxville and regain East Tennessee. To secure Chattanooga and rescue Burnside, Grant had to coordinate the forces of four separate western armies, resupply his troops, and position them to advance for a climactic battle at Chattanooga, all while steeling the skittish Burnside's resolve to hold firm. Dana played key supporting roles in these tasks, in addition to reporting their outcomes to Washington.

Opening the Cracker Line

On the train from Nashville to Stevenson, Alabama, on October 21 Dana updated Grant on the army's supply situation. The rail route eastward was broken at Bridgeport, twenty-seven miles down the Tennessee River from the Army of the Cumberland's encampment in Chattanooga, and Confederates' command of the river made it impossible to send provisions by steamboat or riverside roads. General George Thomas's men had been reduced to half rations, further reductions were in the works, and their animals were starving by the hundreds. "Practically, the Army of the Cumberland was besieged," Grant concluded, no doubt thinking of his own investment of Vicksburg.[1]

At Stevenson General Joseph Hooker sent an officer to Grant's railroad car to invite Grant to his headquarters, in defiance of rank. Grant replied firmly that "if General Hooker wishes to see me he will find me on this train." The incident opened Grant's collaboration with Hooker poorly, according to Dana's report.[2] Grant also had a brief, awkward meeting with General Rosecrans, who had quietly left his army and was passing to the rear to await orders. The two men belittled each other in private conversations with others, but on this occasion they spoke cordially. To Grant, Rosecrans seemed almost cheerful, "as if a great weight had been lifted off his mind." Rosecrans made some suggestions to improve the transport of supplies to Chattanooga; Grant thought them "excellent" but wondered why "he had not carried them out."[3]

The next morning Dana accompanied Grant with his staff on horseback on the wagon route to Chattanooga along and then over Walden's Ridge. "Roads worse than ever," Dana wired Stanton tersely. Rain fell continuously, swollen creeks had washed out embankments, and knee-deep mud slowed the horses. Still on crutches from his mount's fall in New Orleans, Grant had to be carried over soupy spots. He found it impossible to make the journey in one day and rested halfway.[4]

Dana and James Wilson, again inseparable as at Vicksburg, were eager to assess things at Chattanooga before Grant arrived. They took a cutoff road Dana had discovered and proceeded by moonlight to the eastern edge of Walden's Ridge. When darkness gave cover they descended to the road along the Tennessee's north bank. As their horses slopped through the mud, Confederate pickets across the river occasionally fired their way. At the north end of Moccasin Point a ferry carried them across to the town. At midnight they found the quarters of Thomas's aide Horace Porter. Tired and soaked, they received a warm welcome and the best of Porter's larder: a square of fried hardtack, a strip of salt pork, and a cup of black army coffee. The meal spoke more eloquently than words about Chattanooga's supply situation.[5]

The next morning, October 23, they paid respects to General Thomas. "Mr. Dana, you have got me this time," Thomas said as they shook hands. "There is nothing for a man to do in such a case as this but to obey orders." This was Thomas's way of acknowledging Dana's part in his promotion and disclaiming personal ambition. "The government seems to have thought, very properly, that you were not to be consulted," Dana replied suavely. Dana and Wilson next called on several officers, who told them that "the change at headquarters was already perceptible, order prevailing instead of universal chaos." Dana reassured Stanton that Thomas was "firmly resolved to hold [Chattanooga] at all events."[6]

That evening General Grant arrived at Thomas's headquarters "wet, dirty, and well," Dana reported. When Dana and Wilson entered the small house's parlor they encountered an awkward scene. Grant was sitting beside the fireplace, dripping from his uniform and boots. Thomas stood in silence facing him, and staff officers were scattered through the room. Wilson spoke up, pointedly reminding Thomas that Grant needed dry clothes. His suggestion

General Rawlins.   General W. F. Smith.
    Charles A. Dana.   General Wilson.   General Grant.   General Thomas.
                                                                        Captain Porter.

GENERAL GRANT AT THE HEADQUARTERS OF GENERAL THOMAS.

General Ulysses Grant at George Thomas's headquarters, Chattanooga. Grant, *seated*, dries himself by the fireplace; Thomas, *standing*, introduces staff officer Horace Porter as he enters the room. Seated at the table are Charles Dana and his friend James H. Wilson. *Standing, left to right*: John Rawlins, W. F. "Baldy" Smith, Thomas, and Porter. Illustration by C. S. Reinhart. From Horace Porter, *Campaigning with Grant* (New York: Century Co., 1897).

snapped Thomas out of his trance, and he offered a change of outfit to his guest. Although Grant declined, the ice was broken and eventually "a glow of cordiality" warmed the group.[7]

Grant's chilly reception owed much to Thomas's social obtuseness, but Dana and Wilson, always attentive to intrigue, believed it reflected deeper tensions between the two commanders. Thomas remained loyal to Rosecrans, and Grant had chosen Thomas as Rosecrans's replacement without enthusiasm. The two men cooperated without becoming friends, and their staffs followed suit. Eventually Grant turned to Dana and Wilson, who were more polished and less hot-tempered than his chief of staff John Rawlins, to maintain civility between headquarters.[8]

With Grant's and Thomas's staff assembled, Baldy Smith briefed the newcomers on the army's situation. A talented West Point engineer who had ascended in the Army of the Potomac with George McClellan, Smith shone at logistics but had an arrogant streak that erupted periodically to sabotage his career. When Smith finished, Grant took his cigar from his mouth and fired a volley of questions. It was clear that he intended not simply to open a supply line as soon as possible but to take the offensive against the encircling Confederates.[9]

The next day Grant set out with Thomas and Smith to scout positions for establishing a crossing of the Tennessee. While riding along the river on October 19 with Dana, Smith had noticed a promising site at Brown's Ferry at a neck of the river two miles west of Chattanooga. If the Federals could establish a beachhead there they could also take over a road on the south bank and open traffic upriver by small steamers. Whether goods arrived at Brown's Ferry via the Tennessee River or a combined river-and-road route, they could easily be brought overland to Chattanooga. Smith's idea was to seize the crossing with the assistance of Hooker's troops, and Grant quickly approved plans to open what soldiers were now calling the "cracker line."[10] Smith was picked to lead 4,000 men out from Chattanooga to capture and bridge the crossing, while Hooker marched 10,000 men from Bridgeport to Lookout Valley, then up to Brown's Ferry. Dana reported that Hooker "seems to show no zeal in the enterprise," fearing that his troops would be sitting ducks for cannon fire from Lookout Mountain. So Grant ordered Wilson to goad him along, with Dana as reporter.[11]

At dawn on October 27 Dana and Wilson joined the Federals under Hooker as they marched from Bridgeport through rocky country along the disabled Nashville and Chattanooga Railroad. To their astonishment, no significant Confederate force attempted to block them. The next afternoon, booming Confederate cannons from atop Lookout Mountain greeted their arrival, but they were too far away to do damage. Hooker's men arrived too late to assist Smith's attack on Brown's Ferry, but they secured the road along the south shore of the Tennessee. Meanwhile, Smith's capture of the crossing had come off exactly as planned. Landing on the south bank before dawn, the Federals built breastworks against feeble opposition from Confederate pickets while a pontoon bridge was constructed. "Everything perfectly successful," Dana telegraphed Stanton gleefully. The "brilliancy" of Smith's operation "cannot be exaggerated."[12]

Credit for envisioning the Cracker Line through Brown's Ferry was a point of pride that Civil War officers argued over for the rest of their lives. Rosecrans's admirers claimed it was his idea initially, but Dana insisted that Smith deserved the credit, and most historians have agreed. From the coup at Brown's Ferry Dana developed a nearly unshakeable opinion that the brilliant but argumentative Smith deserved a high command.[13]

There was still the danger of a Confederate counterattack on the Union's new positions. Hooker's troops were extended haphazardly along Lookout Valley from Wauhatchie north to Brown's Ferry. Dana and Wilson warned Hooker to concentrate his lines, which, Dana wrote, "invited attack from the enemy." Back at Chattanooga, Grant, although concerned by these reports, decided to do nothing. Shortly after midnight a Confederate division descended from Lookout Mountain to launch an assault on the Union encampments. Hard pressed, the Federals suffered 416 casualties to the Confederates' 408, and the Union general John W. Geary lost his son. Geary's men and General O. O. Howard's troops "behaved splendidly," Dana reported, and the Confederates withdrew before daylight. Despite Hooker's bumbling, the Union troops had held their lines and protected the Cracker Line as well.[14]

By November 1, less than ten days after Grant's arrival, the new supply route was officially in operation. A steamboat and a converted scow unloaded forage for animals and rations for the army at Kelly's Ferry, which were then taken overland to Chattanooga via the Cracker Line. "We have the river," Dana wired Stanton in triumph. There was "no further danger of the Army of the Cumberland being starved out of Chattanooga."[15]

The Federals still faced serious transport challenges, including the balky railroad from Nashville to Stevenson and pontoon bridges on the Tennessee that were ruptured by storms or sabotage.[16] Grant also faced troubles with his subordinate generals. General Thomas inspected Hooker's lines a week after the Confederate attack and found them still "negligently placed," according to Dana. Hooker's foot-dragging, his flawed defense of Lookout Valley, and his inflated battle report—which claimed his "glorious" victory had inflicted 1,500 casualties—lowered him further in Grant's estimation. At the end of October Dana telegraphed Stanton requesting major changes in command: Grant "wishes to have both Hooker and [General Henry] Slocum removed from his command, and the Eleventh and Twelfth Corps consolidated under Howard." Hooker had "behaved very badly since his arrival," Dana explained, and Slocum resented serving under him. Grant believed the change should come from Washington, but Lincoln was unwilling to make it on the eve of battle. Eventually Grant muddled through by assigning Slocum to protect the railroad to Nashville while Hooker remained at Chattanooga.[17]

Grumbling was also heard from generals who vied to head Thomas's XIV Corps after his promotion. John Palmer, miffed at being overlooked, submitted his resignation. Dana recommended that Lincoln and Stanton accept it, and that they pass over Lovell Rousseau, "so unfit that he cannot be considered," for J. J. Reynolds. But Lincoln refused to part with Palmer, a prominent Illinois Republican who had helped him get nominated in 1860, and Grant gave him the command. Dana believed Palmer "a good division general and a sensible man, but hardly equal to this new position," and reported that Rousseau was "deeply grieved." The reshuffling left a lingering residue of hard feelings.[18]

Despite these frustrations Grant remained "very hopeful," he wrote Julia early in November.[19] Solving the army's supply problem had allowed him to shift from defense to offense, where he was much more comfortable. And his favorite, most aggressive subordinate, William T. Sherman, was on the way.

Mission to Burnside

Sherman was taking longer than Grant expected. He advanced from the Mississippi by following the Memphis and Charleston Railroad but was delayed because Henry Halleck ordered him to repair track as he went along. Learning this, Grant wired Sherman on October 24 to drop his railroad rebuilding and direct his 17,000 men to Stevenson. Meanwhile, Grant received scattered reports that Confederates from Bragg's army were being sent toward Knoxville. The rumors were confirmed on the night of November 6, when a Confederate officer crossed over the lines to desert. He was "a northern man," Dana explained, "who had lived in Georgia before the war, and was forced into the service." The officer revealed that two divisions under Longstreet had been sent to Knoxville, instructed to cooperate with a detachment from Robert E. Lee's Virginia army to drive Burnside out of Tennessee. The details "bear the stamp of truth," Dana concluded, and Grant agreed, although Longstreet's total force would reach 16,000, not the 20,000–30,000 Grant and Dana feared from the deserter's testimony. Fortunately for the Federals, Longstreet moved slowly and reluctantly up the Tennessee, constantly calling for more men and supplies.[20]

Grant was convinced that the best way to assist Burnside was to attack Chattanooga so that the Rebels would have to recall Longstreet. But Dana and Baldy Smith persuaded him to drop plans for an immediate move because Thomas's army could not mobilize enough men and animals. A full-scale attack at Chattanooga would have to await Sherman's arrival. Grant penciled in November 21.[21] In the interim, the telegraph line between Chattanooga and Knoxville went dead and Grant was anxious for a reliable assessment of Burnside's condition. He dispatched Wilson to Knoxville to give Burnside instructions and asked Dana to join him as reporter. Dana checked with Stanton, who wired him that he was "at liberty to render any service which General

Grant desires you to perform." The two emissaries started out on the afternoon of November 9.[22]

Dana previewed the expedition for his young daughter in a charming letter:

> I expect to go all the way on horseback, and it will take about five days. About seventy horsemen will go along with their sabers and carbines to keep off the guerillas. Our baggage we shall have carried on pack mules. These are funny little rats of creatures, with the big panniers fastened to their sides to carry their burdens in. I shall put my bed in one pannier and my carpet bag and India-rubber things in the other. Colonel Wilson, who is to go with me, will have another mule for his traps, and a third will carry the bread and meat and coffee that we are to live on. At night we shall halt in some nice shady nook where there is a spring, build a big roaring fire, cook our supper, spread our blankets on the ground, and sleep with our feet toward the fire, while half a dozen of the soldiers, with their guns ready loaded, watch all about to keep the rebels at a safe distance. Then in the morning we shall first wake up, then wash our faces, get our breakfasts, and march on, like John Brown's soul, toward our destination.[23]

Dana's preview was vivid and cozy—except for the John Brown reference—but mostly fanciful. He and Wilson were accompanied by fifteen cavalrymen, not seventy. They slept not in the open but in local houses or tents pitched at the camps of Union detachments. To avoid contact with Confederates, the party followed a roundabout route on the west bank of the Tennessee, meandering through wooded, hilly country with many streams to cross. Free from danger, they relaxed and became expansive. Dana "beguiled our journey with an almost continuous disquisition on history, romance, poetry, and practical life," James Wilson recalled. They loped along for three days, then boarded a train at Lenoir's Station for the final twenty miles to Knoxville.[24]

They arrived on the night of November 12 and the next morning called on Burnside. It was Dana's first meeting with the stout, side-whiskered general who had bravely but foolishly led the Army of the Potomac to slaughter at Fredericksburg. "He was an energetic, decided man, frank, manly, and well educated," Dana later recalled. "When he first talked with you, you would think he had a great deal more intelligence than he really possessed." It didn't take long for Dana to decide that Burnside's showy exterior camouflaged "a weak mind full of vagaries."[25]

Dana and Wilson were alarmed by Burnside's disposition of his troops. Grant had instructed him to hold Knoxville at all costs, but the greater part of

Major General Ambrose Burnside, 1863. Photograph by Mathew Brady. Library of Congress Prints and Photographs Division.

his 25,000 men were scattered from Knoxville to Cumberland Gap, Kentucky, to protect supply lines and cover a retreat. In conversation, Burnside seemed to vacillate between withdrawing and making a stand. Dana and Wilson pressed him to hold Knoxville as long as possible, at least to keep Longstreet engaged there while Grant's army attacked the Rebels facing Chattanooga.[26]

In the early hours of November 14 Burnside learned that the Confederates were bridging the Tennessee near Loudon, thirty miles southwest of Knoxville. The news sent him into a near panic, according to Dana. He drew up orders for his men to leave Lenoir's Station and fall back on Knoxville. If forced to abandon the city, they would destroy workshops and mills and head toward Cumberland Gap. At the same time, Burnside nursed a pet scheme of moving his entire force across the Holston River south of Knoxville, where his army could live off local supplies and forage. Dana protested that the move would cut off his communications and leave the road to Knoxville open to the enemy, and he got Burnside's chief of staff, General John Parke, to agree. After hours of discussion Wilson convinced Burnside by pointing out, according to Dana, that "Grant did not wish him to include the capture of his entire army among the elements of his plan of operations."[27]

By the time Dana and Wilson departed for Chattanooga that morning, Burnside had decided to send troops toward Loudon to verify Longstreet's advance and delay it. Dana and Wilson accompanied Burnside and his staff by train to Lenoir's Station. Skirmishing had already broken out between pickets several miles south, but the Confederate bridges across the Tennessee were not completed. Dana told Stanton there was a reasonable probability that Burnside could hold Knoxville until relieved by forces from Chattanooga. At Lenoir's, Dana and Wilson bade Burnside goodbye, a farewell made solemn by Burnside's threatening situation and the possibility that Confederate cavalry might intercept their own return to Grant.[28]

Grant had less confidence than Dana in Burnside. Knowing that his attack on Chattanooga was at least a week away, he wired Burnside on November 15 to emphasize the necessity of holding Knoxville. Grant wanted Dana and Wilson to remain with Burnside to stiffen his resolve. It was too late. "Dana left Burnside on the 14th to return to you," Halleck informed Grant from Washington. "Burnside was then hesitating whether to fight or to retreat. I fear he will not fight, although strongly urged to do so."[29]

It may not have been Grant's wish, but Dana and Wilson left just in time. They and their cavalry escort had to ride rapidly west from Lenoir's Station toward Kingston to pass around the head of Longstreet's columns. If they had delayed an hour or two they likely would have been cut off and captured.

Once on the western side of the Tennessee they were safe. Over the next three days, riding along country roads to Chattanooga, they enjoyed the hospitality of East Tennessee Unionists. At one farm, the entourage occupied the barn and Dana and Wilson cooked supper in the yard using the family's provisions. Afterward they were invited into the house to socialize. Dana learned something about backwoods customs: "There were two or three young and very pretty girls in the farmer's family, and while we talked they dipped snuff, a peculiar custom that I had seen but once or twice before."[30]

Dana and Wilson also learned about loyal Tennesseans' view of the war. The typical backwoods farmer, they observed, was "plain, simple-minded, and sensible without sham or pretension; loving the Union because he had been taught to love it; hating the slaveholders' rebellion and caring nothing for his 'rights in the territories' because he had no slaves." As for enlisting, he preferred "staying at home when he could and taking no part in the struggle unless he must," since he suspected it was "the rich man's war and the poor man's fight." These hardscrabble farmers provided Dana's contingent with food, shelter, and forage as best as they could. Dana was so impressed by their loyalty that a few weeks later he penned an appeal to New York newspapers urging the public to relieve their "deep distress" by sending food and clothing: "Their country has been repeatedly traversed by both the rebel and the Union armies, and the consequence is that in many portions of it the inhabitants are literally starving."[31]

Dana and Wilson reached Chattanooga the night of November 17. Their return trip, at least at its outset, had "just enough danger and adventure in it to make it romantic," Wilson recalled. They had been out of contact with Grant and the War Department for four days, and rumors claimed they had been taken prisoner. Grant gave them a mixed reception: "Genl. had wished us to remain with Burnside," Wilson recorded in his diary. But Grant also told Wilson that his appointment as interim brigadier general had been approved. Dana received a warm telegram from a relieved Stanton: "I am rejoiced that you have got safely back. My anxiety about you for several days has been very great. Make your arrangements to remain in the field during the winter. Continue your reports as frequently as possible." Stanton wired news of Dana's return and his opinion that Burnside's position was safe to President Lincoln at Gettysburg, where he had been invited to make "a few appropriate remarks" dedicating its soldiers' cemetery.[32]

It took two weeks for Dana to learn whether Burnside held fast. Meanwhile, his mission to Knoxville ended happily for a different reason. By sheer chance—avoiding capture and missing Grant's instructions to remain with

Burnside—Dana was able to witness the Battle for Chattanooga, one of the war's turning points and, by his estimation, "the most spectacular military operation I ever saw."[33]

"An Interposition of God"

During Dana's absence Grant amassed his forces for an attack on the Confederate heights. On November 18 Dana spelled out to Stanton Grant's plans for a three-pronged advance. Sherman's army was to move from Bridgeport into Lookout Valley, pretending to flank Bragg from the west, then stealthily shift to the northeast, out of enemy sight behind the ridge of hills north of the Tennessee River. After crossing the river Sherman would surprise the Rebels at the northern head of Missionary Ridge. Meanwhile, General Gordon Granger would lead 18,000 of Thomas's men to threaten the center of the Confederate lines directly east of Chattanooga. Finally, Hooker would attack the head of Lookout Mountain to pin down the Rebels there and if possible capture the mountain. For the first time in the war, divisions of the Union's three main armies—Hooker's Army of the Potomac, Sherman's Army of the Tennessee, and Thomas's Army of the Cumberland—would co-operate in a single battle. Dana's description was so clear that Stanton had to remind his assistant not to disclose the army's plans by wire: while "the detail of completed operations cannot be too full, there is danger that contemplated or pending movements may fall into the hands of the enemy."[34]

The plan looked good on paper but ran up against frustrating delays in the field. Instead of sending all his troops and artillery first, Sherman had lined up wagon trains in the rear of each of his divisions, slowing the overall advance. Dana called it a "lamentable blunder" in his first telegram critical of Sherman. "Grant says the blunder is his," he reported. "He should have given Sherman explicit orders to leave his wagons behind. But I know that no one was so much astonished as Grant on learning that they had not been left, even without such orders." Had the two men not been warm friends, Dana surmised, Sherman's delays would have elicited a sharp rebuke.[35]

The supply problem at Chattanooga again intervened. The swollen river allowed Confederates to float heavy rafts downriver to smash the Union pontoon bridges at Chattanooga and Brown's Ferry. The railroad between Stevenson and Nashville was badly damaged, Dana told Stanton, and too few cars carrying forage reached Chattanooga. As a result, more than 10,000 camp animals might soon perish.[36] Because of these setbacks the attack on Saturday, November 21, was scuttled. Bragg had fallen for the ruse that

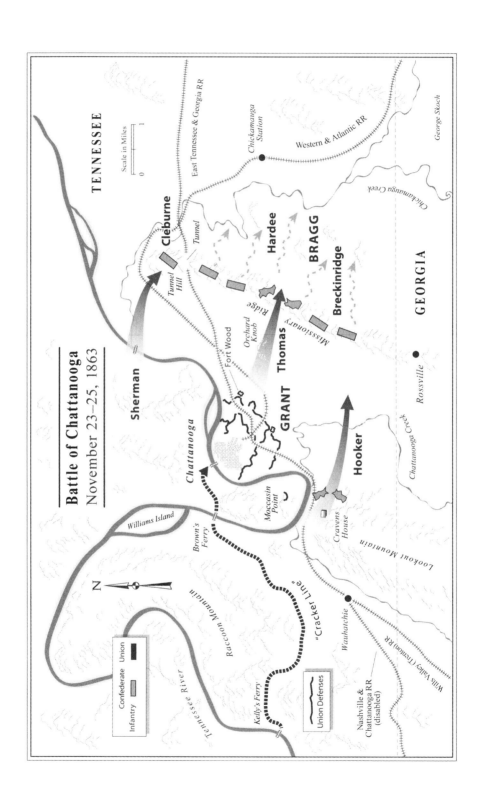

Battle of Chattanooga
November 23–25, 1863

TENNESSEE

GEORGIA

Scale in Miles
0   1

George Skoch

East Tennessee & Georgia RR

Chickamauga Station

Western & Atlantic RR

Chickamauga Creek

Cleburne

Tunnel

Hardee

BRAGG

Tunnel Hill

Breckinridge

Missionary Ridge

Orchard Knob

Fort Wood

Sherman

Thomas

Rossville

GRANT

Chattanooga

Chattanooga Creek

Moccasin Point

Hooker

Williams Island

Brown's Ferry

Cravens House

Lookout Mountain

N

Raccoon Mountain

"Cracker Line"

Wauhatchie

Tennessee River

Kelly's Ferry

Wills Valley (Trenton) RR

Nashville & Chattanooga RR (disabled)

Infantry
Confederate   Union

Union Defenses

Sherman was moving down Lookout Valley into Georgia, but the window of surprise was closing. "I have never felt such restlessness before as I have at the fixed and immovable condition of the Army of the Cumberland," Grant vented to Halleck. The whole operation was "paralyzed," Dana complained on November 23, sounding as restless as the commander himself.[37]

Grant rethought his plan, energized by reports that Bragg had sent additional reinforcements to Longstreet. He decided not to await Sherman's pontoon crossing to find out whether Bragg was vulnerable. On November 23 he ordered Thomas to test the Confederates' strength in his immediate front. The objective was Orchard Knob, a bald, 100-foot hill east of Chattanooga about halfway between the Union lines and the base of Missionary Ridge. Dana rode out to Fort Wood, a defensive work that Rosecrans's army had built in the nervous days after Chickamauga. From there he watched the action with Grant's staff and a constellation of high-ranking generals, including Montgomery Meigs, who had recently arrived from Bridgeport.[38]

Below the fort's parapet the entire field could be seen. Just before one o'clock Thomas's men moved out of camp. Instead of a limited attack, Thomas, to impress Grant or to boost his army's morale, had ordered an all-out display. Nearly 24,000 Federals assembled on the plain, marching into place "with all the precision of a review, the flags flying and the bands playing," Dana wrote. In fact, some Confederate soldiers mistakenly believed a grand review was under way. When the order to advance sounded at 2 P.M. three brigades marched forward at double-quick across the mile and a quarter to Orchard Knob. The Confederates had posted only 650 men around the hill in improvised earthworks, facing several thousand approaching Federals. The Union soldiers opened fire, and the artillery at Fort Wood boomed its support. Within thirty minutes the Federals occupied Orchard Knob and its spur, and the surviving rebel shooters fled to rifle pits at the base of Missionary Ridge. Thomas recognized that his army had seized a valuable promontory that faced Missionary Ridge, and he signaled his men to entrench.[39]

The fight was so brief that by 3:30 P.M. Dana, having returned to Chattanooga headquarters, sent a telegram to Stanton describing the capture. Belatedly, the Confederate artillery atop Missionary Ridge opened fire to assert their presence; Dana counted about a dozen guns. Grant and his staff wondered whether most of Bragg's army was still on Missionary Ridge or had gone to aid Longstreet. "Nothing shows decisively whether the enemy will fight or fly," Dana wired Washington. "Grant thinks latter, other judicious officers think former." If Bragg was still present in force, Grant wanted to give him battle.[40]

Sherman was tabbed to key the Union victory. Grant counted on his flank attack and reserved a supporting role for Hooker's army and Thomas's men. Hooker would have his hands full at Lookout Mountain, and a frontal assault by Thomas on the heights of fortified Missionary Ridge was deemed futile. Besides, Grant told Sherman, Thomas's army "had been so demoralized by the battle of Chickamauga that he feared they could not be got out of their trenches to assume the offensive." According to Dana, Sherman was mortified that he had delayed Grant's offensive and was determined to make up for it.[41]

Grant asked Dana and Wilson to join Sherman for the nighttime crossing five miles upriver from Chattanooga, where 24,000 soldiers were concealed behind hills and prepared to cross the Tennessee undetected. Shortly after midnight, Sherman's advance men floated across on pontoon boats and routed the small Confederate picket. Wilson supervised the ferrying of three divisions across by steamer to secure the bridgehead while the pontoon bridge was built under Baldy Smith's supervision. By the afternoon of November 24, the bridge was completed and the remaining men marched briskly across. Sherman told Dana that he had never seen a stealthy operation done so efficiently. Spanning thirteen hundred and fifty feet, the bridge gave Dana another opportunity to sing Baldy Smith's praises to Stanton.[42]

When Grant expressed anxiety for Sherman's safety, Dana sent reassuring updates by flag-signal relays, which had to be used on the rebel side of the river. So far Sherman's move appeared to be undetected by Confederate commanders. Three columns advanced toward Missionary Ridge, the low clouds and drizzling rain concealing their movements. By 4 P.M., when Dana left to return to Grant, Sherman's troops had clambered up the two northernmost hills of the ridge without much Confederate opposition. Sherman believed he was ideally positioned for the next day's offensive. Dana told Grant, and Grant told Halleck, that Sherman's right extended to the tunnel of the Knoxville railroad.[43]

All were badly mistaken. Sherman's men had taken two hills that were separated from Tunnel Hill and the rest of Missionary Ridge by a steep, narrow saddle. Defective Union maps were the culprit. From studying them, Sherman later wrote, "I had inferred that Missionary Ridge was a continuous hill, but we found ourselves on two high points, with a deep depression between us and the one immediately over the [railroad] tunnel, which was my chief objective point." Instead of a dominant position and clear path down Missionary Ridge, Sherman was faced with the prospect of sending his columns along the narrow ridge path to Tunnel Hill or else descending partway to the valley to attack the fortified northern end of Bragg's line from the west.[44]

As Sherman settled his men on what all believed was the head of Missionary Ridge, Dana hurried back to Chattanooga. He arrived in time to witness the tail end of the Battle of Lookout Mountain. Hooker had orders to gain a foothold on the point of the mountain as a staging ground for attacking the south end of Missionary Ridge. Around noon his forces advanced over heavily wooded terrain to a plateau halfway up the nose of the mountain, where the Cravens House served as rebel headquarters. After heavy fighting the Confederates retreated, but the impenetrable fog, the arrival of rebel reinforcements, and Hooker's cautiousness cut short the battle by late afternoon. From Fort Wood, the Union high command caught intermittent glimpses of the fighting shrouded between the fog below and a cloud bank above. General Meigs christened it memorably, if mistakenly, the "Battle above the Clouds."[45]

At ten o'clock that evening Dana was back at Grant's headquarters in Chattanooga. Standing on the second-story porch with Grant, he admired the spectacle of a nighttime skirmish between federal reinforcements and a fresh Confederate brigade on the Cravens House plateau. The fog had cleared and the bright moon rendered the battlefield "as plain to us in the valley as if it were day," Dana recalled. Flashes of musketry marked the progress of the Federals' advance. Starting at 11 P.M. the dark shadow of the earth crept across the moon's face, an eclipse that made the combatants' rifle shots glow dramatically. Although there was no immediate news, Grant was confident that the Confederates would evacuate the mountain that night and Hooker could position himself for the next day's advance.[46]

The morning of November 25 opened clear, cold, and beautiful. Dana sent his first dispatch to Stanton at half past seven: "No firing at the front," he wired. "This makes it pretty certain Bragg retreated." Visibility was good enough above the smoke and mist that Dana spied an American flag planted on the summit of Lookout Mountain, and he reported its capture to Washington. But it soon became obvious that the Confederates were not leaving. Columns of rebel soldiers from Lookout Mountain were seen in silhouette streaming north along the 500-foot elevation of Missionary Ridge. The fully manned rifle pits at the foot of the ridge also indicated that Bragg's army was massing for a fight.[47]

Dana rode out from town to Fort Wood, where he joined Meigs, and the two proceeded to Orchard Knob, guessing correctly that it would serve as Grant's headquarters for the day. At its round top only a mile west of

Missionary Ridge, Dana and the Union's top brass stood in overcoats behind the low earthworks shielding the Union battery. "We could see the full length of our own and the enemy's lines spread out like a scene in a theater," Dana wrote. The Confederates could see them, too. Dana, Meigs, and Baldy Smith were greeted by a ten-pound shell sent by a cannon on Missionary Ridge. It whizzed and sputtered and dropped into a hole fifteen feet in front of them. For the rest of the day, rebel shells were fired periodically toward the hill to disrupt Union headquarters. Federal batteries behind Orchard Knob responded in kind. Dana later recalled that as the shells burst nearby he hit the ground, face-down, alongside John Rawlins. Most of the officers did the same, except Grant, Thomas, Meigs, and Granger. "It was not according to their dignity to go down on their marrow bones." Remarkably, none of the men on Orchard Knob were hit that day.[48]

It took the whole morning for the battle to develop. At daybreak on the Union left, Grant sent a column of soldiers under General O. O. Howard to assist Sherman, who faced only 6,000 or so Confederates under Generals Patrick Cleburne and Carter Stevenson. But the outnumbered Confederates held formidable defensive positions, with artillery poised to fire downward and soldiers stationed to block Sherman's attacks either southward along the spine of Missionary Ridge or up its steep west face. Before mid-morning Sherman lodged a series of uncoordinated assaults from the two sides of Tunnel Hill. Although Dana's first reports were hopeful, by early afternoon he and the others on Orchard Knob could discern through their spyglasses that Sherman's attacks had failed. "I saw the column sent up [the west face] . . . twice repulsed, falling back the first time in disorder," Dana reported to Stanton. When the Confederates mounted a bayonet charge, the Federals fled down the hill in disarray. In the meantime, Hooker's advance to the southwest ramp of Missionary Ridge was delayed because Confederates had burned the bridge across Chattanooga Creek. It took several hours to construct a replacement, and it seemed unlikely that Hooker would play his part in the planned pincer movement on Missionary Ridge.[49]

Standing in the cold wind on Orchard Knob, Grant's officers clustered in conversation, anxious about the day slipping away. Smith, Wilson, Rawlins, and Dana formed a congenial group "exchanging opinions freely and frequently on every point worthy of notice." After a few hours of indecision, Grant decided to support Sherman by sending Thomas's army to take the rifle pits at the base of Missionary Ridge. The consensus on Orchard Knob—as it turned out, mistaken—was that Bragg had weakened his center to move troops to block Sherman on his right. Perhaps a threat to the rebel center would cause him to recall them. There was little thought of going beyond the rifle pits; if the diversionary attack succeeded, Thomas's men could proceed up the ridge later in concert with moves by Sherman or Hooker.[50]

"Hooker has not come up," Grant remarked to Thomas, "but I think you had better move, on Sherman's account." Thomas, who thought the idea too risky, did nothing until Grant gave him a positive order. Finally, at around three o'clock Thomas's officers began moving their men into the line of battle. Orders were transmitted verbally down the chain of command. General Granger told Thomas Wood to "advance your division and carry the entrenchments at the base of the ridge, if you can, and if you succeed, halt there." Most officers received similar word, though a few believed a full-scale assault was in the works.[51]

Granger stayed behind on Orchard Knob, letting his division commanders place their men. An old artilleryman, Granger busied himself with positioning and sighting the cannons on the hill. A reporter heard Grant reprimand Granger, and Dana noted Rawlins's irritation as well. Dana later told Stanton that Granger's fussing with artillery delayed the transmission of Grant's orders. There were other reasons, including Thomas's hesitation. In any case, Granger's behavior raised Grant's suspicion that he was "a trifler instead of a great soldier" and had the same effect on Dana.[52]

At quarter to four, Granger's cannons signaled the order to advance. "It was a bright, sunny afternoon," Dana wrote, "and the forces marched across the valley in front of us as regularly as if on parade." Four divisions of Thomas's troops, about 23,000 men, moved forward in successive ranks. When they emerged from cottonwood trees into the open plain, cannons roared from both armies' heights. Federal infantrymen trotted across the valley, then broke into a run with whoops and yells as they approached the first line of breastworks. "They took with ease the first rifle-pits at the foot of the ridge as they had been ordered," Dana wrote, "and then, to the amazement of all of us who watched on Orchard Knob, they moved out and up the steep [hill] ahead of them, and before we realized it they were at the top of Missionary Ridge."[53]

The Confederates had made a series of blunders. Confident that the slope of Missionary Ridge could repel a frontal attack, Bragg constructed breastworks and artillery emplacements haphazardly. Confederate cannons were placed at the summit rather than below it—the topographical crest instead of the "military crest"—so that they fired over the heads of the attacking Federals. Rebel forces were divided between the bottom of the ridge and the crest; those below were instructed to retreat after firing on the first wave of attackers. The resulting stampede unnerved soldiers above them who were unaware of the orders. Yet the greatest responsibility—and credit—lay with the attacking Union infantry. Propelled by sheer determination, finding cover in swells and creases to duck enemy fire and regroup, the blue brigades swarmed relentlessly to the top. Emboldened by each success and the enemy's seemingly panicked retreat, Thomas's soldiers carried the fortified ridge against all odds.[54]

In a telegram labeled 4:30 P.M., Dana, breathless with excitement, announced the news to Stanton: "Glory to God! The day is decisively ours. Missionary Ridge has just been carried by a magnificent charge of Thomas' troops, and rebels routed." Grant, Dana, and staff officers immediately started for the front. As Grant rode the lines he received a clamor of hurrahs from soldiers: "We are even with them now for Chickamauga!" one shouted. On Missionary Ridge, Dana recalled, "the ambulance men were picking up the wounded and carrying them to the hospital . . . [but] there did not seem to be many." The assault had hardly been bloodless. Casualties in Wood's and Philip Sheridan's divisions, which were in the thick of the fight, numbered more than 2,500, but the total was minimized by the Confederates' hasty retreat.[55]

The exchange of gunfire continued into evening. Sherman and the Rebels kept up a sporadic duel at their standoff at the north end of Missionary Ridge until Bragg ordered a general retreat. As the Confederates fled, Sheridan pursued them down the east slope of the ridge. He captured one of Bragg's wagon trains, but the Confederates safely crossed Chickamauga Creek and destroyed the bridge, forcing him to give up the chase in the early morning hours.[56]

Later that morning Dana, still amazed by the Federals' feat, wired Stanton: "The storming of the ridge by our troops was one of the greatest miracles in military history. No man who climbs the ascent by any of the roads that wind along its front can believe that 18,000 men were moved up its broken and crumbling face unless it was his fortune to witness the deed. It seems as awful as a visible interposition of God."[57]

When Grant and Sherman wrote their memoirs, they claimed that the battle had gone as intended and that Thomas's assault had been its centerpiece all along. In fact, Grant had put off Thomas's morning charge because he lacked confidence in it; Hooker's advance was delayed; and he expected Sherman to spearhead the victory. In the afternoon Grant ordered the charge more as a way to relieve pressure on Sherman than as a route to victory. Even then, he was angered when he watched Thomas's men climb Missionary Ridge. He demanded to know who had ordered them to continue and promised that "somebody will suffer" if they failed.[58]

Dana's on-the-spot reports confirm that the Union charge up the ridge was improvised. "Neither Grant nor Thomas intended it," he told Stanton. Their orders were to carry the rifle pits and halt there, "but when this was accomplished the unaccountable spirit of the troops bore them bodily up those impracticable steeps, over the bristling rifle-pits on the crest and the thirty cannon enfilading every gully." They clambered "over rocks and through bushes, lifting themselves by thrusting their bayonets into the ground or by catching hold of limbs and twigs."[59]

Dana met up with Sheridan after the battle and asked him why he had ascended the ridge. Joining his men at the line of attack, Sheridan had been unsure whether his men should stop at the base. He sent an aide to Granger on Orchard Knob to clarify; word came back to halt at the rifle pits but then to use his own judgment about pressing on. "When I saw the men were going up," Sheridan told Dana, "I had no idea of stopping them; the rebel pits had been taken and nobody had been hurt, and after they had started I commanded them to go right on."[60]

When Dana's report of the victory reached Washington, Peter Watson, Stanton's assistant secretary, wired the response. Stanton, exhausted by overwork, had retreated to the family homestead in Ohio, and Lincoln was confined to bed with varioloid, a mild version of smallpox. "The Secretary of War is absent and the President is sick," Watson replied, "but both receive your dispatches regularly and esteem them highly, not merely because they are reliable, but for their clearness of narrative and their graphic pictures of the stirring events they describe." As for the soldiers, the "spirited valor exhibited by commanders and men in the last great feat of arms, which has crowned our cause with a glorious success, is making all of us hero worshipers." On his way to the White House Watson recited Dana's "glowing account" of the charge up Missionary Ridge to Lincoln's secretary John Hay, who pronounced it "Titanic."[61]

None of the Washington officials seemed to notice that the triumph at Chattanooga occurred on the eve of the national day of Thanksgiving Lincoln had proclaimed in gratitude for the Union's "advancing armies and navies." Lincoln and Halleck were too fixated on Burnside and East Tennessee to appreciate the magnitude of Grant's achievement. "Well done," Lincoln replied tersely to Grant's report on the capture of Lookout Mountain; "Remember Burnside." Grant and Dana better understood what Chattanooga meant. His army had driven "a big nail in the coffin of rebellion," the general told a friend. The two major Confederate armies west of the Appalachians were divided, Dana exulted. To the north, Longstreet's troops could be chased back to Virginia; to the south, "Bragg was flying toward . . . Atlanta" and the road to the Deep South opened up behind him. Although the victory at Chattanooga was less grandly celebrated by the Northern public than were Vicksburg or Gettysburg five months earlier, it was no less important. Driving Bragg's army from Chattanooga's heights made it possible in the coming months for Sherman to break the Confederacy's back by marching to Atlanta and thence to the sea.[62]

Pursuing the Enemy

On the evening of victory Grant ordered rations loaded into an ambulance so he could follow what one staff officer called "the great Chattanooga skedaddle." The next day Dana accompanied Grant to track the Federals' pursuit. He wired Stanton at 1:30 P.M. from atop Missionary Ridge, where the view was magnificent. Behind him the valley was dotted by thousands of white Union tents, and the Tennessee River wound calmly in the distance. In front, high ascending smoke indicated that "Bragg is in full retreat, burning his depots and bridges." "The Chickamauga Valley, for a distance of 10 miles," Dana reported, "is full of the fires lighted in his flight."[63]

The party descended and rode eastward to Chickamauga Creek. After Baldy Smith's men repaired the railroad bridge, they crossed it and moved on. At Chickamauga Station they viewed the depot's ruins and piles of burning corn that had been torched by the retreating Rebels. At sundown they caught up with Sherman and his staff and examined maps by the light of a campfire. Grant gave orders for Sherman to continue the pursuit toward Ringgold, Georgia, and detached other units eastward to destroy the railroad that connected Bragg and Longstreet. When the moon came up, Grant and his party used its light to ride back to Chattanooga. They passed soldiers bivouacked by the road who mistook them for cavalry and razzed them for heading to the rear. This time they forded Chickamauga Creek, keeping their feet out of the water by resting them on the horses' necks. They climbed the back of Missionary Ridge and descended to town. It was one in the morning on November 27 when Grant, Dana, and the staff arrived at headquarters, exhausted and hungry, and they took dinner at two.[64]

At breakfast that day Grant announced that he was taking the long ride back to the front. Dana stayed behind to compose a wire updating Stanton, then set out with Wilson, Meigs, and Baldy Smith. By the time they arrived at Ringgold at 5 P.M., the Federals' advance under Hooker had been forcibly blocked at a narrow gap where the creek, railroad, and wagon road squeezed through a ridge of hills. Patrick Cleburne again proved the ablest of Bragg's defenders. His troops, making a stand to protect Bragg's retreat, plugged Ringgold Gap and lined the ridges to its north and south. In the morning Hooker's troops had stormed the hills and charged the gap, only to be repulsed by Confederate fire. For four hours Cleburne's 4,100 men turned back Hooker's army of 8,800 and inflicted more than double their own casualties. By one o'clock the deafening gunfire abated and the battle was over. When the Federals edged forward they found that Cleburne's men had left, having covered Bragg's retreating artillery and supply wagons.[65]

Hooker's attack at Ringgold represented "the first great fault in this admirable campaign," Dana declared in his report to Stanton. "It was a very dangerous defile to attack in front, and common sense plainly dictated that it should be turned." Perhaps Hooker was trying to salvage his reputation, but if he had flanked the Confederates he would have lost fewer than fifty men instead of five hundred, in Dana's view. Hooker was unaware of Dana's disapproval. Angered by a *New York Tribune* reporter's opinion that he had made "a very grave mistake" at Ringgold, Hooker asked Stanton to have Dana correct him. Instead, Dana told Stanton that Hooker's subordinate, General Peter Osterhaus, was especially aggrieved because two of his regiments had been ordered up White Oak Ridge at Ringgold and suffered 40 percent casualties, the worst of the fray. Still, the Federals could console themselves that the Confederates had been cleared out of Tennessee and that Union troops were destroying the Rebels' supply wagons and railroad connections.[66]

For Grant and his staff, if not for Hooker and Osterhaus, the mood was relaxed on the rainy night after the fight at Ringgold Gap. Grant's entourage stayed at the two-story brick homestead where Bragg had slept the night before. The family who lived there—an old man, two women, and three children—warmed to the Yankees when Grant patted the little children and an officer played the piano in the parlor. Afterward, Dana joined Rawlins, Ely Parker—the full-blooded Seneca chief on Grant's staff—and three others in a small room, and Dana and Parker began "talking Indian." Dana had picked up the Seneca dialect during his youth near Buffalo. Their chatting amused the group and made a lasting impression on Grant. But Dana's display of erudition, and the fact that he was ceded the room's only bed, set him up for a comeuppance. William Smith, Grant's relative who was traveling with the group, gave Dana a scare by predicting that the Confederates would stage a raid on the house overnight. The ruse gained credibility when one of the party discovered a dead rebel soldier under a blanket in the house opposite. Smith went to sleep chuckling that he had rattled the room's ranking civilian.[67]

The next morning Dana settled the bill with their host, and when the rain ceased he headed with Grant and Wilson back to Chattanooga, passing through Graysville, where Sherman's men were making bonfires of the railroad's track and ties, and then up Missionary Ridge, "looking back to see the smoke and flames of the buildings in which we had a few minutes before been refreshing ourselves." By any reckoning, Grant's pursuit of Bragg had been halfhearted. For a day or two Grant had hopes of overtaking the Confederates' rear guard, but his troops were spread out on too many routes to converge on the task. The repulse at Ringgold Gap put the prize beyond reach. Grant decided not to pursue Bragg further. "The condition of the roads, and the impossibility of getting supplies even as far as Chattanooga, render a movement on Rome and Atlanta impracticable for the moment," Dana told Stanton. Meanwhile, lingering suspicions that Bragg might once again be preparing a counterattack were dispelled when the federals learned that Jefferson Davis had relieved him on November 30. The Army of Tennessee was in disarray and would not return.[68]

Knoxville Secured

Grant had another reason to call off the pursuit: he could now redirect his attention toward rescuing Burnside. Lincoln and Halleck were impatient to secure the hard-pressed Unionist enclave of East Tennessee, and they feared the worst because Longstreet had reached Knoxville. Typically, where Washington officials saw a threat, Grant saw an opportunity. If Burnside could hold off Longstreet, a detachment of Grant's men might pin Longstreet from behind and destroy his army.[69]

Grant sent word for General Granger to move two divisions from the IV Corps as speedily as possible up the south side of the Tennessee River toward Knoxville, 120 miles away. But when Grant returned to Chattanooga on November 28 he found some of Granger's soldiers still gathering supplies; Granger, he was told, had set out toward Knoxville "with reluctance and complaints." Having second thoughts about putting Granger in charge, Grant turned instead to his most trusted subordinate. Sherman, already heading north to protect Granger's flank, was ordered to link up with Granger and take command of the combined forces—in all, more than 30,000 Federals. Because Sherman's men had to move quickly they would have no tents or supply wagons; they would draw food and forage from the country and, if feasible, from two steamers that chugged ahead of them up the Tennessee.[70]

Grant asked Wilson and Dana to carry his orders to Sherman. Wilson joined

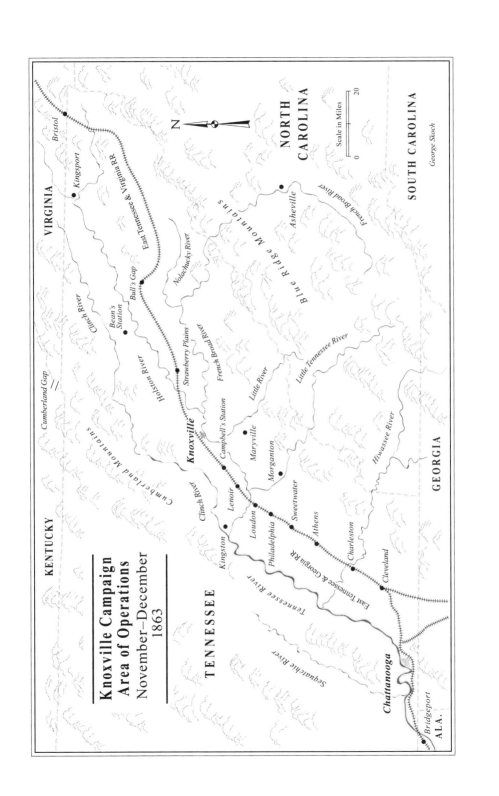

Knoxville Campaign
Area of Operations
November–December
1863

KENTUCKY

VIRGINIA

TENNESSEE

NORTH CAROLINA

SOUTH CAROLINA

GEORGIA

ALA.

N

Scale in Miles

0   20

George Skoch

Cumberland Gap

Cumberland Mountains

Clinch River

Bristol

Kingsport

Bean's Station

Bull's Gap

East Tennessee & Virginia RR

Nolachucky River

Strawberry Plains

Holston River

French Broad River

Blue Ridge Mountains

Asheville

French Broad River

Little Tennessee River

Little River

Knoxville

Campbell's Station

Maryville

Morganton

Kingston

Clinch River

Lenoir

Loudon

Philadelphia

Sweetwater

Athens

Charleston

Hiwassee River

Cleveland

East Tennessee & Georgia RR

Tennessee River

Sequatchie River

Chattanooga

Bridgeport

the expedition as chief engineer and Dana went along to report to Grant via Stanton. The two men, accompanied by a staff member and an orderly, left Chattanooga on the afternoon of November 29 in freezing temperatures. By nightfall they had made only ten miles and took refuge in a deserted house that had been occupied by an extended family of impoverished Unionists. The next morning Dana and Wilson caught up with Sherman and handed him Grant's letter. Sherman sent Grant an opinionated but obedient reply: "Recollect that East Tennessee is my horror," Sherman reminded Grant in the frank, informal tone both men had become accustomed to. But he pledged to move quickly. Burnside would hear his guns "on the 3rd or 4th at furthest."[71]

Pushing on with Dana and Wilson, Sherman reached Charleston on November 30, and the next morning, having repaired the railroad bridge destroyed by the Confederates, crossed the Hiwassee River. For the next three days they marched briskly, passing through fertile fields punctuated by villages with lovely names: Athens, Sweetwater, and Philadelphia, where Sherman planned to junction with Granger. They endured a bitter cold snap but found the eastern Tennessee Valley well supplied with cattle, sheep, corn, and hay, which the soldiers impressed as needed. Meanwhile, Granger's divisions, moving eastward from the Tennessee River to join Sherman, exhausted their rations and fell a day behind.

Instead of waiting, Sherman sent a cavalry brigade ahead under Colonel Eli Long to surprise Longstreet's rear guard and seize his pontoon bridge across the Tennessee at Loudon. The cavalry dashed forward, but at Loudon they found an enemy brigade lined up and artillery poised to fire from behind earthworks. "Long judged it prudent not to attack," Dana deadpanned to Stanton. Before the Rebels left Loudon they destroyed the pontoons, burned the public stores, and ran three locomotives and forty-eight cars into the river. Thwarted at Loudon, Sherman sent Long and his horsemen on a forty-mile dash to ford the Little Tennessee River and enter Knoxville "whatever the cost of life and horse-flesh." His aim was to get word to Burnside to hold on because the Federals' relief column was approaching.[72]

Without the bridge at Loudon, Sherman's main body of troops was forced to turn east to cross the Little Tennessee at Morganton. Riding ahead, Dana and Wilson reached the town on the night of December 3. They found the river several feet deep, two hundred yards across, and almost at freezing point. Wilson supervised construction of a bridge, which proved strong enough to pass Sherman's entire column across on the evening of December 4 and Granger's the next day. Meanwhile, the Federals rummaged through captured Confederate mail to learn news from Knoxville. Letters indicated that the town was being besieged and the writers were despairing of being rescued. Dana forwarded this information to Stanton via field telegraph. He was still at least twenty-five miles from Knoxville.[73]

Burnside, meanwhile, was faring better than his rescuers supposed. Employing the delaying tactics he discussed with Dana and Wilson, he had slowly given ground north of Loudon and adeptly withdrawn his troops into Knoxville on November 16. The next day Longstreet placed the city under siege. Knoxville was perched on a small plateau bounded by two creeks and the Holton River; on its edges Burnside had strengthened a ring of forts and earthworks he inherited from the Rebels. His 12,000 soldiers were outnumbered by Longstreet's 14,000, but they had stout defenses and enough food for the time being. Meanwhile, Longstreet was cut off from Bragg's army and running out of supplies and time. On November 29, the Rebels threw three brigades against the Union redoubt named Fort Sanders, but Burnside's men turned them back easily, inflicting more than 800 casualties compared to the Federals' fifty.[74]

Riding fast and skirting Longstreet's camps, Long's cavalry reached Knoxville at 3 A.M. on December 4 and gave Burnside word that Sherman was near. Sherman's first step in relieving Burnside had been accomplished. The second step—attacking Longstreet's army—never happened. When Sherman, Dana, and Wilson reached Maryville, still more than fifteen miles from Knoxville, on December 5 a messenger from Burnside told them that Longstreet's army had raised the siege. Through a captured message that Grant deliberately planted, Longstreet had learned three days earlier that Sherman was on his way; he also received news that Bragg had been routed at Missionary Ridge. After lingering a couple of days to weigh his options, Longstreet broke off the siege and retreated toward Virginia.[75]

Sherman's relief column arrived too late to trap the Confederates, but his army's march had played its part in rescuing Burnside. "It was a victory achieved by the soldiers' legs," quipped one of Sherman's subordinates. Washington leaders believed it a major accomplishment. "The difference between Burnside saved and Burnside lost is one of the greatest advantages of the war," Lincoln told John Nicolay when he heard that Longstreet had quit Knoxville. "It secures us East Tennessee."[76]

Sherman entered Knoxville on December 6 with his staff and Dana. To their surprise, they found Burnside ensconced in a fine mansion, where all sat down to a dinner of roast turkey served, Sherman noted pointedly, "with clean tablecloth, dishes, knives, forks, spoons, etc." Burnside's rescuers learned that he had three weeks' provisions—more than at the beginning of the siege. As Dana told Stanton, "Longstreet had left open the very avenues which Burnside most desired"—the roads from Knoxville's south side across the Holston River—and loyal Unionists had sent in ample forage and food. Sherman was irritated: "Had I known of this," he wrote, "I should not have hurried my men so fast; . . . I thought his troops there were actually in danger of starvation."[77]

Burnside's men were not starving, but they had faced critical shortages of guns and ammunition, and on short notice they had fortified an impressive series of defenses. Dana toured Knoxville's works with Sherman, who pronounced them "nearly impregnable." Reporting to Stanton, Dana commended Burnside and his troops for their resolve. Despite being outnumbered and closely pressed, "the utmost constancy and unanimity prevailed during the whole siege, from Burnside down to the last private; no man thought of retreat or surrender."[78]

There was less unity in Sherman's patchwork command. Granger's resentment at being replaced by Sherman simmered during the march to Knoxville; once they arrived it came to a boil. When Sherman and Burnside agreed that Granger's divisions should remain to help pursue Longstreet, Granger protested that his men were ill clad and exhausted and should return to Chattanooga like Sherman's. Dana reported that Granger "grumbled and complained so much" that Burnside left Granger's forces deployed locally as his own troops set out against Longstreet. When Grant heard about the episode he agreed with Dana that Granger was "unfit to command." That winter he banished him to an unpromising post in the Department of the Gulf.[79]

Like many officers with thwarted ambitions, Granger never acknowledged the flaws that checked his ascent. Courage in battle could not compensate for his crude behavior and resistance to orders, which alienated several superiors. Writing to William Rosecrans, who had remained his friend, Granger claimed that his lack of an independent command was due to sheer envy. Sherman and all of Grant's "miserable satellites," including "that loathsome Pimp Dana," were allegedly jealous of Granger's troops' successful charge at Missionary Ridge—which Granger claimed he, not Grant, had ordered—and they had set out to destroy him.[80]

Happy to be rid of Granger, Sherman returned to Chattanooga by marching leisurely down the east side of the Tennessee River, distributing his men at strategic points to guard approaches to the city. Dana and Wilson rode with Generals Frank Blair, Jr., and Carl Schurz. An eloquent antislavery orator, Schurz became the most prominent of the "Forty-Eighters" who sought refuge in America and Lincoln's chief campaigner for their votes. Dana and Schurz passed the time conversing in German and English, each complimenting the other's linguistic skill.[81] Dana's relations with Blair, scion of an influential conservative Republican family, were less cordial. Dana's horse gave out on the second day, but when Wilson asked Blair to lend Dana a spare he churlishly declined. Despite not helping Dana, Blair expected Dana to help him. He had been ordered to relinquish the XV Corps to John Logan, and he badgered Dana to press Stanton for another command. Eventually he was given another corps in Sherman's army; like several other Union political generals his pull was too important for the administration to ignore. Meanwhile, Dana somehow got another mount and the group regained the road. They arrived at Grant's headquarters on December 10.[82]

As Dana looked back on the Chattanooga Campaign he concluded that, while its climactic battle was won by an impromptu infantry charge, Grant deserved "infinite credit" for planning and executing the movements that preceded it. The lessons he drew from the victory were simple. First, all the Union armies had to be coordinated "under the leadership of one clear-headed, fearless, and faithful commander." Second, Grant was that man: "It was not till Vicksburg was followed by Chattanooga that the world came to look upon Grant as possessing any merits of his own," Dana wrote. Turning defeat into victory in Tennessee proved that Grant's earlier success was no fluke, and even his detractors now had to recognize him as the preeminent Union general.[83]

Dana played a less vital role in Grant's breakthrough at Chattanooga than he had at Vicksburg, but he assisted Grant by sending frequent updates to Washington (supplementing Grant's meager one-a-day diet for Halleck), relaying battlefield news at Sherman's end of Missionary Ridge, and steadying Burnside's nerves at Knoxville. Dana's reports also served the government well. Always eager to be near the action, he accompanied Grant's various armies and endured their hardships on the march. His vivid dispatches kept Stanton and Lincoln informed and reassured during anxious days about the fate of East Tennessee, and his distribution of praise and blame guided their military appointments and dismissals. Because of Grant and Thomas's victorious sequel to the dismal Rosecrans, Dana emerged from the campaign with his judgment vindicated and his reputation at Washington enhanced.

The cold December weather and General Grant's need to resupply his army prevented a new move against Braxton Bragg. Dana wired Secretary Stanton for permission to return back east. He missed his family after a long absence, and he could be more useful at the War Department than in Tennessee, where "all has become safe, quiet, and regular." When no response came, Dana told Stanton that Grant had asked him to explain his winter plans to administration leaders. He left Chattanooga by train, accompanied by John Rawlins, who was on route to Connecticut to be wed. The two men parted halfway and Dana reached Washington the evening of December 18. His adventures with the Union's western armies had reached their triumphant end.[84]

11 "Organizing Victory"

As the Union's battlefield fortunes rose in the fall of 1863, Washington enjoyed a wartime boom. The city's population of politicians, foreign dignitaries, bureaucrats, and army officers swelled. The district's merchants and manufacturers built fortunes from provisioning the army with clothing, guns, and ammunition. Its Navy Yard filled with vessels under construction or repair. Although street paving remained spotty, Pennsylvania Avenue began to take shape as a vibrant thoroughfare coursed by streetcars and lined by business buildings. Shops and houses sprang up along its numbered side streets. In just a few years, President Lincoln's secretary William Stoddard marveled, the city had become "brilliant and attractive—so well worthy of the destiny which has been literally forced upon it."[1]

The capital's newcomers patronized a growing array of restaurants, hotels, and theaters. Opportunities for political socializing also multiplied. After Treasury Secretary Salmon Chase's daughter Kate married the wealthy Rhode Island senator William Sprague, the widowed Chase moved into rooms attached to the couple's brick mansion at the corner of 6th and E Streets, where he hosted dinners for those who supported his ambitions. Secretary of State William Seward, who rented a spacious house on Lafayette Square overlooking the White House, kept a long list of prominent invitees. Private political dinners were dwarfed by huge fundraising fairs for the United States Sanitary and Christian Commissions that were held in government buildings and attended by thousands. The public's lightened mood carried into the chilly season. Thanks to the Union victories at Gettysburg, Vicksburg, and Chattanooga, "gayety has become as epidemic in Washington this winter, as gloom was last winter," wrote Seward's son Frederick.[2]

Expansion of the Capitol Building moved along as quickly as the federal budget allowed. The new House and Senate wings were being outfitted, and the Capitol's enormous Dome enclosed its wooden scaffolding. Lincoln faced criticism for pushing ahead with construction during wartime, but he saw it as an important symbol: "If people see the Capitol going on," he told one caller, "it is a sign we intend the Union shall go on." On December 2, 1863, the nineteen-foot bronze Statue of Freedom, a helmeted woman leaning on her shield and sword, was lifted into place on top of the completed Dome. Stoddard, who was present at the ceremony, reflected on "a contradiction between the effect of elevation between men and statuary." "The higher you lift the bronze," he wrote, "the smaller it appears, while human beings, especially politicians and generals, expand before our eyes as we . . . hoist them higher." Thinking of George McClellan and his successors atop the Union army, Stoddard mused that "many of them burst like bubbles when we lift them beyond a certain point." Stoddard wondered if this would happen to Ulysses Grant.[3]

Charles Dana, for one, was sure it would not. Arriving from Tennessee, Dana gave little notice to Washington's distractions. Of all the capital's wartime bustle and glitter, he recorded only its high housing prices in letters to friends. The shortage of dwellings enabled real estate agents and landlords to charge exorbitant rates. This inflation, plus uncertainty about how long he would stay, prompted Dana to keep his family in Manhattan and find lodging in a Washington boarding house. Meanwhile, he set about lobbying for General Grant among administration leaders. And in the newly expanded War Department building a short walk from the White House, he joined the busy, growing department he had charged with "organizing victory" in his *Tribune* editorials two years earlier.[4]

Lobbying for Grant

Dana's first task was to sell the Union brass on Grant's plans for a winter campaign to capture Mobile, Alabama, an important Gulf port still under Confederate control. From Chattanooga he had wired a preview to Stanton and asked for the government's go-ahead, adding, "I can see nothing to condemn, but everything to approve, in the scheme." At the capital, Dana sought Lincoln's endorsement. On December 19 Dana walked over to the White House for a private meeting with the president who had anxiously attended his dispatches from the front. Lincoln had entered the war with almost no military experience, but "after three or four years of constant practice in the science and art of war," Dana judged, the president had developed into the Union's best strategist. Lincoln praised Grant's leadership and expressed delight that his army had secured Chattanooga and East Tennessee. He also saw the logic of sending Grant's army south to take Mobile.[5]

Consultations at the war office followed, and on December 21 Dana re-

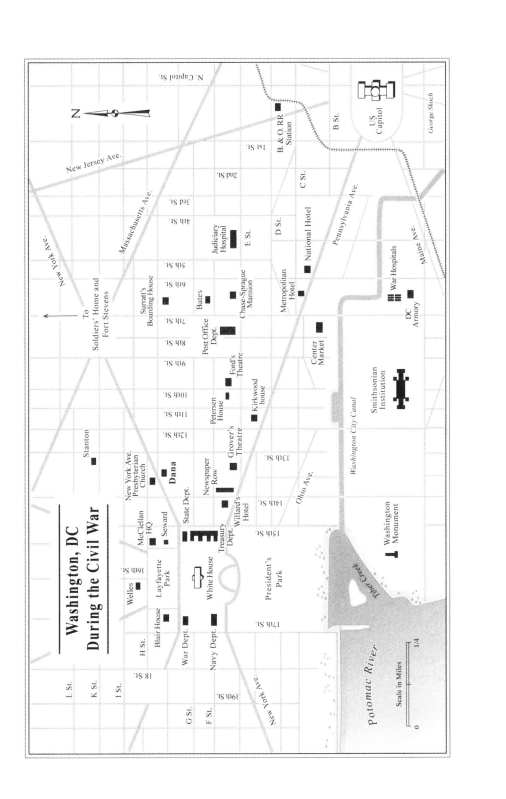

Washington, DC
During the Civil War

N

L St.
K St.
I St.

16th St.

Welles

McClellan HQ

Seward

State Dept.

Dana

New York Ave. Presbyterian Church

Stanton

To Soldiers' Home and Fort Stevens

New York Ave.

Massachusetts Ave.

New Jersey Ave.

N. Capitol St.

H St.

18 St.

G St.

F St.

19th St.

New York Ave.

Blair House

Layfayette Park

White House

War Dept.

Navy Dept.

17th St.

Treasury Dept.

Willard's Hotel

Newspaper Row

15th St.

14th St.

13th St.

Grover's Theatre

12th St.

Kirkwood house

11th St.

Petersen House

10th St.

Ford's Theatre

9th St.

8th St.

Post Office Dept.

7th St.

Bates

Surratt's Boarding House

6th St.

Chase-Sprague Mansion

5th St.

Judiciary Hospital

4th St.

3rd St.

2nd St.

1st St.

E St.

D St.

Metropolitan Hotel

National Hotel

C St.

B St.

B. & O. RR Station

US Capitol

Ohio Ave.

Center Market

Pennsylvania Ave.

Washington City Canal

Smithsonian Institution

War Hospitals

DC Armory

Maine Ave.

President's Park

Washington Monument

Tiber Creek

Potomac River

Scale in Miles

0   1/4

George Skoch

ported to Grant that most Union war leaders had approved the plan. General in Chief Henry Halleck was the main stumbling block. He objected that General James Longstreet's Confederate army might return to Knoxville in Grant's absence, and he wanted the Rebels cleared out of East Tennessee before Union soldiers advanced elsewhere. When Dana suggested that the Army of the Potomac go after Longstreet, the reply was that "from that army nothing is to be hoped under its present commander."[6]

This led to the second proposal Dana brought from Grant: a bid to replace General George Meade as head of the Army of the Potomac with William T. Sherman or Baldy Smith. Washington leaders, frustrated by Meade's recent retreat from Robert E. Lee's front at Mine Run, had been contemplating a move. Secretary of War Edwin Stanton and Halleck told Dana that when a change came Smith would be their first choice. They had some lingering doubts about Smith's "disposition and personal character"—his arrogance and argumentativeness—but Dana helped to clear these up. Lincoln agreed that Smith was a better choice than Sherman. He had more experience with the Army of the Potomac, and Sherman's erratic past made him suspect. For the moment, however, nothing was decided. In giving Grant details of these discussions, Dana admitted that he had "somewhat exceeded" his instructions from Stanton, but he had cast his lot with Grant and wanted him fully informed.[7]

Shortly after updating Grant, Dana departed for New York. His main idea was to spend the Christmas holiday with his wife and children, but he also was sent on an urgent War Department mission to block a secret Confederate operation. A rebel dispatch addressed to a contact in Halifax, Nova Scotia, had been intercepted by authorities at the Manhattan post office and forwarded to the War Department. There, with Lincoln hovering anxiously, Stanton's telegraph clerks succeeded in deciphering it. Rebel agents disguised as crewmen planned to seize a couple of ocean steamers shortly after they left New York Harbor. They would overpower the loyal crews and convert the steamers into privateers. A second captured message confirmed that a large issue of Confederate bonds and notes had been printed in a workshop near New York's Trinity Church. (In a twist worthy of Sherlock Holmes, the cipher used in both letters was based on hieroglyphs found on a tombstone in the church's graveyard.) The bonds and paper currency, along with engraving machines and plates, were scheduled to be shipped by January 1 from New York to Halifax, and then to the Confederacy via the Bahamas.[8]

When the first message was decoded on December 21, Stanton sent orders to prevent all outbound vessels from leaving the Port of New York without being inspected by the United States Marshal. Then he dispatched Dana by train to New York to confer with General John Dix, head of the Department of the East, and to report on the manhunt. The two men acted quickly. By Christmas, several steamers were seized that had been loaded with arms disguised as provisions and packed in hogsheads, and half a dozen rebel conspirators were imprisoned at Fort Lafayette. Pursuit of the counterfeiters progressed more slowly—so much so that Dana grew suspicious that the US Marshal might be colluding with the culprits. Two days later, federal marshals arrested the suspected engraver and lithographer and their accomplices and confiscated the plates. On New Year's Day they seized the machinery and dies along with several million dollars in bonds and notes. The rebel agent who had penned the captured dispatches escaped to Havana, but quick action by the War Department had foiled the plot.[9]

The arrests culminated a "delightful" two weeks in New York, although Dana wished it were longer. "My family I found and left in good health, though not well pleased at my long absence," he reported to James Wilson. Dana entertained his son, Paul, with stories about battles and generals. Looking after Grant's interests, a few days after Christmas he checked on a pontoon bridge that was being prepared for shipment via New Orleans to Chattanooga.[10]

There was one final piece of business in New York. On January 4, 1864, Dana appeared before the American Freedmen's Inquiry Commission, a task force organized by Stanton to investigate conditions among newly freed slaves and make recommendations for their welfare. Stanton's appointees, Samuel Gridley Howe, James McKaye, and Robert Dale Owen, were prominent reformers and early supporters of wartime emancipation. For their investigation they visited several cities and contraband camps in the Union-occupied South; at their headquarters in New York they interviewed those knowledgeable about the freedmen's situation. Owen and McKaye sought out Charles Dana, probably at Stanton's urging, because of his travels with Grant's campaigns through Mississippi and Tennessee.[11]

Although it was not strictly part of their mandate, the commissioners were eager to test Grant's antislavery credentials. "You do know, undoubtedly, how Gen. Grant feels on this matter of emancipation?" they probed Dana. "Gen. Grant is an anti-slavery man," he responded; Grant believed "it would be a great crime to end the war without abolishing slavery." Lest they doubt Grant's sincerity, Dana repeated the mantra he had recited after Vicksburg: "He is a natural democrat—the most disinterested, unpretending, truthful man I ever knew." Hearing that Grant might be given charge of all the Union armies, the commissioners segued to his administrative qualities. Dana offered an admiring but frank appraisal. Grant was "an acute judge of men" and had "a wonderful faculty in getting everything done at the right time." His only flaw was that he sometimes held on to "an inefficient man" longer than he should from "mere unwillingness to hurt his feelings."[12]

On the central matter, the future of the former slaves (now free under the Emancipation Proclamation one year earlier) and the South, Dana's responses provided the most succinct and telling expression of his wartime views of slavery and race. Asked by the commissioners how much guardianship the government should exercise over refugee freedmen, Dana was blunt: "Not much. . . . The only interference you want is the interference of laws to prevent their being abused and overworked." The former slaves were frugal and industrious, and they were well counseled by their preachers. At present they would need help to make labor contracts, but before long they would be "able to make their own bargains, and take care of themselves." The most practical plan, Dana and his interviewers agreed, was to lease captured plantations to private parties and protect the refugee laborers who worked them. As all knew, this policy was already being enacted in the Lower Mississippi Valley under regulations adopted by John Eaton, Grant's supervisor of freedmen.[13]

Like many antislavery Northerners, Charles Dana drew a line between former slaves' right to own property and their right to vote. Fearing that the freedmen would be manipulated by whites, he was reluctant to trust them with the vote. In Massachusetts or New York, "I should vote for allowing the negro his political rights as a matter of abstract principle," Dana said, "but if I had to construct the State of Georgia . . . I would not give the negroes suffrage, except with certain [property] qualifications." Dana's predictions about postwar race relations were similarly hedged. He had "not the least doubt" that Southern blacks and whites would coexist in peace once the rebellion was over. At the same time, he acknowledged that most Southern whites had "no idea of abandoning slavery" and asserted that black Union soldiers would be indispensable after the war as a peacekeeping force.

Commissioner Samuel Howe nursed a pet "scientific" theory that predicted the negro race could not survive "the struggle for existence" and would disappear. Dana disagreed. It was "very possible" the race would become a permanent presence south of the Mason-Dixon Line, although "I don't care a copper whether it can or not." This indifference may have surprised his interviewers, but it was consistent with Dana's conviction that ending the rebellion, and preventing its recurrence, was the top priority. Above all, that meant making its white supporters suffer: "I have not the least objection to reducing the [Southern] white people to the most abject poverty. I want to have them punished, and they are punished," Dana told the commissioners. A month earlier, as Dana rode from Knoxville to Chattanooga with General Sherman, they encountered parties of deserting rebel soldiers who "had got enough of it." Dana told his interviewers that Confederate mailbags captured during Grant's Tennessee campaign contained letters from rebel soldiers' desperate wives, one of whom turned to prostitution to feed her children.

The commissioners asked Dana his opinion of the Proclamation of Amnesty and Reconstruction that Lincoln had just issued. It offered a pardon and restored property rights—"except as to slaves"—to most persons who had engaged in the rebellion once they took an oath of allegiance. Dana thought it an "exceedingly judicious" move that balanced the aims of preserving emancipation, excluding rebel ringleaders from amnesty (Confederate government officials and high military officers were not eligible), and encouraging deserters. He had no illusions that Southern states would call off the war, but he believed Lincoln's offer would siphon men from the rebel armies.[14]

Despite a few differences, Dana and the commissioners agreed that freedmen required temporary supervision and guarantees of legal equality, then should be left alone. During the wartime debate over Reconstruction most abolitionists, including Frederick Douglass, concurred. They feared that guardianship of the freedmen might become a form of perpetual subordination, and they noted that apprenticeship programs undertaken in the British West Indies had failed to raise the former slaves' fortunes or crop totals. Only when truly free could Southern blacks prove their mettle: "The tendency of modern society," Dana declared in the language of nineteenth-century liberalism, "is to let every man fight his own way."[15]

The Freedmen's commissioners' final report, issued four months later, endorsed this philosophy. "The sum of our recommendations is this," they wrote. "Offer the freedmen temporary aid and counsel until they become a little accustomed to their new sphere of life; secure to them, by law, their just rights of person and property; relieve them, by a fair and equal administration of justice, from the depressing influence of disgraceful prejudice; above all, guard them against the virtual restoration of slavery in any form, and let them take care of themselves." The report underlay the establishment of the Freedmen's Bureau under the War Department in March 1865. But its agreement with Dana, and most antislavery Northerners, on temporary and limited federal support for the former slaves meant that their genuine liberation would remain an elusive goal.[16]

The Freedmen's commissioners asked Dana when Grant would rid Tennessee of all Confederate troops. He assured them it would happen in the spring. Meanwhile, Dana hinted that a bolder advance elsewhere would be made "as soon as practicable." Still intent on an Alabama campaign, Grant had developed a plan to divide the Confederate West. He envisioned a pincer movement in which separate Union armies from Tennessee and Mobile Bay (after its capture) converged on Atlanta, severing all rail links in their path. On January 10, Dana, after returning to Washington, "had the happiness" of sending Grant authorization "to go ahead according to his own judgment." As soon as East Tennessee was stabilized he could move troops toward Mobile. Grant immediately ordered General John G. Foster (who had replaced Burnside) to move against Longstreet from Knoxville.[17]

In the end, lingering resistance at the capital and logistical problems in Tennessee combined to stymie Grant's plan. Halleck continued to insist that East Tennessee remain Grant's first priority, although freezing temperatures and lack of supplies made a winter push against Longstreet impossible. If Grant must move south, Halleck urged him to help Nathaniel Banks secure northern Louisiana, then head west along the Red River toward Texas. Lincoln and his cabinet were eager to organize Louisiana's occupied government and to make a show of force in Texas against France's new puppet regime in Mexico.[18]

By now familiar with Henry Halleck's obstructionism, Grant mobilized his allies to flank his superior. James Wilson and Baldy Smith wrote strong letters to Dana supporting operations against Mobile and Atlanta, and Dana handed them with his endorsement to Stanton. To open the path toward Mobile, Grant ordered Sherman to strike east of Vicksburg to destroy rail lines and war materiel. Sherman's Meridian Campaign previewed the devastation his march to Atlanta would later cause. Halleck, however, pulled off his own flanking maneuver. When Sherman returned from Meridian he was informed of an order to send 20,000 men across the Mississippi to cooperate with Generals Banks and Frederick Steele. Grant had opposed such a move, and Dana and Wilson, the general's eyes and ears in Washington, wondered where it came from. Dana asked Lincoln, who told him that "no such order or authority ever came from him, and if any one has given it, he did it without consulting *him*." Halleck was apparently the culprit; he had "requested" that Sherman assist Banks and Steele, thereby undermining the Mobile plan in favor of trans-Mississippi operations.[19]

Grant did not have enough troops at hand for all these operations. Itching to move forward somewhere, he ordered General George Thomas to begin a methodical march south along the corridor from Chattanooga toward Atlanta. Dana, who had expended time and energy lobbying for Grant's plan, was deeply disappointed: "Without jeopardizing our interests in any other quarter," he later wrote, "Grant would have opened the Alabama River and captured Mobile" in three months. This would have forced the Confederate army to leave Tennessee, taken Mobile a year before it surrendered, and threatened Atlanta from its vulnerable south, where Sherman ultimately captured it.[20]

As Grant pondered his army's next move, another kind of campaign was gathering force in Washington: a movement to promote him to the head of all the Union armies. Vicksburg and Chattanooga had made Grant a Union hero and raised hopes that he could reverse the dismal record the federal armies had compiled in the eastern theater. Desperate to bring the war to a close, Congress considered promoting Grant to lieutenant general—a rank not awarded since George Washington. Elihu Washburne, Grant's Illinois congressman, introduced a bill in the US House of Representatives in mid-December reviving the rank and expressly recommending Grant for it.

Because Grant was an unknown entity in Washington, his promotion to such an extraordinary post required a supporting campaign. Dana pitched in eagerly. He lodged in the same boarding house with Washburne, and in late January they were joined by James Wilson. The three formed a cabal that kept Grant's momentum going, despite Dana and Wilson's suspicions that Washburne was cleverly riding Grant's coattails to power. Dana worked on two Republican congressmen who were fellow boarders, and Washburne arranged for Dana to talk with several colleagues who had questions about Grant. Would Grant's antislavery credentials satisfy Radical Republicans? Dana assured Henry Wilson, who chaired the Senate Committee on Military Affairs, that Grant was committed to emancipation, just as he had told the Freedmen's commissioners.[21]

There remained other areas of concern: grumblings, as old as Shiloh, about Grant's ability as a commander; suspicions about his drinking habits; and, most important, fear of the new hero's political ambitions. Some opposition came from what James Wilson called "the Rosecranz interests." James Garfield, who had moved from the army to Congress, defended the general he had privately criticized during the Chickamauga Campaign. Resentment also simmered among supporters of the Army of the Potomac, who read the promotion to imply that Grant would succeed where their protégés had failed. Dana offered tactful reassurance. It might be true that the Virginia front was more complex than campaigns in the West, and General Lee was certainly a formidable foe. But Grant was up to the task of choosing the best strategy and the men to lead—and sticking with them until victory.[22]

Virtually every official who consulted Dana asked about Grant's reputed fondness for the bottle. Continuing his cover-up, Dana repeated his asser-tion to the Freedmen's commissioners that Grant "does not drink at all." He and Wilson privately spread word that as long as Grant's watchdog, John Rawlins, accompanied him as chief of staff there would be no chance for Grant to indulge.[23]

Because 1864 was an election year, political considerations carried a great deal of weight in Congress and the White House. Republicans loyal to Lincoln feared that Grant's promotion would create an instant rival for the top of the ticket, or perhaps a strong War Democrat challenger. Grant discreetly relied on intermediaries to assure Lincoln that he harbored no political aspirations. Dana told Stanton and Lincoln that Grant aimed solely to suppress the rebel-lion. He was "not only not a candidate for the presidency, but was in favor of Lincoln's re-election . . . when the time came around."[24]

Dana's tenure at the *Tribune* and his close association with Grant on cam-paign gave his testimony clout. James Wilson was convinced that Dana swayed several senators and reassured the cabinet about Grant. Six months earlier, Grant had thanked Dana for intervening with Washington authori-ties to keep him in the West; now Grant wanted to move eastward, and Dana helped smooth the way.[25]

On February 29, 1864, Congress passed the lieutenant general bill. President Lincoln signed it and designated Grant general in chief of all the Union armies. On March 8, 1864, a tired and disheveled Grant arrived at Willard's Hotel in Washington. That evening he attended a rowdy reception at the White House, where he was introduced to Lincoln and stood on a sofa to avoid being crushed by the curious and admiring crowd. Charles Dana may have been among those present, but he left no report. The next day, Lincoln handed Grant his commission, and the general, wary of politics and uncomfortable with Washington formalities, left immediately for the Virginia front.[26]

The Business of War

Dana stayed behind. Stanton found him an office in the War Department's brick building across the White House lawn at the corner of 17th Street and Pennsylvania Avenue. By January 1864 the department had mushroomed to employ more than five hundred office workers at the capital. Two stories had been added to the building to consolidate the department's bureaus in one place. Dana's third-floor office, one floor above the telegraph room and Stanton's quarters, shielded him from the clamor in Stanton's reception room,

War Department Building, 1860s. From David Homer Bates, *Lincoln in the Telegraph Office* (New York: Century Co., 1907).

where the secretary emerged twice daily to stand behind a tall desk and listen, scowling with impatience, to the business of a horde of callers. The distance required Dana to shuttle up and down frequently to consult with his boss, but the quiet made it worthwhile.[27]

On January 19, 1864, Lincoln signed a bill to appoint Dana as Stanton's second assistant at a salary of $3,000 per year. Days earlier, Dana had begun signing himself "Acting Assistant Secretary" on letters transmitting orders and information. For the following four months, and then from July 1864 to the end of the war as the sole assistant secretary, Dana followed the methodical routine he had developed at Greeley's *Tribune*. He kept regular hours, arriving before nine in the morning and leaving at five in the afternoon. Chronic eye strain from his college days prevented him from working evenings like Stanton, so he "made it a rule never to go away until my desk was cleared." Dana, his friend Wilson recalled, "disposed of one case after another exactly as a competent mason lays bricks. He hardly got one settled in place before he took another in hand." At night Stanton and the bureau chiefs created much of the next day's pile. "And thus it was all day long, week in and week out."[28]

Wilson, who served under Dana in early 1864, believed him "the best administrator I ever met in public office." His work habits were "the admiration of the department," and because Dana was courteous as well as efficient, unlike Stanton, some petitioners sought him out in preference to his boss. Nevertheless, the majority of the applications, complaints, and requests crossing Dana's desk had been sent to Stanton and passed down the chain for fact-finding and resolution. Dana referred inquiries to the proper department; when a response arrived he summarized the case to Stanton along with his own view, sometimes scribbled on the original letter, but often given orally—that way "he would like better because it was shorter." Stanton then issued an order for Dana to transmit or, less frequently, left it to his assistant to render judgment. Dana sent six or seven thousand such letters and telegrams during his fifteen months in the war office.[29]

This crushing workload had broken the health of Dana's predecessor, Christopher Wolcott, who died in January 1863. First Assistant Secretary Peter Watson suffered various illnesses and lingered on through July 1864 because of Stanton's pleas. Stanton himself was forced to take periodic vacations to prevent his frequent illnesses from escalating to complete collapse. But Dana's general vigor, restricted work hours, and habit of taking exercise spared him from physical breakdowns.[30]

It was "a strenuous life," James Wilson recalled, "devoting our whole time and attention to the public service and to the cause of the country. We accepted but few invitations, in fact, none except such as came to us in the way of duty." Wilson exaggerated in hindsight. At the time, he told Grant he had "met quite a number of young ladies" at the capital. His social invitations included dinners at the White House and excursions to the theater with the president and First Lady, command performances frequently reserved for handsome young officers and high-ranking politicians. Dana fit neither category. It is also possible that his private criticism of Mrs. Lincoln's White House extravagances reached the First Lady. Stanton, a workaholic who entertained sporadically at home and attended few political dinners, provided few social opportunities. Still, Dana's social life in Washington was hardly the void that Wilson remembered. Occasional dinner invitations from Seward and Chase helped fill the evenings, while Dana's wide travels and language skills made him a welcome presence at Seward's receptions for foreign dignitaries. On more routine days, political gossip circulated at the table where Dana and several congressmen boarded, and after-dinner drinks and cigars with Wilson, Adam Gurowski, and military officers lubricated the conversation. During off-hours, outings on horseback provided fresh air and relief from desk work. When the day's duties were done, Dana and Wilson would ride out for an hour or two to the capital's defenses. On Sundays they trotted their mounts to the huge Giesboro cavalry depot and its adjoining camp on the Potomac River five miles south of the capital.[31]

The war was all-consuming, however, and even these jaunts were job-related. One of Dana's earliest assignments as assistant secretary was to re-form administration of the Cavalry Bureau. Its first head, crusty General George Stoneman, Dana called an "expensive failure": "Out of twenty-four thousand cavalry horses brought here under his supervision, less than four thousand are reported as effective for service." Looking for fresh energy, Dana wired Grant asking for Wilson and promising to return him in sixty days. Grant agreed.[32]

Wilson discovered that contractors foisted sick or inferior animals on army quartermasters, who were not trained in judging mounts. With Dana's assistance he organized a system of inspection and contract bidding to speed delivery and reduce fraud.[33] The Cavalry Bureau approved the purchase of nearly five hundred horses per day, but some vendors still violated terms or simply defaulted. Dana, determined to make an example, had them brought to Washington for trial by a military commission. In May three top horse suppliers were found guilty of "willful neglect of duty," given substantial fines, and sentenced to prison until they paid.[34] When their political backers protested, Dana and Stanton stood firm. Lincoln, however, proved more lenient, establishing a pattern that continued through the war. With the president's approval, one convicted contractor was set free on bond and another received a presidential pardon after a senator ally interceded. Still, the arrests and convictions frightened contractors enough that, according to Wilson, frauds became the exception and not the rule.[35]

Much time during Dana's first few months in office was taken up with monitoring tests of new weapons and placing orders for approved guns. When an inventor submitted blueprints for a breech-loading cannon, for example, Dana forwarded them to the Ordnance Bureau for assessment. The bureau found the design faulty, and Dana dictated a polite note of explanation to the applicant. Other replies were more laconic. A projectile designed to simultaneously puncture fort walls and hang ladders for invaders was "impractical and useless," Dana told its inventor. It would be "as dangerous to the person using it as to the enemy." Test-firing a breech-loading rifle, Chief of Ordnance George Ramsay narrowly escaped death when a cartridge exploded in the gun. "Naturally somewhat alarmed," Dana informed the inventor's congressional sponsor, Ramsay "declined giving any further trial" of the gun.[36]

As he ordered a shipment of Springfield rifles, Dana explained to the commander of US Colored Troops at Vicksburg that "it has never been the intention of the Department that the colored soldiers should be armed with inferior weapons." At Wilson's request, Dana also arranged for seven-shot Spencer carbines to be adopted as the standard for the cavalry service. Longer versions of these magazine-loading rifles had proven their worth when used by Colonel John Wilder's brigade at Chickamauga. Supply lagged behind demand, however, and not until early 1865 did James Wilson's cavalry division become the first in the world completely supplied with the carbines.[37]

Horses and guns were only a few of the supplies on the gigantic list of War Department purchases. During the first fiscal year of Dana's appointment (from June 1863 to June 1864) the quartermaster's office paid out nearly $285 million, with another $221 million in bills awaiting examination before being paid. "We bought fuel, forage, furniture, coffins, medicine, horses, mules, telegraph wire, sugar, coffee, flour, cloth, caps, guns, powder, and thousands of other things," Dana recalled. To outfit the huge Union army the department purchased "over 3,000,000 pairs of trousers, nearly 5,000,000 flannel shirts and drawers, some 7,000,000 pairs of stockings, 325,000 mess pans, 207,000 camp kettles, over 13,000 drums, and 14,830 fifes." It was Dana's duty to order, examine, or approve contracts for many of these items.[38]

Such enormous expenditures provided countless opportunities for wrongdoing. "If it was the golden hour of patriotism, so was it equally that of greed," a colleague of Dana recalled. "Money was poured by the million . . . into the pockets of scoundrels and robbers, official and otherwise." The scramble for money became a "Carnival of Fraud." Contractors conspired to rig the bidding process, offered bribes to procurement officials, and delivered adulterated or otherwise inferior products. "Shoddy," as cheap fabric made of reprocessed wool was known, became the general term for substandard goods of all kinds, and Northern war profiteers were lambasted by the press as "shoddy millionaires." These included not only Dana's political enemies like Thurlow Weed, who arranged contracts on commission for blankets and shoes, but also his ally Mayor George Opdyke of New York, a ready-made clothier who was a silent partner in three million dollars' worth of clothing contracts that Thomas Carhart signed with the Quartermaster's Bureau in 1862.[39]

Shortly after Dana settled into his Washington office he told Wilson "a secret, which you may tell General Grant and Rawlins": that affairs in the Quartermaster's Bureau were "in a condition of much disorder and frightful waste." In mid-1862 Congress, with Stanton's cooperation, had begun reforming the contracting process, mandating competitive bidding and making contractors suspected of fraud subject to arrest and court-martial. When Dana arrived he strengthened these regulations. All contracts were to be openly advertised for bids, even those lobbied for by members of Congress. The bidding process was expanded by adding dozens of newspapers to the list of those receiving War Department ads. Records of bids arriving and undergoing review had to be detailed enough that the public could be kept informed of possible wrongdoing.[40]

In pitching in to clean up War Department operations, Dana joined a small but hardworking team. His colleagues included Peter Watson, a former patent attorney and longtime Stanton associate who, according to Dana, had "a great knack" for detecting frauds. Colonel Henry S. Olcott had been a *Tribune* reporter before Stanton, at Dana's urging, hired him to investigate recruitment frauds and quartermaster records in Philadelphia and New York.[41] Special Agent Lafayette C. Baker, whom Dana supervised, was a tireless sleuth whose aggressive methods and constant self-promotion aroused resentment. A veteran of the San Francisco Vigilance Committee of 1856, the compact, dark-eyed Baker developed a nose for intrigue and a habit of taking the law into his own hands. His bragging made it difficult, then and now, to sift his real exploits from his pretended heroics. One intelligence scholar called him "a competent detective of questionable character"; other writers believed him corrupt and an inveterate liar. Over time, Stanton and Dana became aware of Baker's dubious methods, but they valued his pro-Union zeal and the information he gathered. By the time Dana became assistant secretary, Baker, given the rank of colonel, directed a detective force of two dozen men that investigated cases of fraud and corruption in contracts as well as suspected disloyalty and conspiracy against the government.[42]

In addition to his staff, Stanton sent military officers on inspection tours and detailed civilian appointees to investigate offices in the field, as Dana had at Cairo. Once suspects were arrested, their cases were investigated by Judge Advocate Levi Turner, who determined charges, trials, and paroles. A former legal associate of Stanton's, Turner was a portly, avuncular man who, in contrast to Baker's bludgeoning, posed as a kindly inquirer to beguile suspects into damaging admissions. This was the War Department's version of the timeworn "good cop, bad cop" routine.[43]

Dana's duties included soliciting reports and information about suspects, deciding whether to move cases forward, and ordering arrests or releases. The Turner-Baker case files in the war office records, which are incomplete, include more than sixty cases in which Dana had a hand. Among the suspects were quartermasters or contractors accused of fraud in providing goods for the army; blockade runners and others sending contraband goods to the South; officers circulating counterfeit currency in Union camps; and army clerks charged with forging discharge papers.[44]

Although talented and conscientious, Stanton's corps of investigative workers was vastly outnumbered by sharpers and profiteers. Adam Gurowski was appalled at how contractors were busily engaged in twisting "into Uncle Sam's belly their big and little screws and drawing greenbacks therefrom. The honest men in the Departments, such as Stanton, Dana, and a few others, vigilant to the utmost as they are, cannot prevent this phlebotomizing." Olcott recalled that each investigator "crowded at least three years' proper work into one year, and some of us four or five." Based upon his examination of several bureaus, Olcott estimated that up to 25 percent of the government's wartime expenditures were tainted with fraud. Stanton's agents could catch only a few fish from the dirty waters, but they hoped that the exposure and arrest of these bottom-feeders would deter imitators.[45]

The department's internal investigations were supplemented by the Joint Committee on the Conduct of the War, the congressional watchdog group dominated by Radical Republicans. Throughout his tenure Stanton cultivated good relations with this committee, a task made easier because the war secretary and the radicals agreed on most wartime priorities, including attacking waste and corruption. Stanton hated bad publicity for his department, but he could get the committee, with its power of subpoena, to undertake investigations the war office could not, and he could use their exposures to discipline contractors or to press Congress for reforms.[46]

Not all of the committee's investigations were welcome. In early 1864 the committee decided to look into supply contracts the War Department had executed concerning shipments of ice to army hospitals. Trial testimony about irregular purchases during court-martial proceedings against Surgeon General William Hammond probably drew the committee's concern. Stanton had been gathering documents for two weeks when he met with members of the joint committee to discuss procedures—a sequence that suggests the war secretary had been tipped off. In this case, unlike those he initiated, Stanton was anxious to have his agents exonerated. He delegated the case to his newly appointed assistant secretary.[47]

The committee's suspicions centered on a sizeable contract that David L. Magruder, an army medical purveyor at Louisville, had recently signed with J. W. Parrish and Company of St. Louis to provide ice for all US hospitals from Chicago to New Orleans at seemingly inflated rates. After researching market prices, interrogating Parrish and Magruder, and examining the contract, Dana found no evidence of fraud or dishonesty. Given the terms set by the surgeon general's office, Parrish's bid compared favorably with others. The contract was confirmed after more precise wording about compliance was inserted.[48] At the committee's hearings in February, Dana's evaluation of the Parrish deal was inserted into the record. It convinced the committee that no fraud had been committed but also that minor reforms were needed to cut expenses. Thanks to Dana's footwork, Stanton's office emerged unbruised.[49]

Most fraud investigations were performed inside the War Department, where publicity could be controlled and arrests made at once. Even then, officials had to fend off appeals from accused wrongdoers, their influential supporters, and sometimes President Lincoln. Dana's colleague Peter Watson discovered an extensive fraud in forage furnished to the Army of the Potomac. The government purchased a mixture of oats and corn to feed army horses and mules, but by changing the proportions contractors could enhance their profits. Watson arrested those directly involved. Later, when Watson was away on assignment, the president of Philadelphia's corn exchange and his merchant colleagues called on Dana with a thinly disguised proposition. They wrote a check for $33,000 to cover the amount one confessed swindler had taken, plus $32,000 for damages from another. Then they demanded that both prisoners be released and their confiscated papers returned. Dana refused and alerted Watson by telegraph.[50]

The grain merchants' powerful political friends set to work. The former senator David Wilmot of Pennsylvania met with Lincoln and accompanied him to the War Department. While Wilmot waited outside, Watson explained the fraud's gravity to Lincoln and the need for a trial, preferably by military commission. The president reminded Watson that much of the money had been refunded and that Pennsylvania's support was crucial to the war effort, but Watson would release the men only if the president ordered it in writing. Checkmated, Lincoln left the room and told Wilmot he couldn't "do anything with Watson." Dana heard Wilmot curse in reply, but the war office's decision stood.[51]

In addition to contracts and fraud, complaints from military officers about their treatment compelled Dana's attention. One case involving discrimination against a black officer had wide reverberations. In 1863 Dr. Alexander T. Augusta, who received his medical training in Toronto, became the first African American medical officer in the Union army. Given the rank of major, he was assigned as chief surgeon of the Contraband Camp hospital outside Washington. On his way to testifying in court, Augusta was delayed because a street railway driver would not allow him aboard. Dana took up

Augusta's cause. He collected the relevant documents, obtained a statement from Augusta, and forwarded them to Senator Charles Sumner, who had introduced antidiscrimination amendments regarding Washington street railway companies. Sumner read Augusta's complaint into the *Congressional Globe* and called for the District of Columbia Committee to investigate. The committee at first resisted proposing new legislation, but in March 1865 Congress passed a law prohibiting the exclusion of persons on account of color from streetcars in the capital.[52]

Another appeal came to Dana from a group of black contrabands jailed in Maryland. Slavery was abolished by Congress in the District of Columbia in April 1862, but Lincoln's Emancipation Proclamation nine months later exempted the loyal slave states, including neighboring Maryland. As a result, thousands of Maryland slaves fled to the nation's capital, despite resistance from local slave owners. In the case referred to Dana, three former slaves who were federal employees in the District of Columbia procured military passes to retrieve their families from southern Maryland. On their way to the capital, family members were arrested by a local constable and put in chains. When their case reached Dana's desk in June 1864 he ordered the local Union commander to secure their release, overriding the refusal of Maryland's governor to cooperate.[53]

Among the press of supplicants to Dana's office, in person or by letter, were many others requesting permission to enter military zones. These included anxious relatives of wounded soldiers, congressmen visiting home-state brigades, agents of charities, observers from foreign governments, and newspaper reporters. Newspapers were a special concern to Dana, who understood firsthand their influence on public opinion. Under Stanton and Dana the War Department pursued a course that reduced corruption in awarding publishing contracts but still practiced political scorekeeping. Dana ended the disorganized distribution of advertisements for procurement and positions by drafting regulations that included obtaining authorized signatures, providing copies to the assistant secretary, and using all officially recognized local newspapers. At the same time, Dana was not above striking newspapers from the advertiser list if they "abused" the Lincoln administration.[54]

He also took politics into consideration when issuing passes for special correspondents. After the war Dana admitted that he had routinely denied the *New York World*'s reporters passes to the front because their paper was "notoriously treasonous and disloyal." In November 1864 the paper's editor, Manton Marble, appealed to Dana for assistance when one of his reporters was taken prisoner by Confederates. Dana shed crocodile tears, offering the consolation that reporters from a disloyal Northern paper "ought not to be treated with uncommon severity by the rebel authorities." When Marble asked to have another correspondent accredited to Sherman's army, Dana again refused, explaining that the war office did "not consider that paper a proper one to receive such facilities."[55]

Reporters who were denied access or impatient with bureaucracy sometimes tried to forge Dana's signature on passes, but this tactic risked imprisonment. In early 1864 one camp hanger-on was arrested in Tennessee for presenting forged endorsements from Dana certifying him as an Associated Press reporter. General Grant had the imposter released but ordered him not to return to Union lines except as a soldier.[56]

As this case suggests, the final word on passes belonged to Union military commanders. In March 1864 the representative of a Philadelphia charity came to Dana's office seeking permission to take supplies into East Tennessee to relieve Quaker residents who were caught between Union and Confederate armies. Dana, who had firsthand knowledge of Tennessee's beleaguered Unionists, wrote out the necessary passes and sent a letter to Grant urging free transport for charity workers and supplies on government railroads. Grant forwarded the letter to General Sherman, whom he had left in command at Nashville.

Not long afterward, a lengthy reply from Sherman arrived at Dana's desk. Pretending to engage in "a casual conversation, such as we indulged in by the camp fire or as we jogged along by the road" in Tennessee, Sherman lectured Dana on the harsh arithmetic of civil war. As things stood, Sherman told Dana, there were not enough railroad cars to provision his army and prepare it for an offensive into Georgia. At least a hundred worthy citizens presented claims every day to go to the front. Each person taken on a train took the place of two hundred pounds of powder for guns, bread for soldiers, or oats for mules and horses. Sherman gave a pass to the Philadelphian but not his supplies; he "could not promise to feed the suffering Quakers at the expense of our army." "In peace," Sherman perorated, "there is a beautiful harmony in all the departments of life—they all fit together like the Chinese puzzle; but in war all is ajar. . . . [I]t is the struggle between the stronger and the weaker; and the latter, however it may appeal to the better feelings of our nature, must kick the beam. To make war we must and will harden our hearts."[57]

Sherman's respectful but firm reprimand was one of the few wartime letters Dana saved. No doubt he retrieved it from his drawer to answer future applicants for passes. The humanitarian Dana of Brook Farm days might have rejected its brutal logic, but not the War Department agent who had been hardened by several months at the front. The longer the war dragged on, the more Dana adopted Sherman's view of its stern realities.[58]

Stanton, Lincoln, and the War Cabinet

Dana's new position as assistant secretary put him in frequent touch with cabinet leaders and the president and in daily contact with Stanton. Few envied him the latter ordeal. Stanton was notorious for his abrupt manner, suspicious nature, and violent temper. His foes found him an intolerable brute; even his allies, such as Senator Henry Wilson of Military Affairs, described him as "brusque in manner and curt in speech, even to those in whose loyalty . . . he had all confidence." Lincoln's secretary John Hay declared he "would rather make the tour of a small-pox hospital" than be sent to ask Stanton for a favor. When James Wilson, newly appointed to the Cavalry Bureau, presented himself at Stanton's office he was met with a suspicious scowl. "He was rough, overbearing, and outrageous to his inferiors," Wilson learned, and "negligent and contemptuous toward his equals." In retrospect, Wilson believed Dana would have made a better war secretary than Stanton. He was "much better qualified by actual contact with the army and its leading officers, by business experience and natural capacity, as well as by conviction, sanity of temper, and method." Dana told Wilson that Stanton could have become president had he been able to practice common courtesy.[59]

Looking back after the war, Dana sketched a concise portrait of Stanton. He was five foot seven, broad-shouldered and increasingly burly, with Socratic features and a solid frame. Stanton's ordinary expression was grave, but his smile—for children and others fortunate enough to see it—was "exceedingly sweet and tender" and his eyes twinkled in agreement. "Impulsive, warm-blooded, very quick in execution," Stanton was "sometimes harsh and imperious" and "not always infallible in judgment" because his nerves overheated his imagination. Stanton aimed above all "to carry the war efficiently forward to a victorious conclusion. . . . Whoever was not for prosecuting the war most vigorously . . . might be certain to have Mr. Stanton for a critic and an antagonist." In his righteous single-mindedness, Stanton reminded Dana of no one more than Oliver Cromwell.[60]

Unlike most associates, Dana enjoyed friendly relations with Stanton. Stories of Stanton's violent temper, he claimed, were exaggerated: "If Stanton liked a man, he was always pleasant." This was an exacting "if," but Dana evidently met its requirements. Like Stanton, Dana was pragmatic and unsentimental; he focused his energies on winning the war and subordinated all else to that goal. Hardworking, intelligent, and efficient, he was Stanton's ideal assistant. Dana was decisive, possessing (in Senator Wilson's words) "great executive force." He was also durable. Stanton, desperate for men who could handle the heavy department workload, did what he could to keep Dana in his employ, including giving him field assignments, which he knew Dana enjoyed, and holiday leaves more generous than his own.[61]

James Wilson noticed that Dana "was one of the few men in office who did not seem to fear" Stanton. Their similar age helped to equalize relations—Stanton was forty-nine in 1864, Dana forty-four—as did Dana's wider travels and learning, which Stanton respected. As for coping with Stanton's temper, as the *Tribune*'s number-two man Dana had learned to calibrate Greeley's outbursts and handle him with tact, asserting his own opinions while respecting lines of authority. Dana's long-honed skill of exerting influence without upstaging his superiors was surely a key to his compatibility with Stanton.[62]

Long after the war, Dana could recall only one instance when Stanton spoke to him harshly. Myer Strouse, a Democratic congressman from Pennsylvania, had a Virginia friend who wished to leave the Confederacy. Wartime regulations required that his money be confiscated and placed in a Treasury account. Later, Strouse and his associate came to the War Department to demand the money back. Stanton refused, but when pressed he turned the case over to Dana. When Stanton learned that Dana had returned the funds, he exploded: "Did you give that Jew back his money?" he confronted Dana. "I should like to know by what authority you did it." Dana showed his signed instructions to Stanton, who then conceded his mistake.[63]

The intense and humorless Stanton stood at opposite temperamental poles from Lincoln, who was always reminded of a story. In the beginning, Dana wrote, "there was no extraordinary sympathy" between Lincoln and Stanton. "The determined manners and uncompromising earnestness of the Secretary were not attractive to the gentler and more variable nature of the President." But Lincoln's unease wore off, and "though their actions sometimes clashed, and the Secretary did not always yield with grace, . . . relations between them ripened into a warm friendship." Dana attributed this to their "overpowering" interest in Union victory and shared commitment to emancipation. Experiencing the two men's differences firsthand, Dana admired Stanton's zeal and strong personality—so much like his own—but he enjoyed the president's human touch.[64]

In early 1864, during his first winter in the War Department, Dana "had constant opportunities of seeing Mr. Lincoln, and of conversing with him in the cordial and unofficial manner which he always preferred." Lincoln stopped by Dana's office on his frequent visits to the War Department, sometimes accompanied by his son Tad. His humility impressed the assistant secretary. "He never posed, or put on airs, or attempted to make any particular impression." The president's humor also delighted Dana. "His first disposition was to see the funny aspect in anything." You "never saw him but that he would come up and put his arm through yours and go on telling a joke," Dana recalled. "His smile was something most lovely," Dana wrote, and it lit up his face when something amused him. Lincoln's stories and jokes, never unkind, were a salve for the "natural gloom of a melancholy and desponding temperament." And they often expressed a profound point, describing in homespun terms the dilemmas of government decision-making and the foibles of friends or foes.[65]

Angular but not awkward, Lincoln moved slowly but displayed agility when necessary. "The great quality of his appearance was benevolence . . . the wish to do somebody good if he could," Dana recalled. This "philanthropy" was tempered by "solid, hard, keen intelligence." Above all, Dana was impressed by Lincoln's ability to see all sides of a question, then delve beneath appearances to reach the key underlying issue. Unlike politicians committed to fixed positions, misled by theories, or blinded by personal ambition, Lincoln "was the least faulty in his conclusions of any man that I have ever known." Dana cited the Emancipation Proclamation to suggest that Lincoln's timing was politically pitch-perfect. Pressured by abolitionists on one side and conservatives on the other, the president waited to free Southern slaves until Northern opinion was ripe and Kentucky secure. To Dana this "unerring judgment, this patience which waited and knew when the right time had arrived," was the mark of a supreme politician.[66]

Once installed at his desk, Dana engaged in frequent exchanges with Lincoln on war business. Some early correspondence centered on the military implications of loyalty oaths. Did the restored rights of former Confederates under the Proclamation of Amnesty and Reconstruction include the right to become Union army officers? In January 1864 two captains in the Confederate army who deserted asked to be named captains of a Union company they organized in Arkansas. After consulting with General in Chief Halleck, Dana informed Lincoln that the terms of the amnesty proclamation excluded such men. A similar case arose in Tennessee, where Governor Andrew Johnson stepped up recruiting after Union troops occupied the state. A Tennessean named Richard Edwards, who had previously served in the state's Confederate legislature, raised a Union volunteer cavalry regiment and was appointed its colonel. Lincoln sent his appeal to Stanton with an endorsement: "On principle I dislike an oath which requires a man to swear that he has not done wrong. . . . I think it is enough if the man does no wrong hereafter." Stanton, as usual, took a tougher line. "I am directed to say," Dana wrote to Lincoln, "that the oath to which Colonel Edwards objects is verbally the same" as that required of all Union military officers. Edwards was replaced as commanding officer of the 4th Tennessee.[67]

Dana's appointment as assistant secretary of war in 1864 coincided with the opening of an election year, and immediately he began passing to Lincoln information from his party contacts in New York. When the city's Republican Central Committee endorsed Lincoln's renomination, Dana received the news by wire and showed it to Lincoln. A New York insider reported that Secretary Seward and Thurlow Weed planned to put up General Banks for the nomination. Dana sent the note by messenger to Lincoln, asking him to "please burn [it] after reading"—a request Lincoln failed to honor. Throughout the spring Lincoln consulted Dana when political problems arose among New York Republicans, and even between party factions in Pennsylvania.[68]

Apart from transmitting official correspondence and political scuttlebutt, Dana was in a position to perform many small favors for the president. "Will Mr. Dana please see and hear this man and do the best for him he can?" Lincoln scribbled on a typical note. The president had visited a wounded soldier at a Washington hospital and promised to give him an appointment if he recovered. Dana found the veteran a job as a clerk in the pay department. In another case, Lincoln endorsed a request that "an old personal friend & most worthy gentleman" be transferred from the battle zone for health reasons. Dana ordered the man to report to Washington and sit in judgment on courts-martial.[69]

Such requests multiplied as Dana saw Lincoln more frequently. Meanwhile, in February Dana surprised Lincoln by asking for a huge favor of his own: an appointment as customs collector for the Port of New York. Dana had learned from administration insiders that the incumbent, Secretary Chase's friend Hiram Barney, was under fire from all sides. Barney disappointed Radical Republicans by allowing the Seward-Weed faction to control the custom house operations, while the Seward-Weed forces damned him as a Chase-for-president man. Both groups gained ammunition when Barney's subordinates were accused of abetting dealings in contraband goods. Hearing that Barney might have to go, Dana sent Lincoln a carefully worded expression of interest: "I do not ask for this office," he began coyly, "but . . . if you wish to give it to me I should be glad of it." On his own behalf Dana claimed that "there is no man whose appointment would be more likely to please the radicals without offending the conservatives." He pledged to administer patronage according to Lincoln's needs. Dana had mentioned the subject to no one but Stanton, who gave it "no encouragement." He closed by assuring Lincoln that he had "no expectations, nor to say the truth, any great desire" for the position, so he would not be "exposed to disappointment or regret."[70]

The letter's hesitant wording and defeatist tone, so out of character, indicate that Dana knew his case was a long shot. He had become closely identified with Radical Republicans, and his appointment would enrage the Seward-Weed faction. George Opdyke told Chase that the New York radicals opposed dismissing Barney unless someone like Dana could secure the appointment, but "this is supposed to be impracticable." Chase thought so, too. If Barney was to go, Chase and Horace Greeley agreed to support an elder statesman for the post, Daniel S. Dickinson, a War Democrat and former US senator. Even if Lincoln had considered appointing Dana, Stanton would never agree to letting loose so valuable an assistant.[71]

Why, then, did Dana toss his hat in the ring? Money and power were the obvious inducements. Dana's war office salary was much lower than his former *Tribune* earnings, and he kept his eye out for more lucrative opportunities. The New York collectorship was the biggest plum the administration had to offer. Officially the collector's position earned slightly more than $25,000 per year in salary and fees—itself a princely sum—but unofficially Barney grossed $83,600 in 1863, much of it through emoluments from importers or their agents. Wielding control over nearly twelve hundred patronage posts, its incumbent was a powerful party broker with influence over nominations for local and national office. Unlike his mentor Greeley, Dana never longed for elective office, but he harbored a lifelong craving for the fat salary and behind-the-scenes power of the customs collectorship.[72]

There is no record of Lincoln's response. He may have communicated it verbally or let the matter drop quietly. In any case, Lincoln put off dismissing Barney due to Chase's strong opposition. After Chase resigned from the cabinet in June 1864 over another patronage dispute, Lincoln appointed Simeon Draper, a New York merchant and an intimate of Seward and Weed, to the post. Dana nursed no injured feelings and his relation with Lincoln remained warm.

Dana's work at the war office brought him into frequent contact with Lincoln's other cabinet members. In later years he appraised them succinctly and more appreciatively than he had in the friction of war. Secretary of State

President Lincoln and his cabinet adopting the Emancipation Proclamation, September 22, 1862. *Left to right*: Lincoln, Gideon Welles, Salmon P. Chase, Montgomery Blair, William H. Seward, Caleb B. Smith, Edward Bates, and Edwin M. Stanton. Lithograph by Currier & Ives, c. 1876. Library of Congress, Prints and Photographs Division.

Seward, a slight, somewhat stooped man with a beak nose and a shock of gray hair, was an incessant cigar-smoker like General Grant but much more cosmopolitan. Seward had "the most cultivated and comprehensive intellect" in the cabinet, Dana recalled. His skill of "rowing one way and looking another" kept Dana and other radicals off guard, making them fret constantly that he would conciliate the Rebels. Over time, Dana came to appreciate Seward's habit of "indirection" as a way of steering the administration's ship between politically risky extremes while controversial wartime measures like emancipation took hold. Above all, Secretary Seward was a shrewd and forceful orchestrator of Union foreign relations. He faced crisis after crisis "without suffering his feelings to sway his judgment, in beating off the hostile powers eager to pounce upon us." Seward's management of diplomacy "gave us quiet abroad when all our energies were needed at home," Dana later recalled.[73]

Although Seward and his patron Weed kept up their contest for control of New York's Republican machine with the radicals, Dana maintained good relations with the secretary of state. He took no part in the backroom maneuverings of Greeley, Opdyke, and David Dudley Field to have Seward dropped from the cabinet. For his part, Seward remained a genial warrior: although he spent "all his life in controversies," Dana noticed, Seward had "very few personal animosities." Cordial relations between Dana and Seward made practical sense, as they were devoted to the administration's success and could assist each other in their appointed realms. Dana was Seward's main contact in the War Department for matters involving visitors from abroad, foreign volunteers in the Union army, overseas Americans, and information about Confederate sabotage schemes based in Canada, which threatened to disrupt US relations with Great Britain. Meanwhile, Dana was frequently sent by Stanton to Seward's office to convey news or to consult on policy matters. Their positions allowed them to exchange favors, and each found jobs for friends recommended by the other. Dana attended occasional dinners and receptions at Seward's house, where he enjoyed the secretary's urbane wit. "As a companion no one could be more charming," Dana recalled in Seward's 1872 obituary. Seward's humor was dry and biting, and his conversation was "rich with the fruits of reading and of shrewd observation in every sphere of life."[74]

Seward's worldly ease made quite a contrast with the proper, even priggish Treasury secretary, Salmon Chase. Tall and portly, with a large and handsome head, Chase cut an impressive figure. In later years Dana remembered him as "an able, noble, and spotless statesman, a man who would have been worthy of the best days of the old Roman republic." During the war Dana became a frequent guest at the Washington townhouse where Chase and his daughter resided. As was common between political allies, friendship became entwined with business. Dana used his position to procure an honorable discharge for Chase's mentally ill nephew; after the war, Dana tried to recruit Chase as an investor in his newspaper startup.[75]

Despite their friendship, Dana remained well aware of Chase's faults. Behind his correct and formal bearing the secretary was ruled by vanity and an overweening ambition he could never acknowledge. At one dinner in 1864 Chase boasted to Dana that he had single-handedly written the National Banking Act, which "will be a blessing to the country long after I am dead." Highly susceptible to flattery, Chase was obtuse in his judgments of subordinates who supported his political ambitions. At Washington and in the regional customs houses, professedly loyal Chase appointees aggrandized themselves through bribes, embezzling, or involvement in contraband trade. "Of all the eminent men in my acquaintance," Dana wrote a friend, "no one has ever been so unlucky in appointments. Himself a man of strict honesty, he has succeeded in putting into places of importance some of the biggest scamps . . . the country has ever produced."[76]

From his post inside the administration Chase ran a not-so-secret campaign to upstage Lincoln for the 1864 Republican nomination. Dana, despite his radical views, refused to support the insurgency. After a private document distributed by the hard-line Kansas senator Samuel Pomeroy denouncing Lincoln and endorsing Chase became public in February 1864, Chase's boomlet busted. Chase wrote to Lincoln denying any involvement in Pomeroy's circular and asked Ohio friends to withdraw his name from consideration.[77]

The triumvirate of Stanton, Seward, and Chase dominated cabinet discussions, but Dana later recalled others who played supporting roles. Attorney General Edward Bates, the elder Missourian who had been Greeley's favorite candidate for president in 1860, proved to be a skilled but quiet lawyer and adviser. Dana remembered him as a gentle man who occasionally waxed eloquent when an issue aroused him but who otherwise kept in the background. Navy Secretary Gideon Welles, who wore a wig that Dana said made him look like a dour old deacon, was a critical and somewhat suspicious cabinet presence, but he was a hardworking and efficient organizer of his own department. Finally, there was Postmaster General Montgomery Blair, scion of an influential political family and the outspoken voice of conservative Republicans. Shrewd and "a little cranky," Blair was a habitual enemy of Stanton and the radicals, and he eventually tired of Stanton's rude treatment. Whenever he had business at the War Department he approached Dana first.[78]

It was, Dana recalled, a patchwork cabinet, "an incongruous mosaic" composed of fiercely independent men, several of whom had competed with Lincoln for the nomination in 1860. Not all of its members acted as predicted, Dana noted: Blair and Bates quickly betrayed the radicals who had lobbied to get them appointed, while Stanton's predecessor Simon Cameron ended up urging the arming of black soldiers. Cabinet debates often divided into two factions, one headed by Seward and the other by Chase or Stanton. But Dana had no doubt who was in charge. Relations between Lincoln and the members of the cabinet were "perfectly cordial always and unaffected," he recalled. "He treated every one of them with unvarying candor, respect, and kindness." Yet "though there was nothing of selfhood or domination in his manner toward them, it was always plain that he was the master and they the subordinates." They yielded to Lincoln's will when the final decision rested with him, and "if he ever yielded to theirs it was because they convinced him that the course they advised was judicious and appropriate."[79]

In the gauzy retrospect of old age, Dana styled President Lincoln an unflappable cabinet chief: "I fancied during the whole time of my intimate intercourse with him . . . that he was always perfectly prepared to receive the resignation of any one of them." Dana's recollections of Lincoln two decades later tended to sooth wartime distresses with the balm of hindsight. In the spring of 1864, as the war dragged into its fourth year and a massive Union military campaign in Virginia coincided with presidential canvassing, the serene Lincoln that Charles Dana later remembered was in actuality hounded by opponents within his own party and was desperate to defeat Robert E. Lee's Army of Northern Virginia.[80]

12 "A Hand on Lee's Throat"

With Ulysses Grant's promotion to lieutenant general and appointment as commander of all Union armies, the patchwork command structure that had confused relations between Washington and the battlefront was reorganized. The former general in chief Henry Halleck stayed on as chief of staff under Grant, coordinating communications, overseeing the army's moves, and offering advice to war leaders. In his new post Grant directed the armies' grand strategy and campaigns, but he planned to move to the Virginia front and transmit orders to General Halleck at the capital. Charles Dana, never fond of the naysaying Halleck, believed his knowledge of "the technics of armies and of war" compensated for his innate caution and his "habit of picking men and manners to pieces to see what they were worth."[1]

Grant Takes Charge

Although Grant relocated to Virginia, the Army of the Potomac remained under George Meade's direction. An aristocratic Philadelphian, Meade was described by Grant's secretary Adam Badeau as "tall, restless, angular, with piercing eye, aquiline nose, rapid gait, and nervous manner." Proud and high-strung, Meade was quick to take offense and even quicker to give it. Dana found him "agreeable to talk with when his mind was free" but "totally lacking in cordiality toward those with whom he had business." As soon as Grant was put over Meade, Dana and James Wilson opened a private campaign to get Meade dismissed. Dana harped on Meade's failure to pursue Robert E. Lee's defeated Army of Northern Virginia after Gettysburg, which was under investigation by the Joint Committee on the Conduct of the War, and his retreat from Lee's army at Mine Run in December 1863, which made a sorry contrast with Grant's success at Chattanooga. Meade seemed to "lack the boldness that was necessary to bring the war to a close." "Mr Dana and I have had a long talk," Wilson wrote Baldy Smith in mid-February 1864, "and conclude that Meade is not fully nor nearly equal to the occasion."[2]

Dana again pushed for Baldy Smith as the new commander. He remained impressed with Smith's engineering feats at Chattanooga, although he knew of his unsoldierly habit of criticizing superiors over their heads. Grant also knew that Smith was "likely to condemn whatever is not suggested by himself" but still considered him "one of the most efficient officers in service, readiest in expedients and most skillful in the management of troops in action." Smith's prospects brightened with Grant's appointment and Dana and Wilson's lobbying, and he followed Grant to Virginia anticipating an independent command. But when Grant interviewed Meade in March he was pleasantly surprised. Agreeably self-effacing, Meade offered to serve wherever Grant wanted him. Meade's familiarity with the Army of the Potomac and its soldiers' loyalty to him would be indispensable to the transplanted western commander. Cyrus Comstock, Grant's chief engineer, summed up the situation tersely: "Grant, who at Chattanooga thought Baldy Smith should have it—now says no change."[3]

Grant, headquartered just a few miles from Meade, would nevertheless closely oversee the Army of the Potomac's operations, issuing the important orders and leaving details of implementation to his subordinate. The arrangement threatened to produce tensions between Grant and Meade, but Dana allowed that it might work out. Grant was calm and tactful while Meade, though curt and irascible, "had the first virtue of a soldier . . . obedience to orders." Having a fighting commander over him might check Meade's tendency to hesitate in the field, Dana hoped.[4]

Grant's decision on Meade demonstrated that he preferred continuity and had no dramatic personnel changes in mind. In the Military Division of the Mississippi, William T. Sherman was elevated to chief and James McPherson was put in charge of Sherman's old Army of the Tennessee. In the eastern theater there were fewer face cards, but Grant tried to win with the hand he was dealt. Generals Franz Sigel and Benjamin Butler owed their commissions to political influence, and Butler had still not commanded soldiers in battle; Grant trusted that able subordinates would carry them along. He made Baldy Smith one of those subordinates by giving him a corps in Butler's Army of the James. He brought Philip Sheridan from the western armies to lead the Army of the Potomac's Cavalry Corps, and Dana's friend James Wilson was called back from the Cavalry Bureau and assigned to a mounted division under Sheridan.

These moves and others required consultations with Lincoln, Congress, and the War Department. As the spring offensive drew near, Dana shuttled between Washington and Grant's headquarters as war officials considered field and staff assignments and senators required lobbying to confirm appointments.[5] At Vicksburg Dana had found Grant's entourage deficient; changes were necessary to add expertise, especially because Grant's duties had expanded. One mainstay was John Rawlins, whose blunt advice Grant considered indispensable. Dana worried that Rawlins's tubercular disease was worsening: "His loss would be a great misfortune, not only for his friends, but still more for the country," he told Wilson. Grant intervened directly in April 1864 when the Senate held up Rawlins's promotion to brigadier general. Grant then supplemented his staff by appointing young West Pointers with field experience. To complement Comstock he added two engineers, Orville Babcock, who had served under Ambrose Burnside, and Horace Porter, who had been ordnance chief for both George McClellan and William Rosecrans. Dana, familiar with both men from the campaign in Tennessee, pushed for their approval at the War Department. Together with Wilson's friend Badeau, who was named one of Grant's private secretaries, the newcomers added efficiency and decorum to Grant's circle.[6]

Taking charge of Union strategy, Grant planned to enact at last the coordinated advances that President Lincoln had pressed upon previous commanders. Sherman was directed to move toward Atlanta against Joseph Johnston's rebel army, seize the city, then devastate the Southern interior. In the eastern theater, three armies would cooperate in the push toward Richmond. The massive Army of the Potomac—about 115,000 strong—would move south from its camp near Warrenton, Virginia, to stalk the 64,000 men of Lee's Army of Northern Virginia. "Lee's army will be your objective point," Grant wrote succinctly to Meade. "Wherever Lee goes there you will go also." Meanwhile, Sigel would take over the Union forces in West Virginia and push southward through the Shenandoah Valley to prevent its resources and soldiers from coming to Lee's aid and to guard against a Confederate thrust toward Washington. Finally, in a move reminiscent of George McClellan's Peninsula Campaign, Butler was to advance his force of 30,000 men up the James River from Fortress Monroe to cut off Richmond's lines of supply from the south and threaten the capital itself. By pressuring Lee's army from several directions Grant hoped to force him into open combat as Lee moved his defenses or retreated to protect his supply lines and Richmond.[7]

In the weeks before opening the campaign Grant moved swiftly to concentrate troops. He yanked thousands of soldiers from their quarters inside Washington's elaborate fortifications. Commanders of all Northern depart-ments were told to strip their forces as much as possible and send the sur-plus to the capital for assignment. After Dana returned from a trip to Grant's headquarters in late April, Stanton redirected him west, armed with powers to move soldiers "forcibly if necessary" to the front. He was able to pry loose five Indiana regiments totaling 5,500 men, dividing them between infantry and cavalry according to the availability of horses, and sent them to Nashville for forwarding.[8]

On the night of May 4, shortly after Dana returned to Washington, the com-bined forces of the Army of the Potomac and Burnside's IX Corps began their advance against Lee. Crossing the Rapidan River, Grant's men took up posi-tions across two routes that ran through the thick scrub forest known as the Wilderness. Lee, who exactly a year earlier had humiliated General Joseph Hooker there in the Battle of Chancellorsville, sent an advance guard to meet the Federals. When Grant ordered an attack on May 5, two days of vicious fighting broke out in woods so thick and smoky that soldiers fired blindly, whole brigades got lost, and scores of wounded men burned to death in the flaming underbrush.

Both days passed ominously back in Washington without word from the front as an anxious Lincoln and a testy Stanton awaited dispatches in the War Department telegraph office. Lincoln joked gamely with visitors about the taciturn Grant, but black rings under his eyes revealed his strain. The first glimmer of news arrived on Friday evening, May 6—a telegram from Virginia to Assistant Secretary Charles Dana. Henry Wing, a young reporter for the *New York Tribune*, had left Grant's army at four that morning and scratched his way through Confederate territory to a federal post twenty miles from Washington. Eager to file the first report from the Wilderness, Wing learned that only military messages could be sent over the wires and thought of appealing to Dana to get his story forwarded to New York. Dana, however, was at a reception at Secretary Seward's house and did not receive Wing's wire. Instead, Stanton sent Wing a curt reply demanding the news, and when Wing insisted that he first send his story to the *Tribune* the secretary threat-ened to arrest him. At this point Lincoln, on vigil at the telegraph office, in-tervened and accepted Wing's proposal. Wing's brief dispatch, filed at 9 P.M., was vague and inconclusive. The Union had fought a tremendous battle and suffered no disaster; the fighting was still going on and might produce a clear victory if Meade threw in all his troops.[9]

Lincoln and Stanton, dissatisfied with this sketchy report and made uneasy by Grant's silence, decided to send Dana once more as "the government's eyes at the front." Dana eagerly volunteered, brushing aside their concerns for his safety. Around midnight he boarded a train at the Maryland Avenue depot that took him to Alexandria, where a special train was readied with a cavalry escort of a hundred men. By seven the next morning, May 7, Dana reached the Union army's rear guard on the Rappahannock River. Leaving behind a telegraph operator, he wired Stanton that the Battle of the Wilderness was "believed here to be indecisive," then headed south toward Grant's camp. En route Dana stopped at Meade's headquarters, where the general's Boston Brahmin aide, Theodore Lyman, sized him up tartly as "a large man, a combination of scholar and newspaper editor, with a dab of amiability, a large dab of conceit, and another large dab of ultraism." With the last term Lyman associated Dana with Stanton and other Radical Republicans who had pushed to end slavery and pressed for a harder war.[10]

Arriving at Grant's quarters near the Orange Plank Road in mid-afternoon on May 7, Dana was "in fine spirits," according to James Wilson. From Grant and his staff Dana learned about the desperate fighting in the Wilderness the two previous days. The Union artillery was neutralized by the dense forest, but the infantry had fought bravely, repulsing attacks on both flanks. General James Wadsworth, the patrician Democrat whom Dana had backed for New York governor in 1862, had been fatally wounded in James Longstreet's counterattack on May 6, and Longstreet himself had been shot by his own men in the confusion (Longstreet recovered and returned to the army six months later). Dana estimated Union casualties at 12,000; in actuality they totaled 17,000 against about 11,000 Confederates. Lee had used the thickly wooded terrain to offset Grant's superior numbers. Still, the battle appeared to be a draw: Grant reported to Washington that "we can claim no victory over the enemy, neither have they gained a decisive advantage."[11]

What happened after the battle, Dana realized, was more important than the fighting. In the past, bloody encounters with Lee's army had sent Union generals reeling northward toward Washington. This time, Grant ordered a movement south and east toward Spotsylvania Courthouse. When the weary Union veterans marched back from the front lines on the morning of May 8 and were told to turn right instead of left, they let out cheers that resounded as Grant and Meade passed by on their horses. Dana reported that they were in "the highest pitch of animation" and they took up his old *Tribune* cry of "On to Richmond!" The news heartened Lincoln and Stanton, confirming young Henry Wing's message from Grant that "there would be no turning back."[12]

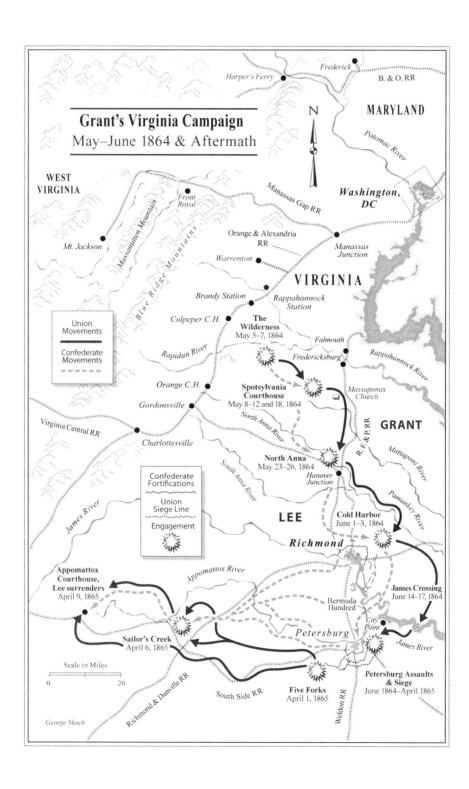

Grant's Virginia Campaign
May–June 1864 & Aftermath

N

MARYLAND

Frederick

Harper's Ferry

B. & O. RR

Potomac River

Washington, DC

WEST VIRGINIA

Front Royal

Manassas Gap RR

Massanutten Mountain

Mt. Jackson

Orange & Alexandria RR

Warrenton

Manassas Junction

Blue Ridge Mountains

VIRGINIA

Brandy Station

Rappahannock Station

Culpeper C.H.

The Wilderness
May 5–7, 1864

Falmouth

Rappahannock River

Rapidan River

Fredericksburg

Orange C.H.

Spotsylvania Courthouse
May 8–12 and 18, 1864

Massaponax Church

Gordonsville

North Anna River

R. F. & P. RR

GRANT

Virginia Central RR

Charlottesville

South Anna River

North Anna
May 23–26, 1864

Hanover Junction

Mattaponi River

James River

LEE

Cold Harbor
June 1–3, 1864

Pamunkey River

Union Movements

Confederate Movements

Richmond

Confederate Fortifications

Union Siege Line

Engagement

Appomattox Courthouse, Lee surrenders
April 9, 1865

Appomattox River

James Crossing
June 14–17, 1864

Bermuda Hundred

City Point

Sailor's Creek
April 6, 1865

Petersburg

James River

Scale in Miles

0   20

Petersburg Assaults & Siege
June 1864–April 1865

Richmond & Danville RR

South Side RR

Five Forks
April 1, 1865

Weldon RR

George Skoch

Spotsylvania and North Anna

At this point Grant's plans crystallized. As Dana explained to Washington authorities, Grant intended to "interpose" his men between Lee's army and Richmond, compelling Lee to leave his entrenchments and shift southward. "If in the collision thus forced Grant found that he could not smash Lee, he meant to make another move to get behind his army." Dana seemed to believe that turning Lee's right might take a week or two, but Lee anticipated Grant's flanking maneuvers and blocked them skillfully. For the next month the opposing armies engaged in a stealthy two-step punctuated by bloody stalemates at each stop. Dana was confident that Grant's determination would prevail, although neither men reckoned the full price in time and lives.[13]

Dana's daily reports not only kept Washington leaders informed; they also reached the Northern public, thanks to an important change in government news policy. Starved for word from the front, several Northern newspapers without special correspondents had urged the War Department to release daily bulletins. Stanton, interested in managing the news as much as informing the public, devised a way to do both. Starting on May 8, telegraphic updates were sent daily from the War Department to General John A. Dix, commander of the Department of the East in New York City, who distributed them to local papers while Stanton fed them to the Associated Press. Concise and authoritative, Stanton's bulletins were based primarily on Dana's reports, summarizing them and sometimes reproducing them verbatim. Although they were more reliable than Stanton's previous press releases, the war secretary reneged on his promise to "withhold nothing from the public." He deleted casualty figures, cherry-picked Dana's telegrams for positive news, and exaggerated it in the telling. On the army's good days Stanton predicted "full and complete success" on the battlefield; on bad days he hid behind what the *New York Tribune* called "Delphic utterances." His bulletins conveyed an unmistakable impression of progress, but they also promoted unrealistic expectations for a quick and painless victory.[14]

The confidence Dana expressed (and Stanton publicized) about flanking Lee's army, for example, turned out to be premature. When the Federals' advance guard arrived at Spotsylvania Courthouse, the crossroads south of the Wilderness where Grant planned to await Lee's army, they found Longstreet's men already entrenching. Grant ordered a general attack, but the Union assaults, sequential rather than simultaneous, proved ineffective. Failure to organize simultaneous attacks would dog the Army of the Potomac throughout the campaign. Grant had inherited a "balky team" of general officers, Dana learned: "The different corps could never be made to act in vigorous concert either on the march or in battle."[15]

Having won the race to Spotsylvania, the Confederates built a five-mile line of breastworks around the town in the shape of an inverted *U*. Determined to find a weak spot, Grant tried flanking movements, then direct assaults. Lee had the advantage of short interior lines that were often concealed by woods, so he could shift his men unnoticed. The heaviest fighting took place on May 10 and 12. On May 10 twelve Union regiments led by Colonel Emory Upton—running across open ground, then "creeping on hands and knees" under obstructing logs, according to Dana—broke through at the northwest face of the *U*. Without adequate backup, they could not hold their position and were forced to retreat under withering Confederate fire. On May 12 Grant ordered two assaults. At dawn General Winfield S. Hancock's II Corps rushed through the rain and fog and overran Confederate trenches at the tip of the *U*, which soldiers dubbed the "Mule Shoe." Pushing forward half a mile, they captured three thousand prisoners before a Confederate counterattack drove them back.[16]

Hancock's Confederate captives included nearly all of General Edward Johnson's division. Dana and staff officers were at headquarters when Johnson was brought to Grant. "He was most horribly mortified at being taken," Meade's aide Lyman noted, "and kept coughing to hide his emotion." Grant gentled him like a skittish horse. Both generals were West Pointers and had served in Mexico. Grant shook Johnson's hand cordially and introduced Dana. Then, to Dana's astonishment, Grant offered Johnson a cigar and the two generals sat down on canvas chairs by a campfire to chat about the past while Union and Confederate soldiers were killing each other a mile away. As they reminisced, a message came from Hancock that he had "finished up Johnson" and was now "going into Early." Seeking to spare Johnson's feelings, Grant handed the message to his staff instead of reading it aloud. Dana marveled at his tact.[17]

While Hancock's men held their ground, the VI Corps under General Horatio Wright attacked the Confederate works where they jutted outward about a quarter-mile down the west side of the Mule Shoe. At this infamous "Bloody Angle" some of the most intense fighting of the war took a horrific toll. All day and into the night the two armies, never more than forty feet apart, traded volleys in a driving rain. Waves of federal soldiers climbed the rebel parapets and fired down until they were shot themselves. Union and Confederate men bayoneted each other through cracks in the logs or fought hand-to-hand with rifle butts. As evening came, the killed and wounded piled atop one another in muddy trenches and a steady hail of bullets cut down trees two feet thick. After midnight the fighting finally subsided and the Confederates pulled back to a newly constructed line. For the day, the Federals had lost about 9,000 men and the Rebels almost as many, the majority along a few hundred yards of trenches.[18]

Dana described the Union assaults at Spotsylvania in succinct, vivid telegrams to Stanton, doling out praise and criticism as he saw fit. General Gouverneur Warren's charges on May 10, Dana wrote, were executed "with the caution and absence of comprehensive *ensemble* which seem to characterize that officer," while Hancock attacked on May 12 "with his customary impetuosity." Dana's information, gathered from his observations and messages to headquarters, was not always accurate. He reported, for example, that General Gershom Mott's division, which was supposed to support Upton's charge, "disgraced" the army by abjectly retreating when faced "without any considerable force." In fact, Mott's men were met with brutal cannon fire that caused them to turn and bolt. Justly or not, Grant and Meade were so disappointed that within a week Mott's division was disbanded.[19]

Overall, the Union men had fought bravely, richly earning a day of rest on May 13. Grant commandeered the yard of a Unionist family for his headquarters, and in the morning Dana sat at mess when the matriarch emerged from the house and "gave us some nice bread, butter & honey with many apologies that she could do no more." The evening made a ghoulish contrast. The fighting safely over, Dana rode out with John Rawlins to inspect the Bloody Angle. The ground around the salient had been soaked by rain and churned so badly by the contending armies that it was soft, "like thin hasty pudding." The two men dismounted and climbed over the outer breastworks. The deafening gunfire had subsided and an eerie silence prevailed as night came on; nothing broke it but the oblivious chirping of a bird in a tree that had somehow not been blasted. Dana and Rawlins stood on a bank looking down at a great pool of mud, its surface as calm as a pond. Suddenly a soldier's leg rose out of the pool and mud dripped off his boot. "It was so unexpected, so horrible," Dana recalled, "that for a moment we were stunned." They summoned the relief corps, whose men tugged at the leg and found a wounded soldier at the other end. Still alive, he was taken to the Union field hospital.[20]

In his preliminary accounting Dana judged Spotsylvania a Union victory. Grant's army had not broken Lee's defenses but had dislodged the opponents from important positions and weakened them by inflicting between nine and ten thousand casualties. Union casualties, however, totaled even higher. One of the losses was a personal blow to Dana. On the first day at Spotsylvania his old friend, General John Sedgwick, leader of the VI Corps, had been killed by a Confederate sharpshooter while inspecting forward lines. Sedgwick had been stationed in Buffalo during the Upper Canada Rebellion of 1837–1838, whose leader, William Lyon Mackenzie, fled to western New York, spurring cross-border raids by both sides. Young Dana, appointed sergeant in a company of Buffalo city guards during the crisis, had befriended Lieutenant Sedgwick. A "solid man, no flummery about him," Sedgwick was "apt to be found where the hardest fighting was," Dana wrote, and he died as he wished.[21]

On May 13 Dana reported to Washington that Lee had abandoned his position during the night — "whether to occupy a new one in the vicinity or to make a thorough retreat is not determined." Stanton released the dispatch to the newspapers, editing out its uncertainty and implying that the Union army would shortly end the war. "We hope to print the announcement — Richmond is Ours! — in a very few days," gushed the *New York Herald*. Dana's next dispatch corrected that impression: Lee's men had simply pulled back to strong new fortifications nearby. That same day, Dana's hopeful speculations created more mischief. An advance of the V and VI Corps against the Confederate right had been planned. "If successful," Dana wired, "this maneuver will put us upon Lee's rear and compel him to retreat toward Lynchburg." Lincoln and Stanton were so eager for good news that they considered it done. The president told his secretaries the news, and Stanton included it in a bulletin to Northern governors. All were disappointed, however, to learn that the attack had been called off due to heavy rains. As the campaign wore on, Dana learned to make fewer sanguine predictions in his dispatches, although his comments continued to relay the buoyant determination prevailing at Grant's headquarters.[22]

After the Spotsylvania battle Grant tried to maneuver the Confederates out of their defenses, first by circling around Lee's right — the advance Dana had counted before it hatched — then by massing toward the Rebels' left. Constant rain and muddy roads frustrated these movements. As the fighting slowed to a halt, field returns of the army's losses came in. The results looked grim, especially when juxtaposed with Stanton's rosy bulletins. Dana estimated that 36,000 men had been killed, wounded, or missing in the two weeks since the army had set out on May 4. Reviewing these figures, Grant expressed regret over the terrible toll. "Well, General, we can't do these little tricks without losses," Dana quoted Meade in reply. The only consolation was that the Rebels suffered similar losses but could afford them less. If it came down to a war of attrition, as seemed increasingly likely, the North could replace more of its fallen men than could the South.[23]

There was additional sobering news at headquarters: Grant's auxiliary armies had bungled their missions. Franz Sigel, ordered to occupy the Shenandoah Valley, was routed on May 15 by a smaller Confederate force at New Market. Benjamin Butler's army, poised only fifteen miles from Richmond, squandered an opportunity to take the capital or destroy its railroads. Instead, defeated at Drewry's Bluff on May 16, Butler retreated to the Bermuda Hundred Peninsula on the James River, where a small Confederate force penned him in like "a bottle strongly corked," Grant wrote. Lee's troops could now be reinforced from western Virginia, and thanks to the hapless Butler, Grant's army would have to go it alone against them.[24]

When the weather improved, Grant made one final attempt to pierce the Confederate defenses at Spotsylvania. Early on May 18 he sent troops against Lee's left, which he supposed had been weakened by Hancock's earlier attack. He was mistaken. The Confederate line was well manned and an impassable abatis held up the Federals while Lee's men let loose what Dana called "a galling fire of canister," taking out as many as 2,000 invaders. "Grant thought it useless to knock our heads against a brick wall," Meade remarked, and he quickly called off the advance.[25]

On May 19 Dana took advantage of the lull in offensive operations to return to Washington. Taking a train to Fredericksburg, then a steamboat at the Belle Plain depot, he hurried back for "a few necessary things." "When I left I brought with me only a toothbrush," he told Stanton, "which proves inadequate to the exigencies of a prolonged campaign." Staying only a day, he rejoined Grant's temporary headquarters at Massaponax Church five miles east of Spotsylvania Courthouse by the morning of May 21. There, in photographs taken from the church's gable window by Timothy O'Sullivan, Grant, Meade, Dana, and various staff officers rest on church pews that had been brought outside and exchange ideas about the army's movements.

In one photo Grant, coiled and pensive, sits near Dana with a fresh cigar in his mouth, awaiting the report of a staff officer who has moved within the circle (see p. 264). Dana, neatly attired in broad-brimmed hat and boots and keeping a respectful distance from Grant, strikes a studiedly casual pose, crossing his legs in the general's direction. The long exposure caught Dana shifting his gaze; his blurred face both looks toward and away from Grant. His left arm rests on the raised knee of John Rawlins, who is unceremoniously slumped in the pew's corner peering down at a newspaper, his dirty

"A Council of War at Massaponax Church," May 21, 1864. Photograph by Timothy O'Sullivan. Ulysses Grant is seated on a church pew with his legs crossed, in front of the two trees. Charles Dana, also with legs crossed, is to his left, flanked by John Rawlins, who is reading a newspaper. Library of Congress Prints and Photographs Division.

boot slammed on the seat. Opposite in bearing but congenial in outlook, Dana and Rawlins were "pretty nearly always together" during the campaign, Dana recalled.[26]

As the parade of wagons in the background of O'Sullivan's photograph indicates, Grant's army was again on the move. After the failed attack of May 18 Grant resumed his plan to sidestep Lee's army southward toward Richmond. Lee, ignoring the chance to attack Grant's elongated line of marching men, hurried his army south, keeping it between the Federals and Richmond. By the afternoon of May 22 Grant and his entourage reached New Bethel Church, where they found Burnside and his aides slouching on the pews. Grant and his staff made camp nearby, beside a stately brick plantation house. On its porch Dana sought relief from the heat with Grant and a few staff members. "Our talk that night was that in all probability we should meet the enemy on the North Anna, a day's march to the south of our position," Dana recorded, and he wired the prediction to Stanton. At last, Grant's soldiers were in open farmland, "a fine, clear country, good to move and fight in." Sure enough, Lee's men were waiting for them. The Union march was slowed by inaccurate maps while Lee's troops, aided by shallower upriver crossings and shorter interior lines, had reached the North Anna River and were entrenching behind its steep banks to protect the road to Richmond and the strategic railroad crossing at nearby Hanover Junction.[27]

Under orders from Grant, Warren's troops forded the North Anna at Jericho Mills, about two miles upriver from the center of Lee's lines. There they were attacked by a Confederate division of A. P. Hill's corps, which they fended off with a hastily placed line of artillery. Dana, four miles away at Grant's headquarters on Moncure's Plantation, said he had never heard such massive cannon fire. Meanwhile, on the Union left Hancock's army overran the Confederate defenses on the north bank and took up positions across the river. Both operations netted about a thousand prisoners, who, according to Dana, were "more discouraged than any considerable number of prisoners ever captured before."[28]

Early the next morning, Grant, Meade, and their staff officers awaited news at Mount Carmel Church. In addition to reports from the North Anna came dispatches from afar. One wire forwarded from General Sherman caused what Meade's aide Theodore Lyman called "a fine blow-up." It was deciphered and handed to Dana, who then read it aloud with all officers present. The western army, Sherman wrote, was pushing toward Atlanta and prepared to "fight like the devil." Not content to stop there, Sherman added: "If General Grant can sustain the confidence [and] . . . the pluck of his army, and impress the Virginians with the knowledge that the Yankees can and will fight fair and square, he will do more good than to capture Richmond or any strategic advantage." On hearing this, Meade grew livid. Eyes bugging and in a voice that sounded like "cutting an iron bar with a handsaw," Meade screeched: "Sir! I consider that dispatch an insult to the army I command and to me personally. The Army of the Potomac does not require General Grant's inspiration or anybody else's to make it fight!" Fuming all day, Meade resented the comparison between Sherman's "armed rabble" in Georgia and his soldiers facing the formidable Lee.[29]

Unintentionally but tactlessly, Dana had brought into the open simmering tensions between Grant and Meade over the Army of the Potomac's command. Since crossing the Rapidan, Meade had fretted that Grant was receiving all the credit for the Union's successes, even though Grant had praised his leadership to Washington authorities. Chastened by Meade's outburst, Grant stepped back. He relinquished control of Burnside's IX Corps and placed it under Meade and, more generally, allowed Meade greater leeway in running the army. These steps smoothed Meade's ruffled feathers for the time being, though they did nothing to improve the armies' coordination.[30]

Meanwhile, it appeared there was ground to be won at North Anna. On May 24 Dana scribbled a familiar message to Stanton on a board laid across the pews in Mount Carmel Church: "The enemy have fallen back, whether to take up a position beyond the South Anna or to go to Richmond is uncertain." Grant, believing he was facing only the scattered forces of Lee's rear guard, renewed the attack. "Everything going on well," Dana reported to Stanton at midday. Burnside was pushing forward at Ox Ford, and "Hancock and Warren will reach the South Anna by nightfall." But Hancock's men were halted by entrenched Confederate troops, and Burnside could not get his men across the river at Ox Ford. By May 25 Dana admitted to Stanton that Union commanders had been mistaken: "It appears very probable that Lee's whole army is here." Lee's defensive entrenchments were impeccable, shaped into a five-mile-long *V* with its apex at Ox Ford. Grant was effectively checkmated: if he drove his army against the point of the wedge or attacked its wings, his army would be cut in two. In fact, Lee had so much the better position that Dana later wondered why he had not attacked. Unbeknown to the Union high command, the Confederate general in chief lay in his tent with a gastrointestinal disorder, unable to seize the opportunity.[31]

Despite the standoff at North Anna, Dana again found cause for optimism. Interviews with Confederate prisoners, plus the fact that Lee's men would not attack even under favorable conditions, seemed to prove that the armies' morale was going in opposite directions. "The Rebels have lost all confidence and are already morally defeated," Dana confided to Stanton, while Grant's army "has learned to believe that it is sure of victory." Grant's spirit had rubbed off on his commanders, who "have ceased to regard Lee as an invincible military genius." "Rely upon it," Dana assured Stanton, "the end is near as well as sure." It was true that Lee's army had assumed a permanently defensive posture, but the bloodletting was far from over.[32]

Cold Harbor

After consulting Meade, Grant decided to make another move across Lee's right, this time a wider swing along the north bank of the Pamunkey River to Hanovertown, where he could draw supplies from White House Landing.

After Philip Sheridan's cavalry seized the crossing, the entire Army of the Potomac crossed the muddy river on newly constructed pontoon bridges on May 28. Grant's long flanking movement was executed "with admirable celerity and success," Dana wired Stanton, and Union soldiers were in high spirits.[33]

Trailing the Union advance, Dana enjoyed a leisurely meander with Cyrus Comstock, twelve years his junior. They slipped away from the main party of staff officers and felt their way down the north bank of the Pamunkey to Hanovertown, "with various adventures now astonishing," Comstock recorded in his diary: "questioning people a long time about roads," stopping to chat "if the young ladies were pretty," and "commiserating with those who had lost chickens, pigs & such wild fowl." Searching for Grant's temporary headquarters, they found him at a Confederate widow's two-story house where, the bachelor Comstock noted, "there were several young ladies — strongly secesh of course, but polite." The army band even serenaded the party.[34]

This sociable respite reflected Grant's confidence as his army approached Totopotomoy Creek without significant resistance. He still believed, as Dana reported, that Lee "had no idea of our coming here." The elation was short-lived. When the Union troops arrived at the Totopotomoy they found Lee on the opposite bank with his entire army drawn up in line of battle. The two armies stared each other down, neither willing to attack. Grant's men needed a rest. He was also awaiting the arrival of Baldy Smith's XVIII Corps, which he had detached from Butler's force at Bermuda Hundred. Lee's army was too depleted for a full-scale attack, and he was pleading with Jefferson Davis for reinforcements. Rather than settle in for a face-off, Grant gradually extended his left flank again, hoping he might finally turn Lee's right. If not, he would be within easy reach of the supply depot at White House Landing and camped at a spot only one river crossing and less than ten miles from the Confederate capital.[35]

In this way Cold Harbor — a dusty hamlet where five roads converged and a ramshackle tavern stood sheltered by a grove of trees — suddenly became vitally important to the warring armies. Sheridan's cavalry arrived on the afternoon of May 31 and held it against a small Confederate force until infantry support arrived. Since Lee was playing catch-up, Grant had ordered a morning attack for June 1, but there were multiple delays. Baldy Smith's reinforcements, which had followed mistaken orders, did not reach Cold Harbor until 3 P.M. Wright's corps was also late, and when he arrived he "reconnoitered, skirmished, and delayed until he found . . . that there were no longer any rebels before him," Dana reported. Not until five in the afternoon did Dana hear cannons indicating that Wright and Smith had assaulted Lee's right. The delay gave the Confederates several hours to slip past General Warren's anemic guard, reach Cold Harbor, and dig in. The attacking Federals were forced to fall back under heavy fire at the second line of rebel entrenchments. Grant and Meade were "intensely disgusted" with these failures, Dana told Stanton. Meade declared that "a radical change must be made, no matter how unpleasant it may be," but Dana doubted that Wright and Warren would be replaced anytime soon.[36]

Despite the reality that the Confederates were now entrenched, Grant prepared a full-scale attack for dawn on the next day. Again there was a damaging delay. It gave Dana a chance to inspect the middle of the Union lines during a cooling afternoon thunderstorm. Much more important, it gave the Confederates another precious day to fortify their works. Early on the morning of June 3, Hancock, Smith, and Wright hurled their men against well-prepared Confederates waiting behind an intricate network of breastworks. The Rebels poured fire from the front and sides upon approaching columns of federal soldiers, who fell in unison as if ordered to lie down. Undaunted, the Union soldiers bravely reformed and charged again until whole brigades were cut down and scattered survivors hugged the earth. By 5:30 A.M. Grant's army had lost perhaps 4,000 men, the majority in the first twenty minutes of the assault.

It happened so quickly that the Union high command did not comprehend it. Around 7 A.M. Meade, finally aware that his army had not broken the Confederate defenses, sought Grant's advice. Grant told Meade to use his own judgment. Perhaps Meade was smarting from Dana's reading of Sherman's telegram a few days earlier and wanted to prove that he could inspire his men to extraordinary feats. In any case, he ordered his corps commanders to attack again on their own. They made halfhearted efforts to comply before giving up. Many soldiers had pinned slips of paper to their uniforms to identify their bodies; those who survived the initial assaults were hemmed in place by Confederate guns, too stunned and grateful to try again.[37]

Just before noon Grant rode to the front to assess the results. After consulting with division commanders, Grant told Meade to call off all attacks. Even then Grant—and Dana with him—seemed strangely unaware of the full extent of the massacre. Grant's first wire told Henry Halleck that the fighting was indecisive. Dana reported that "the fighting was pretty fair along the whole front" and Union troops "gained advantages here and there." According to Dana, Grant estimated the number of Union killed and wounded at 3,000—less than half the entire morning's casualties. Grant believed that Confederate losses were about the same, rather than the horrendous four-to-one ratio against the Union.[38]

What had gone wrong? Grant did not realize that the Confederate defenses at Cold Harbor were elaborate and virtually impenetrable. He also badly miscalculated the state of the Confederate army. Like Dana, Grant believed that after North Anna the Rebels were so worn out and demoralized that they could not withstand a full assault. Cold Harbor was the last chance to crush Lee's army on the north side of the James, and Grant was determined to take it. The battle also exposed gaping fault lines in the Union command. Heeding Meade's desire for autonomy, Grant gave only general orders to attack and left the particulars to his subordinate. Meade, who boasted to his wife that he "had immediate and entire command on the field all day," repeated Grant's orders with little elaboration. No Union corps commander reconnoitered Confederate defenses, no one coordinated lines of attack, and no one discussed what to do should federal troops force an opening. Union officers were only told, as General Wright informed Baldy Smith, to "pitch in." This, Smith complained, was "simply an order to slaughter my best troops."[39]

After the battle Grant compounded the tragedy by engaging Lee in a tangle of miscommunication and punctilio as the two generals warily discussed a truce to retrieve hundreds of wounded soldiers from no-man's-land between the armies. The cries and moans of soldiers dying on the battlefield could be heard as messages passed back and forth between the two commanders fussing over protocol. On June 7, four days after the battle, they agreed to gather the dead and wounded between the lines. Dana counted only two Union men still alive among 434 retrieved; others recorded perhaps a dozen. The inhospitable soil of Cold Harbor, so named because its tavern offered beds but no hot meals, became the final resting ground for thousands of Union bodies.[40]

Cold Harbor marked the low point of the Overland Campaign, and it evoked the first serious criticism of Grant's leadership from all ranks. General Marsena Patrick condemned "this murderous & foolish system of assaulting," while a typical soldier on the Union line railed against "Grant's alleged generalship, which consists of launching men against breastworks." From then on, the image of Grant as a "butcher" who brutally marched Union soldiers to their deaths because he had more of them in reserve tarnished—and for some critics ruined—his reputation.[41]

Where did President Lincoln's field reporter stand in this controversy? Dana's dispatches to Washington betrayed no hint of dissatisfaction with Grant, but privately he was not pleased. As Dana and Wilson discussed the battles at Spotsylvania and Cold Harbor, they agreed that Grant's subordinates had neglected "the details of carrying his general orders into effect," but they also held Grant responsible for "the policy, if not the practice," of making head-on attacks against the enemy's "entrenched and almost impregnable positions." Step by step, Charles Dana, James Wilson, and John Rawlins were forming an informal caucus to push reforms at headquarters. Sitting by Wilson's campfire, they criticized "a certain baleful influence" that had taken over Grant's circle, and Rawlins fingered Cyrus Comstock as the main culprit. Having won Grant's confidence, Comstock was now "leading him and his army to ruin by senselessly advocating the direct attack, and driving it home by the deadly reiteration of 'Smash 'em up! Smash 'em up!'" No doubt Rawlins was worried that newcomers such as Comstock were usurping his own influence over Grant, but Dana agreed with his assessment. The two pledged to work behind the scenes to change Grant's mind, but they were not optimistic because Grant was famously stubborn and there was no authority to appeal to. Years later, James Wilson claimed this lack of recourse explained why "no mention of these criticisms can be found in Dana's dispatches." The fact that Dana kept his misgivings—and those of Grant's officers—from Stanton and Lincoln stemmed from his loyalty to Grant and bedrock confidence in his leadership. After all, the real lack of recourse was not the shortage of authorities to complain to; it was the absence of credible alternatives to Grant at the Union army's helm. Sowing doubts about him in Washington might lead to his replacement and Union disaster.[42]

Looking back after the war, Dana convinced himself that Grant's frontal assaults had been justified. Cold Harbor "has been exaggerated into one of the bloodiest disasters of history, a reckless, useless waste of human life," he told an interviewer, "but it was nothing of the kind." Defeating Lee's army so close to Richmond was worth the risk. To counter the charge of butchery, during the 1868 presidential campaign Dana printed tables comparing the casualties sustained by Grant's army from the Wilderness to Appomattox to those suffered under all Union commanders who preceded him in Virginia. Grant lost 38,000 fewer men. His aggressive generalship was "far more economical of blood than the dawdling mode of some of his colleagues." And Grant succeeded where the others had failed.[43]

It was no coincidence that Grant's most avid defenders, like Dana, were those who had served at headquarters, not officers on the bloody front line. Grant wrote little about Cold Harbor, but in his dying days he conceded that the slaughter had achieved nothing: "I have always regretted that the last assault at Cold Harbor was ever made . . . no advantage whatever was gained to compensate for the heavy loss we sustained."[44]

If Grant had regrets and Dana had doubts about Cold Harbor, they cannot be seen in photographs taken a week later. Just before the army picked up and headed south, Matthew Brady and his assistants took a series of portraits at Cold Harbor. The most famous is that of a tired but determined, almost jaunty General Grant standing in his dusty lieutenant general's coat in front of his tent, leaning against a pine tree with his left fist on his hip and an empty folding chair nearby. A few minutes later Dana was photographed sitting in that chair. With his legs crossed, spectacles put down next to a newspaper on the ground, and his brim raised to expose a tall brow and full beard, Dana fixes his gaze beyond the camera, projecting confidence and physical ease (see pp. 272–273).[45]

Only sporadic skirmishing and trading of volleys took place in the week after Cold Harbor. The lull gave Dana time to catch up on War Department correspondence. Secretary Seward's son William, an officer in a New York regiment, had seen action at Cold Harbor but survived the battle. Dana sent reassuring news for Stanton to pass along. Less reassuring was the list of dismissals that Grant recommended and Dana forwarded. Thomas Crittenden, the Kentucky officer who had performed poorly at Chickamauga, asked to be relieved. "I think he has been in mental trouble for some time," Dana told Stanton, "because his division is small, and also belongs to corps containing Negro troops." J. H. Hobart Ward, who escaped to the rear at the Wilderness and was later found "too drunk to command," would be mustered out. Henry Lockwood, who took his division out of the battle of June 1 by using the wrong road, was relieved for incompetence. General Henry Eustis, who was "said to eat opium," was forced to resign. And so on. The depressing toll only reinforced Dana's low opinion of the eastern army's generals.[46]

The campaign's hiatus also gave George Meade another chance to vent his frustrations. General Meade had been steaming privately about not receiving fair treatment in Northern newspapers, which he read avidly. Early in June a Philadelphia correspondent charged that after the Battle of the Wilderness Meade had advised Grant to retreat across the Rapidan. Enraged, Meade had the reporter paraded through his lines seated backward on a mule displaying a placard labeled "Libeler of the Press," then expelled from the front. Dana approved of Meade's punishment and explained to Stanton that the report was "entirely untrue": Meade had "not shown any weakness of the sort since moving from Culpeper, nor once intimated a doubt as to the successful issue of the campaign." Stanton wired back to assure Meade that "the lying report . . . was not even for one moment believed by the President or myself." Meade felt vindicated, but his satisfaction did not linger long.[47]

As he had after each battle, Dana arranged with General Marsena Patrick to

General Ulysses Grant at his Cold Harbor headquarters, June 11 or 12, 1864. Photograph by Mathew Brady. Library of Congress Prints and Photographs Division.

Charles A. Dana at General Grant's Cold Harbor headquarters, June 11 or 12, 1864. Photograph by Mathew Brady. Taken at the same tent and pine tree as Grant's portrait, probably minutes later. Library of Congress Prints and Photographs Division.

ship thousands of Confederate captives north to Union prisons. Grant maintained the Union policy of refusing to exchange them unless the South included captured black soldiers in the agreements. Grant was convinced that this policy was also militarily sound, for it prevented prisoners from seeping back into the rebel army. Subtractions from Confederate strength became crucial as the conflict degenerated into a war of attrition. Despite horrendous losses, the Union was winning the grim numbers game. At Grant's mess table on the evening of June 12 the conversation turned toward manpower. In forty days Grant's army had lost more than 50,000 killed, wounded, or missing; yet with the addition of reinforcements Dana estimated that Grant's forces still totaled 115,000 fighting men to Lee's maximum of 60,000, including those south of Richmond. The Union army was the same size as when the campaign began; Lee's was shrinking.[48]

On to Petersburg

After Cold Harbor Grant began pulling his army back from the line while pondering his next move. As Dana relayed to Stanton, Grant had "expected that before reaching the Chickahominy he would have a fair chance to crush Lee's army by fair fighting," but this hope had been foiled by Lee's defensive posture. Grant had not been able to maneuver Lee out of his trenches, but he had another flanking action in mind, this time the most daring of all: he would hurry his troops south past Richmond "to strike for the James." The fifty-mile swing would involve grueling forced marches and crossings of two unbridged rivers, the Chickahominy and the James. But once completed it would allow Grant to link up with Butler's men for an attack on Petersburg, a railroad center twenty miles south of Richmond. If the combined Union armies could cut Lee's supply lines, the Confederates would have to abandon Richmond and fight in open terrain; if not, the campaign would settle down to a siege. Either way, as Grant saw it, the Union would emerge victorious.[49]

At sunset on June 12 the main body of the Army of the Potomac headed southeast toward the Chickahominy River. James Wilson's cavalry had been sent ahead to take the landing at Long Bridge and lay a pontoon bridge across the river. When Dana reached Moody's Farm, about ten miles from Cold Harbor, Warren's men were moving past Grant's retinue. They were to feint toward Richmond to deceive Lee into thinking the main attack would be on the Confederate capital. Just down the road from Moody's Farm, the *New York Tribune* reporter Charles A. Page captured the scene at Grant's temporary headquarters that night: "The location of the camp has been fixed, fires built, and inquiries are heard about the headquarters train, which must arrive before tents can be pitched and supper had," Page wrote. "The evening is chilly, and great coats are taken from the pommels of saddles and put on. Boxes and boards are made into seats, or rubber blankets are thrown upon the ground to lie on, and all gather close to the crackling rail-fire, and wait for the wagons." Grant and Meade conversed intermittently while Congressman Washburne, on a visit to the front, slept with his feet to the fire. "Mr. Dana," however, "strides up and down as though the day had not afforded sufficient exercise." Around ten o'clock word arrived that the supply train would be an hour or two longer: while crossing a stream on a narrow dam some wagons had capsized. Dana, venting his impatience by using a pun, remarked that it was "evidently a piece of dam folly." Grant calmly rose and took a brand from the fire. "If we have nothing worse than this . . . ," he trailed off as he lit his cigar. Soon a supply of bread, butter, and gingerbread was procured and all enjoyed a makeshift meal. By midnight the tents arrived and the men turned in until breakfast at four.[50]

Grant's army had little worse than that. "Everything is going prosperously forward," Dana wired Stanton early on June 13. Most of the army had crossed the Chickahominy without casualties or accidents, and its lead columns were pushing on to the James, where ferries would take them across. By the evening Dana and Grant's retinue reached Wilcox's Landing and camped on the north bank of the James. No time was wasted. Early the next morning Dana boarded a steamer with Grant and chugged up the James to confer with Butler at Bermuda Hundred. By afternoon they were back to oversee operations at the bridge site two miles downriver from Wilcox's. There Butler's engineers and Hancock's troops corduroyed the marshy banks and began work on a pontoon bridge spanning the river to Fort Powhatan. The bridge, 2,170 feet long and nearly 12 feet wide, required six schooners and more than a hundred pontoons, many of which had to be anchored because the river reached 80 feet deep. The task was unprecedented in modern military annals—surpassed only by Xerxes's crossing the Hellespont to invade Greece, the Harvard-educated Dana could not resist pointing out. Dana made sure that its designer, chief engineer James C. Duane, received credit in Washington.[51]

By dawn on June 15 the pontoon bridge was finished and the long parade of artillery and wagons began rumbling across. Atop a bluff on the north bank of the river, Grant, Dana, and the staff officers stood watching in silent admiration as troop ferries glided back and forth, gunboats guarded the river, and the rising sun shot brilliant reflections from the cannons drawn by horses across the bridge. Horace Porter noted that Grant's "cigar had been thrown aside, his hands were clasped behind him, and he seemed lost in the contemplation of the spectacle." The gigantic operation proceeded without a hitch. "All goes on like a miracle," Dana wired Stanton at 8 A.M.[52]

The biggest miracle of all was that Robert E. Lee, for once, had not anticipated Grant's move. Learning on June 13 that Grant had abandoned Cold Harbor, Lee reasoned that the Federals were trying to turn his right again, and he shifted his army southward to guard the near approaches to Richmond between the Chickahominy and the James. Dana was right when he told Stanton early on June 15 that "Lee appears to have had no idea of our crossing the James River." To seize this opportunity, Butler and Grant planned a quick attack with their armies. Marching from Bermuda Hundred, the 15,000 Bluecoats of Baldy Smith's XVIII Corps were approaching the thinly manned Petersburg defenses, and Hancock's II Corps was ordered to rush from the pontoon bridge to join them. For a short window of time before Lee could come to the aid of General P. T. Beauregard and his 2,500 men, Petersburg was there for the taking and Grant's plan stood on the verge of spectacular success.[53]

After viewing the crossing with Grant, Dana mounted his horse and rode across the pontoon bridge with Comstock and Babcock. Their objective was City Point, where the Appomattox and James Rivers converged and where Grant had ordered headquarters established on a high bluff overlooking the wharfs and railroad depot on the south bank. Grant, anxious to direct operations, took a steamer upriver. Most of his staff went overland to familiarize themselves with the country and to check on the progress of Hancock's troops. Dana and Babcock had a close call when they lost the road and ran into four rebel soldiers. Both parties wheeled around hastily, a "mutual rapid retreat" that gave the two Union men a good story to tell at camp. When he reached City Point that evening Dana learned that Smith's men had assaulted the entrenchments at Petersburg. Overnight came the heartening news that they had carried the enemy's principal line and taken hundreds of prisoners.[54]

The next morning, June 16, Dana rode with Grant from City Point to see how things stood at Petersburg. Viewing the fortifications from the heights southeast of the town, then inspecting the conquered lines with Grant and his engineers, Dana reported that the works were "more difficult even to take than was Missionary Ridge." Grant believed that the ground Smith took gave the Union military "perfect command of the city and railroad."[55]

Crucial to Smith's advance was the gallant performance of his black soldiers, who according to Dana did "the hardest fighting," captured two batteries, and suffered most of the Union casualties. After the attack Smith commended them. "He says they cannot be exceeded as soldiers, and that hereafter he will send them in a difficult place as readily as the best white troops," Dana reported. Dana was especially pleased because two years earlier Smith had served approvingly under McClellan, a Democrat who opposed emancipating slaves and recruiting black soldiers.[56]

Despite the soldiers' bravery, Dana's reports implying that the Confederates would have to abandon Petersburg proved premature. The position Smith had taken was too far away to command Petersburg, and the Rebels were building an even stronger line of fortifications a mile closer to the city. Over the next few days Grant's staff learned that the Union had squandered a golden opportunity on June 15. Spending hours "reconnoitering what appeared to be empty works" (according to a disgusted Grant), Smith had delayed his advance too long and stopped it before capturing the most extensive ground possible. A cascade of problems, including bad roads, faulty maps, and poor communications, prevented Hancock's troops from arriving until late at night, when Smith had already called off the attack. Meanwhile, back at Bermuda Hundred, Butler failed to take the rebel breastworks when the Union dash to Petersburg caused Confederates to abandon them. Ordering his troops forward to tear up the Richmond & Petersburg Railroad, Butler left behind "not even a line of battle or a cannon placed upon the heights," Dana complained. As a result, the Federals lost the chance to establish an impregnable staging ground a few miles from Richmond's outer defenses. Ruing these developments, Dana, Rawlins, and Wilson agreed that the army was "far too disjointed . . . in the cooperation of its various parts, and far too sluggish in its aggressive movements."[57]

On June 16 Meade took over at Petersburg and directed a twilight assault that carried part of the enemy line but achieved no breakthrough. Lee's men were arriving to reinforce Beauregard. Assaults on June 17 by various Union corps captured a few more positions but suffered heavy losses. On June 18 a general assault was ordered against the Confederates' new line of entrenchments closer to Petersburg, but the Union attack proved so difficult to organize that Meade gave up on fixing an hour for attack and, as at Cold Harbor, ordered corps commanders to "attack at once . . . without reference to each other." The result was predictably disastrous: the Union men, driving forward in fits and starts against strengthened lines, got nowhere. All told, Union casualties for the three days amounted to nearly 10,000, more than twice the Confederate toll.[58]

Dana saw nothing of the fighting on June 17 and 18. Worn out by shuttling between Petersburg, City Point, and the bridge at Fort Powhatan, he took ill and rested at Grant's headquarters. Stanton advised him to return to the capital, but he was determined to recover in camp. There Dana heard from Comstock that the attack at Petersburg had faltered "owing to our heavy loss in superior officers." It was also true, as Meade judged, that Union foot soldiers were exhausted and balked at additional head-on assaults against earthworks. Hoping to head off criticism of Grant, Dana made a not-so-subtle attempt to shift the blame onto Meade. "Attacks of Thursday [June 16] were made by General Grant's orders, those of Friday and Saturday were made by General Meade himself," he wired Stanton. This was technically correct but misleading. "In all this fighting and these operations I had exclusive command," Meade boasted to his wife, and he complained that Stanton's bulletins did not say so. Yet Grant had encouraged him to attack and approved his actions afterward. Grant had not yet shaken his penchant for hurling his men at entrenched foes.[59]

Whatever the causes—and there was plenty of blame to go around—the Union army had bungled its chance to capture Petersburg before Lee reinforced it. Incredibly, even after the failed attacks of June 18 General John G. Barnard, a veteran engineer whom Halleck sent to the front, recommended another assault. Dana told Stanton that "all our experience shows that with the mass of Lee's army to defend the works assailed they cannot be carried," and he warned Grant that the attempt might cost the Union 15,000 men. Meade endorsed Barnard's plan, but this time Grant sided with Dana. He ordered Meade to extend his lines to envelop Petersburg and sent for more troops and artillery to be shipped up the James, preparing for a systematic siege.[60]

Almost overnight, the James River landing at City Point became the busiest port in the United States, with over a mile of wharves receiving boats laden with men and materials to support the Union encirclement of Petersburg. On June 21 City Point received unannounced its most distinguished visitor. As Grant's army settled in for the siege, President Lincoln decided to take a look for himself and ordered a steamship to chug down the Potomac and up the James. Arriving around noon without fanfare, Lincoln suddenly appeared before Grant, Dana, and the staff officers, who were sitting in front of Grant's office tent on the high bluff above the port. Standing tall and alone in his black suit and top hat, the gaunt president looked, according to Horace Porter, "very much like a boss undertaker."[61]

Grant suggested that they visit the Petersburg front, and around 2 P.M. the mounted party, consisting of Grant, Lincoln, Dana, and three officers, rode to General Wright's headquarters. There Lincoln greeted Meade, viewed Petersburg from the Union parapets, and discussed military plans. The ride back took them through the African American soldiers' camps, and Lincoln, remarking that he had read Dana's dispatches on their assault "with the greatest delight," asked to "take a look at those boys." As Lincoln passed on horseback through Baldy Smith's black troops, they were drawn up in double lines on each side of the road. They cheered, shouted, and sang the praises of "Father Abraham" and "Massa Lincoln"; some kissed his hands or tried to touch his clothes. Lincoln doffed his hat and his eyes filled with tears. Even the hard-boiled Dana was moved. "It was a memorable thing," he wrote Stanton, "to behold the President, whose fortune it is to represent the principles of emancipation, passing bareheaded through the enthusiastic ranks of those negroes armed to defend the integrity of the American nation."[62]

Back at City Point, Dana joined Grant and his staff as they relaxed with the president around a campfire. Seated on a low folding chair with his legs crossed, Lincoln asked questions about weaponry and told humorous stories. The next morning Dana joined a party that accompanied Lincoln on the *City of Baltimore* as they headed up the James River to inspect Union fortifications. Along the way they picked up General Butler and Admiral Samuel P. Lee, commander of the Union gunboats. They toured a Union monitor and then went ashore, mounting horses to review the troops and earthworks. Years later, Dana recorded a detail that only an excellent horseman would remember: a tree branch knocked off Lincoln's top hat as he rode along, and Admiral Lee nimbly jumped off his mount to retrieve it.[63]

In the evening the president's boat headed back to Washington, and Dana was aboard again. Lincoln was "sunburnt and fagged" but cheered by the progress that Grant had made. Dana, meanwhile, needed a break. Seizing the chance offered by Lincoln's return, he took a week's furlough to visit his family and to reduce the pile of War Department business that had accumulated on his desk. Not much changed in the interval. When Dana returned to City Point on July 1 he wired Lincoln that Grant's army "occupies about the same position as when you were here." The siege of Petersburg was just getting under way, and the endless efforts to destroy Confederate railroads continued. Grant's Virginia offensive had wound down from rapid marches and frontal attacks to massive digging, and his men had traded muskets for spades.[64]

Yet Dana remained optimistic. Grant "had his hand on Lee's throat, and would keep his hold until he strangled him to death," Dana assured a *New York Tribune* reporter. "It is a mere question of time and of patience," he wrote James Pike, unwittingly echoing Lee's private prediction that if Grant laid siege to Petersburg, Union victory was "a mere question of time." Grant had established a secure base and was poised to cut off Richmond's supply lines from the south and west. Lee's army had hunkered down on defense and was no longer a threat to invade the North, except for nuisance raids. "All of his railroads have been broken up, all of northwest Virginia is destitute, deprived not only of supplies but of laborers, so that the [crops] cannot be harvested." Indeed, Dana judged it "difficult to form an idea of a territory more trampled and blasted by the hoof of war, than the greater part of Virginia." Grant's army was doing its part. Now it was up to politicians in Washington and the public in the North to keep the faith.[65]

"News from Grant's Army"

In two months at the Virginia front Dana sent nearly 120 telegrams to Stanton and Lincoln. Grant's aide Horace Porter judged them "a rare example of perspicuity, accuracy, and vividness of description." To Carswell McClellan, one of Meade's officers (and General George McClellan's cousin), Dana's dispatches were partisan, inaccurate, and (coming from a nonmilitary man) incompetent. The alignment of Grant's man versus Meade's was typical of reactions to Dana. It underscores Dana's identification with Grant's career and his close relations with the lieutenant general's staff, and it reflects the postwar certainty among Grant's men that they had made the right decisions.[66]

Dana's presence was convenient to Grant, who was glad to relinquish the burden of reporting daily to Washington and confident that Dana would represent his situation accurately. "My telegrams would be more frequent but for the fact that Mr Dana keeps you fully advised," Grant explained to Stanton. In addition, Dana inspected operations and conveyed orders in the field; gave advice on army movements, appointments, and dismissals; and served as a conduit for Grant's requests to Lincoln and Stanton. No longer "a sort of spy on Grant" or even "an auxiliary member of Grant's staff," Dana had become an important adviser and the general's primary liaison to Washington authorities.[67]

Although the arrangement worked well it had awkward aspects, chief among them Dana's dual role as both colleague and informer. As Grant explained, Dana's dispatches were not read at headquarters "except as they are seen in the prints of the day." This meant that when Grant, Meade, and their officers read the New York papers and encountered Stanton's news summaries, they wondered how much of Stanton's information had come from his embedded agent. Meade, for one, continued to fret that Stanton's bulletins ignored his contributions. At first he blamed Grant, but then he learned that "it is from Mr. Dana's telegrams that Mr. Stanton's despatches to General

Dix are made up," as he told his wife. This redirected Meade's suspicions toward Dana, and their relations remained distant and formal. Meade's aide Theodore Lyman shared his boss's antipathy, depicting Dana in his journals as "good-natured" but "gossipy," "vain," and—perhaps thinking of the Sherman telegram—"injudicious."[68]

In fact, Stanton bore much greater blame than Dana for squelching Meade. Dana's telegrams gave ample space to Meade's opinions and reports, but Stanton regularly excised references to Meade and inserted additional attributions to Grant. The effect was heightened by headline-writers who referred to "NEWS FROM GRANT'S ARMY." If this was not enough to bruise Meade's ego, the knockout punch was a secret act of retaliation by Northern newspapermen for his previous humiliation and punishment of the "libeler of the press" in June. For the next several months reporters at the front and their bureaus in Washington conspired to omit Meade's name entirely from their accounts— which made the high-strung general more perplexed and angry.[69]

Dana's dispatches accurately reflected the view from Grant's headquarters. Relying upon campfire conversations, his own observations, and reports from the field, he relayed timely and important information about troop placements, battle results, Grant's plans and judgments, and the overall mood at camp. As Adam Badeau noted, although Dana's judgments of men usually concurred with Grant's, they were more severe. By temperament Dana was more critical than Grant, and as Stanton's confidential observer he was freer to express his opinions. If this sometimes meant running roughshod over men's feelings or not pausing to qualify judgments, the decisiveness required by civil war seemed to justify it. "In war, if in no other human pursuit," Dana decreed, "success must be made the sole criterion of merit." Intent on victory and disdainful of second-guessers, Dana made his calls, expressed no regrets, and moved on to the next day's tasks. He had mastered the habit as the *Tribune's* managing editor and never relinquished it.[70]

Dana's hard-boiled newsman's credo suited Stanton and Lincoln perfectly. Wary of military officers' evasions and excuses, they welcomed Dana's clear narratives, sharp opinions of men, and blunt assessments of successes and failures. Tired of generals who penned long telegrams congratulating themselves for puny victories or pleading for more soldiers, they were glad to see Grant concentrate on fighting and to have Dana describe it. Dana's clipped telegrams and crisp sentences matched Grant's reliance upon action rather than words to win the war. His daily updates conveyed Grant's determination to wear down Lee's army with relentless pressure. And his portrayal of Grant as the calm master of the situation sustained the administration's confidence in the lieutenant general in the face of the campaign's waning momentum and staggering casualty lists.

Once or twice a day Lincoln walked over to the War Department to read Dana's dispatches. When a battle was in progress "he almost lived at the telegraph office," one of Stanton's assistants recalled. The president shared Dana's reports from Virginia with his secretary John Hay, showed them to White House visitors, and read them aloud at cabinet meetings. Grant's home-state congressman, Elihu Washburne, read some of them on the House floor, where their good news was greeted with cheers. Incorporated into Stanton's daily bulletins, they gave the Northern press and public the most consistent and reliable military reports the government issued during the war.[71]

Each of Grant's major Civil War victories, Dana wrote in his 1868 campaign biography, revealed a different facet of his military genius. Fort Donelson was won by speed and daring, Shiloh by "two-o'clock-in-the-morning courage," and Vicksburg by "brilliant and original strategy." In the climactic campaign against Robert E. Lee, the determining factor was his "heroic and unshakable resolution." In Virginia Grant faced a formidable opponent and suffered severe setbacks, but he willed the war to a close by his calm and dogged persistence. Of course, while Grant's other victories took days or (in Vicksburg's case) months, the struggle against Lee lasted nearly a year, to April 1865, and it spilled the blood of 80,000 Union soldiers on Virginia soil. After the war, Charles Dana minimized the desperate regularity and the ghastly human toll of Grant's Virginia battles. Yet Dana was essentially repeating what he had written during that campaign, when he deflected criticism from Ulysses Grant to his subordinates and when his battlefront reports projected certainty that the war would end in triumph if only the Northern public remained as patient and determined as its military chief.[72]

13 "The Deepest Shame That Has Yet Befallen Us"

The optimism broadcast from the Virginia front in Charles Dana's dispatches and Edwin Stanton's bulletins was not shared by the entire Northern public. In their cabins at City Point Ulysses Grant and Dana were sheltered from the grief of families who mourned fallen kin and charted the death toll in their towns. In faraway Maine, a newspaper editor denounced "the 'bogus' trash called 'war news' sent North from Washington daily by men in official station." "For eight weeks," he wrote, "one E.M. Stanton has been thus deceiving the people while the fathers, husbands, sons and brothers of northern homes have been perishing by the thousand."[1] Even in Union camps there was palpable disappointment that Grant's mighty offensive had ground to a halt at Petersburg. The mounting frustration triggered mutual recriminations among Grant's commanding officers and led to secret plans hatched by Dana and his allies to reshuffle military positions.

Fighting Generals

When the fighting stopped the finger-pointing began. It happened often during the war, but the problem seemed worse on the Virginia front because victories were scarce, command structures confused, and reporters omnipresent. "The old evil of the Army of the Potomac is appearing in want of harmony among the officers," Dana wrote his friend James Pike overseas. The hot, dry Virginia summer contributed: forty-seven straight days without rain, General George Meade's aide Theodore Lyman recorded on July 19. As the siege of Petersburg commenced, rounds of bickering, backbiting, and scapegoating broke out among the Union generals, aggravating disputes that had been festering for weeks. Dana reported the tiffs to Stanton, but he also took sides. As Dana saw it, internecine warfare gave Grant a golden opportunity to put the right generals in place to break the Confederates' last stand. Failure to seize that chance meant that the momentum his Virginia campaign had built would dissipate in the summer heat.[2]

Politics was to blame in at least two cases. William Rosecrans had been exiled to the Department of the Missouri, but he continued his obstructionist ways by holding up an Iowa regiment ordered east. Then Chief of Staff Henry Halleck reported that Rosecrans was pressing Washington for "twenty thousand men to oppose two thousand" pro-Confederate guerillas in Missouri. Fed up, Grant replied that Rosecrans should be replaced: "It makes but little difference who you assign, it would be an improvement."[3]

When President Lincoln read Grant's telegram he summoned Dana, who had returned temporarily from the Virginia front, to a conference about Rosecrans. Exactly what Lincoln said Dana never revealed, but he likely confided that for political reasons Rosecrans could not be relieved, at least without appointing him elsewhere. "I have in the most informal way communicated to Grant the substance of what you said respecting Rosecrans," Dana wired Lincoln after returning to City Point. "He thinks the most useful way to employ Rosecrans would be to station him . . . on the Northern frontier with the duty of exposing rebel conspiracies in Canada." (Even then, Grant grumbled, Rosecrans would be calling for reinforcements.) Lincoln stood pat. Rosecrans remained popular in the Midwest and claimed to be rooting out conspiracies intended to subvert the 1864 election. Better to keep a loyal War Democrat at work in the army than encourage him to take up political intrigue.[4]

The second case, closer to hand, concerned General Benjamin Butler. The wily Massachusetts politician-turned-general was accustomed to being at the center of controversy. He had caused an uproar in New Orleans by his harsh rule of the occupied city and raised suspicions that he had used his office to enrich himself. Relocated to Virginia, at Bermuda Hundred Butler had bungled his army's role in Grant's campaign. Vain and overbearing, he picked quarrels with subordinates sent to assist him. At the end of June, Dana told Stanton, Butler was "pretty deep in controversial correspondence with Baldy Smith." When Butler reprimanded Smith for "dilatoriness" during a Union advance, Smith copied his reply to Grant's headquarters with a request to be relieved. Grant refused, telling Dana that "Butler is clearly in the wrong." Then Smith asked for a leave of absence and scolded Grant for keeping Butler on: "How can you place a man in command of two army corps who is as helpless as a child on the field of battle and as visionary as an opium-eater in council?"[5]

Out of patience with Butler, Grant hatched plans with Dana to move him elsewhere and replace him with Smith or another West Pointer. Dana agreed to broach the subject with Washington authorities. On board the steamer from

City Point on June 22, or perhaps at the capital itself, Dana aired two proposals to Lincoln. Both involved carving out a new command in the divided midwestern states of Illinois and Indiana, then adding Kentucky or Missouri, and putting Butler in charge. Grant believed that either move would be helpful. Lincoln listened sympathetically enough that Grant followed up. "Mr. Dana Asst. Sec. of War . . . informs me that he called attention to the necessity of sending Gen. Butler to another field of duty," Grant wrote Halleck to encourage the change. A post away from the military front would be a better fit, for despite Butler's ineptness on the battlefield, "as an administrative officer [he] has no superior." If Butler could not be sent off, Grant feared losing Smith, one of his best field generals. Halleck responded bluntly. He had expected that Grant would relieve Butler for "unfitness to command" and his "quarrelsome character." But sending him to Kentucky "would probably cause an insurrection," and putting him in command of Missouri would open a fight with Rosecrans. Halleck suggested bumping Butler up to a desk job, leaving him in administrative charge of the military Department of Virginia and giving Baldy Smith command of the troops in the field.[6]

The truth was that Butler was too politically dangerous to be fired. As the war in Virginia stalled, a coterie of Radical Republicans schemed to dump Lincoln and nominate a more promising man with cross-party appeal. Some War Democrats also trumpeted Butler for their party's nomination. Lincoln could not play into his opponents' hands by releasing a potential rival. Even more than Rosecrans, Butler was untouchable, at least until after the November election.

Halleck's suggestion that Smith assume field command suited Grant and delighted Dana, who remained impressed with Smith despite his fatal hesitation at Petersburg. On July 6 Grant asked Halleck for an order making the changes; he sent Dana to inform Smith and ask him to postpone his leave. Almost immediately, however, the plan began to unravel. To start with, Halleck botched the order. General Orders No. 225 split command of the troops between Butler and Smith instead of keeping Butler in nominal command from his desk. Even worse, Butler refused to be kicked upstairs. Dana was with Grant when Butler barged into the general's cabin at City Point. Brandishing the order, he demanded to know whether Grant had issued it. "No, not in that form," Grant replied evasively. Dana, who tactfully excused himself, never knew what took place between the two men, but he took away the impression that Butler had "cowed his commanding officer." The next day Grant rescinded the order, wiring Halleck that he wanted to put Smith in command of the XVIII Corps as before, other generals in charge of the other

Grant and the generals of the Army of the Potomac. *Left to right, bottom row*: Gouverneur K. Warren, Benjamin F. Butler, George G. Meade, Winfield S. Hancock. *Middle row*: David R. Birney, Ulysses S. Grant, William F. "Baldy" Smith. *Top row*: Horatio G. Wright, John A. Rawlins, Philip H. Sheridan, Ambrose E. Burnside. From Paul F. Mottelay and T. Campbell-Copeland, eds., *The Soldier in Our Civil War: A Pictorial History of the Conflict, 1861–1865* (New York: J. H. Brown, 1885), 2:298–299. Courtesy of Archives and Special Collections, Saint Mary's College of California Library.

two corps, and Butler atop the group from his headquarters. This meant that nothing would change, since Butler insisted upon keeping his headquarters in the field at Bermuda Hundred.[7]

If there was any hope left for change, Baldy Smith destroyed it himself. He had already violated army etiquette by criticizing Butler over his head. Then he visited Grant to denounce Meade. As Smith explained it, he "tried to show him [Grant] the blunders of the late campaign with the Army of the Potomac" and attributed them to "a want of generalship in its present commander." Scheming to take Meade's place, Smith indirectly insulted Grant for tolerating incompetent generals. All this backbiting was too much for Grant, who, Dana wrote, "cannot endure double-dealing or indirectness of any sort." Grant decided that Smith was not worth swapping for two generals, and his carping disposition would worsen relations among corps commanders. Grant left Butler in charge at Bermuda Hundred. Instead, when Baldy Smith returned from his leave, he learned that Grant had relieved *him* of his command.[8]

Smith proceeded to prove that Grant had judged him correctly by plotting public revenge. Using a political surrogate, he circulated the charge that Grant changed his mind because he had been blackmailed by Butler, who supposedly had seen him drunk on a tour of corps headquarters late in June. There was no credible evidence to support the allegation, and by voicing it recklessly after his dismissal Smith talked himself out of the army entirely. Grant never assigned him to another post. Dana, who regretted that Smith's "eminent abilities should be left unemployed," urged Grant to give him another chance, but to no avail. Smith was too critical, Dana told James Wilson, although he admitted—in a rare moment of self-analysis—that he and Wilson had no right to condemn this weakness severely. When Smith complained that Grant had double-crossed him, Dana told him bluntly "that it was very much his own fault, and that if he had no tongue, and had never known how to write, I had no doubt he would now be commanding one of the large armies."[9]

In Dana's view it had turned out all wrong. The brilliant Smith had lost out to the inept Butler. Retaining political generals might help Lincoln's electoral prospects, but not if they lost more battles. "I see that the General has backed down on Butler," Dana wrote John Rawlins from Washington, "but I hope that he will fix it so that military lawyer will not be able to ruin the end of the campaign as he has ruined . . . the beginning."[10]

That left Meade—in Dana's opinion the biggest obstacle to Grant's success—as a candidate for replacement. As Meade's army dug in and the dog days of summer arrived, his eruptions became so frequent and divisive that Grant considered relieving him from command. Meade's wrath initially centered on General Gouverneur Warren, who commanded the V Corps. At Petersburg and elsewhere, Meade alleged, Warren had delayed movements and ignored orders to attack. Dana reported to Grant that Meade contemplated dismissing or court-martialing Warren; Grant then cooled things down by talking with Meade.[11] A few days later, Meade again disturbed the fragile peace in camp by his overbearing treatment of James Wilson, Dana's friend and a favorite at Grant's headquarters. On June 22 Wilson's cavalry had set out on a raid to tear up two rail lines west of Petersburg. Things went well at first, but the Federals unexpectedly ran into a larger force of Confederate cavalry and became trapped behind rebel lines. Although Wilson lost a quarter of his men and had to shed his wagons and artillery, he managed to escape to the Union camp on the James on July 1.[12]

The *Richmond Examiner* charged that during the raid Wilson's men had stolen slaves, silverware, and clothing. Meade demanded an explanation. No slaves had been "stolen," Wilson replied, but several hundred blacks seeking freedom had followed his cavalry, and perhaps 400 reached the Union lines. As for pilfering household items, Wilson had prohibited it but believed Meade should not condemn his men for disturbing "the public enemy." Meade eventually backed off, but his dressing-down of Wilson riled his friends at headquarters.[13] The episode dominated conversation at Grant's campfire on the night of July 6. There were complaints "about Meade's quarrelling with all his subordinates & Rawlins talks wildly," Cyrus Comstock recorded. At first Grant listened calmly, but then he joined in against Meade: according to Wilson, he "more than once said openly that he intended to remove Meade from command." Grant seemed to consider Meade's outburst at Wilson "the final grounds."[14]

Dana wired Washington his confidential prediction: "A change in the commander of the Army of the Potomac now seems probable," he told Stanton. "Grant has great confidence in Meade, and is much attached to him personally, but the almost universal dislike of Meade which prevails among officers of every rank who come in contact with him, and the difficulty of doing business with him felt by everyone except Grant himself, . . . render success under his command so doubtful that Grant seems to be coming to the conviction that he must be relieved." Writing as Meade's accuser more than Stanton's observer, Dana added his own impressions: "I have long known Meade to be a man of the worst possible temper, especially toward his subordinates. I do not think he has a friend in the whole army." Meade's crankiness was no news—associates nicknamed him "Old Snapping Turtle"—but the problem was deeper: Meade's generals had "lost their confidence in him as a commander." Dana heard, for example, that Horatio Wright said Meade led the army "without brains or generalship." Grant had spoken freely about his troubles with Meade and his intention to replace him. In such an event he would put Winfield Hancock in command, Dana told Stanton. This tickled Dana, who regarded the hero of Gettysburg as "a splendid fellow," with "more of the aggressive spirit than almost anybody else" in the Army of the Potomac. Rumors flew around the camps that Meade was about to be relieved. Hancock picked them up and told Meade. But when Meade went to Grant, he was assured that no such change was in the works.[15]

Dana had mistaken campfire grousing for final judgments. He overvalued dissent among Meade's generals, all of whom were unfit for higher command—Ambrose Burnside, Horatio Wright, and Governeur Warren by their abilities and Hancock by his debilitating Gettysburg wound. Dana's colleague Comstock knew better. He had spoken with officers snubbed by Meade, and despite their private grievances he remained their "first choice for Cmding. Genl." under Grant. Dana also misjudged Grant's opinion of Meade. Grant's need for stability in the eastern army would not be served by wholesale changes, and during his frequent travels to Washington he had to leave troops in the competent hands of an obedient subordinate. For all Meade's personal faults, Grant recognized, as he later wrote, that he was "the right man in the right place."[16]

Dana, more impatient than the unflappable Grant, felt differently. As he saw it, Grant had again exposed his Achilles' heel: his reluctance to let go of incompetent subordinates. When Radical Republicans complained that Grant's campaign had gotten nowhere, Dana placed the chief blame on "Meade's blind, unconsidered, fragmentary assaults at Cold Harbor and Petersburg," finding them "deficient in all the elements of generalship." Under further questioning Dana had to admit ruefully that Grant had not removed Meade, nor had he replaced the hapless Butler. As the summer burned on, Dana clung to hopes for a "pretty extensive reorganization" of the Army of the Potomac, but by mid-August he recognized that advocating a purge of Grant's generals was a lost cause. The Virginia campaign had become a war of endurance that would require more patience. In fact, it would sorely test the limits of the Northern public's support for Lincoln.[17]

Rebels at the Gates

While the Union generals quarreled, a genuine military crisis was brewing to their north. Without their knowledge, a column of Confederate troops crossed the Potomac and was approaching Washington. After Cold Harbor General Robert E. Lee reasoned that since the federal army was amassed around Richmond and Petersburg, a clear path to the Union capital might be opened by a quick move up the Shenandoah Valley. For this assignment he chose General Jubal Early, a grizzled, profane West Pointer and Mexican War veteran who took over Stonewall Jackson's old command after Jackson's death at Chancellorsville. On June 13 Lee sent Early from Richmond to the Shenandoah Valley with 14,000 men.[18] Early's immediate objective was to intercept the Union general David Hunter, who was advancing toward Lynchburg, ninety miles west of Richmond. If he could disperse Hunter's forces Early could then push north to threaten and perhaps briefly occupy Washington. This diversion could damage Northern morale and reclaim the local grain harvest for Confederate supplies. Lee hoped it would also prod Grant into a disastrous frontal attack on the Confederate works at Petersburg, or at least loosen Grant's choke hold on the city by forcing him to send troops to Washington.

The rebel plan got off to a fine start. Early's troops checked Hunter and chased his men across the Blue Ridge Mountains, then began their north-ward march on June 23. Rumors that Confederates were sending troops to the Shenandoah Valley circulated in Union camps but were disregarded as deliberate misinformation. Dana reported that Grant and Meade believed that Early's men had rejoined Lee's army after chasing off Hunter. On July 4 he began to backtrack. No recent prisoners taken at Petersburg were Early's men, and a Confederate deserter revealed that Early's corps had gone to Maryland.[19] By the time Union leaders realized the truth, Early's army was crossing the Potomac near Antietam Creek and marching around the Maryland Heights fortifications of Franz Sigel's Union troops. On July 6 Early's divisions con-verged on Frederick, Maryland, their staging ground for cutting off connec-tions from Baltimore and marching on Washington, only thirty-five miles to the southeast.

From Washington Halleck warned Grant that the capital's defenses were undermanned. Grant was not worried, but he took notice when he learned that Hunter's corps had retreated toward West Virginia and might not return in time to confront Early. On July 6 Grant sent General James B. Ricketts's division of Horatio Wright's VI Corps—about 3,300 men—from Petersburg to help intercept Early. On July 9, after more pleas from Halleck, Grant or-dered the rest of Wright's men to Washington with a division from the XIX Corps. These, he told Halleck, should be "forces enough to defeat all that Early has with him" and, if Hunter could cut off his retreat southward, to de-stroy his army.[20]

Early, however, kept a step ahead of the Federals. On July 9 the rebel army, marching east from Frederick to cross the Monocacy River, overpow-ered a smaller patchwork Union force led by General Lew Wallace. Wallace retreated to Baltimore, and Early's troops headed down the wide-open Rockville Pike toward Washington. The Union capital was in imminent dan-ger of being overrun.

Preoccupied with Lee's army, Grant seemed aloof to the peril. He decided against coming to Washington to direct operations; it would have a bad ef-fect on Union morale, he told Lincoln, and it might allow Lee to detach units

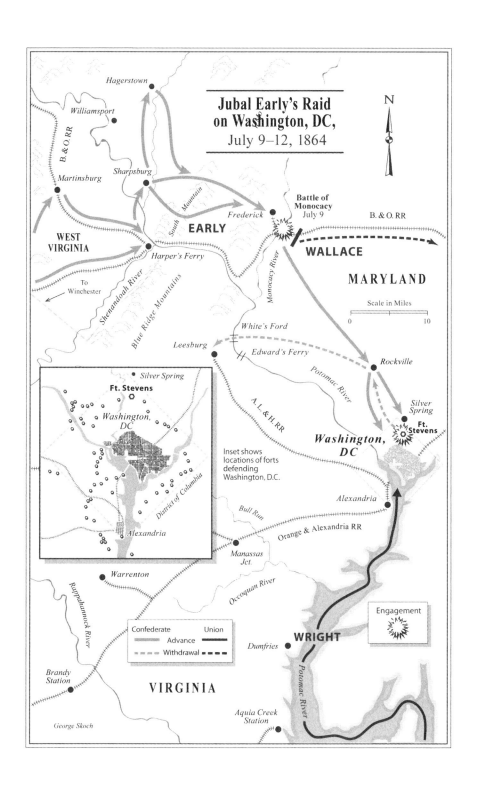

Jubal Early's Raid on Washington, DC, July 9–12, 1864

N

Hagerstown

Williamsport

B. & O. RR

Martinsburg

Sharpsburg

South Mountain

WEST VIRGINIA

Frederick

Battle of Monocacy
July 9

B. & O. RR

EARLY

Harper's Ferry

WALLACE

MARYLAND

To Winchester

Shenandoah River

Monocacy River

Scale in Miles

0   10

Blue Ridge Mountains

White's Ford

Leesburg

Edward's Ferry

Potomac River

Rockville

Silver Spring

Ft. Stevens

Washington, DC

A. L. & H. RR

Silver Spring

Ft. Stevens

Washington, DC

Inset shows locations of forts defending Washington, D.C.

District of Columbia

Alexandria

Alexandria

Bull Run

Orange & Alexandria RR

Manassas Jct.

Warrenton

Rappahannock River

Occoquan River

Confederate   Union

Advance

Withdrawal

Dumfries

WRIGHT

Engagement

Potomac River

Brandy Station

VIRGINIA

Aquia Creek Station

George Skoch

to defend Atlanta against William T. Sherman. Grant believed he had given Washington the necessary troops, and Wright, Hunter, and C. C. Augur (commander of the Washington garrison) were capable generals who could fend off Early. What he lacked was a reliable observer who could investigate the situation at the capital more thoroughly than the deskbound Halleck and relay sound advice. After checking with Stanton, Grant decided to send Dana, who would switch roles by reporting *to* him rather than *about* him.[21]

Before leaving for the capital, Dana wrote his friend James Pike at The Hague, downplaying Early's threat. "The possibility of a campaign by Lee against Washington has been reduced . . . to almost nothing," he assured Pike. Confederate railroads had been broken up, and northwestern Virginia lacked supplies and laborers to harvest crops, making a sustained rebel offensive unlikely. Dana was correct that the only way left for Confederates to harass the North was through nuisance raids like Early's. Yet what he found when he arrived in Washington seemed much more than a nuisance. As Early's troops approached the outskirts of Washington the capital was in a state of anticipation bordering on panic. Lincoln had returned to the White House from his summer residence at the Soldiers' Home. Frightened residents of the surrounding countryside streamed into the capital with household goods piled into wagons. "There was tremendous excitement here yesterday," Dana wrote in his first wire back to Grant's headquarters on July 11, "but all is comparatively calm this morning. The defences of Washington have not yet been attacked."[22]

Within a few hours the calm was broken. By 10 P.M., when Dana summarized the situation for Grant, fighting had broken out at the capital's perimeter. The invaders had apparently destroyed mills, workshops, and factories in western Maryland and had torn up fifty miles of the Baltimore and Ohio Railroad. The Maryland governor's house had reportedly been burned. Rumor had it, Dana told Grant, that Early had more than 20,000 men. He had wheeled his army eastward from Rockville to Silver Spring, where the house of Postmaster General Montgomery Blair was burned to the ground, and then pointed his men south to Washington. In the afternoon, Dana had seen clouds of dust in the distance that he thought were raised by rebel cavalry. Confederate troops appeared to be massing in front of Fort Stevens, which protected the Seventh Street route into the capital from Silver Spring. That evening, Union pickets composed mostly of hundred-day men skirmished with Confederate counterparts in front of the fort.[23]

Dana was alarmed by the disorganized Union defenses. There was no shortage of generals, but the chain of command was utterly confused and no one directed the whole. It seemed that the Union's most incompetent generals had concentrated around the capital. "With Gilmore Couch Wallace McCook and Sigel," Dana sneered to John Rawlins, "we only need Milroy McClernand Rosecrans and Kirby Smith to make us safe—If the General could spare Butler for the Supreme Command all danger would certainly cease." As for Chief of Staff Halleck, Dana's confidant Adam Gurowski scowled that he was so terror-struck that he "cannot even command three broomsticks." Grant himself was too distant to direct matters in detail, and because the telegraph lines to Virginia were cut twice during Early's raid, messages traveled by steamboat and sometimes took several hours to pass between Washington and City Point.[24]

As much as a commanding general, the army defending Washington needed privates. The thirty-seven miles of trenches and earthworks surrounding the capital required 37,000 soldiers to populate them, according to an 1862 report. Only a fraction of that number was in place, few of them trained in using the forts' big cannons. Under Secretary Stanton's orders all able-bodied men—and some questionably fit—were being mobilized. General Augur redeployed soldiers from forts on the south side of town and sent convalescents in Union hospitals from their beds to the trenches. Squads of government clerks, dressed in linen coats or partial uniforms, were hastily drilled in the city's parks by volunteers. Quartermaster General Montgomery Meigs armed 1,500 Quartermaster Bureau employees and marched them to Fort Stevens. At last, during the evening of July 11 these "miscellaneous troops" were bolstered by the six boatloads of men under Wright that Grant had sent from the Army of the Potomac.[25]

They arrived just in time. Early, riding ahead of his infantry, reached Fort Stevens shortly after noon on July 11 and found the Union works thinly manned. Before his foot soldiers could be brought up, Early watched several hundred Union soldiers file out across the works and begin an artillery barrage. As Dana informed Grant, the two sides' skirmishers fought in front of the fort that afternoon, watched for a time by the president himself. Rebel sharpshooters approached close enough to pick off men on the fort's parapet, including a soldier near Lincoln. Early still planned an all-out attack for the next morning. At daylight on July 12 he saw the rifle pits and parapets lined thickly with soldiers. Some were from Wright's VI Corps, recognizable through field glasses by the Greek-cross badges on their caps. Told that more of Grant's men were on the way, Early decided to call off the assault and ordered his men to prepare to retreat after dark. Skirmishing in front of the lines continued through the day, but Washington had been saved.[26]

"No attack either on this city or Baltimore," Dana wired Grant with obvious relief just before noon. Still, authorities at Washington lacked information about the size of Early's forces and whether James Longstreet's corps of Confederates was coming to reinforce them. In search of answers Dana visited "a considerable part" of the Union lines flanking Fort Stevens that afternoon. In charge at the fort he found General Alexander McCook, who had been transferred after his mistakes at Chickamauga. McCook had sent out no reconnaissance force, so Union officers guessed wildly about the army in their front. One general told Dana that the Confederates had built a formidable line of earthworks two miles away, but Dana believed "it exists nowhere but in his imagination." McCook informed Dana that most of Early's infantry had withdrawn. Instead of pursuing them, he ordered his artillery to blast 30-pound shells at a few remaining Confederate sharpshooters, some of whom had taken shelter in a house within range of the fort.[27]

Dana perceived "a lamentable want of intelligence, energy and purpose" in military leaders' overly defensive posture. General Augur, according to Dana, had not visited any part of the lines and knows "as little respecting them as I did before I went out." Halleck, who remained at his desk, was equally out of touch. Navy Secretary Gideon Welles found him "in a perfect maze—without intelligent decision or self-reliance." Dana repeated reports that the chief of staff's mind was "seriously impaired by the excessive use of liquor." Even the usually excitable Stanton seemed passive and incommunicative, holed up in the War Office to await updates on a makeshift telegraph line that had been strung out toward Fort Stevens.[28]

The next morning Dana telegraphed Grant that "the enemy have disappeared along the entire line." Early's infantry pickets had been pulled in the night, and the cavalry departed just before daybreak. The Rebels were apparently heading for the Potomac at Edward's Ferry. Once Early was gone the irregulars at Washington's fortifications began withdrawing. Dana described the return to routine after the scare, injecting drily comic detail for Grant: "Brevet Major-General Meigs marched his division of quartermaster's clerks and employés [back] into town," and Admiral Louis Goldsborough, who had sent sailors from the Navy Yard to Fort Lincoln, "returned to smoke his pipe on his own doorstep." General Abner Doubleday, who commanded the capital's civilian volunteers from the Loyal Leagues, was "still at his post" at the capital's easternmost defenses but "without troops."[29]

The question turned to pursuing Early's retreating army. Again—this time in stronger language—Dana alerted Grant to the lack of coordination among Washington's forces. Augur's job description forbade movements beyond the city, and the other Union generals commanded only their own units. "There is no head to the whole, and it seems indispensable that you should at once appoint one," he wired Grant. Hunter, still unheard from in western Virginia, would be the ranking officer if he arrived, but, according to Dana, "he will not do." In fact, in Stanton's opinion—which he directed Dana to forward— Hunter ought to be relieved for incompetence. "Mere advice or suggestions from you will not be sufficient," Dana told Grant pointedly. Halleck refused to issue any orders, but he blocked others. Wright's men could fight beyond the fortifications, but Halleck opposed sending them and Lincoln was unwilling to overrule him. In short, Dana told Grant, "until you direct positively and explicitly what is to be done, everything will go on in the deplorable and fatal way in which it has gone on for the past week."[30]

Roused by Dana, Grant finally took control and appointed Wright to command the troops pursuing Early. "Boldness is all that is wanted to drive the enemy out of Maryland," he told Dana. Wright went to work right away, but he had to create a unified force from elements of four different army departments, and Halleck made him promise to keep his troops between Early and Washington. In any case, it was too late. By the time Wright set out at midday on July 13 with his corps of 10,000 men, Early's troops were approaching the Potomac. The next day they crossed the river intact with their Union prisoners, more than a thousand Confederate recruits, and wagonloads of plunder in tow. That evening, Lincoln's secretary John Hay asked him for news. "Wright telegraphs that he thinks the enemy are all across the Potomac but that he has halted & sent out an infantry reconnaissance, for fear he might come across the rebels & catch some of them." "The Chief is evidently disgusted," Hay concluded.[31]

Right away the recriminations began. Stanton, Grant, and Dana blamed Halleck for his cautious, bureaucratic ways. His obstructionism continued. On July 15 Cyrus Comstock arrived in Washington with a letter from Grant requesting that Halleck return Wright's men to Petersburg when they stopped chasing Early. Halleck resisted, demanding a formal order. Frustrated, Comstock went to see Dana, awakening him late at night. Dana was reluctant to have Grant's troops leave before a unified local command had been established, and he guessed that Lincoln would agree. But the snail's pace of creating a consolidated command and Halleck's continued stalling drew Dana's ire. With "Old Brains" in mind, Dana told Rawlins that the war would have to be ended by "a younger, more earnest, more manly . . . race of men" than those currently in control.[32]

Dana also had in mind the sixty-two-year-old Hunter, who failed to return from West Virginia in time to cut off Early's retreat. Dana "sentenced Hunter . . . severely," Comstock recorded after their conversation on July 15. Dana complained to Grant, too. Calling Early's escape "the deepest shame that has yet befallen us," he sneered that Hunter had been "engaged in a pretty active campaign against the newspapers in West Virginia." (Hunter had ordered two newspaper editors critical of his generalship jailed and their papers suppressed.) Grant, responding, was sorry to see "such a disposition to condemn so brave an old soldier as General Hunter is known to be without a hearing." To Dana, Grant's reaction typified his loyalty to friends, no matter their competence. But when Early made another move into Maryland three weeks later and Hunter was reported by Comstock to be "doing nothing & not knowing what [the] enemy was doing," Grant ran out of patience. He replaced Hunter with the intrepid Philip Sheridan, with instructions to corral Early and destroy the Shenandoah Valley. Sheridan was only thirty-three, so young that Stanton opposed his appointment to such an important post. But he was a splendid answer to Dana's call for aggressive young war leaders to assume command.[33]

Asked by John Rawlins to sum up the pursuit of Early, Dana wired back that it proved on the whole "an egregious blunder," save for a small success by General William Averell against a detachment of Early's men near Winchester, Virginia. Wright accomplished nothing and returned just when he and Hunter could have combined to destroy railroads and crops. Early escaped from Maryland with thousands of horses, mules, and cattle, a few hundred Union prisoners, and more than $200,000 in ransom extracted from Maryland towns. Total Union losses around Washington amounted to 500 killed and wounded, Dana estimated. This was in addition to some 2,000 casualties at Monocacy and smaller engagements in Maryland.[34]

For Dana, Union casualties and the damage to Maryland were minor compared to the humiliation of having Confederates terrify the Union capital. Rightly or wrongly, public opinion would blame the top Union leaders. "The responsibility for this whole disgraceful affair will be put upon the general's shoulders," Dana wrote privately to Rawlins. Grant's inaction toward the guilty parties—primarily Hunter and Halleck—would only confirm this judgment. Point by point, Dana drew up a prospective indictment of Grant:

In the first place, it will be said, he is the commander in chief, & is bound to provide for the whole field of operations. In the second place it was by his order and request that both Washington and Baltimore have been stripped of troops, so that when the enemy arrived there was nobody but militia to defend either.

In the third place, it was he who sent Hunter to Lynchburg leaving the Valley open for Early. Fourthly, he does nothing to call Hunter to account for retreating to the Ohio river where he could not possibly get his troops up to interfere with Early's movement. And fifthly he does not send troops enough to Washington till it is too late to do anything more than begin a useless pursuit of an enemy whose escape with all his plunder we are impotent to prevent. These are some of the things which are already beginning to be said & which will be said more & more.[35]

Dana's charges reflected some of his own views, especially about Hunter; but by casting them as a warning about criticism to expect, he framed his list as a reality check from a Grant loyalist. He issued a similar alert about Northern public opinion. Since returning to Washington Dana realized how, contrary to the upbeat mood at Grant's headquarters, the long offensive that stalled at Petersburg was viewed by much of the Northern public as a debacle. "I must . . . tell you," he confided to Rawlins, "that I hear from friends of the general & of the cause the decided opinion that the campaign is already a failure and that we are worse off . . . than we were the day you left Culpepper. Seventy thousand men have been killed &d wounded, they say, to produce this net result." Early's raid only capped the campaign's failure. Obviously worked up, Dana extrapolated further: "The black & revolting dishonor of this siege of Washington with all its circumstances of poltroonery & stupidity, is yet too fresh and its brand too stinging for one to have a cool judgment regarding its probable consequences." But "as far as I can now see, they are very likely to be the defeat of Mr Lincoln & the election of Gen[eral] McClellan to the Presidency."[36]

The Wrong Kind of Peace

Dana was now in a better position to monitor political gossip. With a prolonged stalemate developing at Petersburg, Edwin Stanton decided it would be more productive to retain Dana at the capital, where, he wrote, "the pressure of business in the Department requires your assistance." After Early's scare, Dana resumed the office routine he had established before joining Grant in Virginia. Setting up in a rented townhouse on New York Avenue near 14th Street, he sent his family off to the Connecticut shore for the summer and leased out their New York City house. The three-year lease helped compensate for his modest salary and the ravages of wartime inflation. It may also have reflected Dana's growing pessimism about the war. A few weeks before, President Lincoln had vowed before a Philadelphia crowd to see the war through "if it takes three years more."[37]

Seeking a more optimistic prognosis, or at least a respite from the stifling Washington heat, Lincoln, his family, and some Illinois friends boarded the steamer *City of Baltimore* on July 30 to chug down the Potomac and visit General Grant. Assistant Secretary Dana and his navy counterpart Gustavus Fox were invited to go along. At Fortress Monroe on July 31 the party brought Grant aboard. They toured the Norfolk navy yard and set out to sea "to get a sniff of the ocean air." All enjoyed being temporarily away from their cares. Both nights the group "all sat up until after 1 o'clock," Fox wrote his wife.[38]

Yet the war was impossible to escape. A sobering reminder intruded when Grant described to the party the failure of a mine that had just exploded under the rebel earthworks at Petersburg. At dawn on July 30 the tremendous blast killed more than 300 Confederate soldiers and opened a gaping hole in their defenses. But at the last moment the African American soldiers specially prepared for the assault were replaced by untrained white infantrymen, who were soon trapped in the crater and joined by black units sent to rescue them. All were sitting ducks for the regrouped Confederates, who inflicted nearly 4,000 casualties and retook the position. Grant called the Battle of the Crater "the saddest affair I have witnessed in the war." The Union had squandered its best chance to end the siege of Petersburg; instead, there would be eight more months of trench-building and slow encirclement.[39]

The Crater debacle closed a month of bad news for the Union. By the end of July 1864 prospects for a victory by General Sherman that would rescue the Union also looked dim. After fruitless direct assaults on Confederate entrenchments at Atlanta, Sherman moved his army around to the northeast. A counterattack by General John Bell Hood's Confederate army stopped Sherman on July 21, killing his best corps commander, James B. McPherson. Newspapers reported that Sherman was stalled in front of Atlanta just as Grant was before Petersburg. Stunned by the toll of casualties in the two campaigns, the Northern public grew weary of the war. The national debt approached $2 billion—an unthinkable sum—and the government had practically exhausted its credit. On July 18 Lincoln issued a call for 500,000 new volunteers to refill the Union ranks in the wake of the Virginia slaughter, and the draft would restart in September if states' quotas were not filled.

This dreary sequence of events compounded the humiliation of Early's raid and revived the dormant peace movement among Northern Democrats, some of whom called for an immediate armistice followed by a negotiated settlement. Peace Democrats gleefully anticipated nominating one of their own to run against Lincoln and capture the presidency. When a Democratic editor heard about Lincoln's call for more troops he exulted that "Lincoln is *deader* than dead." Lincoln's stock dwindled in his own party. "The people are wild for peace," observed Thurlow Weed, who called Lincoln's reelection "an impossibility." Some of Weed's advisers believed that peace commissioners should be sent to Richmond, offering terms for sectional reunion.[40]

At the head of those who lost the will to continue was Dana's old boss at the *New York Tribune*. Since firing Dana, Horace Greeley had pursued an erratic editorial course, oscillating between militancy and defeatism. The *Tribune*, Adam Gurowski declared, was "an indestructible record of Greeley's uncourageous inconsistencies . . . [and] unmanly despondencies." In the spring of 1864 Greeley supported a movement to nominate Treasury Secretary Salmon P. Chase for president on the Republican ticket, believing Lincoln not forceful enough in prosecuting the war. By midsummer, his pacifist tendencies reemerged. After hearing that Lincoln was preparing a new call for volunteers, Greeley implored the president: "Our bleeding, bankrupt, almost dying country . . . longs for peace—shudders at the prospect of fresh conscriptions, of further wholesale devastations, and of new rivers of human blood." Unless the administration made a peace overture to the Confederates, Greeley warned, there might be a Northern insurrection. At the very least, the Republicans would lose control of Congress and the presidency in November.[41]

This letter set off one of the war's stranger episodes. Through a dubious intermediary Greeley learned that two Confederate emissaries had arrived on the Canadian side of Niagara Falls delegated by Jefferson Davis to negotiate a cessation of hostilities. The gullible editor thought the men (the Confederate senator Clement C. Clay of Alabama and Inspector General Jacob Thompson of Mississippi, formerly a member of James Buchanan's cabinet) were sincere and their go-between (George N. Sanders, a charming, erratic Kentucky schemer) a reliable source. In fact, they were agents of the Confederates' secret service sent by Davis to Canada with a million dollars in bank drafts to plot schemes against the Union and disrupt US relations with Great Britain, perhaps drawing England into the war. The sham negotiations were Sanders's idea to discredit Lincoln and encourage the North's Peace Democrats.[42]

Lincoln, fresh from discussing "rebel conspiracies in Canada" with Grant and Dana, was skeptical but unwilling to bypass an opportunity for peace. He urged Greeley to meet with the "negotiators" at Niagara Falls and—if they were authorized Confederate commissioners—to bring them to Washington, guaranteeing their safe conduct. Greeley went to Canada to transmit Lincoln's offer, but the Confederates backed off, admitting that they were not empowered to negotiate for rebel authorities. At this point Lincoln's secretary John Hay arrived with a letter outlining the president's terms: he would consider any proposal as long as it included "the restoration of peace, the integrity of the whole Union, and the abandonment of slavery." Greeley—duped by the Confederates and unhappy that Lincoln had imposed preconditions—skulked back to New York to face skewering by his rival editors as a naïve fiddler in diplomatic affairs. Embittered by Lincoln's intervention, Greeley felt, a *Tribune* associate remarked, "as if . . . the pit had been digged for him, and he had fallen through the contrivance of the digger."[43]

The Confederate agents leaked Lincoln's terms to the press, charging that the Union president was responsible for continuing the bloodletting since he proposed conditions obviously unacceptable to the South. For his part, Lincoln tried to demonstrate that bargaining with Confederates was useless because recognition of independence was their nonnegotiable demand. Clay and Sanders's real object was to "assist in selecting . . . a candidate and a platform for the [Democrats'] Chicago convention" in August that would commit Northern Democrats to disunion.[44]

Greeley, hopelessly naïve, had been used for propaganda purposes by each side. Looking on from Washington, Dana enjoyed the spectacle of his nemesis making himself a laughingstock. "Horace has distinguished himself in his peace negotiations with George Sanders," he wrote to James Pike. For once, Lincoln flashed a similarly sarcastic sense of humor. Shortly after the incident the president saw Dana at the War Department. "I sent Brother Greeley a commission," he told Dana with a "satirical smile which submerged the ordinary kindness and good nature of his features." "I guess I am about even with him now."[45]

Actually, Lincoln was as much the loser in the affair as Greeley. The president told cabinet members he hoped the episode would not only "shut up Greeley" but "satisfy the people who are clamoring for peace." But Lincoln's terms gave Confederate sympathizers valuable political ammunition. Northern Democrats echoed Clay's claim that there could be peace any day if only the administration would drop its fight to free the slaves. As this sentiment gained ground Lincoln's moderate Republican allies began to waver. Henry Raymond, the *New York Times* editor who published the Niagara Falls correspondence, told friends that the president should have left slavery out of his letter to Greeley. Raymond, who headed the Republicans' National Executive Committee, feared that "the impression that Mr. Lincoln . . . is fighting not for the Union but for the abolition of slavery" would doom the administration in the upcoming election.[46]

Dana disagreed. For Lincoln to drop the demand to end slavery would have "done himself and his party a great injury, hopelessly alienating the Radicals," Dana told Raymond. Lincoln was already "under suspicion of a want of earnestness upon this supreme question," and if he abandoned it "people would have taken for granted that he was willing to sacrifice his emancipation proclamation and let the Southern States come back with their old power."[47]

Raymond's gloom infected the National Executive Committee when they met in Washington in August. Hoping to counter the notion that emancipation alone blocked peaceful reunion, Raymond urged Lincoln to appoint a commission to Richmond that would postpone discussion of slavery and other matters of dispute and require only that the Confederates return to the Union. If Jefferson Davis rejected this offer, as Raymond expected, it would kill the Northern peace movement and reconcile the public to continuing the war. For a few days Lincoln considered Raymond's plan and even began drafting instructions for a delegation that would insist only on "restoration of the Union . . . all remaining questions to be left for adjustment by peaceful modes." John Nicolay, the president's secretary, described the moment as "almost . . . a disastrous panic—a sort of political Bull Run."[48]

In the end Lincoln stood his ground, echoing Dana's and Stanton's advice not to budge on emancipation. At a meeting with Raymond and the cabinet on August 25, the president declared that retreating from emancipation would mean breaking the Proclamation's "promise of freedom," splitting his own party, and "ignominiously surrendering" the presidential contest in advance. Raymond, persuaded by Lincoln that his reelection was possible, went back to New York "encouraged and cheered." The *Times* the next day denied that the administration was considering peace negotiations: "Its sole and undivided purpose is to prosecute the war until the rebellion is quelled."[49] The day of victory, however, remained far off, almost impossible to see through the hot, dusty gloom of summer.

14 "All the Power of the War Department"

The fall 1864 elections loomed as a referendum on the Union government's war record, including emancipation, the draft, arrests for disloyalty, and military successes and failures. Not only was the conduct of the war at stake but also the very existence of the Union, for a victory by Democrats would likely bring negotiations and recognition of secession. There were potential benefits, too. A vote to reelect Lincoln would solidify emancipation, reaffirm the administration's aim to secure the Union, and keep it on course to conquer the rebellion. Either way, a general election was a constitutional requirement and an indispensable democratic ritual. As usual, President Lincoln put it best: "We cannot have free government without elections; and if the rebellion could force us to forego, or postpone a national election, it might fairly claim to have already conquered and ruined us." A "people's war" had to have the people's approval, even if canvassing them risked the chance that they would call it off.[1]

When Charles Dana surveyed the presidential campaign for his overseas friend James Pike in early July 1864, he painted a positive picture. Lincoln had been nominated "without much serious opposition" at the Republicans' Baltimore convention on June 9. To broaden the Republican Party's appeal Andrew Johnson, a War Democrat, replaced Hannibal Hamlin as the vice-presidential nominee. Although most radicals opposed Lincoln on "questions of principle" (mainly the terms of Reconstruction), they failed to agree on an alternative candidate. The Salmon P. Chase boom had imploded when the Treasury secretary withdrew his name in March, embarrassed by revelations that he was campaigning from Lincoln's cabinet. All Republican factions seemed reconciled to Lincoln's nomination, Dana wrote, and unless some unforeseen disaster occurred "this unanimity will be maintained until the election." The Democrats, meanwhile, were "hopelessly split" between peace and war men, some committed to "the white flag," others determined to see the fighting through. Because of this rift their convention was postponed to the end of August, only ten weeks before the election. George McClellan was the frontrunner, but some gravitated toward Ulysses Grant, who, Dana knew, would never consent to run. "Under these circumstances," Dana told Pike, "you can see in Holland quite as plainly as anybody in America, that the election of Mr. Lincoln is more than probable."[2]

A month later things looked much worse. The deadlock at Petersburg, bickering among Union generals, and Jubal Early's raid near Washington had left the Northern public "amply discouraged," Dana told Pike. Opposition was brewing again in the president's own party. Meanwhile, Peace Democrats fed on the country's ill fortune and grew stronger. Some favored former president Franklin Pierce, others the Ohio war dissenter Clement Vallandigham, and still others McClellan. Lately the Democrats, and some Republicans, were lobbying for Lincoln to appoint McClellan to a high army post. Dana considered this a plot to bring a negotiated peace and believed Lincoln would have none of it. Despite Lincoln's resolve, it was obvious to Charles Dana and most other political insiders that his reelection prospects were plummeting.[3]

A Party Divided

It was hard to tell which was more worrisome to Lincoln loyalists: the Democrats' maneuverings or the stirrings of mutiny among Republicans. The anti-Lincoln Republicans were "comprised of all the elements of discontent that a four years administration could produce," Dana wrote. One faction of radicals, supported by New York abolitionists and St. Louis German Americans, had bolted to nominate John C. Frémont at the head of a third-party ticket on May 31. Frémont's coalition called for protection of wartime civil liberties, a constitutional amendment guaranteeing legal equality for former slaves, and the distribution of confiscated rebel lands to "soldiers and settlers." Hoping to align War Democrats with Radical Republicans, the group called itself the "Radical Democratic Party." Despite the initial fanfare, it failed to attract many crossover Democrats or win Republican endorsements. Still, Frémont's loyal following among abolitionists threatened to siphon Republican votes from Lincoln.[4]

A second faction of Radical Republicans, roused by a dispute with Lincoln over Reconstruction in occupied Southern states, also threatened revolt. In July 1864, after nearly five months of debate over terms for readmitting Tennessee, Louisiana, and Arkansas to the Union, congressional Republicans passed a bill sponsored by Representative Henry Winter Davis of Maryland and Senator Benjamin Wade of Ohio. It rejected Lincoln's lenient program by requiring 50 percent of voters to take an oath of allegiance (instead of

Lincoln's proposed 10 percent) and by permitting only previously loyal voters to select delegates to write new state constitutions. Lincoln allowed the measure to die by pocket veto, an unusual tactic that infuriated Wade and Davis. On August 5 they issued a statement warning Lincoln that if he wanted Republicans' support he must suppress the Rebels decisively and "leave political reorganization to Congress." Many observers believed that the "Wade-Davis manifesto" was intended to force Lincoln to withdraw from the race and find someone else who could unify the party.[5]

Still another revolt lurked among those Dana called "the friends of Mr. Chase." Chase had resigned from the cabinet and denied coveting the presidency, but his allies in New York continued to seek alternatives to Secretary of State William Seward and party boss Thurlow Weed. In mid-August a nucleus met at former Mayor George Opdyke's Fifth Avenue mansion to discuss forcing Lincoln off the ticket. Among the attendees were David Dudley Field and Roscoe Conkling, partners of Dana in earlier state and local campaigns. *Tribune* editor Horace Greeley, out of town, sent his endorsement and proposed that a Union general—Ulysses Grant, William Sherman, or Benjamin Butler—be substituted for Lincoln. The group sent messages to persuade Lincoln and Frémont to withdraw—to no avail—and issued a call for a convention to meet in Cincinnati at the end of September. The Opdyke caucus was the faction closest to Dana's views on most issues, but not this one. Once he began working in the War Department Dana became a fierce Lincoln loyalist. The radicals' plan for a Cincinnati convention is "absurd and mischievous," Dana complained to William Bartlett, an administration go-between with New York Republicans. "Can't you do something to break it up?"[6]

None of these movements coordinated activities with the others, and none mustered enough support to dislodge Lincoln. Agreeing only that Lincoln was an unacceptable nominee, they considered several alternatives, but as Dana told Pike, the ideal candidate was still "missing after the most anxious search." Party loyalists believed that changing candidates after the convention could only lead to defeat. Others noted that appeasing the radicals on Reconstruction would alienate moderate voters. For better or worse, the party was stuck with Lincoln.[7]

Many Republican insiders believed it was for worse. Leonard Swett, Lincoln's political friend in Illinois, reported during a visit to New York that "unless material changes can be wrought, Lincoln's election is beyond any possible hope." Thurlow Weed, as well connected as any Republican politico, told Lincoln that his defeat was certain. He had spoken with no one from New York or other states "who authorizes the slightest hope of success." All this pessimism pooled before the Democrats even nominated their candidate. Lincoln himself despaired of being reelected. On August 23 he penned a memorandum acknowledging it "exceedingly probable" that his administration would fail at the polls and pledging to cooperate with the new president-elect "to save the Union between the election and the inauguration." Lincoln asked cabinet members to sign the back of the sheet without reading it, then put it in his desk.[8]

Democratic Rifts and Copperhead Conspiracies

Quite suddenly, the situation began to improve. On the same day as Lincoln's defeatist memorandum, Union admiral David Farragut ran his fleet past naval batteries at the entrance to Mobile Bay and forced the Confederate forts to surrender. The Port of Mobile was closed to rebel blockade runners. Farragut's success "has done much to revive the public mind," Dana wrote Wilson from the capital on August 29.[9]

Dana also told Wilson that Lincoln's nemesis McClellan "will be nominated at Chicago" in a day or two—although not without controversy that Republicans could exploit. After his dismissal from the Army of the Potomac in November 1862 McClellan spread word that he was available for the Democratic nomination. As a Union general, McClellan had opposed emancipating slaves but favored restoring the Union through military victory. His position remained the same in 1864, but this upset the peace wing of the party, which sought an immediate armistice followed by negotiations. At Chicago the party tried to reconcile the two factions by offering the War Democrats McClellan's nomination while allowing Peace Democrats to choose the vice-presidential nominee, George Pendleton of Ohio, and draft the party platform. As approved by the convention, the platform denounced the Lincoln administration's suppression of dissent and its disregard of "State rights"—the right to hold slaves. It declared the Republicans' "experiment of war" a failure and demanded a prompt cessation of hostilities so the Union could be restored through negotiations.[10]

The platform's formula of "peace first, Union second" left the Democrats badly divided, especially after McClellan clarified his stance. The former Union general waited more than a week after the convention to accept the nomination. During the interlude Dana accompanied a New York clergyman to the White House for an audience. When the minister wondered aloud why it was taking McClellan so long to reply to the convention's letter, Dana saw Lincoln's eyes twinkle: "I think he must be entrenching!" McClellan's carefully drafted letter of acceptance reversed the Democratic platform's priorities. Only when "our present adversaries are ready for peace upon the basis of the Union" could a cease-fire and negotiations begin.[11]

Despite McClellan's rejection of a peace-at-any-price policy, most Republicans felt that if he won there would be tremendous pressure to call a truce and negotiate a deal that recognized the Confederacy. Confederate leaders read the situation the same way. "McClellan is under the control of the true peace men," Confederate emissary Clement C. Clay assured Secretary of State Judah Benjamin from Canada. "An armistice will inevitably result in peace. The War cannot be renewed if once stopped, even for a short time."[12]

The Democrats' platform gave Republicans an opening to paint their foes as disloyal advocates of "peace with the rebels but war against their own government." Even before McClellan was nominated, Dana seized an opportunity to smear him with innuendo about treason. A War Department detective coaxed from a former member of the Maryland legislature, Francis Waldron, a story that McClellan had secretly met with General Robert E. Lee at Waldron's house on the night of the Battle of Antietam. This was the eve of "fatal Thursday," when McClellan's failure to renew the attack on Lee's weakened forces disastrously prolonged the war. At their meeting Lee allegedly informed McClellan that his army was retreating across the Potomac, and McClellan agreed to let him withdraw unopposed.[13]

Waldron's story was sent to the War Department, and Waldron himself was brought before Dana to retell it. The tale matched Dana's disgust with McClellan's soft stand on the Rebels and slavery so well that he declared he "believed every word of it." Dana leaked the story to the *New York Tribune*, whose report was widely reprinted, and passed it to the Committee on the Conduct of the War, which subpoenaed Waldron as a witness. By this time in far over his head, Waldron repudiated his story in a signed deposition admitting that he concocted the tale on an alcoholic binge. As usual in such cases, the retraction received less publicity than the initial story, which merged with other tales of McClellan's alleged treachery at Antietam and dogged him during the campaign.[14]

Dana and Stanton found another opportunity to dredge Democratic mud to the surface by publicizing sensational exposés of pro-Confederate conspiracies among Peace Democrats in the Midwest. The potential payoff of stories about seditious secret societies outweighed the two men's misgivings about the source of much of the evidence—their old antagonist, William Rosecrans.

For more than a year there had been conflicting claims about the extent of conspiracies by "Copperheads"—a term of reproach that likened Peace

PLATFORMS ILLUSTRATED.

"Platforms Illustrated." The Republicans' Baltimore platform of 1864 is contrasted with the plank adopted at Chicago by the Democrats. On the left, Lincoln is supported by Senator Charles Sumner, General Ulysses Grant, and Admiral David Farragut. The president holds his Emancipation Proclamation and is endorsed by Lady Liberty. On the right, a dwarfish George B. McClellan is thrust onto a slippery platform of cheese upheld by Copperhead snakes, one holding a Confederate flag labeled "SEPARATION." The reluctant nominee is accompanied by antiblack toughs, an approving John Bull, and notorious Peace Democrats such as Clement Vallandigham and Horatio Seymour. Library of Congress Prints and Photographs Division.

Democrats to poisonous snakes that used camouflage to disguise their approach.[15] Copperheads were especially numerous in the southern belt of the Midwest that stretched from lower Ohio to Missouri, where opposition to Lincoln's war policies often merged with sympathy for the South. Secret societies such as the Knights of the Golden Circle organized chapters to disrupt the war effort, at times encouraged by Confederate agents. There was talk of creating a "Northwest Confederacy" to make a separate peace with the Richmond government.

The existence of secret societies and insurrectionary schemes among zealous Copperheads was no fiction, but war officials and Republican leaders exaggerated the strength of this movement for political purposes. They found an unexpected ally in General Rosecrans, commander of the Department of the Missouri. Like his predecessors, the general stepped into a witches' cauldron of irregular conflict when he arrived in St. Louis. Rival factions of Republicans viciously contended for power, Missouri Democrats organized their own militia to combat Union Leagues, and roving guerrilla bands raided rural settlements. Rosecrans heard talk about conspiracies hatched by local Democrats to resist the draft, free Confederate prisoners, or perhaps overthrow the Unionist state government. Convinced that these Copperhead plots were a dire threat, Rosecrans hoped that exposing them would contribute to Union victory and, not coincidentally, rehabilitate his reputation in Washington.

To build his case, Rosecrans made use of an investigation undertaken by his former aide, Colonel John P. Sanderson. A Pennsylvania lawyer and Cameron protégé, Sanderson had attached himself to Rosecrans's staff during the fighting in Tennessee and became a loyal subordinate. He followed Rosecrans back to Chattanooga during the Battle of Chickamauga and defended the general afterward. Sanderson helped Rosecrans write his self-serving official report on the battle and shared his commander's grudge against Dana and the War Department for the general's dismissal. Rosecrans asked Sanderson to serve as his provost marshal at St. Louis. Fearing Stanton's opposition, he applied directly to the president, and Lincoln wrote out the orders. Dana believed that Sanderson was unqualified for the post and guilty of cowardice at Chickamauga. Behind the scenes the assistant secretary schemed—no doubt with Stanton's approval—to block Sanderson's promotion to colonel. Dana recruited Horace Porter, and both men testified secretly to the Senate Military Committee that Sanderson had left the Chickamauga battlefield without attempting to rally fleeing federal soldiers. Without examining Sanderson, the committee held up his promotion.[16]

When Washington newspapers reported the committee's action, Rosecrans immediately suspected that Dana was behind it, and he received confirmation through intermediaries. Rosecrans wrote Senator Henry Wilson to urge a public hearing where his subordinate could be vindicated. Receiving no reply, Rosecrans sent another aide, Major Frank Bond, to Washington carrying a letter refuting the charges as "unfounded and malicious." Stanton retaliated by placing Bond under arrest, ordering him to return to Missouri, and directing Rosecrans to court-martial him for appearing in Washington on unofficial business without the War Department's permission.[17]

Rosecrans angrily convened a tribunal that quickly exonerated Bond. Meanwhile, Sanderson vented his spleen in his journal, blaming the roadblock on "an infamous libeler . . . no other than the meanest of all knaves and scoundrels, the man of all work that is dirty & stinks in the nostrils of honest men—CHARLES A. DANA." Failing to destroy Rosecrans's career, Dana, according to Sanderson, was trying to take secret revenge on his assistant.[18]

Eventually the full Senate confirmed Sanderson's appointment. Dana's underhanded attack failed to thwart Sanderson. Yet it also led Sanderson to widen his investigation of disloyalty in Missouri to demonstrate his usefulness to the administration. Convinced that Copperhead secret societies were the seedbed of the region's troubles, Sanderson hired investigators, interviewed jailed Confederate sympathizers, and gathered documents from around the Midwest. On this basis he concluded that the Knights of the Golden Circle were still active in Missouri and that an even more dangerous organization, the Order of American Knights (OAK), had been established among Peace Democrats. Sanderson claimed that the OAK had enrolled half a million members in the upper Midwest and that Clement Vallandigham planned to return from Canada during the Chicago Democratic convention and give a speech to inaugurate a rebellion and proclaim a Northwest Confederacy. Like Rosecrans, Sanderson saw an exposé of the OAK as a way both to aid the Union cause and refurbish his reputation.[19]

Sanderson's claims and similar Unionist charges about Copperhead organizations were not a fabrication or "a figment of Republican imagination," as Democratic newspapers (and later pro-Copperhead historians) asserted. Plots to disrupt the draft, free Confederate prisoners, and inaugurate a Northwest Confederacy were real.[20] Some Copperheads cooperated with the enemy, conspiring with Confederate agents in Canada to sway elections or purchase weapons. In April 1864 Phineas C. Wright, whom Sanderson had fingered as the OAK's "Supreme Grand Commander," was arrested by federal authorities in Michigan after he had crossed into Canada to confer with the exiled Vallandigham. Wright sent letters appealing his case to Dana and to Lincoln (who passed his letter to Dana). The assistant secretary denied the appeal, and Wright languished in Northern prisons for the duration of the war.[21]

Vallandigham, the nominal head of the Sons of Liberty (the OAK's successor), consorted with the Confederates' Canadian agents, but by the Chicago Democratic convention he had switched tactics from advocating mob violence to promoting electoral success. Other Sons of Liberty continued to plot mayhem in Chicago, including a plan to free rebel prisoners at nearby Camp Douglas, but the conspirators were so few and disorganized that the Canadian agents canceled the raid and left town. In general, Sanderson's charges, based upon contacts with overzealous secret-society officers, were accurate about

Copperhead conspirators' hopes but vastly overstated their membership and capabilities.[22]

While Sanderson composed his report Rosecrans wrote Lincoln, promising that Sanderson would deliver "detailed information" about a "plot to overthrow the government" if allowed an interview at the White House. Lincoln was skeptical; he was aware of Northern Copperheads, whom he called the "fire in the rear," but he believed that few were capable of treason. "Nothing," he told one senator, "can make me believe that one hundred thousand Indiana Democrats are disloyal." Lincoln also recognized that Rosecrans and Sanderson were deliberately circumventing the War Department, which might create a rift between him and Stanton. Instead of inviting Sanderson to the capital, he sent his secretary John Hay to St. Louis to interview Rosecrans and Sanderson and return with the report.[23]

At St. Louis Rosecrans and Sanderson explained the gist of their findings to Hay. Reporting to Lincoln, Hay found him annoyed that Rosecrans had not handed over papers and suspicious that he and Sanderson were exaggerating the issue to curry favor in Washington. The president, according to Hay, believed the OAK "not especially worth regarding." After another trip to Missouri, Lincoln's other secretary, John Nicolay, bolstered that view. Nicolay reported that Sanderson and Rosecrans had been duped by an unreliable informer and Sanderson was "in a chronic state of stampede." Lincoln promised to write Rosecrans, but he did nothing.[24]

Snubbed by Lincoln, Rosecrans and Sanderson went to the press to get their story out. Sanderson revised his exposé, titled it "Conspiracy to Establish a Northwest Confederacy," and published it at the end of July in influential Republican newspapers from St. Louis to New York. Greeley's *Tribune* proclaimed the OAK guilty of treason and tried to implicate New York Democrats in the conspiracy. A wave of denials by Democratic editors only gave the story more publicity.[25]

Stanton and Dana had no liking for Sanderson, but unlike Lincoln they welcomed his exposé. They opposed Sanderson's promotion, and Stanton even refused to pay the expenses of his detectives because they had ventured beyond his district. But that did not stop them from endorsing his findings. Their motives blended sincerity and opportunism. They dealt daily with cases of disloyalty and were more willing than Lincoln to credit that the contagion had infected midwestern Democrats. Dana monitored the War Department's tracking of Confederate agents in Canada and knew they had met with Vallandigham and encouraged subversive plots by Peace Democrats. Both believed the threat of specific attacks by pro-Confederate conspirators genuine and troubling. Of course, they also understood the political value of tarring the Democrats as traitors and were unabashed about using investigative findings for partisan purposes.[26]

Dana used Sanderson's revelations about the OAK, together with an exposé of the Sons of Liberty by General Henry B. Carrington of Indiana, to send Union commanders on the home front lists of "disloyal persons" with orders to "cause them to be kept under surveillance" and to arrest them "upon their detection in any act of hostility to the United States." His message was followed up by small detachments of troops dispatched by the War Department. Putting them to work, military authorities in the Midwest made dozens of arrests, destroyed weapons cached by Copperhead conspirators, and foiled several plots to release Confederate prisoners of war.[27]

Sanderson's and Carrington's reports also led Stanton to order an official War Department investigation of the secret societies. Dana asked Judge Advocate General Joseph Holt to prepare a report blending Sanderson's and Carrington's findings with Holt's own research. Holt, a Kentucky lawyer who had served in Buchanan's cabinet with Stanton, renounced his sectional sympathies when the Southern states seceded, and then he hounded pro-Confederate sympathizers with the zeal of a convert. In late July Holt embarked on a fact-finding trip to Louisville and St. Louis. After conferring with local investigators and officials, he declared that the evidence pointed to a conspiracy in the border states "looking to an armed rising against the government."[28]

Dana commissioned Chief Detective Lafayette Baker to gather additional information for Holt. After a cursory investigation Baker submitted a one-page list of suspected subversives. Carrington provided further documentation for his exposé, Rosecrans summarized the findings of Sanderson, who was sidelined with illness, and from these materials Holt compiled a 14,000-word report. A mélange of solid information and questionable testimony, it described Copperhead secret societies as larger and more efficiently organized than they were, but it accurately outlined their aims, which ranged from protecting Union deserters to cooperating with Confederates in raids on Union arsenals and prisons. Their grand aim, said Holt, remained the establishment of an independent, pro-Confederate Northwest Confederacy, but an interim goal was to use "foul means" to "prevent the success of the Administration at the coming election." Holt concluded his report with a favorite biblical slur. There was only one Judas Iscariot, he declared, but "there has risen together in our land an entire brood of such traitors . . . all struggling with the same relentless malignity for the dismemberment of our Union."[29]

Completed by October, the Holt Report gave Sanderson's revelations of

Copperhead disloyalty a second public airing, this time with the government's sanction. Stanton turned it over to the press and the Union Congressional Committee, which published it as a pamphlet on "A Western Conspiracy in Aid of the Southern Rebellion." Ten thousand copies were distributed through the Union Leagues. According to historians on both sides of the Copperhead controversy, the reports from Sanderson and Holt contributed powerfully to Lincoln's electoral majority in the Midwest. Charges of Copperhead treason proved to be the Republicans' most effective issue against the Democrats in 1864, and Charles Dana did his partisan best to whip them up.[30]

Sherman and Sheridan Turn the Tide

Even with the split between Peace and War Democrats and sensational revelations of Copperhead conspiracies, a decisive military victory was desperately needed to seal Lincoln's reelection. One possibility was to capture Wilmington, North Carolina, the Rebels' last major blockade-running port east of the Mississippi. On September 1 Dana joined his navy counterpart Gustavus Fox and General Quincy Gilmore on a boat trip from Washington to see General Grant at City Point. They brought a proposal to launch a combined land and sea attack on Fort Fisher, the huge earthwork at the mouth of Cape Fear that guarded Wilmington. A detachment of troops from General Butler's stalemated XIX Corps would march south to support a naval bombardment by Admiral David Porter. Grant approved, and the attack date was set at October 1. Almost immediately, however, the project ran into delays in outfitting and moving the necessary gunboats. As Grant grew impatient he deployed Butler's men at the Virginia front. Not until December, a month after the election, did Butler's troops set out for North Carolina.[31]

Instead, the decisive turn in Republicans' fortunes came when Atlanta succumbed to a flanking movement by William T. Sherman's army. "I am . . . expecting from Sherman news of importance," Dana wrote Wilson on August 29. "It is three days since he took the mass of his army to the south and southeast of Atlanta . . . for the purpose of definitively cutting the connection between Hood and Macon." At Jonesboro, twenty miles south of Atlanta, Sherman's troops broke through Confederate defenses and, by threatening to encircle General John Bell Hood's army holding Atlanta, compelled the Confederates to evacuate the city. Union soldiers marched into Atlanta on September 2, and Sherman telegraphed Washington that "Atlanta is ours, and fairly won."[32] The news revived Northern morale instantaneously. "Union men!" the *Chicago Tribune* shouted, "the dark days are over. We see our way out. . . . Thanks be to God! The Republic is safe!" On September 6 Dana accompanied the New York clergyman Joseph P. Thompson to the White House to congratulate the president. Dana gave Lincoln the additional news that John Hunt Morgan, the rampaging Confederate cavalry leader, had been killed two days earlier during a botched raid in East Tennessee.[33]

Three weeks after Atlanta, more welcome news came from the Shenandoah Valley, where the Union army finally caught up with Jubal Early. After Grant assigned Philip Sheridan to the valley in August, the opposing armies maneuvered and skirmished for a month. Then, after learning that Early's troops had sent a division to reinforce Lee, Sheridan attacked the Confederate defenses around Winchester. His men broke through the rebel lines on September 22 and Early's army retreated far up the valley. When Stanton received a wire announcing the victory he rushed into his anteroom, shouted the news to the swarm of officers waiting there, and gave department employees the day off. Dana was equally elated. "A thousand cheers for the great victory won by the Army of the Shenandoah!" he wrote Wilson. Winchester was "like the battle of Chattanooga in its far-reaching consequence."[34]

"Little Phil" Sheridan did not rest after the victory but pursued Early southward. Grant's orders were to clear out the region: "Take all provisions, forage, and stock wanted for the use of your command. Such as cannot be consumed, destroy." Dana applauded these tactics, but he was concerned that Virginia's loyal Unionists might be caught in the maelstrom. He alerted Grant that Loudon County contained "a considerable settlement of Quakers favorable to the Union" and asked if they could be exempted from pillage and arrest. After Grant modified his orders, Sheridan's 35,000 men proceeded to cut a five-mile-wide gash up the Shenandoah Valley, burning two thousand barns and seventy gristmills, driving off cattle and roasting sheep for their meals. "Sheridan has perfectly destroyed the Valley for a distance of ninety miles from Winchester south," Dana told Wilson after seeing the general's report.[35]

Sheridan's sacking in Virginia was followed by Sherman's scorched-earth march through Georgia. The Civil War had graduated to a new, more destructive phase where farms that supplied hostile armies were targeted and the Northern invaders destroyed anything of potential military use. "We cannot change the hearts of those people of the South," Sherman explained, "but we can make war so terrible . . . [and] make them so sick of war that generations would pass away before they would again appeal to it." These were harsh words, but they were music to Dana's ears: "Sheridan and Sherman are generals after the style I have always looked for in one respect at least," he told Wilson. "They devastate indeed."[36]

Sheridan pulled back his army in mid-October and went to Washington to confer with Chief of Staff Henry Halleck and Dana while Stanton was out of town about returning troops to Grant.[37] Jubal Early, however, refused to concede defeat. While Sheridan was away, the Rebels launched a surprise attack at dawn on October 19 at Cedar Creek, fifteen miles south of Winchester. Seven thousand federal soldiers fled in panic and Early's men pushed back the main body of Sheridan's army four miles. But while the celebrating Confederates broke ranks to plunder the Yankee camps, Sheridan's troops formed a new line. Sheridan, returning from Washington, heard the sounds of battle when he reached Winchester. Mounting his horse, he galloped to the battlefield and rallied his men. By mid-afternoon the counterattack he organized regained the ground lost and drove the Confederates eight miles farther south. The stunning reversal at Cedar Creek scattered Early's army and finished it as an effective fighting force.

Philip Sheridan's ride made him a Union hero. Celebrated in songs, poems, and illustrations, the saga of a general snatching victory from the jaws of defeat seemed to encapsulate the Union's reversal of fortunes that fall of 1864. As a gesture of special recognition, Dana was sent by Stanton to present Sheridan with a letter of promotion to major general. Taking a train to Harper's Ferry, Dana rode from there on horseback with an armed escort to Sheridan's camp, fifty miles up the Shenandoah Valley. When he arrived, Sheridan was in bed, but Dana had him roused and read him the commission by the flare of an army torch in the presence of some staff members. The groggy general mumbled a few words of appreciation.[38]

The next morning Dana and Sheridan rode through camp. Dana was struck by the soldiers' personal affection for their commander: "I had not seen anything like it in either of our great armies." When he asked Sheridan, the general attributed it to his practice of fighting in the front rank with his soldiers: "It would not do for a commanding General to . . . carry on a battle with paper orders, as they do in the Army of the Potomac. These men all know that where it is hottest, there I am, and they like it." Sheridan, Dana wrote Wilson, "appears to me to be the first military genius whom the war has produced on either side." This was a powerful compliment from a man who had seen Grant, Sherman, and Lee in action.[39]

The tide of battle had finally turned, and with it Lincoln's fortunes. Sherman's and Sheridan's victories cleared the remaining political obstacles to Lincoln's reelection. They quieted War Democrats and reunited Republicans behind their candidate. One by one, Lincoln's radical Republican critics returned to the fold. The Opdyke-Field group of New York radicals called off their Cincinnati convention, and Horace Greeley stumped for Lincoln in *Tribune* editorials. In mid-September Salmon P. Chase, no longer in the cabinet, began a speaking tour of Indiana, Ohio, and Kentucky on Lincoln's behalf. On September 22, the same day as Sheridan's victory at Winchester, Frémont withdrew from the race, not to aid Lincoln, he explained, "but to do my part towards preventing the election of the Democratic candidate." The next day Lincoln removed the radicals' nemesis, Postmaster General Montgomery Blair, from his cabinet to seal an arrangement that secured the endorsement of Senator Wade and Representative Davis.[40]

The War Department and the Election

Although Lincoln's reelection seemed likely by October, the War Department left little to chance. "The whole machine was worked in Lincoln's favor for all that it was worth," Dana commented in retrospect. Stanton and his assistants had no idea of remaining neutral in this wartime plebiscite, even if it meant applying double standards and suppressing free speech. All war office employees had a portion of their salaries levied to support Republican campaigning. Some clerks accused of "McClellanism" were dismissed, and several army officers who openly sided with the Democratic ticket faced courts-martial for "disloyalty." Dana suspended payments to a government contractor who was accused of hanging a McClellan banner in front of his shop. Stanton dismissed the superintendent at West Point for inviting McClellan to give an address. Critics complained that such spiteful behavior was "fitting rather to a bad-tempered child than a great and dignified cabinet member."[41]

In an election that many expected to be close, the soldier vote was critical. Republicans wagered that it strongly favored Lincoln. There were Democrats in the western camps and McClellan diehards scattered through the army, but the party's platform and Republican propaganda blunted their impact. Even soldiers who disliked Lincoln or opposed emancipation would not join hands with Copperheads and "peace men." During the war thirteen states passed laws that allowed soldiers to vote in the field; four others provided proxy ballots. Government regulations authorized the state committee for each political party to designate a few agents who, once approved by the war office, distributed ballots to soldiers in camp. No speeches or canvassing were allowed.[42]

Pivotal elections for offices in Ohio, Pennsylvania, and Indiana were scheduled for early October. The results offered a preview of the presidential contest in November and were important in themselves. Governor Oliver Morton of Indiana had waged a two-year battle with the Democratic-controlled state legislature; his defeat would strengthen midwestern Copperheads and probably take Indiana soldiers out of the war. To prevent such an outcome, War Department employees in Washington who were residents of Indiana, Pennsylvania, and Ohio were given leave to return home to vote. Because Indiana did not permit soldiers to vote in the field, Stanton sent home all recuperating Hoosiers from camp hospitals, and officers from Indiana were furloughed to give pro-Republican speeches around the state.[43]

On the night of October 11, when the three swing-state contests were to be decided, Lincoln walked with John Hay to Edwin Stanton's office to await returns on the military telegraph. The president seemed confident, even serene, but Stanton was on edge as he read each telegram brought in and passed it to Lincoln. At about half past eight Dana joined the group. During a lull between dispatches, Lincoln asked Dana if he was a fan of "Petroleum V. Nasby." The Ohio newspaperman David Ross Locke, the president's favorite humorist, regularly skewered Northern Copperheads through comic columns penned by the fictional Nasby, a resident of "Confedrit X Roads, Kentucky" who mouthed dim-witted, traitorous tirades in ragged dialect.

Dana's response—that he was only vaguely familiar with Nasby's writings—gave Lincoln his cue. He motioned Dana to a chair next to him, pulled out a thin yellow-back book from his breast pocket, and read aloud choice snippets with relish, interrupted only by the arrival of new telegrams. Dana and Hay laughed along with Lincoln, but Stanton silently fumed. The merriment went on for half an hour until the arrival of the dour Salmon Chase dampened the mood. When Lincoln put the book aside, Stanton motioned Dana into the next room and shut the door behind them.

"God damn it to hell!" Stanton exploded. "Was there ever such nonsense? Was there ever such inability to appreciate what is going on in an awful crisis? Here is the fate of this whole republic at stake, and here is the man . . . on whom it all depends, turning aside from this momentous . . . issue, to read the God damned trash of a silly mountebank!" Stanton, Dana felt, could never understand Lincoln's need for comic relief to balance his melancholy temperament, so battered by the strain of war. Later that night, Stanton's mood lightened as returns from Ohio and Indiana pointed toward a Republican triumph. Enjoying a victory cigar, he boasted about his midwestern network of army informers who reported on any backsliders.[44]

The results showed the Union ticket victorious in all three states. In Ohio and Pennsylvania the Republicans won huge congressional majorities; in Indiana Morton was handily reelected and Unionists recaptured the legislature. By Hay's reckoning this "rescue[d] Indiana from sedition & civil war" and saved Illinois for November. Lincoln thought the second point more doubtful. When the president jotted down his projections at the telegraph office two evenings later, he put Illinois in McClellan's column and predicted his own reelection by the dangerously slim margin of 117 to 114 electoral votes.[45]

As the November elections approached, once again "all the power and influence of the War Department" was summoned to secure victory for Lincoln, according to Dana. The assistant secretary suggested to Grant that no released Confederate prisoners be allowed to go to the North until after November 8, "as they are all in favor of a cessation of hostilities." Three days before the election a barrage of telegrams from Dana directed the arrest of suspected rebel agents in Cincinnati, Memphis, Nashville, and New York.[46]

Again, the army was mobilized to get out the vote. With the connivance of the White House and the Republican National Committee, an officer was assigned to distribute pro-Republican newspapers free of charge to the Army of the Potomac. Leaves to return home to vote were granted more readily to declared Republican soldiers. A constant stream of telegrams arrived at Dana's desk asking to release men from tossup districts, on detached duty, or convalescing in hospitals. A few days before the November election, Stanton ordered commanders to give two-week furloughs to all midwestern soldiers unfit for field duty. To boost Lincoln's chances in his home state, Stanton told Rosecrans to furlough several regiments of Illinois volunteers. Others being transferred from Missouri to Tennessee were allowed to pause in Illinois to vote.[47]

As soldiers cast their votes, high army officers were pressured to assist Republican state agents and give extra scrutiny to Democratic vote collectors. When stories reached the war office that three New York State agents in Washington appointed by Governor Horatio Seymour had signed blank Democratic ballots to be distributed to Union soldiers, Dana transmitted Stanton's order to arrest them. After the arrests, Dana sent notices to George Meade, Benjamin Butler, and Union generals at the Virginia front to detain suspicious Democratic agents or have them "looked after." He warned General Marsena Patrick, the Army of the Potomac's punctilious provost marshal general, not to favor New York's Democratic vote-gatherers. Patrick, insulted, was left to grumble about Dana's "insolence" and Stanton's "systematic abuse" until he traveled to Washington after the election to give Stanton a piece of his mind.[48]

Meanwhile, the three New York Democratic agents underwent a military trial by the same commission that had convicted state agents in Baltimore of what Dana called "gross frauds and forgeries." One of the defendants, Levi Cohn, wrote Lincoln promising to disclose damaging new information in exchange for his release. On December 1 Cohn met with Lincoln at the White House in the presence of Dana, who recorded his testimony, and John A. Foster, the government's prosecutor. The three agreed that Cohn divulged nothing not already in the trial record, so he was kept in custody. Some of the government's key evidence was tainted, however. After a long trial that ended with a verdict of not guilty, Cohn and his co-defendants were released in early 1865. Like Judge Advocate General Holt, who reviewed the case, Dana believed the three New Yorkers were guilty and claimed they had been freed on a legal technicality.[49]

New York received extra attention from War Department leaders as a swing state evenly divided between McClellan and Lincoln supporters, and it had in Horatio Seymour a vocal antidraft Democratic governor. Union officials also feared that pro-Confederate agents aiming to disrupt the election would cross the New York border from Canada. These anxieties escalated after the raid on St. Albans, Vermont, on October 19, in which a group of rebel soldiers who had escaped Northern prisons and fled to Canada returned to rob the town's banks, killing one townsperson. A few days later, Dana received word from the War Department's spies that Confederate agents in Canada planned additional sabotage.

Captured dispatches between the Canadian agents and Richmond authorities indicated that a series of plots were being hatched. The most threatening, described by Dana years later, was "a scheme for setting fire to New York and Chicago by means of clock-work machines that were to be placed in several of the large hotels and places of amusement." Dana may have added the specific details in hindsight, but the conspiracy to burn New York was corroborated by dispatches from US consuls in Montreal and Halifax to Secretary Seward, which relayed that Confederate agents had scheduled their mayhem for election day. Alerted by Dana, Stanton ordered General John Dix at New York City to set up "a perfect cordon" on the Canadian border and asked Grant to spare a few thousand men to secure the forts in New York Harbor.[50]

Governor Seymour, defying Dix, declared that there was "no necessity, authority, or excuse" for federal intervention. Stanton and Dana suspected that Seymour might use the state's militia to intimidate Republican voters or otherwise tip the political balance. Both men harbored bitter memories of Seymour's conciliation of New York City's draft-rioters the previous summer. Dana believed the threat of riots genuine, but he doubted that Seymour would permit a Democratic mob to take over the city. The plot to burn New York was more credible. Richmond's agent, Jacob Thompson, organized a band of raiders that included two former cavalrymen who had served under John Hunt Morgan and a Louisiana Rebel, Robert Cobb Kennedy, who had escaped from a Union prison on Lake Erie. Traveling in civilian clothes from Toronto to New York in late October, they took rooms in various hotels under assumed names. Their plan was to set fire to several hotels and public buildings, which would stop the election and paralyze the police. The fires would be the signal for a general uprising among New York's Copperheads, who would then take possession of the city and its approaches. This would be the first step toward organizing a Northeast Confederacy that would join the Northwest Confederacy in cooperating with the government in Richmond.[51]

It was a bizarre scheme with virtually no prospect of success. Tipped off by Dana and others, War Department officials took steps to thwart it. Stanton wired Grant to send troops with "loyal, suitable officers" to reinforce Dix, to be led by General Benjamin Butler. Butler could not capably command an army in the field, but his stint as the "Beast" of New Orleans proved that he knew how to subdue rebellious civilians. Joined by 5,000 soldiers from the Army of the James, Butler distributed them on election day on ferryboats and transports floating on the Hudson and East Rivers, from where they could be rushed to shore where needed. Gunboats circled Manhattan to protect key buildings and bridges. Plain-clothed army men were stationed at the polls with direct telegraph connections to the general's hotel headquarters. In place of Seymour's state militia the city's trusted police force beefed up patrols, and volunteer firemen were put on standby duty. The show of force succeeded. The Confederate conspirators, believing their plot had been exposed, postponed it, and their Copperhead allies were cowed. The election proceeded without riots or fires. Butler's dispatch to Washington on November 8 read simply: "The quietest city ever seen."[52]

After Butler's troops departed, the Confederate conspirators carried out their scheme, more out of frustration and revenge than with any clear objective. On the night of November 25 they lit more than a dozen blazes with bottles of "Greek fire"—a mixture of phosphorus in bisulfide of carbon—in several New York hotels and Barnum's Museum. But the fires suffocated quickly and the conspirators' hopes to sow chaos fizzled. Most escaped to Canada, but Kennedy was captured, convicted of spying and irregular warfare, and executed. Even if it had been successful, the arson attack came too late. New York voters had done their part for Lincoln. McClellan outpolled the president two-to-one in the metropolis, but Upstate votes carried the state for Lincoln by a slim margin and ousted Seymour as well.[53]

On election night, Lincoln and Hay again walked from the White House to the War Department telegraph room, splashing through the rain. They were joined in Stanton's office by Secretaries Welles and Bates. Stanton himself was seriously ill at home with a fever, his energy spent on the campaign. Dana was not present, either. The exultant telegrams came in at regular intervals, and by midnight the Republican landslide was apparent. Lincoln took every state except Delaware, Kentucky, and New Jersey, giving him a 212-to-21 electoral vote victory over McClellan. Around two-thirty in the morning the president gave an impromptu speech from Stanton's window, thanking the crowd for "the people's resolution to stand by free government and the rights of humanity."[54]

Stanton and Dana's effort to get out the soldier vote paid off handsomely. Union troops who voted in the field favored Lincoln by more than three to one over McClellan, and the ratio among furloughed soldiers was likely similar. Without these votes, Lincoln would have lost New York, Connecticut, and possibly Indiana, making the national contest much closer. The soldier vote was decisive in several congressional elections, and to Dana's delight it put emancipation over the top in Maryland, where a new state constitution prohibiting slavery passed by only 475 votes out of nearly 60,000. Union soldiers approved it by 2,633 to 163.[55]

Early the next morning Dana called at the White House to offer Lincoln congratulations and escort him to the ailing Stanton. The knowledge that the War Department had contributed to Lincoln's reelection gratified Dana and Stanton, and it probably hastened the latter's recovery. Two nights after the election, President Lincoln stood at the window under the White House North Portico to address a crowd of serenaders. The election, he told them, had "demonstrated that a people's government can sustain a national election, in the midst of a great civil war." The Northern public had proven their resolve to restore the integrity of the Union. But the war for the Union still had to be won. And slavery, the root cause of the war, was not yet outlawed across the land.[56]

15 "Side Politics," Spies, and Swindlers

After the election, public speculation swirled about cabinet changes. The usual talk about fresh faces for a second term was magnified by the toll that war had taken on members' health. A Supreme Court vacancy had been created by the death of Chief Justice Roger Taney in October, and gossip about the Court merged with cabinet rumors because Edwin Stanton, Salmon P. Chase, and Montgomery Blair coveted the judicial post for themselves. "Don't believe any of the reports about approaching changes in the cabinet," Charles Dana warned his friend James Wilson after the election. "If Mr. Stanton is to be Chief-Justice, I don't know it; and I do know that neither General [Benjamin] Butler nor General [Nathaniel] Banks is to be Secretary of War."[1]

The rumors about Stanton and the Court were not unfounded. Stanton had been a brilliant trial lawyer who argued many cases before the Supreme Court, and he longed for the status and security of a judicial appointment. Stanton's friends told President Lincoln he would make a great justice, but Lincoln felt trapped. "Where could I get a man to take Stanton's place?" he asked. "Tell me that, and I will do it." General Ulysses Grant, hearing that Butler might be appointed war secretary, visited Washington to veto such a change.[2]

Lincoln, meanwhile, leaned toward Chase, who was well qualified to join the Court and who had campaigned for him in the end. As chief justice, Chase would uphold the administration's policies on the Emancipation Proclamation and Reconstruction, a path the conservative Blair might not follow. As speculation intensified, Stanton informed Lincoln indirectly that he was withdrawing in favor of his friend Chase, and on December 6 Lincoln sent Chase's name to the Senate. Dana sensed that "this appointment was not made by the President with entire willingness"; Chase, after all, had encouraged the radicals opposing his renomination. Lincoln was "a man who keeps a grudge as faithfully as any other living Christian, and consented to Mr. Chase's elevation, only when the pressure became very general, and very urgent." In particular, Dana told his overseas friend James Pike, the Senate was dead set against Blair's appointment or the elevation of some "second rate man" such as Justice Noah Swayne to chief justice. Lincoln set aside personal feelings and acted in the interest of party harmony and from his belief that Chase would make a first-rate jurist.[3]

There were other changes brewing. Attorney General Edward Bates, who had planned to retire after the election, resigned and was replaced by James Speed, the brother of Lincoln's old Kentucky friend Joshua. A surprise candidate and a man of only "moderate abilities," in Dana's opinion, James Speed nevertheless proved an able officeholder. William Pitt Fessenden at the Treasury and John P. Usher at Interior were replaced by Hugh McCulloch of Indiana and Senator James Harlan of Iowa, respectively. Otherwise, Dana told friends, the two most important cabinet members would stay in place. William Seward at State seemed poised to retire temporarily and regroup for the next presidential contest, but "he is an old and practiced office-holder, and I have observed that men once used to power are very loath to resign it." Dana was certain that Stanton would continue in the War Department as long as his health would allow. In the frenzy of the campaign Stanton had collapsed, but he recovered gradually and returned to his customary sunrise-to-darkness office schedule.[4]

Because Stanton stayed so did Dana, although he kept an eye out for more lucrative posts. In January 1865 Dana told Wilson that he "came near leaving" the previous month to become adjutant general of New York, the chief administrative officer of the state's volunteer forces. The inducements were "complete control of all military appointments" among New York troops, "the opportunity of great political usefulness" to the administration, and—not least—"an amount of pay on which I could live." The costs of housing and food at Washington were "frightful." But Stanton needed Dana and would not approve the appointment. Committed for the duration, Dana pledged that "as soon as the war is so far over that I can properly leave, I shall attend to my own affairs."[5]

Other evidence hints that Dana was growing restless in Stanton's harness. In early January Stanton embarked on a ten-day trip to Savannah and North Carolina. As usual, Dana took on Stanton's routine tasks, such as compiling daily dispatches for the Associated Press. But this time Lincoln formally authorized Dana to perform the duties of the secretary of war. The change was announced in the newspapers and Dana began signing his official letters "Acting Secretary." Lincoln, who probably colluded with Dana, seized the moment to have him promote a favorite colonel to brigadier general, an order that Stanton had refused. "Dana is acting," the president told the colonel's sponsor, "he will attend to it for you." Lincoln reportedly said this "with a manner of relief, as if it was a piece of good luck to find a man there who would obey his orders."[6]

Somehow, Stanton got wind of this subterfuge and telegraphed Dana from Fortress Monroe: "I forgot to mention to you that I shall continue acting as Secretary, issuing orders and making regulations. Your official style and signature will be that of your commission, Assistant Secretary, and not Acting Secretary." Stanton reminded him that "there can be only one Acting Secretary"—himself. Despite the reprimand, Dana continued to use "Acting" when, for example, on January 15 he wired official congratulations to Missouri's governor after the state adopted a new constitution that abolished slavery. Only on January 17, the day before Stanton's return, did Dana's signature line return to "Assistant." A consolation prize arrived a week later, when Peter Watson, who had been on sick leave, resigned as first assistant secretary and Dana was given the title.[7]

This episode, with its whiff of insubordination, calls to mind Dana's earlier tiff with Horace Greeley over control at the *New York Tribune*. Yet Dana's relations with Stanton did not sour in the war's waning months. Stanton valued Dana's work and gave him favorable conditions, and Dana was usually careful not to overstep his authority. During Stanton's trip Grant asked Dana to take an appointment request to Lincoln; Dana replied that nothing would happen "until Mr. Stanton returns." Bound by mutual respect and an understanding about their roles, Stanton and Dana kept their focus on defeating the enemy and avoided potential disputes.[8]

At least Dana was no longer apart from his family. Eunice and their four children joined him at their rented New York Avenue townhouse during the winter of 1864–1865, where the family enjoyed a modest middle-class existence and shared some of the excitement of the wartime capital. With his wife in town Dana's social schedule perked up. In mid-January the couple enjoyed a dinner for a visiting French dignitary at the Chase residence, where they were joined by Charles Sumner. On other occasions the Danas took visitors aboard excursions on the Potomac and comforted wounded soldiers at Union hospitals.[9]

On New Year's Eve Dana was among the guests of honor at a New York dinner to celebrate William T. Sherman's capture of Atlanta and George Thomas's victory at Nashville. Two days later he was in the White House, where the Lincolns held a glittering reception. Cabinet members, Supreme Court justices, diplomats, senators, and congressmen lined up to greet President Lincoln and the First Lady. So did a group of African American men and women, eager to shake hands with the man who signed the freedom proclamation. Dana's ten-year-old daughter Eunice (called "Minnie" by the family) begged to come along and he allowed her to watch the spectacle from a corner. Toward the end of the levee Dana approached the president: "I have a little girl here who wants to shake hands with you." Lincoln lifted Miss Dana for a kiss and a brief conversation. "She will never forget it if she lives to be a thousand years old," Dana told friends. Her next visit to the White House came fifty-two years later, on Bastille Day 1917, when Mrs. Eunice Dana Brannan was arrested while picketing for women's voting rights. "How long must women wait for liberty?" her banner asked Woodrow Wilson.[10]

Lobbying for Lincoln and Emancipation

"The most interesting question just at this moment," Dana wrote James Wilson in early January, "is whether the antislavery amendment of the Constitution will pass the House of Representatives next week. It is hoped that a sufficient number of Democratic members will vote for it . . . but I can't tell whether the hope is well founded." One afternoon about a week later, Lincoln walked over to Dana's office at the War Department and shut the door behind him. The president wanted to talk about the House vote on the Thirteenth Amendment, which had been postponed to January 31. "Dana," he opened, "I am very anxious about this vote. . . . The time is very short. It is going to be a great deal closer than I wish." Dana replied that there were "plenty of Democrats" who would vote for the amendment and named a couple. "But there are some others that I am not clear about," Lincoln responded. "There are three that you can deal with better than anybody else, perhaps, as you know them all. I wish you would send for them." One was from New Jersey and two from New York, according to Dana's recollections. When Dana asked what he could offer in return, Lincoln said he would consent to "whatever promise you make. . . . It is a question of three votes or new armies." With this exchange Lincoln pressed Dana into service to lobby for emancipation.[11]

The amendment to abolish slavery nationwide had passed in the Senate in June 1864 but failed to gain the required two-thirds vote in the House. Republican lawmakers supported it almost unanimously, but only four House Democrats joined them. Republican gains in the November elections made it virtually certain that the amendment would pass once the new 39th Congress started its regular session in December 1865, but Lincoln was unwilling to wait nearly a year. He urged Congress to approve it right away as a gesture of bipartisan loyalty to the principle of freedom. Lincoln was also concerned about the Emancipation Proclamation's fate after the fighting stopped. Issued as a presidential order under "military necessity," would it be operative in peacetime? Would it be enforced by his successors? "A question might be raised whether the proclamation was legally valid," he worried. Opponents could argue that it applied only to slaves fleeing behind Union lines or to children born before it was issued. Passage of a constitutional amendment would be "a King's cure for all the[se] evils," Lincoln told supporters.[12]

Dana believed the amendment was intended not just to abolish slavery, "but as a means of affecting . . . the anticipations of those in rebellion." Its passage would signal definitively that there could be no peace agreement that left slavery intact. Peace Democrats and Confederate sympathizers in the North could no longer charge that only Lincoln's personal demand for emancipation prevented reconciliation, a claim that had dogged him since the Niagara Falls episode. Making emancipation official would solidify the North's pro-Union coalition, "paralyze the enemy," and equal the impact of "new armies in the field."[13]

The amendment's sponsor, Representative James Ashley of Ohio, calculated that more than a dozen additional votes were needed to secure adoption. Most would have to come from Democrats in the border states, the Midwest, and New York. Several lobbying initiatives swung into action. Secretary of State Seward took a leading role, organizing a shady circle of New York and border-state operatives as well as two upstate New York Democratic congressmen. In competition with this "Seward lobby" Montgomery Blair opened his own campaign aimed at building a coalition with moderate Democrats to marginalize Radical Republicans. Ashley himself arranged for Lincoln to meet informally with Democratic congressmen from Missouri, Illinois, and Ohio.[14]

Uncertain whether he had sufficient support, Ashley put off the final vote to the end of January. Meanwhile, Lincoln urged Republican leaders to redouble their efforts and authorized them to use his patronage powers as leverage. He enlisted Charles Dana's help as part of that final push. Dana sent for the three congressmen assigned him and saw them one by one. (Dana withheld their names in his reminiscences.) He found them "afraid of their party" but still amenable to a deal. Two wanted friends appointed as internal revenue collectors and a third sought "a very important appointment about the customhouse of New York." Dana reportedly sealed these agreements on Lincoln's authority in return for their votes.[15]

Or did he? When ghostwriting Dana's *Recollections* three decades later Ida Tarbell mistakenly dated Dana's lobbying efforts to March 1864, when the House voted on Nevada's admission to the Union. Some historians have repeated the error, while others use the confusion as a reason to dismiss Dana's tale.[16] Two of Dana's lobbying deals in January 1865 can be verified, however. Anson Herrick, a New York City Democrat, had been unseated in November. Dana promised that in exchange for his vote for the Thirteenth Amendment his brother Hugh, a Republican who had worked beside Dana in local politics, would be appointed an internal revenue assessor. Herrick changed his vote, and after Congress adopted the amendment Lincoln sent Hugh Herrick's name to the Senate.[17]

Congress adjourned in March without acting on the appointment, however, and after Lincoln was murdered, Seward and President Andrew Johnson turned a deaf ear to Herrick's pleas. Alerted by Roscoe Conkling, Dana tried to intercede with Johnson at the White House. "This is Mr. Lincoln's promise," Dana reminded the new president. "He regarded it as saving the necessity of another call for troops . . . to continue the war." Johnson still balked, lecturing Dana: "I have observed in the course of my experience that such bargains tend to immorality." Political calculations rather than principle may have hardened Johnson's stance, for the incumbent, he was told, was a "most zealous and effective supporter." He did not make the appointment.[18]

The second New York congressman lobbied by Dana was another lame-duck Democrat, Moses F. Odell of Brooklyn. Odell had antagonized party regulars by his criticism of General George McClellan and was not renominated. A few months after Odell voted for the Thirteenth Amendment he was appointed Naval Officer of the Port of New York. In this case, the new president's political calculations aligned with Lincoln's promise. Odell was a former colleague of Johnson's on the Committee on the Conduct of the War and a War Democrat who could help Johnson build a conservative coalition that would promote his lenient plan for Reconstruction.[19]

Dana's third target for lobbying, whom he remembered as a congressman from New Jersey, remains a mystery. No New Jersey Democrat voted for the amendment, but two of the state's Democratic representatives were absent for the final vote, which reduced the number of votes necessary for passage. Dana may have been involved in persuading them.[20]

When Congress gathered before a packed chamber on January 31 for the final vote, no one was certain which way it would go. During a brief time given to speeches, three Democratic converts endorsed the amendment—the last was Anson Herrick—and opponents explained their views. Then the roll was called. The final tally was 119–56, with eight members absent, all Democrats; the amendment passed with two votes to spare. At the announce-

SCENE IN THE HOUSE ON THE PASSAGE OF THE PROPOSITION TO AMEND THE CONSTITUTION, January 31, 1865.

Celebration erupts in the House of Representatives after the passage of the Thirteenth Amendment, January 31, 1865. *Harper's Weekly*, February 18, 1865.

ment the House erupted in the most tumultuous celebration in its history. Victorious congressmen leaped to their feet, cheered, and threw their hats in the air. In the galleries, abolitionist women waved their handkerchiefs and African Americans, including Frederick Douglass's son Charles, shouted for joy. After several minutes of pandemonium the House voted to adjourn "in honor of this immortal and sublime event."[21]

How important had Dana's lobbying been? Without the support of fifteen Democrats who bucked their party, including five who, like Herrick, had voted against the amendment in June 1864, it would have failed. Renegade Democrats supported abolition from a mix of motives, including the decision to vote their conscience (made easier for most by their lame-duck status), fear for their party's prospects if it continued to support slaveholders, and the inducements of patronage posts. There is little doubt that Lincoln's indirect bargaining helped tip the balance, and Dana relished the part he had played. The crusty Thaddeus Stevens, a fierce champion of the amendment, later gloated that "the greatest measure of the nineteenth century was passed by corruption, aided and abetted by the purest man in America." Dana disagreed: "This little piece of side politics was one of the most judicious, humane, and wise uses of executive authority that I had ever assisted in or witnessed." In his view, furthering principles through patronage was not corruption but statesmanship.[22]

As things turned out, it also mattered that the 38th Congress passed the amendment rather than its successor. If Congress waited until its regular session convened, which was not until December 1865, there would have been a long and potentially chaotic interval between the war's end and a definitive prohibition of slavery, especially in light of Lincoln's unexpected death. Without emancipation approved by Congress, Johnson might have allowed Southern states to seek readmission with slavery intact. As things stood, Lincoln called the amendment a fitting adjunct to the war's conclusion and an antidote to its "original cause." He urged Americans to "go forward and consummate by the votes of the states what Congress so nobly began." In December 1865—eight months after his death and shortly after the new Congress convened—they did just that.[23]

As soon as the House vote was tallied, Congressman Ashley left the Capitol and took a fast carriage to the War Department with a list of the aye votes. Stanton ordered a hundred-gun salute in the heart of the city, which shook windows for miles around. Between rounds he read aloud the names of those who had voted for the amendment, declaring that "history will embalm them in great honor." Dana attended the ceremony, but then, and for the next thirty years, he kept his own slice of honor to himself.[24]

Trade with the Enemy

Abraham Lincoln was a master politician, but his judgment was not infallible. His shrewd politicking helped to outlaw slavery, but other backroom deals he orchestrated were more productive of mischief than good. A case in point was his approval of the cotton-for-supplies trade with Confederates in the last year of the war, which Dana and Stanton worked secretly to countermand.

In December 1864 Dana reported to friends that Congress was abuzz over trade with the South. Under Treasury regulations approved by the president, persons within rebel lines who took a loyalty oath could bring products to Union officials and exchange them for supplies. Through this arrangement "rebel agents are now accumulating great quantities of provisions, and count upon being able to feed their armies . . . by means of pork, beef, and flour, which are to be sent to them from New York, St. Louis, and other points in exchange for cotton." This situation, "not yet known but generally suspected," was agitating Congress, especially since "some prominent officials of ours are pretty deep in the speculation."[25]

These exchanges with the enemy flouted Congress's intent to limit the trade when in July 1864 it gave the Treasury Department sole authority to issue licenses. As implemented, the law actually encouraged expanded trade between the lines. Any trader with a permit could take cotton from rebel areas to the Union lines, sell it to a Treasury agent, and immediately receive three-fourths of the New York price. Meanwhile, Lincoln issued an order that allowed cotton sellers to purchase merchandise worth up to one-third of their proceeds and return it to rebel territory. Speculators stood to make substantial profits in both directions. Because the government had no clear definition of "contraband" beyond ordnance, the "supplies" traders shipped to the South often included food and clothing desperately needed by Confederate soldiers.[26]

Lincoln strongly favored the trade, although he was careful to express his support privately. He had been lobbied by Northern textile manufacturers and understood that they badly needed raw cotton. He also accepted the claim that buying Southern cotton would prevent Confederates from selling it abroad at even higher prices in exchange for weapons. "Better give him *guns* for it than let him, as now, get both guns and ammunition for it," he explained to General Edward Canby, a staunch opponent of the trade. As for speculators' profits, "if pecuniary greed can be made to aid us in such effort, let us be thankful that so much good can be got out of pecuniary greed."[27]

These were hardly the sort of noble sentiments Lincoln is now remembered for. They also made little sense. By 1864 the South's cotton exports had been reduced by the Union blockade to one-eighth of their prewar volume and were continuing to decline. Maintaining the permit policy even after all major Confederate ports were shut suggests that aiding Northern business dominated the president's motives. Still, Lincoln convinced himself that he was doing good while allowing friends and supporters to do well. He signed over forty special orders authorizing cotton sales to individuals, and after Treasury Department procedures took effect he used permits to bestow favors on cronies. Among those directly or indirectly involved in cotton speculation were the Republican boss Thurlow Weed, Lincoln's sometime bodyguard Ward Lamon, former Illinois senator Orville Browning, and Lincoln's friend Leonard Swett. The other "prominent officials" Dana referred to in his letter included politicians such as New York senator Edwin Morgan and Customs Collector Simeon Draper, and the Union generals John A. Dix, Napoleon J. T. Dana, and Samuel Curtis. Assistant Secretary Dana was personally familiar with forged permit charges against Captain Lorenzo Thomas, Jr., son of the Union adjutant general. Hanson Risley, the Treasury official overseeing the process, issued permits in late 1864 and early 1865 for almost a million bales of cotton from his Treasury office and his New York headquarters, which happened to be Weed's room at the Astor House.[28]

No doubt fearing opposition, Lincoln did not consult the cabinet or inform Congress about his order permitting exchange of goods. In December 1864 the *New York Herald* broke the story. Many officers and prominent congressmen were appalled. General Grant, who was laboring to starve out Robert E. Lee's army, now had to concern himself with cutting any supply lines coming from the North to support the Rebels. At the War Department, Stanton and Dana resented the regulations and were frustrated by Lincoln's largesse to his allies. After Dana's reversal on cotton speculation in Memphis in early 1863, he had repeatedly opposed trade across the lines. Only a month into office under Stanton, he had a run-in with General Butler in Virginia over issuing permits to trade Confederate corn for lye, a component of gunpowder. "On trade with the rebels my opinion precisely agrees with yours," Dana wrote General Canby. Together with Stanton, Dana conspired to put an end to Lincoln's new policy.[29]

Their first thought was to stall in issuing orders to officers implementing the trade until Congress could convene and change the law, but the delay only led Lincoln to sign the permits himself. Thwarted, they took a more aggressive approach. General Grant's situation in Virginia—fighting the contraband trade at his back and Lee's army in his front—presented an opportunity to enlist his help. By this point in the war it had become common for War Department leaders to ask Grant to "request" the precise actions they had in mind. Dana and Stanton reasoned that Lincoln would listen to Grant more readily than to them and that "military necessity" was a clinching argument against the trade. On January 16 Dana informed Grant that an extensive contraband trade with the Rebels was reportedly being carried on through Norfolk. The War Department sleuth Lafayette Baker, whom Dana set to work on the trade, had uncovered arrangements by which agents with Treasury permits were exchanging cotton upriver from Norfolk for food and clothing that were then traded to the Confederate army. Dana estimated that goods worth $100,000 were being shipped daily. "Please cause the facts at Norfolk to be investigated," Dana wrote Grant, prompting him to "advise this Department what action you deem to be necessary . . . upon military grounds."[30]

Rumors were rife that General Butler and his officers at Norfolk were profiting from the trade, and Baker provided Dana with specific allegations. But Butler was no longer in charge. On January 4 Grant had finally requested Butler's removal from command. His bungled expedition against Fort Fisher in North Carolina was the prime cause, but a second consideration, Grant said, was his lax "administration of the affairs of his department." The investigation Dana ordered may have been part of a campaign to discredit Butler, as the general charged. More likely, once Butler was removed Dana and Stanton believed that they could discover the full extent of the illegal trade he had protected, and the findings could be used to force Lincoln to reverse his stand.[31]

Butler himself played the injured innocent, a role he had rehearsed for Dana a year earlier. While heading northward to await reassignment Butler stopped in Washington to complain about his sacking. He arrived at the War Department just as Dana was writing Grant to investigate the trade. The stage was set for a royal confrontation—which Butler often relished. This time Butler decided that it would serve him better to appear the good soldier. Butler agreed that the trade was helping the enemy, and he showed Dana a captured memorandum from a rebel quartermaster that approved exchanging cotton for provisions. Butler told Dana that he opposed the trade but could do little because it was carried out legally under regulations that allowed supplies to be sent across the lines.[32]

In response to Dana's telegram Grant ordered a three-man military commission led by General George H. Gordon, a Harvard-trained lawyer, to investigate the contraband trade at Norfolk. For six weeks the commission questioned witnesses aggressively. One of Butler's officers wrote him several times in alarm. Describing the commission as an "Inquisition," he warned Butler that "every witness is questioned about your connections with them. . . . From *something* you said to someone in Washington, Dana has built a story which condemns you and your administration." In his reply Butler, conscious that his mail could be used as evidence, washed his hands of the affair. He had done nothing wrong and was "entirely indifferent as to what investigation or inquiries are set on foot." If any of his officers had misbehaved he would certainly not defend them.[33]

Much of the lucrative trade was in fact in the hands of Butler's subordinates, friends, and relatives. After resigning under a cloud, Captain George H. Johnston of Butler's staff used his military contacts to make profits as a civilian merchant. Butler's brother-in-law, Fisher Hildreth, exploited his connection to procure an interest in several ventures and may have funneled money to Butler. According to the most careful historian of the cotton trade scandals, "there can be scant doubt that Butler profited personally from the trade, although he covered his tracks so thoroughly that he could never have been convicted in a court of law."[34]

General Gordon's commission issued its report in mid-March. It recommended that eleven of the traders and their accomplices, including Johnston, Hildreth, and the local US Treasury Agent, be arrested and held for trial. Several of the prisoners petitioned Lincoln to order their release, and Butler himself went to the White House on their behalf. The president apparently prevented a trial, but Gordon kept those charged confined for the duration of the war.[35]

Although it resulted in no trials or convictions, Gordon's commission gave the War Department and Grant ammunition to prohibit trade with Rebels in the eastern theater. Declaring that "military necessity is paramount to all other considerations," Stanton told Grant that "notwithstanding any permit given by the Secretary of the Treasury or President himself, you as Commander may prohibit trade crossing your lines, and may seize goods in transit either way." Grant recommended that the army and navy stop all shipments from Atlantic ports to the Southern interior. Stanton took Grant's request to Lincoln, and the president, who was also facing fierce congressional opposition to the trade, finally relented. "If he [Grant] thought that bacon was of more importance to the enemy at this moment than cotton was to us," Lincoln reportedly said, "why we must do without the cotton." Lincoln authorized Grant "to suspend all operations on the Treasury-trade-permits, in all places South Eastward of the Alleghenies." Stanton, still suspicious of Lincoln, urged Grant to include *all* trade permits, including those signed by the president, "so as to meet the whole mischief." On March 10 Grant issued a special order voiding all trade permits "by whomsoever granted" in southeastern states and prohibiting passage of any supplies beyond Union lines. On paper, at least, the contraband trade was ended.[36]

Just a few days before, Lincoln angered congressional Republicans by refusing to sign a bill that would have restricted trade with the South. It was the product of Elihu Washburne's hearings for the House Commerce Committee, which were held concurrently with Gordon's military commission and examined some of its evidence, including Lafayette Baker's investigations. Washburne's committee cast its net far beyond Norfolk, and it caught a swarm of cotton speculations and trade schemes that embarrassed the Lincoln administration. Congressmen were especially alarmed by Baker's report that Confederate agents in Canada had arranged with Northern speculators for massive exchanges of cotton for pork, with the administration's apparent approval. These revelations vindicated Dana's opposition to the cotton trade, but they put him in an awkward position as a Lincoln loyalist.

In the spring of 1864 Confederate President Jefferson Davis had sent Nathaniel Beverley Tucker, scion of a prominent Virginia family, to Canada to broker the sale of Confederate cotton in exchange for food for the rebel army. Lodging with other Confederates at St. Catherine's near Niagara Falls, Tucker made contacts with Northern speculators. One set of deals involved Thomas C. Durant, vice president of the Union Pacific Railroad, who obtained a Treasury permit and negotiated for 10,000 bales of cotton in exchange for pork, pound for pound. To seal this deal and discuss others, Durant and his associates wanted Tucker to come to New York to sign in person and take the contract to Richmond. Fearing Tucker's arrest, Durant's middlemen approached Lafayette Baker in October with a bribe: if Baker could escort Tucker from Canada to New York for negotiations and then conduct him safely to Virginia, he would receive a one-sixth share in the trade deal. To further sweeten the pot, Durant's men promised to pressure Lincoln to promote Baker from colonel to brigadier general.[37]

After giving a noncommittal response Baker returned to Washington and reported the offer to his chief, Dana. The assistant secretary gave Baker permission to play along in hopes of uncovering the scheme's details and nabbing Tucker as an enemy agent when he crossed the border. Baker told Durant he would cooperate, then headed to Canada with a secret order to arrest Tucker once he set foot on American soil. Baker and Tucker met in Montreal and discussed a deal for half a million bales of cotton, but their talks broke down when Tucker refused to accompany Baker across the border. He distrusted Durant and may also have suspected treachery on Baker's part. The detective returned to Washington alone with news that the plan had fallen through.[38]

All this intrigue went public in February 1865 when Washburne's committee heard Baker's testimony. Dana was also called to appear, but in contrast to Baker's freewheeling storytelling he was guarded and legalistic. Dana confirmed that he had sent Baker to investigate the contraband trade, but he decided that since the evidence against Durant was "all of a hearsay character" he could not press charges. Dana was also eager to arrest Tucker as a Confederate agent, but he claimed—contrary to Baker's testimony—that he had warned that Tucker could be arrested only if he crossed the border voluntarily, not through "deceptive proceedings to seduce him here." Entrapment would not hold up even in a military trial. Dana's clipped replies were meant to assure congressmen that he was vigilant against the contraband trade but would not permit investigators to become complicit in it or overstep legal bounds. Although Dana had secretly schemed with Stanton to stop the cotton trade, he was reluctant to discuss its details in public or face charges that the administration was lax in corralling wrongdoers.[39]

Washburne's committee concluded that the new trade policy had corrupted the army and navy, "led to the prolongation of the war," and "cost the country thousands of lives and millions upon millions of treasure." The bill they reported to the House would abolish the permit system and halt the exchange of cotton for supplies. It passed on the morning of March 3, the day before Lincoln's second inaugural. To Congress's dismay, the president killed the bill by not signing it—a pocket veto. Washburne rushed to the White House in angry protest. A week later he arrived at Grant's headquarters, ostensibly to give him a congressional medal but privately to encourage him to void all trade permits. By then, however, Grant had already received Lincoln's reluctant go-ahead, obtained through Stanton and Dana's intervention, to do so. The War Department duo had bypassed Lincoln's controversy with Congress and circumvented his veto. The exchange of cotton for food was finally stopped, but only one month remained before Grant's army effectively ended the war.[40]

The verdict of historian James Ford Rhodes on the contraband trade seems accurate: "For the South it was a necessary evil; for the North it was an evil and not a necessary one." Dana agreed. After Andrew Johnson succeeded Lincoln, Dana expressed relief to a friend that the new president "is surrounded by a much smaller number of persons who wish to get rich out of contracts or privileges of various kinds conferred by the government. Mr. Lincoln had a vast number of friends who were bent upon making money in various ways, and he was much more willing that they should have favorable opportunities of this sort, than I could have wished." The administration's tolerance of illicit wartime trade set a damaging precedent for the corruption of government by business interests, a practice that would draw Dana's ire in the postwar Gilded Age.[41]

Union Spies and Confederate Plots

Besides supervising the adventurous sleuth Lafayette Baker, Dana was the contact for some of the Union's most important spies. Many were shady characters who worked both sides or who used spying to extort money or as cover for contraband trade. Dana and his colleagues, eager for inside information, were hoodwinked more than once.

In April 1864 Joseph H. Maddox was arrested in Virginia for trading with the enemy. Dana was assured by provost marshals in Baltimore and the Army of the Potomac that Maddox was a valuable spy who had provided useful information about Richmond's defenses, so he ordered the prisoner freed. Several months later evidence surfaced that Maddox was in fact a "true and faithful Confederate" heavily involved in moving contraband tobacco northward from Virginia. Dana ordered Maddox rearrested and sent to Old Capitol Prison.[42]

Another informant, Hiram Rossman, came to Washington to give Dana reports on various plots allegedly hatched by Confederate agents in Canada. Rossman's veracity was questionable: the information he provided was rarely accurate, he failed to warn Dana of the plot to burn New York City, and his handwriting changed between letters. Despite misgivings, Dana provided Rossman with funds, believing it worth keeping his line of communication open on the chance that something valuable might emerge.[43]

James W. Boyd was a captured Confederate officer who told Dana at Old Capitol Prison that he had supervised scouts for John Pemberton's Confederate army and knew the ins and outs of the contraband trade. He offered, if released, to patrol the Mississippi area as a secret detective investigating illegal trade and promised to produce the names of culprits. Dana relayed Boyd's offer to Stanton, and he was released after taking an oath of allegiance. Almost immediately Boyd went to New York City instead of Mississippi to consort with rebel sympathizers. He may have joined one of many conspiracies to kidnap President Lincoln and exchange him for Confederate soldiers held as prisoners.[44]

Some of the Union's most productive spies were double agents or, at least by necessity, professed loyalties to both sides. Richard Montgomery was a star among Dana's stable of undercover agents. A handsome young adventurer with a blurry past and a penchant for deception, Montgomery had been involved in recruiting soldiers in New York early in the war—a business that attracted many sharpers—and may have enlisted fraudulently himself. In August 1862, using the alias "Benjamin Courrier," Montgomery served as a spy for Generals Irwin McDowell and John Pope, made several trips behind Confederate lines, and provided information about Lee's forces and plans. Montgomery's inflated expense account probably got him dismissed, but his intelligence contributions had been genuine.[45]

Returning to Washington, Montgomery found work as a government clerk. In early 1864 he applied for employment as a spy, professing patriotic motives and carrying good recommendations. Montgomery asked for a horse, a pass through Union lines, and some money; he proposed to bring back information from Lee's army and the Richmond government. His offer was accepted. Government records show that he took an oath of office on March 26, 1864. Disguised as a rebel sympathizer named "James Thompson," Montgomery headed to Lee's camp just before Grant's Virginia campaign. From there he went to Richmond, where he impressed Confederate authorities with his ardor. A few weeks later he returned to the War Department with a letter to carry from Jefferson Davis to Clement Clay, the Confederate agent in Canada. By the summer of 1864 "James Thompson" became a regular courier for the Confederates, shuttling back and forth between Richmond and Canada and stopping at Dana's office on the way.[46]

The first rebel messages were not tampered with, and Montgomery was allowed to give Dana a verbal summary. Later dispatches were opened and copied at the war office, then carefully resealed in duplicate envelopes. In October 1864 Montgomery brought Dana a message in cipher to Davis from Jacob Thompson, who judged that Lincoln's reelection was almost certain and that Washington was sufficiently garrisoned to resist another attack from Jubal Early. By then the Confederates may have suspected Montgomery of double-dealing, for the return dispatch from Davis to the Canadian Rebels contained misinformation intended to trick Grant into diverting troops from Lee's front to Sheridan in the Shenandoah Valley.[47]

If the Confederates suspected Montgomery of treachery, they were reassured by an elaborate subterfuge the War Department pulled off to ensure his credibility. On the Sunday before the November election Montgomery arrived at Dana's office bearing a long dispatch from Clement Clay to Judah Benjamin, the secretary of state in Richmond. It indicated that the recent raid on Saint Albans, Vermont, by some escaped Confederate soldiers had been planned in Canada and approved by Clay and Thompson. Clay wanted President Davis to avow official responsibility for their actions so Canadian officials could invoke British neutrality and refuse to extradite the captured raiders to Union authorities.[48]

Dana took the dispatch to Stanton, who sent him to the White House to fetch

Lincoln. When the three convened, Stanton was adamant about confiscating the original letter so that Secretary of State Seward could prove to Britain that Confederates had organized an attack on the United States from British soil. "Well, Dana?" Lincoln turned to the assistant secretary. Dana was reluctant to break Montgomery's cover and lose an important channel of communication. At Lincoln's prompting the three devised a scheme to keep the dispatch and save Montgomery as a source. They sent Montgomery off for Richmond with the letter, staged his capture in Alexandria by federal authorities, "discovered" his secret document, and sent him to Old Capitol Prison. A few days later he was allowed to escape, and advertisements offering a reward for his capture were placed in prominent newspapers. Montgomery gave himself a mild flesh wound, supposedly sustained when prison guards fired at him as he fled. When Montgomery told his story to Clay and Thompson they apparently swallowed it whole and entrusted him with more errands.[49]

Montgomery's other coup—documented only by memoirs and thus open to question—was to return from Canada with information about Confederate agents' plans to disrupt the election in New York by setting fire to hotels. A few weeks later, according to another War Department source, Montgomery reported that the action had been postponed until after Thanksgiving. There is reason to doubt these claims, and even if they are true Montgomery's warnings joined a chorus of alerts that were transmitted to Dana around election time.[50]

Despite Confederates' later claims that Montgomery had been outed early on as a Union spy he continued to carry messages between Richmond and Canada, and he remained on the War Department's secret-service pay books, his disbursements approved by Dana, until the end of the war. Although some of Montgomery's claims about contacts with the Canadian Confederates are suspect, Dana never doubted his young spy's truthfulness or his devotion to the Union. "His style of patriotic lying was sublime; it amounted to genius," Dana marveled. He was confident—too confident—that Montgomery's "habit of lying" had been practiced only on Confederates.[51]

The New York City arson fires showed that Confederate conspiracies in Canada were not imaginary plots but genuine threats meant to terrorize Northerners. When informers told Dana of a plan to spring Confederate soldiers from western New York's Elmira Prison, he took it seriously enough to make his own inspection trip. Meanwhile, War Department agents pooled information to thwart similar activities. There were military drills of Confederate partisans in Ontario, an attempted train hijacking near Buffalo during the transfer of imprisoned Confederate generals, and plans to conduct additional cross-border forays in New York and Vermont. Dana shared all suspicious reports with General John Dix in New York and directed the chief of ordnance to furnish the Vermont militia with guns and ammunition to bolster the state's defenses. When a Confederate officer was arrested during a raid from Canada to free rebel prisoners, Dana obtained legal opinions from War Department insiders and the jurist Francis Lieber that he and others like him should be tried as spies before military tribunals.[52]

In the summer of 1864 coastal residents of Maine reported seeing organized teams sketching the shore. They were Confederate topographers who had run the Union blockade and were making detailed maps of inlets where two armed Confederate steamers could take refuge during a land and sea raid originating from New Brunswick, Canada. This far-fetched scheme had little chance of success, and one of the conspirators, Francis Jones, wrote to Stanton attempting to defect. Prompted by Stanton, Dana sent a terse refusal but ordered Jones's movements monitored. When Jones joined a raid from Quebec on a bank in Calais, Maine, local officials were ready and he was captured. To save himself Jones agreed to talk, and Dana sent Levi Turner to get a complete confession. Jones not only detailed the plot against Maine but also described places in Northern cities where Confederate sympathizers had hidden guns and medicine, and he divulged the names of leading Confederate operatives. Dana's men found that Jones's report "checked in minute detail," and on November 24 War Department agents swooped in to make arrests in Portland, Boston, New York, Baltimore, Cincinnati, and St. Louis. Caches of arms were captured and plans of federal buildings targeted by the group were found. Several Confederate operatives were charged with treason, and all, including Jones, languished in prison until the end of the war.[53]

As Union officials stepped up their surveillance the likelihood of successful raids from Canada decreased. But information about these schemes was also valuable to Union diplomatic maneuvering. Dana sent summaries to Seward, who transmitted them to the US minister in London, Charles Francis Adams, to lay before the British foreign minister Lord Russell with demands that Britain curtail such activity in its colony. Russell was initially more concerned about Americans' pursuit of perpetrators on neutral Canadian soil than machinations by the Confederates' "Canadian cabinet." But after Sherman's March to the Sea and Lincoln's reelection convinced him that the Union would triumph, he slyly shifted tack. In mid-February 1865 Russell wrote three Confederate envoys named Mason, Slidell, and Mann a letter accusing the Confederates in Canada of violating British neutrality and demanding that their operations cease. Russell gave Seward a copy to send to Richmond through Grant's lines, and Dana organized its delivery under a flag of truce. It mattered little that General Lee, under instructions from Richmond, refused to receive the letter. By passing his "private" missive through Union channels Lord Russell succeeded in reassuring federal authorities that Britain had moved decisively from intervention to reconciliation.[54]

In January 1865 Dana became concerned about the growing number of suspect messages that ran in the personal columns of major Northern newspapers. His suspicions were confirmed when Jacob Thompson referred in a captured letter to Judah Benjamin's "personals" in the "New York News." Confederate partisans in the North and South used personal notices to communicate, bypassing the regular exchanges of flag-of-truce mail, which were intermittent and subject to inspection. It was a lucrative business for the newspapers, and for an additional fee some offered to deliver messages directly to the addressee. Written in terse and sometimes coded language, these personal notices, Dana believed, were being used to transmit encouragement, information, and material aid across enemy lines. Dana sought a legal opinion from the Union's hard-line judge advocate general, Joseph Holt, who concluded that the practice was a potentially dangerous evasion of government rules. Proprietors of the offending newspapers should be notified to discontinue the ads and brought to trial before a military commission if they did not. The *New York Daily News*, openly sympathetic to Confederates, was ordered by General Dix to stop the personal ads. Dana soon noticed that personals directed to Southerners had migrated to the *New York World* and the *Herald*, and he had Dix change the orders to include all newspapers in the Department of the East.[55]

Cleaning the War Machine

During and after the 1864 election campaign Dana resumed his daily routine at the War Department, arriving by nine, dispatching dozens of business items, and clearing his desk by the time he departed for dinner. Adam Gurowski, the dyspeptic Polish exile, classified public men as patriots, incompetents, or scoundrels as he scribbled in his war diary. Charles Dana was honored in the ever-shrinking first column as "the incarnation of integrity, patriotism, and of an almost peerless capacity to run the most complicated and the largest administrative machinery." His opinion was widely shared but not unanimous. One department clerk recalled after the war that Edwin Stanton's arrogance was adopted by Dana and the other "petty tyrants" chosen as assistants. Captain Charles Francis Adams, Jr., of the Army of the Potomac's cavalry, son of the US minister to Britain, went to the war office in August 1864 with a plan to procure unfit horses and rehabilitate them. For the next week Adams "went through all the disgusting routine of one who waits upon those in power, dangling my heels in ante-rooms" as officials "shoved me from one to another." Dana, the third man on his itinerary, "suggested Colonel This or General That, but distinctly disapproved of my scheme." General Henry Halleck said no and slammed his door in Adams's face. Between the runaround and the refusal, Adams preferred the latter because it was quicker. Eventually his papers were taken to Stanton, who signed them only because Grant endorsed the scheme.[56]

In addition to petitioners like Adams, letters from cabinet members and congressmen arrived daily on Dana's desk. There were inquiries about constituents in the armed forces, words of advice on appointments and promotions, requests to clarify War Department policies, appeals to release prisoners, and applications for passes to visit the South. For his part, Dana sent government officials directives about war business, information concerning persons accused of corruption or disloyalty, and orders to arrest the most egregious suspects.

Dana continued to be the War Department's conduit to the Committee on the Conduct of the War. In September 1864 Senator Sumner sent Dana materials about alleged irregularities at the US Arsenal in Watertown, Massachusetts, which Dana then passed to the committee with a suggestion for "a full hearing, with subsequent recommendations to the War Department." Major Thomas J. Rodman, the commander at Watertown and inventor of the huge Rodman gun used at federal forts, was charged with excessive spending on his residence, the construction of which cost more than $63,000. An inquiry was held but Rodman escaped penalty. In March 1865 he was promoted and later reassigned to the arsenal at Rock Island, Illinois, where he built an even more imposing commander's residence.[57]

Lincoln frequently referred petitions to Dana. Union cannon fire from Fort Stevens during Jubal Early's raid had destroyed a widow's house that sat between the two armies. Lincoln learned of her plight and sought relief from Dana, who gave her nephew a clerkship in the War Department for her maintenance. Many referrals related to prisoners. A petition from Thurlow Weed and other influential New York Republicans explained that a captured rebel blockade runner was ill; Lincoln forwarded it and asked Dana to "mingle humanity in the case as far as consistent with his security." A Virginia woman traveled to the White House seeking the release of her fiancé and his associate. "Will Mr Dana please see this young lady," Lincoln scribbled, "and let her know the grounds on which her friends are detained at Fort-Warren." After investigating, Dana reported that the men had been ordered confined "as bushwackers, guerrillas, and persons who cannot be at large consistently with the public safety." In another case a Union soldier from Vermont was charged with desertion. "His *wife* says that *he* says he did not intend to desert," Lincoln's secretary noted. Lincoln added a note: "Can Mr. Dana give me any account of this case?" Dana learned from the military governor that the defendant was to be sent to his regiment for trial. Lincoln may have pardoned the soldier, for less than a week later he was back on duty.[58]

Shortly before Lincoln's second inauguration his friend Joshua Speed sat in the president's office amid a throng of petitioners. After nearly all had been seen Lincoln turned to two plainly dressed women, the wife and mother of a young man from western Pennsylvania who had been arrested for resisting the draft. They had no written petition because they could neither write nor afford an attorney. Taking pity, Lincoln sent a messenger to Dana requesting a list of all draft-resisters imprisoned in the region. When Dana arrived, Lincoln asked whether there were any serious criminals in the group, and Dana replied that he knew of none. "Well then," Speed recalled Lincoln saying, "these fellows have suffered long enough, and I have thought so for some time, and now that my mind is on the subject I believe I will turn out the whole flock." He had Dana draw up an order releasing all the men and signed it.[59]

In these and other cases the compassion of the "Pardoner-in-Chief" tested the patience of generals and War Department officials, including Dana. Learning that Lincoln ordered a wounded Confederate major released on parole, General Lew Wallace sent Dana an angry telegram protesting that the officer had joined in the infamous attack on Massachusetts troops passing through Baltimore during the first week of the war. Dana reported this to Lincoln, who apparently retracted the order. Lincoln's leniency sometimes came at Dana's expense. After the war Dana described an incident when General C. C. Augur, commander of Washington's forces, asked him to sign a hasty death warrant for a convicted spy. The man was to be executed the next morning and Lincoln would be out of town until the afternoon. Dana agreed with Augur that the spy should be made an example and signed the order. The next morning Dana encountered the general, who told him that Lincoln had returned at two in the morning and "stopped it all."[60]

By the summer of 1864 the prisoner exchange system between belligerents had broken down, partly due to Confederate violations of paroles issued at Vicksburg, but mainly because Southerners refused to treat black

Union soldiers as prisoners of war rather than recaptured property. Northern prisons began to fill beyond capacity with tens of thousands of rebel soldiers, and Dana's inbox swelled with requests related to them. Dana stuck to Stanton's hard line. He reminded army officers that captured generals were to be treated exactly like other prisoners, and he prescribed retaliatory measures for Confederate officers if their Union counterparts were mistreated. He refused to release Edward Pollard, editor of the *Richmond Examiner*, who had been taken on a Confederate blockade runner. Dana made it clear that he was not simply obeying his superiors' orders. Junius Browne and Albert Richardson, *New York Tribune* reporters whom Dana had sent to the South during the secession crisis, spent years in Confederate prisons. Released at the war's end, they complained that the administration's policy had sacrificed the lives of thousands of white Union prisoners to the rights of a "handful" of blacks. Dana responded sharply that Stanton and Grant had been right to insist on principles of justice and racial equality.[61]

In the war's final year the War Department stepped up its attempts to halt swindling in the government's procurement and recruitment systems. Dana took over ailing Assistant Secretary Peter Watson's watchdog role in July 1864. "Much of my time at this period was spent in investigating charges against defaulting contractors and dishonest agents," he recalled. His agents uncovered frauds among providers of harnesses, hospital tents, and coffee, and they found collusion by quartermaster employees. Determined to root out in-house graft, Dana convinced Stanton to approve a general order requiring army quartermasters to provide delegated investigators with complete access to their books.[62]

Opportunities for fraud were legion in the system of recruiting men for Union service. Vast numbers of soldiers and sailors were needed, record-keeping was sloppy, and private brokers could receive as much as $300 per recruit—a substantial sum. Lafayette Baker, who tracked many cases in Brooklyn and New York City, recounted incidents where brokers presented fictitious names or allowed recruits to desert in transit to their reporting station. Dana examined Baker's cases and found the frauds "astounding, both in their extent and ingenuity." He had the culprits tried in New York and recommended a new system of checks to minimize fraud.[63]

As with military convictions, Dana's own efforts could be frustrated by Lincoln's leniency. In February 1865 New York City police arrested John N. Eitel, a well-connected clothing merchant who had opened a side business as a recruitment broker and kept most of the bounty owed to recruits' families. After a stream of letters from New York politicos arrived at the War

Department urging Eitel's release, Dana referred the case to Holt, who found the evidence "full & entirely satisfactory" and denied parole. Lincoln, however, was persuaded by Eitel's prominent associates to review the decision and reverse it. "Let this man be bailed, Mr. Dana to fix the amount," Lincoln penned atop the file. Dana set the bail at $10,000, and Abraham Wakeman, a New York Customs House official, sent a check to spring Eitel.[64]

"Ordering arrests of persons suspected of disloyalty to the government" was another of Dana's tasks. He was especially unforgiving toward Northerners with Confederate sympathies. After Jubal Early's Confederate troops retreated across the Potomac following his alarming raid, Dana called for a military investigation of Marylanders suspected of aiding the invaders. By telegram Dana directed General Grenville Dodge in Missouri to assess local secession sympathizers for rebuilding a Union man's house destroyed by guerrillas. But Dodge's superior, General John Pope, protested to Stanton that such an order would reimpose martial law and invite thousands of similar claims, and Stanton rescinded the order.[65]

Among the more surprising disloyalty suspects was the photographer Mathew Brady, who had taken images of Grant and Dana at Cold Harbor. According to Lafayette Baker, an informer charged that Brady had arranged with Wall Street brokers to send coded messages from Grant's headquarters at City Point to guide speculation on the gold and stock markets. Baker urged Dana to tell Grant "he is being deceived by one to whom he has granted various privileges and favors." The volatile markets during Grant's Virginia campaign led many observers to suspect conspiracies, but the complaint against Brady was almost certainly malicious gossip. Brady arrived at the Union lines outside Petersburg after battle reports had already reached New York, and he sent no telegrams to the North. Dana had known Brady for years and had no reason to harbor distrust. He referred Baker's letter skeptically to Grant, who apparently agreed.[66]

Investigations of fraud and disloyalty became entangled with Dana's task of supervising War Department spies, who were duplicitous by profession. A case involving exchanges of contraband goods by one of Dana's secret agents resulted in nearly a hundred civilian arrests, among the largest War Department sweeps during the war. It began in the summer of 1864 when the agent, Pardon Worsley, developed a ruse for obtaining information behind Confederate lines by shopping for clothing in Baltimore and reselling it in Virginia, where he picked up valuable information about Confederate troop movements. In October Worsley and a female companion went on an unusually expensive shopping spree. Lafayette Baker, who detained Worsley and examined the goods for the War Department, found brass buttons, percussion caps, uniforms, and other contraband items worth more than $25,000. Worsley, exposed as a double agent, was imprisoned, and Dana used his testimony and receipts to widen the dragnet. On October 17 federal authorities swept down on several of Baltimore's most respected commercial establishments, closing their doors and arresting clerks and managers alike. The suspects were conducted by a special train to their cells in Old Capitol Prison.

Shortly after the raid an outraged deputation of a dozen Baltimore bankers and merchants called at the White House to demand the prisoners' release. Lincoln sent them to Stanton's office, where the war secretary, accompanied by Dana with the incriminating receipts in hand, launched into one of the most eloquent speeches Dana had ever heard, reviewing the war's cost in lives and describing the contraband goods that Worsley had purchased at their stores and their potential to prolong the killing. According to Dana, when Stanton finished his lecture the Baltimore men, properly shamed, filed out of his office without a word. The firms' principals were tried by a military commission; most of the clerks were paroled, but several merchants were fined heavily and given sentences of one to five years in New York's Albany penitentiary. According to the historian who uncovered the case, the War Department was especially intent on exposing prominent wrongdoers and using them as examples.[67]

The businessmen's influential friends still had Lincoln to appeal to, with his soft heart and shrewd judgment about cultivating political support. The president told Judge Advocate Holt: "It is very unsatisfactory to me that so many men of fair character should be convicted principally on the testimony of one single man & he of not quite fair character. It occurs to me that they have suffered enough, even if guilty, and enough for example." Lincoln asked Holt to give them "a jubilee," and the next day Stanton ordered ten merchants released, exempting one who had attempted a bribe. Worsley himself was set free for turning government's witness.[68]

Years later Dana claimed that despite the merchants' release the arrests successfully broke up the contraband business. They also soured Dana's view of Baltimore merchants enough to produce another complaint to the White House. "I have the honor to ask you to remove Mr Dana Assistant Secretary of War from his office," an attorney wrote Lincoln in a huff a few weeks after the Baltimore arrests. He had called on Dana at the war office to obtain a large Treasury requisition for a Baltimore supplier, A. M. White, "whereupon Mr. Dana stated in a loud voice so that all could hear Mr. White is a damned rascal & has been guilty of fraud." Fuming that "an officer of the government has no right to curse the citizen when he applies for payment of his dues," the attorney wanted Dana "instantly dismissed." No reply from Lincoln has survived. The president frequently brushed off complaints from callers offended by Stanton's outbursts, often with humor. He probably chuckled when he received similar complaints about Dana.[69]

Desk General

As Grant's encircling of Petersburg crept along in the fall of 1864, Dana spewed a steady stream of telegrams from the War Department informing him of army promotions and placements, the state of the capital's defenses, and details of military engagements outside Virginia. Occasionally he visited Grant's headquarters. On September 25 Dana joined Secretary Seward and Congressman Washburne aboard the steamer *City of Baltimore* for an outing to City Point and, once transferred to a smaller boat, an inspection tour with Grant and Butler up the James River toward the Union front. As they approached Dutch Gap their boat was shelled by an enemy battery. Seward quipped that with his pen as his only weapon he was not prepared to reply to cannon fire. Their boat promptly turned about and the group reboarded the steamer for the capital.[70]

In early November, when Sherman was about to embark on his March to the Sea, it fell to Dana to notify the general that information about his plans was leaking from his own headquarters to the newspapers. In reply, Sherman—who had a long history of battling the press—blithely suggested that War Department officials should deliberately release false information. For example: "Sherman's destination is not Charleston, but Selma, where he will meet an army from the Gulf." Dana wisely did not follow Sherman's advice, nor did he prolong the exchange.[71]

From his desk in Washington Dana's most directly military role that autumn of 1864 was overseeing aspects of army logistics during the war's final phase. This duty mixed the mundane with the momentous. In the first category was arranging for the transport of tens of thousands of Thanksgiving turkeys to troops stationed in Virginia.[72] A more critical task was transporting men and supplies to enable the clinching Union military victories. The long war of attrition had set the stage for the Union's superior numbers and arms to finish off the enemy, but this required the right concentrations of men and weapons at the proper locations.

Fort Fisher was one such place. In November 1864 Union plans coalesced for a combined land and sea assault on the Confederate's last major blockade-running port at Wilmington, North Carolina, and Fort Fisher, the formidable earthwork at Cape Fear that protected its approach. Grant ordered a force from General Butler's Army of the James to land near the fort while Admiral David Porter's navy bombarded it. Butler nursed a pet scheme of stuffing an old flat-bottomed vessel with two hundred tons of gunpowder and guiding it to explode next to the fort. Ulysses Grant did "not believe a particle" in the plan, but he asked Dana to get an opinion from General Richard Delafield, the War Department's chief engineer. Delafield reported that an explosion hundreds of yards from the fort would leave the fort's earthworks untouched; it would be like "firing feathers from muskets."[73]

Porter favored the plan, however, and he and Butler were allowed to pursue it. Dana scrambled to have the required shiploads of powder sent from New York and Boston to Fortress Monroe. Eager to prove himself after many military failures, Butler headed the expedition. When the powder-boat was exploded on the night of December 23 it did no damage to the fort. Butler landed his troops but decided that the fort remained too strong for an assault to succeed. On Christmas Day he ordered his men to withdraw, ignoring Grant's explicit orders to establish a beachhead and await a full-scale naval bombardment.

After Butler was relieved, the Fort Fisher fiasco was reversed when a second Union attack led by General Alfred Terry easily captured the fort in mid-January 1865. At the time, Stanton was in Savannah visiting Sherman. The welcome news was telegraphed from the battle scene to Dana by his old *Tribune* "special," E. H. House; Dana shared it with Lincoln and, via General Dix and the Associated Press, with the entire nation.[74]

Another happy reversal occurred at Nashville. General George Thomas, a stout defender who was often slow to attack, tested Grant's and Stanton's patience by hesitating to advance against General John Bell Hood's Confederate army as it pushed into central Tennessee in November 1864. For two weeks Grant and Union officials pressed Thomas to attack Hood's underfed troops, while "Old Slow Trot" insisted his preparations were not complete. Out of patience, Grant started for Nashville with the intention to relieve Thomas, but on the way he learned from a telegram that Thomas had attacked successfully. The two-day Battle of Nashville ended in a complete rout, and the remnant of Hood's army was sent reeling back to Mississippi.[75]

After Thomas's big victory Dana set about smoothing things over between him and Grant. Writing to James Wilson, recently made a corps commander under Thomas, Dana announced that Stanton had promoted Thomas to major general, with Grant's "hearty concurrence." "I hope," Dana wrote, "that it will obliterate all unpleasant feeling in the general's mind. . . . In my judg-ment, there is no man in whom . . . confidence can more safely be placed, nor one who would fill the highest station with superior dignity and wisdom." No doubt Thomas had good reasons to delay, Dana explained, but Stanton and Grant had found them "too much like those so often urged by Buell and McClellan to be satisfactory." Fortunately, the prolonged wait worked in the Union's favor, as a devastating ice storm brought Hood's men to the brink of starvation before the attack. In any case, Dana concluded, "without looking too curiously into the past, let us admit that everything has turned out for the best."[76]

After the victory at Nashville Grant figured that Thomas would make no more offensive movements that winter. Inclined to waste neither time nor men, Grant approved plans for Wilson to make a daring cavalry raid through Alabama and Georgia. Dana arranged for his friend's cavalry to be outfit-ted with seven-shot, breech-loading Spencer carbines, which allowed them to outgun Nathan Bedford Forrest's mounted Confederates. Setting out in March, Wilson took 13,000 troopers on the longest and most destructive cav-alry raid of the war. Union horsemen picked apart Forrest's once-proud cav-alry and destroyed railroads, factories, arsenals, and cotton fields along their 500-mile path.[77]

Grant would also use Thomas's infantry if the Rock of Chickamauga was staying put. In January 1865 he ordered General John Schofield's XXIII Corps, more than 16,000 men, transferred as quickly as possible from Tennessee to the Potomac, where they could then set off to join Sherman's army in North Carolina. Dana was designated to plan the move and super-vise it from his office. He sent Colonel Lewis Parsons, the War Department's chief of rail and river transportation, to take charge of arrangements along the route. Constantly in touch by telegraph with Dana, Parsons floated trans-ports to Cincinnati, where he arranged for local railroads to take the soldiers to Bellaire and then across the Ohio River to connect with the B&O line. Dana ordered the army to close all liquor shops along the rail route, and Parsons supplemented soldiers' rations with hot coffee as an alternate anti-dote to the freezing weather. By February 2 the transfer to Virginia was com-plete. Within a few days Schofield's corps then boarded steam transports to North Carolina, where they joined Sherman at Goldsboro to ensure his final victory over General Joseph E. Johnston's army.

On the first leg of the journey the soldiers traveled 1,400 miles from Tennessee to the Potomac camp, over a route equally divided between land and water, at an average time of eleven days, with only one fatality. Parsons's report boasted that the successful transfer had no "parallel in this eventful war, nor, indeed, in the history of warfare." The only move that compared with it was the rapid shipment of Joseph Hooker's two corps to Tennessee in September 1863 to reinforce Rosecrans. Dana's involvement with both episodes made him one of the War Department's resident experts on logistics. The rapid transfers demonstrated how efficient rail transport gave the Union a foundational military advantage over the Confederacy and how thoroughly it had revolutionized the practice of warfare.[78]

16 "The Rebellion Finished"

"Neither party expected for the war the magnitude or the duration which it has already attained," Abraham Lincoln acknowledged in his second inaugural address in 1865. "Neither anticipated that the cause of the conflict might cease with or even before the conflict itself should cease." It had rained the morning of March 4, but as Lincoln stood to speak on the steps of the Capitol East Portico the sun broke through—a hopeful omen. The newly completed Capitol Dome reminded spectators of his promise to see the war through. Turning to the future, Lincoln resolved that the Union government and its armies would "finish the work we are in," acting "with firmness in the right as God gives us to see the right." Then, "with malice toward none, and with charity for all," they would heal the nation's wounds and build a lasting peace. In the compass of seven hundred memorable words Lincoln spurred the Union's righteous armies to victory and offered their enemies peace without rancor.[1]

Just before Lincoln's address Charles Dana sat among department officials in the crowded Senate chamber to witness Vice President Andrew Johnson's rambling, boastful inauguration speech, which Dana called "semi-insane." It confirmed Dana's already low estimate of the new vice president. Some listeners believed Johnson had taken too much brandy; Dana wondered whether he might be under "the inspiration of opium." Shortly before noon Dana walked with officials under the Capitol Rotunda to the East Portico to attend the inaugural address. He can be glimpsed in Alexander Gardner's panoramic photo of the event, standing where the porch railing met the Capitol steps, some thirty feet behind the president, about fifteen feet away from another spectator whom some scholars have identified as John Wilkes Booth (see p. 350).[2]

Of Lincoln's two inaugural agendas—completing the Union victory and offering charity to the enemy—Dana found the first more to his liking than the second. When General Ulysses Grant's troops finally broke through at Petersburg at the beginning of April, Dana focused his energies on capturing and securing Richmond. At the same time, he was determined that the North

Lincoln's second inauguration, March 4, 1865. Photograph by Alexander Gardner. Charles Dana and John Wilkes Booth are visible (with magnification) on the Capitol's balcony behind the standing president. Library of Congress Prints and Photographs Division.

take possession of the rebel South, punish high-ranking Confederate officials, and prevent their resurgence. Surely, Dana thought, those most responsible for promoting treason and prolonging the killing deserved malice. Two weeks late, Lincoln's assassination by a pro-Confederate fanatic compounded the war's toll and amplified Dana's call for retribution.

Richmond at Last

As the cherry trees blossomed in the Union capital, news of Grant's push against Robert E. Lee's badly attenuated lines west of Petersburg verified that the four years of bloodletting was coming to an end. Grant invited President Lincoln and Edwin Stanton to his headquarters before the final drive. Illness from overwork prevented Stanton from going, but aboard the *River Queen* at City Point Lincoln met with Grant, General William T. Sherman, and Admiral

David Porter for long conversations about postwar relations between the rebellious states and the Union. According to Porter, Lincoln suggested that "the most favorable terms" be offered for surrender and no one be punished; little or nothing was said about changing the racial order of the South. As the talks ended the president wired Stanton that he would remain in Virginia to follow Grant's progress.[3]

Stanton chafed in Washington. Frustrated not to have a firsthand look at the war's end, he found the suspense excruciating. On April 1 Sheridan pushed back Lee's endangered right wing at Five Forks, and the next day Grant's assaults along the front finally broke through into Petersburg. Stanton spent the entire night of April 2 in the telegraph rooms of the War Department. Early the next morning Lincoln flashed him the news that Lee had evacuated Petersburg. Certain that Richmond had also been abandoned, Grant was rushing troops to cut off a Confederate retreat westward. Elated, Stanton warned Lincoln by wire not to come close to combat lines and risk capture by the enemy.[4]

A few hours later a telegram announced that Union troops had entered Richmond. Stanton gave his employees the rest of the day off and ordered flags to decorate the War Department. He and Secretary of State William Seward made impromptu speeches to a crowd from the balcony of the building. Stanton led them in singing "The Star-Spangled Banner" and ordered an eight-hundred-gun salute that boomed through the city. Plans were also set in motion for occupying the Confederate capital. Stanton and Dana sent a steamer with medical personnel to attend to the wounded, as well as judges to set up temporary courts. Wary of press interference, they refused passes to reporters, but a few newsmen evaded Dana's inspectors by hiding belowdecks as boats departed the Sixth Street wharf.[5]

Stanton was convinced that victory had to be safeguarded with an exacting occupation. Once again he asked Dana to act as his agent in Virginia. At Richmond Dana was to impound all available records of the Confederate government and keep Stanton apprised of events and conditions. Lincoln, too, needed to be watched, not only because he might expose himself to danger but also because the soft-hearted president might relinquish what Stanton called "the scepter of the conqueror" by offering a quick and lenient peace to Virginia's crushed Confederates.[6]

Dana departed Washington by steamboat. The trip was serious business, but the long-awaited victory lent it a festive air, for occupied Richmond instantly became a tourist attraction for Northern officials. Dana brought along his wife, his twelve-year old son, and New York politico Roscoe Conkling.

When the group landed at City Point on the morning of April 5 Dana reported what he learned from officers there. Richmond had been torched by the retreating Confederates and all leading rebel officials had escaped. The Confederate ironclad CSS *Virginia* lay sunk in the James River. Union soldiers had suffered only minor losses in taking the capital. Grant commanded the armies in person during the final offensive, "having got disgusted with General [George] Meade's stickling about his own dignity." And Lincoln, whom Dana had expected to see, was no longer at City Point: he had departed on the *River Queen* for Richmond the morning before.[7]

Dana was unaware that in Richmond Lincoln had already opened talks with the Confederates. On April 4 Lincoln enjoyed a triumphant tour through the half-ruined city accompanied by the cheers of Richmond's freedpeople. In Jefferson Davis's former residence—a boxy brick mansion often called the Confederate White House—Lincoln had met with John A. Campbell, a former US Supreme Court justice and the Confederacy's assistant secretary of war. Campbell had stayed behind to play a mediating role in restoring peace and order. He secured Lincoln's agreement not to confiscate property or otherwise punish the capital's residents. To solve the larger issues of restoring Virginia to the Union, Campbell suggested that Lincoln confer with moderate leaders of the state, who now believed that "submission was a duty and a necessity."[8]

On the morning of April 5 Lincoln sat in Admiral Porter's barge as it was towed down the James to City Point while Dana steamed upriver to Richmond. Their boats probably passed as they dodged wrecked vessels and sunken mines, grim reminders of the war's destruction. Landing in Richmond, Dana searched out General Godfrey Weitzel, the young corps commander in charge of Union forces in the city, who had established headquarters at the Confederate White House. All signs pointed to a hasty evacuation. Davis, most of the Confederate cabinet, and Congress had slipped away by train the evening of April 2.[9]

The tremendous destruction in Richmond complicated Dana's search for Confederate documents. Nearly the entire business district, between Main Street and the James River, had been burned by retreating Confederates. The war department building was destroyed, the state house ransacked and its documents scattered. Most records of the Confederate States Congress and the departments had been removed with the evacuation. Yet important files survived. The state house contained cases of Confederate military and political papers. Confederate government mailbags were seized at the post office, and a partially destroyed cache of treasury papers was found behind the

railroad depot. Most important, a search of the Confederate telegraph office yielded copies of half of the rebel government's dispatches. Dana turned
these records over to Colonel Richard D. Cutts, whom Henry Halleck had
appointed to manage transport, and during the next few weeks Cutts shipped
more than ninety crates to the War Department offices in Washington. These
were shortly supplemented by eighty-one boxes of papers captured in North
Carolina by General John Schofield. In July Stanton appointed the celebrated
jurist Francis Lieber to organize the "Rebel Archive."[10]

Dana doubted that these papers contained much of value, but he and Halleck
hoped to find "important links of testimony against prominent traitors," especially the Confederates' Canadian agents. Halleck, for example, found a
letter from Beverley Tucker in Montreal that seemed to suggest Richmond's
approval of the Canadians' various sabotage schemes. In any case, the documents would "prove of great value to those who may hereafter write the history of this great rebellion." Eventually they filled several volumes of the
Official War Records the federal government began publishing in the 1880s.[11]

Dana held on to a few finds he considered worthwhile: a letter from General
Lee to Richmond that reviewed the Confederate army's desperate straits, and
a couple of cipher codes found in Secretary of State Judah Benjamin's office.
One of these aligned the alphabet to six sets of hieroglyphs; it had been used
for dispatches between Richmond authorities and their Canadian agents. The
second cipher, a simple alphabet square mounted on a wooden cylinder, later
figured prominently in the trial of President Lincoln's assassins.[12]

Dana reported that there was little resistance to the Union occupation.
General Weitzel said his men were "greeted with a hearty welcome from the
mass of the people," and Lincoln's reception had been "enthusiastic in the
extreme." Still, the task of returning Richmond to normal life was formidable. Rubble from the fire had to be cleared and a military police system established to stop looting. The Tredegar Iron Works, mostly undamaged, were
taken over by Union soldiers, and Libby Prison and Castle Thunder were
filled with rebel prisoners. Dana estimated the city's remaining population at
20,000, virtually all without food. Weitzel issued rations to those who would
take a Union oath. The public responded avidly, but Dana was skeptical: "I
do not think the Union feeling here is half as sincere as Weitzel believes it to
be, but there is a great throng of people after victuals."[13]

Secretary Stanton, also suspicious of sudden rebel conversions, was grudging with Union supplies. He wired Dana demanding to know by whose authority Weitzel was distributing food, and he ordered Weitzel to furnish daily
reports of rations given to persons unconnected to the Union military. He was

appeased only when Dana reported that Weitzel had proper orders from superiors and was paying for the rations by selling confiscated tobacco. Recipients
of rations were put to work clearing debris from the streets and repairing public utilities. Despite some insincerity among the oath-takers, Dana thought the
program was useful. "Unless some [such] system . . . be established," he told
Stanton, "many persons must die of absolute starvation."[14]

Weitzel's troubles were just beginning, for Stanton was convinced he was
unfit for the job of subduing Richmond. Stanton probably recalled that Weitzel
had opposed arming freedmen in Louisiana and now had black soldiers in his
command. More recently Weitzel had been General Benjamin Butler's faithful subordinate at corruption-plagued Norfolk. Right away Stanton suggested
that Grant replace him and his chief of staff, George Shepley, another Butler
protégé. Always opposed to compromises with the Rebels, Stanton became
hypersensitive once the Confederate capital was occupied and peace terms
were being discussed.[15]

Dana, who shared Stanton's fears, provided him with an unlikely pretext
for a showdown: a dispute over prayer in Richmond's churches. On Friday,
April 7, Weitzel authorized the opening of Richmond's churches the following Sunday, on the condition that ministers read a prayer for the president of
the United States. (During the war they had prayed for the Confederate president.) But on Saturday evening Shepley asked Dana to approve revising the
prayer requirement to omit a reference to either president. This, according to
Shepley, was Judge Campbell's request and Weitzel's preference. Dana replied that he had no instructions from Washington and Weitzel must act on
his own. Handed this rope, Weitzel then wrapped it around his neck by dilut-
ing the prayer order. Dana reported the change to Stanton, confessing that "it
shakes a good deal my confidence in Weitzel."[16]

On Sunday morning no Richmond minister invoked blessings upon Lincoln,
although prayers were offered for "all those in authority," an evasive phrase
that neither Dana nor Stanton liked. Weitzel's explanation only made things
worse. He believed the Union president should have been remembered, but
he had left the decision to Shepley, although he "doubted its wisdom." When
he heard this Stanton was livid. The War Department "strongly condemned"
this "omission of respect" to the US president. Stanton ordered Weitzel to discontinue meeting with Campbell unless specifically authorized by superiors.
On this matter as well as larger issues of Reconstruction, Stanton feared that
Weitzel was being pulled by Campbell's strings.[17]

Weitzel explained to Stanton that he had not discussed prayers with
Campbell, but he had been advised by Lincoln to "make concessions in

small matters." Shepley, he claimed, had misunderstood Dana's response and thought he approved the change. Dana denied this but softened his criticism of Weitzel. It was Shepley who had talked with Campbell about prayers, and Weitzel deferred to him. Weitzel's consent was, Dana allowed, "the result of the President's verbal direction to him, to let them down easy." None of this appeased Stanton, who found Weitzel's explanation unsatisfactory. He directed Weitzel to make the Richmond clergy show "no less respect for the President of the United States" than they had demonstrated toward Jefferson Davis. Only when Lincoln intervened did the bickering cease. He did not recall speaking about prayers, he told Weitzel, but he had no doubt that "you have acted in what appeared to you to be the spirit and temper manifested by me while there."[18]

Lincoln was right, but this was precisely why Stanton's fur was up. The prayer issue was symbolic of more important concessions that Lincoln and his go-between Weitzel were on the verge of making to Virginia Confederates. Before he left Richmond Lincoln met again with Campbell, this time accompanied by the Richmond attorney Gustavus Myers, a member of the Virginia legislature, to discuss the terms of Virginia's reentry into the Union. Dana, who arrived after the conference was over, learned from Weitzel that the Confederate representatives suggested that a general amnesty would dissolve the Rebels' army and return their states to the Union. Lincoln did not promise amnesty but told them he could use pardons to "save any repentant sinner from hanging." What Weitzel did not tell Dana was that Lincoln had offered the Virginians an even more ominous concession. Because Jefferson Davis was unwilling to take the Confederacy out of the war, Lincoln suggested that Virginia's rebel legislature could meet and vote to withdraw the state from the Confederate States of America. This was a risky plan that Stanton and the United States Congress would surely disapprove. It violated the policy of not recognizing Confederate governments that Union leaders had carefully followed for four years, and it ignored the existing Unionist government, set up in western Virginia, which Congress recognized as legitimate. Once the Confederate state legislature met, there was no telling what other resolutions it might pass or negotiations it might pursue.[19]

Campbell and Myers jumped on Lincoln's offer. They assured him that the Virginia legislature would repeal its ordinance of secession. This would effectively recall Lee's troops and prompt similar resolutions in the other Confederate states, leading to "perfect peace in the shortest possible time." Lincoln promised the Virginians a decision once he returned to City Point. There Dana finally caught up with the president on the morning of April 7.

Lincoln showed Dana two carefully worded documents he had sent upriver to Richmond. The first, a memorandum addressed to Campbell, outlined the terms Lincoln considered indispensable to peace: resumption of federal authority, "no receding by the Executive of the United States on the slavery question," and the disbanding of all forces hostile to the Union. If these terms were agreed to, he promised to consider others "in a spirit of sincere liberality." Lincoln's second document ordered Weitzel to permit "the gentlemen who have acted as the Legislature of Virginia" to convene in Richmond to withdraw the state from the Confederacy. If they attempted any business hostile to the United States they were to be disbanded.[20]

Campbell and a group of five Virginia notables conferred over Lincoln's letter, then met with Weitzel and Shepley on April 8. Dana was present and sent a report to Stanton. The Richmond men were "conscious that they are whipped and sincerely anxious to stop all further bloodshed and restore peace, law, and order." If they wished to call a convention of prominent citizens in order to restore Union authority they would be allowed to bring them to Richmond. Dana assured Stanton that Weitzel had acted "with caution and discretion" and said nothing to compromise the government. This was true enough. But the position paper Campbell handed to Weitzel at the meeting extended Lincoln's proposition into perilous territory. Campbell proposed that the Confederate "legislature of Virginia" act as the rightful governing body of the state. It would convene to restore the Union "by consent of the seceding States" and to negotiate with the Union government such matters as taxes, oaths, congressional representation, and even "the condition of the slave population." Once agreement with the Union government was reached, the South Carolina legislature, scheduled to meet in May, could follow Virginia's example. Dana saw warning flags all over Campbell's memorandum, which he forwarded to Stanton.[21]

Another onlooker suspicious of this turn of events was Andrew Johnson. The vice president had spoken at a rally in Washington after the fall of Richmond. "Treason must be made odious," he shouted; he prescribed "leniency for the masses" but "*halters* for the leaders." A few days later Johnson joined the stream of Union officials southward. Lincoln, perhaps miffed by Johnson's inflammatory speech, snubbed him at City Point, and Johnson proceeded to Richmond. At the Spotswood Hotel Johnson buttonholed Dana and launched into a twenty-minute harangue on denying the Confederates reentry into the Union "without some conditions or . . . some punishment" for their enormous "sins." Dana, who agreed, urged Johnson to talk to the president.[22]

That is exactly what the alarmed Secretary of War Edwin Stanton did when

Lincoln returned to Washington on April 9. Stanton feared that Virginia's rebel legislature, if allowed to meet, could steal the fruits of Union victory by reestablishing the prewar political and racial order. He leaked Dana's reports to fellow cabinet members Attorney General James Speed and Postmaster General William Dennison, Jr. He met with Lincoln the morning after the president's return, declaring "vehemently" that it was a mistake to extend recognition to the Virginia Confederates and urging that Lincoln revoke his instructions to Weitzel.[23]

Fortunately for Stanton and the Radical Republicans, events on the battle-field were overtaking political negotiations in Richmond. While Grant pursued Lee to Appomattox, the Virginia lawmakers took their time finalizing the call to convene. As Lincoln told Dana, the Union army seemed to be "getting Virginia soldiers out of the war faster than the legislature could think." Lee's surrender to Grant on April 9 removed the Virginians' main bargaining chip. Even then, Lincoln continued to contemplate a session of the Virginia legislature as the best way to make the transition to peace. On April 12 he polled cabinet members informally. Nobody favored the plan, and Edwin Stanton, James Speed, and Gideon Welles spoke up against it. Lincoln began to think, he told Navy Secretary Welles, that "he had perhaps made a mistake." That evening Lincoln read Campbell's memorandum, which Dana had sent Stanton, and agreed that any plan to empower the Confederate legislature of Virginia to negotiate terms of reunion crossed an unmistakable line.[24]

Dana's report finally brought Lincoln around. Immediately the president telegraphed Weitzel to call off the negotiations, now speaking as a conqueror imposing terms. He had no intention to recognize the "insurgent legislature of Virginia" as a rightful body; he intended that they meet solely to withdraw Virginia from the Confederacy in return for concessions on confiscated property. Now that they overstepped their bounds and Grant had captured the Virginia troops, no such deal was approved. "Do not allow them to assemble," Lincoln ordered Weitzel. Thanks to Stanton and Dana, and also to the galloping course of events, Lincoln's plans for Reconstruction had toughened. The war secretary was delegated to draw up a plan for temporary military rule in Virginia.[25]

Kept in Richmond to monitor Weitzel, Dana always regretted that he had not accompanied Grant at Lee's surrender. It would have been a fitting climax to their collaboration, which had begun exactly two years earlier at Vicksburg. Instead, Dana took the news from Appomattox Court House over the wires on April 10. He reported to Stanton that Confederate diehards in the capital finally acknowledged their "defeat is perfect and the rebellion finished" and

merely cling to the "hope that their individual property may escape confiscation."[26]

The next morning an order came from Stanton to proceed to City Point.
There Dana gathered from Grant and his staff the details of Lee's capitulation. It appeared that about 20,000 men had surrendered, but Lee's army was
in such disarray that he could only guess at the number. The day after the
surrender Lee told Grant he would devote himself to pacifying the country
and bringing Southerners back to the Union. Already the myth of Lee the
reluctant Confederate was being constructed: Dana passed along Lee's alleged statement—whose accuracy is disputed—that "he had always been for
the Union in his heart and could find no justification for the politicians who
had brought on the war, whose origin he believed to have been in the folly of
extremists on both sides." Dana also heard that Lee's men were relieved that
the war was over and gratified by Grant's generous terms, which spared them
from arrest and allowed them to claim their horses. According to Dana, Grant
believed such concessions were important for "securing a thorough peace and
undisturbed submission to the government." Privately Dana favored harsher
treatment of rebel soldiers, but he said nothing to Stanton. At least Grant had
confined his terms to military matters and left the restoration of government
to the executive and Congress.[27]

After filing his account of the surrender, Dana accompanied Grant on a
steamer to Washington. Before he left City Point on April 13 he telegraphed
Stanton news of one final victory: Weitzel had been removed from command
in Richmond, and Shepley would no longer be military governor. Control of
the Confederate capital was entrusted to General Marsena Patrick, a strict dis-
ciplinarian, with Henry Halleck as his superior. Grant had ordered the change
after consulting Dana, and it made the assistant secretary's return even more
satisfying. As their boat reached the capital it was saluted with a salvo of cannons, church bells sang out greetings, and flags flapped at the landing.[28]

Assassination and Manhunt

On the night of April 13 Dana and his family witnessed the grand illumina-
tions of government buildings to celebrate the Union victory. Dana joined
Grant and dozens of War Department employees for a rare party at Stanton's
home. By the next day—Good Friday—Dana was back at his desk. Among
the incoming dispatches was a telegram from the provost marshal in Portland,
Maine, informing him that Jacob Thompson, ringleader of the Confederates
in Canada, reportedly would pass through the city to catch a steamer for

Halifax and then England. The provost marshal asked for instructions. Should Thompson be apprehended before he escaped? Dana consulted Stanton, who ordered the arrest. But as Dana was leaving Stanton's office the secretary had second thoughts. No doubt he recalled Lincoln's remark at the cabinet meeting earlier in the day that he would be glad to see Confederate leaders slip abroad. "No, wait; better go over and see the President." Dana walked across the lawn to the White House and ascended unnoticed to the executive office. It was mid-afternoon, and Dana found the president with his coat off and his sleeves rolled up, washing his hands in a small closet off his office.

"Hallo, Dana! What is it? What's up?" Dana read Lincoln the telegram and told him that Stanton wanted to arrest Thompson but referred the question to the president. "Well no," said Lincoln slowly, wiping his hands with a towel, "I rather think not. When you have got an elephant by the hind leg, and he's trying to run away, it's best to let him run." "Oh, stuff!" Stanton reportedly snapped when Dana told him Lincoln's answer. His language was no doubt stronger than that.[29]

Late that night Dana was awakened at home by a messenger sent from Stanton. Lincoln had been shot during a performance at Ford's Theatre; Stanton needed Dana in a boarding house across the street from the theater where the wounded president lay unconscious. In the rain Dana ran the half-dozen blocks from his lodging on New York Avenue to the shabby brick Petersen House on Tenth. Arriving shortly after midnight Dana found the president comatose, placed diagonally on a tiny bed in the small backroom, and breathing heavily. Clearly the wound would be fatal. In the front parlor members of the cabinet and Chief Justice Salmon P. Chase arranged themselves in a silent pall. They seemed "almost as much paralyzed" as Lincoln himself, Dana recalled.[30]

Only Stanton was functioning. The sometimes panicky secretary was calm and in complete control, directing the manhunt and keeping the business of government in motion. Stanton had set up a makeshift office in the back parlor, where he and the federal district court judge David Kellogg Cartter had begun interrogating witnesses. James Tanner, an army corporal who boarded next door, took down testimony in shorthand. Stanton briefed Dana on what had happened, and both men listened to witnesses who implicated the actor John Wilkes Booth. Immediately Stanton began dictating orders. "It seemed as if Mr. Stanton thought of everything," Dana remembered, "and there was a great deal to be thought of that night. . . . The safety of Washington must be looked after. Commanders all over the country had to be ordered to take extra precautions. The people must be notified of the tragedy. The assassins must be captured." On a little stand in the room adjoining Lincoln's death chamber Dana wrote out several of Stanton's dispatches. Major Thomas Eckert, chief of Stanton's telegraph staff, set up a relay of mounted messengers who carried them to the War Department telegraph office a mile away.[31]

The first wires went to General Grant, who had left by train to New Jersey with his wife Julia to see their children. Stanton recalled Grant to Washington to take charge of its security. It occurred to Dana that Grant might also have been targeted for assassination, for he had been expected to attend the theater with the Lincolns. The assistant secretary telegraphed Grant at Philadelphia warning against saboteurs or attackers. "Permit me to suggest to you to keep a close watch on all persons who come near you in the cars or otherwise; also, that an engine be sent in front of the train to guard against anything being on the track." Grant and Julia took a train north to Burlington, New Jersey, with a scapegoat engine running ahead on the track; then Grant had a contingent of soldiers meet his southbound train at Baltimore and accompany him to Washington. A second group of telegrams went to General John A. Dix, the Union commander in New York, describing the assassination attempt at Ford's Theatre and the related attack on Secretary of State Seward. "It is not probable," Stanton dictated, "that the President will live through the night." This was the first of four dispatches to Dix that were released to the Associated Press, providing the American public with the first official news of the tragedy. Not until the second dispatch was filed at 3:00 A.M. did they indicate Booth as the probable assassin.[32]

"The extent of the conspiracy was, of course, unknown," Dana recalled, "and the horrible beginning which had been made naturally led us to suspect the worst." An attack on Seward and indications that other government leaders had been marked for death seemed to point toward a large-scale, coordinated plot to paralyze the Union government. Stanton and Dana suspected that the murder of Lincoln was part of a larger conspiracy that included Confederate agents in Montreal and Richmond. Stanton's first words when Lafayette Baker arrived from New York were revealing: "Well, Baker, they have performed what they have long threatened to do; they have killed the President." Thinking this way, Stanton countermanded Lincoln's order of the previous day. "Arrest Jacob Thompson and his companion, . . . who are either in Portland or on the way to Portland from Montreal en route to Europe," Dana wired the United States Marshal at 4:40 A.M. Thompson had drawn up an alternative escape plan to sail a schooner from St. John's, New Brunswick; Dana wired all Union border commands to track the schooner and "arrest all Rebels aboard." But Thompson stayed away from both Portland and St.

John's. Several weeks after the assassination he took a Canadian route to Halifax and departed for London.[33]

Shortly before daylight Dana was dismissed by Stanton and returned to his house to sleep. He had hardly drifted off when around eight o'clock there was a rapping on a ground-floor window: his War Department colleague Louis Pelouze told him that the president was dead. Back on the job before 9 A.M. Dana sent wires to police officials in Washington, Philadelphia, New York City, and Buffalo. These confirmed that Booth, "well known to all theatrical people," was the assassin, as newspapers had already printed, and implicated G. A. Atzerodt, a hard-drinking German immigrant who worked in Port Tobacco, Maryland, before he joined Booth's conspiracy, as the assailant of Secretary Seward. The descriptions were accurate, but Stanton and Dana did not yet realize that Atzerodt had been assigned to kill Vice President Johnson and had fled after losing his nerve. The attack on Seward was made by Lewis Powell (a.k.a. Paine), a quiet but physically imposing Confederate warrior who had served with Mosby's Rangers, drifted northward to Maryland, and attached himself to the charismatic Booth. By noon on April 15, when Dana wrote out a long telegram to Charles Francis Adams, the American minister in London, he and Stanton had gathered enough evidence to declare that "these horrible crimes were committed in execution of a conspiracy deliberately planned and set on foot by rebels, under pretense of avenging the South and aiding the rebel cause."[34]

For the next twenty days Dana was immersed in the War Department's attempt to track down the suspects, gather evidence, and determine the extent of the conspiracy. The testimony of Louis Weichmann, a War Department clerk who boarded at Mary Surratt's H Street home, threw suspicion on Mary's son John, described as "a red-hot Rebel." Several witnesses placed John Surratt in Washington on April 14, and some claimed he had attacked Seward and fled north. Police detective James McDevitt showed up at Dana's house late on Saturday night, April 15, to demand a special train to Baltimore for him and Weichmann to pursue Surratt. Dana refused; he doubted McDevitt's story and suspected—correctly—that Stanton did not want a key witness like Weichmann to leave the capital. The policeman did not wait. Considering Dana's response an "insult to him and his errand," McDevitt took a morning train with Weichmann to Baltimore. They failed to locate Surratt but obtained a military order permitting them to go to Canada to find him.[35]

Newspaper critics charged that Dana had obstructed McDevitt and prevented Surratt's capture. Surratt, however, had not been in Baltimore or Washington. Two weeks before the assassination he left Richmond for

Montreal carrying dispatches, and on the night of the assassination Surratt was in Elmira, New York, casing the Union prison camp for a potential raid. McDevitt and Weichmann arrived in Montreal on April 20, but Surratt eluded them and found sanctuary in a Catholic rectory in a village east of the city. Eventually he escaped to Europe, where he enlisted as a papal guard at the Vatican under a false name, and was not apprehended until 1867.[36]

Most of Booth's accomplices were rounded up more easily. On April 16 Dana received a wire from the provost marshal in Baltimore who traced the author of an incriminating letter signed "Sam" found in Booth's room at the National Hotel. Samuel Arnold, Booth's old schoolmate who had conspired with him to kidnap Lincoln but grown impatient, had recently taken a job as a store clerk at Fortress Monroe. Dana sent orders to Virginia to arrest him. On the morning of April 17 Michael O'Laughlen, another childhood friend of Booth's in on the kidnapping plot, surrendered in Baltimore. Dana ordered him brought to Washington in irons as inconspicuously as possible and arranged for a closed carriage to await him at the train station.[37]

Lewis Powell was captured on April 17 at Mrs. Surratt's boarding house. O'Laughlen, Powell, Arnold, and George Atzerodt, who was apprehended on April 20 at a relative's farm in Maryland, were taken to ironclad monitors berthed near the Washington Navy Yard. Onboard the *Saugus* Powell was put in wrist irons and fitted with a heavy canvas hood to prevent communication with other prisoners. Stanton sent Dana and Major Eckert to pry some testimony from him. Dana stayed a few hours before giving up and returning to his office. Eckert persisted; a gentle giant who sometimes served as Lincoln's bodyguard, he evidently felt a kinship with the silent gladiator Powell. Winning Powell's confidence through various kindnesses, Eckert eventually got enough information from him to assure officials they had the identities of all of Booth's immediate co-conspirators.[38]

Meanwhile, the chief culprit had taken an escape route through southern Maryland lined with Confederate sympathizers. Booth and his companion David Herold evaded pursuers for twelve days. By coincidence, Dana's younger brother, Lieutenant David D. Dana, who was stationed at Fort Baker in Washington, was put in charge of a contingent of the 13th New York Cavalry to march into southern Maryland and sniff for clues on Booth's whereabouts. Around noon on April 15 Lieutenant Dana arrived in Bryantown, set up headquarters at its tavern, and began scouring for information. He was less than five miles from Dr. Samuel Mudd's house, where Booth rested overnight and had his broken leg treated. Mudd's cousin told Lieutenant Dana about two strangers who had stayed with Mudd, but Dana delayed acting on the tip until Washington detectives arrived the next day. This mistake and other holdups gave the fugitives a head start in their flight across the Potomac into Virginia.[39]

Finally on April 26 Union troops trapped Booth and Herold in a barn near Port Royal, Virginia. Herold surrendered but Booth was fatally wounded by a bullet to the neck. Stanton had Booth's body brought to Washington and, determined not to make a shrine of his grave, ordered it secretly buried in an unmarked spot at the Old Arsenal penitentiary. Stanton also vowed that Ford's Theatre would never house entertainment again. To ward off souvenir hunters Dana ordered the chair in which Lincoln was shot brought to the War Department. Stanton closed the theater and had its proprietor John Ford, a longtime friend of Booth's, arrested at his home in Baltimore. On April 21 Ford wrote Dana from prison asking his help to "induce an early examination" and release. A week later Dana had Ford interrogated, but Stanton kept him in Old Capitol Prison until June. Eventually the government purchased the theater, gutted its interior, and housed its Pension Bureau there.[40]

Just before noon on April 19 Dana was among the 600 dignitaries and guests who crowded into the East Room of the White House to attend Lincoln's funeral service. Lincoln's ornate coffin rested on a raised platform, above which hovered a canopy draped in black. Seated closest to the catafalque were Lincoln's relatives, his secretaries, and General Grant. Dana and other assistant secretaries followed the procession of governors into the room and took their seats beside them. The presiding minister, Phineas D. Gurley, described Lincoln as a universally beloved, religiously devout, and morally pure leader, free of any guile or racial prejudice. Together with a stack of newspaper editorials commemorating the slain president, Gurley's sermon laid the foundation for Lincoln's rapid transformation by death into a martyr for freedom and a national saint. Dana, despite misgivings about converting Lincoln into "a legendary figure," later joined the chorus, calling him "the greatest man in the modern history of mankind."[41]

When the service ended, Dana took his place in the long procession that accompanied Lincoln's horse-drawn hearse for a mile and a half down Pennsylvania Avenue to the Capitol. After lying in state beneath the Capitol Rotunda, Lincoln's body left Washington by train for a ceremonial tour through the Northern states on the way to its final resting place in Springfield, Illinois. General E. D. Townsend of Stanton's staff was designated to accompany the casket and oversee its reception at cities on the route. Stanton stayed behind to continue the hunt for the assassins, with Dana to assist him. Even so, the two kept close tabs on the obsequies at each location.[42]

Stanton learned from newspapers that General Townsend had allowed a photographer to take an image of Lincoln's open coffin as the president lay in state in New York's City Hall. He wired an order to seize and destroy the plates. Dana became involved when the photographer, Thomas Gurney, who knew him from the *Tribune*, appealed to him to have Stanton reconsider. Dana's intervention, backed by endorsements from Henry Raymond of the *Times* and Reverend Henry Ward Beecher, resulted in the glass-plate negatives being sent to the War Department for review. The negatives have not survived, but a print was discovered in Stanton's files in 1952. It is the sole surviving photograph of Lincoln in death.[43]

Elaborate events staged at each stop along the route allowed different groups to pay their respects to the slain president. Not all citizens were invited, however. In New York City the organizing committee, fearing a repeat of the draft-riot violence, announced that black residents would be excluded from the procession accompanying Lincoln's coffin. Angry black New Yorkers gathered at Cooper Union, where they heard Frederick Douglass denounce the ban as a "disgraceful" repudiation of Lincoln's legacy. Back in Washington Dana learned about the controversy through his New York contacts and brought it to Stanton's attention. They drafted a strong response: "It is the desire of the Secretary of War that no discrimination respecting color should be exercised in admitting persons to the funeral procession in New-York tomorrow," Dana wired on April 24, adding that a black regiment "formed part of the escort" in Washington's cortege. At the eleventh hour the parade organizers reversed their decision. Hundreds of black New Yorkers formed lines under police protection at the rear of the procession, and the crowds on Fifth Avenue gave them a prolonged ovation.[44]

Trying the Conspirators

The Senate chaplain, Edwin H. Gray, closed the White House funeral ceremony by beseeching "the God of justice, and Avenger of the nation's wrong" to punish the perpetrators of assassination. Dana and War Department officials suspected that these included others besides Booth and his arrested associates. Back at his desk, Dana recalled two suspicious letters from the previous fall. In November 1864 General Dix had forwarded to the War Department an envelope found on a New York City streetcar. An undated letter inside, from "Charles Selby" to "Louis," declared that "Abe must die, and now." Lots had been cast and Louis had been selected; he should perform the deed "within the fortnight." Another letter, from Louis's wife, revealed little.

After reading the letters, Dana had taken them to Lincoln, who made no special remark but held on to them. A few days after Lincoln died Dana went through the president's desk at the White House and discovered them in an envelope marked "Assassination" in Lincoln's hand. Dana took them to John A. Bingham, the government's prosecutor in the conspiracy trial, and wired for Mrs. Mary Hudspeth, the widowed storekeeper who had found them on the streetcar, to come to Washington to be interrogated.[45]

Another piece of evidence Dana found suggested a link between Booth and Richmond. While searching through the Confederate secretary of state Judah Benjamin's abandoned office in Richmond on April 6 Dana retrieved a cipher sheet pasted on a cylinder. On the paper was an alphabet square (called a Vigenère cipher after its sixteenth-century French inventor), which gridded the alphabet in a table of 26 letters across and 27 down. A key phrase was used to encrypt and decipher messages by tracing where the coded and decoded letters intersect. The cipher alphabet scheme on Benjamin's sheet appeared to match the one found among the papers in Booth's trunk at the National Hotel. The mysterious "Sam" letter found in Booth's trunk also hinted at a link to Confederate officials. In it, Arnold advised Booth not to "act rashly or in haste" but to "go and see how it will be taken at R— —d."[46]

Clues like these matched suspicions voiced throughout the North that Richmond Confederates and their agents in Canada shared responsibility for the assassination. This assumption dominated the War Department's investigation. Judge Advocate Joseph Holt, the loyal Kentuckian who was in charge of assessing the government's case, had developed a fierce hatred for Jefferson Davis and his circle, many of them former friends. From the outset Holt and Stanton were convinced that Davis and other high Confederate leaders were responsible together with Booth's immediate accomplices for Lincoln's murder. If Dana rushed to judgment in his readiness to believe in a Confederate "grand conspiracy" despite questionable evidence, it was a fault he shared with Stanton, Holt, and the government's team of "Lincoln's avengers" in the rage-filled weeks after Lincoln's murder.[47]

One disappointment to Union officials was that Francis Lieber and his staff, whom Stanton had charged with combing the captured rebel archives, found no evidence that incriminated Confederate leaders, only crank assassination offers and "unspecified threats" to the Union government. Nevertheless, tantalizing bits gathered by Holt's agents, local police, and private detectives crowded the War Department inbox along with tips from the public at large. Reports of disloyal conversations overheard among Confederates in Northern states or Canada, names of known acquaintances of the conspirators, alleged foreknowledge of the plot—many such leads found their way to Dana's desk. Some of this information was worthless, but much required further investigation. After consulting with Stanton and Holt, Dana used incoming tips and reports to order witnesses interrogated, suspects arrested, and evidence seized. According to Holt, Dana supervised the interrogation of several ancillary witnesses.[48]

There were plenty of false leads. Testimony by suspects and loyal informers mentioned a Confederate secret operative named "Lamar." Stanton and Dana remembered Gazaway Bugg Lamar—an unforgettable name—a Georgia businessman then New York City banker who left for Savannah after secession, where he engaged in cotton speculation and blockade-running. Dana had Lamar arrested and transported to Old Capitol Prison. He was held for three months without charges before it was concluded that he had no part in the assassination. (Lamar subsequently sued Dana claiming false arrest and seeking damages of $100,000, but a federal circuit court ruled in 1873 that Dana had acted by authority of President Andrew Johnson under martial law.)[49] Another suspect Dana ordered arrested was Francis Tumblety, an Irish-born mountebank who earned a living as "The Indian Herb Doctor," most recently in St. Louis. Because Booth's companion David Herold had briefly worked for Tumblety, the "Doctor" was mistakenly suspected of involvement in Booth's plot. Tumblety was released at the end of May 1865. Two decades later he resurfaced, after a stay in London, as a prime suspect in the unsolved Whitechapel murders of prostitutes that were blamed on "Jack the Ripper." He remains a leading candidate today.[50]

While pursuing these red herrings Dana also gathered evidence to implicate Jefferson Davis and other Confederate leaders not only in Lincoln's killing but also in the cross-border raids undertaken by rebel agents based in Canada. The implication was that if Richmond officials, in concert with their Canadian agents, approved sabotage, arson, and deadly attacks on Northern civilians it was a short step to condoning political assassination.[51]

As they reviewed the mass of materials investigators had collected, Dana, Holt, and Stanton found the grand conspiracy they expected. The evidence might not meet a court's standard of proof, Dana told James Pike, but it left "no possible doubt" that high Confederate officials "were accessory to the murder before the fact, gave it their approval, and even furnished the funds by which the enormous number of actors in the plot were supported and enabled to carry out their design." On May 2, after receiving Holt's advice, President Johnson issued a proclamation naming Jefferson Davis and the Confederacy's Canadian representatives—Jacob Thompson, Clement Clay, George Sanders, and Beverley Tucker—among those who "incited, concerted, and procured" Lincoln's murder. The government offered a reward of $100,000 for Davis's arrest and $25,000 each for Clay, Thompson, Sanders and Tucker.[52]

While these men were still at large the government put the immediate conspirators on trial. They were taken before a military tribunal rather than the civil courts, a decision that Stanton had persuaded Johnson to adopt. Charges were drawn up against Herold, Atzerodt, Powell, Arnold, O'Laughlen, Samuel Mudd, Mary Surrat, and Edmund Spangler, a stagehand who assisted Booth's escape from Ford's Theatre. The specification added that Davis, the Confederate agents in Canada, and "others unknown" had "incited and encouraged" the assassination plot. (Davis and his agents thus became what would later be called "unindicted co-conspirators.") On May 9 a commission of nine military officers headed by General David Hunter began hearing the evidence in a crowded room on the third floor of the Old Penitentiary Building, close by where Booth's body had been secretly buried. Holt served as the government's lead prosecutor, assisted by Colonel Henry Burnett, who had spearheaded the crackdown on midwestern Copperheads a year earlier, and Ohio Congressman John A. Bingham, a pugnacious attorney and long-time Stanton associate.[53]

Despite the absence of Confederate officials, the prosecution went to extraordinary lengths to prove that Davis, his cabinet, and their Canadian agents were as guilty as Booth and his immediate accomplices. Dozens of witnesses provided evidence—not always credible—about the Confederacy's "Canadian cabinet," their secret operations in the North, and Davis's reaction to Lincoln's death. Charles Dana testified twice at the trial, both times attempting to back the existence of a wider conspiracy. On May 20 he identified the alphabetic cipher square he had found in Secretary of State Benjamin's offices in Richmond. Subsequent witnesses declared it identical to the one found in Booth's trunk and the same one that Confederate agents in Canada had used. In fact, it was not an exact match: the first line in Booth's table began with "Z" instead of the customary "A" of Benjamin's. But the fact that Booth possessed such a cipher linked him to the secret communication network among Confederate officials.[54]

Dana's second appearance, on June 9, concerned the suspicious letters found by Mrs. Hudspeth on the New York City streetcar. Earlier Mrs. Hudspeth told the court that she had overheard a conversation between the two men who left the envelope behind. The younger one, with delicate hands and false whiskers, had a pistol in his belt and said he was leaving for Washington in two days. Hudspeth did not identify the young man as Booth, but her description suggested the possibility. Dana told the commissioners how these letters had reached him. He suggested that Lincoln "seemed to attach more importance" to them than to other threats, since he had saved them in his desk. Under cross-examination Dana acknowledged that menacing letters were received frequently by the War Department. Nor did it help the government's case that General Dix had called the letters "obviously a manufacture" when he forwarded them to Washington.[55]

During closed sessions of the commission two informants offered testimony that appeared to back the government's conspiracy claims in more direct and startling ways. One was Dana's spy Richard Montgomery, who had served as a courier between authorities in Richmond and Confederate agents in Canada. After Lincoln was killed, Dana sent Montgomery to Colonel Burnett for questioning; producing him as a star witness was Dana's most important contribution to the prosecution. Montgomery's testimony opened the trial with a bang: "I visited Canada in the summer of 1864," he told the commission, "and excepting the time I have been going backward and forward have remained there." He described several meetings with Thompson, Clay, and other Confederates in Montreal, Toronto, Niagara Falls, and St. Catherine's. At Montreal in January 1865, Montgomery claimed, Jacob Thompson told him that he had endorsed an assassination plot against Union leaders but was waiting for approval from the Richmond government. Montgomery also claimed to have seen Lewis Powell in Canada conferring with Clement Clay. On a mission to Canada a few days after the assassination Montgomery learned additional incriminating facts. John Wilkes Booth had visited Canada more than once in the fall of 1864 to consult with Thompson. Booth, Montgomery was told by Thompson's secretary, was one of the men who had proposed to put Lincoln "out of his way." During the same post-assassination mission Beverley Tucker gave Montgomery the impression that Richmond officials had approved the plot.[56]

The testimony of a second Union secret agent, one "Sandford Conover," was especially sensational and incriminating. Conover, whose real name was Charles A. Dunham, was a journalist, con man, and self-proclaimed spy who adopted several aliases during the war to dupe both Union and Confederate authorities into paying for his stories. Conover testified that he went to Canada in 1864 as an undercover journalist for Horace Greeley's *Tribune*. Assuming the alias "James Watson Wallace," he became a confidant of all the Confederate agents. Conover told commissioners that Jacob Thompson had approved an assassination attempt by Booth against Lincoln, Johnson, and the cabinet, and that Richmond authorities had given their assent to it: he was in Thompson's office in early April 1865 when letters of approval arrived from Jefferson Davis and Judah Benjamin. Conover said he divulged the plot to the *Tribune* in February 1865, but Greeley's paper did not publish it.[57]

Conover's secret testimony was leaked to the press and his claims were disputed in several Canadian depositions and newspaper articles. After the trial his credibility sank rapidly when meetings he described were shown not to have happened and it was proven he had lied about his own identity. Some of the witnesses Conover produced for the assassination trial and for a House Judiciary Committee investigation a year later recanted, admitting that Conover had made up their stories, coached them on delivering them, and paid them for cooperating. In February 1867 Conover was tried for lying under oath and encouraging others to do so during the House investigation of Confederate officials' role in the assassination. He was convicted and sentenced to ten years' imprisonment.[58]

Richard Montgomery was also called a perjurer, but his case was less clear-cut. The Confederates claimed that Montgomery had been dropped as a courier after July 1864, but his later work for Dana refuted this. Charges that Conover coached Montgomery's testimony also appear unfounded: the two had no connection and their stories contained important discrepancies. And there was a genuine nugget of truth among Montgomery's testimonial fool's gold: his story that Booth visited Montreal before December 1864, although he went there fewer times than Montgomery claimed.[59]

Still, Montgomery's murky past and his wartime adventures as a double agent do not inspire confidence. Published rebuttals asserted that Thompson was elsewhere when Montgomery claimed to meet him in Montreal. Montgomery's sighting of Powell in Canada was a fabrication and his post-assassination trip to Montreal dubious. After the war Montgomery was given a position in Holt's Bureau of Military Justice, but, according to Dana, he did not last long because he could not shed the "habit of lying" he acquired as a spy. He was apparently involved in attempting to procure false testimony against John Surratt during the latter's civil trial in 1867. The following year Holt dismissed him, explaining there were complaints about "bad debts and shady deals." Several years later Montgomery, faced with likely conviction in a fraudulent claim over a government-confiscated vessel, left his family and disappeared from the historical record.[60]

Laced with fabrications and coming from a habitual liar, Montgomery's testimony must be considered tainted; but at the time Dana trusted his spy's reports. Privately he corroborated Montgomery's story about Jacob Thompson's involvement. In a letter to James Pike written a few days before

Montgomery's testimony Dana confided that he was "well aware at the time [of Lincoln's death] that Thompson had some two months previously entertained favorably a project for Mr. Lincoln's assassination," but he "had no imagination that the scheme was still entertained and was so soon to be put in execution." Dana did not say who had informed him. Later he wrote that "our secret agents in Canada" had "repeatedly" reported that Thompson and his associates in Canada were considering assassination plans. His main source was Montgomery, although he may also have been referring to Conover.[61]

Montgomery's reports and similar allegations were likely the basis on which Stanton ordered Jacob Thompson's arrest after Lincoln was shot. However, if the War Department was specifically warned earlier about a Confederate-sanctioned assassination plot, why wasn't the tip treated more urgently? According to Nicolay and Hay, Lincoln's secretaries, investigations of assassination alerts were always concluded "without substantial result": "Warnings that appeared to be most definite, when they came to be examined proved too vague and confused for further attention." Perhaps Stanton and Dana believed that Jefferson Davis would not approve the assassination plan, or that Thompson's men would limit undercover operations to the states bordering Canada. In any case, by mid-April concern for Lincoln's safety was waning. The president had survived the second inaugural on March 4 as well as a walk through Richmond only a day after the Confederate capital fell. Lee's army had surrendered and Confederate leaders were returning to their homes or trying to leave the country. Lincoln's associates felt that the danger to the president had passed. Hence Dana's surprise that the murder scheme was still afoot.[62]

Historians continue to debate whether a grand Confederate conspiracy existed to assassinate Lincoln. It is plausible that Jacob Thompson would second the idea of assassinating Lincoln, for he approved deadly schemes of sabotage against Union cities. But no evidence has been produced that Thompson's men presented Jefferson Davis with such a plan. In the summer of 1864, in response to failed Union raids against Richmond and a desperate manpower shortage, Davis may have authorized a plot by the Confederate secret service to kidnap Lincoln and exchange him for Confederate prisoners. (The plan fizzled.) Political assassination remained another matter, especially when undertaken by a private citizen, and Davis apparently refused to cross that line.[63]

It is also doubtful that John Wilkes Booth developed an assassination plot in concert with Confederate officials. Booth visited Montreal for ten days in October 1864, met with Confederate agents who were involved in plotting cross-border raids, and returned with a sizeable bank draft and letters of introduction to members of the Confederate underground in southern Maryland who could assist his escape from Washington. This conspiracy, however, contemplated kidnapping Lincoln, not murdering him. Until April 1865 Booth's fuzzy plan was a variant of several Confederate plots that had hatched separately to abduct Lincoln and take him to Richmond to exchange for rebel prisoners.[64]

Stanton and Holt, though aware that Booth originally plotted a kidnapping, believed that the evidence implicating Confederate leaders in Lincoln's death was compelling enough to sway a military tribunal, if not a criminal jury. In fact, Conover's and Montgomery's vivid disclosures at the trial made a profound impression. One commissioner noted in his diary that the prosecution's evidence "very strongly implicates the rebels in Canada," while a lawyer for the defense told a French observer he believed Jefferson Davis guilty of assassination. John A. Bingham, summing up the government's case, presented a detailed closing argument that blended facts and speculation but seemed to clinch the question. Drawing heavily upon Conover's and Montgomery's testimony, he recited a chain of events that showed Davis, Thompson, and Sanders "as clearly proven guilty of this conspiracy as is John Wilkes Booth." When the trial ended the commissioners might well have condemned Davis and the Canadian Confederates if they had been formally charged. Those who *were* charged were convicted on June 30: Arnold, Mudd, and O'Laughlen were sentenced to life in prison; Spangler received a six-year sentence; and Powell, Herold, Atzerodt, and Mary Surratt were condemned to death.[65]

Still, it appears that government prosecutors harbored doubts about their case against Davis. If they had truly considered it unassailable, Holt and Stanton could have brought the Confederate president to face charges, for he was taken into custody two days after the commission convened.

Elephant by the Leg

Charles Dana's friend James H. Wilson, newly promoted to major general, was headquartered at Macon, Georgia, in early May 1865 when he heard rumors that Jefferson Davis was fleeing south through the Carolinas. Wilson sent a mounted division to find Davis, and on the morning of May 10 a detachment of the 4th Michigan Cavalry captured Davis's small entourage near Irwinville in southern Georgia. Two days later Wilson's dispatch to Stanton flashed the news to Washington.

Wilson's telegram reported that Davis had slipped into "one of his wife's dresses" as a disguise. This stretched the truth: as Davis fled his accosters he put on his wife's waterproof cloak and wrapped around his neck her borrowed shawl. Dana and Stanton, eager to impugn the Confederate president's manhood, sent Wilson's description to the newspapers and ordered the "dress" brought to the War Department. The story provided a field day for Northern cartoonists, who produced gleeful caricatures depicting Davis in a frilly bonnet and petticoats as he slinked away from his Union stalkers, his true identity given away by his boots. At his New York museum P. T. Barnum displayed a wax figure of Davis in costume as "the Belle of Richmond." Stanton and Dana did nothing to correct the record after they learned the prosaic truth. When the captured garments arrived Stanton hid them away to perpetuate the tale in its most embroidered form. Dana repeated the story that Davis was caught disguised as an old woman, and he wanted the garments used to discredit Davis at a treason trial. For Dana, as for Barnum and the cartoonists, the story provided an irresistible chance to mock the rebel aristocrats' claims to manliness, chivalry, and courage.[66]

Davis and Clement Clay, who surrendered to federal authorities in Georgia the same day Davis was captured, were taken by rail to Savannah and then by boat to Fortress Monroe in Virginia. General Nelson Miles was put in charge of the prisoners. The young Miles was a Union hero, having fought at key Virginia battles and suffered several wounds. Despite Miles's stellar credentials Edwin Stanton fretted that rebel guerrillas might attempt to free Davis or that he might commit suicide rather than face trial. Once again he sent Charles Dana to the field on short notice. He was to report firsthand on security provisions at Fortress Monroe and was authorized to have Davis shackled in irons if necessary.

Dana arrived on May 22, in time to witness the transfer of Davis and Clay from the gunboat *Clyde* to the prison. A procession of cavalrymen was followed by General Miles, who held Davis by the arm, then by Clay, accompanied by the cavalry commander. "The arrangements were excellent and successful," Dana wired Stanton, "and not a single curious spectator was anywhere in sight." "Davis marched," Dana wrote to a friend, "with as haughty and defiant an air as Lucifer, Son of the Morning, bore after he was expelled from heaven." His sure steps seemed to belie reports that the Confederate president had been physically and psychologically broken. Dana learned from Miles that this was play-acting for the occasion: Davis was in fact dazed and physically weakened.[67]

After consulting Miles and visiting the prisoners' cells Dana wired Stanton that the situation was secure. Clay and Davis occupied inner rooms of sep-

Jefferson Davis in prison at Fortress Monroe, 1865, as sketched by Albert R. Waud. Morgan Collection of Civil War Drawings, Library of Congress.

arate casemates with windows that were heavily barred. Dana inspected Davis's cell and pronounced it "clean and fit to live in." The cells were surrounded by chambers full of guards, and these in turn were circled by a moat. If this were not enough, Dana wrote out an order for Miles to use "manacles and fetters" on the prisoners if needed. After Dana left, Miles decided to have a pair of iron anklets placed on Davis for a few days while his cell's wooden doors were being replaced with grated iron.[68]

This precaution backfired. Press reports of a manacled Davis in declining health fueled outrage in the South. They also fed a growing sense among some Northern politicians and journalists that Jefferson Davis was being made the victim of the government's passion for revenge. The longer Holt and Stanton delayed filing formal charges, the more public sympathy grew for the jailed Confederate leaders. By the fall of 1865 the case against them had weakened considerably as information surfaced that government witnesses had lied profusely at the conspiracy trial. Eventually Stanton and Holt were forced to realize that their evidence was too incomplete and tainted to implicate the Confederate president in Lincoln's murder, though Holt still fervently believed Davis guilty and Stanton and Dana doubted his innocence.[69]

For a while the government considered a plan to try Davis, Clay, and General Robert E. Lee in civil courts for treason rather than assassination.

On June 7 a federal grand jury in occupied Norfolk, Virginia, returned an indictment for treason against Lee. General Grant intervened on Lee's behalf, declaring that his terms of surrender at Appomattox—which Lincoln had approved and which Grant believed had prevented prolonged guerrilla warfare—precluded prosecution as long as Lee and his men did not violate their parole. In mid-June President Johnson's cabinet discussed the possibility of a treason trial for Lee. Johnson wanted Lee's prosecution to go forward, but when Grant threatened to resign over the issue his view prevailed. Two weeks after the indictment, Attorney General James Speed instructed officials in Norfolk not to arrest any paroled Confederates.[70]

Not long after Speed's decision, Charles Dana—by then free to speak out after having left the War Department in early July—protested publicly. Intent on avenging Union blood, he found it "intensely galling" that Grant's surrender terms were "so loosely worded as to afford a loophole for the escape of such a traitor from the clutches of the law." If the commander of the notorious Andersonville Prison, Henry Wirz, could be tried for treason, then so could Lee.[71]

An additional obstacle to a treason trial was the possibility of acquittal. As Navy Secretary Gideon Welles pointed out when the cabinet debated Jefferson Davis's fate in mid-July, Davis would have to be tried for treason in Virginia because Richmond was the Confederacy's headquarters. Attorney General Speed issued a formal opinion confirming this. The civil courts were not yet open in that unreconstructed state, and there was no clear indication when Davis could be tried there. Dana, observing from the sidelines, continued to urge a treason trial for Davis, but he added ruefully that a Southern jury would likely acquit Davis or that Johnson would pardon him.[72]

As the government's options against Davis dwindled to an assassination inquiry based on tainted evidence or a treason trial that had to be postponed and might end in acquittal, the possibility of punishing Confederate leaders receded. In November 1865 Johnson revoked the reward offers for the capture of Jacob Thompson and the other Canadian Confederates. Pressure was also building for Jefferson Davis's release. His wife, Varina, led a resourceful campaign to free him, enlisting the aid of sympathetic Northerners, including Horace Greeley. The *Tribune* editor had never accepted the grand conspiracy theory, and he argued that postwar clemency would secure white Southerners' assent to emancipation. Acting through an intermediary, Mrs. Davis told Greeley that her husband had tried to improve conditions for Union prisoners. Soon *Tribune* editorials called for Davis's release, claiming that it would "powerfully contribute to that juster appreciation of the North at the South which is the first step toward a beneficial and perfect consolation." In May 1867 Greeley was among those who posted bail when the Johnson administration ordered Davis released from military custody. The next year Davis was freed from prosecution by Johnson's proclamation of amnesty to all Confederates.[73]

To Dana, who never relinquished the idea that Davis was connected to the assassination, Greeley's opposition was all too familiar. The war ended for the two rivals as it had begun: three years after Greeley fired Dana, they were replaying their roles of the secession winter, with Dana clamoring to punish Davis for treason and Greeley advising to let him go in peace. Disgusted, Dana called Greeley a "secessionist" and in September 1865 reminded *New York Times* readers that Greeley had fallen for various rebel peace schemes and proposed France's mediation to end the war: "It is impossible to find a more deplorable catalogue of unpatriotic, useless, and discreditable vagaries than his during these four years."[74]

Yet by 1867 Greeley's call for reconciliation was probably more in tune with the public's war weariness than Dana's thirst for revenge. Certainly it accorded better with the martyred Union president's wishes. During the summer of 1865, while the cabinet debated how to handle Davis's case, Salmon Chase recalled that Lincoln had hoped Union authorities would look the other way while Davis fled. The chief justice urged Stanton to dismiss the problem: "Lincoln wanted Jefferson Davis to escape. And he was right. His capture was a mistake. His trial will be a far greater one. . . . Secession is settled. Let it stay settled." Chase proved prescient. Instead of Jacob Thompson, Jefferson Davis became the elephant whose leg Lincoln had advised Stanton and Dana not to shackle.[75]

Grand Review

Dana returned to Washington on May 23 after his mission to monitor Davis's imprisonment. He found the city's streets swarming with detachments of Union soldiers and thousands of visitors. The Grand Review comprising the Armies of the Potomac and of the Tennessee, arranged for May 23 and 24, featured vast columns of Union soldiers who marched from Capitol Hill down Pennsylvania Avenue. Dana took his place on the official reviewing stand erected in front of the White House. Under its roof President Johnson occupied the center, flanked by cabinet members Stanton and Dennison as well as General Grant; along the same front row a seat was reserved for the corps commander whose troops were passing.

Reporting to a friend, Dana was struck by the precise order and the sheer volume of Union troops, whose officers saluted smartly as they passed the reviewing stand. It was foolish for the Rebels to think that they could have outlasted the men in blue; by fighting a war of attrition they had actually played into the Union's strength. The saviors of the Union were now sending a message to more distant foes. Foreign observers would "now distinctly understand," Dana wrote in syntax echoing Thucydides, "that, as a warlike people the Americans are not to be despised."[76]

On May 24 it was the Army of the Tennessee's turn to march. For their commander William T. Sherman, the luster of victory had been tarnished by bitter controversy over the terms of peace. On April 18, nine days after Appomattox and just a few days after Lincoln's assassination, Sherman had finalized terms of the surrender of Joseph E. Johnston's Confederate army in North Carolina. But Sherman offered such broad and easy conditions that his truce threatened to give away the Union's hard-won advantages. Although he had assured Stanton that he would "accept the same terms as General Grant gave Lee and be careful not to complicate any points of civil policy," his agreement granted recognition to existing Confederate legislatures once they had sworn allegiance to the Union; restored franchise and property rights to all Southerners; and proclaimed a general amnesty.[77]

When word of Sherman's action reached Washington, Stanton was alarmed by the agreement's pro-Confederate cast. He fumed to Dana that this was not a military surrender but the Copperhead armistice the Democrats had campaigned for in 1864. At the April 21 cabinet meeting Stanton condemned Sherman's agreement and secured President Johnson's and Grant's disapproval. Stanton sent Grant to North Carolina with orders to have Sherman notify General Johnston that the agreement had been countermanded. Grant tactfully won Sherman's cooperation—no mean feat, since Sherman had been humiliated—and within a few days Sherman accepted from Johnston a simple military surrender like that at Appomattox.[78]

There the matter might have ended had not Stanton, acting unwisely and "in hot haste," Dana admitted, sent the details of Sherman's blunder to the *New York Times* with an indignant, point-by-point repudiation. Stanton implied that Sherman had deliberately disobeyed President Lincoln's instructions and that his truce could allow Jefferson Davis to escape with Confederate gold. In effect, he hinted that Sherman had colluded with the Rebels as well as committed insubordination.[79]

Charles Dana understood the politics involved. At issue were strong differences between Sherman and Stanton (along with his deputy Dana) over policy toward the conquered South and the former slaves. Sherman supported emancipation begrudgingly, and only a few weeks earlier he had refused to send soldiers to capture Jefferson Davis. Bungling the surrender and coddling the Rebels had taken Sherman "out of the category of possible candidates for the presidency," in Dana's opinion. Still, he believed Stanton's judgment "too severe." Sherman did not collude with Confederate negotiators but was used by them. And Stanton's fury was intensified by personal animosity: "The two men were antagonistic by nature. Sherman was an effervescent, mercurial, expansive man," and the dour, suspicious Stanton "could not accommodate himself to this temperament." They had one thing in common, however: a quick temper.[80]

Sherman was enraged at Stanton's public dressing-down, and he carefully planned public revenge. At the Grand Review, a band played "Marching through Georgia" as Sherman reached the White House grounds, dismounted, then strode up the stairs of the reviewing stand. Johnson, Grant, and the other dignitaries stood to greet him. With all watching intently, Sherman shook hands with the president, then deliberately refused to take Stanton's proffered hand, looking away and slipping past him to greet his friend Ulysses Grant. Dana was seated directly behind Stanton. Ever loyal, he insisted afterward that the war secretary had not been bested: Stanton, he said, had only offered Sherman a nod of recognition.[81]

The Grand Review marked the end of Washington's victory celebrations. Except for the assassination trial, Dana's next month was occupied with the routine work of winding down the Union war machine: processing discharges and reassignments, overseeing the mustering out of regiments, reviewing contractors' claims, and arranging the return of war prisoners.

One task with broader implications for the postwar era was drawing up a plan to return Southern railroads to their private owners. Because of his wartime experience with railroads Dana was asked to review Quartermaster General Montgomery Meigs's plan for relinquishing railroads seized during the conflict. Meigs, eager to demobilize quickly, proposed that they be transferred to their prior private owners or state boards of public works under generous terms and with as few requirements as possible. Dana suggested changes that exempted the Union government from damage claims and made the railroads purchase rolling stock. Meigs accepted these recommendations but not Dana's proposal that Southerners pay for wartime improvements. Generous terms would restore the South's prosperity quickly and promote goodwill toward the Union. As a result, less than a year after the war ended, regular rail service was restored in most of the South. Dana eventually approved of this policy. Despite his hard line against Confederate leaders, he put aside retribution to help remake the South's economy in the North's image.[82]

As War Department business slowed, Dana left his desk periodically to prepare for his next career move or to make up for lost family time. One Sunday in mid-June he commandeered the *River Queen* for an outing to Mount Vernon, where his family, accompanied by members of the French legation, toured George Washington's mansion and admired a glorious sunset from the Potomac. On July 1, two days after the military commission convicted Booth's co-conspirators, Dana resigned his post as assistant secretary. He stayed an additional week to accommodate Stanton, who was ill. Across town on his last day at work, Booth's co-conspirators were hanged in the Old Penitentiary prison yard. Like other government officials, Dana did not dignify the assassins by attending their execution. The next day, July 8, he departed Washington to join his family on the Connecticut shore. Dana's Civil War career was officially over.[83]

17 "Grantism" and Retreat

The war was over, at a staggering cost of lives and money, but the task of securing the Union's victory remained. How would the former Confederate states be restored to the Union, and who would oversee the process? How thoroughly should the Northern victors restructure the South's politics and its racial order after emancipation? The questions were hotly debated as political control veered between the president and Congress, between the states and the national government. Like many Radical Republicans, Charles Dana was determined to ensure that the victorious North not lose the peace through a settlement that was too soft on treasonous slave owners. From the outset of President Andrew Johnson's administration, Dana warned that "restoration" and "Reconstruction" were at odds: a quick and lenient return of rebel states to the Union meant abandoning racial equality, whereas revolutionizing the South's social and political order would take a long and grueling struggle. In the immediate postwar years Dana chose the latter course, but in an abrupt and puzzling turnabout he soon switched sides.

Chicago and Radical Reconstruction

At the war's end Dana was again in debt, having borrowed money to supplement his government salary, but he was not without prospects. Job offers from newspapers came before he left the War Department; most originated in the booming Midwest, where former Union generals and eastern businessmen were organizing railroads and insurance companies. At the urging of prominent Illinois Republicans and with an attractive financial inducement, Dana took charge of a new morning paper, the *Chicago Republican*. He agreed to serve as chief editor for five years at an annual salary of $7,500. The paper's publisher was A. W. Mack, an Illinois businessman who had organized a Union regiment in 1862 and supported the Lincoln administration's policies as a state senator.[1]

The venture aimed to rival the *Chicago Tribune*, a pro-Republican sheet that editor Joseph Medill had developed into the city's leading newspaper. The *Republican* was organized with a nominal capital investment of $500,000, and Dana was slated to receive $100,000 in shares. Its prospects looked promising. In less than a generation Chicago had established itself as a railroad hub where stockyards, warehouses, and grain elevators gathered the bounty of the nation's interior, and its population reached 200,000 during the war. Dana believed he would "be able not only to make a livelihood there, but to gain a political position in many respects agreeable as well as useful."[2]

The first issue of the *Republican* rolled off the press on May 30, 1865, with Charles Dana listed as editor in chief, but that was two months before he actually ran the paper. He arrived in Chicago on July 20; four days later his inaugural editorial promised readers early and accurate news, backing for the industrial and commercial interests of the region, and loyalty to the Union. The *Republican* pledged the Johnson administration its "cordial, but independent and discriminating support." It would champion the tough-minded Unionist policies that had saved the nation in wartime and would secure its triumph during postwar Reconstruction.[3]

Dana poured his energy into the *Republican*, infusing it with crisp and decisive commentary that bore his imprint. The paper covered local, national, and international stories, while special correspondents contributed news from Washington, New York, and several midwestern cities. Dana lured Isaac England from Horace Greeley's *New York Tribune* to be his managing editor and recruited Stanton's personal secretary Frederick Hall as a reporter. He gave the *Republican* a clean, sophisticated look, changing its four dense and massive ten-columned pages to a tidy eight-page, six-column format modeled on the *New York Times*. His editorials used short, direct paragraphs, repetitive phrasing, and humorous jabs at rival editors to woo readers, and the paper's reputation and appeal grew quickly. According to Dana, its circulation reached more than 30,000, eclipsing the *Chicago Times* and approaching the *Chicago Tribune*'s 40,000.[4]

Dana took to Chicago right away, finding its boosterish rhetoric in tune with his newspaper's aspirations. When his family arrived in the fall, he purchased a spacious Victorian house at Calumet Avenue and 22nd Street on Chicago's South Side, only a block from Lake Michigan. The house looked out on a "deep expanse of green water, dotted over by the white sails of vessels, and spotted by the clouds of smoke shot up by many steamers," Dana told a friend. Mary Todd Lincoln, boarding at a downtown Chicago hotel while her son Robert studied law, envied Dana's "handsome residence, costing $28,000," as she bemoaned her reduced circumstances after her husband's death.[5]

Postwar demobilization handed Dana a host of specific policy decisions to comment on through firsthand knowledge, from the return of Southern railroads to civilian control to the disbanding of army units such as the Signal Corps. Punishment for the Confederacy's ringleaders loomed large on his agenda. Intent on avenging the blood of Union soldiers, he applauded the execution of Captain Henry Wirz, the Confederate commander at the notorious Andersonville Prison in Georgia. As was discussed earlier, Dana also called for treason trials for Jefferson Davis and Robert E. Lee, pressuring Johnson to follow through on his dictum that "treason is a crime and must be made odious."[6]

On the central issues of Reconstruction Dana sided with Radical Republicans. Restoring the South without reconstructing its politics and society meant that the traitors who split the Union would be allowed to return with their dominance intact. During the summer and fall of 1865 the *Republican* published stories almost daily confirming that Southern whites had not changed their views about secession, slavery, or racial supremacy and therefore could not be safely readmitted to the Union. The South's political and social order had to be recast, even if this meant years of military rule.[7]

Dana and the radicals at first believed they had an ally in Andrew Johnson, but increasingly they were at odds. The new president wanted a swift and painless restoration of the Union on terms conciliatory to white Southerners. Elections in the Southern states that reorganized under Johnson's plan sent ten Confederate generals to the US Congress. Dana was appalled. "After being crushed and conquered," the *Republican* fumed, "these men are now crawling back into a Union they hate, with the design of reconstructing, under the banner of states' rights, a party that shall restore to them all their lost power." Reseated in Congress, former Confederates would reverse Republican wartime legislation and force Congress to assume the Confederacy's debts. Given a free hand at home, they would return the freedmen who were the South's true Unionists to semislavery.[8]

Dana urged Republicans to draw up a more stringent plan of Reconstruction and to give Congress the power to enforce it. "Loyal negroes must not be put down, while disloyal white men are put up," he declared to Charles Sumner. The arithmetic of postwar politics led Dana and most congressional Republicans to advocate some form of black voting. Dana understood that for many this was a distasteful expedient. "As for negro suffrage," he wrote a colleague, "the mass of Union men in the Northwest do not care a great deal.

What scares them is the idea that the rebels are all to be let back . . . and made a power in the government again, just as though there had been no rebellion." For Dana, however, black suffrage was not just a pawn in the sectional power game. As he told Sumner, "I don't intend to be a party to any arrangement of the Southern States which shall leave justice out of view." His *Republican* editorials praised black Union soldiers, condemned Black Codes that aimed to reduce freed people to dependent laborers, and protested blacks' exclusion from state constitutional conventions.[9]

The *Republican* demanded that to reenter the Union the Southern states had to ratify the Thirteenth Amendment, repudiate secession and the Confederate debt, accord civil rights and suffrage to the freedmen, and exclude high-ranking Confederate officials from office. If a literacy test were required, it should be applied equally to both races. Dana believed that this had been President Abraham Lincoln's program in essence. At the time Lincoln was assassinated, Dana told former Chicago congressman Isaac N. Arnold, he was leaning toward advocating equal suffrage for all loyal men, white and black, as new state constitutions were being drafted. Less plausibly, Dana assured *Republican* readers that Johnson privately agreed, despite his public courting of Southern whites. To preserve party unity, Dana aligned his paper with Johnson "as far and as much as possible."[10]

His patience ran out quickly, however. By background and ideology Dana had little in common with the backcountry Tennessee politician-turned-president, except a desire to punish the former Rebels. Even that vanished as Johnson pardoned thousands of prominent Confederate slaveholders and politicians. A showdown between Congress and Johnson loomed, as Dana admitted to friends: "The plan of rushing the South back into the Union, so that she will vote for a friend of ours [Johnson] in 1868 won't work. . . . The rebel states will have to stay out until they give evidence of a more complete regeneration."[11]

As Johnson's stock went down among Republicans, Ulysses Grant's soared. Dana continued to champion the war hero after the guns fell silent. In August he joined a delegation of notables who accompanied the general on the final railroad leg of his homecoming tour and described him in glowing terms for *Republican* readers. Grant, "the chief military hero of the century," returned to Galena, Illinois, just as he left, "a simple, upright, unambitious citizen, desiring everything for his country and nothing for himself." Nevertheless, there were omens of future tension between Dana and Grant. One lingering sore was Grant's preemptive pardon of Lee at Appomattox. This lapse "tarnishes what would otherwise have been the spotless glory of the surrender, on the part of our great General." A second disagreement arose when Grant was nominated for promotion to the rank of General of the Army, a title previously held only by George Washington. Publicly, Dana opposed the upgrade "for reasons of economy alone." Pay raises should be off the table, the *Republican* decreed, as long as high taxes were needed to support Reconstruction. Privately, Dana was torn between loyalty to Grant and concern for the war hero's reputation. He considered the bill "a dreadful mistake" that "exhibits a desire for rank and money that detracts from the general's greatness in a fatal way." Congress, however, approved the promotion in July 1866 with no apparent damage to Grant's political prospects.[12]

These were Dana's first public criticisms of Grant. There is no solid evidence that they rankled the general, but Dana's friend James Wilson reported that there were "signs of a change of feeling" about Dana among Grant's coterie; a few staffers were spreading rumors that he had turned against Grant. Dana's response was sharp: "As for my being unfriendly to the general, that is too absurd to be thought by any but a fool. There seem to be some gentlemen who don't realize the difference between a friend and a lackey." Dana asked Wilson to show his letter to another wartime friend (and Grant confidant), John Rawlins, who might squelch malicious gossip and smooth things with the general. Politically, Dana remained firmly in Grant's corner: *Republican* editorials vindicated Grant's wartime record against critics, defended his acceptance of money and houses from grateful citizens, and applauded a move to nominate him for president in 1868.[13]

Meanwhile, Dana ran out of kind words for Andrew Johnson. After months of denying that Johnson was deserting the freedmen and Republicans, Dana joined the rising chorus of disgust. The break followed a series of presidential misdeeds in February 1866. When Johnson spoke out against black suffrage in the South, the *Republican* declared that he had "abandoned the negro race to its old taskmasters and oppressors." When Johnson vetoed Congress's bill to extend the Freedmen's Bureau, Dana fumed that the president had "deserted the flag" and joined the Copperheads in "atrocious sin." The final straw was Johnson's impromptu diatribe at the White House on Washington's birthday, in which he condemned congressional Radical Republicans Sumner and Thaddeus Stevens as traitors and accused them of plotting a coup and assassination. The *Republican*'s headline the next day screamed that the nation had been "disgraced" by Johnson's "revolutionary harangue." Dana hurled back Johnson's charge of treason, declaring that former Confederates "look more confidently to Andrew Johnson at Washington as their leader, than they ever did to Jeff Davis at Richmond." The president had the choice of siding with the Union or the Rebels, and "in an evil hour for himself he clearly chose the latter."[14]

Dana's break with the president synchronized with mainstream Northern Republicans' outrage at Johnson's "betrayal." The defectors included many Republican editors and Senator Lyman Trumbull of Illinois, one of the *Republican*'s chief backers. But Dana's enemies suggested that he had ulterior motives for turning against the president: specifically, Johnson's refusal to reward him with a political appointment.

With the endorsement of Henry Raymond, the *New York Times* editor and leader of Johnson's allies in the House, Dana had written Johnson in January 1866 seeking to be named New York customs collector. The post had become vacant two months earlier when the incumbent, Preston King, jumped to his death off the Hoboken ferry. After noting that "friends in the New York delegation" favored his candidacy, Dana listed his qualifications: As a *New York Tribune* editor before the war he knew the city's merchants and politicians; his wartime post had kept him out of the factional squabbles that plagued New York Republicans; and he would administer the office fairly. Dana closed by suggesting that Johnson consult Secretary of War Edwin Stanton as a personal reference. Johnson, however, had no intention of giving the post to Dana, who had been outside New York for years and was identified as a Grant man and a Radical Republican. Nor would the president consult Stanton over the appointment when the two were at bitter odds over Reconstruction.[15]

Dana's bid for office remained private until March, when Johnson published the letter in retaliation for the editor's political defection. By releasing it, the thin-skinned president tried to paint Dana's opposition as the revenge of a disappointed office-seeker, a tactic he used against other newspaper critics.[16] Opponents—and later historians—pounced on Dana's letter to explain his turn against Johnson and accuse him of hypocrisy. Dana replied that he sought the post when Johnson still enjoyed Republican support and afterward "took very good care to have himself counted out." He had not expected the appointment—his diffident letter resembled the trial balloon he had floated past Lincoln two years before—partly because, as he told a friend, Johnson had "taken some sort of miff against me, as also against many of [his] other friends." Such slim hopes gave Dana little reason to respond with outrage when Johnson passed him over.[17]

Dana had the better of the argument. The timing and tone of his editorials demonstrate that his break with Johnson was triggered by the presidential vetoes and tirades of February, not his failed job application. Still, Dana's persistent thirst for the New York collectorship exposed him to the charge that his attacks on Johnson—and later on Grant—were those of a frustrated claimant for patronage. In the postwar years Dana needled his former boss Horace Greeley mercilessly for his desperate and indiscriminate office-seeking. Dana set his sights on only one plum, but his repeated requests for it compromised his journalistic integrity.

Once Johnson revealed his true colors, the *Republican* pursued him like a shark after blood—with Dana's teeth sharpened by his embarrassment over the collectorship episode. Dana reminded readers that Johnson had persuaded Lincoln to exempt Tennessee from the Emancipation Proclamation. He condemned Johnson's veto of the Civil Rights Act of 1866, which guaranteed birthright citizenship and equal legal protection to the freed people. And he gathered evidence that Johnson had plotted all along to desert the Republicans and form a centrist Union party to nominate him in 1868. "The President is an obstinate, stupid man, governed by preconceived ideas, by whiskey, and by women," Dana wrote Wilson. "He means one thing to-day and another to-morrow, but the glorification of Andrew Johnson all the time."[18]

The struggle between Johnson and Congress over Reconstruction energized Dana's editorials, but it failed to make his paper solvent. Rumors spread that the *Republican*'s shareholders found Dana's attacks too venomous and decided to "Johnsonize" the paper. They and Dana denied this, although his willingness to relocate to New York for the collectorship surely damaged the relationship. In the end, money proved the key bone of contention. The paper's backers raised less than half of the $500,000 promised, and most of it went into paying a running deficit. Dana blamed the crisis on the "rascality and mismanagement" of publisher A. W. Mack, who was bent on reducing expenses. According to the paper's night editor, the owners decided they could not afford Dana and were "working a game to freeze [him] out." Dana held on until the annual shareholders' meeting on May 22 where a resignation agreement was approved. He had edited the paper for a mere ten months and left before the fight between Johnson and Congress reached its climax.[19]

Despite his disappointment, Dana emerged with his finances improved. On parting, he received $10,000 for the stock promised him in addition to his salary, and he eventually won a judgment for another $10,000. In July 1866 he sold his house at a profit in Chicago's tight real estate market. He had counted on the *Republican*'s success to pay his debts and build his assets, but its failure did the job. The Chicago proceeds allowed Dana to resettle his family comfortably in New York and begin planning another newspaper venture.[20]

Dana and the *Sun* Turn on Grant

Charles Dana departed Chicago as a staunch Republican committed to radical Reconstruction, but within a few years everything changed. Between January 1868 and the end of 1869 four developments decisively altered the course of Dana's career, his politics, and, not incidentally, his relationship to his Civil War past. First, Dana acquired his own newspaper, the *New York Sun*. At last he was able to imprint his own notions of popular journalism on a big-city daily. Second, after supporting Ulysses Grant for president in 1868, Dana broke bitterly with him during Grant's first year in office. Third, with passage of the Reconstruction amendments, Dana declared that the questions of reunion and emancipation had been settled and that political corruption was now the "supreme issue" threatening the republic. Fourth, although Dana described the *Sun* as a paper independent of political parties, he tilted its editorial allegiance to its traditionally Democratic readers.[21]

These changes overlapped and mutually reinforced, and they coincided with national trends in the Gilded Age. As the hotly contested project of reconstructing the South dragged on, many Republicans retreated from their commitment to enforcing racial equality. Meanwhile, more and more big-city newspapers cut their ties with political patrons and cast themselves as independent watchdogs of the people's purse. Their exposés of political corruption raised public outrage and led to party shifts and splits. Dana was an early leader on all these fronts, but his change of tone and views was extreme even by the loose standards of the Gilded Age "press gang." Journalistic independence cut Dana loose from his Civil War allegiances and led him to a brand of sensationalized, exposé journalism that attracted mass readership and found Grant's administration a ready target. Less than a decade after the Civil War he faced charges of betraying his friends, his ideals, and his past.[22]

On his return to New York Dana pursued plans to start another paper. He was prepared to use his own funds and solicited backers among the city's Republican stalwarts and professional elite. At first he hoped to position his paper to the left of existing New York Republican dailies, including the *Times* and *Tribune*. Early reports indicated that he was starting a Radical Republican morning paper that would back Andrew Johnson's impeachment and black suffrage. But potential investors held back, including political allies such as Salmon Chase. By September 1867 a new plan took shape. Dana and seven associates, including Frederick Conkling, incorporated the New York Evening Telegraph Association. The venture would be an evening sheet, backed by New York's two Republican senators, Roscoe Conkling (Frederick's brother) and Edwin Morgan, and furthering their faction in state and national politics. But this project stalled when negotiations for access to Associated Press reports broke down. Evidence suggests that Greeley and the *Herald*'s James Gordon Bennett, fearing competition, were behind the AP's refusal.[23]

Just when Dana's plans ran aground, luck intervened. New York's Tammany Society, the control center of the city's Democratic machine, moved its headquarters to a larger building uptown and put up for bid the old five-story Tammany Hall at the corner of Nassau and Frankfort Streets. It was an ideal location for an aspiring New York daily: fronting Printing House Square, the building stood just two doors north of Greeley's *Tribune*. Dana's group had to invest $220,000 to purchase the nondescript red-brick structure. Shortly afterward, Moses Beach, editor of the *New York Sun*, offered to sell Dana his paper for $175,000. Founded in 1835, the *Sun* was a four-page, two-penny morning daily that had won a large and loyal readership among the city's mechanics and small merchants. The *Sun* was already profitable and owned an Associated Press franchise. Beach sweetened the offer by including new presses and the commitment of the *Sun*'s advertisers, and Dana readily accepted.[24]

Observers assumed that Dana would transform the paper into a Radical Republican daily. Among his founding stockholders were prominent New York Republicans and Grant supporters, including the Conklings, Morgan, and George Opdyke. However, Dana had purchased a paper that depended on street sales from working-class readers, not political subsidies, and that had leaned Democratic. One of the first self-proclaimed "independent" papers, the *Sun* had found a winning formula by emphasizing timely news presented concisely, coverage of the labor movement, sensationalized crime stories, and human interest narratives. From the outset Dana faced the problem of squaring his prior Republican views and those of his stockholders with the *Sun*'s history and its readers' Democratic allegiances.[25]

Dana's prospectus, printed on January 27, 1868, announced his approach. The *Sun* would continue as an independent newspaper, "wearing the livery of no party." While supporting Grant for president it would advocate frugality in public expenditures and "the speedy restoration of the South" to the Union. It would present "all the news" but "study condensation, clearness, point, and will endeavor to present its daily photograph of the whole world's doings in the most luminous and lively manner." There was something for everyone in this mix. The paper's Republican sponsors were reassured by its Unionist rhetoric and endorsement of Grant, while lower taxes and retrenchment meshed with Democrats' call to curb the federal government, which they charged had been bloated by railroad subsidies and military Reconstruction. Instead of "reconstructing" the South, Dana advocated its speedy "restoration" to the Union, a formula the Democrats favored. "All the news" echoed the *Times*'s authoritative tone, while Dana's promise to produce a cheap, lively paper aimed to please working-class audiences. This hybrid program touted "independence," but there was no mistaking that Dana was leaving Republican dogma behind for an opportunistic strategy that would retain his readers and tilt his paper to the Democrats.[26]

Among the first signs of Dana's moderated views was his newfound reticence on Andrew Johnson's impeachment. Whereas the *Chicago Republican* had been outspoken in its attacks on Johnson, the *New York Sun* was calm. Dana vetoed the partisan reports of his Washington correspondent, Uriah Painter: "I want to avoid the appearance of too much partiality for the Republicans in your dispatches, as in every other part of the paper." In the end he decided that the Senate had done the right thing by not removing the president. The *Sun* commended the seven Republicans who bucked their party to acquit Johnson, calling their action "the highest instance of impartiality and honesty in all political history."[27]

During the run-up to the 1868 campaign the *Sun* affected a nonpartisan air quite alien to the *Chicago Republican*. Expressing concern for the Democrats' future, Dana urged them to nominate his friend Salmon Chase, but when they chose Horatio Seymour the *Sun* defended him against charges of Copperheadism. Once Grant was nominated, Dana followed through on his pledge of support. Approached to write a campaign biography, he and James Wilson quickly produced a hefty book with a rose-tinted take on Grant's life. Advertisements credited Dana as the main author, but he wrote only three of the book's thirty-nine chapters. In them Dana made a virtue of Grant's lack of political experience. Neither an "office-seeker" nor a "partisan politician," Grant would rely on prudent judgment and common sense to provide trustworthy leadership in civil affairs.[28]

The *Sun* reprinted excerpts from the campaign biography and shielded Grant against criticisms Democratic papers hurled at his war record. Continuing his cover-up of Grant's drinking, Dana proclaimed that in camp the general never broke "his rule not to touch or taste anything alcoholic." The *Sun* assured readers that Grant's spotless character guaranteed an honest administration. In words that would seem ironic a year later, Dana wrote that Grant "never made a cent of money himself, nor ever allowed any relative or friend to make any by his help, from the day he entered the army to the present."[29]

After Grant won the election handily the *Sun* offered congratulations but immediately charged him with its impossible mandate to reconcile Republican and Democratic programs. The new president was expected not only to speedily complete the work of Reconstruction and secure the freedmen's rights but also to win over Southern whites and rein in the federal government. Dana tendered Grant cautious support, not the effusive praise he voiced during the campaign. Then, within weeks of the inauguration, all praise of Grant's actions evaporated and the *Sun*'s tone became uniformly critical. In the most dramatic and controversial episode of his long journalistic career, Dana turned abruptly and implacably against Grant.

What had happened? The simplest and most obvious explanation was Dana's bitterness at being denied once again the New York customs collectorship. Dana's earlier requests for the position from Lincoln and Johnson were long shots, but he fully expected it from Grant as a reward for assisting him during and after the war. It appeared he had been promised the appointment. Shortly after the election James Wilson, who relished his insider role, met with John Rawlins to put forward Dana's name. The two agreed that Dana "had rendered both Grant and the government most important service; that he was a vital, able man; and that having a metropolitan newspaper fast rising in popularity and influence, he could be of great benefit to the new administration." In a second meeting Rawlins confirmed that Grant would offer Dana the collectorship, and rumors of the pending appointment were printed in newspapers across the country. But the offer never came.[30]

Why Grant passed over Dana is something of a mystery. George Boutwell, Grant's pick for Treasury secretary and Dana's colleague on the wartime Cairo Claims Commission, urged his appointment but learned that Grant had settled on Moses Grinnell, a Seward-Weed protégé. "Moreover," Boutwell recalled, "the President had formed an unfavorable opinion of Mr. Dana, arising from some intercourse during the war." What this "intercourse" was, the sphinx-like Grant never said directly. Most likely it was one of Dana's private complaints during the Virginia campaign about Grant's futile frontal assaults, the general's retention of the snappish George Meade, or his sluggish response to Jubal Early's raid that had reached the general's ears. Years later Grant told a journalist that during the Overland Campaign "an official of the War Department came down and spent some time in the camp." "Grant took his measure at once [the reporter wrote], for he seemed to understand war better than the General. When this man applied for an important commission under the government, Grant refused the appointment, and has been heartily hated by that gentleman ever since." Those close to Grant testified that he considered criticism from friends as evidence of disloyalty. "Despite the

Appomattox legend," the historian Allan Nevins wrote, Grant "bore grudges and was a vengeful hater."[31]

Yet Dana could also be thin-skinned, and he was quicker to anger than Grant. Publicly he was gracious about Grinnell, whom he praised in the *Sun*; privately, however, Dana considered Grant's snub "a personal insult and never forgave him," according to his brother David and close associates. The incident resurrected the bitterness Dana had tasted when his patron Horace Greeley suddenly dropped him from the *Tribune*. Like Greeley, Grant did not communicate his reasons or acknowledge responsibility. And just as Greeley had sent word through others that Dana could stay on in a lesser post, Grant allowed Boutwell to offer Dana the job of New York customs appraiser. The *Sun* reprinted Dana's haughty reply: "I already hold an office of responsibility as the conductor of an independent newspaper," and "to abandon it or neglect it for the functions you offer me would be to leave a superior duty for one of lesser importance." He could perform a greater public service "by denouncing and exposing political immorality" in the *Sun* than by assessing the customs honestly as appraiser.[32]

Even before the offer, Dana had expressed skepticism about Grant's appointments and published allegations that he made them based on contributions to his campaign or, even worse, his personal funds. On these grounds he called for Navy Secretary Adolph Borie to resign. When George Robeson succeeded Borie, Dana reprinted a Brooklyn paper's charge that Robeson was appointed "for the same reason that Mr. Dana wasn't appointed Collector." "Mr. Robeson gave General Grant five hundred dollars . . . toward the purchase of his Philadelphia house," Dana wrote, while he (Dana) "never gave him any money at all, but only supported him during the war—when his friends were not so many nor so rich as at present—worked for his elevation to the command of our armies, and promoted his election to the Presidency."[33]

Dana was miffed that Grant appointed several wartime staff members—including John Rawlins, Horace Porter, Orville Babcock, Adam Badeau, and Ely Parker—to official posts while passing him over. To escape the contradiction of opposing cronyism while resenting being denied its favors, Dana criticized the influence of Grant's "military circle." More righteously, he condemned the blatant nepotism of Grant's appointments. By one historian's count Grant doled out offices to at least twenty-five relatives by blood or marriage, from diplomatic posts and customs positions to military and White House staff appointments. Nepotism touched a raw nerve in Dana, who had received no help from his widowed father, attributed his success to his own effort, and preached self-reliance. David Dana, Charles's younger brother, offered a revealing insight after a Boston paper claimed that Charles provided him with a monthly stipend in retirement: "My brother has never helped me," he snapped at a visiting reporter. "If ever there was a monomaniac, Charles Anderson Dana was one on the subject of assisting relatives. That was why he pitched into General Grant so fiercely about putting his relatives into office — he believed it was a wrong principle altogether."[34]

Although Dana denied personal motives for his about-face, his resentment of Grant was obvious and his timing synchronized too closely with the customs flap to be a coincidence. Yet even without the snub Dana likely would have turned on the Grant administration, although perhaps not so quickly or viciously. His self-serving rhetoric about the superiority of journalism to politics was not just sour grapes. He and other "independent" editors of the Gilded Age attracted readers by setting themselves up as guardians of political morality and the public purse. Turning down Grant's offer ostentatiously was part of Dana's larger program of repositioning the *Sun* to maximize its readership and political clout. In the Grant era a campaign to ferret out political corruption was irresistible, and it proved to be just what Dana needed to grow his newspaper.[35]

Dana had long targeted political corruption, but in the postwar years exposure of malfeasance became an obsession, not just for him but for much of the press and public. The Union's victory generated high expectations for clean government that were mocked by the sordid reality of cronyism, bribery, and profiteering. The distance between wartime sacrifice and the postwar feeding frenzy was dramatized when the Union's greatest military hero tolerated blatant dishonesty. "At least four-fifths of the American people," the journalist-historian Henry Adams estimated, had drawn a hopeful parallel between George Washington and Grant: the former restored moral order after the Revolution; the latter was expected to redeem the war's bloodletting with a high-minded administration. Dana, knowing Grant's need for money and having witnessed his leniency toward subordinates, doubted that he could withstand unscrupulous influences. "The only hope for Grant," Dana wrote a wartime colleague to defend the *Sun*'s attacks, "is in the free and unsparing criticism of the press. But for that, he would soon get hopelessly in the mud."[36]

Although it was not as pervasive as critics claimed, corruption was real. Opportunities increased as postwar rebuilding commenced, powerful business trusts sought influence, and the federal government expanded its reach into railroad promotion, Indian reservations, and oversight of the South. Dana's initial break with Grant had little to do with the president's Southern agenda, but as stories circulated about extravagant expenses and electoral fraud in reorganized states Reconstruction became tainted as well. Fighting corruption became a winning journalistic tactic to sway voters who were impatient to end the attempt to overhaul the South and return to "frugal and honest" government. Last but not least, charges of fraud and scandal sold papers and won readers' allegiance. "The multitudes," the journalist James Parton quipped, "enjoy their morning villain."[37]

Dana began by laying into Grant's cabinet selections, then moved to other appointments. He claimed that Secretary of State Hamilton Fish, like Borie and Robeson, was chosen because he gave Grant "presents." Fish was hostile to Cuban independence—a favorite cause of Dana's—and too friendly to imperial Spain's government, which employed his son-in-law Sydney Webster as an attorney. Grant's appointments to minor posts and the diplomatic corps were similarly tainted by gift-giving, nepotism, or shady deals, according to Dana's unrelenting attacks. The *Sun* began labeling Grant the "Great Gift-taker" and unloosed a stream of sarcasm and personal abuse. "It is announced that Mrs. Grant will receive every Tuesday afternoon during the winter," the *Sun* declared. "President Grant will receive anytime and anything whenever anything is offered."[38]

Exposures of scandals and frauds became Dana's bread and butter, and Grant's associates obligingly set the table. Dana took a special interest in two controversies that arose out of Civil War–era expenditures. In the winter of 1872 the *Sun*, acting on an inside tip, charged that Navy Secretary Robeson had reopened a claim for payment of three ironclad monitors produced during the war and paid Secor and Company, the builders, an additional $93,000. Dana alleged that this money was stolen from the Treasury and added more charges of procurement fraud against the man the *Sun* dubbed "Secor Robberson." Because of the uproar a congressional inquiry was convened and Dana was called to testify. Under examination Dana refused to name his informants and admitted that his allegation of plunder was based on "inference." Reaction was predictably partisan. The committee's Republican majority report vindicated Robeson, and the *New York Times* editorialized that Dana's testimony was a "humiliating confession of ignorance" that demonstrated his "reckless abuse of his position." Yet Dana's suspicions about Robeson's shady methods were echoed on the witness stand by the former wartime navy secretary, Gideon Welles, whom Dana had consulted. The committee's Democratic minority contended that the Secor payment was illegal and chided Robeson for skirting the law. Dana stretched his allegations into undocumented territory, but he had exposed a pattern of rule-bending and favoritism in Robeson's operations and, by extension, in Grant's.[39]

Dana had more facts on his side when the *Sun* broke the story of the "King of Frauds," the Crédit Mobilier scandal, in September 1872, just weeks before the presidential election. "It is the most damaging exhibition of official and private villainy ever laid bare to the gaze of the world," the *Sun* exclaimed. During the Civil War, congressional Republicans took advantage of the Confederates' absence to authorize construction of a transcontinental railroad on a northern route from Iowa to California. The Union Pacific Railroad was given government loans, vast grants of public lands, and permission to issue stock. The railroad's directors set up an associated construction company, the Crédit Mobilier, as a ruse to overcharge the government. To avoid exposure, in 1867 the company doled out $9 million in discounted shares and cash as bribes to powerful Washington lobbyists and politicians. Included among those the *Sun* named as recipients were Schuyler Colfax, Grant's vice president; James G. Blaine, Speaker of the House of Representatives; three powerful Senate committee chairs; Senator James Garfield, the future president; and others—seventeen men in all.[40]

As usual Dana overshot—he wildly overestimated the number of shares offered to lawmakers—but the *Sun* uncovered undeniable wrongdoing. A congressional investigation focused on thirteen members, two of whom were censured. Circumstantial evidence implicated several more, including Senators Garfield, John Sherman, and John Bingham. Colfax had to be dropped from the Republican ticket that fall and replaced by Henry Wilson. Dana's exposé failed to prevent Grant's reelection, but it did lasting damage to the Republican Party and Grant's administration. Grant's later defense of his private secretary Orville Babcock, who was implicated in the Whiskey Ring tax fraud, and his lenient treatment of Secretary of War William Belknap, who had sold rights to trading posts in Indian Territory, sealed the president's association with scandal. During the war Dana had told his boss Edwin Stanton that Grant's loyalty to incompetent or corrupt staff members crippled his headquarters' operations. The pattern continued in the White House, the *Sun* pointed out: even when Grant's associates were proven to be involved in wrongdoing he defended them and protected their careers.[41]

Most of Dana's allegations against Grant were "more fabulous than true," a historian of Gilded Age plunder concludes, "but Dana was readily believed when he was wrong because so often he was right, or nearly so." Dana used his success at uncovering scandals to argue against the president's reelection,

The press and the Crédit Mobilier scandal, portrayed by cartoonist Thomas Nast, a staunch defender of Ulysses Grant. Charles Dana lurks as the lowest, sneakiest member of the press gang that condemns politicians implicated in the scandal. Lady Justice rebukes the press for hypocrisy: "Let him that has not betrayed the trust of the People, and is without stain, cast the first stone." *Harper's Weekly*, March 15, 1873. Courtesy Florida Center for Instructional Technology, University of South Florida.

which would only entrench "Grantism," a shorthand term for corruption that the *Sun* adopted during the campaign of 1872. The *Sun*'s personal abuse of Grant reached its height that fall. Dana conjured the ghosts of John Rawlins and Edwin Stanton—both of whom had died in 1869—to testify that they had warned him Grant would make a poor president. Editorials in the *Sun* accused Grant of attempting to perpetuate a family dynasty, and when money went missing from a trust fund set up for Rawlins's widow, Dana implied that Grant was responsible. Grant, he wrote, had done much to "destroy in the public mind all distinction between right and wrong, to make it appear that the great object in life and the chief purpose of official authority is to acquire riches."[42]

This abuse was bound to vex Grant. The plainspoken president was famously silent about his feelings, but he was a habitual reader of newspapers and was stung when Dana began to assail him in the *Sun*. Grant was intent on revenge. Joined by Hamilton Fish, who was also exercised by Dana's "malignant and abusive attacks," Grant denied the government's advertising business to the *Sun* and terminated patronage appointments recommended by the paper's proprietors. Grant also secretly aided Dana's detractors. In 1870 the president learned about a sensational pamphlet that accused Dana (falsely) of blackmailing politicians and accepting bribes. Grant heard that a *Sun* reporter who had fed evidence to the anonymous author feared for his safety, and he conferred with Fish about helping him. According to Fish's diary Grant wanted to appoint the informer, Antonio Soteldo, a Venezuelan by birth and a naturalized citizen, US minister to Venezuela. (Grant was unaware that Soteldo had admitted accepting bribes as the *Sun*'s Albany correspondent and had been fired by Dana.) Fish talked him out of it. To avoid a blatant quid pro quo and another administration scandal, the secretary of state suggested a minor, less visible post, and Soteldo was packed off to Key West, Florida, as a Special US Treasury Agent.[43]

At his second inaugural Grant surely had the *Sun* in mind when he told his audience that he had been "the subject of abuse and slander scarcely ever equaled in political history," but now he could disregard these attacks thanks to his electoral "vindication." Perhaps; but Dana had gotten under the president's skin. Over the next decade Grant frequently mentioned the *Sun* in speeches and correspondence, using it as a benchmark for partisan abuse. Despite his stoic exterior he was tormented by Dana's editorial stabs to the very end. One of the last notes the Union hero wrote as he was dying of throat cancer in 1885 was a scribbled slip to his physician: "Get me the N.Y. Sun." It was a sad coda to a relationship that had thrived during the war but descended to bitter animosity afterward.[44]

When the *Sun* turned abruptly from Grant supporter to vicious critic Dana's rivals scolded him. For six months after Dana had taken over the *Sun*, the *Times* declared, he made it reputable, but then "an imposter appeared on the scene, and under the name of CHARLES ASSASSIN DANA, began abusing every respectable man in the community, from the President downward. . . . He has wantonly defamed private character, . . . sacrificed every honorable friendship he possessed, and earned the distinction of telling more untruths in a more cowardly fashion than any man alive." Henry Adams, sizing up the New York dailies, found that Dana "had made the *Sun* a very successful as well as a very amusing paper" but at the price of infusing it with "a strong dash of blackguardism."[45]

Dana came to be regarded as a traitor to his past by former associates in reform and antislavery. George Templeton Strong, the patrician New Yorker whom Dana had impressed after Vicksburg, complained that the *Sun* was "the lowest sensational newspaper in the city," adding that "Dana knows better, is capable of better things, and ought to be ashamed of himself." Several of Dana's cherished companions from Brook Farm and the *Tribune*, including George Ripley and George W. Curtis, cut their ties. E. L. Godkin of the *Nation*, once Dana's admirer, wrote that the *Sun* reveled in "falsehood, indecency, levity, and dishonesty," much "to the horror of Dana's friends." New York's Century Club, which Dana had quit during the war, and its upper-crust Union League banished the *Sun* from their reading rooms.[46]

Although James Wilson maintained his friendship with Dana, he regretted that the editor was "so hard upon Grant." His course "has been marked by exceeding censoriousness and injustice," Wilson confided to Orville Babcock. Writing to another colleague, Wilson put a better face on Dana's attacks: "I think [Dana] is mistaken in the means he has adopted for serving the public. Grant isn't easily driven—and yet he may be goaded into doing what he ought to do of his own free will. But . . . he will probably hate the person who has goaded him." To his credit Wilson voiced his disapproval directly to Dana: he was the "intimate friend of the war days" who tried to persuade Dana that he was carrying his attack on Grant too far. Dana listened but replied firmly: "I am not unmindful of what you say, nor of the good opinion of my friends, and my motives may not be as good as I think they are, but, having taken my course conscientiously, I shall follow it to the end."[47]

Although the *Sun*'s course alienated Dana's former colleagues and caused some stockholders to sell shares, the paper's personal attacks captured its working-class and shop-owner readers. The *Sun* expressed readers' sense that their lives were being controlled by "politicians and manipulators," the shadowy powers the paper's masthead disavowed. In Dana's first two years as editor the *Sun*'s circulation nearly doubled, to 90,000 copies, and by the election of 1872 it reached 160,000. Through the 1870s the *Sun* had the largest circulation of any New York daily. The paper earned hefty annual dividends and made its editor rich. Critics charged that Dana had made a "diabolical compact, by which he sold his soul . . . for newspaper success."[48]

Dana had not simply shifted political allegiances. He had always been shrewd and combative, but by the 1870s his suspicions and snap judgments tipped over into cynicism about human nature. Colleagues noted that Dana privately "never failed to charm even [the] enemies" he made through his paper, but in public Dana shifted without explanation from a reform-friendly editor to a hardened misanthrope. Dana's friend Walt Whitman had decided that his "hissing, hating side" was "not the chief thing in the man, and when his total is made up cuts only a small figure." But a street encounter in the

1870s made him wonder: "It was at a period when Dana's public utterances were particularly irascible," Whitman recalled. "He was finding fault with all things, all people, . . . Grant, particularly." Whitman made directly for Dana and accosted him loudly: "What in hell is the matter with you, Dana, . . . that you keep up an everlasting growl about everybody?" To Whitman's surprise, Dana grabbed the poet by his coat lapels: "See here, Walt: have you spent all these years in the world and not known, not learned, what a sorry, mean lot mankind is anyhow?"[49]

Abandoning Reconstruction

One new weapon in Dana's editorial arsenal was a malicious, mocking sense of humor. For selected targets, including Tammany Hall's Boss Tweed, Dana made up jeering epithets and proposed public offices and honorific statues. This ridicule was nowhere more evident than in Dana's tormenting of his old employer and nemesis, Horace Greeley. "Dana was always possessed by an irresistible inclination to let the world know the profound depths of Greeley's innocence," a *Sun* reporter recalled. The *Sun* belittled the whirl of reform proposals that emanated from "The Philosopher of Chappaqua." With cruel persistence, Dana proposed Greeley for a bewildering series of offices, from the presidency and various foreign ministries to congressman, state comptroller, and prison inspector. The *Sun*'s campaign to make Greeley president began before Grant was nominated in 1868 and continued until late 1871, when Dana, stunned that Greeley's nomination on an anti-Grant ticket was being taken seriously, belatedly expressed second thoughts. Dana's insincere praise was his perverse way of spiking lingering affection for Greeley with personal revenge and the sarcasm of a born-again cynic.[50]

What began as a joke became a reality, proving the adage that politics makes strange bedfellows. As Grant's administration became mired in corruption and entangled in civil rights enforcement in the South, a group of Liberal Republicans split from the party. Adopting a platform promising civil service reform, free trade, and sectional reconciliation, they settled on Greeley as their alternative to Grant. Astonishingly, the Democrats joined with the Republican bolters in July 1872 to nominate Greeley. "Uncle Horace" was pro-tariff and for decades had led the Republican press against Democratic slave owners and Copperheads, but in recent years the *Tribune* had joined the anti-Grant chorus and advocated amnesty for the defeated Confederates. It was time, Greeley famously declared, for Americans North and South to "shake hands across the bloody chasm" that had divided them.

"Splitting the Party: The Entering Wedge." In this Currier & Ives political cartoon of 1872, Carl Schurz and his Liberal Republican colleagues use Horace Greeley as a wedge to split the Republican Party as Grant warns prophetically that "your Mallet will kill the Man." Charles Dana is portrayed cowering at the lower right, advocating "Anything to beat Grant, he would not make me Collector for New York." Library of Congress Prints and Photographs Division.

Dana agreed with the Liberal Republicans' opposition to Grantism and was delighted that they cast their lot with the Democrats. Dead set against a second term for Grant, he chose to endorse Greeley, although he believed him unfit for office. The *Sun*'s support for Greeley was ostentatious, but it was undercut by the same satirical edge Dana had used to propose his candidacy in the first place. The *Sun* insisted on calling its candidate "Doctor Greeley" and touted his farming skills, homespun wisdom, and temperance creed— the last anathema to Wet Democrats. Dana pumped Greeley for president in leaders that sounded like sales pitches for a quack elixir: as an antidote to "Useless S. Grant," "Useful H. Greeley" was "The Man who never Lived an Idle, Useless, or Dishonest Day." One of many *Sun* poems about the weekend "Woodchopper of Chappaqua" declared that "corruption and vice are rife in the land," but "Old Horace" will "chop it all up, with an axe in his hand." The *Sun*'s readers were certain that Dana hated Grant, but they also had to question his praise for Greeley.[51]

Horace Greeley took his own candidacy very seriously. "The Man in the White Coat" wore himself out on speaking tours in New England, the Midwest, and the South while Grant sat in the White House. A week before the election Greeley's sickly wife, Mary, passed away, leaving him distraught with guilt for being absent often. On election day Greeley was soundly defeated by Grant, who won 56 percent of the popular vote and carried all but six Southern states. The *Sun*'s attacks had done little to drain Grant's reservoir of goodwill among the Northern public or to move Southern whites to trust their old nemesis Greeley. Overwhelming popular rejection was the last blow to Greeley's fragile state of mind. Three weeks after the 1872 election, broken in health and spirit, he became delirious and was taken to an asylum, where he died on November 29 at age sixty-one.

Dana attended Greeley's massive funeral at a Fifth Avenue church. For once he put aside mockery to write a moving tribute in the *Sun* expressing dismay at Greeley's tragic end and professing "respectful affection" for the celebrated editor:

> There have been journalists who as such . . . have surpassed him. Minds not
> devoted to particular doctrines, not absorbed in the advocacy of cherished
> ideas—in a word, minds that believe little and aim only at the passing success
> of a day—may easily excel one like his in the preparation of a mere newspaper.
> Mr. Greeley was the antipodes of all such persons. He was always absolutely
> in earnest. His convictions were intense; he had that peculiar courage, most
> precious in a great man, which enables him to adhere to his own line of action
> despite the excited appeals of friends and menaces of variable public opinion;
> and his constant purpose was to assert his principles, to fight for them, and
> present them to the public in a way most likely to give them the hold upon other
> minds which they had upon his own.[52]

Dana noted that Greeley was the last survivor of New York's great triumvirate of newspaper editors, which included Henry Raymond of the *Times* and James Gordon Bennett of the *Herald*. Although Dana had been mentored by Greeley, over the next two decades he grew to prefer Bennett, whom he called "the most brilliant, original, and independent journalist I have ever known." Bennett, Dana told an audience of newspapermen, was "a great news collector and editor, a man of enormous enterprise who was never tired, who never

flinched from his duty. His sarcasm, his satire, his jeers, his eccentricities per-
petually made his newspaper readable. He was a newspaper genius."[53]

With every year at the *Sun*'s helm Dana seemed to become more like the
mercurial and cynical editor of the *Herald*. Like Bennett, Dana set aside larger
principles and elevated the production of a "mere newspaper" to an art form.
The *Sun* thrived as a brisk, iconoclastic, and entertaining daily, "the best edited and most thoroughly interesting paper in the United States," according to
the *Washington Post*. Increasingly Dana made himself—not a particular political party or viewpoint—the paper's main story, and he relished the notoriety of libel suits and no-holds-barred controversies. The *Sun* covered politics
with hefty doses of suspicion and skepticism, heaped scorn on its opponents,
and declared its allegiances forcefully, even when they shifted inexplicably.[54]

Dana's defection to the Democrats in 1872 would not be the last of his piv-
ots. In 1884 he advised *Sun* readers to support Benjamin Butler's third-party
bid rather than Democratic nominee Grover Cleveland, whom he detested,
allegedly because Cleveland while New York governor had ignored Dana's
patronage request for a friend. After Cleveland's second term Dana opposed
the Democrat William Jennings Bryan's free-silver platform and endorsed
the Republican William McKinley. "Rather than the editor of an organ of the
opposition," one journalist quipped, "Dana was usually an opposition party
in himself." Historians' efforts to find a coherent philosophy beneath Dana's
postwar political swings have proven unconvincing. Edward P. Mitchell, his
longtime associate on the *Sun*, concluded that "personal feeling" lay behind
Dana's editorial stands: "I never could see that he was governed by any principle in attacking or defending any case or any man," he told James Wilson.
Mitchell and Wilson agreed that Dana's unpredictability damaged his influence in party circles and prevented his appointment to office. Yet it also kept
the *Sun*'s readers coming back: Dana reportedly told subordinates that no
New Yorker should "go to bed at night with the certainty that he can foretell
the *Sun*'s editorial course the next morning on any given topic."[55]

Dana's journalistic success came at the expense of consistency, sincerity,
and principle—the very qualities he stressed in his eulogy of Greeley. In 1872
his sly subversion of Greeley's candidacy actually worked against the causes
both men favored, especially the call to scale back Reconstruction. Dana and
Greeley had ended the war as allies of the Republican Congress, but by the
early 1870s they lost patience with carpetbagger rule in the South, and their
growing sympathy with Southern whites eclipsed their desire for racial equality. Anxious to return to sectional peace, Greeley endorsed full amnesty for
former Confederates before Dana did, while Dana, adopting the Democrats'

call to curb federal power, preceded Greeley in turning against congressional acts that enforced black civil rights. By 1872, however, they had arrived at essentially the same position, and they were not alone: the Liberal Republican and Democratic platforms of that year, which were identical, declared that "local self-government, with impartial suffrage, will guard the rights of all citizens more securely than any centralized power," and called for "universal amnesty." Liberal Republicans like Greeley, former Republicans like Dana, and much of the Northern voting public retreated from their commitment to secure freedom for the former slaves when Southern whites' resistance to it hardened.

During the *Sun*'s first year Dana took the position, as he had in the *Chicago Republican*, that restoring the South to the Union hinged on guaranteeing civil rights for the freedmen. White defiance made temporary military rule of the South a necessary evil. The *Sun* endorsed Congress's Reconstruction plan and blamed delays in completing it on Southern states' opposition. In December 1869 Dana applauded when Congress passed the Fifteenth Amendment, which outlawed denying the vote on racial grounds, and he backed lawmakers when they compelled the holdout Southern states to ratify it before they could be readmitted.[56]

But he stopped short there. Once ratified by the states, Dana declared, the amendment would represent the final settlement of the issues bequeathed by emancipation and bitterly contested by all parties. "LET US HAVE PEACE," the *Sun* pleaded, echoing Grant, and its editor saw the amendment as the key: "The right to vote being safe, the right to hold office will take care of itself." This position was consistent with Dana's wartime recommendation to the Freedmen's Commission that the former slaves should simply be left alone after they secured legal rights. But it struck an ominous note amid the reality of Southern whites' violent response to black voting and office-holding in the postwar years. Like many moderate Republicans, including Greeley, Dana clung to laissez-faire doctrines and the unrealistic hope that Southern whites would accept colorblind justice even as the facts showed otherwise.[57]

After Grant took office it became apparent that speedy restoration of the South meant accepting Southern states' return to Democratic rule, regardless of its implications for the freedmen. When an 1869 election in Virginia returned a conservative majority Dana predicted the beginning of a "Solid South": "The money and brains of the white rebels will be more than a match for the negroes and scattering of white Republicans in the former Slave States." Yet he seemed unfazed by the prospect. The *Sun* chastised Grant for postponing elections in Texas and Mississippi to secure further guarantees for

black voters, claiming that "the peace of the country demands an early settlement" of Reconstruction.[58]

When Republican regimes in the South began to fall in 1870, Dana distanced himself from the Reconstruction program and Grant's support for it.
"For a time after the war the rule of the carpet baggers in the South was
a matter of necessity," the *Sun* editorialized. But when the South's ruling
class rejected the Republican agenda an unscrupulous "governing element
from the North" took charge. The result was a series of "corrupt carpet-bag
usurpations" that were sustaining Grant by African American votes while he
"maintains them by his bayonets." In recent decades historians have begun
to reassess Grant's Reconstruction record, noting that as president he vigorously supported black Southern officeholders, sent troops to suppress riots
by revanchist White Leaguers, and took strong measures to smash the Ku
Klux Klan. The Democratic convert Dana saw only political opportunism
and fraud in these moves. Dana's critique of Reconstruction emerged later
than his attacks on the administration's corruption, but it gained traction by
being linked to the scandals that engulfed Grant's cabinet and his cronies. As
Dana switched parties he began to interpret federal intervention in Southern
state conventions and elections as partisan plots to maintain the Republicans'
political control by any means necessary. Reconstruction became Grantism
imposed on Southern states.[59]

This skepticism supported a corollary argument for limiting the scope of
the national government. During the war Dana had justified expanding federal powers to protect the Union from rebellious Southerners and Northern
Copperheads. Afterward, like Democrats and many Republican moderates,
he advocated abandoning "excessive taxation" and returning authority to the
states. The *Sun* joined critics who argued that federal enforcement of the
Fourteenth Amendment to protect civil rights was unnecessary and unconstitutional; intimidation of black voters was a matter for states to adjudi-
cate. The Klan's outrages were exaggerated, Dana claimed, used as an excuse
by Grant's administration to invade the South and prop up its puppet allies.
During the 1872 election the *Sun* accused Republicans of manufacturing evidence to make arrests under the Klan Act, inflaming blacks to hate their former masters, and deliberately provoking Southern whites to riot so their votes
could be discounted.[60]

Such charges gained a hearing not simply because they stoked suspicions
of political manipulators; they also fed prevalent racial stereotypes about the
ill effects of supposed "Negro supremacy" in the Republican South. Some
reconstructed Southern states had honest governments, but in others, such

as South Carolina, Louisiana, and Florida, bribery, embezzlement, and profiteering thrived as state governments made deals with railroads, awarded
contracts to repair war-damaged roads, and built new schools and hospitals.
Political corruption was probably no more prevalent than in the Gilded Age
North, but in the South it could be linked to the evils of supposed black majority rule, even though state governments were controlled by white carpetbaggers and their local white "scalawag" allies.

In company with its newspaper rivals, including the *Times* and Greeley's
Tribune, the *Sun* swallowed whole the tales of "black rule" and "barbarism"
told by white journalists touring the South. Dana's *Tribune* friend James S.
Pike filed newspaper reports from South Carolina that were collected into
a bestselling book, *The Prostrate State* (1874). Before the war Dana had
denounced Pike's Negrophobia, but the *Sun* adopted Pike's vicious rhetoric when describing the situation in reconstructed South Carolina: "A more
ragged, worthless, and demoralized set of human beings cannot probably be
found than lazy, thriftless freedmen who have the supreme control of affairs
in the State of South Carolina. In their case it appears quite evident that the
exercise of the freedmen's privilege has not proved much of a blessing either
to them or to the white neighbors."[61]

Instead of indicting Southern whites for clinging violently to white supremacy, Dana came out for a general amnesty for former Confederates in 1871 and
expressed sympathy for their hardships under the "outrageous robberies" of
carpetbag rule. Except for "the most ignorant and degraded class of whites,"
the Southern people "are animated by friendly feelings toward the colored
race," the *Sun* declared. They accept former slaves' right to vote, but they
only want to exercise "their fair share of power." As Southern whites seized
local power their party gained influence in Washington. In the congressional
elections of 1874 the Democrats won control of the House for the first time
since the 1850s, proof to Dana that the public was fed up with both Grantism
and Reconstruction. When the newly elected president Rutherford Hayes removed the last federal troops from the South in 1877 and gave disputed gov-
ernorships in Louisiana and South Carolina to the Democratic candidates,
Dana felt vindicated. Yet he remained bitter that Hayes and the Republicans
had wrested the presidency from his favorite Democrat, Samuel Tilden, by an
irregular special Electoral Commission and partisan vote-counting.[62]

After military Reconstruction and carpetbagger rule ended, Dana continued to attack congressional Republicans who sought judicial action to prevent
black disfranchisement. Federal intervention was not only unconstitutional,
said the *Sun*; it was designed by Republicans to use the "ignorant black vote"

of the South to cancel the "intelligent white vote." This alleged ploy "was the thing surest to make Dana's blood boil," his assistant Edward Mitchell recalled, and it became "one of *The Sun's* foremost and most special issues in Presidential elections from 1876 to 1892." "NO FORCE BILL! NO NEGRO DOMINATION!" blazoned the *Sun* repeatedly as it successfully opposed versions of the Federal Elections Bill, which would have placed monitoring of congressional elections under federal circuit courts instead of state officials. These racially charged campaigns dramatized the enormous distance Dana had traveled from his former support for the freedmen.[63]

Looking back twenty years after Appomattox, Dana declared that the Reconstruction experiment had been undermined not by Southern Democrats but by Republican leaders, who "never tried to win any moral support" among Southern whites but "depended upon frauds at the ballot boxes or upon force." Well-meaning Northerners wanted to "secure the rights of the colored race," but they were tricked by the Republicans, whose "main idea . . . was to secure the permanent ascendancy of the Republican Party." In the South this meant relying on carpetbaggers and scalawags, who "made tools of the Negro to plunder States, fill their own pockets, and send Administration Senators and Representatives to Washington." It was no surprise, Dana concluded, that Southern whites overthrew the Republican regimes and restored Democratic rule. With few changes this view became the consensus narrative among leading American historians of Reconstruction in the early twentieth century. Scholars of the so-called Dunning School labeled the North's agenda of empowering unprepared blacks badly mistaken, harped on carpetbagger corruption, and justified the restoration of white supremacy as a precondition for sectional reconciliation.[64]

Dana convinced himself that the white South's return to "home rule" was benign. When Grover Cleveland took the oath of office in 1885 as the first Democratic president since the Civil War, Dana predicted a new "era of good feeling" between the races.[65] By then he was more than willing to proclaim sectional peace between whites at the expense of former slaves. The harsh truth was that, although the North had won the war, by defeating Reconstruction where it mattered most the South had won the peace. And by ceding power to white Southern "Redeemers," former Radical Republicans like Charles Dana betrayed the ideals they had championed in saving the Union.

Epilogue: Remembering (and Forgetting) the War

As the editor of a timely compendium of the day's news at the *New York Sun*, Charles Dana was not keen to rehash the Civil War. But because assessments of the war's major figures and controversies permeated postwar politics and the popular press, he became a significant player in the nation's collective remembering almost in spite of himself.

Until the century's end, serving in the Civil War was practically a prerequisite for political success. From Andrew Johnson to William McKinley seven Union veterans were elected president in the postwar period. The sole exception was Grover Cleveland, who paid for a substitute when drafted in order to take care of his widowed mother. When a politician was nominated or gave an important speech the *Sun* usually hauled out his Civil War record for critical inspection. The presidential campaign of 1880 pitted two prominent Union soldiers as contenders: the Democrat Winfield Hancock and the Republican James Garfield. Dana could not resist contrasting their records: "About the time that Gen. Hancock fought the battle of Gettysburg," the *Sun* pointed out, "Gen. Garfield turned his back to the front and went into politics." Twelve years later General Russell Alger of Michigan emerged as a potential Republican presidential candidate. Dana circulated the unfounded claim that Alger, who was wounded four times in the war, had been dismissed in 1864 for deserting his command. The absence of a military record could also be used against candidates: Dana slyly wondered aloud why the Republican hopefuls James G. Blaine and Roscoe Conkling, who were barely over thirty in 1861, had not volunteered.[1]

Dana's ad hominem appraisals in the Gilded Age *Sun* were dictated by current political preferences and personal vendettas more than his wartime opinions. This produced some stark reversals. Dana had admired General Philip Sheridan for his fearless leadership in battle, but he condemned Sheridan in 1875 when he assumed military control of Louisiana to enforce congressional Reconstruction. William T. Sherman, whom Dana praised lavishly during the

THE REPUBLICAN PRESIDENTIAL CANDIDATE NOW ON VIEW.
CHARLES A. DANA:—"Come and see! Two cents a sight! Great Sun Microscope! Magnifies 100,000,000,000 Diameters."

"The Republican Presidential Candidate Now on View." Dana puts James Garfield's record under the *Sun*'s microscope, as he had with President Ulysses Grant, and reveals the ugly results. *Puck*, August 11, 1880. Author's collection, gift of Jay Gordon.

war, had "never won a single important battle," the *Sun* declared in retaliation for the general's criticism of an editorial.[2]

This postwar revisionism worked in reverse as well, mainly because after 1868 Dana favored Democrats, his reviled wartime opponents. During the campaign of 1872 the *Sun* dismissed Horace Greeley's wartime dalliance with peaceful secession and French mediation as harmless trial balloons. Benjamin Butler, the hapless general whom Dana pilloried for incompetence and corruption during the war, became, during his third-party bid in 1884, a "brave, frank, original, and above all an honest and independent man." Most dramatically, the Democrat Samuel J. Tilden, whom Dana had called out for "encouraging treason and stimulating Disunion" during the secession crisis, was lionized in the *Sun* as the victim of the "Fraud of 1876," an incorruptible statesman, and Dana's perennial presidential hopeful.[3]

Political partisanship aside, public life in the Gilded Age created endless opportunities to reassess the war's heroes, villains, battles, and turning points. Aging generals published memoirs to defend their war records, fix their places in history, and, like Grant, leave royalties to their families. Veterans' organizations, Union Leagues, and historical societies invited old soldiers and officials to share war stories. When notable war heroes died, obituaries and appreciations gauged their importance and offered personal anecdotes or new revelations.

If this were not enough, a vast trove of wartime documents became available as the government published the official Union and Confederate war records between 1881 and 1901. Dana gave the compilers permission to reprint his dispatches from the battle front, which the series editor called "the most remarkable, interesting, and instructive collection of official documents relating to the Rebellion." Their publication kept the war's embers flickering around Dana, especially over General William Rosecrans's dismissal, the most debated incident of Dana's war career. Yet apart from that episode Dana almost never discussed his wartime telegrams in public, preferring to leave them to future historians to assess.[4]

Instead, Dana was generally content to take potshots at politicians with questionable Civil War records, reprint unpublished wartime letters sent to the *Sun*, add a few memories to obituaries, or weigh in on topics others brought up. Union generals' deaths or the publication of their memoirs called forth cursory assessments—positive in the cases of George Thomas and Philip Sheridan, more critical toward William Sherman and George McClellan. The most important exceptions occurred when Dana conjured up extended first-hand recollections of Abraham Lincoln, Edwin Stanton, and Ulysses Grant, who remained his war heroes to the end.[5]

According to the government's Civil War archivist, Leslie J. Perry, the aging Dana "loved and reverenced" Lincoln and Stanton. "He could not bear to have either of these two men criticized even in the mildest form. No doubt he knew they had not been right in all things, but, having achieved the greatest work in the history of the nation, . . . they were, somehow, above the reach of criticism." Editorial references to the martyred president tapered off after Dana aligned with the Democrats, but they resumed during the Civil War publishing boom of the 1880s, when Dana was asked to contribute reminiscences of Lincoln. His first set appeared in the *New York Tribune* in 1885; he amplified them for a commemorative volume in 1886 and again for a lecture on "Lincoln and His Cabinet" in 1896.[6]

Two decades after the war, hindsight made its outcome seem inevitable and Lincoln had ascended to the height of the political pantheon. These changes swept aside Dana's earlier criticisms. In his memory Lincoln was not the slow-moving president he had berated in the *Tribune* or the tenderhearted commander in chief he and Stanton had pushed into crackdowns on Copperheads and cotton traders, but instead a master of military strategy and political calculation. Far from the "guileless and mushy philanthropist" of popular imagination, Dana wrote, Lincoln had been a "shrewd and all-considering politician." He hired and fired generals wisely, timed the Emancipation Proclamation exactly right, and effortlessly orchestrated balky cabinet members into agreement. While disposing of one romanticized version of the martyred president—Lincoln as secular saint—Dana's reminiscences helped to build up another: Lincoln as the unerring mastermind of Union victory.[7]

Dana visited the ailing Edwin Stanton at his Washington home in May 1869 and got his promise to write on a controversial Civil War issue. "If I get well," Stanton quipped, "I will write you an article; and if I don't, you will write me one." When Stanton died at the year's end Dana escorted his widow to the gravesite ceremony in Georgetown, then penned a long eulogy. The *Sun* praised the war secretary's dedication to Union victory and contrasted his integrity with Gilded Age grasping. Stanton "wielded an immense power with perfect disinterestedness and spotless honesty; and in a time when the pursuit of gain and the worship of wealth inspire men with a kind of frenzy, he lived nobly and died poor."[8]

Throughout the postwar decades Dana defended Stanton's record against detractors. When critics blamed Stanton for the breakdown of prisoner exchanges and the grisly fate of Union captives, Dana responded sharply: Confederate leaders had shut down exchanges by refusing to treat black Union soldiers the same as white captives. Addressing Sherman's resentment that the cabinet voided his surrender agreement with General Joseph E. Johnston after the March to the Sea, Dana declared that Stanton correctly pointed out that the truce overstepped Sherman's authority and could have perpetuated slavery. Sherman did not reply publicly but told his brother that "the idea of Dana raking in the embers of 1865 for a personal attack on me . . . struck me as the act of a Hyena." If he came across Dana he would "trash him as a 'Cur.'" In 1886 the former Confederate general Joseph Wheeler, elected to Congress from Alabama, attacked Stanton in a long harangue on the House floor. Wheeler revived old charges that Stanton had sabotaged McClellan's

Peninsula Campaign by detaching a corps from the Army of the Potomac to bolster Washington's defenses. Dana wrote a letter defending Stanton's wartime service that was read into the *Congressional Record*. Without Stanton's energy and focus, he declared, "the Union would not have been saved."[9]

The same could be said of General Grant. Despite Dana's fierce political opposition to Grant, he consistently defended his war record. The *Sun*'s assessment and that of many observers afterward—until the recent historical rehabilitation of Grant's record as president—was that Grant was a great general but a poor chief executive: "The man who saved the nation as a soldier covered it with shame as a President." This formula allowed Dana to remain a faithful camp follower of the general even while he attacked Grant's conduct in the White House.[10]

Dana weighed in on several controversies. He repeated his declaration—at least until Grant died—that the general had avoided alcohol during the war. He denied charges that Grant spilled Union soldiers' blood needlessly during the campaign in Virginia against Lee. He even claimed that Grant, not Sherman, conceived the devastating March to the Sea. Yet there were times when his postwar break led Dana to take unfair swipes at Grant. During the customs appointment flap Dana sniped that he had single-handedly saved Grant from being fired while the general dug canals fruitlessly at Vicksburg.[11]

After Grant died, Dana, honoring his generalship, agreed to serve as a trustee of the association formed to build a memorial in New York City. He called on James Wilson to write a long obituary for the *Sun*. Without stinting on praise for Grant, Wilson, like Dana, credited John Rawlins for much of Grant's steadiness and strategic success.[12] Wilson was just getting warmed up: once retired from the military after the Spanish-American War he became a prolific recorder of history at Grant's headquarters, publishing lives of Baldy Smith (1904) and John Rawlins (1916), his own two-volume memoir (1912), and a flattering biography of Dana (1907).

Dana was happy to leave the chronicling to Wilson, much as he had in their joint 1868 campaign biography of Grant. Not only did their views dovetail on most matters; Dana's commitment to daily journalism precluded historical projects, and his habit of discarding letters made writing a book of his own nearly impossible. Dana "talks much less than one would expect about his experiences during the war," the *Sun*'s Edward Mitchell reported in the 1890s, "and has shown no signs of a disposition to put in permanent form . . . his personal recollections of that period." Mitchell found Dana's indifference to history and his own place in it "curious." He attributed it to Dana's journalistic cast of mind, which regarded events a few weeks earlier as "old news."[13]

Dana himself told friends that he lacked the time to compose his war memoirs. Even so, by the 1880s he began to take extended absences for leisure and travel, leaving his paper in the hands of his son Paul. The *Sun* and the *American Cyclopedia* had made Dana rich; one estimate put his income at $150,000 a year. In 1873 Dana purchased a rambling estate at Dosoris on the North Shore of Long Island; a decade later he built an elegant Manhattan townhouse at the corner of Madison Avenue and East 60th Street. He became a connoisseur of wine and orchids, collected rare Chinese porcelains, and experimented with imported trees and shrubs on his island property grounds, which were designed by his friend Frederick Law Olmsted. In the late 1880s Dana enjoyed a kind of semiretirement. He traveled to Europe in search of works of art and new languages to acquire. He presided as the family patriarch at Dosoris and was photographed with his grandchildren on the grounds or sitting on the veranda.[14]

As the Civil War receded into the distant past and Dana's politics became more conservative, his attitude toward Confederates began to soften. In 1890 Dana told a Richmond reporter that Robert E. Lee had been "a man of ideal personal character" who exhibited "the noblest qualities of human nature." He endorsed plans for a joint Grant and Lee monument in Tennessee and contributed to publicity for the dedication of the Chickamauga battlefield site in 1895, as did his former nemesis Rosecrans.[15]

These conciliatory gestures climaxed when Dana took the lead in proposing a massive United Veterans Blue and Gray Parade for New York City, to be held on July 4, 1896. Joint Union and Confederate military reunions began to be held in the late 1870s, but they were not universally popular. Even those who participated attributed divergent meanings to the event. Many celebrated the soldiers' shared fellowship of valor regardless of their cause. Some former Confederates saw such reunions as validation for the "Lost Cause." Other attendees proclaimed that sectional differences had been reconciled—often, as historians have pointed out, by excluding African American veterans from marching and otherwise participating in full citizenship rights.[16]

Dana declared the Blue and Gray movement proof that sectional bitterness had passed and was being replaced by a shared "Americanism." Most New York veterans' organizations supported his proposal, but the Grand Army of the Republic (GAR) announced its opposition. Welcoming veterans in Confederate uniforms, the GAR's commander in chief claimed, offended those who fought for the Union: "The sooner those who wore the gray shall cease trying to symbolize the 'lost cause' . . . and . . . refrain from representing themselves as a distinct part of the people, the sooner will a full realization of patriotism and fraternity be brought about."[17]

Dana saw it differently. "It is precisely because the cause of secession is dead and buried that those who fought for it are welcome to march with those who fought against it," he editorialized, overlooking the issue of separate flags and uniforms. Dana had something else in mind: reconciliation of Northerners and Southerners would bolster their common quest to spread American-style liberty abroad. Anticipating a war with Spain over Cuban independence, Dana believed that a celebration of American unity "could come at no better time for our relations with foreign lands." The GAR's opposition forced Dana to cancel the march, but he pledged to try again.[18]

Dana's impulse to leave behind sectional animosities was abetted by his failing memory. Old wartime controversies lost their bite when their details blurred. In 1889, when Lincoln's former secretary John Hay published a first-hand account of the October 1864 elections, Dana printed a rejoinder that Hay had not been present at the gathering in Stanton's office. Hay produced clinching evidence from his wartime diary, grumbling privately that Dana was a "conceited old man with a bad memory." A few months later Grover Cleveland, who was frequently the target of the *Sun*'s barbs but had not responded in kind, dismissed Dana's conjectures about his personal life as emanations of "a senile liar, with one foot in the grave." As rumors of Dana's failing powers circulated, Dana's subordinates at the *Sun* insisted that "when he was obliged to leave his post, there was not a younger mind or body in the office."[19]

Senile or not, by the 1890s Civil War notables were dying by the day, and publishers scrambled to record their recollections. Samuel McClure, editor of the popular monthly magazine of the same name and Dana's friend, visited the *Sun* office and persuaded him to provide his war story in a series of interviews if a reporter would write them up. The memoirs would then be serialized in the magazine.[20]

McClure assigned Ida M. Tarbell to the job. Later to win acclaim for her muckraking exposé of John D. Rockefeller's Standard Oil Company, Tarbell had just published a series for *McClure's* on the early life of Lincoln that earned praise from Dana and ratcheted up the journal's circulation. Still, she was wary. A prim reporter half Dana's age, Tarbell knew him only from the *Sun*'s "relentless pursuit of fakers" and reformers and feared he was "too clever, too quick-witted, too malicious . . . to get on with."[21]

Tarbell got hold of Dana's dispatches from the field and his brief published reminiscences. She drew up a list of questions and made an appointment. Appearing at the *Sun* building at the end of Dana's workday, Tarbell climbed to the third story and found a bald, white-bearded, curmudgeonly newsman

Ida M. Tarbell. Library of Congress Prints and Photographs Division.

of seventy-seven sitting behind a desk cleared of work. An old photograph of Horace Greeley reading the *Tribune* hung on the wall, and a photo of Lincoln rested on the mantel. Dana seemed to regret his promise to McClure. "I am not interested in what I did in the past," he complained. Tarbell persisted. She proposed to interview him three times a week, accompanied by a stenographer, at the *Sun* office. Dana reluctantly agreed, and in December 1896 Tarbell recorded a dozen interviews about his involvement in the Civil War's decisions and campaigns.[22]

Years later Tarbell remembered it as "the most impersonal job I ever had."

Dana in his office at the *Sun*. Engraving by Henry Wolf, based on an 1894 painting by C. K. Linson. From *Human Documents: Portraits and Biographies of Eminent Men* (New York: S. S. McClure, 1896).

Dana answered her questions bluntly, occasionally fell into a longer narrative, responded to follow-up queries, and lapsed into silence. His clipped, meandering, and often vague replies disappointed Tarbell. "Probably it was his way of punishing me for being afraid of him," she surmised. It was also a symptom of Dana's decline, for his responses included many slips of memory and showed him grasping for names and places. Dana's kind words for virtually all Union generals and officials suggested that he had mellowed late in life; his characterizations of them as "pleasant" or "unpretentious" indicated that his sharp descriptive powers had vanished.[23]

Early in 1897 Tarbell set to writing. She relied mainly on the war records and Dana's published pieces, supplementing them with a few private letters, Grant's memoirs, and Dana's impressions from the interviews. Using these materials she stitched together a narrative told in Dana's voice. It was, Tarbell recalled, "the most important piece of ghost writing I ever did." The ghost was not credited in the published work, which *McClure's* presented as "a series of articles by him [Dana] on his life as the private war reporter of Mr. Lincoln and Mr. Stanton."[24]

Dana never lived to read his own so-called memoir. As Tarbell completed the manuscript Dana asked only to see the proofs. Bothered by an undisclosed illness, he was convalescing at Dosoris, where he read the first of nine installments and returned it with minor changes. It was all he would see. His illness, diagnosed as cirrhosis of the liver, deepened, and when the second episode of "Reminiscences of Men and Events of the Civil War" appeared in *McClure's* in December it came with a notice that Dana had died on October 17.[25]

The following year Tarbell's articles were published in book form as *Recollections of the Civil War*. Like the *McClure's* series it was a mélange of Dana's reminiscences, Tarbell's inferences, and wartime documents rephrased in the first person. Key episodes were left out, and some that were included were distorted by Dana's memory lapses or Tarbell's errors. Yet the book was received as an authentic memoir "written . . . in Mr. Dana's inimitable English."[26] Even Dana's confidant James Wilson did not know that *Recollections* was ghosted, and he relied heavily on it for his biography of Dana. Not until Tarbell published her own memoirs in 1939 did the public learn the book's real authorship. Long after that, Civil War historians continued to cite and quote it as Dana's own narrative.

Of all Dana's achievements, he wished to be remembered for his newspaper success in the postwar decades. As he instructed, the day after his death a simple notice appeared at the top of the *Sun*'s editorial columns: "CHARLES

ANDERSON DANA, Editor of THE SUN, died yesterday afternoon." Across the nation newspaper obituaries marked Dana's death and editorials assessed the career of the "Great Editor." To the reading public, press professionals, and most historians, Dana's leadership of the *Sun* became his "best title to remembrance," marking him as one of the last of the great nineteenth-century newspaper editors.[27]

Yet whatever later chroniclers judged and the proud newspaperman proclaimed, the Civil War, not the Gilded Age, was Dana's finest hour. Dana may have glimpsed this himself. In January 1895 he delivered a nostalgic remembrance of his fellow Brook Farmers and a stirring tribute to antebellum abolitionists at the University of Michigan. Both groups envisioned a "genuine emancipation" that wanted democracy "raised up into life and made social"; but whereas the utopians disbanded in failure, the abolitionists prevailed when wartime emancipation "struck the fetters from every slave."[28] The Civil War culminated two decades of the young Dana's dedication to social change. It harnessed his prodigious energy and ambition to the dual cause of preserving the Union and ending slavery. Its termination set him adrift and landed him in a journalistic career of personal notoriety, political adventurism, and mocking cynicism that mirrored the excesses of the Gilded Age. Along the way, like many other Northern victors, Dana lost sight of the promise of freedom for Southern blacks, left them to their former masters, and sacrificed them for the advantages of sectional reconciliation.

A Chicago reporter who covered Dana's funeral at St. Paul's Church in Glen Cove, Long Island, summarized the long-winded eulogies and listed the celebrated politicians and newspaper editors who attended. Only James H. Wilson was there to represent Dana's nearly forgotten Civil War career. Then the reporter spied an aged figure who harked back to the 1840s, when Dana first linked social progress with loosening the stranglehold of all forms of slavery:

> Standing apart from the grave was an old bent man, with long white beard and hair. He was John W. Hutchinson, one of the [Hutchinson Family Singers] whose abolitionist songs mightily stirred New England audiences before the war. He had known Mr. Dana for more than half a century, and today, with a quavering voice, joined in the hymns at the graveside. "I sang for him when he was a college lad," he said. "He sent for us to come and sing at Brook Farm."[29]

It was the day's simplest and most affecting remembrance.

Notes

Abbreviations

AFIC Records	American Freedmen's Inquiry Commission Records, National Archives, Washington, DC
AJP	*The Papers of Andrew Johnson*, ed. Paul H. Bergeron, Leroy P. Graf, and others, 16 vols. (Knoxville: University of Tennessee Press, 1967–2000).
AL	Abraham Lincoln
AL Papers	Abraham Lincoln Papers, Library of Congress, online edition.
Badeau, *Military History*	Adam Badeau, *Military History of Ulysses S. Grant, From April, 1861, To April, 1865*, 3 vols. (New York: D. Appleton & Co., 1868–1881).
Battles and Leaders	Robert U. Johnson and Clarence C. Buel, eds., *Battles and Leaders of the Civil War* (New York: Century Co., 1884–1888).
BT	Bayard Taylor
CAD	Charles A. Dana
Comstock, *Diary*	*The Diary of Cyrus B. Comstock*, ed. Merlin E. Sumner (Dayton, OH: Morningside House, 1987).
CR	*Chicago Republican*
CU	Cornell University, Division of Rare and Manuscript Collections
CWL	*The Collected Works of Abraham Lincoln*, ed. Roy P. Basler, 9 vols. (New Brunswick, NJ: Rutgers University Press, 1953).
Dana, *Recollections*	Charles A. Dana, *Recollections of the Civil War* (New York: D. Appleton & Co., 1898).
Dana and Wilson, *Life of Grant*	Charles A. Dana and J. H. Wilson, *The Life of Ulysses S. Grant, General of the Armies of the United States* (Springfield, MA: Gurdon Bill, 1868).
EMS	Edwin M. Stanton
FRUS	US Department of State, *Papers Relating to Foreign Affairs* (Washington, DC: Government Printing Office, 1864 and 1865).
Grant, *Memoirs*	Ulysses S. Grant, *Memoirs and Selected Letters* (New York: Library of America, 1990).
Hay, *Diary*	*Inside Lincoln's White House: The Complete Civil War Diary of John Hay*, ed. Michael Burlingame and John R. Turner Ettlinger (Carbondale: University of Southern Illinois Press, 1997).
HG	Horace Greeley
HL	Huntington Library, San Marino, CA

HL-HU	Houghton Library, Harvard University
HSD	Historical Society of Delaware, Wilmington
HSP	Historical Society of Pennsylvania, Philadelphia
HWH	Henry W. Halleck
JHW	James H. Wilson
JSP	James S. Pike
LC	Library of Congress, Washington, DC
MHS	Massachusetts Historical Society, Boston
NARA	National Archives and Records Administration, Washington, DC
NYH	*New York Herald*
N-YHS	New-York Historical Society, New York, NY
NYPL	New York Public Library, New York, NY
NYS	*New York Sun*
NYT	*New York Times*
NYTr	*New York Tribune*
OR	US War Department, *The War of the Rebellion: A Compilation of the Official Records of the Union and Confederate Armies* (Washington, DC: Government Printing Office, 1880–1901). Entries are followed by series, volume, part, and page numbers.
Pike Papers	James S. Pike Papers, University of Maine, Orono
PUSG	*The Papers of Ulysses S. Grant*, ed. John Y. Simon, 32 vols. (Carbondale: Southern Illinois University Press, 1967–2012).
RG	Record Group (in National Archives)
Sanderson Journal	Journal, John P. Sanderson Papers, Ohio Historical Library, Columbus
SPCP	*The Salmon P. Chase Papers*. 5 vols., ed. John Niven (Kent, OH: Kent State University Press, 1993–1998).
Strong, *Diary*	*The Diary of George Templeton Strong*, ed. Allan Nevins and Milton Halsey Thomas, 4 vols. (New York: Macmillan, 1952).
Tarbell Papers	Ida Tarbell Papers, Allegheny College Library, Meadville, PA
USG	Ulysses S. Grant
Welles, *Diary*	*The Civil War Diary of Gideon Welles, Lincoln's Secretary of War*, ed. William E. Gienapp and Erica L. Gienapp (Urbana and Chicago: University of Illinois Press, 2014).
Wilson, *Dana*	James Harrison Wilson, *The Life of Charles A. Dana* (New York: Harper & Bros., 1907).
Wilson, *Flag*	James Harrison Wilson, *Under the Old Flag*, 2 vols. (D. Appleton & Co., 1912).

Introduction: "The Eyes of the Government at the Front"

1. Strong, *Diary*, 3:442; Brooks D. Simpson, "Great Expectations: Ulysses S. Grant, the Northern Press, and the Opening of the Wilderness Campaign," in *The Wilderness Campaign*, ed. Gary W. Gallagher (Chapel Hill: University of North Carolina Press, 1997), 15.

2. The first published account of this story is in Albert D. Richardson, *A Personal History of Ulysses S. Grant* (Hartfield, CT: American Publishing Co., 1868), 399–400. Quotations are from Dana, *Recollections*, 188–189.

3. Leslie J. Perry, quoted in *NYS*, October 22, 1897. A historical novel by Thomas Fleming, *The Secret Trial of Robert E. Lee* (New York: Forge Books, 2006), combines fictional and conspiracy-theory approaches. Fleming imagines Dana as an abolitionist fanatic, the hidden power behind Secretary Stanton's throne, and—in the book's main plot—the instigator of a postwar treason trial of Robert E. Lee, which ends when Lee is acquitted by a Union military commission.

4. *OR* I, v. 24, pt. 1, 93; Ida M. Tarbell, *The Life of Abraham Lincoln* (New York: Lincoln History Society, 1924), 3:213. See also Tarbell, "Charles A. Dana in the Civil War," *McClure's Magazine* 9 (October 1897): 1087–1088.

5. *Civil War Monitor* 3 (Winter 2013): 32.

6. For a wide-ranging survey of newspapers' "war for public opinion," see Harold Holzer, *Lincoln and the Power of the Press* (New York: Simon & Schuster, 2014).

7. Allan Nevins, *The War for the Union* (New York: Charles Scribner's Sons, 1971), 3:331.

8. Sylvanus Cadwallader to JHW, December 2, 1907, Wilson Papers, LC; Wilson, *Dana*, xi; Sanderson Journal, March 25, 1864.

9. For positive and critical views of Dana from Stanton biographers, see, respectively, Benjamin P. Thomas and Harold M. Hyman, *Stanton: The Life and Times of Lincoln's Secretary of War* (New York: Alfred A. Knopf, 1962), and William Marvel, *Lincoln's Autocrat: The Life of Edwin Stanton* (Chapel Hill: University of North Carolina Press, 2015). Among historians of Vicksburg who compliment Dana are Brooks D. Simpson, *Ulysses S. Grant: Triumph over Adversity, 1822–1865* (Boston: Houghton Mifflin, 2000); and Edwin C. Bearss, *The Campaign for Vicksburg*, 3 vols. (Dayton, OH: Morningside Books, 1991). Chickamauga accounts highly critical of Dana include Glenn Tucker, *Chickamauga: Bloody Battle in the West* (Indianapolis: Bobbs-Merrill, 1961); and William M. Lamers, *The Edge of Glory: A Biography of General William S. Rosecrans, U.S.A.* (New York: Harcourt, Brace & World, 1961).

10. Letter from A. K. McClure, reprinted in *McClure's Magazine* 10 (February 1898): 385.

11. This was the opinion of historian Paul M. Angle, who nevertheless accepted the book as "an accurate representation of his [Dana's] own experience." Angle, "Introduction" to Dana, *Recollections* (reprint; New York: Collier Books, 1963), 6–7.

12. Mention should be made of three useful studies of the last half-century. Harry J. Maihafer, *The General and the Journalists: Ulysses S. Grant, Horace Greeley, and Charles Dana* (Washington, DC: Brassey's, 1998), describes Grant's relationship with Greeley and Dana, using Dana's *Recollections* as the main source for him. Janet E. Steele, *The Sun Shines for All: Journalism and Ideology in the Life of Charles A. Dana* (Syracuse: Syracuse University Press, 1993), is a journalism biography that is informative for Dana's *Tribune* and postwar years. Charles V. Spaniolo, "Charles Anderson Dana: His Early Life and Civil War Career" (PhD diss., Michigan State University, 1965), first explored Dana's service on the Cairo Claims Commission.

Chapter 1. "The Responsible Editor of the *Tribune*"

1. James Parton, *The Life of Horace Greeley, Editor of the New York Tribune* (New York: Mason Brothers, 1855), 411.

2. Bayard Taylor, quoted in Louis M. Starr, *Bohemian Brigade: Civil War Newsmen in Action* (New York: Alfred A. Knopf, 1954), 17; *Boston Courier*, quoted in *Vermont Phoenix*, January 14, 1860.

3. John Russell Young, *Men and Memories: Personal Reminiscences* (New York and London: F. Tennyson Neely, 1901), 119.

4. Charles Congden, quoted in Starr, *Bohemian Brigade*, 18; Richard Kluger, *The Paper: The Life and Death of the New York Herald Tribune* (New York: Alfred A. Knopf, 1986), 70; Adam Tuchinsky, *Horace Greeley's New-York Tribune: Civil War–Era Socialism and the Crisis of Free Labor* (Ithaca, NY: Cornell University Press, 2009), 145; Parton, *Greeley*, 411.

5. The account that follows is based on Parton, *Greeley*, 391–411, supplemented with details from Starr, *Bohemian Brigade*, 13–14; and Kluger, *The Paper*, 13–19.

6. Parton, *Greeley*, 403.

7. Parton, *Greeley*, 404–405.

8. Wilson, *Dana*, 159; Young, *Men and Memories*, 115.

9. Dana quoted in Starr, *Bohemian Brigade*, 16; CAD to Marianne Orvis, December 31, 1895, Borneman Papers, University of Illinois.

10. HG to Schuyler Colfax, January 20, 1852, Greeley Papers, NYPL; Starr, *Bohemian Brigade*, 19; *Boston Courier*, quoted in *Vermont Phoenix*, January 14, 1860.

11. Wilson, *Dana*, 16–17. The following details are drawn mainly from Wilson's biography.

12. Eventually Dana was granted Harvard degrees in recognition of his *Tribune* work: an honorary master's in 1861, and two years later a bachelor's retroactive to the Class of 1843.

13. Wilson, *Dana*, 19, 27.

14. Ripley to Emerson, November 9, 1840, in Octavius Brooks Frothingham, *George Ripley* (Boston: Houghton Mifflin, 1882), 307–308; Wilson, *Dana*, 31, 51.

15. Thomas Wentworth Higginson, *Cheerful Yesterdays* (Boston and New York: Houghton Mifflin, 1898), 84.

16. Lindsay Swift, *Brook Farm: Its Members, Scholars, and Visitors* (New York: Macmillan, 1900), 151–152; John Thomas Codman, *Brook Farm: Historic and Personal Memoirs* (Boston: Arena Publishing Co., 1894), 17; Higginson, *Cheerful Yesterdays*, 83–84.

17. Codman, *Brook Farm*, 18; Marianne Dwight, *Letters from Brook Farm, 1844–1847*, ed. Amy L. Reed (Poughkeepsie, NY: Vassar College, 1928).

18. Carl J. Guarneri, *The Utopian Alternative: Fourierism in Nineteenth-Century America* (Ithaca, NY: Cornell University Press, 1991), 58–59, 395.

19. HG to CAD, August 29, 1842, Greeley Papers, LC.

20. Guarneri, *Utopian Alternative*, 51–59.

21. Sterling F. Delano, *The Harbinger and New England Transcendentalism: A Portrait of Associationism in America* (Rutherford, NJ: Fairleigh Dickinson University Press, 1983).

22. *The Harbinger* 1 (November 15, 1845): 362; (September 6, 1845): 205.

23. Elizabeth Ellery Dana, *The Dana Family in America* (Cambridge, MA.: n.p., 1956), 117–118, 147–151, 395; *Dallas Morning News*, February 3, 1898.

24. Wilson, *Dana*, 57; Codman, *Brook Farm*, 189.

25. CAD to Dwight, March 1846, in Zoltan Haraszti, *The Idyll of Brook Farm* (Boston: Trustees of the Public Library, 1937), 38.

26. Codman, *Brook Farm*, 136; Dwight, *Letters from Brook Farm*, 171.

27. CAD to Parke Godwin, August 18, 1846, Bryant-Godwin Papers, NYPL; Wilson, *Dana*, 59.

28. Godwin to CAD, November 16, 1846, Bryant-Godwin Collection, NYPL; CAD to John Dwight, January 26, 1847, Anthony Collection, NYPL.

29. Wilson, *Dana*, 61; CAD to Hannah Ripley, September 5, 1847, John S. Brown Papers, Kansas State Historical Society.

30. Sterling F. Delano, *Brook Farm: The Dark Side of Utopia* (Cambridge, MA: Harvard University Press, 2004), 302; CAD to BT, November 27, 1857, Taylor Papers, CU; CAD to Hannah Ripley, September 6, 1849, John S. Brown Papers, Kansas State Historical Society.

31. *The Harbinger* 6 (April 22, 1848): 195; Wilson, *Dana*, 63; Frank M. O'Brien, *The Story of* The Sun (New York: George H. Doran Company, 1918), 210.

32. *NYS*, March 16, 1883; Wilson, *Dana*, 62–63. For Dana and the 1848 Revolutions, see Guarneri, *Utopian Alternative*, 337–342; and Tuchinsky, *Greeley's Tribune*, 95–101.

33. CAD to Elizur Wright, February 15, 1849, Samuel J. May Collection, CU. See Dana, *Proudhon and His "Bank of the People"* (New York: B. F. Tucker, 1896).

34. W. H. Channing, "Revolution—Reaction—Reorganization," *Spirit of the Age* 1 (July 14, 1849): 26; Dana, "The European Revolutions," *Spirit of the Age* (August 18, 1849): 98.

35. Wilson, *Dana*, 71, 81–82; *NYTr*, October 23, 1848.

36. Dana, "The Newspaper Press" (1850), reprinted in Frederic Hudson, *Journalism in the United States, From 1690 to 1872* (New York: Harper & Brothers, 1873), 679–681.

37. *The Harbinger* 7 (July 22, 1848): 89; Wilson, *Dana*, 74, 78, 86; *The Harbinger* 7 (August 12, 1848): 117.

38. Allan Nevins, "Charles Anderson Dana," *Dictionary of American Biography* (New York: Charles Scribner's Sons, 1930), 5:50.

39. CAD to Karl Marx, July 15, 1850, in Morten Borden, ed., "Five Letters from Charles A. Dana to Karl Marx." *Journalism Quarterly* 36 (Summer 1959): 315; Jenny Marx to Karl Weydemeyer, February 13, 1852, quoted in Karl Marx and Friedrich Engels, *Collected Works* (New York: International Publishers, 1975), 39:35. On Marx's relationship with the *Tribune*, see Morten Borden, "Some Notes on Horace Greeley, Charles Dana and Karl Marx," *Journalism Quarterly* 34 (Fall 1957): 457–465; and *The American Journalism of Marx & Engels: A Selection from the New York Daily Tribune*, ed. Henry M. Christman (New York: New American Library, 1966).

40. CAD to Marx, March 8, 1860, quoted in Gareth Stedman Jones, *Karl Marx: Greatness and Illusion* (Cambridge, MA: Harvard University Press, 2016), 345; *NYTr*, April 7, 1853; Marx to Engels, December 2, 1853, *Collected Works*, 39:404.

41. CAD to Hannah Ripley, September 6, 1849, John S. Brown Papers, Kansas State Historical Society; Janet E. Steele, *The Sun Shines for All: Journalism and Ideology in the Life of Charles A. Dana* (Syracuse: Syracuse University Press, 1993), 33–34; Robert C. Williams, *Horace Greeley: Champion of American Freedom* (New York: New York University Press, 2006), 166; CAD to BT, June 7, 1853, Taylor Papers, CU.

42. CAD to BT, August 15, 1849, Taylor Papers, CU; CAD to JSP, April 8, 1851, in James S. Pike, *First Blows of the Civil War: The Ten Years of Preliminary Conflict in the United States from 1850 to 1860* (New York: American News Company, 1879), 87–88; Wilson, *Dana*, 159; Ownership Ledger in Tribune Association Minute Book, 1849–1860, Whitney Family Papers, Yale University Library.

43. CAD to JSP, April 8, 25, 1851, in Pike, *First Blows*, 88–89; Alfred Habegger, *The Father: A Life of Henry James, Sr.* (New York: Farrar, Straus & Giroux, 1994), 322; Tribune Association Minutes, June 30, 1854, Whitney Family Papers, Yale University Library.

44. CAD to JSP, June 25, 1856, and November 12, 1857, Pike Papers; CAD to BT, September 25 and October 13, 1857, Taylor Papers, CU.

45. CAD to BT, November 5, 1857, Taylor Papers, CU; CAD to William Henry Huntington, November 24, 1857, in Wilson, *Dana*, 174; CAD to JSP, February 14, 1859, Pike Papers.

46. CAD to JSP, June 14, 1859, Pike Papers; CAD to William Henry Huntington, November 24, 1857, in Wilson, *Dana*, 174.

47. Edwin L. Godkin, *Life and Letters of Edwin Lawrence Godkin*, ed. Rollo Ogden (New York: Macmillan, 1907), 1:168.

48. CAD to JSP, July 14, 1855, July 24, 1856, in Pike, *First Blows*, 296, 346. For Dana's

Fourierist critique of the "isolated family," see Charles A. Dana, *A Lecture on Association, in Its Connection with Religion* (New York: B. H. Greene, 1844), 37; *The Harbinger* 1 (September 27, 1845): 251–253.

49. CAD to BT, January 21, 1858, Taylor Papers, CU; *NYH*, November 25, 1860; Edward P. Mitchell, *Memoirs of an Editor: Fifty Years of American Journalism* (New York : Charles Scribner's Sons, 1924), 45–46; *Nick-Nax*, March 1, 1860. For one carriage race, see *NYTr*, June 5, 1862.

50. Whitman, *New York Dissected* (New York: Rufus Rockwell Wilson, Inc., 1936), 132.

51. Whitman, *The Correspondence*, ed. Edwin Haviland Miller (New York: New York University Press, 1961), 1:40–41; *NYTr*, July 23, October 10, 1855. For Whitman's recollections of the episode, see Horace Traubel, *With Walt Whitman in Camden (July 16, 1888– October 31, 1888)* 1908 (1908; reprint ed., New York: Rowman & Littlefield, 1961), 467–468; and Whitman, *Prose Works 1892. Vol. III: Collect and Other Prose*, ed. Floyd Stovall (New York: New York University Press, 1964), 774.

52. CAD to BT, April 14, 1857, Taylor Papers, CU; Dana, *The Household Book of Poetry* (New York: D. Appleton & Co., 1858), Preface; Grant Overton, *Portrait of a Publisher* (New York: D. Appleton & Co., 1925), 45; CAD to William Henry Huntington, September 30, 1862, in Wilson, *Dana*, 177.

53. Stedman Jones, *Karl Marx*, 329.

54. CAD to William Henry Huntington, April 6, 1858, in Wilson, *Dana*, 175; Charles Crowe, *George Ripley, Transcendentalist and Utopian Socialist* (Athens: University of Georgia Press, 1967), 236.

55. Parton, *Greeley*, 404.

Chapter 2. "A Party against the Slave Power"

1. CAD to James M. McKim, November 17, 1855, Samuel J. May Collection, CU; CAD to JSP, May 29, 1850, in James S. Pike, *First Blows of the Civil War: The Ten Years of Preliminary Conflict in the United States from 1850 to 1860* (New York: American News Company, 1879), 83; John Russell Young, *Men and Memories: Personal Reminiscences*, ed. May D. Russell Young (New York and London: F. Tennyson Neely, 1901), 114; Edwin L. Godkin, *Life and Letters of Edwin Lawrence Godkin*, ed. Rollo Ogden (New York: Macmillan, 1907), 1:168.

2. Robert C. Williams, *Horace Greeley: Champion of American Freedom* (New York: New York University Press, 2006), 152–155; *NYTr*, March 9, 1850.

3. CAD to JSP, May 29, 1850, in Pike, *First Blows*, 83; Jeter Allen Isely, *Horace Greeley and the Republican Party, 1853–1861* (Princeton, NJ: Princeton University Press, 1947), 37–38.

4. HG to Schuyler Colfax, March 17, 1850, Greeley-Colfax Correspondence, NYPL; CAD to JSP, April 25, 1851, Pike Papers; CAD to JSP, October 1852, in Pike, *First Blows*, 153.

5. Eric Foner, *Gateway to Freedom: The Hidden History of the Underground Railroad* (New York: W. W. Norton & Co., 2015), 9–10, 131, 210; Glyndon G. Van Deusen, *Horace Greeley: Nineteenth-Century Crusader* (Philadelphia: University of Pennsylvania Press, 1953), 170.

6. Wilson, *Dana*, 116.

7. Isely, *Greeley and the Republican Party*, 67; *NYTr*, May 24, 1854, in Pike, *First Blows*, 235.

8. Henry Wilson, *History of the Rise and Fall of the Slave Power in America* (Boston: James R. Osgood & Co., 1874), 2:407; *NYS*, December 5, 1872. For Pike's provocative role, see Joanne B. Freeman, *The Field of Blood: Violence in Congress and the Road to Civil War* (New York: Farrar, Straus & Giroux, 2018), 193–198.

9. See Van Deusen, *Greeley*, 116–143, 167–192, on his alliance with Seward and Weed.

10. CAD to BT, June 7, 1853, Taylor Papers, CU; HG to Seward, November 11, 1854, in Greeley, *Recollections of a Busy Life* (New York: J. B. Ford, 1868), 315–320; Van Deusen, *Greeley*, 190.

11. *NYTr*, June 16 and 28, 1854; Adam Gurowski to JSP, June 8, 1854, in Pike, *First Blows*, 253–254; *NYTr*, January 17, 1856.

12. *NYTr*, quoted in Williams, *Greeley*, 173; Carl J. Guarneri, *The Utopian Alternative: Fourierism in Nineteenth-Century America* (Ithaca, NY: Cornell University Press, 1991), 372–373; John R. Wennersten, "Parke Godwin, Utopian Socialism, and the Politics of Antislavery," *New-York Historical Society Quarterly* 60 (July–October 1976): 107–127; Wilson, *Dana*, 136.

13. CAD to JSP, November 22, 1854, in Pike, *First Blows*, 261; *NYTr*, March 19, 1855.

14. Isely, *Greeley and the Republican Party*, 116–117; *NYTr*, June 2, 1855; William E. Gienapp, *The Origins of the Republican Party, 1852–1856* (New York: Oxford University Press, 1987), 182–187.

15. *NYTr*, June 15, October 31, 1855; CAD to JSP, August 23, 1855, in Pike, *First Blows*, 298; Isely, *Greeley and the Republican Party*, 138.

16. Young, *Men and Memories*, 113; *NYS*, December 5, 1872.

17. HG to CAD, January 7, 28, 30, February 3, March 2, April 11, 1856, and undated; in Joel Benton, *Greeley on Lincoln, With Mr. Greeley's Letters to Charles A. Dana and a Lady Friend* (New York: Baker & Taylor, 1893), 89–90, 101–103, 107, 111, 123–124, 134, 149–150; *NYTr*, December 29, 1855; Freeman, *Field of Blood*, 216–217.

18. HG to CAD, January 30, February 1, 6, 1856, in Benton, *Greeley on Lincoln*, 107, 109, 112–113; CAD to JSP, June 4, 1858, Pike Papers.

19. HG to CAD, February 1, 1856, in Benton, *Greeley on Lincoln*, 109.

20. Dana quoted in Wilson, *Dana*, 133, 152; *NYTr*, June 10, September 29, 1856. For 1848 and the struggle in Kansas, see Timothy Mason Roberts, *Distant Revolutions: 1848 and the Challenge to American Exceptionalism* (Charlottesville: University of Virginia Press, 2009), 168–186.

21. Isely, *Greeley and the Republican Party*, 131; Pike, *First Blows*, 321; John R. McKivigan, *Forgotten Firebrand: James Redpath and the Making of Nineteenth-Century America* (Ithaca, NY: Cornell University Press, 2008), 28–33, photo, 31.

22. *NYTr*, June 10, 1856; October 1; January 27, 1857; Kluger, *The Paper*, 89; Wilson, *Rise and Fall*, 2:538–539.

23. Tribune Association Minutes, June 24, 1856, Whitney Family Papers, Yale University Library; Craig Miner, *Seeding Civil War: Kansas in the National News, 1854–1858* (Lawrence: University Press of Kansas, 2008), 81, 114; CAD to JSP, [Summer 1856], Pike Papers.

24. HG to CAD, April 2, 1856, in Benton, *Greeley on Lincoln*, 141; HG to JSP, February 15, 1856, in Pike, *First Blows*, 306.

25. *NYTr*, May 28, 1856, in Pike, *First Blows*, 342–343; Robert Franklin Durden, *James Shepherd Pike: Republicanism and the American Negro, 1850–1882* (Durham, NC: Duke University Press, 1957), 24–28, 31–35.

26. CAD to JSP, June 5, July 24, October 5, 1856, Pike Papers. Williams, *Greeley*, 216, erroneously places Dana on the disunionists' side.

27. CAD to JSP, [May] 1856; June 11, 1856, Pike Papers.

28. CAD to Henry C. Carey, June 14, 1856, Carey Papers, HSP; CAD to JSP, October 5, 1856, in Pike, *First Blows*, 349. For Dana's campaign speeches, see *NYTr*, July 1, 8, 23, 24, 28, 30, August 2, September 23, 25, 27, October 1, 17, 20, 1856.

29. CAD to BT, November 10, 1856, Taylor Papers, CU; CAD to JSP, July 24, October 5, 1856, in Pike, *First Blows*, 346, 349.

30. CAD to BT, November 10, 1856, Taylor Papers, CU; CAD to Henry C. Carey, November 27, 1856, Carey Papers, HSP.

31. Isely, *Greeley and the Republican Party*, 214–215; 230–232, 260–261; *NYTr*, April 1, 1857.

32. Van Deusen, *Greeley*, 225.

33. *NYTr*, May 17, 1858; Isely, *Greeley and the Republican Party*, 238–239; Harlan Hoyt Horner, *Lincoln and Greeley* (Urbana: University of Illinois Press, 1953), 135, 138, 158; Harold Holzer, *Lincoln and the Power of the Press* (New York: Simon & Schuster, 2014), 171.

34. CAD to JSP, June 11, 1856, Pike Papers; HG to Colfax, April 1858, Greeley Papers, NYPL; CAD to JSP, November 15, 1858, Pike Papers.

35. Isely, *Greeley and the Republican Party*, 248–252; CAD to JSP, September 6, 1858, in Pike, *First Blows*, 425; Van Deusen, *Greeley*, 222–225.

36. *NYTr*, July 25, August 17, 1859; CAD to JSP, September 1, 1859, in Pike, *First Blows*, 444.

37. Van Deusen, *Greeley*, 240–241; CAD to JSP, March 20, 1860, Pike Papers; *NYTr*, May 26, 1860; Mark Wahlgren Summers, *The Plundering Generation* (New York: Oxford University Press, 1987), 267–273. Greeley claimed that he "carried none of New-York's dirty linen to the Chicago laundry," but Summers, "'A Band of Brigands': Albany Lawmakers and Republican National Politics, 1860," *Civil War History* 30 (June 1984): 112, finds that Greeley used the Albany corruption issue to influence delegates.

38. *NYTr*, February 20, 1860; CAD to JSP, September 1, 1859, in Pike, *First Blows*, 444.

39. CAD to JSP, August 9, 1856, Pike Papers; CAD to JSP, June 23, 1859; August 26, 1859; in Pike, *First Blows*, 441, 443; CAD to JSP, August 25, 1859, Pike Papers; CAD to Henry C. Carey, March 9, 1860, Carey Papers, HSP.

40. *CWL*, 3:550; *NYTr*, February 28, 1860.

41. Harold Holzer, *Lincoln at Cooper Union: The Speech That Made Abraham Lincoln President* (New York: Simon & Schuster, 2004); *NYTr*, March 7, 12, 1860.

42. Isely, *Greeley and the Republican Party*, 268–274.

43. Fitz Henry Warren to JSP, February 25, 1860, in Pike, *First Blows*, 496–497.

44. *NYTr*, June 6, 1859; CAD to JSP, September 1, 1859, in Pike, *First Blows*, 444; CAD to Colfax, July 10, 1859, quoted in Bates, *Diary of Edward Bates*, ed. Howard K. Beale (Washington, DC: Government Printing Office, 1933), 37; CAD to JSP, August 25, 1859, Pike Papers.

45. CAD to JSP, March 15, 1860, Pike Papers.

46. *NYTr*, May 18, 1860.

47. *NYTr*, May 19, 1860.

48. *NYTr*, May 22, 1860.

49. Van Deusen, *Greeley*, 247–250.

50. *NYTr*, June 18, 1860. For the "manifesto" of the "Volunteer Fremont National Committee," see CAD to Henry C. Carey, November 6, 1856, Carey Papers, HSP.

51. Horace Greeley and John F. Cleveland, *A Political Text-book for 1860, Comprising a Brief View of Presidential Nominations and Elections* (New York: Tribune Office, 1860); Tribune Association minutes, September 24, 1860, Whitney Family Papers, Yale University Library.

52. Horner, *Lincoln and Greeley*, 182–183; *NYTr*, August 21, 1860.

53. William M. Dickson to AL, June 9, 1860, AL Papers.

54. *NYTr*, September 22, October 23, 1860.

55. *NYTr*, June 14, 29, 30, October 31, November 3, 1860; *NYH*, August 17, 1860.

56. *NYTr*, October 13, 1860.

57. Emmet Crozier, *Yankee Reporters, 1861–65* (New York: Oxford University Press, 1956), 18–19.

58. *NYTr*, November 9, 1860; Isely, *Greeley and the Republican Party*, 301.

59. Frank H. Moore, ed. *The Rebellion Record, a Diary of Events with Documents, Narratives, Illustrative Incidents, Poetry, etc.* (New York: G. P. Putnam, 1861–1869), 1:3–4.

60. *NYTr*, November 9, 1860.

Chapter 3. "Forward to Richmond!"

1. Albert D. Richardson, *The Secret Service, the Field, the Dungeon, and the Escape* (Hartford, CT: American Publishing Co., 1865), 18–19.

2. Richardson, *Secret Service*, 66, 79.

3. Louis M. Starr, *Bohemian Brigade: Civil War Newsmen in Action* (New York: Alfred A. Knopf, 1954), 8; J. Cutler Andrews, *The North Reports the Civil War* (Pittsburgh: University of Pittsburgh Press, 1955), 17; Richardson, *Secret Service*, 57–58.

4. Glyndon G. Van Deusen, *Horace Greeley: Nineteenth-Century Crusader* (Philadelphia: University of Pennsylvania Press, 1953), 261–263; *NYTr*, November 9, December 17, 1860.

5. Jeter Allen Isely, *Horace Greeley and the Republican Party, 1853–1861* (Princeton, NJ: Princeton University Press, 1947), 309; *OR* IV, v. 1, 47; David M. Potter, *The South and the Sectional Conflict* (Baton Rouge: Louisiana State University Press, 1968), 236; Thomas N. Bonner, "Horace Greeley and the Secession Movement, 1860–1861," *Mississippi Valley Historical Review* 38 (1951): 425–444.

6. George C. Fogg to CAD, December 18, 1860, Greeley Papers, LC; Fogg to AL, December 22, 1860, AL Papers.

7. HG to AL, December 22, 1860, AL Papers; Van Deusen, *Greeley*, 267; David M. Potter, *Lincoln and His Party in the Secession Crisis* (New Haven, CT: Yale University Press, 1942), 235.

8. Isely, *Greeley and the Republican Party*, 324; Robert Carter, letter in *NYT*, April 29, 1867. Greeley told Lincoln's law partner William Herndon that "our friends will not listen to anything but fight, so I shall have to let them have their own way." HG to Herndon, December 26, 1860, AL Papers.

9. *NYTr*, December 22, 28, 1860, January 23, 1861.

10. *NYTr*, January 26, 1861, December 22, 1860. Historian Allan Nevins was badly mistaken when he wrote that "there is no question that Dana acquiesced in Greeley's willingness to let the erring sisters depart in peace." Nevins, "Charles Anderson Dana," *Dictionary of American Biography* (New York: Charles Scribner's Sons, 1930), 5:50.

11. For the theme of sonship to the "Founding Fathers," see George B. Forgie, *Patricide in the House Divided: A Psychological Interpretation of Lincoln and His Age* (New York: W. W. Norton and Co., 1979); and Richard Brookhiser, *Founders' Son: A Life of Abraham Lincoln* (New York: Basic Books, 2014).

12. For Dana's "more virile temperament and much greater moral steadiness" than Greeley, see Mayo W. Hazeltine, "Charles Anderson Dana," *North American Review* 185 (July 5, 1907): 508.

13. *NYTr*, January 16, 17, 1861.

14. *NYTr*, January 24, 31, February 13, 1861.

15. *NYTr*, January 31, February 14, 1861; William H. Russell, *My Diary North and South* (1863; reprint ed. New York: McGraw-Hill, 1988), 38.

16. *NYTr*, January 24, February 26, 1861; Daniel W. Crofts, *Lincoln and the Politics of Slavery: The Other Thirteenth Amendment and the Struggle to Save the Union* (Chapel Hill: University of North Carolina Press, 2016), 25, 222; CAD to Schuyler Colfax, February 5, 1861, Colfax Papers, Indiana State Library.

17. CAD to Schuyler Colfax, February 5, 1861, Colfax Papers, Indiana State Library; Harold Holzer, *Lincoln and the Power of the Press* (New York: Simon & Schuster, 2014), 276; *NYTr*, January 17, 1861, February 7, 1861; Isely, *Greeley and the Republican Party*, 327.

18. *NYTr*, January 18, 1861.

19. *NYTr*, February 18, 1861.

20. *NYTr*, February 21, 1861; Joseph Nye to William Seward, February 23, 1861, quoted in Isely, *Greeley and the Republican Party*, 329.

21. Horace Greeley, *Recollections of a Busy Life* (New York: J. B. Ford, 1868), 404; *NYTr*, March 5, 12, 16, 1861.

22. *NYTr*, January 17, April 3, 1861.

23. *NYTr*, April 13, 1861.

24. Adam Gurowski, *Diary, From March 4, 1861, to November 12, 1862* (Boston: Lee & Shepard, 1862), 17.

25. HG to Beman Brockway, November 17, 1860, Greeley Papers, LC; Crofts, *Lincoln and the Politics of Slavery*, 107–109; Glyndon G. Van Deusen, *William Henry Seward* (New York: Oxford University Press, 1967), 238–239.

26. *NYTr*, December 3, 1860; Potter, *Lincoln and His Party*, 84–85, 161; Seward to Weed, December 3, 1860, in Thurlow Weed Barnes, *Memoir of Thurlow Weed* (Boston: Houghton Mifflin, 1884), 308; Burton J. Hendrick, *Lincoln's War Cabinet* (Garden City, NY: Doubleday & Co., 1961), 160; *NYTr*, December 5, 1861.

27. Barnes, *Memoir of Weed*, 323; *NYH*, January 25, February 2, 1861; Glyndon G. Van Deusen, *Thurlow Weed: Wizard of the Lobby* (Boston: Little, Brown & Co., 1947), 262–264.

28. *NYTr*, January 14, February 19, March 2, 6, 1861; CAD to Henry C. Carey, October 26, 1860, Carey Papers, HSP; CAD to Chase, November 7, 1860, Chase Papers, HSP; Chase to CAD, November 10, 1860, *SPCP*, 3:32–33.

29. Chase to JSP, January 10, 1861, *SPCP*, 3:47; Harry James Carman and Reinhard H. Luthin, *Lincoln and the Patronage* (New York: Columbia University Press, 1943), 35–36; Van Deusen, *Greeley*, 258; CAD to Chase, January 22, 1861, Chase Papers, HSP.

30. Carman and Luthin, *Lincoln and the Patronage*, 49; Chase to CAD, March 1, 1861, Chase Papers, HSP; *NYS*, February 12, 1869.

31. *NYTr*, December 29, 1860; Carmen and Luthin, *Lincoln and the Patronage*, 60.

32. H. B. Stanton to Thomas B. Carroll, n.d., Stanton MSS, N-YHS; *NYS*, February 23, 1869; CAD to Chase, February 22, March 6, 8, 1861, Chase Papers, HSP; Frank M. O'Brien, *The Story of the Sun* (New York: George H. Doran Company, 1918), 179.

33. *NYS*, February 23, 1869; Dana, *Recollections*, 2–4.

34. *NYTr*, March 12, 1861; Ward Hill Lamon, *Recollections of Lincoln, 1847–1865*, ed. Dorothy Lamon Teillard (Lincoln: University of Nebraska Press, 1994), 214; Benton, *Greeley on Lincoln*, 41–42; Stanton to Carroll, n.d., Misc. MSS, N-YHS; Carroll to AL, March 23, 1861, AL Papers; *CWL*, 4:300; Carl Sandburg, *Abraham Lincoln* (New York: Charles Scribner's Sons, 1943), 1:179.

35. *CWL*, 4:325, 334; Supplement: 68; Carman and Luthin, *Lincoln and the Patronage*, 63–64; CAD to Hiram Barney, November 21, 1861, Barney Papers, HL; CAD to Chase, December 28, 1861, Chase Papers, HSP.

36. Isely, *Greeley and the Republican Party*, 331; Emmet Crozier, *Yankee Reporters, 1861–65* (New York: Oxford University Press, 1956), 22.

37. *NYTr*, April 17, May 1, 1861.

38. *NYTr*, May 16, April 25, May 2, 1861.

39. Starr, *Bohemian Brigade*, 34–35.

40. William A. Croffut, *An American Procession, 1855–1914: A Personal Chronicle of Famous Men* (Boston: Little, Brown & Co., 1931), 123; HG to Margaret Allen, June 17, 1861, Greeley Papers, LC; Van Deusen, *Greeley*, 277; Greeley, *Recollections*, 402–403.

41. Starr, *Bohemian Brigade*, 36; Crozier, *Yankee Reporters*, 81.

42. Van Deusen, *Greeley*, 277.

43. *NYTr*, July 23, 1861; Fitz Henry Warren to CAD [1861], Seward Papers, University of Rochester; CAD to Henry C. Carey, August 6, 1861, Carey Papers, HSP; *NYTr*, July 28, 1861; Frank Blair, Jr., to Montgomery Blair, August 8, 1861, AL Papers.

44. *Vanity Fair*, July 27, 1861; *Harper's Weekly*, August 3 and 10, 1861; John Hay, *Lincoln's Journalist: John Hay's Anonymous Writings for the Press, 1860–1864*, ed. Michael Burlingame (Carbondale: Southern Illinois University Press, 1998), 77.

45. CAD to William Huntington, August 6, 1861, in Wilson, *Dana*, 175; Frank Blair, Jr., to Montgomery Blair, August 8, 1861, AL Papers.

46. HG to AL, July 29, 1861, reprinted in Horner, *Lincoln and Greeley*, 233–235; *NYTr*, July 25, November 16, 1861.

47. *NYH*, October 5, 1861, April 3, 1862; HG to Beman Brockway, quoted in William Harlan Hale, *Horace Greeley: Voice of the People* (New York: Harper & Brothers, 1950), 250; HG to Samuel Wilkeson, August 24, 1861, Greeley Papers, NYPL.

48. CAD to Adams Hill, August 7, 1861, Hill Papers, Duke University; Starr, *Bohemian Brigade*, 54; Tribune Association Minutes, September 2, November 18, 1861, Whitney Family Papers, Yale University; CAD to JSP, November 8, 1861, Pike Papers; HG to Brockway, n.d., quoted in Hale, *Greeley*, 250.

49. CAD to JSP, November 8, 1861; January 4, 1862, Pike Papers.

Chapter 4. "A Printing House Divided"

1. CAD to Charles Sumner, April 4, 1862, Sumner Papers, HL-HU; Marx's letters in *NYTr*, December 19 and 25, 1861; *NYTr*, September 6, 1861.

2. Allan Nevins, *Frémont: Pathmarker of the West* (Lincoln: University of Nebraska Press, 1992), 473–549.

3. *NYTr*, October 28, November 8, 26, 1861; January 1, 27, 1862; CAD to JSP, January 4, 1862, Pike Papers.

4. Harold Holzer, *Lincoln and the Power of the Press* (New York: Simon & Schuster, 2014), 377–378; CAD to JSP, January 4, 1862, Pike Papers.

5. *NYTr*, November 12, December 4, 1861.

6. *NYTr*, March 7, 8, 1862; CAD to JSP, January 4, 1862, Pike Papers. Dana later recalled encountering a delegation of clergymen on their way to persuade Lincoln to proclaim rebel slaves free. The president waited until public opinion was ripe; otherwise, "the consequence of it might have been our entire defeat." Dana, *Recollections*, 180–181.

7. CAD to JSP, January 4, 1862, Pike Papers; *OR* III, v. 1, 722–723; *NYTr*, December 13, 1861; CAD to Cameron, December 29, 1861, Cameron Papers, LC.

8. CAD to JSP, [February 1861]; November 8, 1861; January 4, 1862, Pike Papers; Michael

Burlingame, *Abraham Lincoln: A Life* (Baltimore: Johns Hopkins University Press, 2008), 2:273–280.

9. *NYTr*, September 10, 1861.

10. *NYTr*, December 9, 12, 1861; CAD to JSP, January 4, 1862, Pike Papers; *NYTr*, January 13, 1862.

11. *NYTr*, February 22, March 12, 15, 1862; Bernard A. Weisberger, *Reporters for the Union* (Boston: Little, Brown & Co., 1953), 193.

12. Louis M. Starr, *Bohemian Brigade: Civil War Newsmen in Action* (New York: Alfred A. Knopf, 1954), 8; J. Cutler Andrews, *The North Reports the Civil War* (Pittsburgh: University of Pittsburgh Press, 1955), 17; Albert D. Richardson, *The Secret Service, the Field, the Dungeon, and the Escape* (Hartford, CT: American Publishing Co., 1865), 57–58.

13. Tribune Association Minutes, March 23, 1861, Whitney Family Papers, Yale University; *Tribune* quoted in Starr, *Bohemian Brigade*, 33; Charles A. Page, *Letters of a War Correspondent* (Boston: L. C. Page, 1899), v; CAD to Adams S. Hill, August 7, 1861, Hill Papers, Duke University; Frederic Hudson, *Journalism in the United States, From 1690 to 1872* (New York: Harper & Brothers, 1873), 483.

14. & W. Smalley, "Chapters in Journalism," *Harper's Monthly* 89 (August 1894): 426; CAD to JSP, May 28, 1862, Pike Papers; Weisberger, *Reporters for the Union*, 126.

15. See Starr, *Bohemian Brigade*, 33, 67–68, 123–124, for profiles of Warren, Wilkeson, and Hill.

16. CAD to Mr. Robinson, May 24, 1861, reprinted in William Roscoe Thayer, *The Life and Letters of John Hay* (Boston: Houghton Mifflin, 1908), 2:40; Andrews, *North Reports the Civil War*, 95; *NYTr*, July 22, 1861; *OR* III, v. 1, 324. For accounts of shifting Union government censorship policies, see Weisberger, *Reporters for the Union*, 74–124; Ford Risley, *Civil War Journalism* (Santa Barbara, CA: Praeger, 2012), 83–105; and, for the war's first year, Richard B. Kielbowicz, "The Telegraph, Censorship, and Politics at the Outset of the Civil War," *Civil War History* 40 (June 1994): 95–118.

17. *NYTr*, July 13, 1861.

18. Weisberger, *Reporters for the Union*, 86–88; *OR* II, v. 2, 246; Wilkeson testimony, January 31, 1862, Hearings on "Telegraphic Censorship of the Press," House Judiciary Committee Papers, RG 233, NARA.

19. Starr, *Bohemian Brigade*, 85; *NYTr*, February 27, 1862.

20. *NYTr*, July 26, 1861; Andrews, *North Reports the Civil War*, 91; Hill testimony, February 3, 1862, Hearings on "Telegraphic Censorship of the Press," House Judiciary Committee Papers, RG 233, NARA.

21. Starr, *Bohemian Brigade*, 88; Richard Kluger, *The Paper: The Life and Death of the New York Herald Tribune* (New York: Alfred A. Knopf, 1986), 102; George W. Smalley, *Anglo-American Memories* (New York: G. P. Putnam's Sons, 1911, 129–130; *NYTr*, November 15, 1861.

22. John Russell Young, quoted in *NYT*, July 15, 1867; William A. Croffut, *An American Procession, 1855–1914: A Personal Chronicle of Famous Men* (Boston: Little, Brown & Co., 1931), 265; Smalley, *Anglo-American Memories*, 130; Gay to Thomas B. Gunn, in Andrews, *North Reports the Civil War*, 197.

23. CAD to Adams S. Hill, December 8, 1861, Hill Papers, Duke University; Samuel J. Tilden, *Letters and Literary Memorials of Samuel J. Tilden*, ed. John Bigelow (New York: Harper & Brothers, 1908), 2:657.

24. CAD to Simon Cameron, August 15, 1861, Cameron Papers, LC; Starr, *Bohemian Brigade*, 68; *NYTr*, November 5, 1861.

25. Smalley, *Anglo-American Memories*, 131; Cameron, quoted in Starr, *Bohemian Brigade*, 70; Wilkeson to HG, October 15, 1861, Greeley Papers, NYPL.

26. Starr, *Bohemian Brigade*, 71–72; Andrews, *North Reports the Civil War*, 131.

27. *NYTr*, October 30, 1861; Starr, *Bohemian Brigade*, 72–73.

28. *NYTr*, December 4, 6, 1861; *CWL*, 5:97–98.

29. *NYTr*, January 14, 1862; Carl Sandburg, *Abraham Lincoln* (New York: Charles Scribner's Sons, 1943), 3:440; CAD to Wilkeson, January 19, 1862, Cameron Papers, LC.

30. Tribune Association Minutes, April 9, 1862, Whitney Family Papers, Yale University.

31. CAD to JSP, April 9, 1862, Pike Papers.

32. CAD to JSP, April 9, 1862, Pike Papers; Wilson, *Dana*, 172; Tribune Association Minutes, March 28, 1862, Whitney Family Papers, Yale University.

33. CAD to William Henry Huntington, April 11, 1862, in Wilson, *Dana*, 176.

34. Sidney Howard Gay to BT, April 7, 1862, Taylor Papers, CU; CAD to Henry C. Carey, April 8, 1862, Carey Papers, HSP.

35. Dana, *Recollections*, 2; HG to H. Orr, April 15, 1862, Greeley Misc. MSS, N-YHS; CAD to Charles Sumner, April 7, 1862, Sumner Papers, HL-HU.

36. *Vanity Fair*, October 19, 1861; *NYTr*, March 12, 13, 17, 18, 1862; HG to Wilkeson, December 9, 1862, quoted in Starr, *Bohemian Brigade*, 53.

37. *Harper's Weekly*, March 29, 1862; *Vanity Fair*, March 15, 1862.

38. BT to Sidney H. Gay, April 1, 1862, in Taylor, *Selected Letters of Bayard Taylor*, ed. Paul C. Wermuth (Lewisburg, PA: Bucknell University Press, 1997), 176; CAD to JSP, April 9, 1862, Pike Papers; Gay to BT, April 7, 1862, Taylor Papers, CU.

39. CAD to JSP, April 9, 1862, Pike Papers; Sidney H. Gay to A. S. Hill, May 23, 1862, Hill Papers, Duke University.

40. *Washington Evening Star*, April 4, 1862; Gareth Stedman Jones, *Karl Marx: Greatness and Illusion* (Cambridge, MA: Harvard University Press, 2016), 330; Karl Marx, *On America and the Civil War*, ed. Saul K. Padover (New York: McGraw-Hill, 1972), xix. For a sampling of commentary on Dana's dismissal, see *NYT*, April 6, 1862.

41. *Vanity Fair*, September 7, 1861, April 26, 1862; Starr, *Bohemian Brigade*, 196; Hill to Sidney H. Gay, December 26, 1863, Gay Papers, Columbia University; Oliver Johnson to CAD, May 27, 1865, in Wilson, *Dana*, 171. For Greeley's meandering editorial course, see Glyndon G. Van Deusen, *Horace Greeley: Nineteenth-Century Crusader* (Philadelphia: University of Pennsylvania Press, 1953), 274–312; and Ralph Ray Fahrney, *Horace Greeley and the Tribune in the Civil War* (Cedar Rapids, IA: Torch Press, 1936), 75–210.

42. CAD to Henry Carey, April 8, 1862, Carey Papers, HSP; CAD to JSP, May 28, 1862, Pike Papers.

43. *NYH*, April 5, 1862; Tribune Association Minutes, May 19, June 2, 1862, Whitney Family Papers, Yale University; Kluger, *The Paper*, 107.

44. CAD to JSP, May 28, 1862, Pike Papers; CAD to T. B. Carroll, April 23, 1862, Dana Misc. MSS, N-YHS.

45. CAD to William Henry Huntington, April 11, 1862, CAD to Robert Carter, April 18, 1862, in Wilson, *Dana*, 176.

Chapter 5. "Several Propositions"

1. CAD to William Henry Huntington, April 11, 1862, in Wilson, *Dana*, 176.

2. Benjamin P. Thomas and Harold M. Hyman, *Stanton: The Life and Times of Lincoln's Secretary of War* (New York: Alfred A. Knopf, 1962), 136.

3. CAD to Charles Sumner, February 21, 1862, Sumner Papers, HL-HU. On Stanton's contradictory antislavery opinions, see Thomas and Hyman, *Stanton*, 141, 229–250, and William Marvel, *Lincoln's Autocrat: The Life of Edwin Stanton* (Chapel Hill: University of North Carolina Press, 2015), 148–157.

4. *NYTr*, January 21, 1862; EMS to CAD, January 24, 1862, Dana Papers, LC; *NYTr*, January 31, 1862; EMS to CAD, February 2, 1862, Stanton Collection, Yale University Library.

5. *NYTr*, January 1, 27, 1862; CAD to JSP, January 4, 1862, Pike Papers; Benjamin Wade to CAD, February 3, 1862, CAD Papers, LC.

6. EMS to CAD, February 1, 1862, CAD Papers, LC; *NYTr*, March 4 and 7, 1862.

7. Bruce Tap, *Over Lincoln's Shoulder: The Committee on the Conduct of the War* (Lawrence: University Press of Kansas, 1998), 93–96; EMS to CAD, February 23, 1862, CAD Papers, LC; Dana, *Recollections*, 157–158.

8. Louis M. Starr, *Bohemian Brigade: Civil War Newsmen in Action* (New York: Alfred A. Knopf, 1954), 88; *NYTr*, February 18, 20, 1862; Dana, *Recollections*, 7.

9. Strong, *Diary*, 3:208; Marsena Rudolph Patrick, *Inside Lincoln's Army: The Diary of Marsena Rudolph Patrick, Provost Marshal General, Army of the Potomac*, ed. David S. Sparks (New York: Thomas Yoseloff, 1964), 45; John Hay, *Lincoln's Journalist: John Hay's Anonymous Writings for the Press, 1860–1864*, ed. Michael Burlingame (Carbondale: Southern Illinois University Press, 1998), 227; *Washington Star*, February 26, 1862.

10. Dana, *Recollections*, 9; EMS to CAD, February 23, 1862, CAD Papers, LC.

11. EMS to CAD, January 24, 1862, CAD Papers, LC; *CWL*, 5:115.

12. CAD to Adams S. Hill, April 2, 1862, Hill Papers, Duke University; CAD to Charles Sumner, April 7, 1862, Sumner Papers, HL-HU; *Washington Evening Star*, April 14, 1862; Wilson, *Dana*, 172, 182.

13. EMS to CAD, February 19, 1862, CAD Papers, LC; Dana, *Recollections*, 2.

14. Anthony Trollope, *North America* (London: Chapman & Hall, 1862), 2:101, 104, 105–106.

15. EMS to CAD, June 16, 1862, CAD Papers, LC; *CWL*, 5:177n.

16. *CWL*, 4:461.

17. The following paragraphs build upon Charles V. Spaniolo, "Charles Anderson Dana: His Early Life and Civil War Career" (PhD diss., Michigan State University, 1965), 84–98, the first attempt to uncover the Cairo Commission's history.

18. *House Reports* 2, 37 Cong., 2nd sess., Serial 1143, p. 138; *Chicago Tribune*, December 12, 1861; W. S. Hillyer to USG, December 22, 1861, Cairo Claims Commission File, RG 92, NARA; *PUSG*, 3:351; J. F. Lee to M. C. Meigs, January 8, 1862, Cairo Claims Commission File, RG 92, NARA; *PUSG*, 4:79.

19. *Report of the St. Louis Claims Commissioners*, March 10, 1862, Holt Papers, HL.

20. *PUSG*, 3:352; Scott to EMS, February 12, 1862, Stanton Papers, LC.

21. *PUSG*, 4:80; *House Reports* 37 Cong., 2nd sess., Serial 1143, lii, 1090–1137.

22. John G. Nicolay, *With Lincoln in the White House: Letters, Memoranda, and Other Writings of John G. Nicolay, 1860–1865*, ed. Michael Burlingame (Carbondale: Southern Illinois University Press, 2000), 68; *CWL*, 5:116; *PUSG*, 4:82–83.

23. Meigs to J. F. Lee, February 3, 1862, AL Papers, LC; Meigs to EMS, March 26, 1862, RG 107, NARA; *CWL*, 5:177.

24. George S. Boutwell, *Reminiscences of Sixty Years in Public Affairs* (New York: McClure, Phillips & Co., 1902), 1:293–294; *Proceedings*, Cairo Commission File, RG 92, NARA.

25. Dana, *Recollections*, 13–14.

26. *Proceedings*, July 2, 1862; Hatch to CAD, July 25, 1862, Cairo Commission File, RG 92, NARA.

27. CAD to John G. Nicolay, February 6, 1864, Cairo Commission File, RG 92, NARA.

28. *Proceedings*, July 10, 1862; P. Clark to CAD, August 27, 1862; CAD to Boutwell, September 3, 1862, Cairo Commission File, RG 92, NARA.

29. *PUSG*, 4:59; CAD to JSP, July 24, 1863, Pike Papers; Dana, *Recollections*, 14–15.

30. Dana, *Recollections*, 12; Shelby M. Cullom, *Fifty Years of Public Service: Personal Recollections of Shelby M. Cullom*, 2nd ed. (Chicago: A. C. McClurg & Co., 1911), 97; *PUSG*, 7:297.

31. O. Hatch to AL, August 11, 1862, Cairo Commission File, RG 92, NARA; William Richardson to AL, August 29, 1862, and Orville Browning to AL, n.d., RG 107, NARA; AL to Meigs, August 15, 1862, Cairo Commission File; AL to EMS, September 27, 1862, *CWL, Supplement*, 154; Meigs to Gen. Lorenzo Thomas, November 8, 1862, RG 94, NARA.

32. AL to EMS, January 14, 1864, RG 94, NARA, quoted in *PUSG*, 7:298n; Meigs, endorsement on CAD to Nicolay, February 6, 1864, Cairo Commission File, RG 92, NARA.

33. Jerry O. Potter, *The Sultana Tragedy: America's Greatest Maritime Disaster* (Gretna, LA: Pelican Publishing Co., 1992), 158, 178; Gene Eric Salecker, *Disaster on the Mississippi: The Sultana Explosion, April 27, 1865* (Annapolis, MD: Naval Institute Press, 1996), 197. For Grant and Lincoln's recommendations, see *PUSG*, 11:357.

34. In June 1865 Dana transmitted to General Grant letters relating to the *Sultana* investigation, but he did not mention Hatch. *PUSG*, 15:533.

35. Dana, *Recollections*, 15; Albert D. Richardson, *A Personal History of Ulysses S. Grant* (Hartfield, CT: American Publishing Co., 1868), 265; *PUSG*, 5:383.

36. *CWL*, 6:423; Boutwell, *Sixty Years*, 1:294.

37. Grenville M. Dodge, *Biography of Major-General Grenville M. Dodge from 1831 to 1871: Written and Compiled by Himself at Different Times and Completed in 1914*, typescript, Council Bluffs, IA, Library, 1:65–66; J. R. Perkins, *Trails, Rails and War: The Life of General G. M. Dodge* (Indianapolis: Bobbs-Merrill, 1929), 100–101; James Patrick Morgans, *Grenville Mellen Dodge in the Civil War: Union Spymaster, Railroad Builder and Organizer of the Fourth Iowa Volunteer Infantry* (Jefferson, NC: McFarland & Co., 2016), 91.

38. Edward P. Mitchell, "Mr. Dana of 'The Sun,'" *McClure's Magazine* 3 (October 1894): 376.

39. Gurowski to JSP, August 19, 1858, in James S. Pike, *First Blows of the Civil War: The Ten Years of Preliminary Conflict in the United States from 1850 to 1860* (New York: American News Company, 1879), 424; Perry Miller, *The Raven and the Whale: The War of Words and Wits in the Era of Poe and Melville* (New York: Harcourt, Brace & World, 1956), 341; *New Orleans Daily Delta*, January 17, 1863; Octavius Brooks Frothingham, *George Ripley* (Boston: Houghton Mifflin, 1882), 218–223.

40. CAD to Chase, October 17, 1862, Chase Papers, HSP; CAD to EMS, December 19, 1862, Stanton Papers, LC; *NYT*, October 10, 15, 29, 1862; CAD to AL, October 30, 1862, AL Papers.

41. CAD to JSP, January 4, 1862, Pike Papers; Glyndon G. Van Deusen, *Thurlow Weed: Wizard of the Lobby* (Boston: Little, Brown & Co., 1947), 301–302.

42. CAD to EMS, December 19, 1862, Stanton Papers, LC; *CWL*, 5:490–491; CAD to Thomas Carroll, October 29, November 25, 28, December 1, 25, 1862, Dana Misc. Mss., N-YHS; CAD to Gerrit Smith, December 4, 1862, Smith Papers, Syracuse University.

43. George Dawson to Thurlow Weed, November 5, 1862, Weed Papers, University of Rochester; CAD to JSP, December 30, 1862, Pike Papers.

44. Watson to CAD, November 14, 1862, RG 107, NARA; William O. Stoddard, *Dispatches from Lincoln's White House: The Anonymous Civil War Journalism of Presidential Secretary William O. Stoddard*, ed. Michael Burlingame (Lincoln: University of Nebraska Press, 2002), 133; Dana, *Recollections*, 16–17.

45. *NYT*, November 20, 1862; *NYTr*, November 20, 1862; *NYH*, November 24, 1862.

46. CAD to JSP, December 30, 1862, Pike Papers.

47. Adam Gurowski, *Diary: 1863–'64–'65* (Washington, DC: W. H. & O. H. Morrison, 1866), 295; CAD to JSP, May 28, 1862, Pike Papers; CAD to Robert Carter, April 18, 1862, quoted in Wilson, *Dana*, 172, 183; CAD to Thomas B. Carroll, December 25, 1862, Dana Misc. MSS, N-YHS.

48. *CWL*, 5:139; Allan Nevins, *The War for the Union* (New York: Charles Scribner's Sons, 1971), 3:350.

49. Dana, *Recollections*, 17; *PUSG*, 8:287.

50. CAD to EMS, January 21, 1863, reprinted in Dana, *Recollections*, 18–19.

51. Sylvanus Cadwallader, *Three Years with Grant*, ed. Benjamin P. Thomas and Brooks D. Simpson (Lincoln: University of Nebraska Press, 1996), 23; *OR* I, v. 17, pt. 2, 424; William S. McFeely, *Grant: A Biography* (New York: W. W. Norton, 1981), 123–124; Dana interview, undated [December 1896], Tarbell Papers. Dana's plan for government purchasing may have been based upon one Grant had sent to the War Department a month earlier. See *OR* I, v. 17, pt. 2, 421–422.

52. Dana interview, undated [December 1896], Tarbell Papers; Dana, *Recollections*, 20. CAD to Frank A. Burr, June 23, 1885, Dana Papers, Duke University, mentions a meeting with Stanton but not Lincoln.

53. *CWL*, 5:157, 159–160, 307; Dana, *Recollections*, 20; Wilson, *Dana*, 198.

54. Nevins, *War for the Union*, 3:363; USG to Chase, July 31, 1863, in Bruce Catton, *Grant Moves South* (Boston: Little, Brown & Co., 1960), 351.

55. John Eaton, *Grant, Lincoln and the Freedmen: Reminiscences of the Civil War* (New York: Longmans, Green & Co., 1907), 30–31; Dana interview, undated [December 1896], Tarbell Papers.

56. *NYTr*, November 1, December 4, 5, 6, 1861; CAD to JSP, January 4, 1862, Pike Papers; *NYTr*, March 7, 1862.

57. Swett interview, March 14, 1878, in John G. Nicolay, *An Oral History of Abraham Lincoln: John G. Nicolay's Interviews and Essays*, ed. Michael Burlingame (Carbondale: Southern Illinois University Press, 1996), 58.

58. Glyndon G. Van Deusen, *William Henry Seward* (New York: Oxford University Press, 1967), 332; Kevin Peraino, *Lincoln in the World: The Making of a Statesman and the Dawn of American Power* (New York: Crown Publishers, 2013), 210; Michael Burlingame, *Abraham Lincoln: A Life* (Baltimore: Johns Hopkins University Press, 2008), 2:417. A carping letter sent to Secretary Seward after Lincoln issued his Preliminary Emancipation Proclamation is identified by the Library of Congress as Dana's, but it was written by the New York merchant Charles A. Davis. It criticized the timing of Lincoln's announcement and worried that the proclamation would encourage slave revolts. See Charles A. Davis to William H. Seward, September 23, 1862, AL Papers.

59. Wilson, *Dana*, 117.

60. CAD to JSP, December 30, 1862, Pike Papers; Van Deusen, *Weed*, 300–302; CAD to EMS, December 19, 1862, Stanton Papers, LC.

61. CAD to JSP, December 30, 1862, Pike Papers; *NYT*, February 22, 1863.

62. CAD to JSP, May 28, 1862, August 18, 1863, Pike Papers.

Chapter 6. "Mr. Stanton's Spy"

1. CAD to William H. Huntington, April 13, 1863, in Wilson, *Dana*, 212.

2. CAD to William H. Huntington, April 13, 1863, in Wilson, *Dana* 212–213.

3. David Dixon Porter, *Incidents and Anecdotes of the Civil War* (New York: D. Appleton & Co., 1885), 95–96.

4. *PUSG*, 7:479.

5. *PUSG*, 7:234, 274.

6. Brooks D. Simpson, *Ulysses S. Grant: Triumph over Adversity, 1822–1865* (Boston: Houghton Mifflin, 2000), 177, 178, 181.

7. Shelby Foote, *The Civil War: A Narrative* (New York: Random House, 2006), 2:217; *CWL*, 6:83, 100, 350.

8. Dana, *Recollections*, 21–22.

9. *PUSG*, 7:339.

10. CAD to EMS, March 16, 1863, Dana Papers, LC; CAD to EMS, March 19, 1863, AL Papers; *OR* I, v. 24, pt. 1, 64; EMS to AL, March 19, 1863, AL Papers.

11. *CWL*, 6:142; *OR* I, v. 24, pt. 1, 64.

12. Dana, *Recollections*, 22–24; David Homer Bates, *Lincoln in the Telegraph Office: Recollections of the United States Military Telegraph Corps during the Civil War* (New York: Century Company, 1907), 49–56; Anson Stager, *Cipher for Telegraphic Correspondence; Arranged Expressly for Military Operations, and for Important Government Despatches* (Cipher Book #9) (Washington, DC: n.p., 1861 and 1862), 11, 18; Cipher Book #5 [1864–1865], 34, Eckert Papers, HL.

13. Charles V. Spaniolo, "Charles Anderson Dana: His Early Life and Civil War Career" (PhD diss., Michigan State University, 1965), 111–112; Tom Wheeler, *Mr. Lincoln's T-Mails: How Abraham Lincoln Used the Telegraph to Win the Civil War* (New York: HarperCollins, 2006), 130–135.

14. *OR* I, v. 24, pt. 1, 64–68; Dana, *Recollections*, 26–27.

15. *OR* I, v. 24, pt. 1, 69, 70.

16. *OR* I, v. 24, pt. 1, 66–67.

17. JHW to Adam Badeau, March 22, 1867, Wilson Papers, LC; *NYT*, May 31, 1914; Sylvanus Cadwallader, *Three Years with Grant*, ed. Benjamin P. Thomas and Brooks D. Simpson (Lincoln: University of Nebraska Press, 1996), 61.

18. James Harrison Wilson, *The Life of John A. Rawlins* (New York: Neale Publishing Co., 1916), 121; Wilson, *Dana*, 201–202; Dana, *Recollections*, 28.

19. Simpson, *Grant*, 184; *OR* I, v. 24, pt. 1, 71.

20. Dana, *Recollections*, 61.

21. *PUSG*, 8:534–535, 54.

22. *PUSG*, 9:396, 587; Wilson, *Dana*, 203.

23. Wilson, *Dana*, 203.

24. Dana, *Recollections*, 62; Wilson, *Life of Rawlins*, 124.

25. JHW to Badeau, March 22, 1867, Wilson Papers, LC; Wilson, *Dana*, 202; Wilson, *Flag*, 1:215. For Wilson's biography, see Edward G. Longacre, *From Union Stars to Top Hat: A Biography of the Extraordinary General James Harrison Wilson* (Harrisburg, PA: Stackpole Books, 1972).

26. W. T. Sherman to John Sherman, April 10, 26, 1863, in *Sherman's Civil War: Selected Correspondence of William T. Sherman, 1860–1865*, ed. Brooks D. Simpson and Jean V. Berlin (Chapel Hill: University of North Carolina Press, 1999), 450, 461; Dana interview, undated

[December 1896], Tarbell Papers; W. T. Sherman to John Sherman, April 10 and 23, 1863, in Simpson and Berlin, eds., *Sherman's Civil War*, 450, 459; *PUSG*, 8:59n.

27. W. T. Sherman to John Sherman, April 23, 26, 1863, in Simpson and Berlin, eds., *Sherman's Civil War*, 456, 461, 462. For Sherman's stormy relations with newspapers, see John F. Marszalek, *Sherman's Other War: The General and the Civil War Press* (Kent, OH: Kent State University Press, 1999).

28. *OR* I, v. 24, pt. 1, 72.

29. William Tecumseh Sherman, *Memoirs of General W. T. Sherman* (1885; New York: Library of America, 1990), 359; Richard L. Kiper, *Major General John Alexander McClernand: Politician in Uniform* (Kent, OH: Kent State University Press, 1999), 183; W. T. Sherman to John Sherman, April 10, 1863, in Simpson and Berlin, eds., *Sherman's Civil War*, 450.

30. Dana, *Recollections*, 35–36; Dana to W. H. Huntington, April 13, 1863, in Wilson, *Dana*, 213; Wilson, *Flag*, 1:188–189; Wilson, *Dana*, 213; Dana, *Recollections*, 29.

31. Dana, *Recollections*, 32; *OR* I, v. 24, pt. 1, 71; Edwin C. Bearss, *The Campaign for Vicksburg* (Dayton, OH: Morningside Books, 1991), 2:48–49; Wilson, *Dana*, 213–214; *OR* I, v. 24, pt. 1, 73–75; Wilson, *Dana*, 215.

32. *OR* I, v. 24, pt. 1, 73.

33. Sherman *Memoirs*, 339; Dana, *Recollections*, 32; *OR* I, v. 24, pt. 1, 74.

34. *OR* I, v. 24, pt. 1, 74, 75, 78.

35. Wilson, *Dana*, 212–213; *OR* I, v. 24, pt. 1, 76.

36. Dana, *Recollections*, 37; Grant, *Memoirs*, 307; Wilson, *Flag*, 1:164; *OR* I, v. 24, pt. 1, 76; *PUSG*, 9:396.

37. *OR* I, v. 24, pt. 1, 76; Dana, *Recollections*, 38.

38. *OR* I, v. 24, pt. 1, 78; Dana, *Recollections*, 38–39; Earl Schenck Miers, *The Web of Victory: Grant at Vicksburg* (New York: Knopf, 1955), 144; Bearss, *Campaign for Vicksburg*, 2:79.

39. Dana, *Recollections*, 39–41; *OR* I, v. 24, pt. 1, 79–80.

40. Dana, *Recollections*, 41–42; *OR* I, v. 24, pt. 1, 81–82.

41. OR I, v. 24, pt. 1, 82–83; Grant, *Memoirs*, 317; Frederick D. Grant, "A Boy's Experience at Vicksburg," in *Personal Recollections of the War of the Rebellion: Addresses Delivered before the Commandery of the State of New York, Military Order of the Loyal Legion of the United States, 3rd Series*, ed. A. Noel Blakeman (New York: G. P. Putnam's Sons, 1907), 88; Bearss, *Campaign for Vicksburg*, 2:314–315.

42. Dana, *Recollections*, 43–44.

43. Grant, *Memoirs*, 318, 321; Dana, *Recollections*, 44; *OR* I, v. 24, pt. 1, 83.

44. *OR* I, v. 24, pt. 1, 83.

45. Dana, *Recollections*, 44–45.

46. Dana, *Recollections*, 45–46; Samuel Carter III, *The Final Fortress: The Campaign for Vicksburg, 1862–1863* (New York: St. Martin's Press, 1980), 184; Fred Grant, "Boy's Experience," 90; Albert D. Richardson, *A Personal History of Ulysses S. Grant* (Hartfield, CT: American Publishing Co., 1868), 308; Grant, *Memoirs*, 325; Wilson, *Flag*, 1:194.

47. *NYTr*, December 9, 1868. Reporter Albert Richardson remembered it somewhat differently: Richardson, *Personal History*, 309.

48. Grant, *Memoirs*, 327; *OR* I, v. 24, pt. 1, 84.

49. Dee Alexander Brown, *Grierson's Raid* (Urbana: University of Illinois Press, 1954); Winston Groom, *Vicksburg, 1863* (New York: Alfred A. Knopf, 2009), 195.

50. Grant, *Memoirs*, 327–328; *OR* I, v. 24, pt. 1, 84.

51. Dana, *Recollections*, 48; *PUSG*, 8:159, 183; *CWL*, 6:326.

52. CAD to JSP, July 24, 1863, Pike Papers; Dana, *Recollections*, 48–49.

53. *PUSG*, 8:196.

54. Wilson, *Flag*, 1:194–195; Richardson, *Personal History*, 310; Wilson, *Dana*, 222; James Harrison Wilson, "A Staff Officer's Journal of the Vicksburg Campaign, April 30 to July 4, 1863," *Journal of the Military Service Institution of the United States* 43 (1908): 95–109.

55. Dana, *Recollections*, 50–51; Wilson, *Dana*, 222, 224.

56. Wilson, *Flag*, 1:198–200.

57. Wilson, *Flag*, 1:200–201; Grant, *Memoirs*, 332; *OR* I, v. 24, p. 1, 59.

58. Wilson, *Dana*, 222; Dana, *Recollections*, 51–52.

59. *OR* I, v. 24, pt. 1, 84; Wilson, *Dana*, 211; Wilson, *Flag*, 1:174–176.

60. Wilson, "Staff Officer's Journal," 105; Grant, *Memoirs*, 338; Dana, *Recollections*, 53.

61. Wilson, "Staff Officer's Journal," 108.

62. Dana, *Recollections*, 54–55.

63. Catton, *Grant Moves South*, 445; Wilson, "Staff Officer's Journal," 108; Grant, *Memoirs*, 347.

64. Wilson, "Staff Officer's Journal," 109.

65. *OR* I, v. 24, p. 1, 86; *CR*, August 31, 1865; Wilson, "Staff Officer's Journal," 109.

66. Wilson, *Dana*, 223; Wilson, "Staff Officer's Journal," 261; Sherman, *Memoirs*, 349.

67. Wilson, "Staff Officer's Journal," 262–263; *OR* I, v. 24, p. 1, 86; Catton, *Grant Moves South*, 448.

68. Wilson, "Staff Officer's Journal," 264; *OR* I, v. 24, p. 1, 86. Hovey, believing his role at Champion's Hill had been understated, sent a letter of protest up the chain of command. *OR* I, v. 24, pt. 2, 46–48.

69. Wilson, "Staff Officer's Journal," 264.

70. Groom, *Vicksburg 1863*, 347; Wilson, "Staff Officer's Journal," 264.

71. Wilson, "Staff Officer's Journal," 265.

72. Sherman, *Memoirs*, 353; Cadwallader, *Three Years with Grant*, 92.

73. Wilson, "Staff Officer's Journal," 265; *OR* I, v. 24, p. 1, 86–87; *PUSG*, 8:261.

74. *OR* I, v. 24, p. 1, 87.

75. *OR* I, v. 24, p. 1, 87.

76. Wilson, *Dana*, 224.

77. Welles, *Diary*, 195, 203; *CWL*, 6:350.

Chapter 7. "At the Side of the Conqueror"

1. *OR* I, v. 24, pt. 1, 89; Earl Schenck Miers, *The Web of Victory: Grant at Vicksburg* (New York: Knopf, 1955), 222.

2. Dana, *Recollections*, 57.

3. Dana, *Recollections*, 79–80.

4. Wilson, *Dana*, 230; Dana, *Recollections*, 78.

5. Wilson, *Dana*, 229–230; Dana, *Recollections*, 79.

6. Wilson, *Flag*, 1:214; Wilson, *Dana*, 230–231.

7. Wilson, *Dana*, 212; Dana, *Recollections*, 57; *OR* I, v. 24, pt. 1, 110.

8. Dana, *Recollections*, 58.

9. Dana, *Recollections*, 58; Wilson, *Dana*, 245.

10. Dana, *Recollections*, 59–60.

11. Dana, *Recollections*, 57; *OR* I, v. 24, pt. 1, 87, 89.

12. *OR* I, v. 24, pt. 1, 93; Stanton, Letter of Appointment, June 6, 1863, RG 107, NARA; JHW to Cadwallader, February 27, 1897, Cadwallader Papers, LC; *Emporia Daily Gazette*, October 1, 1897. There is no evidence to support William Marvel's suspicion that Stanton made the military appointment to circumvent restrictions on naming Dana an assistant secretary. William Marvel, *Lincoln's Autocrat: The Life of Edwin Stanton* (Chapel Hill: University of North Carolina Press, 2015), 279.

13. *OR* I, v. 24, pt. 1, 87, 90; *PUSG*, 8:294–295; *OR* I, v. 24, pt. 1, 90–91.

14. *OR* I, v. 24, pt. 1, 92–93.

15. Wilson, *Flag*, 1:210; Brooks D. Simpson, *Ulysses S. Grant: Triumph over Adversity, 1822–1865* (Boston: Houghton Mifflin, 2000), 206.

16. Rawlins to USG, June 6, 1863, reprinted in *NYS*, January 23, 1887. Rawlins's letter is included with other relevant documents in *PUSG*, 8:322–325.

17. Dana, *Recollections*, 83; *NYS*, January 28, 1887; Wilson Diary, June 7, 1863, HSD; JHW to Cadwallader, November 8, 1889, Cadwallader Papers, LC.

18. Wilson, "Draft of Biography of John A. Rawlins," 118, Wilson Papers, LC. For concurrence by a reliable Grant biographer, see Simpson, *Grant*, 207–208.

19. CAD to William H. Huntington, April 13, 1863, in Wilson, *Dana*, 214.

20. Dana, *Recollections*, 83; CAD to Wilson, January 18, 1890, Wilson Papers, LC; Edwin C. Bearss, *The Campaign for Vicksburg* (Dayton, OH: Morningside Books, 1991), 3:1029.

21. Dana, *Recollections*, 83.

22. Dana entry in Wilson Journal, June 7, 1863, Wilson Papers, LC; *OR* I, v. 24, pt. 1, 94.

23. CAD to JHW, January 18, 1890, Wilson Papers, LC. Dana interview, December 9, 1896, Tarbell Papers; Sylvanus Cadwallader, *Three Years with Grant*, ed. Benjamin P. Thomas and Brooks D. Simpson (Lincoln: University of Nebraska Press, 1996), 105–109.

24. Michael B. Ballard, *Grant at Vicksburg: The General and the Siege* (Carbondale: Southern Illinois University Press, 2013), 53–54. Biographers who accept the Cadwallader account include William S. McFeely, *Grant: A Biography* (New York: W. W. Norton, 1981), 132–134, and Jean Edward Smith, *Grant* (New York: Simon and Schuster, 2001), 231–232. Among the skeptics are Bruce Catton, *Grant Moves South* (Boston: Little, Brown & Co., 1960), 462–464, Simpson, *Grant*, 207–208, and Ron Chernow, *Grant* (New York: Penguin Press, 2017), 273–277. For a strong argument that Cadwallader fabricated his tale, see Simpson, "Introduction," in Cadwallader, *Three Years With Grant*, v–xix.

25. Three decades after the war Dana, Cadwallader, and Wilson exchanged letters in an attempt to square the two accounts but failed. See the string of letters among Dana, Wilson, and Cadwallader, November 1889–January 1890, in Wilson Papers and Cadwallader Papers, LC.

26. JHW to Cadwallader, September 8, 1904, Cadwallader Papers, LC; Badeau to Cadwallader, and USG to Cadwallader, September 23, 1864, Cadwallader Papers, LC.

27. Strong, *Diary*, 3:352.

28. *NYS*, January 28, 1887; John Eaton, *Grant, Lincoln and the Freedmen: Reminiscences of the Civil War* (New York: Longmans, Green & Co., 1907), 90.

29. *NYS*, January 28, 1887; Dana, *Recollections*, 62.

30. *OR* I, v. 24, pt. 1, 96.

31. *OR* I, v. 24, pt. 1, 105; *PUSG*, 8:400–401, 468–469.

32. *OR* I, v. 24, pt. 1, 96.

33. *OR* I, v. 24, pt. 1, 106.

34. Brooks D. Simpson, "Quandaries of Command: Ulysses S. Grant and Black Soldiers," in *Union and Emancipation: Essays on Politics and Race in the Civil War Era*, ed. David W.

Blight and Brooks D. Simpson (Kent, OH: Kent State University Press, 1997), 124, 126–127; *PUSG*, 8:92.

35. Ballard, *Grant at Vicksburg*, 82–84; *PUSG*, 8:343n. Three of Grant's corps commanders assented to the new policy, but a vocal outlier was Sherman, who held strong racist views. "I won't trust niggers to fight," Sherman told his brother after Thomas "made a speech to my command about the Negroes." *PUSG*, 8:94n, 91; W. T. Sherman to John Sherman, April 26, 1863, in *Sherman's Civil War: Selected Correspondence of William T. Sherman, 1860–1865*, ed. Brooks D. Simpson and Jean V. Berlin (Chapel Hill: University of North Carolina Press, 1999), 461.

36. *OR* I, v. 24, pt. 1, 92, 98–99.

37. *OR* I, v. 24, pt. 1, 99; Dana, *Recollections*, 89.

38. Catton, *Grant Moves South*, 466–467.

39. Wilson, *Flag*, 1:185–186.

40. *OR* I, v. 24, pt. 1, 103.

41. *PUSG*, 9:146; *OR* I, v. 24, pt. 1, 110–111.

42. Grant, *Memoirs*, 368; Winston Groom, *Vicksburg, 1863* (New York: Alfred A. Knopf, 2009), 382, 395–396; Catton, *Grant Moves South*, 469–470; *OR* I, v. 24, pt. 1, 105.

43. *OR* I, v. 24, pt. 1, 109, 111, 113; Ballard, *Grant at Vicksburg*, 134.

44. Dana, *Recollections*, 93; *OR* I, v. 24, pt. 1, 112, 114.

45. *OR* I, v. 24, pt. 1, 283–284; Dana, *Recollections*, 96.

46. Dana, *Recollections*, 96; Grant, *Memoirs*, 379–380; *OR* I, v. 24, pt. 1, 112, 114; James Harrison Wilson, "A Staff Officer's Journal of the Vicksburg Campaign, April 30 to July 4, 1863," *Journal of the Military Service Institution of the United States* 43 (1908): 273; Miers, *Web of Victory*, 286.

47. Grant, *Memoirs*, 375–376; Dana, *Recollections*, 97; John C. Pemberton, "The Terms of Surrender," *Battles and Leaders*, 3:544.

48. Grant, *Memoirs*, 376–377; *OR* I, v. 24, pt. 1, 114–115.

49. *PUSG*, 8:470n; Welles, *Diary*, 242–244; *OR* I, v. 24, pt. 1, 114, 62.

50. *OR* I, v. 24, pt. 1, 115; Wilson, *Dana*, 237; Wilson, *Flag*, 1:221–222; Dana, *Recollections*, 100; Bearss, *Campaign for Vicksburg*, 3:1310–1311.

51. Dana, *Recollections*, 100.

52. Dana, *Recollections*, 99; Wilson, *Flag*, 1:223; Albert D. Richardson, *A Personal History of Ulysses S. Grant* (Hartfield, CT: American Publishing Co., 1868), 334; Frederick D. Grant, "A Boy's Experience at Vicksburg," in *Personal Recollections of the War of the Rebellion: Addresses Delivered before the Commandery of the State of New York, Military Order of the Loyal Legion of the United States, 3rd Series*, ed. A. Noel Blakeman (New York: G. P. Putnam's Sons, 1907), 99; Strong, *Diary*, 3:352.

53. Bearss, *Campaign for Vicksburg*, 3:1295; David Dixon Porter, *Incidents and Anecdotes of the Civil War* (New York: D. Appleton & Co., 1885), 200–201.

54. *OR* I, v. 24, pt. 1, 97; Dana, *Recollections*, 100; Grant, *Memoirs*, 384–385; CAD to EMS, July 13, 1863, Seward Papers, University of Rochester; CAD to JSP, July 24, 1863, Pike Papers.

55. Emerson Opdyke, *To Battle for God and the Right: The Civil War Letterbooks of Emerson Opdyke*, ed. Glenn V. Longacre and John E. Haas (Urbana: University of Illinois Press, 2003), 119; Dana and Wilson, *Life of Grant*, 413.

56. Welles, *Diary*, 243, 248.

57. *OR* I, v. 24, pt. 1, 62, 63; *CWL*, 6:409, 326.

58. Dana, *Recollections*, 101–102; *OR* I, v. 24, pt. 3, 542; *PUSG*, 9:71; Wilson, *Flag*, 1:223; *OR* I, v. 24, pt. 1, 116.

59. Dana, *Recollections*, 102; *PUSG*, 8:483; 9:3; Catton, *Grant Moves South*, 481; Benjamin P. Thomas and Harold M. Hyman, *Stanton: The Life and Times of Lincoln's Secretary of War* (New York: Alfred A. Knopf, 1962), 269.

60. Dana, *Recollections*, 102; *OR* I, v. 52, 379.

61. CAD to EMS, July 12 and 13, 1863, reprinted in Dana, *Recollections*, 63–77 (quotations, 65, 68, 70, 71). The originals in the Dana Papers, LC, provide the names deleted in published versions.

62. Dana, *Recollections*, 64, 67–69.

63. Dana, *Recollections*, 65; Wilson, *Flag*, 1:177; Wilson, *Dana*, 253.

64. Dana, *Recollections*, 65–67, 73, 75.

65. Dana, *Recollections*, 74–75; *PUSG*, 9:475–476n; Dana, "Reminiscences of Men and Events of the Civil War," *McClure's Magazine*, 10 (January 1898): 254n.

66. Wilson, *Dana*, 246; Cadwallader, *Three Years with Grant*, 61, 70–71. Dana alerted Stanton when his statements reflected superior officers' opinions rather than his own.

67. David Work, *Lincoln's Political Generals* (Urbana: University of Illinois Press, 2009), 97.

68. James Harrison Wilson, *The Life of John A. Rawlins* (New York: Neale Publishing Co., 1916), 122–123.

Chapter 8. Interlude: "Some Duty Not Yet Explained"

1. CAD to EMS, July 10, 1863, RG 107, NARA.

2. CAD to JHW, July 21, 1863, in Wilson, *Dana*, 249; CAD to JSP, July 29, 1863, Pike Papers.

3. *PUSG*, 9:147–148. Dana's arguments can be inferred from Henry Wilson to Elihu Washburne, July 25, 1863, Washburne Papers, LC, and *PUSG*, 9:217–218.

4. *PUSG*, 9:145–148. Grant repeated his thanks in the postwar years. See John Russell Young, *Around the World with General Grant*, ed. Michael Fellman (Baltimore: Johns Hopkins University Press, 2002), 387–388.

5. *PUSG*, 9:218.

6. *CWL*, 6:374; *PUSG*, 8:343n. In a public letter to James C. Conkling, August 26, 1863, Lincoln wrote that the Vicksburg victory "could not have been achieved *when it was*, but for the aid of black soldiers." *CWL*, 6:409, 423 (emphasis added).

7. Jonathan W. White, *Emancipation, the Union Army, and the Reelection of Abraham Lincoln* (Baton Rouge: Louisiana State University Press, 2014), 44; *PUSG*, 9:148, 196; CAD to JSP, August 18, 1863, Pike Papers; AL to USG, August 9, 1863, AL Papers.

8. Frederick Douglass, *Life and Times of Frederick Douglass, Written by Himself* (reprint, 1892 ed., New York: Collier Books, 1962), 424; Paul Kendrick and Stephen Kendrick, *Douglass and Lincoln: How a Revolutionary Black Leader and a Reluctant Liberator Struggled to End Slavery and Save the Union* (New York: Walker & Company, 2008), 148–154.

9. Douglass, *Life and Times*, 424–425; Kendrick and Kendrick, *Douglass and Lincoln*, 164–167; David W. Blight, *Frederick Douglass: Prophet of Freedom* (New York: Simon & Schuster, 2018), 407–410.

10. CAD to Washburne, August 29, 1863, Henry Wilson to Washburne, July 25, 1863, Washburne Papers, LC.

11. Strong, *Diary*, 3:352.

12. CAD to JSP, July 24, 1863, Pike Papers.

13. For Rawlins's interview with Lincoln and the cabinet, see Welles, *Diary*, 261–262. For McClernand's maneuvering, see Richard L. Kiper, *Major General John Alexander McClernand: Politician in Uniform* (Kent, OH: Kent State University Press, 1999), 274–275.

14. *PUSG*, 9:124–125, 147, 218; CAD to JHW, August 11 and 31, 1863, in Wilson, *Dana*, 252–253.

15. John Strausbaugh, *City of Sedition: The History of New York City during the Civil War* (New York: Twelve Books, 2016), 278–279; Don C. Seitz, *Horace Greeley, Founder of the New York Tribune* (Indianapolis: Bobbs-Merrill, 1926), 211–212; Barnet Schecter, *The Devil's Own Work: The Civil War Draft Riots and the Fight to Reconstruct America* (New York: Walker & Co., 2005), 155, 178–179, 196.

16. Schecter, *Devil's Own Work*, 125–252; Ernest A. McKay, *The Civil War and New York City* (Syracuse: Syracuse University Press, 1990), 195–215.

17. CAD to JHW, July 21, 1863, in Wilson, *Dana*, 250; CAD to JSP, August 18, 1863, Pike Papers.

18. CAD to JSP, July 24, 1863, Pike Papers; *NYTr*, January 9, 1863; William Harlan Hale, *Horace Greeley: Voice of the People* (New York: Harper & Brothers, 1950), 268–270; Warren F. Spencer, "The Jewett-Greeley Affair: A Private Scheme for French Mediation in the American Civil War," *New York History* 51 (1970): 238–268.

19. CAD to JSP, July 24, August 18, 1863, Pike Papers; CAD to William H. Huntington, April 13, 1863, in Wilson, *Dana*, 213.

20. CAD to JSP, July 24, 1863, Pike Papers; CAD to JHW, July 21, August 11, 1863, in Wilson, *Dana*, 249, 252. On Tompkins Square and the riots, see Schecter, *Devil's Own Work*, 373; *NYT*, September 14, 2007.

21. CAD to JSP, August 18, 1863, Pike Papers; Dana, *Recollections*, 103.

22. CAD to Olmsted, August 7, 1863, in *The Papers of Frederick Law Olmsted*, ed. Charles Beveridge and others (Baltimore: Johns Hopkins University Press, 1977–2013), 5:6; Witold Rybczynski, *A Clearing in the Distance: Frederick Law Olmsted and America in the 19th Century* (New York: Scribner, 2013), 221–264.

23. CAD to JHW, August 11, 1863, in Wilson, *Dana*, 251–252.

24. *PUSG*, 9:148; CAD to JSP, August 18, 1863, Pike Papers.

25. McKay, *Civil War and New York City*, 212–213; *OR* III, v. 3, 693; Schecter, *Devil's Own Work*, 255–256.

Chapter 9. "As Fatal a Name as Bull Run"

1. *NYS*, May 28, 1868; *OR* I, v. 23, pt. 2, 518.

2. For biographical details, see William M. Lamers, *The Edge of Glory: A Biography of General William S. Rosecrans, U.S.A.* (New York: Harcourt, Brace & World, 1961).

3. Stephen E. Woodworth, *Six Armies in Tennessee: The Chickamauga and Chattanooga Campaigns* (Lincoln: University of Nebraska Press, 1998), 17.

4. Larry J. Daniel, *Days of Glory: The Army of the Cumberland, 1861–1865* (Baton Rouge: Louisiana State University Press, 2006), 265–282; *OR* I, v. 23, pt. 2, 518; *OR* I, v. 30, pt. 3, 110.

5. *OR* I, v. 23, pt. 2, 518.

6. Lamers, *Edge of Glory*, 277, 297, 298; *OR* I, v. 23, pt. 2, 601–602; *CWL*, 6:378.

7. Lamers, *Edge of Glory; SPCP*, 4:103; Sanderson Journal, August 16, 24, 1863.

8. Stephen E. Ambrose, *Halleck: Lincoln's Chief of Staff* (Baton Rouge: Louisiana State University Press, 1962), 151; EMS to CAD, August 30, 1863, Stanton Papers, LC.

9. *OR* I, v. 30, pt. 1, 182–183.

10. Dana, *Recollections*, 105; Dana interview, December 10, 1896, Tarbell Papers.

11. *OR* I, v. 30, pt. 1, 182–183.

12. OR I, v. 30, pt. 1, 183–184. For assessments of Truesdail, see Peter Mazlowski, *"Treason Must Be Made Odious": Military Occupation and Wartime Reconstruction in Nashville, Tennessee, 1862–65* (Millwood, NY: KTO Press, 1978), 62–64; and William B. Feis, "'There Is a Bad Enemy in This City': Colonel William Truesdail's Army Police and the Occupation of Nashville, 1862–1863," *North & South* 8 (March 2005): 35–45.

13. *OR* I, v. 30, pt. 1, 184; pt. 3, 520.

14. D. H. Hill, in *Battles and Leaders*, 3:644.

15. *OR* I, v. 30, pt. 3, 229; Lamers, *Edge of Glory*, 311–312; Dana, *Recollections*, 107; *NYS*, November 26, 1879.

16. William F. G. Shanks, *Personal Recollections of Distinguished Generals* (New York: Harper & Brothers, 1866), 263.

17. Dana, *Recollections*, 108.

18. *OR* I, v. 30, pt. 1, 185.

19. Woodworth, *Six Armies*, 71–76.

20. Dana, *Recollections*, 109; *OR* I, v. 30, pt. 1, 186–189; Rosecrans to Ann E. Rosecrans, September 16 and 28, 1863, Rosecrans Papers, UCLA.

21. *OR* I, v. 30, pt. 1, 189; Dana, *Recollections*, 110.

22. *OR* I, v. 30, pt. 1, 187, 189.

23. *OR* I, v. 30, pt. 1, 191.

24. Sanderson Journal, September 19, 1863; *OR* I, v. 30, pt. 1, 190–191.

25. *OR* I, v. 30, pt. 1, 191; Woodworth, *Six Armies*, 89; Peter Cozzens, *This Terrible Sound: The Battle of Chickamauga* (Urbana: University of Illinois Press, 1992), 293; Shanks, *Personal Recollections*, 266.

26. *OR* I, v. 30, pt. 1, 191; Cozzens, *Terrible Sound*, 294.

27. Sanderson Journal, September 19, 1863; Cozzens, *Terrible Sound*, 292; David A. Powell, *The Chickamauga Campaign* (El Dorado Hills, CA: Savas Beatie, 2014–2016), 2:15; Shanks, Personal *Recollections*, 267.

28. Cozzens, *Terrible Sound*, 294–295; *NYS*, March 30, 1870; Dana interview, December 12, 1896, Tarbell Papers; Powell, *Chickamauga Campaign*, 2:26.

29. Dana, *Recollections*, 113–114; Gates P. Thruston, "Chickamauga," *Southern Bivouac* 6 (December 1886): 409.

30. Dana, *Recollections*, 114–115; Powell, *Chickamauga Campaign*, 2:183–184.

31. Dana, *Recollections*, 115; *OR* I, v. 30, pt. 1, 192–193; Wilson, *Dana*, 264; Cozzens, *Terrible Sound*, 389.

32. *OR* I, v. 30, pt. 1, 192–193; Cozzens, *Terrible Sound*, 357–367. Powell, *Chickamauga Campaign*, 2:198–203, persuasively defends Wood against charges that he deliberately undermined Rosecrans.

33. Dana, *Recollections*, 116; Cozzens, *Terrible Sound*, 390. For his role in holding off the Confederates long enough to allow most of Sheridan's artillery to escape, Porter was later awarded the Medal of Honor.

34. Cozzens, *Terrible Sound*, 389–390, 403–404; *OR* I, v. 30, pt. 1, 194; Powell, *Chickamauga*

Campaign, 2:313–315; Lamers, *Edge of Glory*, 352–353; Rosecrans to Sylvester Rosecrans, October 9, 1863, Rosecrans Papers, UCLA.

35. Dana interview, December 12, 1896, Tarbell Papers.

36. Cozzens, *Terrible Sound*, 395.

37. John T. Wilder, "Preliminary Movements of the Army of the Cumberland before the Battle of Chickamauga [1908]," in *Sketches of War History, 1861–1865, Vol. 7* (Wilmington, NC: Broadfoot Publishing Co., 1993), 270.

38. *OR* I, v. 30, pt. 1, 449; Cozzens, *Terrible Sound*, 395. The best account of this incident is Powell, *Chickamauga Campaign*, 2:308–313.

39. Glenn Tucker, *Chickamauga: Bloody Battle in the West* (Indianapolis: Bobbs-Merrill, 1961), 319; Cozzens, *Terrible Sound*, 396.

40. Quoted in Cozzens, *Terrible Sound*, 396. For Wilder's various retellings, see Robert E. Harbison, "Wilder's Brigade in the Tullahoma and Chattanooga Campaigns of the American Civil War" (MMAS thesis, US Army Command and General Staff College, Fort Leavenworth, KS, 2002), 83–86; and Powell, *Chickamauga Campaign*, 2:309–310.

41. Dana, *Recollections*, 117; *OR* I, v. 30, pt. 1, 193.

42. Thruston, in *Battles and Leaders*, 3:664; *OR*, I, v. 30, pt. 1, 449; Wilder, "Preliminary Movements," 269; Thruston quoted in Daniel, *Days of Glory*, 331, n.44.

43. *OR* I, v. 30, pt. 1, 194–195.

44. *NYS*, March 30, 1870; Powell, *Chickamauga Campaign*, 2:316–319.

45. Cozzens, *Terrible Sound*, 469–470, 478; Wiley Sword, *Mountains Touched with Fire: Chattanooga Besieged, 1863* (New York: St. Martin's Press, 1995), 14–15.

46. *OR* I, v. 30, pt. 1, 193; Wilson, *Dana*, 264; Powell, *Chickamauga Campaign*, 2:324–327.

47. *OR* I, v. 30, pt. 1, 192–193.

48. Dana, *Recollections*, 24; CAD to General R. S. Granger, October 5, 1863, CAD Papers, LC; *OR* I, v. 30, pt. 1, 207–208, 214.

49. Welles, *Diary*, 294; *OR* I, v. 30, pt. 1, 142–143.

50. *OR* I, v. 30, pt. 1, 193–194.

51. *OR* I, v. 30, pt. 1, 146; David Homer Bates, *Lincoln in the Telegraph Office: Recollections of the United States Military Telegraph Corps during the Civil War* (New York: Century Company, 1907), 202; Hay, *Diary*, 85.

52. *OR* I, v. 30, pt. 1, 193, 195; Sword, *Touched with Fire*, 38–39.

53. *OR* I, v. 30, pt. 1, 195, 199; Robert C. Conner, *General Gordon Granger: The Savior of Chickamauga and the Man Behind "Juneteenth"* (Philadelphia: Casemate, 2013), 106.

54. Powell, *Chickamauga Campaign*, 2:594; Dana interview, December 14, 1896, Tarbell Papers; *OR* I, v. 30, pt. 1, 195–197; Woodworth, *Six Armies*, 136; Daniel, *Days of Glory*, 339; Hay, *Diary*, 86.

55. Sword, *Touched with Fire*, 29–35, 63–69.

56. *OR* I, v. 30, pt. 1, 197–198. Casualty totals are from Powell, *Chickamauga Campaign*, 3:83–84.

57. Bates, *Lincoln in the Telegraph Office*, 204; *OR* I, 30, pt. 1, 199; *NYS*, March 30, 1870.

58. *OR* I, v. 30, pt. 1, 197–198.

59. *OR* I, v. 30, pt. 3, 792; pt. 1, 207; Cozzens, *Terrible Sound*, 523.

60. *SPCP*, 1:450–454; Roger Pickenpaugh, *Rescue by Rail: Troop Transfer and the Civil War in the West* (Lincoln: University of Nebraska Press, 1998), 4–7; *OR* I, v. 29, pt. 1, 150–151.

61. *OR* I, v. 30, pt. 1, 205; Frank S. Bond, in "Correspondence Relating to Chickamauga and Chattanooga," *Papers of the Military Historical Society of Massachusetts, Vol. 8: The*

Mississippi Valley, Tennessee, Georgia, Alabama, 1861–1864 (Boston: Military Historical Society of Massachusetts, 1910), 265; Dana, *Recollections*, 130; Pickenpaugh, *Rescue by Rail*, 73, 130; Woodworth, *Six Armies*, 137; Walter Stahr, *Stanton: Lincoln's War Secretary* (New York: Simon & Schuster, 2017), 311–319.

62. *OR* I, 30, pt. 1, 198; Cozzens, *Terrible Sound*, 294; Sanderson Journal, September 21, 1863; *OR* I, 30, pt. 1, 200, 209.

63. *OR* I, 30, pt. 1, 199–200; Hay, *Diary*, 86. Hay incorrectly attributed the telegram to Rosecrans.

64. Woodworth, *Six Armies*, 134; Sanderson Journal, September 22, 1863.

65. Dana, *Recollections*, 122. For biographies, see Damon R. Eubank, *In the Shadow of the Patriarch: The John J. Crittenden Family in War and Peace* (Macon, GA: Mercer University Press, 2009); and Wayne Faneburst, *Major General Alexander M. McCook, USA: A Civil War Biography* (Jefferson, NC: McFarland, 2012).

66. *OR* I, 30, pt. 1, 201–202, 204; Emerson Opdyke, *To Battle for God and the Right: The Civil War Letterbooks of Emerson Opdyke*, ed. Glenn V. Longacre and John E. Haas (Urbana: University of Illinois Press, 2003), 99; Ethan S. Rafuse, "In the Shadow of the Rock: Thomas L. Crittenden, Alexander M. McCook, and the 1863 Campaigns for Middle and East Tennessee," in *The Chickamauga Campaign*, ed. Steven E. Woodworth (Carbondale: Southern Illinois University Press, 2012), 38–39.

67. *OR* I, v. 30, pt. 3, 946; *OR* I, 30, pt. 1, 212, 962, 996–997.

68. *OR* I, v. 30, pt. 1, 202, 204. Dana had probably overheard Rosecrans's comment that he "hated to injure two such good fellows." Cozzens, *Terrible Sound*, 7. For Dana's "long and frank talk with Garfield," see Edward P. Mitchell, "Mr. Dana of 'The Sun,'" *McClure's Magazine* 3 (October 1894): 383.

69. *OR* I, 30, pt. 1, 202, 204–205; Dana, *Recollections*, 124–125.

70. Welles, *Diary*, 301–302; Lincoln quoted in Lamers, *Edge of Glory*, 408.

71. *OR* I, v. 30, pt. 3, 946; Dana, *Recollections*, 125–126; *OR* I, 30, pt. 1, 211.

72. Opdyke, *To Battle for God and the Right*, 109; 207–213; *OR* I, v. 30, pt. 1, 204–214.

73. *OR* I, 30, pt. 1, 215; Dana, *Recollections*, 121; Woodworth, *Six Armies*, 141.

74. *OR* I, 30, pt. 1, 215; Dana, *Recollections*, 129; *OR* I, 30, pt. 1, 221.

75. Woodworth, *Six Armies*, 144, 146; Daniel, *Days of Glory*, 346.

76. *OR* I, 30, pt. 1, 215–216.

77. Bates, *Lincoln in the Telegraph Office*, 205.

78. David Donald, *Lincoln* (New York: Simon & Schuster, 1995), 455.

79. *OR* I, v. 30, pt. 1, 210; Henry Villard, *Memoirs of Henry Villard, Journalist and Financier, 1835–1900* (New York: Da Capo Press, 1969), 2:184; *OR* I, v. 30, pt. 4, 57, 79; Lamers, *Edge of Glory*, 380.

80. *OR* I, v. 30, pt. 1, 217; Jennifer L. Weber, *Copperheads: The Rise and Fall of Lincoln's Opponents in the North* (New York: Oxford University Press, 2006), 121–122.

81. *OR* I, v. 30, pt. 1, 216–221; OR I, v. 30, pt. 4, 413–414.

82. *OR* I, v. 30, pt. 1, 219; Daniel, *Days of Glory*, 347.

83. *OR* I, v. 30, pt. 1, 210, 218–219; Sanderson Journal, October 14, 1863.

84. Welles, *Diary*, 302; Hay, *Diary*, 98–99.

85. *OR* I, v. 30, pt. 4, 404; Daniel, *Days of Glory*, 353; Lesley Gordon, "The Failed Relationship of William S. Rosecrans and Grant," in *Grant's Lieutenants: From Cairo to Vicksburg*, ed. Steven E. Woodworth (Lawrence: University Press of Kansas, 2001), 127.

86. *OR* I, v. 30, pt. 1, 221.

87. EMS to CAD, October 17, 1863, Eckert Papers, HL; Grant, *Memoirs*, 404, 409; John

Russell Young, *Around the World with General Grant*, ed. Michael Fellman (Baltimore: Johns Hopkins University Press, 2002), 298.

88. Wilson, *Flag*, 1:263; Grant in *OR* I, v. 31, pt. 2, 27; Adam Badeau, *Military History of Ulysses S. Grant, From April, 1861, To April, 1865* (New York: D. Appleton & Co., 1868–1881), 1:424; Dana, *Recollections*, 129, 131. Stahr, *Stanton*, 322, concludes that "perhaps Grant was right in remembering that Stanton was worried that night [October 19], although wrong on some details."

89. W. F. Smith, in *Battles and Leaders*, 3:718; Villard, *Memoirs*, 2:189, 211–212. Dana rode partway with General Baldy Smith on the reconnaissance trip to Williams Island before parting for Nashville. See William F. Smith, *Autobiography of Major General William F. Smith, 1861–1864*, ed. Herbert M. Schiller (Dayton, OH: Morningside House, 1990), 74–75; Smith, "An Historical Sketch of the Military Operations around Chattanooga, Tennessee, September 22 to November 27, 1863," *Papers of the Military Historical Society of Massachusetts, Vol. 8*, 169. For the "deliberate lie" charge, see Albert Castel, *Victors in Blue: How Union Generals Fought the Confederates, Battled Each Other, and Won the Civil War* (Lawrence: University Press of Kansas, 2011), 233.

90. *OR* I, v. 30, pt. 4, 479.

91. Dana, *Recollections*, 130–131.

92. *NYH*, October 23, 1863; Villard, *Memoirs*, 2:210–211; Welles, *Diary*, 301; Hay, *Diary*, 98–99.

93. Gilmore to Rosecrans, May 23, 1864, Rosecrans Papers, UCLA.

94. Villard, *Memoirs*, 2:211.

95. Garfield to Chase, July 27, 1863, in James A. Garfield, *The Wild Life of the Army: Civil War Letters of James A. Garfield*, ed. Frederick D. Williams (East Lansing: Michigan State University Press, 1964), 290; Lamers, *Edge of Glory*, 408; Gilmore, "Why Rosecrans Was Removed," *Atlanta Constitution*, December 22, 1895.

96. *NYS*, December 25, 1869; Francis Darr to Rosecrans, September 16, 1880, Rosecrans Papers, UCLA; Cozzens, *Terrible Sound*, 524.

97. *NYS*, March 8, 1882; Garfield, *Wild Life*, 289–291; Theodore Clarke Smith, *The Life and Letters of James Abram Garfield* (New Haven, CT: Yale University Press, 1925), 2:883–884; CAD to Jacob W. Schuckers, March 31, April 3, 1889, Schuckers Papers, LC; Rosecrans to CAD, March 17, 1882, CAD Papers, LC; Dana interview, December 15, 1896, Tarbell Papers.

98. *Tombstone* (Ariz.) *Epitaph*, March 20, 1882. This is also the judgment of John G. Nicolay and John Hay, *Abraham Lincoln: A History* (New York: Century Co., 1890), 8:117–119; and Smith, *Garfield*, 2:879.

99. Lamers, *Edge of Glory*, 386, 404; Sanderson Journal, March 25, 1864. For charges that Dana colluded with Stanton against Rosecrans, see Cozzens, *Terrible Sound*, 80; Lamers, *Edge of Glory*, 383–389; and Pickenpaugh, *Rescue by Rail*, 159.

100. Opdyke, *To Battle for God and the Right*, 117; Smith, "Operations," 167–168; *PUSG*, 9:557; Grant, *Memoirs*, 410; Sanderson Journal, October 24, 1863.

101. Villard, *Memoirs*, 2:189, 211.

102. Jacob D. Cox, *Military Reminiscences of the Civil War* (New York: Scribner's, 1900), 2:7; Villard, *Memoirs*, 2:189; CAD to Rosecrans, March 18, 1882, Rosecrans Papers, UCLA.

103. For corroborating opinions see Daniel, *Days of Glory*, 343; and Allan Nevins, "Charles Anderson Dana," *Dictionary of American Biography* (New York: Charles Scribner's Sons, 1930), 5:50.

Chapter 10. "Glory to God! The Day Is Decisively Ours"

1. Wilson, *Flag*, 1:264; Grant, *Memoirs*, 414.

2. Oliver Otis Howard, *Autobiography of Oliver Otis Howard* (New York: Baker & Taylor, 1907), 1:460; Wilson, *Dana*, 278; Walter H. Hebert, *Fighting Joe Hooker* (Indianapolis: Bobbs-Merrill, 1944), 257.

3. Wilson, *Flag*, 1:265; John Russell Young, *Around the World with General Grant*, ed. Michael Fellman (Baltimore: Johns Hopkins University Press, 2002), 298; Grant, *Memoirs*, 410.

4. *OR*, I, v. 31, pt. 1, 693; *PUSG*, 9:317; Grant, *Memoirs*, 410–411.

5. Wilson, *Flag*, 1:268–269; Wilson, *Dana*, 278–279.

6. Dana, *Recollections*, 132–133; Albert D. Richardson, *A Personal History of Ulysses S. Grant* (Hartfield, CT: American Publishing Co., 1868), 354; *OR* I, v. 31, pt. 1, 69.

7. *OR* I, v. 31, pt. 1, 70; Wilson, *Flag*, 1:273–275; Wilson, *Dana*, 281.

8. Wilson, *Flag*, 1:275–276; James Harrison Wilson, *The Life of John A. Rawlins* (New York: Neale Publishing Co., 1916), 168. On the Grant-Thomas relationship, see Steven E. Woodworth, "Old Slow Trot: George H. Thomas," in *Grant's Lieutenants: From Chattanooga to Appomattox*, ed. Steven E. Woodworth (Lawrence: University Press of Kansas, 2008), 23–45.

9. Horace Porter, *Campaigning with Grant* (New York: Century Co., 1897), 4–5.

10. *OR* I, v. 31, pt. 1, 70; William F. Smith, *Autobiography of Major General William F. Smith, 1861–1864* (Dayton, OH: Morningside House, 1990), 74–75; William F. Smith, "An Historical Sketch of the Military Operations around Chattanooga, Tennessee, September 22 to November 27, 1863," *Papers of the Military Historical Society of Massachusetts, Vol. 8* (Boston: Military Historical Society of Massachusetts, 1910), 169; Wiley Sword, *Mountains Touched with Fire: Chattanooga Besieged, 1863* (New York: St. Martin's Press, 1995), 60–61.

11. Sword, *Touched with Fire*, 114–116; Grant, *Memoirs*, 417; *OR* I, v. 31, pt. 1, 69, 70, 72; Howard, *Autobiography*, 1:458–459; Wilson, *Dana*, 283–284.

12. Wilson, *Dana*, 284; Sword, *Touched with Fire*, 121; *OR* I, v. 31, pt. 1, 72.

13. See William S. Rosecrans, "The Mistakes of Grant," *North American Review* 141 (December 1885): 580–599; W. F. Smith, *The Relief of the Army of the Cumberland and the Opening of the Short Line of Communication between Chattanooga, Tenn., and Bridgeport, Ala. In October, 1863* (Wilmington: C. F. Thomas & Co., 1891); Smith, *Battles and Leaders*, 3:715–720.

14. *OR* I, v. 31, pt. 1, 72; Wilson, *Dana*, 284; Sword, *Touched with Fire*, 127–144; Stephen E. Woodworth, *Six Armies in Tennessee: The Chickamauga and Chattanooga Campaigns* (Lincoln: University of Nebraska Press, 1998), 167; *OR* I, v. 31, pt. 1, 73.

15. *OR* I, v. 31, pt. 1, 74; *OR* I, v. 31, pt. 2, 53; Dana, *Recollections*, 135.

16. *OR* I, v. 31, pt. 2, 54–55; *PUSG*, 9:328–329.

17. Wilson, *Dana*, 285; *OR* I, v. 31, pt. 2, 52–53, 57; *OR* I, v. 31, pt. 1, 73, 94–95; *CWL*, 6:486; Brian C. Melton, *Sherman's Forgotten General: Henry W. Slocum* (Columbia: University of Missouri Press, 2007), 156–157.

18. *OR* I, v. 31, pt. 1, 69; *OR* I, v. 30, pt. 1, 211; *CWL*, 7:61; *PUSG*, 9:323–324; *OR* I, v. 31, pt. 2, 53–54.

19. *PUSG*, 9:396.

20. Sword, *Touched with Fire*, 153–154; *OR* I, v. 31, pt. 2, 57–58; Woodworth, *Six Armies*, 176–178.

21. *OR* I, v. 31, pt. 2, 57–59; Larry J. Daniel, *Days of Glory: The Army of the Cumberland, 1861–1865* (Baton Rouge: Louisiana State University Press, 2006), 368.

22. Dana, *Recollections*, 137; *OR* I, v. 31, pt. 2, 56, 59; *OR* I, v. 52, 490.

23. Dana, *Recollections*, 137.

24. Wilson, *Diary*, November 10 and 11, 1863, HSD; Wilson, *Flag*, 1:281–283; Wilson, *Dana*, 288; *OR* I, v. 31, pt. 3, 127.

25. Dana, *Recollections*, 138; Wilson, *Dana*, 287.

26. *OR* I, v. 31, pt. 1, 258–259; Dana and Wilson, *Life of Grant*, 143.

27. Earl J. Hess, *The Knoxville Campaign: Burnside and Longstreet in East Tennessee* (Knoxville: University of Tennessee Press, 2012), 40; *PUSG*, 9:392; *OR* I, v. 31, pt. 1, 259–260.

28. Wilson, *Flag*, 1:285; *OR* I, v. 31, pt. 1, 260; William Marvel, *Burnside* (Chapel Hill: University of North Carolina Press, 1991), 309.

29. *OR* I, v. 31, pt. 3, 156, 163. It is not clear whether Grant's initial instructions had been to return on November 14, as Dana and Wilson believed, or to stay at Knoxville "until present dangers are over," as Grant told Halleck. *PUSG*, 9:401; *OR* I, v. 31, pt. 3, 154.

30. Dana, *Recollections*, 138.

31. Wilson, *Flag*, 1:287; *New York Evening Post*, December 30, 1863, reprinted in *Daily National Intelligencer*, January 2, 1864.

32. Wilson, *Dana*, 288; Wilson, *Flag*, 1:286; Wilson, *Diary*, November 17, 1863, HSD; *OR* I, v. 52, 495; *OR* I, v. 31, pt. 3, 190; Joshua Zeitz, *Lincoln's Boys: John Hay, John Nicolay, and the War for Lincoln's Image* (New York: Penguin Books, 2014), 140.

33. Dana, *Recollections*, 143.

34. *OR* I, v. 31, pt. 2, 60, 64; *OR* I, v. 52, 495.

35. *OR* I, v. 31, pt. 2, 64; Wilson, *Flag*, 1:291. On the Grant-Sherman friendship, see John F. Marszalek, "Take the Seat of Honor: William T. Sherman," in Woodworth, ed., *Grant's Lieutenants*, 5–22.

36. *OR* I, v. 31, pt. 2, 61, 63, 66; Sword, *Touched with Fire*, 162; Grant, *Memoirs*, 435.

37. *PUSG*, 9:428; *OR* I, v. 31, pt. 2, 64.

38. Grant, *Memoirs*, 424–425, 433; *OR* I, v. 31, pt. 2, 64; Sword, *Touched with Fire*, 178–180; Dana, *Recollections*, 144.

39. Dana, *Recollections*, 144; *OR* I, v. 31, pt. 2, 65; Sword, *Touched with Fire*, 180–184.

40. *OR* I, v. 31, pt. 2, 65–66.

41. William Tecumseh Sherman, *Memoirs of General W. T. Sherman* (1885; New York: Library of America, 1990), 387; *OR* I, v. 31, pt. 2, 65–66.

42. Wilson, *Flag*, 1:294–295; Dana, *Recollections*, 147.

43. *OR* I, v. 31, pt. 2, 42, 66–67, 108–109; *PUSG*, 9:439; CAD to EMS, November 21, 1863, Dana Telegraph Ledgers, Eckert Papers, HL.

44. *OR* I, v. 31, pt. 2, 573.

45. Sword, *Touched with Fire*, 202–221; *OR* I, v. 31, pt. 2, 78.

46. Dana, *Recollections*, 148; William Wrenshall Smith, "Holocaust Holiday," *Civil War Times Illustrated* 18, no.6 (October 1979): 35.

47. *OR* I, v. 31, pt. 2, 67.

48. Montgomery C. Meigs, "First Impressions of Three Days' Fighting: Quartermaster General Meigs's 'Journal of the Battle of Chattanooga,'" in *Ulysses S. Grant: Essays and Documents*, ed. David L. Wilson and John Y. Simon (Carbondale: Southern Illinois University Press, 1981), 72–73; Dana, *Recollections*, 148–149; Dana interview, December 17, 1896, Tarbell Papers.

49. Sword, *Touched with Fire*, 237–258; *OR* I, v. 31, pt. 2, 68.

50. Wilson, *Flag*, 1:297. Grant had apparently put off attacking the rifle pits when he saw them fully manned. *PUSG*, 9:443; *OR* I, v. 31, pt. 2, 68.

51. Brooks D. Simpson, *Ulysses S. Grant: Triumph over Adversity, 1822–1865* (Boston: Houghton Mifflin, 2000), 240; Thomas J. Wood, "The Battle of Missionary Ridge," in *Sketches of War History 1861–1865, Vol. 4.*, ed. W. H. Chamberlin (Cincinnati: Robert Clarke Co., 1896), 35; Sword, *Touched with Fire*, 268–269.

52. Sylvanus Cadwallader, *Three Years with Grant*, ed. Benjamin P. Thomas and Brooks D. Simpson (Lincoln: University of Nebraska Press, 1996), 153–154; Dana interview, December 17, 1896, Tarbell Papers; *OR* I, v. 31, pt. 2, 68; Robert C. Conner, *General Gordon Granger: The Savior of Chickamauga and the Man Behind "Juneteenth"* (Philadelphia: Casemate, 2013), 122–123; Wilson, *Dana*, 293.

53. Dana, *Recollections*, 149–150; Cadwallader, *Three Years with Grant*, 149–150.

54. Woodworth, *Six Armies*, 198–199; Sword, *Touched with Fire*, 272–281.

55. *OR* I, v. 31, pt. 2, 68–69; Dana and Wilson, *Life of Grant*, 149; Dana interview, December 15, 1896, Tarbell Papers; Conner, *Granger*, 129; Peter Cozzens, *The Shipwreck of Their Hopes: The Battles for Chattanooga* (Urbana: University of Illinois Press, 1994), 389.

56. Sword, *Touched with Fire*, 303, 315–317; *OR* I, v. 31, pt. 2, 69.

57. *OR* I, v. 31, pt. 2, 69.

58. Sherman, *Memoirs*, 390; Grant, *Memoirs*, 446; Cozzens, *Shipwreck*, 282.

59. *OR* I, v. 31, pt. 2, 69.

60. Dana, *Recollections*, 150–151; *OR* I, v. 31, pt. 2, 190–191.

61. Benjamin P. Thomas and Harold M. Hyman, *Stanton: The Life and Times of Lincoln's Secretary of War* (New York: Alfred A. Knopf, 1962), 292; Michael Burlingame, *Abraham Lincoln: A Life* (Baltimore: Johns Hopkins University Press, 2008), 2:578–579; Dana, *Recollections*, 151–152; Hay, *Diary*, 118–119.

62. *CWL*, 6:496–497, 7:30; *PUSG*, 9:479–480; Dana, *Recollections*, 152.

63. Sword, *Touched with Fire*, 325; *OR* I, v. 31, pt. 2, 70.

64. Smith, "Holocaust Holiday," 37–38; Wilson, *Flag*, 1:302.

65. Smith, "Holocaust Holiday," 38; *OR* I, v. 31, pt. 2, 70; Sword, *Touched with Fire*, 331–343.

66. J. Cutler Andrews, *The North Reports the Civil War* (Pittsburgh: University of Pittsburgh Press, 1955), 488–489; *OR* I, v. 31, pt. 2, 70–71, and v. 32, pt. 2, 468; Sword, *Touched with Fire*, 338, 344.

67. Smith, "Holocaust Holiday," 39–40; Wilson, *Dana*, 5.

68. Smith, "Holocaust Holiday," 40; *PUSG*, 9:455–456; *OR* I, v. 31, pt. 2, 26, 72.

69. *OR* I, v. 31, pt. 3, 256–257; *PUSG*, 9:465.

70. *PUSG*, 9:457–458, 467, 473–474; *OR* I, v. 31, pt. 2, 35, 47; Conner, *Granger*, 134–135; *OR* I, v. 31, pt. 1, 264–265.

71. Wilson, *Diary*, November 29, 1863, HSD; Wilson, *Flag*, 1:307–309; *OR* I, v. 31, pt. 3, 297.

72. Wilson, *Flag*, 1:309, 313; *OR* I, v. 31, pt. 1, 262; Sherman, *Memoirs*, 407.

73. *OR* I, v. 31, pt. 3, 316; Dana, *Recollections*, 153–154; Wilson, *Flag*, 1:314; Wilson, *Diary*, December 3 and 4, 1863, HSD; Sherman, *Memoirs*, 407–408; *OR* I, v. 31, pt. 1, 263.

74. Marvel, *Burnside*, 314–321; *OR* I, v. 31, pt. 1, 278–279; Hess, *Knoxville Campaign*, 170–171, 249, 252.

75. Sherman, *Memoirs*, 393, 408; Wilson, *Diary*, December 5, 1863, HSD; *PUSG*, 9:466; *OR* I, v. 31, pt. 1, 462; Hess, *Knoxville Campaign*, 181; James Longstreet, *From Manassas to Appomattox: Memoirs of the Civil War in America* (Philadelphia: J. B. Lippincott, 1896), 505–509. In his *Memoirs*, 455, Grant implied that Dana and Wilson were entrusted with the letters intended to be captured; Marvel, *Burnside*, 325, repeats the error.

76. Carl Schurz, *The Reminiscences of Carl Schurz*, ed. Frederic Bancroft and William A. Dunning (New York: McClure, 1908), 3:80; Nicolay Memorandum, December 7, 1863, quoted in Lincoln, *Recollected Words of Abraham Lincoln*, ed. Don E. Fehrenbacher and Virginia Fehrenbacher (Stanford: Stanford University Press, 1996), 347.

77. Sherman, *Memoirs*, 394; *OR* I, v. 31, pt. 1, 263; Longstreet, *Manassas to Appomattox*, 497; Marvel, *Burnside*, 332.

78. Sherman, *Memoirs*, 408; *OR* I, v. 31, pt. 1, 263.

79. Sherman, *Memoirs*, 393; *OR* I, v. 31, pt. 1, 264–265; *OR* I, v. 31, pt. 3, 358–359.

80. Granger to Rosecrans, June 6, 1864, Rosecrans Papers, UCLA.

81. Wilson, *Flag*, 1:315; Wilson, *Diary*, December 7, 1863, HSD; Wilson, *Dana*, 36, 296; *NYTr*, March 7, 1862.

82. Schurz, *Reminiscences*, 3:80–84; Wilson, *Dana*, 296; *OR* I, v. 31, pt. 3, 353–354; *OR* I, v. 31, pt. 1, 264; Wilson, *Diary*, December 9, 1863, HSD.

83. Dana and Wilson, *Life of Grant*, 150, 157, 400–401.

84. *OR* I, v. 31, pt. 1, 264; *OR* I, v. 31, pt. 2, 73; CAD to USG, December 18, 1863, Grant Papers, LC.

Chapter 11. "Organizing Victory"

1. William O. Stoddard, *Inside the White House in War Times: Memoirs and Reports of Lincoln's Secretary*, ed. Michael Burlingame (Lincoln: University of Nebraska Press, 2000), 155.

2. John Niven, *Salmon P. Chase: A Biography* (New York: Oxford University Press, 1995), 340–343; Margaret Leech, *Reveille in Washington, 1860–1865* (New York: Harper & Brothers, 1941), 351.

3. Ernest B. Furgurson, *Freedom Rising: Washington in the Civil War* (New York: Alfred A. Knopf, 2004), 53–54, 275; Leech, *Reveille*, 345; William O. Stoddard, *Dispatches from Lincoln's White House: The Anonymous Civil War Journalism of Presidential Secretary William O. Stoddard*, ed. Michael Burlingame (Lincoln: University of Nebraska Press, 2002), 194.

4. CAD to JHW, January 11, 1864, Wilson, *Dana*, 303; CAD to JSP, December 12, 1864, Pike Papers; Ida M. Tarbell, *The Life of Abraham Lincoln* (New York: Lincoln History Society, 1924), 2:80.

5. *OR* I, v. 31, pt. 2, 72; EMS to AL, December 19, 1863, Stanton Papers, LC; Dana, *Recollections*, 181.

6. *OR* I, v. 31, pt. 3, 457–458; *PUSG*, 9:501–502.

7. *OR* I, v. 31, pt. 3, 458.

8. David Homer Bates, *Lincoln in the Telegraph Office: Recollections of the United States Military Telegraph Corps during the Civil War* (New York: Century Company, 1907), 71–75.

9. Welles, *Diary*, 328–329; Bates, *Lincoln in Telegraph Office*, 75, 78; Bates, *The Telegraph Goes to War: The Personal Diary of David Homer Bates, Lincoln's Telegraph Operator*, ed. Donald E. Markle (Hamilton, NY: Edmonston Publishing, Inc., 2003), 49; Bates, "A Rebel Cipher Dispatch," *Harper's Monthly* 97 (June 1898): 109; *NYT*, January 1, 1864; Robin W. Winks, *The Civil War Years: Canada and the United States*, 4th ed. (Montreal and Kingston: McGill-Queen's University Press, 1998), 258–259; Report from Robert Murray, January 5, 1864, Turner-Baker Files, Case 611B, RG 94, NARA.

10. CAD to JHW, January 11, 1864, in Wilson, *Dana*, 303; *PUSG*, 9:650.

11. *OR* III, v. 3, 73–74. On the Freedmen's Commission, see John G. Sproat, "Blueprint for Radical Reconstruction," *Journal of Southern History* 23 (February 1957): 25–44.

12. Ira Berlin, Barbara J. Fields, Thavolia Glymph, Joseph P. Reidy, and Leslie S. Rowland, eds., *Freedom: A Documentary History of Emancipation, 1861–1867, ser. 1, vol. 1, The Destruction of Slavery* (Cambridge, UK: Cambridge University Press, 1985), 3:771; Dana unpublished testimony, Records of the American Freedmen's Inquiry Commission (AFIC), RG 94, NARA.

13. Berlin et al., *Freedom*, ser. I, 3:766–767; John Cimprich, *Slavery's End in Tennessee, 1861–1865* (Tuscaloosa: University of Alabama Press, 1985), 46–80.

14. Berlin et al., *Freedom*, ser. I, 3:766–773, and Dana unpublished testimony, Records of the AFIC, RG 94, NARA. On Howe's racial theories, see Matthew Furrow, "Samuel Gridley Howe, the Black Population of Canada West, and the Racial Ideology of the 'Blueprint for Radical Reconstruction,'" *Journal of American History* 97 (September 2010): 352–366.

15. James M. McPherson, *The Struggle for Equality: Abolitionists and the Negro in the Civil War and Reconstruction* (Princeton, NJ: Princeton University Press, 1964), 187–188; Berlin et al., *Freedom*, ser. I, 3:768.

16. *OR* III, v. 4, 382.

17. Dana unpublished testimony, Records of the AFIC, RG 94, NARA; *PUSG*, 10:15–16; CAD to JHW, January 11, 1864, in Wilson, *Dana*, 301; *OR* I, v. 32, pt. 2, 58.

18. *PUSG*, 10:17.

19. JHW and W. F. Smith to CAD, January 15, 1864, Stanton Papers, LC; *PUSG*, 10:18n, 128, 141.

20. Dana, *Recollections*, 157.

21. *PUSG*, 10:37; Wilson, *Dana*, 311; Henry Wilson to Washburne, July 25, 1863, Washburne Papers, LC.

22. *PUSG*, 10:142; William M. Lamers, *The Edge of Glory: A Biography of General William S. Rosecrans, U.S.A.* (New York: Harcourt, Brace & World, 1961), 413; Dana and Wilson, *Life of Grant*, 411–412.

23. Wilson, *Flag*, 1:346; Dana, unpublished testimony, Records of the AFIC, RG 94, NARA.

24. Brooks D. Simpson, *Ulysses S. Grant: Triumph over Adversity, 1822–1865* (Boston: Houghton Mifflin, 2000), 257; Wilson, *Dana*, 311–312.

25. Henry Wilson to Washburne, July 25, 1863, Washburne Papers, LC; Wilson, *Dana*, 312.

26. Noah Brooks, *Washington, D.C., in Lincoln's Time* (1895; reprint ed. Athens: University of Georgia Press, 1989), 134–136. Benjamin Thomas, *Abraham Lincoln: A Biography* (New York: Alfred A. Knopf, 1952), 417, places Dana at the White House reception and quotes his description of Grant. However, it was Richard H. Dana, Jr., who was present and described the scene in his journal.

27. Noah Brooks, *Sacramento Union*, January 7, 1864, cited in Allan Nevins, *The War for the Union* (New York: Charles Scribner's Sons, 1971), 3:279; Dana interview, December 18, 1896, Tarbell Papers.

28. Frank J. Welcher, *The Union Army: Organization and Operations* (Bloomington: Indiana University Press, 1989–1993), 2:Appendix 1; Dana, unpublished testimony, Records of the AFIC, RG 94, NARA; *OR* III, v. 4, 43–44, 1035; Dana, *Recollections*, 161; Wilson, *Flag*, 1:342.

29. Wilson, *Flag*, 1:342; Dana interview, December 18, 1896, Tarbell Papers; Wilson, *Dana*, 305. For the bulk of Dana's voluminous correspondence, see Records of the Secretary of War, RG 107, NARA.

30. Benjamin P. Thomas and Harold M. Hyman, *Stanton: The Life and Times of Lincoln's Secretary of War* (New York: Alfred A. Knopf, 1962), 162, 267; Henry Wilson, "Edwin M. Stanton," *Atlantic Monthly* 25, no. 148 (February 1870): 240.

31. Wilson, *Flag*, 1:343, 345, 348–350; *PUSG*, 9:489n; CAD to JSP, January 4, 1862, Pike Papers.

32. CAD to JHW, January 11, 1864, in Wilson, *Dana*, 303; *PUSG*, 10:45n.

33. Wilson, *Dana*, 307; Edward G. Longacre, *From Union Stars to Top Hat: A Biography of the Extraordinary General James Harrison Wilson* (Harrisburg, PA: Stackpole Books, 1972), 98.

34. CAD to General John A. Dix, March 30, 1864, CAD to Col. L. C. Baker, April 1, 1864, RG 107; Baker to CAD, April 18, 1864, RG 94, NARA; Wilson, *Dana*, 307–308; Mark R. Wilson, *The Business of Civil War: Military Mobilization and the State, 1861–1865* (Baltimore: Johns Hopkins University Press, 2006), 188–189.

35. Wilson, *Business of Civil War*, 199; Wilson, *Dana*, 307–308; Wilson, *Flag*, 1:330; Longacre, *Union Stars to Top Hat*, 100; Stephen Z. Starr, *The Union Cavalry in the Civil War* (Baton Rouge: Louisiana State University Press, 1979–1985), 2:69; Russell F. Weigley, *Quartermaster General of the Union Army: A Biography of M. C. Meigs* (New York: Columbia University Press, 1959), 295–296.

36. Dana, "Reminiscences," *McClure's Magazine* 10, no.5 (March 1898): 440; Charles V. Spaniolo, "Charles Anderson Dana: His Early Life and Civil War Career" (PhD diss., Michigan State University, 1965), 212–213; CAD to Daniel Goddard, March 26, 1864, CAD to M. L. Galley, March 12, 1864, CAD to Senator J. M. Howard, March 30, 1864, RG 107, NARA.

37. CAD to Gen. J. P. Hawkins, March 2, 3, 1864, CAD to Gov. John Andrew, February 24, 1864, CAD to Gen. George Ramsey, August 12, 1864, RG107, NARA; Wilson, *Flag*, 1:331.

38. Dana, *Recollections*, 161–162.

39. Henry S. Olcott, "The War's Carnival of Fraud," *The Annals of War* (Philadelphia: Times Publishing Co., 1879), 706, 708; John Strausbaugh, *City of Sedition: The History of New York City in the Civil War* (New York: Twelve Books, 2016), 118, 202–203; Wilson, *Business of Civil War*, 176, 180–181.

40. Thomas and Hyman, *Stanton*, 156; CAD to JHW, January 11, 1864, in Wilson, *Dana*, 303; CAD to Gen. George Ramsey, March 28, 1864, RG107, NARA.

41. Dana, *Recollections*, 162; Howard Murphet, *Yankee Beacon of Buddhist Light: The Life of Col. Henry S. Olcott* (Wheaton, IL: Theosophical Publishing House, 1988), 8–17; Stephen Prothero, *The White Buddhist: The Asian Odyssey of Henry Steel Olcott* (Bloomington: Indiana University Press, 1996), 29–35.

42. Edwin C. Fishel, *The Secret War for the Union: The Untold Story of Military Intelligence in the Civil War* (Boston: Houghton Mifflin, 1996), 604n.27; Lafayette C. Baker, *History of the United States Secret Service* (Philadelphia: L. C. Baker, 1867).

43. Fischel, *Secret War*, 27; Carman Cumming, *Devil's Game: The Civil War Intrigues of Charles A. Dunham* (Urbana and Chicago: University of Illinois Press, 2004), 201.

44. Turner-Baker Case Files, RG 94, NARA. For a well-documented case involving a Georgia attorney arrested while carrying funds for a blockade-running operation, see Thomas G. Dyer, *Secret Yankees: The Union Circle in Confederate Atlanta* (Baltimore: Johns Hopkins University Press, 1999), 115–134.

45. Adam Gurowski, *Diary, 1863–'64–'65* (Washington, DC: W. H. & O. H. Morrison, 1866), 276; Olcott, "War's Carnival of Fraud," 715, 723.

46. Thomas and Hyman, *Stanton*, 151; Bruce Tap, *Over Lincoln's Shoulder: The Committee on the Conduct of the War* (Lawrence: University Press of Kansas, 1998), 2.

47. *Report of the Joint Committee on the Conduct of the War at the Second Session, Thirty-Eighth Congress* (Washington: Government Printing Office, 1865), 1: ix–x; 3:69–70.

48. CAD to D. L. Magruder, January 23, 1864, RG 107, NARA; *Report of the Joint Congressional Committee on the Conduct of the War*, 1865, 3:57, 78–79; CAD to EMS, January 27, 1864, in *Congressional Serial Set*, Vol. No. 2603, Session Vol. 6, 50th Cong., 1st session, House Report 1992, 8–9.

49. CAD to Benjamin Wade, February 19, 1864, RG 107, NARA; and *Report of the Joint Congressional Committee on the Conduct of the War*, 1865, 1: xiv–xv. For the eventual resolution of the Parrish claims, see Senate Committee on Claims, 56th Congress, 1st Session, *Senate Report No. 1628* (1900), and 57th Congress, 1st Session, *Senate Report No. 351* (1902); *Parrish v. Macveagh*, 214 U.S. 124 (1909); *McGowan v. Parrish*, 237 U.S. 285 (1915).

50. L. C. Baker to CAD, February 13, 1864, RG 94, NARA; CAD to P. W. Watson, February 15, 1864, RG 107, NARA.

51. Dana, *Recollections*, 162–164; Mark E. Neely, Jr., *The Fate of Liberty: Abraham Lincoln and Civil Liberties* (New York: Oxford University Press, 1991), 98–99.

52. CAD to Col. J. Howard Willets, February 6, 1864, CAD to Dr. Augusta, February 8, 1864, RG 107, NARA; Dr. Augusta to CAD, February 8, 1864, RG 94, NARA; *Congressional Globe*, 38th Congress, 1st Session (1864), 553–555, 784, 816–818; *U.S. Statutes at Large*, XIII, 536–537. For Augusta's career, see Heather M. Butts, "Alexander Thomas Augusta—Physician, Teacher and Human Rights Activist," *Journal of the National Medical Association* 97 (January 2005): 106–109.

53. Berlin et al., *Freedom*, ser. 1, 1:379–381.

54. US War Department, *Accounts for Newspaper Advertising*, May 20, 1864, American Antiquarian Society; CAD to J. M. Spellissy, November 25, 1864, RG 107, NARA.

55. *CR*, September 20, 1865; *NYS*, December 25, 1869; CAD to Manton Marble, November 29, 1864, Marble Papers, LC; Bernard A. Weisberger, *Reporters for the Union* (Boston: Little, Brown & Co., 1953), 254.

56. *NYT*, March 13, 1864; *PUSG*, 10:543–544.

57. CAD to Frederick Collins, March 11, 1864, RG 107, NARA; Dana, *Recollections*, 165–166.

58. Spaniolo, "Charles Anderson Dana," 218.

59. Henry Wilson, "Stanton," 240; Hay quoted in Doris Kearns Goodwin, *Team of Rivals: The Political Genius of Abraham Lincoln* (New York: Simon & Schuster, 2005), 511; Wilson, *Flag*, 1:327, 338, 539; Wilson, *Dana*, 305.

60. *NYS*, December 25, 1869; Dana, *Lincoln and His Cabinet* (Cleveland and New York: De Vinne Press, 1896), 26; CAD to W. P. Hepburn, June 17, 1886, in *Chicago Inter-Ocean*, July 5, 1886.

61. Dana, *Recollections*, 159; Henry Wilson, "Stanton," 240.

62. Wilson, *Flag*, 1:338; EMS to CAD, February 19, 1862, CAD Papers, LC.

63. Dana, *Recollections*, 159–161; Dana interview, December 18, 1896, Tarbell Papers.

64. *NYS*, December 25, 1869; *NYTr*, May 29, 1868.

65. Dana, *Recollections*, 168, 173; Dana interview, December 21, 1896, Tarbell Papers; Dana, "Reminiscences of Lincoln," 373.

66. Dana, *Lincoln and His Cabinet*, 32–33, 35; Dana, *Recollections*, 174, 181.

67. CAD to AL, February 17, 1864, Edwards to EMS, January 29, 1864, with Lincoln endorsement of February 5, CAD to AL, February 19, 1864, AL Papers. Richard Nelson Current, *Lincoln's Loyalists: Union Soldiers from the Confederacy* (Boston: Northeastern University Press, 1992), 54–55, apparently unaware of Dana's response, claims that Lincoln's view prevailed.

68. John A. Hardenbrook to CAD, January 23, 1864, Frederick A. Conkling to CAD, February 15, 1864, AL Papers; Dana, "Reminiscences of Lincoln," 368–369.

69. *CWL*, 7:166, 277.

70. Harry James Carman and Reinhard H. Luthin, *Lincoln and the Patronage* (New York: Columbia University Press, 1943), 245, 264–266; John Niven, *Salmon P. Chase: A Biography* (New York: Oxford University Press, 1995), 345, 351–352; Ernest A. McKay, *The Civil War and New York City* (Syracuse: Syracuse University Press, 1990), 236; CAD to AL, February 25, 1864, AL Papers.

71. Opdyke to Chase, January 15, 1864, *SPCP*, 4:256; Chase to HG, January 14, 1865, Greeley Papers, LC; *SPCP*, 4:284–285.

72. *Frank Leslie's Illustrated Newspaper*, July 18, 1863; William Hartman, "Custom House Patronage under Lincoln," *New-York Historical Society Quarterly* 41 (October 1957): 450.

73. Dana, *Recollections*, 169; Dana interview, December 22, 1896, Tarbell Papers; *NYS*, August 22, 1868; October 23, 1868.

74. Hay, *Diary*, 104; Dana interview, December 22, 1896, Tarbell Papers; CAD to Frederick W. Seward, November 3, 1864, John Fitch to CAD, September 14, 1864, Seward Papers, University of Rochester; *NYS*, October 11, 1872.

75. Dana, *Recollections*, 169; *SPCP*, 1:513–514, 638; CAD to Chase, February 13, 1865, Chase Papers, HSP.

76. Dana, *Recollections*, 170; CAD to JSP, July 10, 1864, Pike Papers.

77. Dana, *Recollections*, 169; Niven, *Chase*, 360–361.

78. Dana, *Lincoln and His Cabinet*, 17; Dana, *Recollections*, 170–171; Henry Wilson, "Stanton," 240; Dana interview, December 22, 1896, Tarbell Papers.

79. Dana, *NYS*, March 1869, quoted in *Portland Morning Oregonian*, March 24, 1869; Dana interview, December 21, 1896, Tarbell Papers; Dana, *Recollections*, 171.

80. Dana, *Recollections*, 171–172.

Chapter 12. "A Hand on Lee's Throat"

1. Dana, *Recollections*, 187.

2. Badeau, *Military History*, 2:369; Dana, *Recollections*, 189–190; JHW to W. F. Smith, February 19, 1864, Wilson Papers, LC.

3. Theodore Lyman, *Meade's Headquarters, 1863–1865: Letters of Colonel Theodore Lyman from Wilderness to Appomattox*, ed. George R. Agassiz (Boston: Atlantic Monthly Press, 1922), 140; *OR* I, v. 36, pt. 3, 43; *PUSG*, 11:155; *OR* I, v. 31, pt. 3, 457–458; JHW to Smith, February 27, 1864, Wilson Papers, LC; Bruce Catton, *Grant Takes Command* (Boston: Little, Brown & Co., 1969), 131–132; Comstock, *Diary*, 260.

4. Dana, *Recollections*, 189–190.

5. *PUSG*, 10:220, 358–359; James H. Wilson Diary, April 26–27, 1864, HSD; Marsena R. Patrick, *Inside Lincoln's Army: The Diary of Marsena Rudolph Patrick, Provost Marshal General, Army of the Potomac*, ed. David S. Sparks (New York: Thomas Yoseloff, 1964), 358.

6. CAD to EMS, July 13, 1863, CAD Papers, LC; CAD to JHW, January 11, 1864, in Wilson, *Dana*, 302–303; Brooks D. Simpson, *Ulysses S. Grant: Triumph over Adversity, 1822–1865* (Boston: Houghton Mifflin, 2000), 278–280; James H. Wilson, *The Life of John A. Rawlins* (New York: Neale Publishing Co., 1916), 193; *NYTr*, January 26, 1884.

7. *PUSG*, 10:273–275; Simpson, *Grant*, 268–272.

8. *PUSG*, 10:240, 335, 370–372; *OR* I, v. 36, pt. 2, 328–329; *OR* I, v. 39, pt. 2, 5.

9. Strong, *Diary*, 3:442; Brooks D. Simpson, "Great Expectations: Ulysses S. Grant, the Northern Press, and the Opening of the Wilderness Campaign," in *The Wilderness Campaign*, ed. Gary W. Gallagher (Chapel Hill: University of North Carolina Press, 1997), 15; *NYTr*, May 7, 1864. Louis M. Starr, *Bohemian Brigade: Civil War Newsmen in Action* (New York: Alfred A. Knopf, 1954), 299–302, sifts the facts from Henry Ebeneser Wing, *When Lincoln Kissed Me: A Story of the Wilderness Campaign* (New York and Cincinnati: Abingdon Press, 1913).

10. Ida M. Tarbell, *The Life of Abraham Lincoln* (New York: Lincoln History Society, 1924), 3:213; Dana, *Recollections*, 188–189; CAD to Thomas Eckert, May 7, 1864, AL Papers; *OR* I, v. 36, pt. 1, 63; Theodore Lyman, *Meade's Army: The Private Notebooks of Lt. Col. Theodore Lyman*, ed. David W. Lowe (Kent, OH: Kent State University Press, 2007), 142.

11. Gaillard Israel Hunt, *Elihu and Cadwallader Washburn: A Chapter in American Biography* (New York: Macmillan, 1925), 214; Wilson, *Dana*, 318; *OR* I, v. 36, pt. 1, 63–64; *PUSG*, 10:405–406.

12. *OR* I, v. 36, pt. 1, 64; Wing, *Lincoln Kissed Me*, 39.

13. Dana, *Recollections*, 193; *OR* I, v. 36, pt. 1, 63.

14. Starr, *Bohemian Brigade*, 307; *OR* III, v. 4, 278; *NYTr*, May 9 and 28, 1864; Crompton Burton, "'No Turning Back': The Official Bulletins of Secretary of War Edwin M. Stanton," in *Words at War: The Civil War and American Journalism*, ed. David B. Sachsman, S. Kittrell Rushing, and Roy Morris, Jr. (West Lafayette, IN: Purdue University Press, 2008), 284–291.

15. *OR* I, v. 36, pt. 1, 64; Dana and Wilson, *Life of Grant*, 185.

16. *OR* I, v. 36, pt. 1, 65–68.

17. Lyman, *Meade's Headquarters*, 111; Dana, *Recollections*, 195–196; Simpson, *Grant*, 310.

18. Catton, *Grant Takes Command*, 228–232; Gordon C. Rhea, *The Battles for Spotsylvania Court House and the Road to Yellow Tavern, May 7–12, 1864* (Baton Rouge: Louisiana State University Press, 1997), 311–312.

19. *OR* I, v. 36, pt. 1, 67; Rhea, *Battles for Spotsylvania*, 167–168; Catton, *Grant Takes Command*, 220–221. Grant used similar descriptors for Warren and Hancock, which suggests that his views influenced Dana's. Grant, *Memoirs*, 554, 559, 701–702.

20. Comstock, *Diary*, 267; Gordon C. Rhea, *To the North Anna River: Grant and Lee, May 13–25, 1864* (Baton Rouge: Louisiana State University Press, 2000), 8–9; Dana, *Recollections*, 196–197.

21. *OR* I, v. 36, pt. 1, 68; Dana, *Recollections*, 190.

22. *OR* I, v. 36, pt. 1, 69; Simpson, "Great Expectations," 26; *OR* I, v. 36, pt. 1, 70.

23. *OR* I, v. 36, pt. 1, 71; Dana, *Recollections*, 199; *PUSG*, 11:19.

24. Grant, Report, in *Memoirs*, 791.

25. *OR* I, v. 36, pt. 1, 73; Meade to Margaret Meade, May 19, 1864, in George Gordon Meade, *The Life and Letters of George Gordon Meade, Major-General United States Army* (New York: Charles Scribner's Sons, 1913), 1:197.

26. *OR* I, v. 36, pt. 1, 74; 36. William A. Frassanito, *Grant and Lee: The Virginia Campaigns, 1864–1865* (New York: Charles Scribner's Sons, 1983), 116–121; Dana interview, December 22, 1896, Tarbell Papers. In the *Harper's Weekly* engraving of this photo, July 9, 1864, Dana is outfitted as an anonymous military officer.

27. Rhea, *To the North Anna River*, 277–278; Dana, *Recollections*, 202–203; *OR* I, v. 36, pt. 1, 75–76.

28. *OR* I, v. 36, pt. 1, 76–78.

29. Theodore Lyman journal, May 24, 1864, MHS; *OR* I, v. 38, pt. 4, 294; Lyman, *Meade's Headquarters*, 126.

30. Simpson, *Grant*, 316–317.

31. *OR* I, v. 36, pt. 1, 77–78; Mark Grimsley, *And Keep Moving On: The Virginia Campaign, May–June 1864* (Lincoln: University of Nebraska Press, 2002), 145.

32. *OR* I, v. 36, pt. 1, 79.

33. *OR* I, v. 36, pt. 1, 80–81.

34. Comstock, *Diary*, 270; Gordon C. Rhea, *Cold Harbor: Grant and Lee, May 26–June 3, 1864* (Baton Rouge: Louisiana State University Press, 2002), 90.

35. *OR* I, v. 36, pt. 1, 81; James H. Wilson Diary, May 16, 1864, HSD; Comstock, *Diary*, 269–270; Catton, *Grant Takes Command*, 250.

36. *OR* I, v. 36, pt. 1, 84–86; Rhea, *Cold Harbor*, 193, 227; Dana, *Recollections*, 191.

37. Gregory Jaynes, *The Killing Ground: Wilderness to Cold Harbor* (Alexandria, VA: Time-Life Books, 1986), 164; Horace Porter, *Campaigning with Grant* (New York: Century Co., 1897), 174–175; Ernest Furgurson, *Not War But Murder: Cold Harbor, 1864* (New York: Alfred A. Knopf, 2000), 134–168; Rhea, *Cold Harbor*, 318–379. Like many previous historians, Furgurson, 278, puts Union losses in the morning assaults at around 7,000, but Rhea (362, 382) revises the figure downward to 4,700. Ethan S. Rafuse, "Wherever Lee Goes . . . : George G. Meade," in *Grant's Lieutenants: From Chattanooga to Appomattox*, ed. Steven E. Woodworth (Lawrence: University Press of Kansas, 2008), 227, n.41, speculates on the impact of the Dana incident on Meade.

38. *OR* I, v. 36, pt. 1, 87–88; *PUSG*, 11:9.

39. Porter, *Campaigning with Grant*, 172; Furgurson, *Not War But Murder*, 239; Meade to Margaret Meade, June 4, 1864, in Meade, *Life and Letters*, 2:200; Smith, quoted in Rhea, *Cold Harbor*, 352.

40. William S. McFeely, *Grant: A Biography* (New York: W. W. Norton, 1981), 171–173; Gordon C. Rhea, *On to Petersburg: Grant and Lee, June 4–15, 1864* (Baton Rouge: Louisiana State University Press, 2017), 114–121, 123; *OR* I, v. 36, pt. 1, 93–94.

41. Patrick, *Inside Lincoln's Army*, 380; Simpson, *Grant*, 327.

42. James H. Wilson Diary, June 4, 10, 19, 1864, HSD; Wilson, *Flag*, 1:439, 443–445; Wilson, *Dana*, 325, 327; Wilson, *Life of Rawlins*, 227–228.

43. Dana, *Recollections*, 209; *NYS*, June 23, 30, 1868. Three decades later Dana's *Recollections* (210–211) reduced the difference to 19,500.

44. Furgurson, *Not War But Murder*, 235; Grant, *Memoirs*, 588.

45. Frassanito, *Grant and Lee*, 178. Two weeks later Brady displayed Dana's photograph next to those of Grant and generals of the Army of the Potomac in his New York gallery. *NYTr*, July 28, 1864.

46. Walter Stahr, *Seward: Lincoln's Indispensable Man* (New York: Simon & Schuster, 2012), 398; *OR* I, v. 36, pt. 1, 65, 86, 92, 96; *PUSG*, 11:431; Furgurson, *Not War But Murder*, 139, 144; Wilson, *Flag*, 1:400.

47. *OR* I, v. 36, pt. 1, 94; *OR* I, v. 36, pt. 3, 722; J. Cutler Andrews, *The North Reports the Civil War* (Pittsburgh: University of Pittsburgh Press, 1955), 546–547. For Dana's defense of Stanton against another outspoken journalist, see Sylvanus Cadwallader, *Three Years with Grant*, ed. Benjamin P. Thomas and Brooks D. Simpson (Lincoln: University of Nebraska Press, 1996), 222–224.

48. Patrick, *Inside Lincoln's Army*, 372, 378, 381–82; James M. McPherson and James K. Hogue, *Ordeal by Fire: The Civil War and Reconstruction*, 4th ed. (Boston: McGraw-Hill, 2009), 491; Porter, *Campaigning with Grant*, 191–192; *OR* I, v. 36, pt. 1, 89–90.

49. *OR* I, v. 36, pt. 1, 89, 91.

50. Porter, *Campaigning with Grant*, 195; *OR* I, v. 36, pt. 1, 96; Charles A. Page, *Letters of a War Correspondent* (Boston: L. C. Page, 1899), 111–112.

51. *OR* I, v. 40, pt. 1, 18–19, 21; Dana, *Recollections*, 219; Rhea, *On to Petersburg*, 240. See Brian Holden Reid, "Another Look at Grant's Crossing of the James, 1864," *Civil War History* 39 (1993): 291–316.

52. Porter, *Campaigning with Grant*, 199; *OR* I, v. 40, pt. 1, 19.

53. *OR* I, v. 40, pt. 1, 20.

54. Comstock, *Diary*, 273; *OR* I, v. 40, pt. 1, 20.

55. *OR* I, v. 40, pt. 1, 21.

56. *OR* I, v. 40, pt. 1, 21; McPherson and Hogue, *Ordeal by Fire*, 459; William F. Smith, *Autobiography of Major General William F. Smith, 1861–1864*, ed. Herbert M. Schiller (Dayton, OH: Morningside House, 1990), 57–58.

57. Grant, *Memoirs*, 600; David M. Jordan, *Winfield Scott Hancock: A Soldier's Life* (Bloomington: Indiana University Press, 1988), 141–146; A. Wilson Greene, *A Campaign of Giants—The Battle for Petersburg* (Chapel Hill: University of North Carolina Press, 2018), 1:112–120; Catton, *Grant Takes Command*, 287; *OR* I, v. 40, pt. 1, 24; Wilson, *Flag*, 1:454.

58. *OR* I, v. 40, pt. 2, 205; Bruce Catton, *A Stillness at Appomattox* (New York: Doubleday & Co., 1953), 198.

59. EMS to CAD, June 19, 1864, Stanton Papers, LC; CAD to EMS, June 20, 1864, RG 107, NARA; *OR* I, v. 40, pt. 1, 24–25; Meade to Margaret Meade, June 21, 1864, in Meade, *Life and Letters*, 205–206; *PUSG*, 11:78.

60. *PUSG*, 11:32n; *OR* I, v. 40, pt. 1, 33–34, 36.

61. Catton, *Grant Takes Command*, 305.

62. Porter, *Campaigning with Grant*, 218–220; *OR* I, v. 40, pt. 1, 27.

63. Porter, *Campaigning with Grant*, 222–223; *NYH*, June 25, 1864; Dana, *Recollections*, 224–225.

64. Hay, *Diary*, 210; *OR* I, v. 40, pt. 1, 28, 36.

65. *NYTr*, June 28, 1864; CAD to JSP, July 10, 1864, Pike Papers; Lee quoted in Ethan S. Rafuse, *Robert E. Lee and the Fall of the Confederacy, 1863–1865* (Lanham, MD: Rowman & Littlefield, 2009), 166.

66. Porter, *Campaigning with Grant*, 83; Carswell McClellan, *The Personal Memoirs and Military History of U.S. Grant Versus the Record of the Army of the Potomac* (Boston: Houghton Mifflin, 1887), 101–120.

67. *PUSG*, 11:27; Lyman, *Meade's Army*, 170; Geoffrey Perret, *Ulysses S. Grant: Soldier and President* (New York: Random House, 1997), 250.

68. *PUSG*, 11:146; Porter, *Campaigning with Grant*, 168; Meade to Margaret Meade, June 12, 1864, in Meade, *Life and Letters*, 203–204; Lyman, *Meade's Army*, 170, 173.

69. EMS to Gen. John A. Dix, in *NYTr*, May 9–June 21, 1864; Cadwallader, *Three Years with Grant*, 209–210; Andrews, *North Reports the Civil War*, 547–548.

70. Badeau, *Military History*, 2:277; Dana and Wilson, *Life of Grant*, 402.

71. David Homer Bates, *Lincoln in the Telegraph Office: Recollections of the United States Military Telegraph Corps during the Civil War* (New York: Century Company, 1907), 42; Hay, *Diary*, 198; *NYTr*, May 14, 1864; Andrews, *North Reports the Civil War*, 544; Benjamin P. Thomas and Harold M. Hyman, *Stanton: The Life and Times of Lincoln's Secretary of War* (New York: Alfred A. Knopf, 1962), 301. There were disappointed outcries from newspaper editors when Stanton's bulletins all but ended after Dana returned from the Virginia front. Burton, "'No Turning Back,'" 291–292.

72. Dana and Wilson, *Life of Grant*, 412–414. Wilson, *Dana*, 385, credits Dana with penning this assessment of Grant.

Chapter 13. "The Deepest Shame That Has Yet Befallen Us"

1. G. W. Drisko of the *Machias* (Maine) *Union*, quoted in Crompton Burton, "'No Turning Back': The Official Bulletins of Secretary of War Edwin M. Stanton," in *Words at War: The Civil War and American Journalism*, ed. David B. Sachsman, S. Kittrell Rushing, and Roy Morris, Jr. (West Lafayette, IN: Purdue University Press, 2008), 289.

2. CAD to JSP, August 8, 1864, Pike Papers; Theodore Lyman, *Meade's Army: The Private Notebooks of Lt. Col. Theodore Lyman*, ed. David W. Lowe (Kent, OH: Kent State University Press, 2007), 235.

3. *PUSG*, 10:382; 11:124–125.

4. *OR* I, v. 40, pt. 1, 28; *PUSG*, 11:124–125. Rosecrans was not relieved until December 1864, after Lincoln was reelected.

5. *OR* I, v. 40, pt. 1, 28; Butler to Smith, June 21, 1864, in *Private and Official Correspondence of Gen. Benjamin F. Butler during the Period of the Civil War* (Norwood, MA: Plimpton Press, 1917), 4:426; Benjamin F. Butler, *Autobiography and Personal Reminiscences of Benjamin F. Butler: Butler's Book* (Boston: A. M. Thayer & Co., 1892), 1085–1086; *OR* I, v. 40, pt. 2, 301; *PUSG*, 11:163.

6. *PUSG*, 11:155–156; Bruce Catton, *Grant Takes Command* (Boston: Little, Brown & Co., 1969), 327. On the Grant-Butler relationship, see Mark Grimsley, "A Lack of Confidence: Benjamin F. Butler," in *Grant's Lieutenants: From Chattanooga to Appomattox*, ed. Steven E. Woodworth (Lawrence: University Press of Kansas, 2008), 105–131.

7. *PUSG*, 11:176; CAD to JHW, July 7, 1864, in Wilson, *Dana*, 334; *OR* I, v. 40, pt. 2, 594; William F. Smith, *From Chattanooga to Petersburg under Generals Grant and Butler* (Boston: Houghton Mifflin, 1893), 175; *OR* I, v. 40, pt. 3, 69; Wilson, *Dana*, 335–336; *PUSG*, 11:205, 252.

8. Smith, *From Chattanooga to Petersburg*, 176; Dana and Wilson, *Life of Grant*, 406; Brooks D. Simpson, *Ulysses S. Grant: Triumph over Adversity, 1822–1865* (Boston: Houghton Mifflin, 2000), 358.

9. *PUSG*, 11:207–209; CAD to JHW, August 29, 1864, and October 10, 1864, in Wilson, *Dana*, 343, 345; JHW to Smith, August 4, 1864, Wilson Papers. L. C. Simpson, *Grant*, 349–350, 358, finds Smith's allegations about Grant's drunkenness lacking in evidence and logic.

10. *PUSG*, 11:210.

11. *OR* I, v. 40, pt. 1, 26, 28; *PUSG*, 11:104–106; Emerson Gifford Taylor, *Gouverneur Kemble Warren: The Life and Letters of an American Soldier, 1830–1882* (Boston: Houghton Mifflin, 1932), 181–182.

12. Stephen Z. Starr, *The Union Cavalry in the Civil War* (Baton Rouge: Louisiana State University Press, 1979–1985), 2:176–207; Edward G. Longacre, *From Union Stars to Top Hat: A Biography of the Extraordinary General James Harrison Wilson* (Harrisburg, PA: Stackpole Books, 1972), 134–144.

13. CAD to JHW, July 2, 1864, in Wilson, *Dana*, 334; *OR* I, v. 40, pt. 2, 632; *OR* I, v. 40, pt. 1, 33–34, 37; Starr, *Union Cavalry*, 2:202; *OR* I, v. 40, pt. 3, 15–16; Wilson, *Flag*, 1:528–530.

14. Comstock, *Diary*, 279; Wilson, *Flag*, 1:530; Dana, *Recollections*, 227–228.

15. *OR* I, v. 40, pt. 1, 35–36; George Gordon Meade, *The Life and Letters of George Gordon Meade, Major-General United States Army* (New York: Charles Scribner's Sons, 1913), 2:212, 215–216.

16. Comstock, *Diary*, 279; Badeau, *Military History*, 2:190; Grant, *Memoirs*, 788. On the Grant-Meade relationship, see Ethan S. Rafuse, "Wherever Lee Goes . . . : George G.

Meade," in *Grant's Lieutenants: From Chattanooga to Appomattox*, ed. Steven E. Woodworth (Lawrence: University Press of Kansas, 2008), 47–83.

17. *PUSG*, 11:253; CAD to JSP, August 8, 1864, Pike Papers; CAD to JHW, November 14, 1864, in Wilson, *Dana*, 348.

18. Benjamin Franklin Cooling, *Jubal Early's Raid on Washington 1864* (Baltimore: Nautical & Aviation Publishing Co. of America, 1989), 22–23, gives various estimates of Early's strength.

19. *OR* I, v. 37, pt. 2, 16, 33; Dana, *Recollections*, 228.

20. *OR* I, v. 37, pt. 2, 134.

21. *PUSG*, 11:203; *OR* I, v. 40, pt. 3, 111; Wilson, *Dana*, 336.

22. CAD to JSP, July 10, 1864, Pike Papers; *PUSG*, 11:210.

23. *OR* I, v. 37, pt. 2, 192–194.

24. *PUSG*, 11:210; Adam Gurowski, *Diary, From November 12, 1862, to October 18, 1863* (New York: Carleton, 1864), 280; Horace Porter, *Campaigning with Grant* (New York: Century Co., 1897), 239.

25. Margaret Leech, *Reveille in Washington, 1860–1865* (New York: Harper & Brothers, 1941), 409; Noah Brooks, *Washington, D.C., in Lincoln's Time* (1895; reprint ed. Athens: University of Georgia Press, 1989), 159; *OR* I, v. 37, pt. 2, 193.

26. Jubal Early, "Early's March," *Battles and Leaders*, 4:497–498; *OR* I, v. 37, pt. 2, 193.

27. *OR* I, v. 37, pt. 2, 223; *PUSG*, 11:228–232.

28. Welles, *Diary*, 442; *PUSG*, 11:228–232; Benjamin P. Thomas and Harold M. Hyman, *Stanton: The Life and Times of Lincoln's Secretary of War* (New York: Alfred A. Knopf, 1962), 321; William Marvel, *Lincoln's Autocrat: The Life of Edwin Stanton* (Chapel Hill: University of North Carolina Press, 2015), 340. On Halleck's drinking and use of opium, see John F. Marszalek, *Commander of All Lincoln's Armies: A Life of General Henry W. Halleck* (Cambridge, MA: Harvard University Press, 2004), 148, 152, 173, 252; John Y. Simon, *The Union Forever: Lincoln, Grant, and the Civil War* (Lexington: University Press of Kentucky, 2012), 86–87.

29. *OR* I, v. 37, pt. 2, 259, 303.

30. *OR* I, v. 37, pt. 2, 223; *PUSG*, 11:244.

31. *OR* I, v. 37, pt. 2, 222–223; *PUSG*, 11:228; Hay, *Diary*, 223.

32. Welles, *Diary*, 449; Simpson, *Grant*, 356; Thomas and Hyman, *Stanton*, 319–320; Comstock, *Diary*, 282; *PUSG*, 11:253.

33. Comstock, *Diary*, 282, 285; *OR* I, v. 37, pt. 2, 332; Edward A. Miller, Jr., *Lincoln's Abolitionist General: The Biography of David Hunter* (Columbia: University of South Carolina Press, 1997), 218–219.

34. *OR* I, v. 37, pt. 2, 332, 427.

35. *PUSG*, 11:253.

36. *PUSG*, 11:253.

37. EMS to CAD, July 8, 1864, Stanton Papers, LC; CAD to JSP, July 10, 1864, Pike Papers; *CWL*, 7:395.

38. Ari Hoogenbloom, *Gustavus Vasa Fox of the Union Navy: A Biography* (Baltimore: Johns Hopkins University Press, 2008), 244–245. For the trip's beginning and end, see *CWL*, 7:470, and *Washington Evening Star*, August 1, 1864.

39. Hoogenbloom, *Gustavus Vasa Fox*, 244–245; *PUSG*, 11:361; Richard Slotkin, *No Quarter: The Battle of the Crater, 1864* (New York: Random House, 2009); A. Wilson Greene, *A Campaign of Giants—The Battle for Petersburg* (Chapel Hill: University of North Carolina Press, 2018), 1:419–516.

40. Frank L. Klement, *The Copperheads in the Middle West* (Chicago: University of Chicago Press, 1960), 233; *CWL*, 7:515.

41. Gurowski, *Diary* (1864), 240; HG to AL, July 7, 1864, AL Papers, LC.

42. William A. Tidwell, *April '65: Confederate Covert Action in the American Civil War* (Kent, OH: Kent State University Press, 1995), 107–159.

43. *OR* I, v. 40, pt. 1, 28; *CWL*, 7:451; John Russell Young, *Men and Memories: Personal Reminiscences* (New York and London: F. Tennyson Neely, 1901), 51.

44. *CWL*, 7:461.

45. CAD to JSP, August 8, 1864, Pike Papers; Dana, *Recollections*, 179–180; *NYS*, July 8, 1891.

46. Harold Holzer, *Lincoln and the Power of the Press* (New York: Simon & Schuster, 2014), 516; Francis Brown, *Raymond of the Times* (New York: W. W. Norton, 1954), 259–260.

47. CAD to Raymond, July 26, 1864, George Jones Papers, NYPL.

48. *CWL*, 7:517–518; John G. Nicolay, *With Lincoln in the White House: Letters, Memoranda, and Other Writings of John G. Nicolay, 1860–1865*, ed. Michael Burlingame (Carbondale: Southern Illinois University Press, 2000), 152–154.

49. *CWL*, 7:500, 518; Brown, *Raymond*, 261.

Chapter 14. "All the Power of the War Department"

1. *CWL*, 8:101. See James A. Rawley, *Turning Points of the Civil War* (Lincoln: University of Nebraska Press, 1989), 171–173, on the stakes of the 1864 election. Jefferson Davis's six-year presidential term avoided such a crisis in the Confederacy.

2. CAD to JSP, July 10, 1864, Pike Papers; EMS to CAD, June 7, 1864, RG 107, NARA.

3. CAD to JSP, August 8, 1864, Pike Papers.

4. CAD to JSP, August 8, 1864, Pike Papers.

5. *NYTr*, August 5, 1863.

6. CAD to JSP, August 8, 1864, Pike Papers; HG to Opdyke, August 18, 1864, quoted in John C. Waugh, *Reelecting Lincoln: The Battle for the 1864 Presidency* (New York: Crown Publishers, 1997), 270; CAD to William O. Bartlett, September 3, 1864, Bartlett Family Papers, Columbia University.

7. CAD to JSP, August 8, 1864, Pike Papers.

8. Waugh, *Reelecting Lincoln*, 265; *CWL*, 7:514.

9. Wilson, *Dana*, 342–343.

10. The platform is reprinted in David E. Long, *The Jewel of Liberty: Abraham Lincoln's Re-Election and the End of Slavery* (Mechanicsburg, PA: Stackpole Books, 1994), 283–284.

11. Charles Carleton Coffin, *Abraham Lincoln* (New York: Harper & Brothers, 1893), 443; Abraham Lincoln, *Recollected Words of Abraham Lincoln*, ed. Don E. Fehrenbacher and Virginia Fehrenbacher (Stanford: Stanford University Press, 1996), 446; *Frank Leslie's Illustrated Newspaper*, November 25, 1865; McClellan to Horatio Seymour and others, September 8, 1864, reprinted in Long, *Jewel of Liberty*, 275–277.

12. *OR* IV, v. 3, 637–638.

13. General Robert Schenck quoted in William Frank Zornow, *Lincoln and the Party Divided* (Norman: University of Oklahoma Press, 1954), 139; *NYTr*, March 10, 1864.

14. *NYTr*, March 10, 1864; *Baltimore Sun*, March 21, 1864. For McClellan's denials, see *The Civil War Papers of George B. McClellan*, ed. Stephen W. Sears (New York: Ticknor & Fields, 1989), 568–570.

15. In July 1861 Dana's *Tribune* had been among the first papers to popularize this nick-

name for the North's Confederate sympathizers. Charles H. Coleman, "The Use of the Term 'Copperhead' during the Civil War," *Mississippi Valley Historical Review* 25 (September 1938): 264.

16. Frank L. Klement, *Dark Lanterns: Secret Political Societies, Conspiracies, and Treason Trials in the Civil War* (Baton Rouge: Louisiana State University Press, 1984), 75; Rosecrans to AL, February 20, 1864, AL Papers; *CWL*, 7:198; Sanderson Journal, March 18, 21, 1864.

17. Rosecrans to James Garfield, March 22, 1864, quoted in Stephen E. Towne, *Surveillance and Spies in the Civil War: Exposing Conspiracies in America's Heartland* (Athens: Ohio University Press, 2015), 184; William M. Lamers, *The Edge of Glory: A Biography of General William S. Rosecrans, U.S.A.* (New York: Harcourt, Brace & World, 1961), 419; John P. Sanderson to AL, March 31, 1864, AL Papers.

18. Sanderson Journal, March 25, 1864.

19. Towne, *Surveillance and Spies*, 184, 221–224, 228–232; *OR* II, v. 8, 228–239.

20. Frank L. Klement, *The Copperheads in the Middle West* (Chicago: University of Chicago Press, 1960), 205. Klement dismisses Copperhead threats, but Jennifer L. Weber, *Copperheads: The Rise and Fall of Lincoln's Opponents in the North* (New York: Oxford University Press, 2006), 148–151, and Towne, *Surveillance and Spies*, judge them substantial and serious.

21. Frank L. Klement, "Phineas C. Wright, the Order of the American Knights, and the Sanderson Exposé," *Civil War History* 18 (March 1972): 15; John A. Marshall, *American Bastille: A History of the Arrests and Imprisonment of American Citizens in the Northern and Border States, On Account of their Political Opinions, During the Late Civil War* (Philadelphia: Thomas W. Hartley, 1881), 227; *CWL*, 8:547; CAD to Gen. S. P. Heintzelman, August 2, 1864, RG 107, NARA.

22. Larry E. Nelson, *Bullets, Ballots, and Rhetoric: Confederate Policy for the United States Presidential Contest of 1864* (Tuscaloosa: University of Alabama Press, 1980), 110–111; Long, *Jewel of Liberty*, 131–152.

23. Rosecrans to AL, June 2, 1864, AL Papers; Lincoln quoted in James M. McPherson, *Battle Cry of Freedom: The Civil War Era* (New York: Oxford University Press, 2005), 591; John G. Nicolay and John Hay, *Abraham Lincoln: A History* (New York: Century Co., 1890), 8:13; *CWL*, 7:386n.

24. Hay, *Diary*, 207; John G. Nicolay, *With Lincoln in the White House: Letters, Memoranda, and Other Writings of John G. Nicolay, 1860–1865*, ed. Michael Burlingame (Carbondale: Southern Illinois University Press, 2000), 149.

25. Klement, *Dark Lanterns*, 88.

26. Klement, *Dark Lanterns*, 82, 86; Hiram Rossman to CAD, October 18, 1864, Holt Papers, LC.

27. CAD to Generals Burbridge, Heintzelman, Dix, Augur, Butler, Washburn, Slocum, and Thomas, August 1 and 5, 1864, RG107, NARA; Towne, *Surveillance and Spies*, 246–275.

28. Holt to EMS, July 29, 1864, Stanton Papers, LC, quoted in Towne, *Surveillance and Spies*, 244. For Holt's biography, see Elizabeth D. Leonard, *Lincoln's Forgotten Ally: Judge Advocate General Joseph Holt of Kentucky* (Chapel Hill: University of North Carolina Press, 2011).

29. L. C. Baker to CAD, September 3, 1864, Holt Papers, LC; *OR* II, v. 7, 930–953. Towne, *Surveillance and Spies*, 282–287, provides an excellent summary.

30. US War Department, *Report of the Judge Advocate General on the "Order of American Knights" or "Sons of Liberty," a Western Conspiracy in Aid of the Southern Rebellion*

(Washington, DC: Chronicle Print, 1864); Klement, *Dark Lanterns*, 145–146; Klement, *Copperheads*, 205; Long, *Jewel of Liberty*, 152.

31. *PUSG*, 12:141–142 and 32:185; Bruce Catton, *Grant Takes Command* (Boston: Little, Brown & Co., 1969), 386–387, 392–393; Grant, *Memoirs*, 635, 663.

32. CAD to JHW, August 29, 1864, in Wilson, *Dana*, 343; William Tecumseh Sherman, *Memoirs of General W. T. Sherman* (1885; New York: Library of America, 1990), 583.

33. Waugh, *Reelecting Lincoln*, 297; Coffin, *Lincoln*, 442, 444.

34. William O. Stoddard, *Inside the White House in War Times: Memoirs and Reports of Lincoln's Secretary*, ed. Michael Burlingame (Lincoln: University of Nebraska Press, 2000), 194; CAD to JHW, September 21, 1864, in Wilson, *Dana*, 344.

35. *PUSG*, 11:242–243; Grant quoted in Philip Sheridan, *Personal Memoirs of P. H. Sheridan* (New York: Charles L. Webster & Company, 1888), 1:465; *PUSG* 12:63–64; *OR* I, v. 43, pt. 1, 30–31; Wilson, *Dana*, 345.

36. *OR* I, v. 17, pt. 2, 261; Wilson, *Dana*, 348.

37. CAD to EMS, October 17, 1864, *OR* I, v. 43, pt. 2, 393.

38. CAD to EMS, October 22, 1864, RG 107, NARA.

39. *NYS*, August 8, 1888; Dana, *Recollections*, 249; Wilson, *Dana*, 348.

40. Zornow, *Lincoln and the Party Divided*, 142–143; *NYTr*, September 27, 1864; Waugh, *Reelecting Lincoln*, 305.

41. CAD to Thomas B. Carroll, April 28, 1887, Dana Miscellaneous Manuscripts, N-YHS; Charles F. Benjamin, "Recollections of Secretary Stanton," *Century Magazine* 33 (March 1887): 763; *Washington Evening Star*, January 1, 1866; Jonathan W. White, *Emancipation, the Union Army, and the Reelection of Abraham Lincoln* (Baton Rouge: Louisiana State University Press, 2014), 120–121; Theodore Lyman, *Meade's Army: The Private Notebooks of Lt. Col. Theodore Lyman*, ed. David W. Lowe (Kent, OH: Kent State University Press, 2007), 248.

42. White, *Emancipation*, 109–110; Long, *Jewel of Liberty*, 217–220; *PUSG*, 12:212–215; *OR* III, v. 4, 751–752.

43. EMS to Meigs, Andrews, Foster, and others, October 4, 1864, RG 107, NARA; Zornow, *Lincoln and the Party Divided*, 204; Benjamin P. Thomas and Harold M. Hyman, *Stanton: The Life and Times of Lincoln's Secretary of War* (New York: Alfred A. Knopf, 1962), 329.

44. Dana's first recounting of this episode was in *NYS*, December 25, 1869. See also *Rocky Mountain News*, September 22, 1889, quoting from *NYS*; Hay, *Diary*, 239–240; David Homer Bates, *Lincoln in the Telegraph Office: Recollections of the United States Military Telegraph Corps during the Civil War* (New York: Century Company, 1907), 277. Dana, *Lincoln and His Cabinet* (Cleveland and New York: De Vinne Press, 1896), 61–63, correctly dated this episode to the October state elections, but Ida Tarbell mistakenly moved it to the November elections in Dana's ghostwritten *Recollections*, 261–262.

45. Hay, *Diary*, 240; Bates, *Lincoln in the Telegraph Office*, 279.

46. Dana, *Recollections*, 261; *PUSG*, 12:458; CAD to Generals Joseph Hooker, C. C. Washburn, J. F. Miller, and John A. Dix, November 5, 1864, James William Eldridge Papers, HL.

47. John G. Nicolay to HG, September 15, 1864, Greeley Papers, LC; Harold Holzer, *Lincoln and the Power of the Press* (New York: Simon & Schuster, 2014), 530; *OR* I, v. 39, pt. 3, 603; *OR* III, v. 4, 871–872.

48. Marshall, *American Bastille*, 561–563; Joseph George, Jr., "The North Affair: A Lincoln Administration Civil War Trial, 1864," *Civil War History* 33 (September 1987): 200; Edward G. Longacre, "The Union Army Occupation of New York City, November 1864," *New York History*

65 (April 1984): 135; *OR* I, v. 42, pt. 3, 435–436, 455, 596; L. C. Baker to CAD, October 29 and November 1, 1864, RG 107, NARA; Marsena Rudolph Patrick, *Inside Lincoln's Army: The Diary of Marsena Rudolph Patrick, Provost Marshal General, Army of the Potomac*, ed. David S. Sparks (New York: Thomas Yoseloff, 1964), 435, 440–441, 464.

49. Scott Sumpter Sheads and Daniel Carroll Toomey, *Baltimore during the Civil War* (Linthicum, MD: Toomey Press, 1997), 75–76; George, Jr., "North Affair," 216; *CR*, September 20, 1865.

50. Bates, *Lincoln in the Telegraph Office*, 295–296; Charles A. Dana, "The War—Some Unpublished History," *North American Review* 153 (August 1891): 242–243; *OR* III, v. 4, 872; CAD to Seward, November 4, 1864, RG 107, NARA; *OR* I, v. 43, pt. 2, 452–453, 463–464.

51. Benjamin F. Butler, *Autobiography and Personal Reminiscences of Benjamin F. Butler: Butler's Book* (Boston: A. M. Thayer & Co., 1892), 671–672; Nat Brandt, *The Man Who Tried to Burn New York* (Syracuse: Syracuse University Press, 1986), 65–102; Oscar A. Kinchen, *Confederate Operations in Canada and the North* (North Quincy, MA: Christopher Publishing House, 1970), 148–161.

52. *OR* I, v. 42, pt. 3, 470; Butler, *Autobiography*, 757–760; Longacre, "Union Army Occupation," 139–142, 145–154; Brandt, *Man Who Tried to Burn New York*, 88–90; Hay, *Diary*, 243.

53. Brandt, *Man Who Tried to Burn New York*, 105–244.

54. Hay, *Diary*, 243–246; *CWL*, 8:96.

55. Zornow, *Lincoln and the Party Divided*, 201; Long, *Jewel of Liberty*, 257–258; White, *Emancipation*, 167–170.

56. Hay, *Diary*, 246; *CWL*, 8:101.

Chapter 15. "Side Politics," Spies, and Swindlers

1. CAD to JHW, November 23, 1864, in Wilson, *Dana*, 348–349.

2. Benjamin P. Thomas and Harold M. Hyman, *Stanton: The Life and Times of Lincoln's Secretary of War* (New York: Alfred A. Knopf, 1962), 336–338.

3. CAD to JSP, December 12, 1864, Pike Papers.

4. CAD to JSP, December 12, 1864, Pike Papers; CAD to JHW, January 24, 1865, in Wilson, *Dana*, 354.

5. CAD to JHW, January 4, 1865, in Wilson, *Dana*, 352; CAD to JSP, December 12, 1864, Pike Papers.

6. Lincoln endorsement, January 5, 1865, RG 107, NARA; *CWL*, 8:575; *NYH*, January 8, 1865; Alexander K. McClure, *Lincoln Yarns and Stories* (New York: Western W. Wilson, 1901), 236–237.

7. *OR* I, v. 42, pt. 2, 52; CAD to Gov. Thomas Fletcher, January 15, 1865, RG 107, NARA; *Boston Daily Advertiser*, January 24, 1865; William Marvel, *Lincoln's Autocrat: The Life of Edwin Stanton* (Chapel Hill: University of North Carolina Press, 2015), 319.

8. *PUSG*, 13:501.

9. *SPCP*, 1:517; Auguste Laugel, *The United States during the Civil War*, ed. Allan Nevins (Bloomington: Indiana University Press, 1961), 316; CAD to Capt. J. C. Lee, February 11, 1865, RG 107, NARA.

10. *NYH*, January 1, 1865; Dana, *Lincoln and His Cabinet* (Cleveland and New York: De Vinne Press, 1896), 42; *Chicago Tribune*, July 18, 1917.

11. CAD to JHW, January 4, 1865, in Wilson, *Dana*, 352; Dana, *Lincoln and His Cabinet*, 54–56.

12. *CWL*, 8:149, 254.

13. Dana, *Lincoln and His Cabinet*, 52.

14. Michael Vorenberg, *Final Freedom: The Civil War, the Abolition of Slavery, and the Thirteenth Amendment* (Cambridge, UK: Cambridge University Press, 2001), 180–185; LaWanda Cox and John H. Cox, *Politics, Principle, and Prejudice, 1865–1866: Dilemma of Reconstruction America* (New York: Free Press, 1963), 6–17. The Seward lobby was a focal point of the 2012 dramatic film "Lincoln," which centered on the amendment's passage.

15. Vorenberg, *Final Freedom*, 199; Dana, *Lincoln and His Cabinet*, 52–58; Dana, *Recollections*, 176.

16. Compare Dana, *Lincoln and His Cabinet*, 53, and Tarbell's version in Dana, *Recollections*, 175–177. Earl S. Pomeroy, "Lincoln, the Thirteenth Amendment, and the Admission of Nevada," *Pacific Historical Review* 12 (1943): 362–368, helps straighten out the confusion.

17. Leonard L. Richards, *Who Freed the Slaves? The Fight over the Thirteenth Amendment* (Chicago: University of Chicago Press, 2015), 205–206; Vorenberg, *Final Freedom*, 199; Dana, *Lincoln and His Cabinet*, 57; Christian G. Samito, *Lincoln and the Thirteenth Amendment* (Carbondale: Southern Illinois University Press, 2015), 95–98. For Hugh Herrick's Republican service in New York, see *NYT*, December, 18, 1861.

18. *AJP*, 8:32; Herrick to Seward, August 8, 1865, Seward Papers, University of Rochester; Dana, *Lincoln and His Cabinet*, 585–589; *AJP*, 7:648. In the *Daily National Intelligencer*, August 1, 1867, Johnson insisted that Hugh Herrick got the appointment, but Anson Herrick corrected him.

19. Richards, *Who Freed the Slaves?*, 181–182; Cox and Cox, *Politics, Principle, and Prejudice*, 29, 69; *NYT*, June 14, 1866.

20. Vorenberg, *Final Freedom*, 199–201; William Gillette, *Jersey Blue: Civil War Politics in New Jersey, 1864–1865* (New Brunswick, NJ: Rutgers University Press, 1995), 300–301. It is also possible that Dana lobbied fellow Harvard alumnus John Ganson of Buffalo, another lame-duck Democrat who switched his vote in January 1865.

21. Noah Brooks, *Washington, D.C., in Lincoln's Time* (1895; reprint ed. Athens: University of Georgia Press, 1989), 185–187; *Congressional Globe*, quoted in James M. McPherson and James K. Hogue, *Ordeal by Fire: The Civil War and Reconstruction*, 4th ed. (Boston: McGraw-Hill, 2009), 467.

22. James M. Scovel, "Thaddeus Stevens," *Lippincott's Monthly Magazine* (April 1898): 550; Dana, *Lincoln and His Cabinet*, 58.

23. Cox and Cox, *Politics, Principle, and Prejudice*, 30; *CWL*, 8:254.

24. Frank Abial Flower, *Edwin McMasters Stanton: The Autocrat of Rebellion, Emancipation, and Reconstruction* (Akron, OH: Saalfield Publishing Co., 1905), 190.

25. CAD to JSP, December 12, 1864, Pike Papers.

26. Ludwell H. Johnson, "Contraband Trade during the Last Year of the Civil War," *Mississippi Valley Historical Review* 49 (1963): 636–638; *CWL*, 8:20–22.

27. *CWL*, 8:163–164; David G. Surdam, "Traders or Traitors: Northern Cotton Trading during the Civil War," *Business and Economic History* 28 (1999): 303–304; Johnson, "Contraband Trade," 640.

28. US House of Representatives, *Trade with Rebellious States*, House Report No. 24, 38th Congress, 2nd session (Washington, DC, 1864–1865), 2; Surdam, "Traders or Traitors," 304–308; Ludwell H. Johnson, "Northern Profit and Profiteers: The Cotton Rings of 1864–65,"

Civil War History 12 (1966): 102–114. For the Thomas, Jr., case, see *OR* I, v. 36, pt. 1, 96; Brian C. Melton, *Sherman's Forgotten General: Henry W. Slocum* (Columbia: University of Missouri Press, 2007), 164–165; and *OR* I, v. 39, pt. 2, 189–194.

29. Johnson, "Northern Profit," 101; Johnson, "Contraband Trade," 642–643; Benjamin F. Butler, *Private and Official Correspondence of Gen. Benjamin F. Butler during the Period of the Civil War* (Norwood, MA: Plimpton Press, 1917), 3:428–434; CAD to Gen. E.R.S. Canby, February 16, 1865, Charles Henry Ray Papers, HL.

30. Johnson, "Northern Profit," 111; *PUSG*, 13:508; Baker to CAD, January 20, 1865, Washburne Papers, LC; Baker to USG, January 22, 1865, George H. Gordon Papers, MHS; *OR* I, v. 46, pt. 2, 144–145. An additional case was the Union navy's capture of the steamer *Philadelphia*, which had left Norfolk loaded with salt, sugar, boots, and shoes bound for Lee's men. See Johnson, "Contraband Trade," 650; *OR Navies* I, v. 11, 410, 422–423.

31. Bruce Catton, *Grant Takes Command* (Boston: Little, Brown & Co., 1969), 403; Baker to CAD, January 20, 1865, Washburne Papers, LC; *PUSG*, 13:223; Butler, *Private and Official Correspondence*, 5:504.

32. *OR* I, v. 46, pt. 2, 144–145.

33. Butler, *Private and Official Correspondence*, 563–565.

34. Johnson, "Contraband Trade," 641. See also L. C. Baker to CAD, January 20, 1865, Turner-Baker Files, RG 94, NARA.

35. *PUSG*, 13:509; draft report in Gordon papers, MHS; Butler, *Private and Official Correspondence*, 5:593, 633; telegram exchange of April 11, 1865, between Gordon and Lincoln, Gordon Papers, MHS. When Gordon was reassigned in June 1865 the prisoners were released and all charges dismissed. See *PUSG*, 13:511; Gen. O. C. Ord to Gordon, June 7, 1865, Gordon Papers, MHS.

36. *PUSG*, 14:113, 114, 119; Abraham Lincoln, *Recollected Words of Abraham Lincoln*, ed. Don E. Fehrenbacher and Virginia Fehrenbacher (Stanford: Stanford University Press, 1996), 16.

37. Johnson, "Northern Profit," 92; US House, *Trade with Rebellious States*, 93, 101.

38. Baker to CAD, October 25, 1864, Turner-Baker Files, RG 94, NARA; US House, *Trade with Rebellious States*, 102, 187–194. Baker apparently played his role straight in this episode, but in early 1866 he was dismissed from the War Department amid unrelated charges of extortion. See Stephen E. Towne, *Surveillance and Spies in the Civil War: Exposing Conspiracies in America's Heartland* (Athens: Ohio University Press, 2015), 401, n. 125.

39. US House, *Trade with Rebellious States*, 192–193.

40. US House, *Trade with Rebellious States*, 2, 4; Ward Hill Lamon, *Recollections of Lincoln, 1847–1865*, ed. Dorothy Lamon Teillard (Lincoln: University of Nebraska Press, 1994), 185; *PUSG*, 14:132.

41. Rhodes, quoted in McPherson and Hogue, *Ordeal by Fire*, 416; CAD to JSP, May 10, 1865, Pike Papers.

42. Letter from Secretary of War (1890), in *Congressional Serial Set*, Vol. No. 2686, Session Vol. 9, S. Exec. Doc. 101, 100.

43. Transcript of Rossman interview with State Department, September 1864, Rossman to Whom It May Concern, September 29, 1864, Rossman to CAD, October 13, November 17, 30, December 7, 1864, Holt Papers, LC.

44. Boyd to EMS, February 14, 1865, Turner-Baker files, RG 94, NARA; Leonard F. Guttridge and Ray A. Neff, *Dark Union: The Secret Web of Profiteers, Politicians, and Booth Conspirators That Led to Lincoln's Death* (Hoboken, NJ: John Wiley & Sons, 2003), 94–97,

122–123, 257n. Guttridge and Neff make the far-fetched claim that Boyd joined John Wilkes Booth's escape after Lincoln's assassination and was killed in his place.

45. Edwin C. Fishel, *The Secret War for the Union: The Untold Story of Military Intelligence in the Civil War* (Boston: Houghton Mifflin, 1996), 187, 192, 204; Joseph George, Jr., "The Conspiracy Trial's 'Suppressed Testimony': An Attempt to Implicate Jefferson Davis in Lincoln's Assassination," *Lincoln Herald* 111 (June 2009): 100; Montgomery to Gen. Irwin McDowell, October 29, 1862, Secret Service files, RG 110, NARA.

46. Montgomery file, Secret Service records, RG 110, NARA; Charles Dana, "The War—Some Unpublished History," *North American Review* 153 (August 1891): 240–241; David Homer Bates, *Lincoln in the Telegraph Office: Recollections of the United States Military Telegraph Corps during the Civil War* (New York: Century Company, 1907), 79; Bates, *The Telegraph Goes to War: The Personal Diary of David Homer Bates, Lincoln's Telegraph Operator*, ed. Donald E. Markle (Hamilton, NY: Edmonston Publishing, Inc., 2003), 158. Dana's interviews with Ida Tarbell confirm that the unnamed spy in his published story was Montgomery.

47. Bates, *Lincoln in the Telegraph Office*, 79, 295; Fishel, *Secret War*, 187.

48. *OR* I, v. 43, pt. 2, 914–917. In fact, Thompson had not been informed of the raid until after it occurred; see *OR* I, v. 43, pt. 2, 934.

49. Dana, "Reminiscences of Abraham Lincoln," in *Reminiscences of Abraham Lincoln, by Distinguished Men of His Time*, 5th edition, ed. Allen Thorndike Rice (New York: North American Review, 1888), 373–375; Dana, "The War," 243–245; Bates, *Lincoln in the Telegraph Office*, 80–82; Carman Cumming, *Devil's Game: The Civil War Intrigues of Charles A. Dunham* (Urbana: University of Illinois Press, 2004), 276, n. 31; George, Jr., "Conspiracy Trial," 101–102.

50. Dana, "The War," 242; Bates, *Lincoln in the Telegraph Office*, 299–304. Oscar A. Kinchen, *Confederate Operations in Canada and the North* (North Quincy, MA: Christopher Publishing House, 1970), 157, writes that it is "well known" that Montgomery tipped federal authorities about the election day plot, but Nat Brandt, *The Man Who Tried to Burn New York* (Syracuse: Syracuse University Press, 1986), 90–91, notes that several sources gave warnings. John Boyko, *Blood and Daring: How Canada Fought the American Civil War and Forged a Nation* (Toronto: Alfred A. Knopf Canada, 2013), 188, names Godfrey Hyams as the double agent who betrayed the New York City sabotage mission.

51. Cumming, *Devil's Game*, 138; *PUSG*, 14:471; Montgomery file, Secret Service Records, RG 110, NARA; Dana, "The War," 245.

52. *Frank Leslie's Illustrated Newspaper*, September 17, 1864; Dana endorsement, December 12, 1864, reprinted in *Congressional Serial Set*, Vol. No. 3346, Session Vol. 2, House Report 1957, 22; *PUSG*, 15:37. The captured Confederate, Captain John B. Castleman, was released after the war and exiled to Canada. See *PUSG*, 15:39; and *AJP*, 8:196. For other Confederate plots around the time of the St. Albans raid, see Kinchen, *Confederate Operations in Canada and the North*, 104–147; Boyko, *Blood and Daring*, 189–193; and James D. Horan, *Confederate Agent: A Discovery in History* (New York: Crown Publishers, 1954), 226–228.

53. Horan, *Confederate Agent*, 113–116, 118–20, 224–229; Robin W. Winks, *The Civil War Years: Canada and the United States*, 4th ed. (Montreal and Kingston: McGill-Queen's University Press, 1998), 284–286; Alan Axelrod, *The War Between the Spies: A History of Espionage during the American Civil War* (New York: Atlantic Monthly Press, 1992), 233–235.

54. *FRUS 1864*, 360, 812–813; Frank L. Owsley, *King Cotton Diplomacy: Foreign Relations of the Confederate States of America* (Tuscaloosa: University of Alabama Press, 2008), 536–537; *FRUS 1865*, pt. 1, 253, 296–297; *OR* (Navy) II, v. 3, 1265–1270; *PUSG*, 14:166–168.

55. *OR* I, v. 43, pt. 2, 935; *OR* III, v. 4, 1064–1068; CAD to General Dix, February 1, 1865, RG 107, NARA.

56. Adam Gurowski, *Diary, 1863–'64–'65* (Washington, DC: W. H. & O. H. Morrison, 1866), 378; Charles Benjamin quoted in Marvel, *Lincoln's Autocrat*, 159; Worthington Chauncey Ford, ed., *A Cycle of Adams Letters, 1861–1865* (Boston and New York: Houghton Mifflin, 1920), 2:186.

57. CAD to Sumner, September 5, 1864; CAD to D. W. Gooch, September 5 and October 15, 1864, RG 107, NARA; www.commandersmansion.com/history.html.

58. *PUSG*, 18:457; AL to CAD, October 8, 1864, RG 249, NARA, reproduced in the Papers of Abraham Lincoln Digital Library (papersofabrahamlincoln.org); Thurlow Weed to AL, November 5, 1864, AL Papers; Maggie K. Ryan to AL, September 28, 1864, with endorsements by Lincoln and Dana, AL Papers; John Hay memorandum and AL to CAD, August 4, 1864, in *CWL*, 7:479.

59. Memorandum of Joshua F. Speed, December 6, 1866, reprinted in William H. Herndon, *Herndon's Life of Lincoln*, ed. Paul M. Angle (Cleveland: World Publishing Co., 1942), 423–424. Speed mistakenly called Charles Dana "General Dana," but the reference is clear.

60. Wallace to CAD, November 15, 1864, Robert A. Gray to AL, December 8, 1864, AL Papers; Dana, *Recollections*, 183–184.

61. *OR* II, v. 7, 457, 925, 1195, 1207; *OR* II, v. 8, 31, 146, 257, 485, 575, 580; Edward Pollard, *Observations in the North: Eight Months in Prison and on Parole* (Richmond: E. W. Ayres, 1865), 129–130; *NYT*, July 28, 1865; *CR*, August 18, 1865; *NYTr*, September 15, 1865; *NYS*, August 29, 1868.

62. Dana, *Recollections*, 235; Henry Olcott to CAD, February 14 and 18, 1865; CAD to Olcott, February 16 and 20, 1865, Turner-Baker Files, RG 94, NARA.

63. Mark E. Neely, Jr., *The Fate of Liberty: Abraham Lincoln and Civil Liberties* (New York: Oxford University Press, 1991), 95–96; Lafayette C. Baker, *History of the United States Secret Service* (Philadelphia: L. C. Baker, 1867), 398–399; CAD to EMS, March 13, 1865, James H. Wilson Papers, LC.

64. Neely, *Fate of Liberty*, 95–98. Eitel later sued Wakeman for charging him $3,500 for his services. *NYTr*, April 28, 1869.

65. Dana, *Recollections*, 235; CAD to John A. Bingham, July 25, 1864, RG 107, NARA; *OR* I, v. 48, pt. 2, 395–397, 609.

66. *PUSG*, 11:85–86; Robert Wilson, *Matthew Brady: Portraits of a Nation* (New York: Bloomsbury, 2013), 199–203.

67. Dana, *Recollections*, 237–238; *NYS*, December 25, 1869; Neely, *Fate of Liberty*, 100.

68. Neely, *Fate of Liberty*, 100–102; *CWL*, 8:251, 303.

69. John Joliffe to AL, November 3, 1864, AL Papers; Marvel, *Lincoln's Autocrat*, 267.

70. *PUSG*, 12:205n; Walter Stahr, *Seward: Lincoln's Indispensable Man* (New York: Simon & Schuster, 2012), 410; *NYH*, September 29, 1864.

71. Edward P. Mitchell, "Mr. Dana of 'The Sun,'" *McClure's Magazine* 3 (October 1894): 382–383; *OR* I, v. 39, pt. 3, 727; *PUSG*, 12:403–404, 410–411.

72. Dana, *Recollections*, 252; Mitchell, "Mr. Dana of 'The Sun,'" 387.

73. *PUSG*, 13:56, 401; *OR* I, v. 42, pt. 3, 641.

74. *OR* I, v. 42, 708, 775; Horace Porter to CAD, January 17, 1865, Stanton Papers, LC; E. H. House to CAD, January 17, 1865, Eckert Papers, HL; *Washington Evening Star*, January 17, 1865. The scene in the 2012 movie "Lincoln," in which the president and Stanton hold hands in the War Department telegraph office while anxiously awaiting news from Fort Fisher, is fictitious.

75. *PUSG*, 13:124.

76. Wilson, *Dana*, 350–351.

77. Wilson, *Dana*, 351–353; James Pickett Jones, *Yankee Blitzkrieg: Wilson's Raid through Alabama and Georgia* (Athens: University of Georgia Press, 1976).

78. *OR* I, v. 47, pt. 2, 214–247, 275; *OR* I, v. 46, pt. 2, 167, 175; Thomas Weber, *The Northern Railroads in the Civil War, 1861–1865* (New York: King's Crown Press of Columbia University Press, 1952), 212–214; Earl J. Hess, *Civil War Logistics: A Study of Military Transportation* (Baton Rouge: Louisiana State University Press, 2017).

Chapter 16. "The Rebellion Finished"

1. *CWL*, 8:332–333; Ronald C. White, Jr., *Lincoln's Greatest Speech: The Second Inaugural* (New York: Simon & Schuster, 2002), 39–42.

2. *Washington Evening Star*, March 4, 1865; *NYS*, August 2, 1875.

3. Benjamin P. Thomas and Harold M. Hyman, *Stanton: The Life and Times of Lincoln's Secretary of War* (New York: Alfred A. Knopf, 1962), 350; William S. McFeely, *Grant: A Biography* (New York: W. W. Norton, 1981), 212–213; *CWL*, 8:377.

4. Thomas and Hyman, *Stanton*, 351; *CWL*, 8:384–385.

5. Walter Stahr, *Seward: Lincoln's Indispensable Man* (New York: Simon & Schuster, 2012), 429–430; Ernest B. Furgurson, *Freedom Rising: Washington in the Civil War* (New York: Alfred A. Knopf, 2004), 367; Emmet Crozier, *Yankee Reporters, 1861–65* (New York: Oxford University Press, 1956), 414–415.

6. Stanton quoted in Thomas and Hyman, *Stanton*, 355; Dana, *Recollections*, 263.

7. Dana, *Recollections*, 263–264; Marsena Rudolph Patrick, *Inside Lincoln's Army: The Diary of Marsena Rudolph Patrick, Provost Marshal General, Army of the Potomac*, ed. David S. Sparks (New York: Thomas Yoseloff, 1964), 488; *NYTr*, April 10, 1865; *OR* I, v. 46, pt. 3, 574.

8. David Donald, *Lincoln* (New York: Simon & Schuster, 1995), 578.

9. *OR* I, v. 46, pt. 3, 574–575, 594; Patrick, *Inside Lincoln's Army*, 488; Marquis Adolphe de Chambrun, *Impressions of Lincoln and the Civil War: A Foreigner's Account* (New York: Random House, 1952), 74.

10. Dana, *Recollections*, 265; CAD to EMS, April 6, 1865, Stanton Papers, LC; *OR* I, v. 46, pt. 3, 593, 659, 698, 944, 1132, 1158; Edward H. Ripley, "Final Scenes at the Capture and Occupation of Richmond, April 3, 1865," in *Personal Recollections of the War of the Rebellion*, 3rd ser., Military Order of the Loyal Legion of the US, New York Commandery (New York: G. P. Putnam's Sons, 1907), 491. Inventories of records sent are in Cutts to CAD, May 2, 3, 4, 5, 10, 12, 13, 15, and 20, 1865, RG 109, NARA. For Lieber's work at the Archive Office, see Dallas D. Irvine, "The Archive Office of the War Department: Repository of Captured Confederate Archives, 1865–1881," *Military Affairs*, 10 (Spring 1946): 93–111; and Carl L. Lokke, "The Captured Confederate Archives under Francis Lieber," *American Archivist* 9 (October 1946): 277–319.

11. *OR* I, v. 46, pt. 3, 594, 1132, 1152. For captured Confederate documents in the published *Official Records*, see *OR* I, vols. 43, 46, 51; *OR* IV, vols. 2 and 3; Yael A. Sternhell, "The Afterlives of a Confederate Archive: Civil War Documents and the Making of Sectional Reconciliation," *Journal of American History* 102 (March 2016): 1025–1050.

12. *OR* I, v. 46, pt. 3, 1295–1296; Dana, *Recollections*, 280; David Homer Bates, *Lincoln in the Telegraph Office: Recollections of the United States Military Telegraph Corps during the Civil War* (New York: Century Company, 1907), 76, 83–84, 283 (see 77 for a facsimile of the

first cipher). For an explanation of the alphabet square, see David Homer Bates, *The Telegraph Goes to War: The Personal Diary of David Homer Bates, Lincoln's Telegraph Operator*, ed. Donald E. Markle (Hamilton, NY: Edmonston Publishing, Inc., 2003), 232–233.

13. *OR* I, v. 46, pt. 3, 575, 594.

14. Dana, *Recollections*, 266; *OR* I, v. 46, pt. 3, 619, 658.

15. *OR* I, v. 46, pt. 3, 573.

16. *OR* I, v. 46, pt. 3, 619, 677; Godfrey Weitzel, *Richmond Occupied: Entry of the United States Forces into Richmond, Va., April 3, 1865*, ed. Louis H. Manarin (Richmond, VA: Civil War Centennial Committee, 1965), 62.

17. *OR* I, v. 46, pt. 3, 684, 678.

18. *OR* I, v. 46, pt. 3, 684, 697, 712.

19. *OR* I, v. 46, pt. 3, 575, 711, 712, 724.

20. Donald, *Lincoln*, 579; *CWL*, 8:386–387, 389; *OR* I, v. 46, pt. 3, 593.

21. *OR* I, v. 46, pt. 3, 655, 657; Nelson Lankford, *Richmond Burning: The Last Days of the Confederate Capital* (New York: Viking Penguin, 2002), 206. Shepley later claimed he had advised Weitzel against the "madness" of allowing the Virginia legislature to convene. George F. Shepley, "Incidents of the Capture of Richmond," *Atlantic Monthly* 46 (July 1880): 27; Weitzel, *Richmond Occupied*, 58.

22. *AJP*, 7:545; Furgurson, *Freedom Rising*, 367; Dana, *Recollections*, 269–270.

23. Donald, *Lincoln*, 589; Thomas and Hyman, *Stanton*, 354; Walter Stahr, *Stanton: Lincoln's War Secretary* (New York: Simon & Schuster, 2017), 411.

24. *OR* I, v. 46, pt. 3, 619; Russell F. Weigley, *A Great Civil War: A Military and Political History, 1861–1865* (Bloomington: Indiana University Press, 2004), 444–445; Welles, *Diary*, 622; Stahr, *Stanton*, 413.

25. *CWL*, 8:406–407.

26. Wilson, *Dana*, 357; *OR* I, v. 46, pt. 3, 683–684.

27. *OR* I, v. 46, pt. 3, 716; Wilson, *Dana*, 373.

28. *OR* I, v. 46, pt. 3, 717–718, 728; John F. Marszalek, *Commander of All Lincoln's Armies: A Life of General Henry W. Halleck* (Cambridge, MA: Harvard University Press, 2004), 227; Patrick, *Inside Lincoln's Army*, 494; Julia Dent Grant, *The Personal Memoirs of Julia Dent Grant*, ed. John Y. Simon (New York: G. P. Putnam's Sons, 1975), 153.

29. Michael W. Kauffman, *American Brutus: John Wilkes Booth and the Lincoln Conspiracies* (New York: Random House, 2004), 214–215; *NYS*, March 14, 1870; Dana, *Recollections*, 273–274.

30. Dana, *Recollections*, 275.

31. Mark A. Plummer, "The Last Hours of Lincoln: The Haynie Diary," *Journal of Illinois History* 4 (Spring 2001): 36; Dana, *Recollections*, 275; W. Emerson Reck, *A. Lincoln: His Last 24 Hours* (Columbia: University of South Carolina Press, 1994), 141.

32. *OR* I, v. 46, pt. 3, 756–757, 780–781; Dana, *Recollections*, 275.

33. Dana, *Recollections*, 275; Lafayette C. Baker, *History of the United States Secret Service* (Philadelphia: L. C. Baker, 1867), 525; *OR* II, v. 8, 493; James D. Horan, *Confederate Agent: A Discovery in History* (New York: Crown Publishers, 1954), 264, 270.

34. Dana, *Recollections*, 276; *OR* I, v. 46, pt. 3, 782; EMS to C. F. Adams, April 15, 1865, RG, NARA 107 (the copy in Stanton Papers, LC, transmitted to the telegraphers is in Dana's hand.)

35. Elizabeth D. Leonard, *Lincoln's Avengers: Justice, Revenge, and Reunion after the Civil War* (New York and London: W. W. Norton, 2004), 88; *Washington National Republican*, July

31, 1866; Louis J. Weichmann, *A True History of the Assassination of Abraham Lincoln and of the Conspiracy of 1865*, ed. Floyd E. Risvold (New York: Alfred A. Knopf, 1975), 219–221.

36. *Washington National Republican*, July 31, 1866; Roy Z. Chamlee, Jr., *Lincoln's Assassins: A Complete Account of Their Capture, Trial, and Punishment* (Jefferson, NC: McFarland, 1990), 72–76; Edward Steers, Jr., *Blood on the Moon: The Assassination of Abraham Lincoln* (Lexington: University Press of Kentucky, 2001), 173–174; Andrew C. A. Jampoler, *The Last Lincoln Conspirator: John Surratt's Flight from the Gallows* (Annapolis, MD: Naval Institute Press, 2008), 45–49, 200–206.

37. CAD to James McPhail, *Congressional Serial Set*, Vol. 1626, Session Vol. 4, House Report 742, 2; *OR* I, v. 46, pt. 3, 806, 821.

38. Bates, *Lincoln in the Telegraph Office*, 379–386; Edward Steers, Jr., and Harold Holzer, *The Lincoln Assassination Conspirators: Their Confinement and Execution, as Recorded in the Letterbook of John Frederick Hartranft* (Baton Rouge: Louisiana State University Press, 2009), 72–75, 84, 106, 114, 125, 142–144; Chamlee, *Lincoln's Assassins*, 90, 329.

39. William A. Tidwell, "April 15, 1865," *Civil War History* 42 (Spring 1996): 226–228; James L. Swanson, *Manhunt: The Twelve-Day Chase for Lincoln's Killer* (New York: Harper-Collins, 2006), 186, 208–212, 234–239; Benn Pitman, ed., *The Assassination of President Lincoln and the Trial of the Conspirators* (New York: Moore, Wilstach & Baldwin, 1865), 88.

40. Swanson, *Manhunt*, 355, 381; CAD to Gen. C. C. Augur, April 22, 1865, RG 107, NARA; William C. Edwards and Edward Steers, Jr., *The Lincoln Assassination: The Evidence* (Urbana and Chicago: University of Illinois Press, 2009), 530–531, 73.

41. *NYH*, April 20, 1865; *NYT*, April 20, 1865; Charles A. Dana, *Lincoln and His Cabinet* (Cleveland and New York: De Vinne Press, 1896), 60, 65.

42. James L. Swanson, *Bloody Crimes: The Funeral of Abraham Lincoln and the Chase for Jefferson Davis* (New York: HarperCollins, 2010), 201–203.

43. Swanson, *Bloody Crimes*, 234–241; *OR* I, v. 46, pt. 3, 952, 965–967; Steers, *Blood on the Moon*, 283.

44. Victor Searcher, *The Farewell to Lincoln* (New York and Nashville: Abingdon Press, 1965), 138–140; Philip Foner, *History of Black Americans* (Westport, CT: Greenwood Press, 1983), 3:449–450; *NYT*, April 25, 1865.

45. Steers, *Blood on the Moon*, 273; Dana, *Recollections*, 276–279; Edwards and Steers, *Lincoln Assassination*, 439–440.

46. Dana, *Recollections*, 280–281; Edwards and Steers, *Lincoln Assassination*, 1011; Kaufmann, *American Brutus*, 66–67.

47. Thomas Reed Turner, *Beware the People Weeping: Public Opinion and the Assassination of Abraham Lincoln* (Baton Rouge: Louisiana State University Press, 1982), 46–48, 61–62, 125; William Hanchett, *The Lincoln Murder Conspiracies* (Urbana and Chicago: University of Illinois Press, 1983), 62–63; Leonard, *Lincoln's Avengers*.

48. Lieber quoted in Sternhell, "Afterlives," 1032; Dana, *Recollections*, 281–282; *OR* II, v. 8, 977. For some of Dana's inquiries, see Edwards and Steers, *Lincoln Assassination*, 102–103, 577, 1063–1064.

49. CAD to Gen. N. Jeffries, April 22, 1865, Andrew Johnson Papers, LC; Testimony of John H. Patten, Holt Papers, LC; Carman Cumming, *Devil's Game: The Civil War Intrigues of Charles A. Dunham* (Urbana and Chicago: University of Illinois Press, 2004), 163, 188; *OR* II, v. 8, 937–938; Richard C. Marsh, "The Military Trial of Gazaway Bugg Lamar," *Georgia Historical Quarterly* 85 (Winter 2001): 560–561. For Lamar's lawsuit, see *PUSG*, 17:309–310; *AJP*, 8:255, 422; *Lamar v. Dana*, 71 U.S. 250 (1865).

50. Steers, *Blood on the Moon*, 46–51; Edwards and Steers, *Lincoln Assassination*, 105–107, 1010; Stewart Evans and Paul Gainey, *Jack the Ripper: First American Serial Killer* (New York: Kodansha America, 1998), 188–247.

51. Edwards and Steers, *Lincoln's Assassination*, 440, 916–917.

52. CAD to JSP, May 10, 1865, Pike Papers; *AJP*, 8:15–16.

53. Pitman, *Assassination and Trial*, 18–19.

54. Pitman, *Assassination and Trial*, 41. On the difference between Booth's and Benjamin's copies, see Terry L. Jones, "The Codes of War," *NYT*, March 14, 2013.

55. Pitman, *Assassination and Trial*, 40–41.

56. Pitman, *Assassination and Trial*, 24–27; Edwards and Steers, *Lincoln's Assassination*, 269. For Montgomery's contacts with Dana in early 1865, see *OR* I, v. 46, pt. 2, 170; v. 46, pt. 3, 62; USG to CAD, February 23, 1865, Grant Papers, LC.

57. *OR* II, v. 8, 932; Pitman, *Assassination and Trial*, 28–30; Hanchett, *Lincoln Murder Conspiracies*, 72; Cumming, *Devil's Game*, 113–114, 130–135.

58. Cumming, *Devil's Game*, 160–212; Hanchett, *Lincoln Murder Conspiracies*, 81; Leonard, *Lincoln's Avengers*, 226–227.

59. Hanchett, *Lincoln Murder Conspiracies*, 73; Turner, *Beware the People Weeping*, 213; [F. A. St. Lawrence], *Testimony of Sandford Conover, Dr. J.B. Merritt, and Richard Montgomery Before Military Court at Washington, Respecting the Assassination of President Lincoln, and Proofs Disproving their Statements, and Showing their Perjuries* (Toronto: Lovell & Gibson, 1865), 52–61; Joseph Holt, *Reply of J. Holt to Certain Calumnies of Jacob Thompson* (n.p., 1883), 15; Cumming, *Devil's Game*, 124, 135, 138.

60. Joseph George, Jr., "The Conspiracy Trial's 'Suppressed Testimony': An Attempt to Implicate Jefferson Davis in Lincoln's Assassination," *Lincoln Herald* 111 (June 2009): 102–103, 120–121, 127, n. 73; Dana interview, December 21, 1896, Tarbell Papers; Cumming, *Devil's Game*, 138.

61. CAD to JSP, May 10, 1865, Pike Papers; *NYS*, March 14, 1870; *NYTr*, June 6, 1865.

62. John G. Nicolay and John Hay, *Abraham Lincoln: A History* (New York: Century Co., 1890), 10:286; CAD to Gen. John Dix, April 13, 1865, RG 107, NARA; Turner, *Beware the People Weeping*, 69–73.

63. William A. Tidwell, with James O. Hall and David Winfred Gaddy, *Come Retribution: The Confederate Secret Service and the Assassination of Lincoln* (Jackson: University Press of Mississippi, 1988), 418–421; Steers, *Blood on the Moon*, 55–58, 88–89; Hanchett, *Lincoln Murder Conspiracies*, 32; Donald, *Lincoln*, 677.

64. Hanchett, *Lincoln Murder Conspiracies*, 44; William A. Tidwell, *April '65: Confederate Covert Action in the American Civil War* (Kent, OH: Kent State University Press, 1995), 144; Steers, *Blood on the Moon*, 71–74.

65. Kauffman, *American Brutus*, 367; General August Kautz quoted in Turner, *Beware the People Weeping*, 210; Walter S. Cox quoted in Chambrun, *Impressions of Lincoln*, 138; Pitman, *Assassination and Trial*, 380, 339–347.

66. *NYT*, May 15, 1865, July 13, 2015; *OR* I, v. 49, pt. 1, 538, pt. 2, 888; *OR* II, vol. 8, 569; Chester D. Bradley, "Was Jefferson Davis Disguised as a Woman When Captured?" *Journal of Mississippi History* 36 (August 1974): 246; *CR*, May 11, 1866. Wilson belatedly corrected the record in his official report, *OR* I, v. 49, pt. 1, 378–379, and *Flag*, 2:329–335.

67. *OR* II, v. 8, 563–564; CAD to JHW, May 30, 1865, in Wilson, *Dana*, 364–365.

68. *OR* II, v. 8, 564–565, 577; *NYS*, quoted in *Troy Weekly Times*, February 12, 1891; CAD to EMS, May 22, 1865, Stanton Papers, LC.

69. Hanchett, *Lincoln Murder Conspiracies*, 74–79; Cumming, *Devil's Game*, 160–180.

70. John Reeves, *The Lost Indictment of Robert E. Lee: The Forgotten Case against an American Icon* (Lanham, MD: Rowman & Littlefield, 2018), 80–85; William A. Blair, *With Malice toward Some: Treason and Loyalty in the Civil War Era* (Chapel Hill: University of North Carolina Press, 2014), 239–241; Elizabeth R. Varon, *Appomattox: Victory, Defeat, and Freedom at the End of the Civil War* (New York: Oxford University Press, 2014), 197–206; *PUSG*, 15:149–150, 204.

71. *CR*, August 15, 1865, November 9, 1865. Dana's call for a treason trial of Lee is the premise of a fanciful historical novel by Thomas Fleming, *The Secret Trial of Robert E. Lee* (New York: Forge Books, 2006).

72. Leonard, *Lincoln's Avengers*, 147–149, 205–06; *CR*, September 12, 1865, April 16, 1866, May 24, 1866. For detailed analysis of the case, see Roy Franklin Nichols, "The United States v. Jefferson Davis, 1865–1869," *American Historical Review* 31 (1926): 266–284; and Cynthia Nicoletti, *Secession on Trial: The Treason Prosecution of Jefferson Davis* (Cambridge, UK: Cambridge University Press, 2017).

73. Leonard, *Lincoln's Avengers*, 189; *NYTr*, April 13, May 2, 1865; Burke Davis, *The Long Surrender* (New York: Vintage Books, 1985), 206–207, 219–223.

74. *NYT*, September 4, 1865.

75. Davis, *Long Surrender*, 204. For Chase's role in putting off a treason trial for Davis, see Nicoletti, *Secession on Trial*, 192–204.

76. CAD to JHW, May 30, 1865, in Wilson, *Dana*, 362.

77. *OR* I, v. 47, pt. 3, 221.

78. Undated memo of Dana interview, Tarbell Papers; Thomas and Hyman, *Stanton*, 405–414.

79. Dana, *Recollections*, 289; *NYT*, April 23 and 24, 1865.

80. CAD to JHW, May 30, 1865, in Wilson, *Dana*, 364; *NYS*, June 15, 1875; Dana, *Recollections*, 289. On the politics of the episode, see Thomas and Hyman, *Stanton*, 402–414; and Michael Fellman, *Citizen Sherman: A Life of William Tecumseh Sherman* (New York: Random House, 1995), 238–254.

81. William Tecumseh Sherman, *Memoirs of General W. T. Sherman* (1885; New York: Library of America, 1990), 866; CAD to JHW, May 30, 1865, in Wilson, *Dana*, 363; *NYS*, June 15, 1875; Dana, *Recollections*, 288–290. For historians' accounts of the episode, see Thomas and Hyman, *Stanton*, 416, and William Marvel, *Lincoln's Autocrat: The Life of Edwin Stanton* (Chapel Hill: University of North Carolina Press, 2015), 379.

82. *OR* III, v. 5, 26–28, 235; William G. Thomas, *The Iron Way: Railroads, the Civil War, and the Making of Modern America* (New Haven, CT: Yale University Press, 2011), 182–186; Thomas Weber, *The Northern Railroads in the Civil War, 1861–1865* (New York: King's Crown Press of Columbia University Press, 1952), 217–219; *CR*, September 9, 1865. Dana's report is reprinted in his *Recollections*, 255–260.

83. Chambrun, *Impressions of Lincoln*, 162–164; *NYTr*, June 8, 1865; CAD to A. W. Mack, June 30, 1865, and July 6, 1865, RG 107, NARA.

Chapter 17. "Grantism" and Retreat

1. CAD to JHW, May 30, 1865, in Wilson, *Dana*, 361; Elmer Gertz, "Charles A. Dana and the *Chicago Republican*," *Journal of the Illinois State Historical Society* 45 (Summer 1952): 125; *NYT*, January 7, 1871.

2. CAD to JHW, May 30, 1865, in Wilson, *Dana*, 362.

3. CAD to A. W. Mack, June 30, 1865, RG 107, NARA; *CR*, July 24, 1865.

4. Gertz, "Dana and the *Chicago Republican*," 127–128; *CR*, December 4, 1865.

5. CAD to JSP, November 10, 1865, Pike Papers; Mary Todd Lincoln to Mary Jane Welles, October 14, 1865, in *Mary Todd Lincoln: Her Life and Letters*, ed. Justin G. Turner and Linda Levitt Turner (New York: Fromm International Publishing Corporation, 1987), 277–278.

6. *CR*, September 9, August 22, 1865; *Army and Navy Journal* 3 (September 2, 1865), 26, 71; *CR*, September 12, November 9, 1865.

7. *CR*, July 30, October 12, November 28, 1865.

8. *CR*, September 8, 1865.

9. CAD to Charles Sumner, September 1, 1865, Sumner Papers, HL-HU; CAD to Isaac Sherman, September 17, 1865, quoted in Eric Foner, *Reconstruction: An Unfinished Revolution, 1863–1877* (New York: Harper & Row, 1988), 225; CAD to Charles Sumner, September 1, 1865, Sumner Papers, HL-HU.

10. *CR*, August 5, September 8, October 5, 1865; CAD to Isaac N. Arnold, November 13, 1866, Stanton Papers, LC; CAD to Charles Sumner, September 1, 1865, Sumner Papers, HL-HU.

11. CAD to JHW, November 6, 1865, Wilson, *Dana*, 372; CAD to JSP, November 10, 1865, Pike Papers.

12. *CR*, August 15, 21, 1865; January 3, 1866; CAD to JHW, undated, Wilson, *Dana*, 373.

13. Wilson, *Dana*, 373–374; *CR*, April 13, March 13, March 23, 1866. Grant's aide Orville Babcock may have been one of those badmouthing Dana to Grant. See *PUSG*, 19:179n.

14. *CR*, February 10, 22, 26, 28, 1866; April 16, 1866; *AJP*, 10:145–157.

15. CAD to Raymond, December 20, 1865, George Jones Papers, NYPL; LaWanda Cox and John H. Cox, *Politics, Principle, and Prejudice, 1865–1866: Dilemma of Reconstruction America* (New York: Free Press, 1963), 113–127; *AJP*, 9:612.

16. Mark Wahlgren Summers, *The Press Gang: Newspapers and Politics, 1865–1878* (Chapel Hill: University of North Carolina Press, 1994), 34–35. Johnson's publication of Dana's letter was triggered by partisan misrepresentation. Dana's rivals at the *Chicago Tribune* had jokingly proposed him for the Chicago customs collectorship. Dana responded that "the scheme to buy off the present managers of *The Republican* with collectorships . . . is very smart, but it won't win." Democratic newspapers ripped Dana's words out of context, making him appear to accuse Johnson of trying to buy his support with an appointment. *CR*, March 21, 1866.

17. *CR*, March 19, 1866; CAD to William Bartlett, January 27, 1866, Bartlett Family Papers, Columbia University. For portrayals of Dana as a frustrated office-seeker taking revenge on Johnson, see Harry J. Maihafer, *The General and the Journalists: Ulysses S. Grant, Horace Greeley, and Charles Dana* (Washington, DC: Brassey's, 1998), 222; and William Marvel, *Lincoln's Autocrat: The Life of Edwin Stanton* (Chapel Hill: University of North Carolina Press, 2015), 398. Janet E. Steele, *The* Sun *Shines for All: Journalism and Ideology in the Life of Charles A. Dana* (Syracuse: Syracuse University Press, 1993), 68–73, mistakenly connects the Johnson customs flap to Dana's earlier lobbying for the Thirteenth Amendment.

18. *CR*, March 6, 7, 8, 23, 30, April 10, 30, May 3, 7, 9, 1866; CAD to JHW, July 19, 1866 in Wilson, *Dana*, 377.

19. *New York Independent*, June 14, 1866, quoted in Gertz, "Dana and the *Chicago Republican*," 134; *Washington National Republican*, August 11, 1866; CAD to JHW, April 30, 1866, Wilson, *Dana*, 376; *Chicago Inter-Ocean*, October 18, 1897.

20. Gertz, "Dana and the *Chicago Republican*," 135; *Washington National Republican*, August 11, 1866; Wilson, *Dana*, 377.

21. *NYS*, November 1871, quoted in Charles J. Rosebault, *When Dana Was the Sun* (New York: R. M. McBride & Co., 1931), 198.

22. For an excellent overview of these trends, see Summers, *Press Gang*, 4–6, 314–318.

23. *NYS*, January 31, 1867; *San Francisco Bulletin*, January 31, 1867; *SPCP*, 1:638; Frederic Hudson, *Journalism in the United States, From 1690 to 1872* (New York: Harper & Brothers, 1873), 678–679; Steele, *Sun Shines for All*, 76–77.

24. CAD to JHW, January 8, 1868, quoted in Wilson, *Dana*, 378; Steele, *Sun Shines for All*, 77–78.

25. Candace Stone, *Dana and the* Sun (New York: Dodd, Mead, & Co., 1938), 31.

26. *NYS*, January 27, 1868.

27. CAD to Uriah H. Painter, February 1, 1868, Painter Collection, HSP; *NYS*, May 19, 1868.

28. Stone, *Dana and the* Sun, 60–62; Dana and Wilson, *Life of Grant*, 417. For the authors' division of labor, see Wilson, *Dana*, 385.

29. *NYS*, quoted in *Portland Oregonian*, June 17, 1868; *NYS*, August 15, 1868.

30. Wilson, *Dana*, 406–407; JHW to Barney, December 29, 1868, Barney Collection, HL; *Cincinnati Daily Gazette*, February 10, 1869.

31. George S. Boutwell, *Reminiscences of Sixty Years in Public Affairs* (New York: McClure, Phillips & Co., 1902), 1:294; J. F. Packard, *General Grant's Tour Around the World* (Cincinnati: Forshee & McMakin, 1880), 30; Allan Nevins, *Hamilton Fish: The Inner History of the Grant Administration* (New York: Dodd, Mead, & Co., 1937), 136.

32. *Dallas Morning News*, February 3, 1898; *NYS*, April 19, 1869. The post of appraiser reportedly carried a salary of $4,000 a year.

33. *NYS*, April 1, 8, 17, 1869; *Brooklyn Union*, quoted in Steele, *Sun Shines for All*, 92; *NYS*, July 6, 1869.

34. Mark Wahlgren Summers, *The Era of Good Stealings* (New York: Oxford University Press, 1993), 96; *Dallas Morning News*, February 3, 1898.

35. Steele, *Sun Shines for All*, 92.

36. Henry Adams, *The Education of Henry Adams: An Autobiography* (1918; reprint ed. Boston: Houghton Mifflin, 1961), 260; CAD to Marsena Patrick, November 20, 1869, Anthony Collection, NYPL.

37. Summers, *Era of Good Stealings*, 16–29, 81.

38. Charles W. Calhoun, *The Presidency of Ulysses S. Grant* (Lawrence: University Press of Kansas, 2017), 188; *NYS*, June 17, 1869; January 8, 1870; January 9, 13, 1871.

39. *Select Committee Report on Charges against the Navy Department*, House Misc. Doc. No. 210, 42nd Congress, 2nd Session (Washington, DC, 1872), 139–152; Stone, *Dana and the* Sun, 97–99; *NYT*, April 8, 1872; *NYTr*, May 23, 1872; CAD to Gideon Welles, October 27, 1870, Brown Collection of Greeley MSS, N-YHS; CAD to Edgar Welles, June 8, 1872, and draft reply, Gideon Welles Papers, LC.

40. *NYS*, September 4, 1872; Donald A. Ritchie, *Press Gallery: Congress and the Washington Correspondents* (Cambridge, MA: Harvard University Press, 1991), 102–105. Uriah Painter, the *Sun*'s part-time Washington correspondent, had secretly received shares. See Ritchie, *Press Gallery*, 92–112; and Summers, *Press Gang*, 109–122.

41. *NYS*, March 17, 29, 1876.

42. Summers, *Press Gang*, 240; *NYS*, quoted in *New Orleans Daily Picayune*, October 14, 1869, and *Cincinnati Daily Gazette*, June 10, 1872; CAD to A. H. Markland, January 29, 1887, Dana Miscellaneous Manuscripts, N-YHS; *NYS*, October 14, 1872; Wilson, *Dana*, 426.

43. Nevins, *Hamilton Fish*, 582; *PUSG*, 22:152; Calhoun, *Presidency of Grant*, 89; Steele,

Sun *Shines for All*, 103; *PUSG*, 21:100 (reprinting Fish's diary of December 5 and 21, 1870). For the pamphlet, see [James B. Mix], *The Biter Bit, or the Robert Macaire of Journalism; Being a Narrative of Some of the Black-Mailing Operations of Charles A. Dana's "Sun"* (Washington, DC, 1870). For Soteldo's appointment, see *NYTr*, February 11, 1882, confirming suspicions Dana had expressed in letters to Uriah H. Painter, March 3 and 13, 1871, Painter Collection, HSP.

44. *PUSG*, 24:64, 25:52; 31:391.

45. *NYT*, February 2, 1871; Adams, *Education*, 244.

46. Strong, *Diary*, 4:287; Wilson, *Dana*, 432; Rosebault, *When Dana Was the Sun*, 185, 286; Edwin L. Godkin, *Life and Letters of Edwin Lawrence Godkin*, ed. Rollo Ogden (New York: Macmillan, 1907), 1:305; Edward P. Mitchell, *Memoirs of an Editor: Fifty Years of American Journalism* (New York: Charles Scribner's Sons, 1924), 126–128.

47. *PUSG*, 19:257; JHW to Hiram Barney, June 21, 1869, Barney Papers, HL; JHW to CAD, October 21, 1869, Wilson Papers, LC; Wilson, *Dana*, 432.

48. Stone, *Dana and the* Sun, 380–384; *Cincinnati Daily Gazette*, November 16, 1878.

49. Mitchell, *Memoirs of an Editor*, 124; Horace Traubel, *With Whitman in Camden (July 16, 1888–Oct. 31, 1888)* (1908; reprint ed., New York: Rowman & Littlefield, 1961), 79, 467–468.

50. Rosebault, *When Dana Was the Sun*, 200; *NYS*, September 9, 1870; Stone, *Dana and the* Sun, 115, 118–119.

51. Stone, *Dana and the* Sun, 122; Rosebault, *When Dana Was the Sun*, 176–177; *NYS*, July 10, 1872.

52. *NYS*, December 5, 1872.

53. Wilson, *Dana*, 485; *Philadelphia Inquirer*, February 15, 1890.

54. *Washington Post*, May 19, 1885, quoted in Stone, *Dana and the* Sun, 393.

55. Mitchell, *Memoirs of an Editor*, 327–330; Stone, *Dana and the* Sun, 115, 157; Frank M. O'Brien, *The Story of the Sun* (New York: George H. Doran Company, 1918), 420; Mitchell to JHW, undated, Wilson Papers, LC. Despite abundant evidence of Dana's volatility, Steele, Sun *Shines for All*, 1–6, claims to detect a consistent "producerist ideology" beneath his editorial zigzags.

56. Stone, *Dana and the* Sun, 56–57; *NYS*, March 5, December 20, 1869.

57. *NYS*, February 4, 15, 1869.

58. *NYS*, April 3, July 22, 1869.

59. *NYS*, August 9, 1870. Reassessment of Grant's record on Reconstruction gained momentum with Brooks D. Simpson, *Let Us Have Peace: Ulysses S. Grant and the Politics of War and Reconstruction, 1861–1868* (Chapel Hill: University of North Carolina Press, 1991), and has been summarized in Ron Chernow, *Grant* (New York: Penguin Press, 2017), and Calhoun, *Presidency of Grant*.

60. Wilson, *Dana*, 424, 466; *NYS*, March 29, 1871, October 21, 1872.

61. *NYS*, January 18, 1873.

62. Stone, *Dana and the* Sun, 69, 87–89; *NYS*, May 10, March 27, November 14, 1872.

63. Mitchell, *Memoirs of an Editor*, 323; Stone, *Dana and the* Sun, 239–241.

64. *NYS*, May 4, 1885; Foner, *Reconstruction*, xvii–xxii.

65. *NYS*, November 18, 1884.

Epilogue: Remembering (and Forgetting) the War

1. *NYS*, August 2, October 7, 1880; *Duluth Daily News*, February 15, 1892. At the war's

end, Dana set off a prolonged feud between Conkling's Republican "Stalwarts" and Blaine's "Half-Breeds" by appointing Conkling to investigate bounty frauds in western New York. The move prompted charges of cronyism and corruption from the War Department's James B. Fry and his ally, Blaine. See CAD to Roscoe Conkling, April 3, 1865, RG 107, NARA; US House of Representatives, *Select Committee Report on Hon. Roscoe Conkling and Provost Marshal Gen. Fry*, House Report No. 93, 39th Congress, 1st Session (Washington, DC, 1866); and in his defense, see James B. Fry, *The Conkling and Blaine-Fry Controversy, in 1866* (New York: A. G. Sherwood & Co., 1893). Dana's view was printed in *NYS*, January 21, 1890.

2. *NYS*, May 21, 1872; Candace Stone, *Dana and the* Sun (New York: Dodd, Mead, & Co., 1938), 83–84; *NYTr*, February 20, 1886.

3. *NYS*, August 17, 1872, November 8, 1876, January 12, 1893; *Boston Daily Journal*, February 13, 1891; *NYTr*, November 5, 1860. Dana used Greeley's example to excuse Thomas Bayard of Delaware, an advocate of "peaceable separation" after Fort Sumter, when he sought the Democratic presidential nomination in 1884. *NYS*, June 18, 1884.

4. *NYS*, October 22, 1897. In 1890 Dana supplemented the official published records by re-printing in the *Sun*, without comment, the blunt assessments of Grant's staff and subordinate officers he sent to Stanton after Vicksburg. He was able to recover copies from Stanton's papers. See *NYS*, July 27, 1890, and, for their recovery from Stanton's papers, Ida M. Tarbell, "Charles A. Dana in the Civil War," *McClure's Magazine* 9 (October 1897): 1088.

5. *NYS*, March 30, 1870, May 19, 1875, December 9, 1886, August 8, 1888.

6. *NYS*, October 22, 1897; *NYTr*, June 7, 1885; Dana, "Reminiscences of Abraham Lincoln," in *Reminiscences of Abraham Lincoln, by Distinguished Men of His Time*, 5th edition, ed. Allen Thorndike Rice (New York: North American Review, 1888), 362–376; Dana, *Lincoln and His Cabinet* (Cleveland and New York: De Vinne Press, 1896).

7. *NYS*, July 8, 15, 1891; Dana, *Lincoln and His Cabinet*.

8. Benjamin P. Thomas and Harold M. Hyman, *Stanton: The Life and Times of Lincoln's Secretary of War* (New York: Alfred A. Knopf, 1962), 640; *NYS*, December 25, 1869.

9. *CR*, August 18, 1865; *NYS*, August 29, 1868; *NYTr*, February 20, 1886; William T. Sherman to John Sherman, February 23, 1886, W. T. Sherman Papers, LC; *NYS*, June 8, 9, 1886; *Chicago Inter-Ocean*, July 5, 1886.

10. *NYS*, June 20, 1870.

11. *NYS*, January 21, 1869, June 20, 1870, December 2, 1870, April 17, 1871; *NYH*, May 19, 1875. Dana's denials about Grant's drinking applied only to the war years. During the campaign of 1872 he charged that Grant, as president, indulged in monthly drunken sprees at the White House. *NYS*, August 17, 1872.

12. Joan Waugh, *U. S. Grant: American Hero, American Myth* (Chapel Hill: University of North Carolina Press, 2009), 274; *NYS*, July 24, 1885.

13. Edward P. Mitchell, "Mr. Dana of 'The Sun,'" *McClure's Magazine* 3 (October 1894): 388. Dana toyed with plans to write a political history of the half-century from 1835 to 1885 but put them aside. See Samuel J. Tilden, *Letters and Literary Memorials of Samuel J. Tilden*, ed. John Bigelow (New York: Harper & Brothers, 1908), 2:657.

14. CAD to A. H. Markland, November 25, 1886, Dana Miscellaneous Manuscripts, N-YHS; Janet E. Steele, *The Sun Shines for All: Journalism and Ideology in the Life of Charles A. Dana* (Syracuse: Syracuse University Press, 1993), 125; Wilson, *Dana*, 495–508.

15. *New Haven Register*, January 22, 1890; *Springfield Republican*, June 15, 1890; *Chicago Inter-Ocean*, September 18, 1895.

16. *NYS*, December 4, 6, 1895. On the reunions, see Caroline E. Janney, *Remembering the Civil War: Reunion and the Limits of Reconciliation* (Chapel Hill: University of North

Carolina Press, 2013), 160–163; David W. Blight, *Race and Reunion: The Civil War in American Memory* (Cambridge, MA: Belknap Press of Harvard University Press, 2001), 198–206, 356, 385–387; John R. Neff, *Honoring the Civil War Dead: Commemoration and the Problem of Reconciliation* (Lawrence: University Press of Kansas, 2005), 214–220. As early as 1877 Dana praised sentiments of reconciliation voiced by Memorial Day orators in New York City. *NYS*, May 31, 1877.

17. *NYH*, February 27, 28, 1896.

18. *NYS*, February 27, April 9, 1896.

19. *Rocky Mountain News*, September 22, 1889; Joshua Zeitz, *Lincoln's Boys: John Hay, John Nicolay, and the War for Lincoln's Image* (New York: Penguin Books, 2014), 259; *Washington Critic*, April 17, 1890; *McClure's Magazine* 10 (December 1897): 194.

20. Ida M. Tarbell, *All in the Day's Work: An Autobiography* (New York: Macmillan, 1939), 175.

21. Tarbell, *Day's Work*, 175; *New Haven Register*, March 11, 1896.

22. Tarbell, *Day's Work*, 175–176; Mitchell, "Mr. Dana of 'The Sun,'" 372–373. Typed transcriptions of most of the interviews are in the Tarbell Papers, Allegheny College Library, Meadville, PA.

23. Tarbell, *Day's Work*, 177.

24. Tarbell, *Day's Work*, 174; Tarbell, "Charles A. Dana in the Civil War," 1088.

25. *McClure's Magazine* 10 (December 1897): 193–194.

26. *Boston Journal*, quoted in *Book Reviews* 7 (January 1899): 25.

27. Mayo W. Hazeltine, "Charles Anderson Dana," *North American Review* 185 (July 5, 1907): 505; Allan Nevins, "Charles Anderson Dana," *Dictionary of American Biography* (New York: Charles Scribner's Sons, 1930), 5:50. See the survey of editorial tributes in the *Chicago Tribune* and *Chicago Inter-Ocean*, October 18, 1897.

28. Wilson, *Dana*, 518, 521.

29. *Chicago Tribune*, October 21, 1897. For the Hutchinsons' visit to Brook Farm in April 1843, see *Excelsior: Journals of the Hutchinson Family Singers, 1842–1846*, ed. Dale Cockrell (Stuyvesant, NY: Pendragon Press, 1989), 102–104, 389; and James Wallace Hutchinson, *Story of the Hutchinsons* (Boston: Lee & Shepard, 1896), 1:80–85.

Bibliography

Manuscripts

Abraham Lincoln Presidential Library, Springfield, IL
  Papers of Abraham Lincoln Digital Library (papersofabrahamlincoln.org)
Allegheny College Library, Meadville, PA
  Ida M. Tarbell Papers
Columbia University, New York, NY
  Willard Bartlett Family Papers
  Sidney Howard Gay Papers
  Allan Nevins Collection
Cornell University, Division of Rare and Manuscript Collections, Ithaca, NY
  Samuel J. May Collection
  John P. Sanderson Diary (typescript)
  Bayard Taylor Papers
Duke University, Durham, NC
  Charles A. Dana Papers
  Adams S. Hill Papers
Gilder Lehrman Institute of American History, New York, NY
  Letterbook of telegrams from Dana to Edwin M. Stanton, 6 September 1863–8 November
    1863
Historical Society of Delaware, Wilmington
  James Harrison Wilson Collection
Historical Society of Pennsylvania, Philadelphia
  Henry C. Carey Papers
  Salmon P. Chase Papers
  Uriah H. Painter Collection
Houghton Library, Harvard University, Cambridge, MA
  Charles Sumner Papers
Huntington Library, San Marino, CA
  Samuel L. M. Barlow Papers
  Hiram Barney Collection
  Thomas T. Eckert Papers
  James William Eldridge Papers
  Ulysses S. Grant Papers
  Joseph Holt Papers
  Charles H. Ray Papers

Indiana State Library, Indianapolis
    Schuyler Colfax Papers
Kansas State Historical Society, Topeka
    John Stillman Brown Family Papers, microfilm edition
Library of Congress, Manuscript Division, Washington, DC
    David Homer Bates Diary
    Simon Cameron Papers
    Salmon P. Chase Papers
    Cyrus B. Comstock Papers
    Charles A. Dana Papers
    Ulysses S. Grant Papers (online)
    Horace Greeley Papers
    Joseph Holt Papers
    Andrew Johnson Papers
    Abraham Lincoln Papers (online)
    Manton Marble Papers
    Montgomery Meigs Papers
    Jacob W. Schuckers Papers
    William T. Sherman Papers
    Edwin M. Stanton Papers
    George Hay Stuart Collection
    Horatio Nelson Taft Diary
    Elihu B. Washburne Papers
    Gideon Welles Papers
    James H. Wilson Papers
Massachusetts Historical Society, Boston, MA
    Dana Family Papers
    George Gordon Papers
    Theodore Lyman Papers
National Archives and Records Administration, Washington, DC
        House Judiciary Committee Papers, Record Group 233
        Hearings on "Telegraphic Censorship of the Press"
        Records of the Adjutant General, Record Group 94
            Case Files of Investigations by Levi C. Turner and Lafayette C. Baker (M797)
            Individual Service Records
    Records of the Commissary General of Prisoners, Record Group 249
        Records of the Judge Advocate General, Record Group 153
        Investigation and Trial Papers Relating to Suspects in the Lincoln Assassination
            (M599)
        Records of the Office of the Secretary of War, Record Group 107
        Letters Received by the Secretary of War, Main Series (M221)
        Letters Received by the Secretary of War, Irregular Series (M492)
        Letters Received by the Secretary of War from the President, Executive
            Departments, and War Department Bureaus, 1862–1870 (M494)
        Letters Sent by the Secretary of War Relating to Military Affairs (M6)
        Letters Sent by the Secretary of War to the President (M127 and M421)
        Letters Sent to the President (M127)
        Orders and Endorsements Sent by the Secretary of War (M444)

    Telegrams Collected by the Office of the Secretary of War, Bound, 1861–1882 (M473)
    Telegrams Collected by the Office of the Secretary of War, Unbound, 1860–1870 (M504)
  Records of the Provost Marshal General, Record Group 110
    Accounts of Secret Service Agents
  Records of the Quartermaster General, Record Group 92
    Cairo Claims Commission File
  Records Received by the Headquarters of the Army, Record Group 108 (M1635)
  War Department Collection of Confederate Records, Record Group 109
New-York Historical Society, New York, NY
  James Wright Brown Collection of Horace Greeley Manuscripts
  Charles A. Dana Miscellaneous Manuscripts
  Henry B. Stanton Papers
New York Public Library, New York, NY
  Alfred W. Anthony Collection
  Bryant-Godwin Papers
  Charles A. Dana Papers
  Goddard-Roslyn Collection
  Horace Greeley Papers
  George Jones Papers
  Henry J. Raymond Papers
Ohio Historical Society, Columbus, OH
  John P. Sanderson Papers
Syracuse University Library, Syracuse, NY
  Gerrit Smith Papers
University of California, Los Angeles
  William S. Rosecrans Papers
University of Illinois, Champaign-Urbana
  Henry S. Borneman Papers, microfilm edition
University of Maine, Orono
  James S. Pike Papers
University of Rochester, Rochester, NY
  William H. Seward Papers
  Thurlow Weed Papers
Yale University Library, New Haven, CT
  Civil War Manuscripts Collection
  Edwin D. Stanton Collection
  John Hay Whitney and Betsey Cushing Whitney Family Papers

Court Cases

Lamar v. Dana, 71 U.S. 250 (1865)
Parish v. Macveagh, 214 U.S. 124 (1909)
McGowan v. Parish, 237 U.S. 285 (1915)

Newspapers and Periodicals

Boston Courier
Chicago Inter-Ocean

Chicago Republican
Chicago Tribune
Frank Leslie's Illustrated Newspaper, New York
The Harbinger, Boston and New York
Harper's Weekly, New York
National Republican, Washington, DC
New York Daily Tribune
New York Herald
New York Sun
New York Times
Spirit of the Age, New York
Vanity Fair, New York
Washington Evening Star
Note: Other papers are cited when they reprinted articles from Dana's newspapers or wrote noteworthy reports about Dana or New York journalism.

Government Documents

US Congress. *Congressional Globe*. 26th–42nd Congress.
———. *Congressional Serial Set, Fiftieth Congress* (1887–1889).
———. Joint Committee on the Conduct of the War. *Report of the Joint Committee on the Conduct of the War at the Second Session, Thirty-Eighth Congress*. Washington, DC: Government Printing Office, 1865.
US Department of State. *Papers Relating to Foreign Affairs, Accompanying the Annual Message of the President to the Second Session Thirty-Eighth Congress*. Washington, DC: Government Printing Office, 1864. Cited as *FRUS* 1864.
———. *Papers Relating to Foreign Affairs, Accompanying the Annual Message of the President to the First Session Thirty-Ninth Congress, Part 1*. Washington, DC: Government Printing Office, 1865. Cited as *FRUS* 1865.
US House of Representatives. *Committee on War Claims*. House Report No. 55, 45th Congress, 3rd Session. Washington, DC, 1879.
———. *Committee on War Claims*. House Report No. 250, 46th Congress, 3rd Session. Washington, DC, 1881.
———. *Select Committee Report on Charges against the Navy Department*. House Misc. Doc. No. 210, 42nd Congress, 2nd Session. Washington, DC, 1872.
———. *Select Committee Report on Hon. Roscoe Conkling and Provost Marshal Gen. Fry*. House Report No. 93, 39th Congress, 1st Session. Washington, DC, 1866.
———. *Trade with Rebellious States*. House Report No. 24, 38th Congress, 2nd session. Washington, DC, 1864–1865.
US Senate. *Committee on Claims*. Senate Report No. 1628, 56th Congress, 1st Session. Washington, DC, 1900.
———. *Committee on Claims*. Senate Report No. 351, 57th Congress, 1st Session. Washington, DC, 1902.
US War Department. *Accounts for Newspaper Advertising*. Broadside. Washington, DC, May 20, 1864.
———. *List of Newspapers Authorized by the Secretary of War to Publish Advertisements for All the Bureaus of the War Department*. Broadside. Washington, DC, 1864.
———. *Report of the Judge Advocate General on the "Order of American Knights" or "Sons*

of Liberty," a Western Conspiracy in Aid of the Southern Rebellion. Washington, DC, Chronicle Print, 1864.

———. *The War of the Rebellion: A Compilation of the Official Records of the Union and Confederate Armies.* 128 vols. Prepared under the direction of the Secretary of War by Robert N. Scott. Washington, DC: Government Printing Office, 1880–1901.

Other Published Primary Sources

Adams, Henry. *The Education of Henry Adams: An Autobiography.* 1918; Boston: Houghton Mifflin, 1961.

Baker, Lafayette C. *History of the United States Secret Service.* Philadelphia: L. C. Baker, 1867.

———. *Spies, Traitors and Conspirators of the Late Civil War.* Philadelphia: John E. Potter & Company, 1894. [Mainly an abridged version of the title above.]

Barnes, Thurlow Weed. *Memoir of Thurlow Weed.* Boston: Houghton Mifflin, 1884.

Bates, David Homer. *Lincoln in the Telegraph Office: Recollections of the United States Military Telegraph Corps during the Civil War.* New York: Century Company, 1907.

———. "A Rebel Cipher Dispatch." *Harper's Monthly* 97 (June 1898): 105–109.

———. *The Telegraph Goes to War: The Personal Diary of David Homer Bates, Lincoln's Telegraph Operator.* Edited by Donald E. Markle. Hamilton, NY: Edmonston Publishing, Inc., 2003.

Bates, Edward. *Diary of Edward Bates.* Edited by Howard K. Beale. Washington, DC: Government Printing Office, 1933.

Battles and Leaders of the Civil War. 4 vols. Edited by Robert U. Johnson and Clarence C. Buel. New York: The Century Co., 1884–1888.

Benjamin, Charles F. "Recollections of Secretary Stanton." *Century Magazine* 33 (March 1887): 758–768.

Benton, Joel. *Greeley on Lincoln, With Mr. Greeley's Letters to Charles A. Dana and a Lady Friend.* New York: Baker & Taylor, 1893.

Berlin, Ira, Barbara J. Fields, Thavolia Glymph, Joseph P. Reidy, and Leslie S. Rowland, eds. *Freedom: A Documentary History of Emancipation, 1861–1867, ser. 1, vol. 1, The Destruction of Slavery.* Cambridge, UK: Cambridge University Press, 1985.

Black, Jeremiah S. "Senator Wilson and Edwin M. Stanton." *The Galaxy* 9, no. 6 (June 1870): 817–831.

Borden, Morten, ed. "Five Letters from Charles A. Dana to Karl Marx." *Journalism Quarterly* 36 (Summer 1959): 314–316.

Boutwell, George S. *Reminiscences of Sixty Years in Public Affairs.* 2 vols. New York: McClure, Phillips & Co., 1902.

Brooks, Noah. *Washington, D.C. in Lincoln's Time.* 1895; reprint ed. Athens: University of Georgia Press, 1989.

Butler, Benjamin F. *Autobiography and Personal Reminiscences of Benjamin F. Butler: Butler's Book.* Boston: A. M. Thayer & Co., 1892.

———. *Private and Official Correspondence of Gen. Benjamin F. Butler during the Period of the Civil War.* 5 vols. Norwood, MA: The Plimpton Press, 1917.

Cadwallader, Sylvanus. *Three Years with Grant.* Eds. Benjamin P. Thomas and Brooks D. Simpson. Lincoln: University of Nebraska Press, 1996.

Chambrun, Marquis Adolphe de. *Impressions of Lincoln and the Civil War: A Foreigner's Account.* New York: Random House, 1952.

Chase, Salmon P. *Diary and Correspondence of Salmon P. Chase*. Edited by George S. Denison and Samuel H. Dodson. Washington, DC: American Historical Association, 1903.

———. *The Salmon P. Chase Papers*. 5 vols. Edited by John Niven. Kent, OH: Kent State University Press, 1993–1998.

Cist, Henry M. "Comments on General Grant's 'Chattanooga.'" *Battles and Leaders of the Civil War*. New York: Century, 1888. 3:717–718.

Cockrell, Dale, ed. *Excelsior: Journals of the Hutchinson Family Singers, 1842–1846*. Stuyvesant, NY: Pendragon Press, 1989.

Codman, John Thomas. *Brook Farm: Historic and Personal Memoirs*. Boston: Arena Publishing Co., 1894.

Coffin, Charles Carleton. *Abraham Lincoln*. New York: Harper & Brothers, 1893.

Comstock, Cyrus B. *The Diary of Cyrus B. Comstock*. Edited by Merlin E. Sumner. Dayton, OH: Morningside House, 1987.

"Correspondence Relating to Chickamauga and Chattanooga." *Papers of the Military Historical Society of Massachusetts, Vol. 8: The Mississippi Valley, Tennessee, Georgia, Alabama, 1861–1864*. Boston: Military Historical Society of Massachusetts, 1910. 249–271.

Cox, Jacob D. *Military Reminiscences of the Civil War*. 2 vols. New York: Scribner's, 1900.

Croffut, William A. *An American Procession, 1855–1914: A Personal Chronicle of Famous Men*. Boston: Little, Brown & Co., 1931.

Cullom, Shelby M. *Fifty Years of Public Service: Personal Recollections of Shelby M. Cullom*. 2nd ed. Chicago: A. C. McClurg & Co., 1911.

Dana, Charles A. *The Art of Newspaper Making: Three Lectures*. New York: D. Appleton & Co., 1895.

———. *The Household Book of Poetry*. New York: D. Appleton & Co., 1858.

———. *A Lecture on Association, in Its Connection with Religion*. New York: B. H. Greene, 1844.

———. *Lincoln and His Cabinet*. Cleveland and New York: De Vinne Press, 1896.

———. *Proudhon and His "Bank of the People."* New York: B. F. Tucker, 1896.

———. *Recollections of the Civil War*. New York: D. Appleton & Co., 1898.

———. "Reminiscences of Abraham Lincoln." In *Reminiscences of Abraham Lincoln, by Distinguished Men of His Time*. 5th ed. Edited by Allen Thorndike Rice. New York: North American Review, 1888. 362–376.

———. "Reminiscences of Men and Events of the Civil War." *McClure's Magazine* 10 (November 1897–April 1898): 21–31, 150–164, 253–266, 347–360, 431–442, 561–571; and 11 (May–August 1898): 28–40, 172–177, 380–392.

———. "The War—Some Unpublished History." *North American Review* 153 (August 1891): 240–245.

———, and J. H. Wilson. *The Life of Ulysses S. Grant, General of the Armies of the United States*. Springfield, MA: Gurdon Bill, 1868.

Dodge, Grenville M. *Biography of Major-General Grenville M. Dodge from 1831 to 1871: Written and Compiled by Himself at Different Times and Completed in 1914*. Typescript. 6 vols. Council Bluffs (Iowa) Library. archive.org.

Douglass, Frederick. *Life and Times of Frederick Douglass, Written by Himself*. Reprint of 1892 ed. New York: Collier Books, 1962.

Dwight, Marianne. *Letters from Brook Farm, 1844–1847*. Edited by Amy L. Reed. Poughkeepsie, NY: Vassar College, 1928.

Eaton, John. *Grant, Lincoln and the Freedmen: Reminiscences of the Civil War*. New York: Longmans, Green & Co., 1907.

Edwards, William C., and Edward Steers, Jr. *The Lincoln Assassination: The Evidence*. Urbana and Chicago: University of Illinois Press, 2009.

"Extracts from the Journal of Henry J. Raymond." *Scribner's Monthly* 19, no. 3 (January 1880): 419–424.

Ford, Worthington Chauncey, ed. *A Cycle of Adams Letters, 1861–1865*. 2 vols. Boston and New York: Houghton Mifflin, 1920.

Fox, Gustavus V. *Confidential Correspondence of Gustavus Vasa Fox, Assistant Secretary of the Navy, 1861–1865*. Edited by Richard Means Thompson and Richard Wainwright. 2 vols. New York: Naval History Society, 1918–1919.

Fry, James B. *The Conkling and Blaine-Fry Controversy, in 1866*. New York: A. G. Sherwood, & Co., 1893.

Fullerton, Joseph S. "The Army of the Cumberland at Chattanooga." *Battles and Leaders of the Civil War*. New York: Century, 1888. 3:719–726.

Garfield, James A. *The Diary of James A. Garfield, 1848–1874*. 2 vols. Edited with an Introduction by Harry James Brown and Frederick D. Williams. East Lansing: Michigan State University Press, 1967.

———. *The Wild Life of the Army: Civil War Letters of James A. Garfield*. Edited by Frederick D. Williams. East Lansing: Michigan State University Press, 1964.

Godkin, Edwin L. *Life and Letters of Edwin Lawrence Godkin*. 2 vols. Edited by Rollo Ogden. New York: Macmillan, 1907.

Grant, Frederick D. "A Boy's Experience at Vicksburg." In *Personal Recollections of the War of the Rebellion: Addresses Delivered Before the Commandery of the State of New York, Military Order of the Loyal Legion of the United States*. 3rd series. Edited by A. Noel Blakeman. New York: G. P. Putnam's Sons, 1907. 86–100.

Grant, Julia Dent. *The Personal Memoirs of Julia Dent Grant*. Edited by John Y. Simon. New York: G. P. Putnam's Sons, 1975.

Grant, Ulysses S. *Memoirs and Selected Letters*. New York: Library of America, 1990.

———. *The Papers of Ulysses S. Grant*. Edited by John Y. Simon. 32 vols. Carbondale: Southern Illinois University Press, 1967–2012.

———. *The Papers of Ulysses S. Grant. Vol. 32: Supplement*. Edited by John F. Marszalek. Carbondale: Southern Illinois University Press, 2012.

———. *Report of Lieutenant-General U. S. Grant, of the United States Armies—1864–'65*. (dated July 22, 1865). In Julia Dent Grant, *Personal Memoirs*, Appendix, 2:555–632.

Greeley, Horace. *Recollections of a Busy Life*. New York: J. B. Ford, 1868.

———, and John F. Cleveland, *A Political Text-book for 1860, Comprising a Brief View of Presidential Nominations and Elections*. New York: Tribune Office, 1860.

Gurowski, Adam. *Diary, From March 4, 1861, to November 12, 1862*. Boston: Lee & Shepard, 1862.

———. *Diary, From November 12, 1862, to October 18, 1863*. New York: Carleton, 1864.

———. *Diary: 1863–'64–'65*. Washington, DC: W. H. & O. H. Morrison, 1866.

Hartranft, John Frederick. *The Lincoln Assassination Conspirators: Their Confinement and Execution, As Recorded in the Letterbook of John Frederick Hartranft*. Edited by Edward Steers, Jr., and Harold Holzer. Baton Rouge: Louisiana State University Press, 2009.

Hay, John. *Inside Lincoln's White House: The Complete Civil War Diary of John Hay*. Edited by Michael Burlingame and John R. Turner Ettlinger. Carbondale: Southern Illinois University Press, 1997.

———. *Lincoln's Journalist: John Hay's Anonymous Writings for the Press, 1860–1864*. Edited by Michael Burlingame. Carbondale: Southern Illinois University Press, 1998.

Hazeltine, Mayo W. "Charles Anderson Dana." *North American Review* 185 (July 5, 1907): 505–514.

Herndon, William H. *Herndon's Life of Lincoln.* Introduction and Notes by Paul M. Angle. Cleveland: World Publishing Co., 1942.

Higginson, Thomas Wentworth. *Cheerful Yesterdays.* Boston and New York: Houghton Mifflin, 1898.

Holt, Joseph. *Reply of J. Holt to Certain Calumnies of Jacob Thompson.* n.p., 1883.

Howard, Oliver Otis. *Autobiography of Oliver Otis Howard.* 2 vols. New York: Baker & Taylor, 1907.

Hutchinson, James Wallace. *Story of the Hutchinsons.* 2 vols. Boston: Lee & Shepard, 1896.

Johnson, Andrew. *The Papers of Andrew Johnson.* 16 vols. Edited by Paul H. Bergeron, Leroy P. Graf, and others. Knoxville: University of Tennessee Press, 1967–2000.

Lamon, Ward Hill. *Recollections of Lincoln, 1847–1865.* Edited by Dorothy Lamon Teillard. Lincoln: University of Nebraska Press, 1994.

Laugel, Auguste. *The United States during the Civil War.* Edited by Allan Nevins. Bloomington: Indiana University Press, 1961.

Lincoln, Abraham. *The Collected Works of Abraham Lincoln.* Edited by Roy P. Basler. 9 vols. New Brunswick, NJ: Rutgers University Press, 1953.

———. *The Collected Works of Abraham Lincoln. Supplement, 1832–1865.* Edited by Roy P. Basler. Westport, CT: Greenwood Press, 1974.

———. *Recollected Words of Abraham Lincoln.* Compiled and edited by Don E. Fehrenbacher and Virginia Fehrenbacher. Stanford: Stanford University Press, 1996.

Lincoln, Mary Todd. *Mary Todd Lincoln: Her Life and Letters.* Edited by Justin G. Turner and Linda Levitt Turner. New York: Fromm International Publishing Corporation, 1987.

Livermore, Thomas L. "The Siege and Relief of Chattanooga." *Papers of the Military Historical Society of Massachusetts, Vol. 8: The Mississippi Valley, Tennessee, Georgia, Alabama, 1861–1864.* Boston: Military Historical Society of Massachusetts, 1910. 273–339.

Longstreet, James. *From Manassas to Appomattox: Memoirs of the Civil War in America.* Philadelphia: J. B. Lippincott, 1896.

Lyman, Theodore. *Meade's Army: The Private Notebooks of Lt. Col. Theodore Lyman.* Edited by David W. Lowe. Kent, OH: Kent State University Press, 2007.

———. *Meade's Headquarters, 1863–1865: Letters of Colonel Theodore Lyman from the Wilderness to Appomattox.* Edited by George R. Agassiz. Boston: Atlantic Monthly Press, 1922.

McClellan, Carswell. *The Personal Memoirs and Military History of U. S. Grant versus the Record of the Army of the Potomac.* Boston: Houghton Mifflin, 1887.

McClellan, George. *The Civil War Papers of George B. McClellan.* Edited by Stephen W. Sears. New York: Ticknor & Fields, 1989.

McClure, Alexander K. *Lincoln Yarns and Stories.* New York: Western W. Wilson, 1901.

Marx, Karl. *On America and the Civil War.* Edited and translated by Saul K. Padover. New York: McGraw-Hill, 1972.

———, and Friedrich Engels. *The American Journalism of Marx & Engels: A Selection from the New York Daily Tribune.* Edited by Henry M. Christman. New York: New American Library, 1966.

———, and Friedrich Engels. *The Civil War in the United States.* 3rd ed. New York: International Publishers, 1961.

———, and Friedrich Engels. *Collected Works.* Vols. 38–40. New York: International Publishers, 1975.

Meade, George. *The Life and Letters of George Gordon Meade, Major-General United States Army*. 2 vols. Edited by George Gordon Meade. New York: Charles Scribner's Sons, 1913.

Meigs, Montgomery C. "First Impressions of Three Days' Fighting: Quartermaster General Meigs's 'Journal of the Battle of Chattanooga.'" Edited by John M. Hoffman. In *Ulysses S. Grant: Essays and Documents*. Edited by David L. Wilson and John Y. Simon. Carbondale and Edwardsville: Southern Illinois University Press, 1981. 59–76.

———. "General M. C. Meigs on the Conduct of the Civil War," *American Historical Review* 26, no. 2 (January 1921): 285–303.

Mitchell, Edward P. *Memoirs of an Editor: Fifty Years of American Journalism*. New York: Charles Scribner's Sons, 1924.

———. "Mr. Dana of 'The Sun.'" *McClure's Magazine* 3 (October 1894): 370–396.

[Mix, James B.] *The Biter Bit, or the Robert Macaire of Journalism; Being a Narrative of Some of the Black-Mailing Operations of Charles A. Dana's "Sun."* Washington, DC, 1870.

Moore, Frank H., ed. *The Rebellion Record, a Diary of Events with Documents, Narratives, Illustrative Incidents, Poetry, etc.* 12 vols. New York: G. P. Putnam, 1861–1869.

Nicolay, John G. *An Oral History of Abraham Lincoln: John G. Nicolay's Interviews and Essays*. Edited by Michael Burlingame. Carbondale: Southern Illinois University Press, 1996.

———. *With Lincoln in the White House: Letters, Memoranda, and Other Writings of John G. Nicolay, 1860–1865*. Edited by Michael Burlingame. Carbondale: Southern Illinois University Press, 2000.

Olcott, Henry S. "The War's Carnival of Fraud." *The Annals of War*. Philadelphia: Times Publishing Co., 1879.

Olmsted, Frederick Law. *The Papers of Frederick Law Olmsted*. 8 vols. Edited by Charles Beveridge and others. Baltimore: Johns Hopkins University Press, 1977–2013.

Opdyke, Emerson. *To Battle for God and the Right: The Civil War Letterbooks of Emerson Opdyke*. Edited by Glenn V. Longacre and John E. Haas. Urbana and Chicago: University of Illinois Press, 2003.

Packard, J. F. *General Grant's Tour around the World*. Cincinnati: Forshee & McMakin, 1880.

Page, Charles A. *Letters of a War Correspondent*. Boston: L. C. Page, 1899.

Palmer, John M. *Personal Recollections of John M. Palmer*. Cincinnati: Robert Clarke, 1901.

Parton, James. *The Life of Horace Greeley, Editor of the New York Tribune*. New York: Mason Brothers, 1855.

Patrick, Marsena Rudolph. *Inside Lincoln's Army: The Diary of Marsena Rudolph Patrick, Provost Marshal General, Army of the Potomac*. Edited by David S. Sparks. New York: Thomas Yoseloff, 1964.

Pike, James S. *First Blows of the Civil War: The Ten Years of Preliminary Conflict in the United States from 1850 to 1860*. New York: American News Company, 1879.

———. *The Prostrate State: South Carolina under Negro Government*. New York: D. Appleton & Co., 1874.

Pitman, Benn, ed. *The Assassination of President Lincoln and the Trial of the Conspirators*. New York: Moore, Wilstach & Baldwin, 1865.

Plummer, Mark A. "The Last Hours of Lincoln: The Haynie Diary." *Journal of Illinois History* 4 (Spring 2001): 25–40.

Pollard, Edward. *Observations in the North: Eight Months in Prison and on Parole*. Richmond: E. W. Ayres, 1865.

Porter, David Dixon. *Incidents and Anecdotes of the Civil War*. New York: D. Appleton & Co., 1885.

Porter, Horace. *Campaigning with Grant.* New York: Century Co., 1897.

Rice, Allen Thorndike, ed. *Reminiscences of Abraham Lincoln, by Distinguished Men of His Time.* 5th ed. Edited by Allen Thorndike Rice. New York: North American Review, 1888.

Richardson, Albert D. *A Personal History of Ulysses S. Grant.* Hartfield, CT: American Publishing Co., 1868.

———. *The Secret Service, the Field, the Dungeon, and the Escape.* Hartford, CT: American Publishing Co., 1865.

Ripley, Edward H. "Final Scenes at the Capture and Occupation of Richmond, April 3, 1865." In Military Order of the Loyal Legion of the US, New York Commandery, *Personal Recollections of the War of the Rebellion*, 3rd ser. (New York: G. P. Putnam's Sons, 1907), 491.

Robinson, Stuart. *Infamous Perjuries of the "Bureau of Military Justice" Exposed.* Toronto: n.p., 1865.

Rosecrans, William S. "The Mistakes of Grant." *North American Review* 141 (December 1885): 580–599.

Russell, William H. *My Diary North and South.* London: Bradbury & Evans, 1863. Reprint ed. New York: McGraw-Hill, 1988.

Schurz, Carl. *The Reminiscences of Carl Schurz.* Edited by Frederic Bancroft and William A. Dunning. 3 vols. New York: McClure, 1908.

Scovel, James M. "Thaddeus Stevens." *Lippincott's Monthly Magazine* 61 (April 1898): 545–551.

Shanks, William F. G. *Personal Recollections of Distinguished Generals.* New York: Harper & Brothers, 1866.

Shepley, George F. "Incidents of the Capture of Richmond." *Atlantic Monthly* 46 (July 1880): 18–29.

Sheridan, Philip. *Personal Memoirs of P. H. Sheridan.* 2 vols. New York: Charles L. Webster & Company, 1888.

Sherman, William Tecumseh. *Memoirs of General W. T. Sherman.* 1885; New York: Library of America, 1990.

———. *Sherman's Civil War: Selected Correspondence of William T. Sherman, 1860–1865.* Edited by Brooks D. Simpson and Jean V. Berlin. Chapel Hill: University of North Carolina Press, 1999.

Slater, Joseph, ed. *The Correspondence of Emerson and Carlyle.* New York: Columbia University Press, 1964.

Smalley, George W. *Anglo-American Memories.* New York: G. P. Putnam's Sons, 1911.

———. "Chapters in Journalism." *Harper's Monthly* 89 (August 1894): 426–435.

Smith, William F. *Autobiography of Major General William F. Smith, 1861–1864.* Edited by Herbert M. Schiller. Dayton, OH: Morningside House, 1990.

———. "Comments on General Grant's 'Chattanooga.'" *Battles and Leaders of the Civil War.* New York: Century, 1888. 3:715–718.

———. *From Chattanooga to Petersburg under Generals Grant and Butler.* Boston: Houghton Mifflin, 1893.

———. "An Historical Sketch of the Military Operations around Chattanooga, Tennessee, September 22 to November 27, 1863." *Papers of the Military Historical Society of Massachusetts, Vol. 8: The Mississippi Valley, Tennessee, Georgia, Alabama, 1861–1864.* Boston: Military Historical Society of Massachusetts, 1910. 149–272.

———. *The Relief of the Army of the Cumberland and the Opening of the Short Line of Communication between Chattanooga, Tenn., and Bridgeport, Ala. in October, 1863.* Wilmington: C. F. Thomas & Co., 1891.

Smith, William Wrenshall. "Holocaust Holiday." *Civil War Times Illustrated* 18, no. 6 (October 1979): 28–40.

Stager, Anson. *Cipher for Telegraphic Correspondence; Arranged Expressly for Military Operations, and for Important Government Despatches.* Washington, DC: n.p., 1861 & 62.

[St. Lawrence, F. A.]. *Testimony of Sandford Conover, Dr. J. B. Merritt, and Richard Montgomery Before Military Court at Washington, Respecting the Assassination of President Lincoln, and Proofs Disproving their Statements, and Showing Their Perjuries.* Toronto: Lovell & Gibson, 1865.

Stoddard, William O. *Dispatches from Lincoln's White House: The Anonymous Civil War Journalism of Presidential Secretary William O. Stoddard.* Edited by Michael Burlingame. Lincoln: University of Nebraska Press, 2002.

———. *Inside the White House in War Times: Memoirs and Reports of Lincoln's Secretary.* Edited by Michael Burlingame. Lincoln: University of Nebraska Press, 2000.

Strong, George Templeton. *The Diary of George Templeton Strong.* Edited by Allan Nevins and Milton Halsey Thomas. 4 vols. New York: Macmillan, 1952.

Sumner, Arthur. "A Boy's Recollections of Brook Farm." *New England Magazine* 10 (March–August 1894): 309–313.

Swinton, John. "Memoranda as to the Late Charles A. Dana." *Chautauquan* 26 (March 1898): 610–613.

Swinton, William. *Campaigns of the Army of the Potomac.* New York: C. B. Richardson, 1866.

Tarbell, Ida M. *All in the Day's Work: An Autobiography.* New York: Macmillan, 1939.

Taylor, Bayard. *Selected Letters of Bayard Taylor.* Edited by Paul C. Wermuth. Lewisburg, PA: Bucknell University Press, 1997.

———. *The Unpublished Letters of Bayard Taylor in the Huntington Library.* Edited by John Ritchie Schultz. San Marino, CA: Huntington Library, 1937.

Thruston, Gates P. "Chickamauga." *Southern Bivouac* 6 (December 1886): 406–415.

Tilden, Samuel J. *Letters and Literary Memorials of Samuel J. Tilden.* 2 vols. Edited by John Bigelow. New York: Harper & Brothers, 1908.

Traubel, Horace. *With Walt Whitman in Camden (July 16, 1888–October 31, 1888).* 1908; reprint ed. New York: Rowman & Littlefield, 1961.

———. *With Walt Whitman in Camden (November 1, 1888–January 20, 1889).* 1908; reprint ed. New York: Rowman & Littlefield, 1961.

Trollope, Anthony. *North America.* 2 vols. London: Chapman & Hall, 1862.

Villard, Henry. *Memoirs of Henry Villard, Journalist and Financier, 1835–1900.* 2 vols. 1904; reprint ed. New York: Da Capo Press, 1969.

Weichmann, Louis J. *A True History of the Assassination of Abraham Lincoln and of the Conspiracy of 1865.* Edited by Floyd E. Risvold. New York: Alfred A. Knopf, 1975.

Weitzel, Godfrey. *Richmond Occupied: Entry of the United States Forces into Richmond, Va., April 3, 1865.* Edited by Louis H. Manarin. Richmond, VA: Civil War Centennial Committee, 1965.

Welles, Gideon. *The Civil War Diary of Gideon Welles, Lincoln's Secretary of War.* Edited by William E. Gienapp and Erica L. Gienapp. Urbana and Chicago: University of Illinois Press, 2014.

Whitman, Walt. *The Correspondence, Volume 1: 1842–1867.* Edited by Edwin Haviland Miller. New York: New York University Press, 1961.

———. *New York Dissected.* Introduction and Notes by Emory Holloway and Ralph Adimari. New York: Rufus Rockwell Wilson, Inc., 1936.

———. *Prose Works 1892. Vol. III: Collect and Other Prose.* Edited by Floyd Stovall. New York: New York University Press, 1964.

Wilder, John T. "Preliminary Movements of the Army of the Cumberland before the Battle of Chickamauga [1908]." In *Sketches of War History, 1861–1865*, vol. 7. Wilmington, NC: Broadfoot Publishing Co., 1993. 263–272.

Wilson, Henry. "Edwin M. Stanton." *Atlantic Monthly* 25, no. 148 (February 1870): 234–245.

———. *History of the Rise and Fall of the Slave Power in America*. 2 vols. Boston: James R. Osgood & Co., 1874.

Wilson, James Harrison. "A Staff Officer's Journal of the Vicksburg Campaign, April 30 to July 4, 1863." *Journal of the Military Service Institution of the United States* 43 (1908): 93–109, 261–275.

———. *Under the Old Flag*. 2 vols. New York: D. Appleton & Co., 1912.

Wilson, Rufus Rockwell. *Intimate Memories of Lincoln*. Elmira, NY: Primavera Press, 1945.

Wing, Henry Ebeneser. *When Lincoln Kissed Me: A Story of the Wilderness Campaign*. New York and Cincinnati: Abingdon Press, 1913.

Winter, William. *Old Friends; Being Literary Recollections of Other Days*. New York: Moffat, Yard & Company, 1909.

Wood, Thomas J. "The Battle of Missionary Ridge." In *Sketches of War History, 1861–1865: Papers Prepared for the Ohio Commandery of the Military Order of the Loyal Legion of the United States*. Vol. 4. Edited by W. H. Chamberlin. Cincinnati: Robert Clarke Co., 1896. 23–51.

Young, John Russell. *Around the World with General Grant*. Abridged and edited by Michael Fellman. Baltimore: Johns Hopkins University Press, 2002.

———. *Men and Memories: Personal Reminiscences*. Edited by May D. Russell Young. New York and London: F. Tennyson Neely, 1901.

Books, Dissertations, and Theses

Ambrose, Stephen E. *Halleck: Lincoln's Chief of Staff*. Baton Rouge: Louisiana State University Press, 1962.

Andrews, J. Cutler. *The North Reports the Civil War*. Pittsburgh: University of Pittsburgh Press, 1955.

Atkins, Smith D. *Chickamauga: Useless, Disastrous Battle*. Freeport, IL: Journal Printing Co., 1907.

Axelrod, Alan. *The War between the Spies: A History of Espionage during the American Civil War*. New York: Atlantic Monthly Press, 1992.

Badeau, Adam. *Military History of Ulysses S. Grant, From April, 1861, To April, 1865*. 3 vols. New York: D. Appleton & Co., 1868–1881.

Ballard, Michael B. *Grant at Vicksburg: The General and the Siege*. Carbondale: Southern Illinois University Press, 2013.

———. *Vicksburg: The Campaign That Opened the Mississippi*. Chapel Hill: University of North Carolina Press, 2010.

Bearss, Edwin C. *The Campaign for Vicksburg*. 3 vols. Dayton, OH: Morningside Books, 1991.

Bentley, George R. *A History of the Freedmen's Bureau*. Philadelphia: University of Pennsylvania Press, 1955.

Blair, William A. *With Malice toward Some: Treason and Loyalty in the Civil War Era*. Chapel Hill: University of North Carolina Press, 2014.

Blight, David W. *Frederick Douglass: Prophet of Freedom*. New York: Simon & Schuster, 2018.

———. *Race and Reunion: The Civil War in American Memory*. Cambridge, MA: Belknap Press of Harvard University Press, 2001.

Borchard, Gregory A. *Abraham Lincoln and Horace Greeley*. Carbondale: Southern Illinois University Press, 2011.

Boyko, John. *Blood and Daring: How Canada Fought the American Civil War and Forged a Nation*. Toronto: Alfred A. Knopf Canada, 2013.

Brady, Kathleen. *Ida Tarbell: Portrait of a Muckraker*. Pittsburgh: University of Pittsburgh Press, 1989.

Brandt, Nat. *The Man Who Tried to Burn New York*. Syracuse: Syracuse University Press, 1986.

Brookhiser, Richard. *Founders' Son: A Life of Abraham Lincoln*. New York: Basic Books, 2014.

Brown, Dee Alexander. *Grierson's Raid*. Urbana: University of Illinois Press, 1954.

Brown, Francis. *Raymond of the Times*. New York: W. W. Norton, 1954.

Burlingame, Michael. *Abraham Lincoln: A Life*. 2 vols. Baltimore: Johns Hopkins University Press, 2008.

Calhoun, Charles W. *The Presidency of Ulysses S. Grant*. Lawrence: University Press of Kansas, 2017.

Carman, Harry James, and Reinhard H. Luthin. *Lincoln and the Patronage*. New York: Columbia University Press, 1943.

Carter, Samuel III. *The Final Fortress: The Campaign for Vicksburg, 1862–1863*. New York: St. Martin's Press, 1980.

Castel, Albert, with Brooks D. Simpson. *Victors in Blue: How Union Generals Fought the Confederates, Battled Each Other, and Won the Civil War*. Lawrence: University Press of Kansas, 2011.

Catton, Bruce. *Grant Moves South*. Boston: Little, Brown & Co., 1960.

———. *Grant Takes Command*. Boston: Little, Brown & Co., 1969.

———. *A Stillness at Appomattox*. New York: Doubleday & Co., 1953.

Chamlee, Roy Z., Jr. *Lincoln's Assassins: A Complete Account of Their Capture, Trial, and Punishment*. Jefferson, NC: McFarland, 1990.

Chernow, Ron. *Grant*. New York: Penguin Press, 2017.

Cimprich, John. *Slavery's End in Tennessee, 1861–1865*. Tuscaloosa: University of Alabama Press, 1985.

Conner, Robert C. *General Gordon Granger: The Savior of Chickamauga and the Man behind "Juneteenth."* Philadelphia: Casemate, 2013.

Cooling, Benjamin Franklin. *Jubal Early's Raid on Washington, 1864*. Baltimore: Nautical & Aviation Publishing Co. of America, 1989.

Cox, LaWanda, and John H. Cox. *Politics, Principle, and Prejudice, 1865–1866: Dilemma of Reconstruction America*. New York: Free Press, 1963.

Cozzens, Peter. *The Shipwreck of Their Hopes: The Battles for Chattanooga*. Urbana and Chicago: University of Illinois Press, 1994.

———. *This Terrible Sound: The Battle of Chickamauga*. Urbana: University of Illinois Press, 1992.

Crofts, Daniel W. *Lincoln and the Politics of Slavery: The Other Thirteenth Amendment and the Struggle to Save the Union*. Chapel Hill: University of North Carolina Press, 2016.

Crowe, Charles. *George Ripley: Transcendentalist and Utopian Socialist*. Athens: University of Georgia Press, 1967.

Crozier, Emmet. *Yankee Reporters, 1861–65*. New York: Oxford University Press, 1956.

Cumming, Carman. *Devil's Game: The Civil War Intrigues of Charles A. Dunham*. Urbana and Chicago: University of Illinois Press, 2004.

Current, Richard Nelson. *Lincoln's Loyalists: Union Soldiers from the Confederacy*. Boston: Northeastern University Press, 1992.

Dana, Elizabeth Ellery. *The Dana Family in America*. Cambridge, MA: n.p., 1956.

Daniel, Larry J. *Days of Glory: The Army of the Cumberland, 1861–1865*. Baton Rouge: Louisiana State University Press, 2006.

Davis, Burke. *The Long Surrender*. New York: Vintage Books, 1985.

Delano, Sterling F. *Brook Farm: The Dark Side of Utopia*. Cambridge, MA: Belknap Press of Harvard University Press, 2004.

———. *The Harbinger and New England Transcendentalism: A Portrait of Associationism in America*. Rutherford, NJ: Fairleigh Dickinson University Press, 1983.

Donald, David. *Lincoln*. New York: Simon & Schuster, 1995.

Durden, Robert Franklin. *James Shepherd Pike: Republicanism and the American Negro, 1850–1882*. Durham, NC: Duke University Press, 1957.

Dyer, Thomas G. *Secret Yankees: The Union Circle in Confederate Atlanta*. Baltimore: Johns Hopkins University Press, 1999.

Einolf, Christopher J. *George Thomas: Virginian for the Union*. Norman: University of Oklahoma Press, 2007.

Eubank, Damon R. *In the Shadow of the Patriarch: The John J. Crittenden Family in War and Peace*. Macon, GA: Mercer University Press, 2009.

Evans, Stewart, and Paul Gainey, *Jack the Ripper: First American Serial Killer*. New York: Kodansha America, 1998.

Fahrney, Ralph Ray. *Horace Greeley and the Tribune in the Civil War*. Cedar Rapids, IA: Torch Press, 1936.

Faneburst, Wayne. *Major General Alexander M. McCook, USA: A Civil War Biography*. Jefferson, NC: McFarland, 2012.

Fellman, Michael. *Citizen Sherman: A Life of William Tecumseh Sherman*. New York: Random House, 1995.

Fenton, Alfred H. *Dana of the Sun*. New York: Farrar & Rinehart, 1941.

Fishel, Edwin C. *The Secret War for the Union: The Untold Story of Military Intelligence in the Civil War*. Boston: Houghton Mifflin, 1996.

Flower, Frank Abial. *Edwin McMasters Stanton: The Autocrat of Rebellion, Emancipation, and Reconstruction*. Akron, OH: Saalfield Publishing Co., 1905.

Foner, Eric. *Gateway to Freedom: The Hidden History of the Underground Railroad*. New York: W. W. Norton & Co., 2015.

———. *Reconstruction: An Unfinished Revolution, 1863–1877*. New York: Harper & Row, 1988.

Foner, Philip. *History of Black Americans*. 3 vols. Westport, CT: Greenwood Press, 1983.

Foote, Shelby. *The Civil War: A Narrative*. 3 vols. New York: Random House, 2006.

Forgie, George B. *Patricide in the House Divided: A Psychological Interpretation of Lincoln and His Age*. New York: W. W. Norton & Company, 1979.

Frassanito, William A. *Grant and Lee: The Virginia Campaigns, 1864–1865*. New York: Charles Scribner's Sons, 1983.

Freeman, Joanne B. *The Field of Blood: Violence in Congress and the Road to Civil War*. New York: Farrar, Straus & Giroux, 2018.

Frothingham, Octavius Brooks. *George Ripley*. Boston: Houghton Mifflin, 1882.

Furgurson, Ernest B. *Ashes of Glory: Richmond at War*. New York: Alfred A. Knopf, 1996.

———. *Freedom Rising: Washington in the Civil War*. New York: Alfred A. Knopf, 2004.

———. *Not War But Murder: Cold Harbor, 1864*. New York: Alfred A. Knopf, 2000.

Gienapp, William E. *The Origins of the Republican Party, 1852–1856*. New York: Oxford University Press, 1987.

Gillette, William. *Jersey Blue: Civil War Politics in New Jersey, 1864–1865*. New Brunswick, NJ: Rutgers University Press, 1995.

Goodwin, Doris Kearns. *Team of Rivals: The Political Genius of Abraham Lincoln*. New York: Simon & Schuster, 2005.

Gragg, Rod. *Confederate Goliath: The Battle of Fort Fisher*. New York: HarperCollins, 1991.

Greene, A. Wilson. *A Campaign of Giants—The Battle for Petersburg: Volume 1: From the Crossing of the James to the Crater*. Chapel Hill: University of North Carolina Press, 2018.

Grimsley, Mark. *And Keep Moving On: The Virginia Campaign, May–June 1864*. Lincoln: University of Nebraska Press, 2002.

Groom, Winston. *Vicksburg, 1863*. New York: Alfred A. Knopf, 2009.

Guarneri, Carl J. *The Utopian Alternative: Fourierism in Nineteenth-Century America*. Ithaca, NY: Cornell University Press, 1991.

Guttridge, Leonard F., and Ray A. Neff. *Dark Union: The Secret Web of Profiteers, Politicians, and Booth Conspirators That Led to Lincoln's Death*. Hoboken, NJ: John Wiley & Sons, 2003.

Habegger, Alfred. *The Father: A Life of Henry James, Sr*. New York: Farrar, Straus & Giroux, 1994.

Hale, William Harlan. *Horace Greeley: Voice of the People*. New York: Harper & Brothers, 1950.

Hanchett, William. *The Lincoln Murder Conspiracies*. Urbana and Chicago: University of Illinois Press, 1983.

Haraszti, Zoltan. *The Idyll of Brook Farm*. Boston: Trustees of the Public Library, 1937.

Harbison, Robert E. "Wilder's Brigade in the Tullahoma and Chattanooga Campaigns of the American Civil War." MMAS thesis, US Army Command and General Staff College, Fort Leavenworth, KS, 2002.

Harris, M. Keith. *Across the Bloody Chasm: The Culture of Commemoration among Civil War Veterans*. Baton Rouge: Louisiana State University Press, 2014.

Hatfield, Mark O., with the Senate Historical Office. *Vice Presidents of the United States, 1789–1993*. Washington, DC: US Government Printing Office, 1997.

Hebert, Walter H. *Fighting Joe Hooker*. Indianapolis and New York: Bobbs-Merrill, 1944.

Hendrick, Burton J. *Lincoln's War Cabinet*. Garden City, NY: Doubleday & Co., 1961.

Hess, Earl J. *Civil War Logistics: A Study of Military Transportation*. Baton Rouge: Louisiana State University Press, 2017.

———. *The Knoxville Campaign: Burnside and Longstreet in East Tennessee*. Knoxville: University of Tennessee Press, 2012.

Holzer, Harold. *Lincoln and the Power of the Press*. New York: Simon & Schuster, 2014.

———. *Lincoln at Cooper Union: The Speech That Made Abraham Lincoln President*. New York: Simon & Schuster, 2004.

Hoogenbloom, Ari. *Gustavus Vasa Fox of the Union Navy: A Biography*. Baltimore: Johns Hopkins University Press, 2008.

Horan, James D. *Confederate Agent: A Discovery in History*. New York: Crown Publishers, 1954.

Horner, Harlan Hoyt. *Lincoln and Greeley*. Urbana: University of Illinois Press, 1953.

Hudson, Frederic. *Journalism in the United States, From 1690 to 1872*. New York: Harper & Brothers, 1873.

Hunt, Gaillard Israel, *Elihu and Cadwallader Washburn: A Chapter in American Biography*. New York: Macmillan, 1925.

Isely, Jeter Allen. *Horace Greeley and the Republican Party, 1853–1861*. Princeton, NJ: Princeton University Press, 1947.

Jampoler, Andrew C. A. *The Last Lincoln Conspirator: John Surratt's Flight from the Gallows*. Annapolis, MD: Naval Institute Press, 2008.

Janney, Caroline E. *Remembering the Civil War: Reunion and the Limits of Reconciliation*. Chapel Hill: University of North Carolina Press, 2013.

Jaynes, Gregory. *The Killing Ground: Wilderness to Cold Harbor*. Alexandria, VA: Time-Life Books, 1986.

Jones, James Pickett. *Yankee Blitzkrieg: Wilson's Raid through Alabama and Georgia*. Athens: University of Georgia Press, 1976.

Jordan, David M. *"Happiness Is Not My Companion": The Life of General G. K. Warren*. Bloomington: Indiana University Press, 2001.

———. *Winfield Scott Hancock: A Soldier's Life*. Bloomington: Indiana University Press, 1988.

Kauffman, Michael W. *American Brutus: John Wilkes Booth and the Lincoln Conspiracies*. New York: Random House, 2004.

Kendrick, Paul, and Stephen Kendrick. *Douglass and Lincoln: How a Revolutionary Black Leader and a Reluctant Liberator Struggled to End Slavery and Save the Union*. New York: Walker & Company, 2008.

Kinchen, Oscar A. *Confederate Operations in Canada and the North*. North Quincy, MA: Christopher Publishing House, 1970.

Kiper, Richard L. *Major General John Alexander McClernand: Politician in Uniform*. Kent, OH: Kent State University Press, 1999.

Kirkland, Edward Chase. *The Peacemakers of 1864*. New York: Macmillan, 1927.

Klement, Frank L. *The Copperheads in the Middle West*. Chicago: University of Chicago Press, 1960.

———. *Dark Lanterns: Secret Political Societies, Conspiracies, and Treason Trials in the Civil War*. Baton Rouge: Louisiana State University Press, 1984.

Kluger, Richard. *The Paper: The Life and Death of the New York Herald Tribune*. New York: Alfred A. Knopf, 1986.

Lamers, William M. *The Edge of Glory: A Biography of General William S. Rosecrans, U.S.A.* New York: Harcourt, Brace & World, 1961.

Lankford, Nelson. *Richmond Burning: The Last Days of the Confederate Capital*. New York: Viking Penguin, 2002.

Leech, Margaret. *Reveille in Washington, 1860–1865*. New York: Harper & Brothers, 1941.

Leonard, Elizabeth D. *Lincoln's Avengers: Justice, Revenge, and Reunion after the Civil War*. New York and London: W. W. Norton, 2004.

———. *Lincoln's Forgotten Ally: Judge Advocate General Joseph Holt of Kentucky*. Chapel Hill: University of North Carolina Press, 2011.

Lewis, Lloyd. *Sherman: Fighting Prophet*. New York: Harcourt Brace, 1932.

Long, David E. *The Jewel of Liberty: Abraham Lincoln's Re-Election and the End of Slavery*. Mechanicsburg, PA: Stackpole Books, 1994.

Longacre, Edward G. *From Union Stars to Top Hat: A Biography of the Extraordinary General James Harrison Wilson*. Harrisburg, PA: Stackpole Books, 1972.

Maihafer, Harry J. *The General and the Journalists: Ulysses S. Grant, Horace Greeley, and Charles Dana*. Washington, DC: Brassey's, 1998.

Marshall, John A. *American Bastille: A History of the Arrests and Imprisonment of American Citizens in the Northern and Border States, On Account of Their Political Opinions, During the Late Civil War*. Philadelphia: Thomas W. Hartley, 1881.

Marszalek, John F. *Commander of All Lincoln's Armies: A Life of General Henry W. Halleck.* Cambridge, MA: Harvard University Press, 2004.

———. *Sherman's Other War: The General and the Civil War Press.* Kent, OH: Kent State University Press, 1999.

Marvel, William. *Burnside.* Chapel Hill, NC: University of North Carolina Press, 1991.

———. *Lincoln's Autocrat: The Life of Edwin Stanton.* Chapel Hill: University of North Carolina Press, 2015.

Matter, William D. *If It Takes All Summer: The Battle of Spotsylvania.* Chapel Hill: University of North Carolina Press, 1988.

Mazlowski, Peter. *"Treason Must Be Made Odious": Military Occupation and Wartime Reconstruction in Nashville, Tennessee, 1862–65.* Millwood, NY: KTO Press, 1978.

McFeely, William S. *Grant: A Biography.* New York: W. W. Norton, 1981.

McKay, Ernest A. *The Civil War and New York City.* Syracuse: Syracuse University Press, 1990.

McKivigan, John R. *Forgotten Firebrand: James Redpath and the Making of Nineteenth-Century America.* Ithaca, NY: Cornell University Press, 2008.

McPherson, James M. *Battle Cry of Freedom: The Civil War Era.* New York: Oxford University Press, 2005.

———. *The Struggle for Equality: Abolitionists and the Negro in the Civil War and Reconstruction.* Princeton, NJ: Princeton University Press, 1964.

———, and James K. Hogue, *Ordeal by Fire: The Civil War and Reconstruction.* 4th ed. Boston: McGraw-Hill, 2009.

Melton, Brian C. *Sherman's Forgotten General: Henry W. Slocum.* Columbia: University of Missouri Press, 2007.

Miers, Earl Schenck. *The Web of Victory: Grant at Vicksburg.* New York: Knopf, 1955.

Miller, Edward A., Jr. *Lincoln's Abolitionist General: The Biography of David Hunter.* Columbia: University of South Carolina Press, 1997.

Miller, Perry. *The Raven and the Whale: The War of Words and Wits in the Era of Poe and Melville.* New York: Harcourt, Brace & World, 1956.

Miner, Craig. *Seeding Civil War: Kansas in the National News, 1854–1858.* Lawrence: University Press of Kansas, 2008.

Mitchie, Peter S. *The Life and Letters of Emory Upton, Colonel of the Fourth Regiment of Artillery, and Brevet Major-General, U.S. Army.* New York: D. Appleton & Co., 1885.

Mogelever, Jacob. *Death to Traitors: The Story of General Lafayette C. Baker, Lincoln's Forgotten Secret Service Chief.* Garden City, NY: Doubleday, 1960.

Morgans, James Patrick. *Grenville Mellen Dodge in the Civil War: Union Spymaster, Railroad Builder and Organizer of the Fourth Iowa Volunteer Infantry.* Jefferson, NC: McFarland & Co., 2016.

Murphet, Howard. *Yankee Beacon of Buddhist Light: The Life of Col. Henry S. Olcott.* Wheaton, IL: Theosophical Publishing House, 1988.

Neely, Mark E., Jr. *The Fate of Liberty: Abraham Lincoln and Civil Liberties.* New York: Oxford University Press, 1991.

Neff, John R. *Honoring the Civil War Dead: Commemoration and the Problem of Reconciliation.* Lawrence: University Press of Kansas, 2005.

Nelson, Larry E. *Bullets, Ballots, and Rhetoric: Confederate Policy for the United States Presidential Contest of 1864.* Tuscaloosa: University of Alabama Press, 1980.

Nevins, Allan. *Frémont: Pathmarker of the West.* Lincoln: University of Nebraska Press, 1992.

———. *Hamilton Fish: The Inner History of the Grant Administration.* New York: Dodd, Mead, & Co., 1937.

———. *The War for the Union.* 4 vols. New York: Charles Scribner's Sons, 1971.

Nicolay, John G., and John Hay. *Abraham Lincoln: A History.* 10 vols. New York: Century Co., 1890.

Nicoletti, Cynthia. *Secession on Trial: The Treason Prosecution of Jefferson Davis.* Cambridge, UK: Cambridge University Press, 2017.

Niven, John. *Salmon P. Chase: A Biography.* New York: Oxford University Press, 1995.

O'Brien, Frank M. *The Story of the Sun.* New York: George H. Doran Company, 1918.

O'Harrow, Robert, Jr. *The Quartermaster: Montgomery C. Meigs, Lincoln's General, Master Builder of the Union Army.* New York: Simon & Schuster, 2016.

Overton, Grant. *Portrait of a Publisher.* New York: D. Appleton & Co., 1925.

Owsley, Frank L. *King Cotton Diplomacy: Foreign Relations of the Confederate States of America.* Tuscaloosa: University of Alabama Press, 2008.

Peraino, Kevin. *Lincoln in the World: The Making of a Statesman and the Dawn of American Power.* New York: Crown Publishers, 2013.

Perkins, J. R. *Trails, Rails and War: The Life of General G. M. Dodge.* Indianapolis: Bobbs-Merrill, 1929.

Perret, Geoffrey. *Ulysses S. Grant: Soldier and President.* New York: Random House, 1997.

Pickenpaugh, Roger. *Rescue by Rail: Troop Transfer and the Civil War in the West.* Lincoln: University of Nebraska Press, 1998.

Potter, David M. *Lincoln and His Party in the Secession Crisis.* New Haven, CT: Yale University Press, 1942.

———. *The South and the Sectional Conflict.* Baton Rouge: Louisiana State University Press, 1968.

Potter, Jerry O. *The Sultana Tragedy: America's Greatest Maritime Disaster.* Gretna, LA: Pelican Publishing Co., 1992.

Powell, David A. *The Chickamauga Campaign.* 3 vols. El Dorado Hills, CA: Savas Beatie, 2014–2016.

Pratt, Fletcher. *Stanton: Lincoln's Secretary of War.* New York: W. W. Norton, 1953.

Prothero, Stephen. *The White Buddhist: The Asian Odyssey of Henry Steel Olcott.* Bloomington: Indiana University Press, 1996.

Quatman, G. William. *A Young General and the Fall of Richmond: The Life and Career of Godfrey Weitzel.* Athens: Ohio University Press, 2015.

Rafuse, Ethan S. *Robert E. Lee and the Fall of the Confederacy, 1863–1865.* Lanham, MD: Rowman & Littlefield, 2009.

Rawley, James A. *Turning Points of the Civil War.* Lincoln: University of Nebraska Press, 1989.

Reck, W. Emerson. *A. Lincoln: His Last 24 Hours.* Columbia: University of South Carolina Press, 1994.

Reeves, John. *The Lost Indictment of Robert E. Lee: The Forgotten Case against an American Icon.* Lanham, MD: Rowman & Littlefield, 2018.

Rhea, Gordon C. *The Battle of the Wilderness, May 5–6, 1864.* Baton Rouge: Louisiana State University Press, 1994.

———. *The Battles for Spotsylvania Court House and the Road to Yellow Tavern, May 7–12, 1864.* Baton Rouge: Louisiana State University Press, 1997.

———. *Cold Harbor: Grant and Lee, May 26–June 3, 1864.* Baton Rouge: Louisiana State University Press, 2002.

———. *On to Petersburg: Grant and Lee, June 4–15, 1864.* Baton Rouge: Louisiana State University Press, 2017.

———. *To the North Anna River: Grant and Lee, May 13–25, 1864*. Baton Rouge: Louisiana State University Press, 2000.

Richards, Leonard L. *Who Freed the Slaves? The Fight over the Thirteenth Amendment*. Chicago: University of Chicago Press, 2015.

Risley, Ford. *Civil War Journalism*. Santa Barbara, CA: Praeger, 2012.

Ritchie, Donald A. *Press Gallery: Congress and the Washington Correspondents*. Cambridge, MA: Harvard University Press, 1991.

Roberts, Timothy Mason. *Distant Revolutions: 1848 and the Challenge to American Exceptionalism*. Charlottesville: University of Virginia Press, 2009.

Rosebault, Charles J. *When Dana Was the Sun*. New York: R. M. McBride & Co., 1931.

Rybczynski, Witold. *A Clearing in the Distance: Frederick Law Olmsted and America in the 19th Century*. New York: Scribner, 2013.

Salecker, Gene Eric. *Disaster on the Mississippi: The Sultana Explosion, April 27, 1865*. Annapolis, MD: Naval Institute Press, 1996.

Samito, Christian G. *Lincoln and the Thirteenth Amendment*. Carbondale: Southern Illinois University Press, 2015.

Sandburg, Carl. *Abraham Lincoln*. 7 vols. New York: Charles Scribner's Sons, 1943.

Sarna, Jonathan D. *When General Grant Expelled the Jews*. New York: Schocken, 2012.

Schecter, Barnet. *The Devil's Own Work: The Civil War Draft Riots and the Fight to Reconstruct America*. New York: Walker & Co., 2005.

Searcher, Victor. *The Farewell to Lincoln*. New York and Nashville: Abingdon Press, 1965.

Seitz, Don C. *Horace Greeley, Founder of the New York Tribune*. Indianapolis: Bobbs-Merrill, 1926.

Sheads, Scott Sumpter, and Daniel Carroll Toomey. *Baltimore during the Civil War*. Linthicum, MD: Toomey Press, 1997.

Simon, John Y. *The Union Forever: Lincoln, Grant, and the Civil War*. Lexington: University Press of Kentucky, 2012.

Simpson, Brooks D. *Let Us Have Peace: Ulysses S. Grant and the Politics of War and Reconstruction, 1861–1868*. Chapel Hill: University of North Carolina Press, 1991.

———. *Ulysses S. Grant: Triumph over Adversity, 1822–1865*. Boston: Houghton Mifflin, 2000.

Slotkin, Richard. *No Quarter: The Battle of the Crater, 1864*. New York: Random House, 2009.

Smith, Jean Edward. *Grant*. New York: Simon & Schuster, 2001.

Smith, Theodore Clarke. *The Life and Letters of James Abram Garfield*. 2 vols. New Haven, CT: Yale University Press, 1925.

Spaniolo, Charles V. "Charles Anderson Dana: His Early Life and Civil War Career." PhD diss., Michigan State University, 1965.

Stahr, Walter. *Seward: Lincoln's Indispensable Man*. New York: Simon & Schuster, 2012.

———. *Stanton: Lincoln's War Secretary*. New York: Simon & Schuster, 2017.

Starr, Louis M. *Bohemian Brigade: Civil War Newsmen in Action*. New York: Alfred A. Knopf, 1954.

Starr, Stephen Z. *The Union Cavalry in the Civil War*. 3 vols. Baton Rouge: Louisiana State University Press, 1979–1985.

Stedman Jones, Gareth. *Karl Marx: Greatness and Illusion*. Cambridge, MA: Harvard University Press, 2016.

Steele, Janet E. *The Sun Shines for All: Journalism and Ideology in the Life of Charles A. Dana*. Syracuse: Syracuse University Press, 1993.

Steers, Edward, Jr. *Blood on the Moon: The Assassination of Abraham Lincoln*. Lexington: University Press of Kentucky, 2001.

Stoddard, Henry Luther. *Horace Greeley: Printer, Editor, Crusader*. New York: G. P. Putnam's Sons, 1946.

Stone, Candace. *Dana and the Sun*. New York: Dodd, Mead & Co., 1938.

Strausbaugh, John. *City of Sedition: The History of New York City during the Civil War*. New York: Twelve Books, 2016.

Summers, Mark Wahlgren. *The Era of Good Stealings*. New York: Oxford University Press, 1993.

———. *The Plundering Generation*. New York: Oxford University Press, 1987.

———. *The Press Gang: Newspapers and Politics, 1865–1878*. Chapel Hill: University of North Carolina Press, 1994.

Swanson, James L. *Bloody Crimes: The Funeral of Abraham Lincoln and the Chase for Jefferson Davis*. New York: HarperCollins, 2010.

———. *Manhunt: The Twelve-Day Chase for Lincoln's Killer*. New York: HarperCollins, 2006.

Swift, Lindsay. *Brook Farm: Its Members, Scholars, and Visitors*. New York: Macmillan, 1900.

Sword, Wiley. *Mountains Touched with Fire: Chattanooga Besieged, 1863*. New York: St. Martin's Press, 1995.

Tap, Bruce. *Over Lincoln's Shoulder: The Committee on the Conduct of the War*. Lawrence: University Press of Kansas, 1998.

Tarbell, Ida M. *The Life of Abraham Lincoln*. 10 vols. New York: Lincoln History Society, 1924.

———. *A Reporter for Lincoln: The Story of Henry E. Wing, Soldier and Newspaperman*. New York: Macmillan, 1927.

Taylor, Emerson Gifford. *Gouverneur Kemble Warren: The Life and Letters of an American Soldier, 1830–1882*. Boston: Houghton Mifflin, 1932.

Thayer, William Roscoe. *The Life and Letters of John Hay*. 2 vols. Boston: Houghton Mifflin, 1908.

Thomas, Benjamin P. *Abraham Lincoln: A Biography*. New York: Alfred A. Knopf, 1952.

———, and Harold M. Hyman. *Stanton: The Life and Times of Lincoln's Secretary of War*. New York: Alfred A. Knopf, 1962.

Thomas, William G. *The Iron Way: Railroads, the Civil War, and the Making of Modern America*. New Haven, CT: Yale University Press, 2011.

Tidwell, William A. *April '65: Confederate Covert Action in the American Civil War*. Kent, OH: Kent State University Press, 1995.

———, with James O. Hall and David Winfred Gaddy. *Come Retribution: The Confederate Secret Service and the Assassination of Lincoln*. Jackson: University Press of Mississippi, 1988.

Towne, Stephen E. *Surveillance and Spies in the Civil War: Exposing Conspiracies in America's Heartland*. Athens: Ohio University Press, 2015.

Trudeau, Noah Andre. *Bloody Roads South: The Wilderness to Cold Harbor, May–June, 1864*. Boston: Little, Brown & Co., 1989.

———. *The Last Citadel: Petersburg, Virginia, June 1864–April 1865*. Boston: Little, Brown & Co., 1991.

Tuchinsky, Adam. *Horace Greeley's New-York Tribune: Civil War–Era Socialism and the Crisis of Free Labor*. Ithaca, NY: Cornell University Press, 2009.

Tucker, Glenn. *Chickamauga: Bloody Battle in the West.* Indianapolis: Bobbs-Merrill, 1961.

Turner, Hy B. *When Giants Ruled: The Story of Park Row, New York's Great Newspaper Street.* New York: Fordham University Press, 1999.

Turner, Thomas Reed. *Beware the People Weeping: Public Opinion and the Assassination of Abraham Lincoln.* Baton Rouge: Louisiana State University Press, 1982.

Van Deusen, Glyndon G. *Horace Greeley: Nineteenth-Century Crusader.* Philadelphia: University of Pennsylvania Press, 1953.

———. *Thurlow Weed: Wizard of the Lobby.* Boston: Little, Brown & Co., 1947.

———. *William Henry Seward.* New York: Oxford University Press, 1967.

Vandiver, Frank E. *Jubal's Raid: General Early's Famous Attack on Washington in 1864.* New York: McGraw-Hill, 1960.

Varney, Frank P. *General Grant and the Rewriting of History: How the Destruction of General William S. Rosecrans Influenced Our Understanding of the Civil War.* El Dorado Hills, CA: Savas Beatie, 2013.

Varon, Elizabeth R. *Appomattox: Victory, Defeat, and Freedom at the End of the Civil War.* New York: Oxford University Press, 2014.

Vorenberg, Michael. *Final Freedom: The Civil War, the Abolition of Slavery, and the Thirteenth Amendment.* Cambridge, UK: Cambridge University Press, 2001.

Waugh, Joan. *U. S. Grant: American Hero, American Myth.* Chapel Hill: University of North Carolina Press, 2009.

Waugh, John C. *Reelecting Lincoln: The Battle for the 1864 Presidency.* New York: Crown Publishers, 1997.

Weber, Jennifer L. *Copperheads: The Rise and Fall of Lincoln's Opponents in the North.* New York: Oxford University Press, 2006.

Weber, Thomas. *The Northern Railroads in the Civil War, 1861–1865.* New York: King's Crown Press of Columbia University Press, 1952.

Weigley, Russell F. *A Great Civil War: A Military and Political History, 1861–1865.* Bloomington: Indiana University Press, 2004.

———. *Quartermaster General of the Union Army: A Biography of M. C. Meigs.* New York: Columbia University Press, 1959.

Weisberger, Bernard A. *Reporters for the Union.* Boston: Little, Brown & Co., 1953.

Welcher, Frank J. *The Union Army: Organization and Operations.* 2 vols. Bloomington: Indiana University Press, 1989–1993.

Wheelan, Joseph. *Terrible Swift Sword: The Life of General Philip H. Sheridan.* Cambridge, MA: Da Capo, 2012.

Wheeler, Tom. *Mr. Lincoln's T-Mails: How Abraham Lincoln Used the Telegraph to Win the Civil War.* New York: HarperCollins, 2006.

White, Jonathan W. *Emancipation, the Union Army, and the Reelection of Abraham Lincoln.* Baton Rouge: Louisiana State University Press, 2014.

White, Ronald C., Jr. *Lincoln's Greatest Speech: The Second Inaugural.* New York: Simon & Schuster, 2002.

Williams, Robert C. *Horace Greeley: Champion of American Freedom.* New York: New York University Press, 2006.

Williams, T. Harry. *Lincoln and the Radicals.* Madison: University of Wisconsin Press, 1941.

Wills, Brian Steel. *George Henry Thomas: As True As Steel.* Lawrence: University Press of Kansas, 2012.

Wilson, James Harrison. *The Life and Services of General Smith.* Wilmington, DE: John M. Rogers, 1904.

————. *The Life of Charles A. Dana.* New York: Harper & Bros., 1907.

————. *The Life of John A. Rawlins.* New York: Neale Publishing Co., 1916.

Wilson, Mark. R. *The Business of Civil War: Military Mobilization and the State, 1861–1865.* Baltimore: Johns Hopkins University Press, 2006.

Wilson, Robert. *Mathew Brady: Portraits of a Nation.* New York: Bloomsbury, 2013.

Winks, Robin W. *The Civil War Years: Canada and the United States.* 4th ed. Montreal and Kingston: McGill-Queen's University Press, 1998.

Woodworth, Steven E. *Chickamauga: A Battlefield Guide.* Lincoln: University of Nebraska Press, 1999.

————. *Nothing but Victory: The Army of the Tennessee, 1861–1865.* New York: Knopf, 2005.

————. *Six Armies in Tennessee: The Chickamauga and Chattanooga Campaigns.* Lincoln: University of Nebraska Press, 1998.

————, ed. *Grant's Lieutenants: From Chattanooga to Appomattox.* Lawrence: University Press of Kansas, 2008.

————, and Charles D. Grear, eds. *The Chattanooga Campaign.* Carbondale and Edwardsville: Southern Illinois University Press, 2012.

Work, David. *Lincoln's Political Generals.* Urbana: University of Illinois Press, 2009.

Zeitz, Joshua. *Lincoln's Boys: John Hay, John Nicolay, and the War for Lincoln's Image.* New York: Penguin Books, 2014.

Zornow, William Frank. *Lincoln and the Party Divided.* Norman: University of Oklahoma Press, 1954.

Articles and Essays

Blondheim, Menahem. "'Public Sentiment is Everything': The Union's Public Communication Strategy and the Bogus Proclamation of 1864." *Journal of American History* 89 (2002): 869–899.

Bonner, Thomas N. "Horace Greeley and the Secession Movement, 1860–1861." *Mississippi Valley Historical Review* 38 (1951): 425–444.

Borden, Morten. "Some Notes on Horace Greeley, Charles Dana and Karl Marx." *Journalism Quarterly* 34 (Fall 1957): 457–465.

Bradley, Chester D. "Was Jefferson Davis Disguised as a Woman When Captured?" *Journal of Mississippi History* 36 (August 1974): 243–268.

Burton, Crompton. "'No Turning Back': The Official Bulletins of Secretary of War Edwin M. Stanton." In *Words at War: The Civil War and American Journalism.* Edited by David B. Sachsman, S. Kittrell Rushing, and Roy Morris Jr. West Lafayette, IN: Purdue University Press, 2008. 281–292.

Butts, Heather M. "Alexander Thomas Augusta—Physician, Teacher and Human Rights Activist." *Journal of the National Medical Association* 97 (January 2005): 106–109.

Carleton, Philip G. "Eyes of the Union." *Harvard Alumni Bulletin* 54 (October 27, 1951): 113–115, 122–124.

Coleman, Charles H. "The Use of the Term 'Copperhead' during the Civil War." *Mississippi Valley Historical Review* 25 (September 1938): 263–264.

Feis, William B. "'There Is a Bad Enemy in This City': Colonel William Truesdail's Army Police and the Occupation of Nashville, 1862–1863." *North & South* 8 (March 2005): 35–45.

Frank, Seymour J. "The Conspiracy to Implicate Confederate Leaders in Lincoln's Assassination." *Mississippi Valley Historical Review* 40, no. 4 (March 1954): 629–636.

Furrow, Matthew. "Samuel Gridley Howe, the Black Population of Canada West, and the Racial Ideology of the 'Blueprint for Radical Reconstruction.'" *Journal of American History* 97 (September 2010): 344–370.

George, Joseph, Jr. "The Conspiracy Trial's 'Suppressed Testimony': An Attempt to Implicate Jefferson Davis in Lincoln's Assassination." *Lincoln Herald* 111 (June 2009): 94–127.

———. "The North Affair: A Lincoln Administration Civil War Trial, 1864." *Civil War History* 33 (September 1987): 199–218.

Gertz, Elmer. "Charles A. Dana and the *Chicago Republican.*" *Journal of the Illinois State Historical Society* 45 (Summer 1952): 124–135.

Gordon, Lesley. "The Failed Relationship of William S. Rosecrans and Grant." In *Grant's Lieutenants: From Cairo to Vicksburg.* Edited by Steven E. Woodworth. Lawrence: University Press of Kansas, 2001. 109–128.

Grimsley, Mark. "A Lack of Confidence: Benjamin F. Butler." In *Grant's Lieutenants: From Chattanooga to Appomattox.* Edited by Steven E. Woodworth. Lawrence: University Press of Kansas, 2008. 105–131.

Hartman, William. "Custom House Patronage under Lincoln." *New-York Historical Society Quarterly* 41 (October 1957): 440–457.

Irvine, Dallas D. "The Archive Office of the War Department: Repository of Captured Confederate Archives, 1865–1881." *Military Affairs* 10 (Spring 1946): 93–111.

Johnson, Ludwell H. "Beverly Tucker's Canadian Mission, 1864–1865." *Journal of Southern History* 29 (1963): 88–99.

———. "Commerce between Northeastern Ports and the Confederacy." *Journal of American History* 54 (1967): 30–42.

———. "Contraband Trade during the Last Year of the Civil War." *Mississippi Valley Historical Review* 49 (1963): 635–652.

———. "Northern Profit and Profiteers: The Cotton Rings of 1864–65." *Civil War History* 12 (1966): 101–115.

Jones, Evan C. "A 'Malignant Vindictiveness': The Two-Decade Rivalry between Ulysses S. Grant and William S. Rosecrans." In *Gateway to the Confederacy: New Perspectives on the Chickamauga and Chattanooga Campaigns, 1862–1863.* Edited by Evan C. Jones and Wiley Sword. Baton Rouge: Louisiana State University Press, 2014. 172–226.

Kielbowicz, Richard B. "The Telegraph, Censorship, and Politics at the Outset of the Civil War." *Civil War History* 40 (June 1994): 95–118.

Klement, Frank L. "Phineas C. Wright, the Order of the American Knights, and the Sanderson Exposé." *Civil War History* 18 (March 1972): 5–23.

Lokke, Carl L. "The Captured Confederate Archives under Francis Lieber." *American Archivist* 9 (October 1946): 277–319.

Longacre, Edward G. "The Union Army Occupation of New York City, November 1864." *New York History* 65 (April 1984): 133–158.

Maihafer, Harry J. "Mr. Grant and Mr. Dana." *American History* 35 (December 2000): 24–32.

Mallam, William D. "The Grant-Butler Relationship." *Mississippi Valley Historical Review* 41 (September 1954): 259–276.

Marsh, Richard C. "The Military Trial of Gazaway Bugg Lamar." *Georgia Historical Quarterly* 85 (Winter 2001): 555–591.

Mathis, Robert Neil. "The Ordeal of Confiscation: The Post–Civil War Trials of Gazaway Bugg Lamar." *Georgia Historical Quarterly* 63 (Fall 1979): 339–352.

Morris, Roy, Jr. "A Bird of Evil Omen: The War Department's Charles Dana." *Civil War Times Illustrated* 25 (January 1987): 20–29.

Nevins, Allan. "The Effects of Greeley on Dana." *Journalism Quarterly* 5 (1928): 1–5.

Nichols, Roy Franklin. "The United States v. Jefferson Davis, 1865–1869." *American Historical Review* 31 (1926): 266–284.

Pomeroy, Earl S. "Lincoln, the Thirteenth Amendment, and the Admission of Nevada." *Pacific Historical Review* 12 (1943): 362–368.

Rafuse, Ethan S. "In the Shadow of the Rock: Thomas L. Crittenden, Alexander M. McCook, and the 1863 Campaigns for Middle and East Tennessee." In *The Chickamauga Campaign*. Edited by Steven E. Woodworth. Carbondale and Edwardsville: Southern Illinois University Press, 2012. 5–49.

———. "Wherever Lee Goes . . . : George G. Meade." In *Grant's Lieutenants: From Chattanooga to Appomattox*. Edited by Steven E. Woodworth. Lawrence: University Press of Kansas, 2008. 47–83.

Reid, Brian Holden. "Another Look at Grant's Crossing of the James, 1864." *Civil War History* 39 (1993): 291–316.

Rives, Timothy. "Grant, Babcock, and the Whiskey Ring." *Prologue* 32 (Fall 2000). www.archives.gov/publications/prologue/2000/fall/whiskey-ring-1.html.

Simpson, Brooks D. "Great Expectations: Ulysses S. Grant, the Northern Press, and the Opening of the Wilderness Campaign." In *The Wilderness Campaign*. Edited by Gary W. Gallagher. Chapel Hill: University of North Carolina Press, 1997. 1–35.

———. "Quandaries of Command: Ulysses S. Grant and Black Soldiers." In *Union and Emancipation: Essays on Politics and Race in the Civil War Era*. Edited by David W. Blight and Brooks D. Simpson. Kent, OH: Kent State University Press, 1997. 123–149.

Spencer, Warren F. "The Jewett-Greeley Affair: A Private Scheme for French Mediation in the American Civil War." *New York History* 51 (1970): 238–268.

Sproat, John G. "Blueprint for Radical Reconstruction." *Journal of Southern History* 23 (February 1957): 25–44.

Sternhell, Yael A. "The Afterlives of a Confederate Archive: Civil War Documents and the Making of Sectional Reconciliation." *Journal of American History* 102 (March 2016): 1025–1050.

Summers, Mark W. "'A Band of Brigands': Albany Lawmakers and Republican National Politics, 1860." *Civil War History* 30 (June 1984): 101–119.

Surdam, David G. "Traders or Traitors: Northern Cotton Trading during the Civil War." *Business and Economic History* 28 (1999): 301–312.

Tarbell, Ida M. "Charles A. Dana in the Civil War." *McClure's Magazine* 9 (October 1897): 1085–1088.

Tidwell, William A. "April 15, 1865." *Civil War History* 42 (Spring 1996): 220–239.

Wennersten, John R. "Parke Godwin, Utopian Socialism, and the Politics of Antislavery." *New-York Historical Society Quarterly* 60 (July–October 1976): 107–127.

Woodworth, Steven E. "Old Slow Trot: George H. Thomas." In *Grant's Lieutenants: From Chattanooga to Appomattox*. Edited by Steven E. Woodworth. Lawrence: University Press of Kansas, 2008. 23–45.

Index